TERRORISM
AND
HOMELAND SECURITY

THE BUTTERWORTH-HEINEMANN HOMELAND SECURITY SERIES

Series Editors:
George Haddow and Jane A. Bullock
Institute for Crisis, Disaster and Risk Management
George Washington University

Other titles in the Series
- **Introduction to Homeland Security, Second Edition** (2006)
  ISBN: 0-7506-7992-1
  Jane Bullock, et al.
- **Introduction to Emergency Management, Second Edition** (2006)
  ISBN: 0-7506-7961-1
  George Haddow and Jane Bullock
- **Emergency Response Planning for Corporate and Municipal Managers, Second Edition** (2006)
  ISBN: 0-12-370503-7
  Paul Erickson

Other related titles of interest:
- **Introduction to International Disaster Management** (2006)
  ISBN: 0-7506-7982-4
  Damon Coppola
- **Vulnerability Assessment of Physical Protection Systems** (2006)
  ISBN: 0-7506-7788-0
  Mary Lynn Garcia
- **Risk Analysis and the Security Survey, Third Edition** (2006)
  ISBN: 0-7506-7922-0
  James Broder
- **Introduction to Security, Seventh Edition** (2003)
  ISBN: 0-7506-7600-0
  Robert J. Fischer and Gion Green
- **High-Rise Security and Fire Life Safety** (2003)
  ISBN: 0-7506-7455-5
  Geoff Craighead
- **Transportation Disaster Response Handbook** (2002)
  ISBN: 0-12-445486-0
  Jay Levinson and Hayim Granot
- **Investigative Data Mining for Security and Criminal Detection** (2002)
  ISBN: 0-7506-7613-2
  Jesus Mena
- **The Design & Evaluation of Physical Protection Systems** (2001)
  ISBN: 0-7506-7367-2
  Mary Lynn Garcia

Visit **http://books.elsevier.com/security** for more information on these titles and other resources.

TERRORISM

AND

HOMELAND SECURITY

An Introduction with Applications

Philip P. Purpura

AMSTERDAM • BOSTON • HEIDELBERG • LONDON
NEW YORK • OXFORD • PARIS • SAN DIEGO
SAN FRANCISCO • SINGAPORE • SYDNEY • TOKYO

Butterworth-Heinemann is an imprint of Elsevier

Senior Acquisitions Editor: Mark Listewnik
Assistant Editor: Kelly Weaver
Senior Marketing Manager: Christian Nolin
Project Manager: Jeff Freeland
Cover Designer: Eric DeCicco
Compositor: CEPHA Imaging Private Limited
Cover Printer: Phoenix Color Corp.
Text Printer/Binder: The Maple-Vail Book Manufacturing Group

Butterworth–Heinemann is an imprint of Elsevier
30 Corporate Drive, Suite 400, Burlington, MA 01803, USA
Linacre House, Jordan Hill, Oxford OX2 8DP, UK

Library of Congress Cataloging-in-Publication Data
Purpura, Philip P.
    Terrorisim and homeland security : an introduction with applications / Philip P. Purpura.
        p.   cm. – (Butterworth-Heinemann homeland security series)
    Includes bibliographical references and index.
    ISBN 13:   978-0-7506-7843-8 (alk. paper)
    ISBN 10:   0-7506-7843-7 (alk. paper)
 1.   Terrorism–United States–Prevention–Textbooks. 2.   National security–United
States–Textbooks. 3.   Internal security–United States–Textbooks. I. Title. II. Series.

    HV6432. P87 2007
    363.325'160973–dc22

                                                                                    2006048392

British Library Cataloguing-in-Publication Data
A catalogue record for this book is available from the British Library.

ISBN 13:   978-0-7506-7843-8
ISBN 10:   0-7506-7843-7

For information on all Butterworth–Heinemann publications
visit our Web site at www.books.elsevier.com

Transferred to Digital Printing 2010

To My Family

To the United States and its allies, to the victims of terrorism, and to the millions of military, public safety, security, and other professionals and volunteers who strive to create a safe and secure world.

About the Author

Philip Purpura, Certified Protection Professional, is Director of the Security Training Institute and Resource Center and Coordinator of the Security for Houses of Worship Project in South Carolina. He has taught security and criminal justice courses for over 25 years. He serves on the ASIS International Council on Academic Programs. Pupura has practical experience as an expert witness, consultant, security manager, investigator, and police officer. He served as a member of the National Defense Executive Reserve. Purpura is the author of six other books: *Security and Loss Prevention: An Introduction*, 4th ed. (Boston, MA: Butterworth-Heinemann, 2002); *Security Handbook*, 2nd ed. (Boston, MA: Butterworth-Heinemann, 2003; Albany, NY: Delmar Pub., 1991); *Police and Community: Concepts and Cases* (Needham, MA: Allyn & Bacon, Pub., 2001); *Criminal Justice: An Introduction* (Boston, MA: Butterworth-Heinemann, 1997); *Retail Security and Shrinkage Protection* (Boston, MA: Butterworth-Heinemann, 1993); and *Modern Security and Loss Prevention Management* (Boston, MA: Butterworth, 1989). Purpura was contributing editor to three security periodicals, wrote numerous articles published in journals, magazines and newsletters, and has been involved in a variety of editorial projects for publishers. He holds bachelor's and master's degrees in criminal justice from the University of Dayton and Eastern Kentucky University, respectively. He also studied in Europe, Asia, and the former Soviet Union.

Table of Contents

Preface

This book is the result of much thought, research, and writing following the 9/11 attacks, recent natural and accidental disasters, and government and private sector action and inaction in response to a multitude of hazards. At the same time, the United States and its allies are faced with conflict in Iraq, Afghanistan, and other regions, while facing old and emerging state competitors and the proliferation of weapons of mass destruction.

Unfortunately, the 9/11 attacks were immensely successful and cost effective for the terrorists. With a loss of 19 terrorists and expenses between $400,000 and $500,000, the attackers were able to kill about 3000 people, cause hundreds of billions of dollars in economic damage and spending on counterterrorism, and significantly impact global history. With such a huge kill ratio and investment payoff, governments and the private sector must succeed in controlling terrorism.

The events of September 11, 2001 became a wake-up call to an ancient method of warfare that has reenergized itself through history. Terrorism is becoming a more powerful and serious threat due to a number of factors: it is more lethal, there is the proliferation of weapons of mass destruction, there is the potential for mass casualties and severe economic harm, there is opportunity to exploit mass media, and there are successes in causing change.

Although common through history, this new century has also recorded huge natural disasters that—along with the problem of terrorism—necessitate a rethinking of emergency management. Hurricanes Katrina and Rita, in 2005, devastated Gulf-coast states and flooded New Orleans. The December 2004 Sumatran Tsunami killed almost 300,000 people and impacted 18 countries around the Indian Ocean. The human and financial strain on nations to prepare and respond to natural and accidental threats is overwhelming. These challenges require global cooperation, a broad base of knowledge, skills from many disciplines, and continued research.

Terrorism and Homeland Security: An Introduction with Applications provides an overview of the problem of terrorism, public and private sector counterterrorism, "all hazards" emergency management, and many controversial issues. This book contains key terms and definitions, examples and illustrations, and theories from many disciplines. The theoretical foundation is multidisciplinary because many fields of study hold answers to the challenges we face. The study of terrorism has been multidisciplinary for many years. However, the study of homeland security and its body of knowledge are both in a stage of infancy and the debate rages over its definition and meaning. The disciplines that support this book include architecture, business, criminal justice, emergency management, fire protection, government, public health and medicine, history, international relations, law, life safety, military science, politics, psychology, religion, risk management, security, sociology, and structural engineering. Other disciplines within engineering, sciences, and social sciences also support homeland security.

The controversial issues in this book are both national and international in scope. America has been under great strain since the 9/11 attacks, while confronting an elusive, crafty and patient enemy, as it recovers, responds, and seeks to protect itself under the United States Constitution. Although many positive changes have occurred since the 9/11 attacks, weaknesses remain that must be studied and corrected.

In addition to providing theory from several disciplines, this book offers explanations of problems and countermeasures to assist both practitioners searching for answers to complex questions and students seeking to bridge theory to practice. The pedagogical features of this book are as follows.

- **Learning objectives** and **key terms** at the beginning of all chapters guide the reader on chapter content and the topics to understand.

- **Bold type** is used to identify key terms, concepts, theories, names, laws, and other topics throughout the book. This helps the reader to master the body of knowledge on terrorism and homeland security and prepare for examinations and academic projects.
- **Scenarios** are placed at the beginning of each chapter to offer the reader a dose of reality and to increase interest in chapter content.
- **Examples, illustrations, and figures** help explain concepts and relate theory to practice.
- **Boxed topics** are contained in each chapter to extend the depth of the information and to offer additional perspectives on issues.
- **"Reality Check" boxes** expose thorny events and issues, pose controversial questions, offer answers, and seek to differentiate law, policy, and plans from reality.
- **Critical thinking boxes** throughout the book help the reader to formulate alternative perspectives on issues and to seek creative and improved solutions to problems.
- **Discussion questions** at the end of each chapter reinforce content and provide an opportunity for the reader to review, synthesize, and debate major concepts and issues.
- **Web sites** at the end of each chapter provide direction for additional resources, information, and research.
- An **Interdisciplinary research base** was developed from books, journals, newsletters, magazines, professional associations and groups, government, training programs, and other sources.
- **Applications** are located at the end of chapters to be used as learning and skill-building tools. The purpose of the applications is to (1) bridge theory to practice; (2) help us to understand ourselves and our adversaries, including ideologies, organizational structures, and methods of operation; (3) expose weaknesses in our systems and methods and those of our adversaries; (4) gain insight into the challenges faced by both homeland security practitioners and terrorists; (5) improve decision making during planning, counterterrorism, investigations, research, dilemmas, and emergencies; and (6) improve global security and safety while working toward peace.
- An **Instructor's Manual** offers an outline and objective questions for all chapters.

The applications can be applied in a classroom environment where small groups of students can think critically and creatively, while receiving feedback from other students and an educator/facilitator. The author field-tested select applications in college courses and in security training with officers and management. The applications were shown to stimulate critical thinking and debate; an understanding of our adversaries; the consideration of numerous variables that no individual is likely to produce alone; creative solutions; knowledge and skills; and preparation for assessment centers in the workplace.

The applications apply assessment center and red team techniques. The former have been used widely for decades to improve organizational selection of both job candidates and employees seeking promotion. The assessment center process begins with job analysis and behaviors relevant to the job. "In-basket" exercises are used to simulate what occurs on the job (e.g., daily duties, emergencies) to see how candidates respond and justify their decisions. The assessment center techniques used in this book seek to develop a mind-set in the reader to "think like a Homeland Security practitioner."

Red team techniques involve a friendly side (blue) viewing a problem or challenge through the eyes of an adversary or competitor (red). The technique varies in purpose, scope, and nobody "owns it." It was noted as a major initiative of the *National Strategy for Homeland Security* and is applied by the military, law enforcement agencies, risk management service firms, and other groups. The military seeks to anticipate an enemy's actions. Security specialists search for vulnerabilities in physical security and information technology. A police officer "thinks like a thief." A business proposal can be challenged from a competitor's perspective. The technique is applicable to marketers, grant writers, and job applicants, among others. Red team techniques serve to not only anticipate an adversary's action and test defenses, but to prioritize threats and train. Essentially, red team techniques are used in this book to view the United States from the perspective of terrorists, thereby understanding their mind-set, planning, methods, means, and target selection. "Thinking like a terrorist" improves counterterrorism.

The applications vary in level of difficulty; introductory students are capable of answering certain applications, whereas more difficult applications are appropriate for advanced students and practitioners. The reader will notice either assessment center or red team techniques in the applications, and some applications contain both techniques.

> A note of caution: A major purpose of the applications is to assist the reader in understanding the mind-set of terrorists and their thought processes when they plan and prepare for attacks. We are seeking to "think like a terrorist" because knowing one's enemy is a vital prerequisite to investigating terrorists, interrupting their plans, designing countermeasures, and taking other action. The reader is cautioned to not violate any laws or policies/procedures of any organization or to become involved in any unethical activity while engaged in the chapter applications or in the use of the educational and training materials contained in this book.

Part I of this book provides an historical foundation. Chapter 1 introduces the reader to the problems of international and domestic terrorism. It includes topics on history, religion, politics, typologies, and causes of terrorism. The chapter helps us to understand how we think about terrorism, because such perceptions influence our views on causes and solutions. Chapter 2 explains how terrorist groups are organized and their educational resources, training, methods of operation, and weapons. Part II concentrates on government and private sector action against terrorism. Chapter 3 provides an overview of U.S. government action against terrorism. It presents information on measuring terrorism, superpower status, the Cold War, the U.S. response to the 9/11 attacks, war and foreign policy, government and terrorist options, and *The 9/11 Commission Report*. Chapter 4 explains the development of the Department of Homeland Security, national strategies against terrorism, state and local government missions, intelligence, counterterrorism, and evaluation of nation strategies. Chapter 5 addresses constitutional issues, legislation and court decisions guiding government investigations, the rights of noncitizens, racial profiling, and civilian and military justice. Chapter 6 focuses on private sector action against terrorism. It includes the business of homeland security, privatizing counterterrorism, the private security industry, professional associations and industry groups, public–private sector partnerships, and citizen volunteer groups. Part III explains a wide variety of protection methods against "all hazards," besides terrorism. Chapter 7 concentrates on the processes and tools of risk management and emergency management, and the chapter shows how both are linked together in an "all hazards" approach to protect people and assets. Business and government perspectives on risk management and emergency management are discussed. The chapter includes the national response plan, the national incident management system, the national preparedness goal, and the role of the military in emergency management. Chapter 8 describes life safety and public safety and explains how both are linked together and merge during an emergency. Chapter topics cover regulations, standards, codes, building design, public safety agencies, and response to WMD. Chapter 9 concentrates on security, loss prevention, and "target-hardening" methods to protect people, buildings, and other assets from a variety of internal and external threats. Chapter 10 focuses on protecting critical infrastructures and key assets. An emphasis is placed on government efforts and cooperation between public and private sectors. Chapter 11 explains border and transportation security and covers major initiatives of the federal government. Part IV discusses the future. Chapter 12 anticipates the future of terrorism, technology, research, and education. A variety of viewpoints and tools are presented for anticipating future events. Chapter topics include antiterrorism technologies, how terrorists use technology, how research is assisting the Department of Homeland Security and the war against terrorism, and the development of academic programs. A glossary is located at the end of the book.

The author hopes students and practitioners improve their understanding of terrorism, other risks, and homeland security and seek creative, global solutions. The safety and security of many people are depending on these efforts.

Acknowledgments

I am thankful for the many people who supported the writing of this book. My family is at the top of the list. The typing and editorial work on the first draft was led by Laura Ashley Purpura, who was very helpful. The superb editorial team at Elsevier, specifically, Jenn Soucy, Mark Listewnik, and Kelly Weaver, are recognized for their intelligence, skills, and support. I am thankful for the many Homeland Security practitioners who answered questions and provided information. The reviewers who provided helpful feedback to improve this book are Richard Hill (University of Houston), Dr. Thomas O'Connor (Austin Peay State University), and Theodore Glickman (George Washington University). I am grateful to colleagues, counterterrorism instructors, librarians, and so many others who provided input for this book.

PART I

HISTORICAL FOUNDATION

CHAPTER 1

THE PROBLEM OF TERRORISM

OBJECTIVES

The study of this chapter will enable you to:
1. Trace the history of terrorism.
2. Examine the connection among religion, politics, and terrorism.
3. Appreciate the difficulty in defining terrorism.
4. List, explain, and compare typologies of terrorism.
5. Discuss the explanations and causes of terrorism.
6. Describe international terrorism.
7. Describe domestic terrorism.

KEY TERMS

Sicarii
Zealots
Assassins
Thugees
French Revolution
Reign of Terror
Ku Klux Klan
state terrorism
guerrilla warfare
Palestinian Liberation Organization
Fundamentalism
Islam
Prophet Muhammad
Muslims
Allah
Jesus
Koran
bible
Jihad
Sunni

Shiite
Crusades
domestic terrorism
international terrorism
classical ideological continuum
right-wing extremism
left-wing extremism
dissident terrorism
genocide
psychopathic personality disorder
social learning models
rational choice approach
structural theories
multiple marginality theory
relative deprivation theory
globalization
asymmetrical warfare
Abu Nidal organization
HAMAS
Hizballah

KEY TERMS

al-Qaida	extremism
internal state terrorism	Ruby Ridge incident
external state terrorism	Christian Identity
anarchism	Waco incident
ecoterrorism	Oklahoma City bombing
Animal Liberation Front	Patriot movement
Earth Liberation Front	

THE 9/11 ATTACKS

September 11, 2001 began as a typical workday in the United States. During the morning hours, commuters from across the nation hurried to their jobs. Airports were busy as passengers boarded flights to distant cities. Unfortunately, four flights in particular would be remembered in American history as fatal flights resulting in almost 2800 deaths, scores of injuries, and billions of dollars in property damage because four teams of al-Qaida terrorists were able to hijack the planes. Two of the flights took off from Logan Airport in Boston bound for Los Angeles. One was United Airlines Flight 175 that departed at 7:58 AM. The other was right behind it, American Airlines Flight 11 that took off at 7:59 AM. After entering New York State, Flight 11 suddenly turned south, followed the Hudson River to New York City and then at 8:45 AM. slammed into the North Tower of the World Trade Center. Many first thought the crash was an accident, but 20 minutes later opinions changed when, as many eyes and cameras were focused on the disaster, Flight 175 struck the South Tower. The shocking video of Flight 175 disappearing inside the South Tower, with an explosion on the opposite side, seemed surrealistic. Each jet was traveling about 300 mph and carrying about 60,000 lbs. of fuel upon impact. Witnesses on the street were shocked as both 110-story office buildings were burning and bodies, body parts, furniture, and assorted debris fell to the ground. Some leaped to their deaths or were thrown out by the explosions from the jet fuel. One man tried to climb down the outside of the building, was successful at first, but lost his grip and fell to his death. As office workers scrambled down the stairs to escape, many had horrendous injuries. Several were badly burned with skin peeling off their body as they somehow found the strength to keep moving. Those trapped in the floors above the fires had no choice but to pray and await their fate. As the intense heat bent the steel supporting the buildings, upper floors began to collapse onto lower floors. Eventually, both towers came crashing down, killing those trying to escape and the brave rescue workers (Figure 1-1).

A third flight involved in the attack, United Airlines Flight 93, took off from Newark International Airport at 8:01 AM en route to San Francisco. Near Cleveland, the flight abruptly headed toward Pittsburgh. Passengers on this flight had used their cell phones to talk to love ones who informed the passengers about the other attacks. As brave passengers fought to take back the plane, it crashed nose-first in an empty field 80 miles from Pittsburgh at 10:10 AM, killing all those on board. We can only imagine the struggle that ensued before the crash as passengers tried to save their lives. It was surmised that the target of this flight was the White House or the U.S. Capitol building.

The fourth plane, Flight 77, departed from Dulles International Airport in Virginia at 8:10 AM and headed toward Los Angeles. In a dive toward the Pentagon, it struck at 9:40 AM, killing 189 people and injuring many.

The 9/11 attacks are perhaps the most creative and most spectacular terrorist attacks that ever occurred in history. It is known that these suicide bombers were armed with box cutters, small knives and pepper spray, and claimed to have a bomb. Some passengers and crew had their throats slit as a way to terrorize and control the passengers and crew. The terrorists knew that the four planes would

THE 9/11 ATTACKS—Cont'd

Figure 1-1 ■ Ground Zero (World Trade Center, New York City) following 9/11 Attacks. U.S. Navy photo by Photographer's Mate 2nd Class Aaron Peterson. http://www.news.navy.mil/view_single.asp?id=137

be fully loaded with fuel because of the cross-country destinations, thus transforming each plane into a powerful suicide bomb, something like a "poor person's cruise missile." The 19 hijackers in the four teams received various training in, for example, the martial arts and flight training. In summary, the terrorists were successful in infiltrating the United States, avoiding police and intelligence services, coordinating and executing their plan, and bringing al-Qaida and its goals to the attention of the global community. At the same time, al-Qaida underestimated the reaction of the global community to the attacks. It unleashed a global war against terrorism and two regimes fell (Afghanistan and Iraq) from military action, primarily by the United States.

THE HISTORY OF TERRORISM

Terrorism has a long history. Interestingly, early examples of terrorism have roots in religious convictions (Laqueur, 2001; Rapoport, 1984). Ancient terrorists were "holy warriors" as we see with certain terrorists today. During the first century in the Middle East, the **Sicarii** and the **Zealots**, Jewish groups in ancient Palestine, fomented revolution against the occupying forces of Rome. The Sicarii instilled fear by using a dagger to stab Romans and Roman sympathizers during the day at crowded holiday festivities. The throngs provided cover for the killers and heightened terror because people never knew when an attacker would strike. The Zealots–Sicarii believed that by confronting the Romans, the Messiah would intervene and save the Jewish people. Between 66 and 70 AD, revolution became a reality. However, it ended in disaster for the Zealots–Sicarii. With thousands of Jews killed and the Jewish state in shambles, the survivors fled to the top of Masada where their abhorrence to being subjected to control by the Romans, who surrounded them, resulted in mass suicide. Today, we have the term "zealot," meaning fanatical partisan.

In analyzing the methods of the Zealot–Sicarii, and drawing parallels to modern-day terrorism, Poland (2005: 26–27) writes that "the primary purpose of the Sicarii terrorist strategy, like so many terrorist groups today, seems to be the provocation of indiscriminate countermeasures by the established political system and to deliberately provoke repression, reprisals, and counterterrorism." Poland refers to Northern Ireland where, for hundreds of years, Catholics have battled Protestants. Simonsen and Spindlove (2004: 70–75) explain that during the 16th century, James I, King of England, offered land in Ireland to Scottish settlers for the purpose of establishing the Protestant church in Ireland. Conflict ensued with Catholics, but the Protestant landowners prevailed. Catholics were regulated to a life of poverty. Poland cites incidents during the 20th century when Catholics, protesting peacefully against Protestants and British rule, were killed and wounded when police and British Security Forces overreacted. In one illegal march, on January 30, 1972, thirteen people were killed and twelve were wounded. A government investigation blamed demonstrators for creating a highly dangerous situation leading to inevitable violence. The deliberate provocation resulted in retaliation by the Provisional Irish Republican Army against Protestants and the British Army. Scores were killed or wounded by bombings and shootings.

Poland draws another parallel from the Zealot–Sicarii movement to recent times. The Irgun Zvai Leumi-al-Israel, led by Menachem Begin, terrorized the British military government of Palestine between 1942 and 1948 in an effort to establish a Jewish state. The Irgun perpetrated many bombings and assassinations, leading to a cycle of terror and counterterror. Manifestos of the Irgun argued "No Masada." Irgun fighters had actually studied terrorist methods of the Sicarii and the Irish Republican Army. Eventually, the British turned the problem over to the United Nations, and in 1948, the country of Israel was born.

The **Assassins** were another religious sect that used terrorism to purse their goals (Weinzierl, 2004: 31–32). This group gave us the term "assassin," which literally means "hashish-eater," a reference to the drug taking that allegedly occurred (perhaps rumor) prior to murdering someone. During the 11th and 12th centuries, this group evolved from the Shiites of the present-day Mideast and they believed that the Muslim community needed the purified version of Islam to prepare for the arrival of the Inman, the Chosen of God and leader of mankind. The Assassins waged a war against the majority Sunni Muslim population. Their terror strategies consisted of using unconventional means, establishing mountain fortifications from which terror attacks were launched, and using daggers like the Sicarii. *Although the Assassins were not successful in reforming the Islamic faith or in recruiting many converts, they are remembered for their innovations in terrorist strategies, namely the suicide mission and using disguise and deception.* Acting under God, they were promised a place in paradise for their ultimate sacrifice as they sought out and killed Sunni religious and political leaders.

We can see that contemporary terrorists have followed in the footsteps of the Assassins. Poland (2005: 28) writes: "This program of terror by a small religious sect to maintain its religious autonomy succeeded in terrorizing the Mideast for two centuries." He also notes that the Assassins inspired subsequent generations in a campaign of suicide bombings beginning in the 1980s to today by Hizballah, HAMAS, al Aqsa Martyrs Brigades, al-Qaida, and Islamic Jihad.

Thugees, from which the word "thug" originated, terrorized India for hundreds of years until the mid-19th century. This religious cult used a silk handkerchief to ritually terrorize and strangle victims who were chosen at random. This violence served as an offering to the Hindu goddess of destruction called Kali.

We can see that religion played a major role in early terrorism, as it does today. Weinzierl (2004: 32) notes the numerous religious wars through history, but emphasizes: "There are no examples of terrorism equaling the sustained campaign of the Zealots or the Assassins."

Secular motivations for terrorism can be seen in the **French Revolution**, a major historic milestone in the history of terrorism. The French Revolution ended absolute rule by French kings and strengthened the middle class. The **"Reign of Terror"** (1793–1794), from which the word "terrorism" evolved, saw leadership from Maximilien Robespierre, who led the Jabcobin government in executing, by guillotine, 12,000 people declared enemies of the Revolution. During the "Reign of Terror," terrorism was viewed in a positive light and Robespierre declared that terrorism is prompt justice and a consequence of democracy applied during a time of urgent need. In 1794, when Robespierre prepared a new list of traitors of the revolution, those fearing their names were on the list, executed him at the guillotine, and thus, the "Reign of Terror" ended. By this time, terrorism was beginning to be characterized in a negative light. Edmund Burke, a British statesman and writer, criticized the French Revolution and popularized the term "terrorism" in the English language as a repulsive action. This state terrorism of the French government was significant in the history of terrorism because the terror was not justified by religion or God, but by the masses to promote a political ideology (Weinberg and Davis, 1989: 24–25). Greenberg (2001: 1) writes: "Over the next century the Jacobin spirit infected Russia, Europe and the United States." Anarchist terrorist groups worked to foment revolution. In Russia, the Narodnaya Volya (meaning "people's will") was born in 1878 to destroy the Tsarist regime. They assassinated Alexander II in 1881, but the success sealed their fate because they were crushed by the Tsarist regime. This group did inspire other anarchists. During an anarchist-led labor protest at Chicago's Haymarket Square in 1886, a bomb was thrown into the crowd as police intervened. A riot ensued and several police and demonstrators were killed or injured. This incident hurt the labor movement. The anarchists were tried and sentenced to be hanged or imprisoned. A few years later the surviving anarchists were pardoned by the governor of Illinois. There had been insufficient evidence.

As the 19th century gave way to the 20th century, anarchists and others dissatisfied with established order adopted terrorism as a strategy to reach their goals (Laqueur, 1999). Terrorist attacks and assassinations occurred in France, Italy, Spain, Germany, Ireland, India, Japan, the Balkans, and the Ottoman Empire, among other areas. Bombs were detonated in cafes, theaters, and parades. In the United States, two Presidents were assassinated—Garfield (1881) and McKinley (1901). This era also saw an increase in nationalism and struggles for statehood as native groups revolted and used terrorism to free themselves from imperial control and European colonialism. The assassination of Archduke Ferdinand, the Austrian heir, in 1914, is a famous illustration of how terrorism was used for nationalistic goals. Gavrilo Princip, a member of the Pan-Serbian secret group called the Black Hand, planned to kill Ferdinand to help southern Slavs. The assassination actually became the precipitating incident that triggered World War I and doomed the Austrian Empire. We can see that terrorism can sometimes have a profound impact on world affairs.

Weinzierl (2004: 34–35) writes that before World War I, global terrorism was primarily left-wing oriented (see Dyson in subsequent pages). Then, conservative, right-wing groups also formed to maintain the status quo and prevent change. In the United States, the **Ku Klux Klan** (KKK), a right-wing group, was formed before World War I.

KU KLUX KLAN

The KKK was formed in 1865 by Confederate Army veterans who believed in the superiority of whites (Chalmers, 1981). The major goal of the KKK is to hinder the advancement of blacks, Catholics, Jews, and other minority groups. Klan methods include wearing white robes and hoods, burning crosses (at meetings and to frighten nonmembers), intimidation, tar and feathering, lynching, and murder.

The KKK evolved through periods of strength and weakness. In 1871, Congress passed the Force Bill that empowered the President to direct federal troops against the KKK. The Klan then disappeared. By the 1920s, it grew to 2 million members and used violence to further its goals. However, most members at the time were peaceful and saw the value of voting for political candidates most aligned with Klan doctrine. Public criticism of Klan violence and internal conflict led to another collapse of the Klan. During the mid-20th century, it was revived to oppose racial integration and it applied terrorist strategies, such as murder and bombing. Because of infighting, splits, court cases, FBI infiltration, and imprisonment, membership declined to about 5000 by the early 1970s. Since that time, the Klan has yet to see a major resurgence. However, *The Year in Hate*, published by the Southern Poverty Law Center (2004), a private group that collects intelligence on hate groups, claimed a surge in Klan rallies and cross-burnings in 2003. The Law Center's Web site reports a variety of news on hate activity, such as the White Knights official in Ohio who posted pipe bomb-making instructions on the Internet in response to organizers of a Martin Luther King celebration.

Because of the spread of communism, especially the Bolshevik Revolution of 1917 in Russia that overthrew the Czar, many political leaders worldwide became fearful and took brutal steps to eliminate communists, socialists, and other left-wing activists within their own countries. Repressive regimes included the Nazis led by Adolph Hitler in Germany and the fascists led by Benito Mussolini in Italy, both becoming allies during World War II. Violence by a government to repress dissidence among its own population, or supporting such violence in another country, is called **state terrorism**. The communist regime of the Soviet Union, existing for most of the 20th century, failed to produce the utopia and equality proclaimed by Karl Marx's theories, it created a consumer-starved population and economic disaster that eventually caused its own collapse, and it was the superpower that battled the United States in a Cold War for decades after World War II. Its leader, Joseph Stalin, ruled the Soviet Union from 1929 to 1953 and was responsible for state terrorism in the form of millions of Soviet citizens either being executed or sent to labor camps.

Following the end of World War II in 1945, a resurgence of nationalism among European colonies in the Middle East, Asia, and Africa resulted in violent uprisings. A combination of **guerrilla warfare** and terrorism occurred, with the former being characterized by larger units resembling the military and operating from a geographic area over which they controlled and the latter involving smaller groups blending into the population and planning spectacular attacks for maximum media attention.

Examples of successful guerrilla wars aiming for national liberation or social revolution can be seen with Mao Tse-tung in China, Ho Chi Minh in Vietnam, and Fidel Castro in Cuba. In contrast, the Irgun, led by Menachem Begin, in an effort to force the British from Palestine, used a bombing campaign. The Irgun's most spectacular attack was the 1946 bombing of Jerusalem's King David Hotel, the site of British Army headquarters. This devastating attack killed 91 people, and within 2 years, the country of Israel came into existence. Later, Begin became prime minister of Israel, an illustration of a terrorist gaining legitimate political power (Weinzierl, 2004: 35).

According to Greenberg (2001), it was Algeria's Front de Liberation Nationale (FLN), fighting for independence from France in the 1950s, that set the tone for terrorism to come. The FLN raised the cost to France for its colonialism by bombing coastal tourist resorts, thereby randomly killing French families on vacation. By the 1960s, this precedent was copied worldwide by Palestinian and Irish nationalists, Marxists in Africa and Latin America, the Weather Underground in the United States, the Marxist Baader–Meinhoff Gang in Germany, and the Red Brigades in Italy. Terrorist methods were being applied not only by nationalists seeking independence, but also by those with ethnic and ideological agendas.

RED BRIGADES MURDER ALDO MORO

Aldo Moro was a famous politician who served as premier of Italy five times. He was influential in both his life and his death. One of his greatest accomplishments was as President of the Christian Democratic party when he worked out a deal for a new government in Italy whereby the communists would be supporting their traditional enemies—Christian Democrats. Following this political success, he was accused of being a Trojan horse for communism (Drake, 1995).

Aldo Moro was a classic case of a creature of habit. Moro was extremely predictable. He would leave his home in the morning to attend mass at a nearby church. Shortly after 9:00 AM he was en route to his office. The route was the same each morning, even though plans existed for alternatives. Although five armed men guarded Moro, he met an unfortunate fate. On the morning of March 16, 1978, an attack characterized by military precision enabled terrorists to block Moro's vehicle and a following police car. Then, on the narrow street, four gunmen hiding behind a hedge opened fire. Moro's bodyguard turned around from the front seat and pushed him down as the gun battle erupted. Eighty rounds hit the police car. Three policemen, Moro's driver, and a bodyguard were killed. Moro was dragged by his feet from the car. Almost 2 months later Moro was found dead in a car in Rome. The Red Brigades who killed Moro hoped that his death would cause the collapse of the capitalist establishment in Italy and clear a path for a Marxist–Leninist revolution. It never happened.

It was during the 1970s that Yasser Arafat's **Palestinian Liberation Organization** (PLO), and its splinter groups, while locked in a cycle of shocking violence with Israel, pioneered the hijacking of jet airlines to publicize their goal of Palestinian statehood. Black September, as one splinter group was known, staged an outrageous attack at the 1972 Munich Olympics in Germany and murdered 11 Israeli athletes (Figure 1-2). This attack, which became a major, global media event, inspired other terrorists.

During the mid-1980s, state-sponsored terrorism grew again and supported terrorist attacks against Western targets in the Middle East. Sponsors of terrorism included Syria, Libya, Iran, Iraq, and North Korea. More recently, the religion–terrorism mixture has grown in intensity.

RELIGION, POLITICS, AND TERRORISM

The relationship between religion and terrorism deserves special attention. We have seen in the long history of terrorism that this mixture has appeared over and over again, and many wars have been fought because of religious differences. At the same time, confusion may arise over whether a terrorist group has a religious agenda, a political agenda, or both. Wilkinson (2003: 124) writes that Osama bin Laden and his al-Qaida network portray themselves as fighting a holy war and use religious language to legitimize their terrorist attacks. However, their political agenda is to force the U.S. military to withdraw from the Middle East, they want to overthrow regimes that side with the West and fail to follow "true" Islam, and they seek to unite all Muslims.

Figure 1-2 ■ PLO terrorists disguised themselves as athletes and used gym bags to smuggle weapons (e.g., AK-47) into the 1972 Munich Olympics before killing Israeli athletes, as depicted here by Munich Police.

Al-Qaida uses the Muslim communities and mosques in the West to recruit, seek aid, and conduct covert operations, even though the majority of Muslims who live in the West reject terrorism. Jordan and Boix (2004) write that the methods and terrorism of al-Qaida could endanger the social relationships between Muslims and non-Muslims in the same country.

In an article entitled "Why Do They Hate Us?," Peter Ford (2001) presents numerous opinions and perceptions of the United States by Arabs and others. Many Arabs see the carnage of 9/11 as retribution for unjust policies by America. The Israeli–Palestinian conflict is a primary topic of contention. The perception is that Israel can get away with murder and the United States will turn a blind eye. Arab media shows countless photos of Israeli soldiers killing and wounding Palestinians and Israeli tanks plowing through Palestinian neighborhoods. Ford refers to the dominance of state-run media in the Middle East and how it often fans the flames of anti-American and anti-Israeli feelings because it helps divert citizens away from the shortcomings of their own government.

Ford goes on to cover widespread resentment from around the globe toward America and its policies. It is common knowledge that the United States has provided billions of dollars of military and economic aid to Israel and other regional allies to strengthen U.S. interests in the oil-rich region. Ford refers to the popular sympathy that Osama bin Laden draws when bin Laden speaks about injustices to Palestinians and Iraqis, the presence of U.S. troops in Saudi Arabia, and the repressive and corrupt regimes of U.S.-backed Gulf states.

Ford quotes an Indonesian sociologist and talk-show host who says [referring to America] "you are a superpower, you are a military superpower, and you can do whatever you want. People don't like that, and this is dangerous."

Another Ford interviewee states that if Americans are concerned about the deaths from 9/11, they should also remember the deaths in Palestine, Chechnya, Bosnia, and Kashmir. Ford writes: "It is this double standard that creates hatred." According to Ford, Middle Easterners argue that if the United States does not rethink the policies that cause anti-American sentiment, trying to root out terrorism will fail.

Greenberg (2001) notes that as the PLO distanced itself from using terrorism in order to convince others that they could lead a new government, Islamic fundamentalism grew in the Middle East. (**Fundamentalism** refers to a strict adherence to the basic tenants of a belief system to reach purity in that belief system as defined by its leaders; it fosters intolerance of others' beliefs and it can generate terrorism.) Greenberg points out that the causes of this growth include the 1979 Israel–Egypt peace agreement, the Iranian revolution, and the Soviet invasion of Afghanistan. He adds that Islamic fundamentalists fear the spread of satanic Western values and influence and they believe that "to destroy America is to do God's work." Of great concern is how dangerous this mixture of religion and terrorism has become, as evidenced by the al-Qaida attacks of September 11, 2001. Future attacks might be more devastating and include weapons of mass destruction. Although al-Qaida has received much attention, we should not lose sight of the "big picture" of global terrorism and the need for broad solutions as covered in subsequent chapters.

Bruce Hoffman (1998) compares eras of terrorism as a way to further understand the relationship between religion and terrorism. He points to terrorism during the Cold War that was motivated by communist ideologies (Red Brigades of Italy and Japanese Red Army) and ethnonationalist and separatist movements (Irish Republican Army and Basque Separatists). Hoffman claims that these groups sought to avoid mass casualties to prevent a public backlash or intense government reaction. When the Cold War ended with the breakup of the Soviet Union, communist ideology lost its popularity. According to Hoffman, a new era of terrorism emerged with a variety of agendas and limited regard for public image and mass casualties. His examples include the 1995 sarin nerve gas attack in a Tokyo subway by Aum Shinrikyo (a Japanese religious cult) and the truck bombing of the Alfred P. Murrah Federal Office Building in Oklahoma City in 1995 by the Christian Patriots (an antigovernment Christian White Supremacist group). Hoffman writes that terrorism is not just a strategy of Islamic militants. Extremists from other religions are involved in terrorism.

ISLAM

Griset and Mahan (2003: 49) write that many Americans and Europeans equate Islam with terrorism. These authors emphasize that this is incorrect and that most Muslims, even most fundamentalists, are not terrorists.

Griset and Mahan explain the victimization of Muslims in numerous conflicts through history. Hundreds of thousands were killed in the war between Iran and Iraq, the civil wars in Afghanistan and Algeria, and the war between Chechnya and Russia. Indonesia and Africa are other locations marked by the death of Muslims. Griset and Mahan note: "Terrorism has destroyed the lives of many Muslims and non-Muslims throughout the world."

Continued

ISLAM—Cont'd

Islam is one of the world's largest religions and refers to the religious doctrine preached by the **Prophet Muhammad** during the AD 600s. Those who believe in this doctrine are called **Muslims**. Over one-fifth of the global population is Muslim and they reside in countries throughout the world, including Pakistan, Bangladesh, Indonesia, India, Turkey, Egypt, Iran, England, and the United States.

Muhammad was an Arab born in Mecca who believed he was God's messenger and his calling was to guide his people to worship God (**Allah**). Like Christianity and Judaism, Islam emphasizes that there is only one God. **Jesus** and other religious leaders are recognized as prophets, but Muhammad is worshipped by Muslims as the last and greatest prophet. Islam has the **Koran** and, like the **bible**, it forbids lying, stealing, adultery, and murder. It teaches honor for parents, kindness, honesty, honor, courage, and generosity. The Koran condemns mistrust and cruelty. Muslims are required to affirm the faith, pray five times a day while facing Mecca, give alms, fast during the month of Ramadan, and make a pilgrimage to Mecca. Angels in heaven record behavior on earth. Death is the gate to eternal life. When the judgment day arrives, Muslims will go to heaven or hell. One doctrine of Islam is the **jihad** or holy war, wherein Muslims who perish defending Islam are rewarded in heaven.

Like Jesus, when Muhammad began preaching, the progress was slow. Some plotted to kill him. Eventually, Islam spread throughout the Middle East and North Africa, with conquests begun from Mecca and Medina. When Muhammad died in AD 632, Abu Bakr was elected caliph (Muslim ruler). He favored the jihad, as did subsequent generations of caliphs who ruled empires and were religious/political leaders. Conflicts among Muslims over the rightful succession of caliphs led to disputes within Islam. Civil war resulted in two Muslim sects that remain today, along with a history of conflict. The **Sunni** branch is the larger of the two sects and members dominate the Middle East. They are followers of the teachings of Muhammad. Al-Qaida is primarily Sunni. **Shiite** is the minority sect. They believe that Ali, cousin and son-in-law of Muhammad, is the Prophet of Islam. Shiite activism promoted the Iranian revolution of 1979 and emphasized that Islam should be lived as a tool of the oppressed, besides being a religious doctrine. Although Iraq is mostly Shiite, as is Iran, Iraq was ruled by the Sunni minority in Iraq under Saddam Hussein, until his regime was toppled by U.S.-led forces in 2003. The conflict that followed pitted the formerly oppressed Shiites (supported by coalition forces to establish a new government) against Sunnis.

In 732 AD, the Muslim empire included land from Spain to India, but when western Europe was threatened, Charles Martel led a victorious army at the Battle of Poitiers, also known as the Battle of Tours (Reich, 1989). Conflict between caliphs and the West, through history, is at the foundation of the doctrine of al-Qaida and other groups. This brings us to the **Crusades** to help us in understanding the long history of religion and violence. These eight major military expeditions originated in western Europe between 1096 and 1270 (during the Middle Ages) with the purpose of recapturing Palestine from the Muslims because it was the area where Jesus had lived. In fact, Jerusalem is considered holy land to Muslims, Christians, and Jews. This was an era when western Europe was expanding its economy and Christianity. Kings, nobles, knights, and peasants joined the Crusades and fought, *not only for Christianity, but also for territory and wealth*. Battles were won and lost, Jerusalem changed hands multiple times, and there was no significant impact, except for expanded trade. Subsequent attempts at organizing crusades failed as Europe turned its attention westward to the Atlantic Ocean toward the New World. The Holy Land was left to the Muslims (Queller, 1989).

CRITICAL THINKING:

Through history, why has there been so much violence in the name of religion?

ISRAELIS AND PALESTINIANS

The conflict between the Israelis and the Palestinians has existed for many years. One significant event for the Jewish people was the 1917 British Balfour Declaration, which helped establish a national homeland for Jewish people in Palestine. The British motivation was to gain Jewish support in the United States and in Britain for the British effort to seize Palestine from the Ottoman Empire during World War I. The British also promised independence to Arab groups in the Middle East for their support. When World War I ended and the Ottomans were defeated, Britain assisted Palestinian Jews in developing their homeland. Controversy arose over Jewish immigration. However, the rise of anti-Semitism before and during World War II caused an increase in Jewish immigration to Palestine. Civil War erupted between Jews and Arab Palestinians under British rule in 1937. In 1947, the United Nations divided Palestine into an Arab state and a Jewish state, with the Holy City of Jerusalem under international control. Arabs disagreed with the plan and fighting erupted again. Britain could not longer deal with the violence and the United Nations continued its involvement. By 1948, the country of Israel was formed but, immediately, Egypt, Syria, Lebanon, Iraq, and Jordan attacked Israel. By the following year, Israeli military successes had gained control of half the land planned for the new Arab state, plus thousands of hostile Arab residents. The violence continued with cross-border fighting by both sides and United Nations intervention in 1956, backed by both the United States and Soviet Union. By 1967, United Nations peacekeepers were removed and then the Six-Day War showed the superiority of the Israeli armed forces. Before their ground forces won over those of the Arabs, Israeli fighter jets destroyed almost the entire air forces of Egypt, Jordan, and Syria. Israel seized more land, including Egypt's Sinai Peninsula, the Gaza Strip, Syria's Golan Heights, and the West Bank, which includes the eastern half of Jerusalem. Israel refused to withdraw from occupied areas unless the Arab countries accepted Israel's right to exist. Within the Gaza Strip and West Bank, Israel controlled about one million angry Palestinians.

We have seen through history that when superior armed forces cannot be defeated by conventional means, guerrilla and terrorist methods are a viable option. Enter the Palestine Liberation Organization that became popular in the Middle East following the Six-Day War. Essentially, the PLO saw that Arab allies were unable to drive Israeli armed forces from occupied lands, so the PLO began a campaign of terrorism. The PLO is supported by Palestinian Arab leaders and groups with the goal of forming an Arab state in Palestine. New rounds of fighting ensued between Arabs and Israelis.

In 1973, the Yom Kippur War broke out when Egypt and Syria attacked Israel. The attack came on the most sacred Jewish holy day of Yom Kippur. Initial Arab successes failed and Israel won the war.

During the late 1970s, President Jimmy Carter met with Egyptian President Anwar Sadat and Israeli Prime Minister Menachem Begin at Camp David, Maryland. The meeting resulted in the Camp David Accords that aimed for peace. Israel and Egypt signed a peace treaty and Israel withdrew from the Sinai Peninsula, but efforts at a broader peace in the Middle East were not successful. Sadat and Begin received the Nobel Peace Prize in 1978. Sadat was assassinated in 1981 during a military parade in Egypt because of his moderation toward Israel. The PLO and other groups continued fighting with Israel (Reich, 1989). During the last few years, as Israeli forces continue to withdraw from occupied lands, withdrawals are marred by violence from both sides.

CRITICAL THINKING:

What is the current state of Israeli–Palestinian relations? What is your opinion of the situation and what solutions can you offer?

WHAT IS TERRORISM?

The definition of terrorism varies over time and among agencies of government, disciplines, and political viewpoints. There is general disagreement over the definition of terrorism and many definitions exist (Poland, 1988: 9–10). The following definitions of terrorism serve as a beginning point as we seek to understand its meaning.

The United States Department of State (April 2003) chooses the definition of terrorism contained in Title 22 of the U.S. Code, Section 2656f(d): "The term 'terrorism' means premeditated, politically motivated violence perpetrated against noncombatant [e.g., civilians; military personnel who are unarmed and/or not on duty] targets by sub national groups or clandestine agents, usually intended to influence an audience."

The United States Department of Defense (Military Periscope, 2004) defines terrorism as follows: "The unlawful use or threatened use of force or violence against individuals or property to coerce or intimidate governments or societies, often to achieve political, religious, or ideological objectives."

The FBI (n.d.) defines terrorism as "the unlawful use of force or violence against persons or property to intimidate or coerce a government, the civilian population, or any segment thereof, in furtherance of political or social objectives."

The United Nations (2003) offers an interesting perspective on the definition of terrorism. United Nations member states have debated definitions of terrorism for decades, and today there is no agreed-upon definition. It has been argued that one state's "terrorism" is another state's "freedom fighter." Simply put, terrorism is a "dirty word" drenched in emotion, and it describes what the "other guy" has done. The lack of agreement on a definition has been a major obstacle to meaningful international countermeasures. A similar problem is faced by the International Criminal Police Organization (INTERPOL). This organization, headquartered in Lyons, France, is not a global police force, but rather a collaborative effort of about 181 nations whose aim is to promote the widest possible mutual assistance to prevent and suppress crime. Although INTERPOL's efforts are minimal when compared to the activities of police agencies of many nations, its constitution forbids action involving political, military, religious, or racial issues. Thus, Western police counterterrorism efforts may conflict with police in Arab nations (Purpura, 1997: 143–144; Deflem and Maybin, 2005: 175–191).

Bruce Hoffman (1998), author of *Inside Terrorism*, explains not only the difficulty of defining terrorism, but also how the meaning of the term has changed over time and how the meaning varies among multiple viewpoints and contexts. Today, for example, terrorism has negative connotations but, as we learned earlier, during the French Revolution, a system of terror was seen in a positive light as a catalyst to promote democratic ideals. The violence between Israel and the Palestinians over the issue of a Palestinian state provides an illustration of the debate over which side practices terrorism. Hoffman argues, like the United Nations, that terrorism is such an ambiguous term, with constantly changing meanings, that the international community is stymied in its efforts to control it.

CONTEXTS OF TERRORISM

White (2003: 5–7) writes: "it is more helpful to list the contexts of terrorism than to memorize a variety of definitions." Here is a summary of White's views, with examples, of how the definition of terrorism has changed under various contexts. He writes that there are an endless number of contextual factors that influence the changing use of the word "terrorism."

CONTEXTS OF TERRORISM—Cont'd

History

Following the French revolution, the meaning of the term referred to violent revolutionaries of the 1800s. During the late 1800s and the 1900s, "terrorism" was a label placed on labor unions, anarchists, and nationalist groups. From the 1960s to early 1980s, the term was applied to left-wing groups. The late 1900s saw the term attached to the hate movement and attackers sponsored by rogue regimes. The beginning of the 21st century has seen the term change again and used to label large groups that are independent of a state, religious fanatics, and violent groups who favor a specific cause.

Conflict

The meaning of terrorism is applied within the context of war and either side of a conflict can employ the label. Examples are devastating commando raids or an attack by an air force that destroys a city and its civilian population. During World War II, Allied and German air forces obliterated each other's cities.

Political Power

Government can justify police and military action, and reduced civil liberties, when an opposition group is labeled as terrorists.

Repression

Governments themselves use domestic terrorism [i.e., state terrorism] to maintain the status quo. Examples include the brutality of Joseph Stalin who ruled the Soviet Union, Latin American dictators, and Saddam Hussein in Iraq, until the US toppled his regime by force.

Media

Journalists sometimes use the term "terrorism" to sensationalize a story. There is no standard that they follow in their use of the term.

Crime

All terrorism is criminal behavior. Exceptions are when government uses repression or during times of conflict. (Here again, we are dealing with perspectives on the use of the term.)

Religion

Religious groups may need to destroy others who are "wrong" in their beliefs. A religious group may become so fanatical about a cause that they establish a surrogate religion and use violence to further their cause.

Specific Forms

The term "terrorism" has been attached to numerous words to produce a specific context. Examples are "cyberterrorism" and "narcoterrorism." (Both terms are explained in the next chapter.)

William Dyson (2001: 17–31), a career FBI agent and terrorism specialist, writes that during the early 1970s the term "terrorism" began to be applied as a new term to acts of extreme political violence and the offenders came to be called "terrorists." Dyson is not clear on who first employed the term, the media or law enforcement. During this time, other terms began to wane. For instance, anti-Vietnam War activists were called "Communists" or "new left radicals," and Ku Klux Klan members were known as "segregationists" or "Klansmen." Once the term "terrorism" gained momentum, it began to be applied broadly to include groups using extreme violence intended to generate fear, with examples being street gangs, motorcycle gangs, and violent labor union members. Dyson does not view these groups as being terrorists.

Dyson notes that the term "terrorism" has been applied by various groups to opposing groups. A freedom-of-choice group might label an antiabortion group as terrorists or a religious or ethnic group may do the same with a group subjecting them to violent victimization.

Dyson (2001: 31) questions whether revolution, civil war, and guerrilla war are terrorism because of the large numbers of people involved. Are the American Revolution for independence from the British or the South's violence during the American Civil War acts of terrorism? Dyson again narrows the definition of terrorism and writes that although terrorism applies extreme violence intended to cause a government or population to modify its direction, terrorists operate as individuals or small groups. Interestingly, White (2003: 5) argues that today terrorism also refers to large groups. Here are elements from definitions of terrorism compiled from government agencies and other sources (Combs, 2003: 17; Simonsen and Spindlove, 2004: 7):

- unexpected, premeditated, unlawful violence
- against innocent persons and property
- often directed at "soft targets" (i.e., innocent persons and property characterized by limited or no security)
- staged to produce media attention and fear beyond the immediate victims
- political, religious, or ideological objectives
- conducted by an organization with a chain of command or conspiratorial cell structure
- conducted by a subnational group or nonstate entity

IS "TERRORISM" A LOOSE LABEL?

Early in the 2004 presidential election year, at a private White House meeting of Republican governors, Education Secretary Rod Paige called the nation's largest teacher's union a "terrorist organization." Prominent Democrats criticized Paige's speech. Reg Weaver, president of the 2.7-million-member National Education Association, denounced Paige's comments as "pathetic" and stated that the words were "not a laughing matter." The union planned to sue the Bush administration over lack of funding under the "No Child Left Behind" schools law (Associated Press, February 24, 2004).

TYPOLOGIES OF TERRORISM

Numerous typologies of terrorism are offered by scholars. White (2003: 10) writes that "a typology is a classification system, and there are as many typologies of terrorism as there are definitions."

Combs (2003: 14–16) provides a critical analysis of typologies. She explains that typologies are problematic because

- among scholars, they offer similar categories with different labels.
- the categories may overlap within an individual scholar's typology and among scholars' typologies.
- a detailed review of typologies would not significantly help us in formulating a definition of contemporary terrorism.
- a wide variety of acts fall under the various typologies.

White (2003: 10–11) writes of advantages of typologies over definitions:

- a typology offers a range of terrorist activities better than most definitions.
- a typology can help pinpoint the level (i.e., local, national, or international) and kind of terrorism to be studied and then the type of response can be determined.
- the specific information gained through typologies helps prevent the heated debates over the meaning of terrorism.

White explains that typologies have weaknesses:

- typologies are generalizations of the constantly changing process of terrorism.
- each terrorist event must be studied in its specific social, historical, and political circumstances.
- reality may be distorted to fit a particular typology (e.g., researcher bias).

Let us review a few typologies of terrorism from scholars so we can compare and contrast their work. Dyson (2001: 20–31) divides terrorism into two broad categories, domestic and international: "**Domestic terrorism** is politically oriented extreme violence that is perpetrated by residents of a country within that country." "**International terrorism** is politically oriented extreme violence that is perpetrated by residents or representatives of one or more countries against the interests of another country, or by members of a violent politically directed organization not affiliated with the country being attacked." Dyson does admit to problems with these two major categories, such as certain types of terrorism overlapping both. Here is a summary of Dyson's other typologies with his examples.

> *Left-wing extremism.* The ideology of this typology is based on communism. In theory, the government owns the means of production and provides for the needs of all citizens in a classless, equal society. [History has shown this ideology to be faulty, as seen in the collapse of the Soviet Union, which had a communist party membership who enjoyed privileges and consumer goods that were unavailable to most Soviet citizens.]

> *Right-wing extremism.* This typology is characterized by hate and prejudice. Representative groups are neo-Nazi and Ku Klux Klan.

> *Single-issue or special interest terrorism.* This typology focuses on a specific issue. Examples of such causes are animal rights, protection of the environment, and abortion. Theodore Kaczynski, dubbed the "Unabomber," feared the loss of human dignity to technology and detonated bombs that killed and maimed people across the country between 1978 and 1995 until the FBI arrested him.

> *Religious terrorism.* Extreme violence is used by religious groups to force changes. Such terrorists see their cause and violence blessed by God.

> *National or ethnic terrorism.* The goal of these terrorists is to use violence to secure a homeland for their group. This is often domestic terrorism in that the terrorist group is battling the government for control of land. Factions in Northern Ireland have fought with the British for many years over the issue of independence; this conflict overlaps religious terrorism because of violence between Catholics and Protestants in Northern Ireland.

> *Race-based or hate terrorism.* This typology is characterized by violence against a hated group. Furthermore, government, businesses, and others who are sympathetic to the hated group may also be victimized by terrorism. Several right-wing terrorist groups espouse hate against non-Whites and Jews. The hate of certain groups also characterizes religious and ethnic terrorists.

RIGHT-WING AND LEFT-WING EXTREMISM DEFINED

Gus Martin (2003: 7, 23) provides helpful explanations for our understanding of extremism. He refers to the **classical ideological continuum** containing extremes on opposite ends. Ideologies are systems of belief from theories that explain human sociopolitical conditions. Martin draws on the French Revolution to explain the roots of the continuum, also called the political spectrum. He refers to the French assembly at the time that was composed of ideological divisions: on the left sat those favoring radical change, on the right sat those favoring the old order or slow change, and in the middle sat those who could not decide on change.

Martin offers these definitions: "**Right-wing extremism** is generally a reaction against a perceived threat to a group's value system, its presumption of superiority, or its sense of specialness. Rightists often try to preserve their value system and special status by aggressively asserting this status."

"**Left-wing extremism** is future oriented, seeking to reform or destroy an existing system prior to building a new and just society."

Ted Gurr (1989) writes of a four-category typology of terrorism. His work is explained by Barkan and Bryjak (2004), who offer historical examples of each category as summarized next.

Vigilante terrorism. This typology is characterized by violence by private citizens against other private citizens to express hatred or to resist social change. One example is the KKK. According to Gurr, issue-oriented terrorism (e.g., abortion, animal rights, and environmental extremists) is included in vigilante terrorism.

Insurgent terrorism. This form of terrorism is committed by private groups against public authorities to seek radical political change. These subgroups are ethnic separatist and émigré groups, left-wing radical organizations, and right-wing, racist, antigovernment, and survivalist type. [This type of terrorism is also called **dissident terrorism** (i.e., against an established political or social order) or "terror from below." The U.S.-led invasion of Iraq in 2003 was followed by an insurgency.]

Transnational terrorism. It begins in one country and culminates in another. In one subcategory, individuals residing in one country attack targets in another country. This is also call international terrorism. An example is the 1988 bombing of Pan American Flight 103 with 289 people on board that exploded over Lockerbie, Scotland. A bomb was hidden in a radio cassette player inside a suitcase. Two Libyan intelligence agents were implicated. In the other subcategory, individuals born and raised in one country move to a target country and prepare for an attack, usually over several months or years. The 9/11 attackers were from four Middle-Eastern countries.

State terrorism. This typology (also called "terror from above") is characterized by a government using violence against its own population to eliminate dissent or to increase political power. The methods include kidnapping, torture, execution, assassination, and mass murder. Because the government makes the law, these acts are "legal." Examples of state terrorism are the victimization of the American Indians by early settlers and the U.S. Army, the mass murder of six million Jews by the Nazis during World War II (Figures 1-3 and 1-4), and the use of nerve gas against the Kurds of Northern Iraq during the regime of Saddam Hussein. These killings are also called **genocide**, defined as the deliberate and systematic extermination of a specific group.

Figure 1-3 ■ Dachau concentration camp, used by the Nazis during World War II in a program of genocide against Jews and other groups.

Figure 1-4 ■ Ovens at Dachau concentration camp used to dispose of corpses.

HOW DO WE ORGANIZE OUR THINKING ABOUT TERRORISM?

With so much debate surrounding terrorism, and what to do about the problem of terrorism, a method is needed to organize our thinking. Kegley (2003: 10–13) offers such a method. He recommends dividing the subject into three parts: (1) definition and characteristics, (2) causes, and (3) methods of control. This approach assists us with both our critical thinking of terrorism and in understanding our biases. Kegley points out that how we define terrorism influences our perceptions of causes and methods of control. He explains that those who view terrorism as a method used by the impoverished or persecuted tend to claim that terrorism is rooted in an environment of oppression and injustice, whereas those who see terrorism as just another mode of violent conflict tie terrorism to ideologies that favor violence to achieve political goals. In reference to the 9/11 attacks, Kegley adds to his illustrations by discussing the perspectives of those who claim that the terrorists were suicidal maniacs and see such terrorists as psychopaths who are difficult to deter.

CRITICAL THINKING:

Do you view the 9/11 terrorists as mentally disturbed? Explain your answer.

EXPLANATIONS AND CAUSES OF TERRORISM

Kegley (2003: 10–11) seeks objectivity and balance in his publication on explanations and causes of terrorism. He writes that to most, terrorism is like a disease requiring a remedy. Conversely, "others see terrorism as a legitimate response to unjustified repression, and accordingly view it not as a curse but as a cure." Kegley emphasizes that we must understand the root causes of terrorism if we are to plan successful solutions. The causes include perceived political, social, and economic inequities, as well as the intrusion of one culture on another. The explanations and causes of terrorism are offered from many perspectives. Three major categories are psychological, rational choice, and structural. What follows here is a summary of research, including the work of Clayton *et al.* (2003).

PSYCHOLOGICAL EXPLANATIONS

Silke (1998: 51–69) writes that most terrorists feel that they are doing nothing wrong when they kill, injure, and destroy property. He claims that terrorists are not mentally ill, but that they share a psychological condition known as **psychopathic personality disorder** (also called antisocial personality disorder), which is the absence of empathy for others. He cites the case of Nezar Hindawi, who in 1986, sent his pregnant Irish girlfriend on an El Al flight to Israel, claiming that he would marry her soon. She apparently was not aware that Hindawi had hid a bomb from the Abu Nidal Organization in her belongings.

According to Reich (1990), because of the complex nature of terrorism, it is futile to attribute generalized psychological characteristics to all terrorists. Research on the personal backgrounds of terrorists shows conflicting results. Research shows that terrorists were unsuccessful in their personal lives, jobs, and educations. At the same time, research shows terrorists from middle-class or upper-class backgrounds with university education (Clayton *et al.*, 2003). Palestinian suicide bombers who terrorized Israel were often poor, with limited education and hope for the future. Their salvation was paradise after killing Jews. Conversely, the 9/11 terrorists were well-educated professionals living middle-class lives.

Several researchers report that terrorists are not mentally disturbed. The recruiting process to obtain new recruits is selective, as psychopathology can result in friction within a terrorist group and when completing missions (Hudson, 1999). Terrorists typically rationalize and minimize their actions by referring to historical events (Bandura, 1990). Clayton *et al.* (2003) note that right-wing separatist groups in the United States argue that the U.S. democratic system was born from violent rebellion. Clayton *et al.* (2003: 21–22) cite additional research results under the psychological category.

- Terrorists generally are not impulsive. They plan carefully and are patient until everything is in place.
- However, terrorists are prone to take risks.
- Many terrorists are stimulus seekers who are attracted to stressful situations and are bored when inactive.
- Terrorist leaders socially "engineer" the emotions of subordinates. The emotions are judged for suitability and norms emerge.
- Violent behavior develops through a process of gradual moral disengagement. Previously abhorrent violence is eventually accomplished callously.

Social learning models offer explanations for terrorism. Bandura (1977) emphasizes learning through observing and modeling the behaviors of others. Many terrorists grow up in locations where violence is both the norm and a daily event. Terrorists also follow family tradition, as is the case with some groups of Palestinians (Silke, 2001: 580–581). The repeated success of aggressive behavior encourages groups to engage in violence. Terrorists capitalize on this association between violence and success, and it is strengthened through brainwashing, modeling, and reinforcement within terrorist groups (Tedeschi and Felson, 1994).

RATIONAL CHOICE EXPLANATIONS

Crenshaw (1990) writes that *terrorism is a logical political choice among alternative actions.* She favors studying terrorism through a **rational choice approach** because terrorist groups can be compared to some standard of rationality. Also, the quality of their decisions can be studied. This approach leads to numerous questions for research. Examples include the following. Can the group judge the consequences of action? What are the true motives of the group? Is the group likely to use weapons of mass destruction? Rational choice explanations help us understand the circumstances surrounding terrorist decisions to choose violence. For instance, global media exposure of terrorist violence and its aims can be beneficial to the terrorist group. However, rational choices can also harm the group's agenda. Terrorism can result in government repression that hinders the group. Conversely, government repression can fuel opposition to the government among the general population and can generate sympathy for the terrorist cause.

Another aspect of rational choice is the timing of terrorist attacks. Terrorists may attack on an anniversary of a significant event or on an enemy's holy day or national holiday. Timothy McVeigh blew up the Alfred P. Murrah Federal Building in Oklahoma City on the second anniversary of the deaths of the Branch Davidians in Waco, Texas, a clash he blamed on the FBI.

STRUCTURAL EXPLANATIONS

Structural theories are a major part of sociological thought. Sociological research (Calhoun *et al.*, 2001: 27 and 429) also shows that terrorism is not the work of deranged individuals who are oblivious to social norms. Sociologists explain terrorism as a form of social action: "behavior which is shaped by a person's understandings, interpretations, and intentions and which is in response to, coordinated with, or oriented toward the actions of others." Terrorists respond to social–structural conditions (i.e., stable, enduring patterns of social relationship or social positions) that they are powerless to deal with through conventional political or military methods.

These conditions include citizen access to services, rights, and protection. The social structures include the laws and policies of government, the role of police and military forces, and the geographic location of the group. Social and political oppression in an environment of weak social structures may result in terrorism and revolution.

Similarly, **multiple marginality theory**, often associated with gangs (Martin, 2005: 325), involves the convergence of several marginalizing factors that result in a group's feeling of alienation, isolation, dislocation, and powerlessness. Marginalizing factors include social, psychological, economic, and political components. History is replete with numerous ethnic, racial, and religious groups that have suffered under the dominance of more powerful groups, while being denied adequate amenities and rights. The realization of being marginalized can create antisocial associations and violence as avenues for change.

Another theory that helps us understand terrorism is **relative deprivation theory** (Barken and Snowden, 2001: 17). Basically, a group's rising expectations and disappointments lead to feelings of deprivation and frustration (Figure 1-5). When group members compare their plight with more fortunate groups, the ill feelings are compounded. Violence is seen as a viable option. The living conditions of Palestinians in and near Israel serve as an example.

Terrorism may also be shaped by efforts to maintain cultural identity and autonomy, with an example being the past violence between Catholics and Protestants in Northern Ireland.

Terror instills fear in a population, disrupts everyday life, and calls into question the ability of a government to protect its citizens. When citizens fear going out in public or to businesses, such as restaurants and retail stores, and when economic conditions suffer, terrorists may succeed in their demands for change.

Clayton *et al.* (2003) emphasize the causal model of Ross (1993: 317–329) under the structural explanations of terrorism. Ross's model consists of three permissive causes and seven precipitant causes.

Figure 1-5 ■ Relative deprivation theory is one of many explanations for terrorism.

Permissive causes	Precipitant causes
Level of modernization	Grievances
Type of political system	Availability of weapons and explosives
Geographical location	Counterterrorist failure
	Support
	Other types of unrest
	Organizational split and development
	Social, cultural, and historical facilitation

In describing Ross's model, Clayton *et al.* (2003) make the following observations.

- Permissive causes facilitate precipitant causes.
- Modernization is the most important permissive factor.
- The characteristics of modern societies that facilitate terrorism are better targets, weapons and technology, mass media, increased literacy, conflicts with tradition, and modern transportation.
- Organizational split and development refers to terrorist groups that break away from other groups because of differences in ideology and strategy and possibly the goal of seeking dominance over competitive groups.
- Social, cultural, and historical facilitation means that heterogeneous subgroups with a variety of beliefs and values may clash.

The U.S. Government (2003), in the National Strategy for Combating Terrorism, describes a building process from which terrorism emerges (Figure 1-6). Underlying conditions include poverty, corruption, and religious and ethnic conflict. Although these conditions may be real or manufactured, terrorists use these problems to legitimize violence and gain support. The belief that terrorism is a means to change is a serious problem. The international environment can facilitate terrorism through, for example, open borders that enable terrorists to seek havens and travel to targets. States around the world—either through ignorance or intent—offer safe houses, training, communications systems, and financial opportunities that support terrorist operations. A terrorist organization can then thrive in a stable environment. Leadership links the components of the building process and provides direction for goals. Because leaders may be apprehended or killed, certain terrorist groups have opted for a decentralized and autonomous cell structure.

Figure 1-6 ■ The Structure of Terror. Source: U.S. Government (2003).

INTERNATIONAL TERRORISM

This section provides an overview of international terrorism to assist the reader in understanding the scope of this problem. In striving for objectivity, refer to the coverage earlier in the chapter pertaining to the difficulties of defining terrorism, the various contexts of terrorism, and Kegley's suggestions on how we can "organize our thinking about terrorism."

Martin (2003: 228) seeks objectivity by comparing perceptions of international terrorism by those from the West and those from developing nations. Western governments are critical of international terrorism because (1) democratic justice is the norm and terrorism is seen as criminal behavior, (2) the West is often a target of terrorism, and (3) the West finds specific methods of warfare to be acceptable and terrorism is not one of them. Developing nations may find terrorism to be acceptable because (1) anticolonial revolutionaries (also called terrorists) have become national leaders, (2) terrorism was the best choice to freedom from colonialism, and (3) many revolutionaries crafted an effective fusion of ideology and terrorism that became justified and legitimate.

CRITICAL THINKING:

Do you think Martin's reasons why developing nations may find terrorism acceptable supports George Washington and the American Revolution? Why or why not?

The FBI (n.d.) defines international terrorism as "the unlawful use of force or violence committed by a group or individual, who has some connection to a foreign power or whose activities transcend national boundaries, against persons or property to intimidate or coerce a government, the civilian population, or any segment thereof, in furtherance of political or social objectives." According to the U.S. Department of State (2004: xii), "the term international terrorism means terrorism involving citizens or the territory of more than one country."

GLOBALIZATION

To assist our understanding of international terrorism, the term globalization is explained. **Globalization** is a process of worldwide changes that are increasingly integrating and remolding the lives of the people of the world (Bailey, 2003: 75). Economic changes are the driving force behind globalization. All labor, goods, and services are bought on the global market. Whether we purchase bread, vehicles, or gasoline, the price is influenced by world prices and global competition. One example of global competition is labor costs, and we have seen many U.S. companies lay off U.S. workers and move manufacturing to plants in other countries where labor and other costs are lower. Citizens of countries throughout the world are seeing their products and services sold globally, and they are buying from other countries. Modern technology and communications have enabled American movies, television programs, and music to reach almost anywhere in the world. McDonald's hamburgers and Kentucky Fried Chicken are sold in cities throughout the world. Likewise, the United States is a huge market for other countries. The ideology of capitalism and its goal of wealth are often seen as the driving forces behind the global economy. This ideology originated from Western (European) cultural beliefs and values. *The process of globalization involves not only economic changes, but also political, social, and cultural changes.* The United States is at the forefront of globalization through its military might, huge economy, power, and influence. Citizens of less developed nations perceive threats to their native culture and society from Western ideas, democratic values, and differences in religion. People in conservative cultures are angered by inequities, injustice, and the age-old problem of the "haves and the have nots." Western industrialized nations are a ripe target for discontent. Barber (1992: 53) writes that the planet is falling apart and coming together at the same time. He calls this phenomenon "Jihad" versus "McWorld." Samuel Huntington (1996), who wrote *The Clash of Civilizations and the Remaking of the World Order*, has often been quoted following the 9/11 attacks. He identified eight civilizations and predicted that in the 21st century wars would be fought, not between nations, but between different cultures and religions. Furthermore, he predicted that the most serious wars would occur with Western nations dominated by Christians versus African and Asian nations dominated by Muslims.

Thus, globalization is important to our understanding of international terrorism. As the forces of globalization continue to change the world dramatically, terrorism seeks to divide and foment discontent among ethnic, religious, political, and economic groups.

INTERNATIONAL TERRORISTS

When terrorists stage an attack domestically that has domestic implications, the attention they receive for their cause may not be as intense as a cross-border attack in another country. Martin (2003: 220, G-24) refers to "the 'spillover effect' that describes terrorist violence that occurs beyond the borders of the countries that are the target of such violence." Terrorists may also select domestic targets that have international connections to enhance global attention to their cause. Examples of international targets include diplomats, tourists, foreign business people, and the locations they inhabit or visit. By bringing their struggle into the international arena, a low-budget, spectacular attack, at a symbolic or well-known target, can reap enormous, immediate publicity. Such political violence has been termed **asymmetrical warfare**, "a term used to describe tactics, organizational configurations, and methods of conflict that do not use previously accepted or predictable rules of engagement" (Martin, 2003: 216, G-3). This means that terrorists, who have an arsenal that is no match to, say, a superpower, can be successful when they apply imaginative, well-planned, low-budget, surprise attacks against a much stronger enemy. This occurred, for example, with the 9/11 attacks, when al-Qaida suicide operatives, using box cutters, commandeered airliners and transformed them into missiles that totally destroyed the Twin Towers in New York City and damaged the Pentagon, while killing almost 3000 people. Many countries, especially the United States, were forced to rethink their war fighting and counterterrorism capabilities because, clearly, the "wake-up call" is that conventional methods of deterrence, security, and war are no match against creative, determined terrorists.

The true number of terrorist organizations is difficult to gauge because these groups are dynamic, splinter groups form, and groups change their names. The U.S. Department of State (2005: 92), in *Country Reports on Terrorism 2004*, lists 40 foreign terrorist organizations (FTOs), followed by "a list of other selected terrorist groups also deemed of relevance in the global war on terrorism." The U.S. Department of State (2004) published a list of 37 FTOs in *Patterns of Global Terrorism 2003*. (The *Country Reports* are the newer version of the *Patterns of Global Terrorism*, as explained at the beginning of Chapter 3. These reports contain U.S. policy, antiterrorism fronts and programs, a variety of data, and summaries of many terrorist organizations.) In 1997, the Secretary of State initially identified 30 FTOs. FTO status expires in 2 years and groups can remain on the list or be deleted. FTOs meet the criteria of the Antiterrorism and Effective Death Penalty Act of 1996. Criteria for designation as an FTO are it must be foreign; engage in terrorism as defined by U.S. law; and the group must threaten U.S. persons, national security, foreign relations, or economic interests. The consequences of being an FTO are it is illegal to provide funds or other material support by a person subject to the jurisdiction of the US; FTO members, if they are aliens, can be denied access to the United States; and financial institutions must block FTO accounts and report this action to the U.S. Department of the Treasury.

Next is a sample summary of FTOs from *Patterns of Global Terrorism 2003*, with updates from *Country Reports on Terrorism 2004*. Through these summaries we learn the background, goals, methods, weapons, and funding of FTOs. Although the sample begins with groups originating in the Middle East, which is a hotbed of violence today and garnering much attention, we should maintain our awareness that many terrorist organizations exist globally, new ones are being formed each year, and any one of these groups may attack unexpectedly.

ABU NIDAL ORGANIZATION (ANO)

a.k.a. Fatah—the Revolutionary Council, Arab Revolutionary Brigades, Black September, and Revolutionary Organization of Socialist Muslims

Description   International terrorist organization founded by Sabri al-Banna (a.k.a. Abu Nidal). Split from PLO in 1974. Made up of various functional committees, including political, military, and financial. In November 2002, Abu Nidal died in Baghdad; the new leadership of the organization is unclear. First designated in October 1997.

Activities   Has carried out terrorist attacks in 20 countries, killing or injuring almost 900 persons. Targets include the United States, the United Kingdom, France, Israel, moderate Palestinians, the PLO, and various Arab countries. Major attacks included the Rome and Vienna airports in December 1985, the Neve Shalom synagogue in Istanbul, the Pan Am Flight 73 hijacking in Karachi in September 1986, and the City of Poros day-excursion ship attack in Greece in July 1988. Suspected of assassinating PLO deputy chief Abu Iyad and PLO security chief Abu Hul in Tunis in January 1991. ANO assassinated a Jordanian diplomat in Lebanon in January 1994 and has been linked to the killing of the PLO representative there. Has not staged a major attack against Western targets since the late 1980s.

Strength   Few hundred plus limited overseas support structure.

Location/Area of Operation   Al-Banna relocated to Iraq in December 1998 where the group maintained a presence, until Operation Iraqi Freedom, but its current status in country is unknown. Has an operational presence in Lebanon, including several Palestinian refugee camps. Authorities shut down the ANO's operations in Libya and Egypt in 1999. Has demonstrated ability to operate over wide area, including the Middle East, Asia, and Europe. Financial problems and internal disorganization have reduced the group's activities and capabilities.

External Aid   Has received considerable support, including safe haven, training, logistic assistance, and financial aid from Iraq, Libya, and Syria (until 1987), in addition to close support for selected operations.

HAMAS

a.k.a. Islamic Resistance Movement

Description   Formed in late 1987 as an outgrowth of the Palestinian branch of the Muslim Brotherhood. Various HAMAS elements have used both violent and political means, including terrorism, to pursue the goal of establishing an Islamic Palestinian state in Israel. Loosely structured, with some elements working clandestinely and others openly through mosques and social service institutions to recruit members, raise money, organize activities, and distribute propaganda. HAMAS's strength is concentrated in the Gaza Strip and the West Bank. First designated in October 1997.

Activities   HAMAS terrorists, especially those in the Izz al-Din al-Qassam Brigades, have conducted many attacks, including large-scale suicide bombings, against Israeli civilian and military targets. HAMAS maintained the pace of its operational activity during 2004, claiming numerous attacks against Israeli interests. HAMAS has not yet targeted U.S. interests, directly, although the group makes little or no effort to avoid targets frequented by foreigners. HAMAS continues to confine its attacks to Israel and the occupied territories. [In 2006 elections, HAMAS won a large majority in the Palestinian parliament; this event could reshape Palestinian relations with Israel and other countries.]

Strength   Unknown number of official members; tens of thousands of supporters and sympathizers.

Location/Area of Operation   HAMAS currently limits its terrorist operations to Israeli military and civilian targets in the West Bank, Gaza Strip, and Israel. The group's leadership is dispersed throughout the Gaza Strip and West Bank, with a few senior leaders residing in Syria, Lebanon, Iran, and the Gulf States.

External Aid   Receives some funding from Iran but relies primarily on donations from Palestinian expatriates around the world and private benefactors, particularly in western Europe, North America, and the Persian Gulf region.

HIZBALLAH (PARTY OF GOD)
a.k.a. Islamic Jihad, Revolutionary Justice Organization, Organization of the Oppressed on Earth, and Islamic Jihad for the Liberation of Palestine

Description   Also known as Lebanese Hizballah, this group was formed in 1982 in response to the Israeli invasion of Lebanon; this Lebanon-based radical Shi'a group takes its ideological inspiration from the Iranian revolution and the teachings of the late Ayatollah Khomeini. The Majlis al-Shura, or consultative council, is the group's highest governing body and is led by Secretary General Hassan Nasrallah. Hizballah is dedicated to liberating Jerusalem and eliminating Israel and has formally advocated ultimate establishment of Islamic rule in Lebanon. Nonetheless, Hizballah has actively participated in Lebanon's political system since 1992. Hizballah is closely allied with, and often directed by, Iran but has the capability and willingness to act alone. Although Hizballah does not share the Syrian regime's secular orientation, the group has been a strong ally in helping Syria advance its political objectives in the region. First designated in October 1997.

Activities   Known or suspected to have been involved in numerous anti-U.S. and anti-Israeli terrorist attacks, including the suicide truck bombings of the U.S. Embassy and U.S. Marine barracks in Beirut in 1983 and the U.S. Embassy annex in Beirut in September 1984. Three members of Hizballah—'Imad Mughniyah, Hasan Izz-al-Din, and Ali Atwa—are on the FBI's list of 22 most-wanted terrorists for the hijacking in 1985 of TWA Flight 847 during which a U.S. Navy diver was murdered. Elements of the group were responsible for the kidnapping and detention of United States and other Westerners in Lebanon in the 1980s. Hizballah also attacked the Israeli Embassy in Argentina in 1992 and the Israeli cultural center in Buenos Aires in 1994. In fall 2000, Hizballah operatives captured three Israeli soldiers in the Shab'a Farms and kidnapped an Israeli noncombatant whom may have been lured to Lebanon under false pretenses.

In 2003, Hizballah appeared to have established a presence in Iraq, but for the moment its activities there are limited. Hizballah Secretary General Hassan Nasrallah stated in speeches that "we are heading ... toward the end and elimination of Israel from the region" and that the group's "slogan is and will continue to be death to America." Hizballah's television station, al-Manar, continued to use inflammatory images and reporting in an effort to encourage the intifadah and promote Palestinian suicide operations.

In 2004, Hizballah launched an unmanned aerial vehicle from Lebanese airspace and it crashed in Israel. This action followed Hizballah statements that it would counter Israeli Air Force violations of Lebanese airspace. In 2004, Hizballah and HAMAS signed an agreement to increase joint efforts at attacking Israel.

In the summer of 2006, the Israeli-Hizballah war began when Hizballah forces entered northern Israel from southern Lebanon and killed and captured Israeli soldiers. Israel responded by using air power to destroy the infrastructure and many homes in Hizballah-controlled southern Lebanon. Hizballah fired hundreds of rockets into northern Israel as the Israeli army invaded southern Lebanon. Both sides sustained hundreds of casualties and claimed victory by the time the one-month war ended as UN peacekeepers created a buffer zone in southern Lebanon.

Strength   Several thousand supporters and a few hundred terrorist operatives.

Location/Area of Operation   Operates in the southern suburbs of Beirut, the Bekaa Valley, and southern Lebanon. Has established cells in Europe, Africa, South America, North America, and Asia.

External Aid   Receives financial, training, weapons, explosives, political, diplomatic, and organizational aid from Iran and diplomatic, political, and logistic support from Syria. Receives financial support from sympathetic business interests and individuals worldwide, largely through the Lebanese diaspora.

AL-QAIDA
a.k.a. Osama bin Ladin Organization

Description   Established by Osama bin Ladin in the late 1980s to bring together Arabs who fought in Afghanistan against the Soviet Union. Helped finance, recruit, transport, and train Sunni Islamic extremists for the Afghan resistance. Current goal is to unite Muslims to fight the United States as a means of defeating Israel, overthrowing regimes it deems "non-Islamic," and expelling Westerners and non-Muslims from Muslim countries, particularly Saudi Arabia. Eventual goal would be to establish an Islamic Caliphate throughout the world by working with allied Islamic extremist groups. Issued statement under banner of "the World Islamic Front for Jihad Against the Jews and Crusaders" in February 1998, saying it was the duty of all Muslims to kill U.S. citizens—civilian or military—and their allies everywhere. Merged with Egyptian Islamic Jihad (Al-Jihad) in June 2001.

Activities   In 2004, the Saudi-based al-Qaida launched 11 attacks, killed over 60 people, including 6 Americans, and wounded over 225 in Saudi Arabia. Other al-Qaida groups are responsible for attacks in Iraq and Afghanistan.

In 2003 carried out the assault and bombing on May 12 of three expatriate housing complexes in Riyadh, Saudi Arabia that killed 30 and injured 216. Assisted in carrying out the bombings on May 16 in Casablanca, Morocco, of a Jewish center, restaurant, nightclub, and hotel that killed 33 and injured 101. Probably supported the bombing of the J.W. Marriott Hotel in Jakarta, Indonesia, on August 5 that killed 12 and injured 149. Responsible for the assault and bombing on November 9 of a housing complex in Riyadh, Saudi Arabia that killed 17 and injured 122. Conducted the bombings of two synagogues in Istanbul, Turkey, on November 15 that killed 20 and injured 300, and the bombings in Istanbul of the British Consulate and HSBC Bank on November 20 that resulted in 41 dead and 555 injured. Has been involved in some attacks in Afghanistan and Iraq.

In 2002, carried out bombing on November 28 of hotel in Mombasa, Kenya, killing 15 and injuring 40. Probably supported a nightclub bombing in Bali, Indonesia, on October 12 that killed over 200. Responsible for an attack on U.S. military personnel in Kuwait, on October 8 that killed 1 U.S. soldier and injured another. Directed a suicide attack on the MV Limburg off the coast of Yemen on October 6 that killed 1 and injured 4. Carried out a firebombing of a synagogue in Tunisia on April 11 that killed 19 and injured 22. On September, 2001, 19 al-Qaida suicide attackers hijacked and crashed four U.S. commercial jets—two into the World Trade Center in New York City, one into the Pentagon near Washington, DC, and a fourth into a field in Shanksville, Pennsylvania, leaving about 3000 individuals dead or missing. Directed the attack on the U.S.S. Cole in the port of Aden, Yemen, on October 12, 2000, killing 17 U.S. Navy members and injuring another 39 (Figure 1-7).

Figure 1-7 ■ U.S.S. Cole. Navy destroyer, was relaunched (September 14, 2001) at Northrop Grumman Ship Systems Ingalls Operations in Pascagoula, MS, after repairs on her hull. The ship was transported to Pascagoula following the October 12, 2000 terrorist attack in Yemen. U.S. Navy Photo. http://www.news.navy.mil/view_single.asp?id=127

Conducted the bombings in August 1998 of the U.S. Embassies in Nairobi, Kenya, and Dares Salaam, Tanzania, that killed at least 301 individuals and injured more than 5000 others. Claims to have shot down U.S. helicopters and killed U.S. servicemen in Somalia in 1993 and to have conducted three bombings that targeted U.S. troops in Aden, Yemen, in December 1992.

Al-Qaida is linked to the following plans that were disrupted or not carried out: to assassinate Pope John Paul II during his visit to Manila in late 1994, to kill President Clinton during a visit to the Philippines in early 1995, to bomb in midair a dozen U.S. transpacific flights in 1995, and to set off a bomb at Los Angeles International Airport in 1999. Also plotted to carry out terrorist operations against U.S. and Israeli tourists visiting Jordan for millennial celebrations in late 1999. (Jordanian authorities thwarted the planned attacks and put 28 suspects on trial.) In December 2001, suspected al-Qaida associate Richard Colvin Reid attempted to ignite a shoe bomb on a transatlantic flight from Paris to Miami. Attempted to shoot down an Israeli chartered plane with a surface-to-air missile as it departed the Mombasa airport in November 2002.

Strength   Al-Qaida's organizational strength is difficult to determine, but it probably has several thousand members and associates. The arrests and deaths of midlevel and senior-level al-Qaida operatives have interrupted some terrorist plots. Also serves as a focal point or umbrella organization for a worldwide network that includes many Sunni Islamic extremist groups, some members of al-Gama'a al-Islamiyya, the Islamic Movement of Uzbekistan, and the Harakat ul-Mujahidin.

Location/Area of Operation   Al-Qaida has cells worldwide and is reinforced by its ties to Sunni extremist networks. Was based in Afghanistan until Coalition forces removed the Taliban from power in late 2001. Al-Qaida has dispersed in small groups across south Asia, southeast Asia, and the Middle East and probably will attempt to carry out future attacks against U.S. interests.

External Aid   Al-Qaida maintains moneymaking front businesses, solicits donations from like-minded supporters, and illicitly siphons funds from donations to Muslim charitable organizations. United States and international efforts to block al-Qaida funding have hampered the group's ability to obtain money.

ELEMENTS OF AL-QAIDA IDEOLOGY

According to the U.S. Department of State (2005), many jihadist groups have adopted the ideology and targeting strategies of al-Qaida. The tenets of this ideology, from al-Qaida public statements, are as follows.

- This is a clash of civilizations. Militant jihad is a religious duty before God. The clash is necessary for the salvation of one's soul and to defend the Muslim nation.
- Only two camps exist and there can be no middle ground in an apocalyptic showdown with both the "West" and Muslims that do not agree with al-Qaida's vision of "true Islam."
- Violence is the only solution; peace is an illusion.
- Many of the theological and legal restrictions on the use of violence by Muslims do not apply to this war.
- The United States power is based on its economy and, thus, large-scale, mass-casualty attacks, especially focused on U.S. and Western economic targets, are a major goal.
- Muslim governments that are religiously unacceptable, and cooperate with the West, must be violently overthrown.

OSAMA BIN LADIN

Osama bin Ladin has been credited with organizing al-Qaida, which has evolved from a terror network to a global movement. He was born in 1957 in Riyadh, Saudi Arabia, and was 1 of 52 children in his family (Bergen, 2001). His father, Sheikh Mohammed bin Ladin, was originally from Yemen, settled in Saudi Arabia, and became a billionaire in the construction industry. Bin Ladin's mother was Syrian who was his father's fourth wife. Information about bin Ladin's early childhood differs among researchers. In 1979, he earned a college degree from King Abdul Aziz University in Jeddah. By this time he had developed radical views because of his distaste for the conditions in his own society. That year was also marked by world events that impacted his ideas and actions: the Iranian revolution, Israeli and Egyptian peace, and the Soviet invasion of Afghanistan. He fought in Afghanistan, against a superpower (i.e., Soviet Union), and viewed the communists and the West with disdain. Ironically, the guerrillas fighting the Soviets in Afghanistan were supported by the United States. During this conflict, bin Ladin gained valuable experience in organizing, funding, and recruiting fighters. In 1989, the Soviets withdrew in defeat from Afghanistan and bin Ladin returned to Saudi Arabia. When Iraq invaded Kuwait in 1990, bin Ladin offered the Afghan guerrillas to the Saudi government to assist in the defense against the threat from Iraq, but the Saudis received assistance from the United States. During 1995, after years of frustration with the Saudi government, bin Ladin used an "open letter" to criticize the

OSAMA BIN LADIN—Cont'd

Saudi royal family by claiming that it was not supporting Islam and it depended on the West for security. He even advocated attacks against U.S. forces in Saudi Arabia. His hatred for the United States grew because U.S. forces remained on Muslim land and he drew references to the Crusades. The Saudi government exiled him to Sudan and then to Afghanistan where he was supported by the Taliban regime while involved in training terrorists and planning attacks, until the 9/11 attacks resulted in the fall of that regime by U.S.-led forces. As of this writing, U.S. authorities are still seeking bin Ladin, who is supposedly hiding in the border area between Afghanistan and Pakistan.

To further illustrate the global nature of terrorism, here are brief summaries of additional FTOs residing in regions outside of the Middle East.

Basque Fatherland and Liberty (ETA). This group, founded in 1959, seeks to establish an independent homeland in northern Spain based on Marxism. It is involved in bombings and assassinations of Spanish officials and is financed primarily through extortion and robbery. Its strength is in the hundreds.

Revolutionary Armed Forces of Columbia (FARC). Established in 1964, the FARC is the military wing of the Columbian Communist Party and has ties to illegal drug trafficking. It is the most powerful Latin American insurgency based on Marxism. In 2002 it launched a mortar attack on the presidential palace during Columbia's presidential inauguration. FARC has 9000 to 12,000 armed combatants and specializes in car bombing, grenade attack, and kidnapping for ransom.

Liberation Tigers of Tamil Eelam (LTTE). Founded in 1976, the LTTE aims to create an independent Tamil state in Sri Lanka. The Tigers are notorious for their suicide bombers called the Black Tigers. In 1991, one such attacker, a female, blew herself up as she stood next to India's Prime Minister Rajiv Gandhi, who did not survive. A similar fate met the President of Sri Lanka. LTTE strength is about 8000 to 10,000 armed combatants, and funds and equipment come from Tamil communities in North America, Europe, and Asia. Between 2003 and 2005 a cease-fire was being observed.

Communist Party of Philippines/New People's Army (CPP/NPA). A Maoist group formed in 1969, this group seeks to overthrow the government through guerrilla warfare and terrorism. It is primarily a rural-based guerrilla group, uses city-based assassination squads, and targets Philippine officials and U.S. troops. Its strength is less than 9000.

Real Irish Republican Army (RIRA). Formed in 1998, the RIRA is dedicated to removing the British army from Northern Ireland and unifying Ireland. Many RIRA members are former members of the Provisional IRA and became dissatisfied with the peace process. This group specializes in bombings, assassinations, and robberies. The RIRA has less than 100 members and funds are obtained from sympathizers in the United States.

STATE TERRORISM

State terrorism has a long history and it takes many forms. **Internal state terrorism** occurs when a nation's government victimizes its own people. Combs (2003: 72) writes "no matter how chilling the atrocities committed by individuals or groups, these crimes pale into insignificance beside the terror inflicted by a state on its own people." Here is a sample list from Barkan and Bryjak (2004: 166–167) and Combs (2003: 73–74).

- Along with settlers, British and U.S. Army troops killed tens of thousands of American Indians during the settlement and westward expansion in North America.
- During World War II, Hitler's Nazi Party murdered six million Jews, Slavs, gypsies, and homosexuals.
- The Soviet Union, under Stalin's rule until his death in 1953, was responsible for sending 40 to 50 million people to Soviet prisons or slave labor camps. Between 15 and 25 million perished from execution, hunger, or disease.
- During the 4-year rule by the Khmer Rouge in the 1970s, in Cambodia, one million people were killed from a population of seven million.
- Between 1971 and 1979, Idi Amin, leader of Uganda, was responsible for the deaths of over 100,000 people.
- Latin America continues to have regimes that practice internal terrorism.
- During the mid-1990s, the Rwandan government (primarily ethnic Hutus) killed about one million Tutsis, many hacked to death.
- Yugoslav president Slobodan Milosevic was responsible for the massacre of tens of thousands of Muslims and Croats between 1992 and 1995.

External state terrorism refers to a nation's efforts in exporting or supporting terrorism against another nation. Conventional wars can result in disadvantages for a nation, such as enormous expense, counterattack, global condemnation and sanctions, economic disruption, and domestic dissent. Consequently, nations may opt for warfare through terrorism. This can be accomplished by covertly supporting a terrorist group, offering a safe haven, and denying involvement with terrorists.

The Secretary of State, U.S. Department of State (2005: 88) is authorized to designate a government as a "State Sponsor of Terrorism" if that government supports international terrorism. U.S. law requires the imposition of sanctions on such countries. These include a ban on arms-related exports and sales, restrictions on exports of dual-use items (e.g., photographic equipment that can be used for military purposes), prohibitions on economic assistance, and various financial restrictions. On October 20, 2004, Iraq's designation as a state sponsor of terrorism was rescinded by the United States, even though the country is a battleground in the war on terrorism. Six state sponsors of terrorism are Iran, North Korea, Syria, Cuba, Sudan, and Libya. During 2004, Sudan and Libya took significant steps to cooperate in the war on terrorism. Iran was the most active promoter of terrorism in 2003 and 2004. It did turn over to foreign governments a number of al-Qaida members, but it provided a safe haven for other al-Qaida members. Iran has encouraged anti-Israeli terrorism and suicide attacks. Its leader referred to Israel as a "cancerous tumor." FTOs supported by Iran with funding, safe haven, training, and weapons include Hizballah, HAMAS, and the Palestine Islamic Jihad. In 2004, senior Iraqi officials expressed concern over Iranian interference in Iraq by supporting insurgents and terrorists.

During 2006, Iran faced a confrontation with the West (Slackman, 2006). The primary issue concerned its ambitions to develop nuclear weapons. Other issues dealt with terrorism and its policies on Israel.

DOMESTIC TERRORISM

The FBI (n.d.) defines **domestic terrorism** as "groups or individuals who are based and operate entirely within the United States and Puerto Rico without foreign direction and whose acts are directed at elements of the U.S. government or population."

Domestic terrorism, also called "homegrown terrorism," is difficult to define, categorize, and research. White (2003: 207–208) offers an analysis of the problems of conceptualizing domestic terrorism. He notes that law enforcement in the United States has historically labeled terrorism or political violence under various crime labels (e.g., arson, homicide). White also writes that the United States has had a long history of political violence, but only recently have more than a few scholars studied the problem under the label of "terrorism."

White refers to three early authors who pioneered publications on domestic (U.S.) terrorism. He praised H. Cooper and coauthors who wrote the *Report of the Task Force on Disorders and Terrorism* in 1976. This publication focused on the civil disorders of the time, the political context of domestic terrorism, and the need for emergency planning.

Two other pioneers are Ted Gurr and J. Bell (1979), who emphasized the historical context of terrorism and how it has been applied by the strong to control the weak and by the weak to fight the strong. Examples in American history include the genocide against American Indians by Europeans, industrialists versus unions, and vigilantism (e.g., KKK).

TYPOLOGIES AND HISTORY

As covered earlier in the chapter, White (2003: 209) "tells it like it is" with typologies of terrorism: "Despite their pejorative nature, typologies of domestic terrorism are inevitably related." ... "No matter how you decide to arrange the categories, you still cover the same ground." He offers five categories of domestic terrorism: (1) foreign groups in America, (2) revolutionary nationalists (e.g., Puerto Rican separatists), (3) the ideological right, (4) the ideological left, and (5) criminal groups using terrorist tactics. There are many other typologies of domestic terrorism.

Griset and Mahan (2003: 85–93) divide homegrown terrorism into a typology of five categories based on ideology as explained next. These researches state that their categories may overlap. Here we will explain each and add historical information from several sources.

STATE-SPONSORED TERRORISM

Government authorities, including Congress and the president, have passed laws and supported policies that have intimidated Americans and fostered violence. The Removal Act of 1830 required the forced march of Indian tribes from the east coast to Oklahoma; many Indians died during the march, and upon reaching reservations, the conditions were poor. In another example, during the late 1800s and early 1900s, many city and state police agencies were formed or expanded to serve as strikebreakers (Holden, 1986: 23).

LEFTIST CLASS STRUGGLES

Identifying with Marxism, the 1960s and 1970s saw leftist groups embroiled in antiwar and civil rights struggles. The Students for a Democratic Society (SDS) began in 1960 to support the "liberal" policies of the Democratic Party. It called for an alliance of blacks, students, peace groups, and liberal organizations. As with many other leftist groups of the time, an "antiestablishment" theme prevailed (i.e., government and business were corrupt and change was needed to help the less fortunate). In 1965, the SDS organized the first anti-Vietnam War march in Washington, DC, which resulted in increased popularity for the SDS among students. The SDS led many campus disturbances and sit-down demonstrations. Military draft resistance became a top priority. As the Vietnam War intensified, the SDS divided into competing groups, each supporting violence and terrorism. One of the most noted splinter groups was the Weather Underground Organization (WUO). This group advocated revolution against capitalism. It was responsible for almost 40 bombings, including those inside the U.S. Capitol and the Pentagon. When the war ended, interest in the WUO waned (Poland, 1988: 91–92).

Violence against nonviolent civil rights workers sparked the Black Power movement during the 1960s. It advocated political, economic, and cultural awakening. One splinter group of this movement was the Black Panthers, formed in 1966, in Oakland, California. A tactic of the Black

Panthers was to dispatch members to police stops to observe. The Panthers would arrive carrying law books and an open display of shotguns and rifles (legal at the time). This paramilitary movement grew and Panthers wore black berets and black leather jackets as they marched and chanted slogans. The FBI viewed the Panthers as a threat to domestic security; gun battles and arrests occurred, and by the late 1970s, the group began its decline (Martin, 2003: 311 and 318).

This period also saw the formation of the Republic of New Africa (RNA) in 1968. The goal was to establish a black nation by annexing the states of Georgia, Louisiana, Alabama, Mississippi, and South Carolina. Following gun battles with police, RNA interest declined. In 1971, the Black Liberation Army (BLA) was formed when the Panthers split. The BLA promoted fear by killing police (often called "pigs"), robbing banks, planting bombs, and organizing prison escapes. BLA members were eventually killed in shootouts with police or imprisoned (Poland, 1988: 91).

During the 1980s, the May 19 Communist Organization (M19CO) emerged from members of the SDS, Black Panthers, and other groups. The group's name came from the birthdays of Ho Chi Minh (North Vietnamese Communist leader) and Malcolm X (American Black Muslim leader). This group sought links to radical black, Hispanic, and women's movements. The overall goal was violent revolution. By the end of the decade, the group split apart and members were imprisoned for crimes such as bombings, murders, and robberies (Poland, 1988: 90).

Following the Spanish–American War in 1898, Puerto Rico was ceded to the United States by the Treaty of Paris. The resolve of Puerto Rican nationalists in seeking independence from the United States was illustrated in 1950 following an uprising that was quickly suppressed by government troops. On November 1, 1950, nationalists tried to assassinate President Truman while he was at Blair House, across from the White House. A gun battle erupted, one police officer was killed, Truman was unharmed, and the independence movement gained national attention. The next attack occurred on March 1, 1954, again in Washington, DC, when several nationalists fired shots at legislators while Congress was in session, wounding five. In 1974, the Armed Forces for National Liberation (FALN) was formed. Its agenda for independence leaned to the far left. The FALN introductory attack consisted of bombing five banks in New York City. Over 200 bombings followed, targeting federal and local government buildings, the military (especially in Puerto Rico), and businesses. The FALN was also known for ambushing and shooting U.S. armed services personnel (Poland, 1988: 72–76).

ANARCHISTS/ECOTERRORISTS

Anarchism is a political ideology that reached America from 19th-century Europe, opposed centralization by government, and favored the poor and working class. Martin (2003: 38–39) argues that anarchists were among the first antiestablishment radicals who opposed both capitalism and Marxism and advocated revolution, although they never offered a plan for replacing a central government. Anarchism in the United States was linked to the labor movement and the advocacy of a bombing campaign against industry and government (Combs, 2003: 163).

The Ecoterror movement in the United States focuses on both the dangers of humans encroaching on nature and preserving wilderness. The FBI (2002) defines **ecoterrorism** as the use or threatened use of violence of a criminal nature against innocent victims or property by an environmentally oriented, subnational group for environmental–political reasons, or aimed at an audience beyond the target, often of a symbolic nature.

An early ecoterror group was the Luddites of England, who were known as the "antimachine" people because they wanted to stop the Industrial Revolution (Sale, 1995). Ted Kaczynski (a.k.a. the Unabomber) was a modern-day ecoterrorist. He was an anti-industrialist who targeted scientists and engineers. In 1996 he was arrested after a 17-year investigation that involved 16 bombings, including three deaths and many injuries. Upon pleading guilty in federal court, he is now serving a life sentence without the possibility of release.

Two major, domestic ecoterrorist groups are the **Animal Liberation Front** (ALF) and the **Earth Liberation Front** (ELF). The FBI (2002) estimates that the ALF and ELF have committed over 600 criminal acts in the United States since 1996, resulting in damage exceeding $43 million. Arson is the most destructive practice of ALF and ELF.

ALF is committed to ending the abuse and exploitation of animals. They seek to cause economic loss or destruction of the victim company's property. Victims include fur companies, mink farms, restaurants, and animal research laboratories. The ALF Web site (http://animalliberationfront.com) claims their campaign is nonviolent.

ELF promotes "monkey wrenching," a euphemism for acts of sabotage and vandalism against companies that are perceived to be harming the environment. An example is "tree spiking," in which metal spikes are hammered into trees to damage logging saws.

ALF and ELF show unity in their activities. The ELF Web site (http://earthliberationfront.com) on May 3, 2004 listed ALF, ELF, and Animal Liberation Brigade (ALB, a more violent type of ALF group) "actions" for the previous year. Examples:

> ALF, February 27, 2003, Berlin, MD: 115 chickens liberated from Merial Labs and rehomed.

> ALF, March 27, 2003, San Diego, CA: Home visit to Claire MacDonald, representative for Huntingdon Life Sciences. Property vandalized with red paint and graffiti. Vehicle tires punctured.

> ELF, August 1, 2003, San Diego, CA: In the largest act of environmental sabotage in U.S. history, ELF claims responsibility for a $50 million fire in San Diego that destroyed an unfinished condominium complex.

> ELF, August 22, 2003, West Covina, CA: Four SUV dealerships attacked, causing damage of $2.5 million.

> ALB, August 28, 2003, Emeryville, CA: Two pipe bombs exploded at the offices of Chiron Corporation, a biotech firm.

RACIAL SUPREMACY

Continuing with the Griset and Mahan (2003: 86) typology of domestic terrorism, they view the racial supremacy and religious extremists classifications as right wing, but separate them based on their aims. Their research from multiple sources shows that "these two categories often overlap, but they have also developed separately—white supremacists without religion, and religious extremists without racism." The KKK, as covered earlier, has advocated hate for over a century. Griset and Mahan (2003: 89) write: "for many white supremacists, though, the swastika now symbolizes their agenda for a pure Aryan race" (Figure 1-8). Griset and Mahan add that there are also black separatist groups (as in the 1960s and 1970s) in the United States calling themselves the "Nation of Islam" and they are followers of the Messenger Elijah Muhammad.

White supremacists are often critical of the U.S. Constitution and our government. These right-wing groups are diversified and include skinheads, neo-Nazi Aryan Nations, militant gun advocates, antitax protesters, and survivalists.

The Southern Poverty Law Center (2004) counted 751 hate group chapters of various kinds in 2003, up 67 from a year earlier. Hate Web sites rose from 443 in 2002 to 497 in 2003. The year 2003 was characterized by realignment and rebuilding for many hate groups. Intergroup and intragroup conflict occurs with many terrorist groups as they are born, split into new groups, disband, and are reborn. For example, the National Alliance, a neo-Nazi group headquartered in West Virginia that runs a white power music operation called Resistance Records, is involved in a bitter

Figure 1-8 ■ The swastika is used by white supremacists to symbolize their aim for a pure Aryan race.

feud with its chief competitor, Minnesota-based Panzerfaust Records. During 2003, Resistance banned other hate groups from a major racist concert in Phoenix called Aryan Fest. Another example is the bad feelings over a stabbing incident between the Keystone State Skinheads of Pennsylvania and the Hammerskin Nation (spread over multiple states).

Other 2003 news from the Southern Poverty Law Center includes activity of black separatist groups, specifically an increase in chapters of the New Black Panther Party. Also, Holocaust denial groups are thriving; The Institute for Historical Review, based in California, held events and revamped its Web site.

Although much attention and resources are focused on international terrorists, domestic terrorists are also a serious threat.

RUBY RIDGE, WACO, AND OKLAHOMA CITY

The history of domestic violence against the federal government shows that this activity is not new. Following the American Revolution in 1791, the first such confrontation occurred when the federal government placed a tax on the production of whiskey. Farmers in western Pennsylvania, whose livelihood depended on whiskey, were especially angered and they rioted. President George Washington responded by sending troops to Pennsylvania to quell the disturbance. Another, more serious, example is the Civil War, when many issues surfaced, one being states rights versus federal government power over the states (White, 2003: 221).

The decade of the 1990s provides an excellent example of how citizen confrontations with the federal government can foment hate and violence from extremists. Martin (2003: G-8) defines **extremism** as follows: "Political opinions that are intolerant toward opposing interests and divergent opinions. Extremism forms the ideological foundation for political violence. Radical and reactionary extremists often rationalize and justify acts of violence committed on behalf of their cause."

RUBY RIDGE, WACO, AND OKLAHOMA CITY — Cont'd

The **Ruby Ridge** (Idaho) **incident** occurred in 1992 when U.S. marshals tried to arrest Randy Weaver for failing to appear in court on charges of trying to sell illegal firearms to federal agents. Weaver was a white supremacist and believer in Christian Identity. Martin (2003: G-5) offers this definition for **Christian identity**: "The American adaptation of Anglo-Israelism. A racial supremacist mystical belief that holds that Aryans are the chosen people of God, the United States is the Aryan 'Promised Land,' non-Whites are soulless beasts, and Jews are biologically descended from the devil." During the siege of Weaver's mountain cabin by federal agents, a U.S. marshal was killed, as well as Weaver's son. An FBI sniper fatally shot Weaver's pregnant wife as she stood in the cabin doorway prior to Randy Weaver's surrender. The Ruby Ridge incident became a symbol and inspiration for the struggle of right-wing extremists.

Another symbolic incident that inflamed right-wing extremists was the **Waco incident**, although it had nothing to do with right-wing extremism. On February 28, 1993, the Bureau of Alcohol, Tobacco, and Firearms (ATF), with numerous agents, tried to serve arrest and search warrants for illegal firearms on Vernon Howell, a.k.a. David Koresh. Koresh led the Branch Davidians at the Mount Carmel compound outside of Waco, Texas. He claimed that the end was near and that he was the second coming of Christ who would save the world. The ATF assault and gun battle involved thousands of rounds being fired from both sides. The media captured the fierce battle and showed, on television, ATF agents on an A-frame roof being hit by rounds fired through the wall from inside the compound as the agents attempted, but failed, to enter a window. Four ATF agents were killed and another 20 were injured, plus an unknown number of casualties on the Branch Davidian side.

Following the failed assault, the FBI was enlisted and a 51-day seize began. Continuous negotiations were unable to resolve the standoff as the Branch Davidians waited for a message from God. The FBI stopped electricity and water to the compound and bright lights and loud music were aimed at the compound at night to force members to leave. Some members did leave. Finally, on April 19, 1993, following unsuccessful negotiations, tear gas was pumped and fired into the compound. Fires began and then explosions from ammunition and combustibles created a huge fire. Seventy-five people, mostly women and children perished; nine survived. The FBI, especially the ATF, received an enormous amount of criticism, from many quarters, over the Waco incident (Combs, 2003: 178–179).

The **Oklahoma City bombing** was a major terrorist incident in the United States that occurred on April 19, 1995, when a powerful truck bomb exploded in front of the Alfred P. Murrah Federal Building. The attack killed 168 people and injured more than 500. The nine-story downtown building contained offices of the ATF, Secret Service, Drug Enforcement Administration, among other federal offices, and a day-care center. A rented Ryder truck served as the delivery weapon and it was converted into a mobile bomb containing ammonium nitrate, fuel oil, and Tovex (i.e., a high explosive that acted as a booster). The truck exploded near supporting columns at the front of the building, and then from the bottom up, floor slabs broke off in a "progressive collapse." The force of the explosion caused damage over several blocks in all directions (Poland, 2005: 184–186).

Initially, it was thought that a Middle East terrorist group targeted the building, but this was not the case. A clean-cut white male named Timothy McVeigh was arrested by authorities and prosecuted, convicted, and sentenced to death. In 2001, he was executed by lethal injection at the U.S. penitentiary in Terre Haute, Indiana.

McVeigh was a member of the **Patriot movement** that developed in the early 1990s. This group believes in "true" American ideals of individualism, armed citizens, and minimum interference from government. They distrust government and view it as no longer reflecting the will of the people, intrusive, and violently oppressive (Martin, 2003: 313).

Continued

RUBY RIDGE, WACO, AND OKLAHOMA CITY—Cont'd

In addition to McVeigh, Terry Nichols, a friend from their service in the U.S. Army, was also arrested and convicted for the bombing. Both were inspired by the fictional book, *The Turner Diaries*, by William Pierce, a noted race-hate domestic extremist with a Ph.D. who worked as a college professor. The book describes an international white revolution and U.S. patriots battling non-Whites, Jews, and a corrupt federal government. Pierce tells the story of this struggle and describes methods of making bombs, mortars, and other weapons. It is a how-to manual for terrorism. McVeigh was arrested with a copy of this book. Interestingly, April 19, 1995, the day of the Oklahoma City attack, was the second anniversary of the law enforcement disaster at Waco.

RELIGIOUS EXTREMISTS

This is the fifth typology of domestic terrorism according to Griset and Mahan (2003: 91–92). As covered earlier in this chapter, global religious terrorism has had a significant impact on terrorism in many countries. Domestically, White (2004: 11) refers to the Christian Identity movement and their claims that Jews are descendants of the devil, non-White people evolved from animals, and Caucasians are created in the image of God. White cites Barkun (1997), who notes that some identity ministers preach the destruction of Jews and nonwhites. White (2003: 59) also cites the work of Bordrero (1999), who identifies four types of American religious extremism: *Apocalyptic cults* believe the world is coming to an end and they may resort to violence to facilitate the end; *Black Hebrew Israelism*, a form of black supremacy, contains a faction that preaches violence (the Miami-based Nation of Yahweh); and *Christian Identity* and a *hodgepodge of white supremacy religions*. Finally, Hoffman (1998) claims that Christian Patriot influence played a role in the Oklahoma City bombing, and those religious extremists, not necessarily of the Islamic faith, are involved in terrorism.

DISCUSSION QUESTIONS

1. How are ancient terrorists similar to contemporary terrorists? How are they different?
2. What are the connections among religion, politics, and terrorism?
3. What produces hate toward American foreign policy and Americans?
4. Why is terrorism so difficult to define?
5. Which typology of terrorism do you favor and why?
6. What are the causes of terrorism?
7. What are the negative and positive outcomes of the 9/11 attacks for the United States? What about for al-Qaida?
8. How do domestic and international terrorism impact you?

APPLICATIONS

1A   YOU BE THE INTELLIGENCE ANALYST

As an intelligence analyst working for a government agency, prepare a threat analysis report by answering the following clusters of questions. Select a terrorist attack that occurred anywhere in the world as a way to focus on one terrorist group.

- *The attack:* What terrorist attack did you select? What is the date of the attack, the location and target of the attack, the methods of attack and weapon(s), the security weaknesses of the target, the number of deaths and injuries, and the amount of property damage?

- *The group:* What group executed the attack and what are their ideology and affiliations? Where are they based and trained? How do they recruit members? How are they organized and funded? What did they aim to accomplish by their attack? How did they use the media to help their cause? If they have a Web site, explain its contents.
- *The history and future:* What is the history of the group, including modus operandi, weapons, successes, and failures? How serious is the threat from this group in the future? What targets are they likely to select and when are they likely to strike?
- *The response:* How have governments responded to the group's actions, including counterterrorism, new laws, and diplomacy?

1B YOU BE THE INTELLIGENCE ANALYST

You work for a government agency as an intelligence analyst. Part of your job is to study terrorist attacks, categorize the attacks, and compile summaries for agency personnel and others. You have been given discretion by your supervisor to design a unique system of studying terrorism because your agency is looking for innovative methods in the war against terrorism.

Design a new typology of terrorism containing at least four categories. Name and explain each category. Select a terrorist group operating anywhere in the world and place the group in the appropriate category of your typology and justify your placement decision.

Why do you think your typology is unique? How can it help counterterrorism efforts?

1C YOU BE THE RESEARCHER

As a researcher for a think tank, you have been assigned the task of preparing a report on whether domestic or international terrorism is the greater threat to the United States. Prepare this report with at least three references and include a defense of your findings.

WEB SITES

Al-Fatah: www.fateh.net
Amnesty International: www.amnesty.org
Center for the Study of Terrorism and Political Violence: www.st-andrews.ac.uk
Earth First: www.earthfirstjournal.org
Human Rights Watch: www.hrw.org
Southern Poverty Law Center: www.splcenter.org
Terrorism Knowledge Base: www.tkb.org
Terrorism Research Center: www.terrorism.com
U.S. Department of State: www.state.gov/s/ct/

NOTES

Associated Press (February 24, 2004). "Paige calls teacher's union 'terrorist organization.'"

Bailey, G. (2003). "Globalization." In A. del Carmen (Ed.), *Terrorism: An Interdisciplinary Perspective*, 2nd ed. Toronto: Thomas Learning, Inc.

Bandura, A. (1990). "Mechanisms of Moral Disengagement." In H. Hall (Ed.), *Terrorism: Strategies for Intervention*. Binghamton, NY: The Haworth Press.

Bandura, A. (1977). *Social Learning Theory*. NY: General Learning Press.

Barber, B. (1992). "Jihad vs. McWorld." *Atlantic Monthly*, 269(3).

Barkan, S., and Bryjak, G. (2004). *Fundamentals of Criminal Justice*. Boston: Allyn and Bacon.

Barkan, S., and Snowden, L. (2001). *Collective Violence*. Boston: Allyn and Bacon.

Barkun, M. (1997). *Religion and the Racist Right: The Origins of the Christian Identity Movement*. Chapel Hill, NC: University of North Carolina Press.

Bell, J., and Gurr, T. (1979). "Terrorism and Revolution in American." In H. Graham and T. Gurr (Eds.), *Violence in America*. Newbury Park, CA: Sage.

Bergen, P. (2001). *Holy War, Inc.: Inside the Secret World of Osama Bin Laden*. New York: Free Press.

Bodrero, D. (1999). Project Megiddo Y2K Paranoia: Extemists Confront the Millennium. Tallahassee, FL: Institute for Intergovernmental Research.

Calhoun, C., Light, D., and Keller, S. (2001). *Understanding Sociology*. New York: Glencoe-McGraw-Hill.

Chalmers, D. (1987). *Hooded Americanism: The History of the Ku Klux Klan*, 3rd ed. Durham, NC: Duke University Press.

Clayton, C., Ballif-Spanvill, B., Barlow, S., and Orton, R. (2003). "Terrorism as Group Violence." In H. Hall (Ed.), *Terrorism: Strategies for Intervention*.

Combs, C. (2003). *Terrorism in the Twenty-First Century*, 3rd ed. Upper Saddle River, NJ: Prentice-Hall.

Crenshaw, M. (1990). "The Logic of Terrorism: Terrorist Behavior as a Product of Strategic Choice." In H. Hall (Ed.), *Terrorism: Strategies for Intervention*.

Deflem, M., and Maybin, L. (2005). "Interpol and the Policing of International Terrorism: Developments and Dynamics Since September 11." In L. Snowden and B. Whitsel (Eds.), *Terrorism: Research, Readings, and Realities*. Upper Saddle River, NJ: Pearson Prentice Hall.

Dickey, C. (2004). "From 9/11 to 3/11." *Newsweek*. March 22.

Drake, R. (1995). *The Aldo Moro Murder Case*. Cambridge, MA: Harvard University Press.

Dyson, W. (2001). *Terrorism: An Investigator's Handbook*. Cincinnati, OH: Anderson Pub.

FBI (n.d.). *Counterterrorism*. http://denver.fbi.gov/inteterr.htm, retrieved January 14, 2004.

FBI (2002). "The Threat of Ecoterrorism." http://www.fbi.gov/congress/congress02/jarboe021202.htm, retrieved May 3, 2004.

Ford, P. (2001). "Why Do They Hate Us?" *The Christian Science Monitor:* September 27.

Greenberg, D. (2001). "Is Terrorism New?" *Slate.com*. http://historynewsnetwork.org, retrieved March 15, 2004.

Griset, P., and Mahan, S. (2003). *Terrorism in Perspective*. Thousand Oaks, CA: Sage.

Gurr, T. (1989). "Political Terrorism: Historical Antecedents and Contemporary Trends." In T. Gurr (Ed.), *Violence in America: Protest, Rebellion, and Reform*. Newbury Park, CA: Sage.

Hoffman, B. (1998). *Inside Terrorism*. New York: Columbia University Press.

Holden, R. (1986). *Modern Police Management*. Englewood Cliffs, NJ: Prentice-Hall.

Hudson, R. (1999). *The Sociology and Psychology of Terrorism: Who Becomes a Terrorist and Why?* Washington, DC: Federal Research Division, Library of Congress. In H. Hall (Ed.), *Terrorism: Strategies for Intervention*.

Huntington, S. (1996). *The Clash of Civilizations and the Remaking of the World Order*. New York: Simon & Schuster.

Jordan, J., and Boix, L. (2004). "Al-Qaida and Western Islam." *Terrorism and Political Violence*, 16 (Spring).

Kegley, C. (2003). *The New Global Terrorism: Characteristics, Causes, Controls*. Upper Saddle River, NJ: Prentice-Hall.

Laqueur, W. (1999). *The New Terrorism: Fanaticism and the Arms of Mass Destruction*. New York: Oxford University Press.

Laqueur, W. (2001). *A History of Terrorism*. New Brunswick: Transaction Pub.

Martin, G. (2003). *Understanding Terrorism: Challenges, Perspectives, and Issues*. Thousand Oaks, CA: Sage.

Martin, G. (2005). *Juvenile Justice: Process and Systems*. Thousand Oaks, CA: Sage.

Military Periscope (2004). *Terrorism*. www.periscope.ucg.com, retrieved January 14, 2004.

Poland, J. (1988). *Understanding Terrorism: Groups, Strategies, and Responses*. Englewood Cliffs, NJ: Prentice-Hall.

Poland, J. (2005). *Understanding Terrorism: Groups, Strategies, and Responses*, 2 nd ed. Englewood Cliffs, NJ: Prentice-Hall.

Purpura, P. (1997). *Criminal Justice: An Introduction*. Boston, MA: Butterworth-Heinemann.

Queller, D. (1989). "Crusades." *World Book*, Vol. 4. Chicago: World Book, Inc.

Rapoport, D. (1984). "Fear and Trembling: Terrorism in Three Religious Traditions." *American Political Science Review*, 78 (September).

Reich, B. (1989). "Israel." *World Book*, 10. Chicago: World Book, Inc.

Reich, W. (1990). *Origins of Terrorism: Psychologies, Ideologies, Theologies, States of Mind*. Cambridge, UK: Cambridge University Press. In H. Hall (Ed.), *Terrorism: Strategies for Intervention*.

Ross, J. (1993). "Structural Causes of Oppositional Political Terrorism: Towards a Causal Model." *Journal of Peace Research*, 30.

Sale, K. (1995). *Rebels Against the Future*. New York: Addison-Wesley. In P. Griset and S. Mahan (2003). *Terrorism in Perspective*.

Silke, A. (1998). "Cheshire-cat logic: The recurring theme of terrorist abnormality in psychological research." *Psychology, Crime and Law*, 4.

Silke, A. (2001). "Terrorism." *The Psychologist*, 14.

Simonsen, C., and Spindlove, J. (2004). *Terrorism Today*, 2nd ed. Upper Saddle River, NJ: Prentice-Hall.

Slackman, M. (2006). "As Syria's Influence in Lebanon Wanes, Iran Moves In (March 13). www.nytimes.com, retrieved March 19, 2006.

Southern Poverty Law Center (2004). *The Year in Hate*. http://www.splcenter.org, retrieved May 5, 2004.

Tedeschi, J., and Felson, R. (1994). *Violence, Aggression, and Coercive Actions*. Washington, DC: American Psychological Association. In Hall (Ed.), *Terrorism: Strategies for Intervention*.

United Nations (2003). *Definitions of Terrorism*. www.unodc.org/unodc/terrorism_definitions.html, retrieved January 14, 2004.

U.S. Department of State (2003). *Patterns of Global Terrorism 2002*. www.state.gov, retrieved October 20, 2003.

U.S. Department of State (2004). *Patterns of Global Terrorism 2003*. www.state.gov, retrieved August 31, 2005.

U.S. Department of State (2005). *Country Reports on Terrorism 2004*. www.hsdl.org, retrieved March 13, 2006.

U.S. Government (2003). *National Strategy for Combatting Terrorism*. www. Whitehouse.gov/, retrieved March 5, 2004.

Weinberg, L., and Davis, P. (1989). *Introduction to Political Terrorism*. New York: McGraw Hill.

Weinzierl, J. (2004). "Terrorism: Its Origin and History." In A. Nyatepe-Coo and D. Zeisler-Vralsted (Eds.) *Understanding Terrorism: Threats in an Uncertain World*. Upper Saddle River, NJ: Pearson Prentice Hall.

White, J. (2003). *Terrorism: An Introduction*, 4th ed. Belmont, CA: Wadsworth/Thomson Learning.

White, J. (2004). *Defending the Homeland: Domestic Intelligence, Law Enforcement, and Security*. Belmont, CA: Wadsworth/Thomson Learning.

Wilkinson, P. (2003). "Why Modern Terrorism? Differentiating Types and Distinguishing Ideological Motivations." In C. Kegley (Ed.), *The New Global Terrorism: Characteristics, Causes, Controls*.

TERRORIST METHODS AND WEAPONS

OBJECTIVES

The study of this chapter will enable you to:

1. Describe the organizational structure of terrorist groups.
2. Explain educational resources and training for terrorists.
3. Define modus operandi and list examples pertaining to specific terrorist groups.
4. List and detail the methods of violence perpetrated by terrorists.
5. Explain the threat of cyberterrorism.
6. Examine how, during terrorist attacks, media reporting is used by terrorists, the government, and the media itself to further the goals of each group.
7. Identify the methods employed by terrorist groups to obtain financial support for their operations.
8. Define narcoterrorism, explain relevant methods, and describe its impact on government.
9. Name and describe conventional terrorist weapons.
10. Name and describe weapons of mass destruction.

KEY TERMS

division of labor	safe area bombing
chain of command	kamikaze
cellular model of organization	targeted killing
leaderless resistance	kidnapping
martyrdom tactics	hostage taking
new terrorism	Munich olympics
modus operandi	Black September Palestinian terrorists
hardened targets	hijacking
soft targets	skyjacking
strategy	cyberterrorism
tactic	cyberwarfare
People for the Ethical Treatment of Animals	built-in escalation imperative
secondary explosion	Al-Jazeera

KEY TERMS

money laundering
hawala system
narcoterrorism
M-19
Revolutionary Armed Forces of Columbia
Shining Path
manufactured firearms
improvised firearms
bored weapons

improvised explosive device
weapon of mass destruction
weapon of mass effect
ethnic targeting
anthrax
ricin
Aum Shinrikyo cult
radiological dispersion device

CRIMES TO SUPPORT TERRORISM

Detective Robert Fromme of the Iredel County Sheriff's Department noticed unusual behavior while moonlighting as a security officer for J. R. Tobacco, a wholesale distributor of tobacco products, in Statesville, North Carolina (Bell, 2004; Broyles and Rubio, 2004). Over several weeks, Fromme observed subjects driving vans with out-of-state license plates making large purchases of cigarette cartons and making payments with bags full of cash. Fromme contacted a friend, who was a federal agent, and a lengthy investigation began that involved over 15 law enforcement and intelligence agencies. Eventually, 26 subjects were arrested and convicted for such crimes as cigarette smuggling, money laundering, racketeering, bank fraud, immigration fraud, and, most importantly, providing "material support" to Hizballah, a terrorist organization. The case showed one way in which terrorist groups raise money illegally and how law enforcement agencies can apply their resources to control the problem.

Hizballah has been an enemy of the United States for several years. It was established in Lebanon in 1982 to oppose Israel and the West. The group has been linked to many attacks, such as the truck bombings of the U.S. Embassy and U.S. Marine barracks in Beirut in 1983 that killed over 200 Marines and the bombing of the U.S. Embassy annex in Beirut in 1994. Hizballah has also kidnapped and murdered Westerners and hijacked airplanes. U.S.-based cells have raised funds, recruited, and spread propaganda.

The group observed by Detective Fromme purchasing large quantities of cigarettes was a Hizballah cell led by Mohamad Hammoud. Family ties, religion, and politics united the cell.

The criminal activities of Hammoud, which are explained next, were typical of cell members. Hammoud sought permanent residence in the United States through sham marriages. After several years of perpetuating such fraud, the U.S. Immigration and Naturalization Service, without knowledge of Hammoud's scheme, granted him conditional lawful permanent residence status. Then, he assumed the identities of other individuals to avoid detection by police and to obtain drivers licenses and credit cards. One cell member associated with Hammoud would "max out" credit cards and make $150,000 annually per identity. One false identity would always be saved until its use was absolutely necessary.

The cell raised funds by purchasing North Carolina cigarettes, taxed at 50¢ per carton, and selling them in Michigan where the tax was $7.50 per carton. A van loaded with 1500 cartons could generate about $10,000 in profit. Between $1.5 and $2.5 million in profits were laundered through fraudulent shells and alias names. Expenses, such as vehicle rentals, gas, lodging, and meals, were charged to the credit cards.

CRIMES TO SUPPORT TERRORISM—Cont'd

Interestingly, the cell members recruited American women, some of whom worked at convenience stores, to drive the vans to Michigan. When rental trucks were used, bicycles were tied to the back to make it look as if a family was moving.

Some of the profits were used to build a gas station that was also financed by the U.S. Small Business Administration. Another way the cell made money was through a Web porn site that double-billed customers who paid by credit card, hoping the victims would not report the fraud. Three law enforcement agents, who were certified public accountants, were required to delineate the money trail through about 500 accounts involving credit cards, banks, and businesses, many with false identities.

The law enforcement methods applied in this case included physical surveillance, seizures, subpoenas, search warrants, cultivation of witnesses, investigative grand jury, analysis of telephone records, cameras, and financial analysis. Court-authorized electronic surveillance produced evidence of cigarette smuggling, money laundering, financial frauds, and ties to Hizballah. Hammoud, for example, was in almost daily contact with individuals in Lebanon, discussing Hizballah military operations.

Electronic surveillance by Canadian intelligence showed a Hizballah procurement cell in Vancouver that was tied to the North Carolina cell. "Dual use" equipment was sought by Hizballah in Lebanon, including night vision devices, laser range finders, ultrasonic dog repellers, aviation software, and photographic gear. It was learned later, for example, that the laser range finders improved the accuracy of shelling of enemies by Hizballah.

In July 2000, law enforcement agents executed 18 search warrants in Charlotte, North Carolina, and arrested 18 subjects. Valuable financial evidence and incriminating correspondence were seized, plus a virtual library on Hizaballah and various weapons.

The safety of those working on the case became an issue. The FBI told Ken Bell, Assistant U.S. Attorney, that Hammoud had asked an informant to "put two bullets into the skull of the arrogant bastard prosecutor." When Bell retired, he was provided with a remote car starter. Robert Fromme came home one day and caught two Arabic-looking men standing in his living room searching through a briefcase. They fled and could not be found.

For Bell to prove the most serious charge, "providing material support" to terrorists, he needed one of the cell members to turn against Hammoud. Agents focused on Said Harb, a high-living individual who was not a devout Muslim. He had maintained multiple identities and his phone had four different rings—each one for a different identity. Faced with a long prison term, he testified against Hammoud once he and his family in Lebanon were provided safe haven in the United States.

The 5-week trial in June 2002 resulted in Hammoud and other cell members being found guilty of multiple charges. As Hammoud "stared daggers through Bell" while sitting in shackles, he was sentenced to 155 years in prison. The case became a model to be used by law enforcement agencies to disrupt terrorist cells and the financing of terrorism.

CRITICAL THINKING:

In reference to the Hizballah case, why do you think this terrorist cell was able to establish itself and operate the smuggling operation without being detected initially?

TERRORIST METHODS

ORGANIZING FOR TERRORISM

Because of the loose, flexible, transnational network structure of modern terrorist organizations, facilitated by modern technology, terrorists can work together on funding, sharing intelligence, training, planning, and executing attacks (U.S. Government, 2003). For example, in 2001, three members of the Irish Republican Army were arrested by Columbian authorities for training the Revolutionary Armed Forces of Columbia (FARC) in how to operate an urban bombing campaign. Figure 2-1 shows how terrorists operate on three levels.

- *State level*: operate primarily within a single country and their reach is limited. Such a group may expand unless it is countered.
- *Regional level*: these groups operate regionally and transcend at least one international boundary.
- *Global level*: their operations cover several regions and their ambitions can be transnational and even global.

Terrorist groups often follow basic, universal characteristics of legitimate (e.g., business or government) or criminal organizations. For example, **division of labor** means that tasks are divided among workers according to such factors as function and clientele. A terrorist organization may have members specialize in recruitment, training, planning, finance, surveillance, bomb making, and assassinations. Smaller groups or cells may require members to specialize in multiple tasks.

Chain of command refers to upward and downward communications within an organized hierarchy to maintain order and control among workers. Superiors communicate tasks to be accomplished to subordinates through the chain of command. For example, terrorist leaders may decide that a suicide bombing is the next plan of action, so a subordinate is contacted to execute the plan. The subordinate then contacts another group member to prepare for the mission and to contact the suicide bomber. If, for instance, a serious problem develops with the preparation for the mission, then the chain of command would be followed so word of the problem would reach the leaders. The chain of command also serves to insulate leaders, as is the case with organized crime. Terrorists may also be organized into cells and characterized by decentralized decision making, as discussed later.

Organizations typically utilize manuals that are like "rule books" containing an organization's mission, philosophy, and policies and procedures. Manuals serve as training tools and assist individuals in learning how they can best serve the organization and its goals.

Figure 2-1 ■ Transnational Terrorist Networks. Source: U.S. Government (2003: 9).

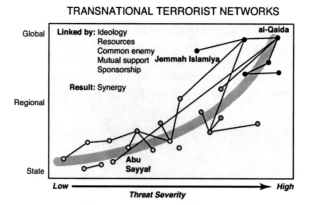

White (2003: 35–36) refers to the work of Fraser and Fulton (1984) to describe similarities in the organizational structure of terrorist groups. Fraser and Fulton divide the hierarchical structure of terrorist groups into four levels arranged as a pyramid.

- *Leadership* is at the top of the pyramid with command responsibilities.
- A *cadre* is at the second level and responsible for executing missions.
- *Active supporters* comprise the third level and provide assistance through safe houses, weapons, and other logistics.
- *Passive supporters* provide political support without actually joining a terrorist group. They are difficult to identify and they may be used by terrorists without their knowledge.

From a law enforcement or military perspective, terrorist groups that follow universal characteristics of organizations generate evidence of terrorist activities that can assist in their arrest. Because a division of labor requires specialized tasks, members must communicate and coordinate their work within a chain of command. Authorities using surveillance equipment can intercept communications. When authorities confiscate terrorist manuals, such information can be valuable for investigations and counterterrorism.

Because of the threat from law enforcement and the military, both transnational and home-grown terrorists are similar in their use of the **cellular model of organization**. This approach is decentralized rather than centralized. A decentralized cell is characterized by more discretion, very little (if any) communication within a larger chain of command, more self-sufficiency, and greater pressure to be creative and resourceful. This approach has also been referred to as **leaderless resistance**. Because a cell consists of a few members, and they know each other well, infiltration by government agents is very difficult. Because communication within a centralized chain of command or between cells is unnecessary, the interception of telephone calls, e-mails, and other forms of communication is less of a risk. Examples of successful cells with leaderless resistance are the al-Qaida network and the McVeigh–Nichols group that bombed the Murrah Federal Building in Oklahoma City.

Terrorist cells may be divided into various types according to functions. A *recruitment cell* serves to identify individuals who may be willing to join the cause. These cell members are active at houses of worship, institutions of higher education, and locations where radical ideas are being espoused. Because terrorists are very concerned about undercover agents infiltrating their cells, extreme caution and screening methods are employed to reduce this threat. A *support cell* provides aid to the mission by securing funds, training, transportation, travel documents, cover stories, disguises, safe houses, weapons, equipment, and so forth. An *intelligence cell* gathers a variety of information through surveillance, countersurveillance, investigation, careful interviewing, Web research, and other methods to increase security and secrecy and to help the mission succeed. A *sleeper cell* remains dormant, while blending into a community, until it is activated for a mission. Such cells present a serious threat and security concern to nations. An *operational cell* executes a mission. Because avoidance of detection is an extremely important objective of terrorists, the number of both cells and cell members is usually very limited. To increase security, a *multifunction cell* performs a variety of tasks while reducing the need to communicate and make contact with other cells.

EDUCATIONAL RESOURCES FOR TERRORISTS

Students studying to be terrorists have access to a wide assortment of readily available resources. The Web offers a huge volume of information on political groups, terrorist groups, targets, methods and tactics of terrorism, bomb making, homeland security, policing, the military, and so forth. For example, Al-Qaida offers its on-line military magazine, *Camp al-Battar*, which contains a variety of instructions on terrorist methods. Publications used to instruct terrorists include *The Terrorist's Handbook, The Anarchist's Cookbook, The Turner Diaries*, and assorted al-Qaida and

AL-QAIDA: CHALLENGING ASSUMPTIONS AND SERVING AS A MODEL FOR TERRORISTS

Before the 9/11 attacks, suicide bombers were thought to be poor, uneducated, unmarried, seeking revenge, and unable to mesh suicidal fanaticism with technical planning and skills (Gueli, 2003). Earlier profiles of suicide bombers did not include pilots or highly educated people capable of long-term, methodical planning. Some of the 19 terrorists who executed the 9/11 attacks had been planning the attacks for several years and even had U.S. Social Security numbers from the 1980s.

AL-Qaida uses loosely connected or indirectly connected cells among indigenous groups and Islamic movements throughout the world, which provide cover and opportunities to covertly gather funds from multiple sources. Al-Qaida exploits modern technology to advance its agenda and to launder money. It has used satellite technology, the Internet, cell phones, and fax machines, among other tools. It has exploited porous borders and weak immigration systems as it blends into communities worldwide. The al-Qaida network is a multinational enterprise with operations in more than 60 countries (U.S. Government, 2003: 7).

Poland (2005) writes that al-Qaida has several traits:

- long-range planning of several years prior to attacks
- the ability to conduct simultaneous attacks
- great emphasis on operational security (e.g., compartmentalized planning)
- flexible, decentralized, command structure of diverse membership that cuts across ethnic, class, and national boundaries
- attacks often follow these stages: intelligence and surveillance of a target; attackers rehearse the operation; a support team organizes safe houses, vehicles, forged documents, and weapons; and mission executed

Since the 9/11 attacks in 2001, a variety of sources have provided a description of al-Qaida operations. These sources include information from intelligence agencies, interrogation of captives, and documents from training camps and safe houses. One subject of interest is the selection of al-Qaida members (Caruso, 2002). To begin with, only Muslim men are considered in the rigorous screening process that covers background checks and interviews with family, friends, and the potential member. Because al-Qaida is acutely aware that government agents are seeking to infiltrate their group, a variety of countermeasures are used, such as never accepting volunteers. Al-Qaida recruits young men (late teens to early 30s), who have patience and discipline, and are willing to follow orders to the point of dying for "the cause." Al-Qaida handpicks recruits from Islamic centers, mosques, and schools. According to *Intelligence Digest* (2003), recruitment goes beyond the conflict areas of the Middle East, into Western countries, and essentially, it is worldwide.

A sworn oath of allegiance and code of silence is required by the group that, if broken, will result in a death sentence. Another method used to protect the group is to not reveal plans for attacks throughout the organization.

Once a prospect has been identified, they may be required to attend a religious or education center that is aligned with the al-Qaida perspective. Afghanistan was a prime location for al-Qaida basic training camps where recruits learned about al-Qaida ideology, weapons and explosives, identifying targets, and a broad range of techniques of terrorism. However, U.S. military action following 9/11 ended the Taliban regime in Afghanistan that supported the terrorist training camps in that country. Because of the global war on terrorism, training must be conducted under greater secrecy, in geographic areas that are isolated and under limited government control, or online.

During 2004, the Congressional commission investigating the 9/11 attacks heard testimony from the Central Intelligence Agency (CIA) about al-Qaida. The CIA noted that although al-Qaida lost some of its

AL-QAIDA: CHALLENGING ASSUMPTIONS AND SERVING AS A MODEL FOR TERRORISTS — Cont'd

high-ranking members and much of its command structure, it is not a spent force. It is adaptable, agile, and capable of lethal attacks in the United States and elsewhere. Diverse, autonomous groups inspired by al-Qaida ideology and successes have replaced the cohesive network of pre-9/11 days. These diverse groups may or may not receive multinational network support for training, financing, and other logistics.

Risk Management Solutions, Inc. (2004a: 2), a service company to the insurance industry and publisher of reports and risk models, emphasizes that al-Qaida is resilient, despite its losses. Al-Qaida is trying to compensate for its losses by turning to dozens of associated groups and the more than 70,000 Muslim youth it trained during the 1990s in Afghanistan, who are spread worldwide. One of al-Qaida's greatest successes is its ability to penetrate local Islamist groups in conflict and co-opt their leaders into expanding local and international struggles. Since 9/11, over 100 attacks have been aborted or disrupted, and al-Qaida's methods, such as its martyrdom tactics, continue to be a serious threat. **Martyrdom tactics** involve sacrificing one's life for a cause, usually in a suicide mission, and becoming a martyr.

Even though police and military action are pressuring al-Qaida, and it is not in the form is was prior to 9/11, it still serves as a model to other terrorists for being fluid, adaptable, creative, and patient. Al-Qaida has spawned and inspired terrorists worldwide.

Al-Qaida is not a centralized terrorist group with one strong leader, but rather a worldwide network of autonomous groups of diverse membership who are at war with the West.

Cold War-era manuals. Libraries and bookstores are other sources of information. Writers from a variety of disciplines have published periodical articles and books on terrorism that can provide helpful information on planning, goals, and strategies of terrorism. To be objective, this book can possibly be of use to terrorists. However, it is hoped that legitimate counterterrorism publications do more to control terrorists than to help them.

CRITICAL THINKING:

What can be done to reduce readily available resources on terrorist methods?

TRAINING FOR TERRORISTS

As covered in the previous chapter, state terrorism has a long history and it takes on many forms. During the last half of the 20th century, the former Soviet Union, for instance, provided aid to terrorists through training camps and arms. It established training camps internally and in eastern Europe, Cuba, and the Mideast. It also conspired with terrorist states, such as Libya, to supply arms and training to terrorists. Cuba was a popular Western training location for terrorists from Lain America, Africa, Palestine, and North America (e.g., Weather Underground). The Soviets tried to be discreet in their support of terrorists by arguing that they were supporting struggles for "liberation." By the 1990s, as the Soviet Union collapsed, this training network became too expensive, both financially and politically (Comb, 2003: 105–107). During the decades of Soviet power, the United States also played a role in supporting groups seeking "liberation." The methods of supporting terrorist groups have changed as Soviet-era support has declined and countries (e.g., Libya, Iran, and Syria) seek to distance themselves from terrorists because of the worldwide war on terrorism that is led by the United States.

Prior to 9/11, the Taliban in Afghanistan permitted Osama bin Laden to operate al-Qaida training camps until the Taliban fell to U.S. forces. Then, the training shifted to "home schooling," on-line training, and on-the-job training in Iraq during the occupation by coalition forces.

AL-QAIDA TRAINING

Following the 9/11 attacks and the war in Afghanistan, several terrorist publications (printed, electronic, and video) were seized from terrorist training camps in Afghanistan and from raids at terrorist residences worldwide. The information that follows is from an al-Qaida training manual that was located by the Manchester (England) Metropolitan Police during a search of an al-Qaida member's house. This manual was found in a computer file described as "the military series" related to the "Declaration of Jihad." The manual was retrieved from a U.S. Department of Justice (n.d.) Web site. The purpose of presenting this information is to improve counterterrorism, security, and investigations by studying the enemy. What follows are al-Qaida methods and tactics. Applications at the end of the chapter provide the reader with an opportunity to apply the information and "think like a terrorist" to understand them. Here are excerpts from the manual.

The Military Organization dictates a number of requirements to assist it in confrontation and endurance. These are:

- Military organization commander and advisory council
- The soldiers (individual members)
- A clearly defined strategy
- Forged documents and counterfeit currency
- Apartments and hiding places
- Communication means
- Transportation means
- Information
- Arms and ammunition

Missions Required of the Military organization The main mission for whom the Military Organization is responsible is: The overthrow of the godless regimes and their replacement with an Islamic regime. Other missions:

- Gathering information about the enemy, the land, the installations, and the neighbors.
- Kidnapping enemy personnel, documents, secrets, and arms.
- Assassinating enemy personnel as well as foreign tourists.
- Spreading rumors and writing statements that instigate people against the enemy.
- Blasting and destroying places of amusement, bridges, embassies, and economic centers.

Security precautions for forged documents:

- The photograph of the brother in these documents should be without a beard.
- When a brother is carrying a forged passport of a certain country, he should not travel to that country. It is easy to detect forgery at the airport, and the dialect of the brother is different from that of the people from that country.

Hiding Places These are apartments, command centers, etc., in which secret operations are executed against the enemy.

- It is preferable to rent apartments on the ground floor to facilitate escape and digging of trenches.
- Prepare secret locations in apartments to hide documents, arms, etc.
- Rent apartments using false names, appropriate cover, and non-Moslem appearance.
- Rent apartments in newly developed areas where people do not know one another. In older quarters, people know one another and strangers are easily identified.
- Prepare special ways of knocking and signs to communicate, such as hanging out a towel or opening a curtain.
- Replace locks and keys with new ones.

Security Plan This is a set of coordinated, cohesive, and integrated measures that are related to a certain activity and designated to confuse and surprise the enemy. The plan should be:

- Realistic and based on fact so it would be credible to the enemy before and after the work.
- Coordinated, integrated, cohesive, and accurate, without any gaps.
- Simple so that the members can assimilate it.
- Creative.
- Flexible.
- Secretive.

Traveling through an airport, the brother might be interrogated so he must be taught the answers to the following questions:

- What are the reasons for your travel?
- How did you get the money to travel?
- What will you be doing in the arrival country?
- Do you belong to a religious organization?
- With whom will you be staying?

When your true travel plans are discovered:

- Who trained you?
- On what weapons were you trained?
- Who are your contacts?
- What is your mission?

Security measures when gathering information:

- Walking down a dead-end street and observing who is walking behind you. Beware of traps.
- Casually dropping something out of your pocket and observing who will pick it up.
- Stopping in front of a store window and observing who is watching you.
- Agreeing with one of your brothers to look for whoever is watching you.
- Do not accept events at their face value. Do not overlook a quick friendship or an apparent dispute.
- Covert means of gathering information include surveillance, theft, interrogation, excitement, drugging, and recruitment.

- Collecting information from a military base should include fortifications, guard posts, lighting, numbers of soldiers, and sleeping and waking times. Start a friendship with soldiers by giving them rides to bus or train stations.

Many other topics were included in the manual, such as communications, transportation, meetings, weapons, assassinations, and guidelines for beating and killing hostages.

AL-QAIDA ASSASSINATION TRAINING

Prior to the fall of the Taliban, the Tarnak Farm in Afghanistan served as a training location for al-Qaida assassins. The 4- to 6-week curriculum consisted of instruction and group projects that involved planning an assassination. Training materials found at this facility covered such topics as motorcades, what drivers are taught, where the victim would be located in a motorcade, the weapons and procedures to be followed by the protection team, terrorist warning teams (i.e., people on the street ready to signal of an approaching motorcade), and diversionary tactics. Targets of opportunity were also covered, including visiting diplomats and corporate executives, victims with minimal or no security detail, and victims on foot. Interestingly, a seized training video showed a two-man team with a rocket-propelled grenade (RPG) on a makeshift golf course fire the weapon at a simulated golfer while students at the camp observed (Bauer, 2004).

ISLAMIC MOVEMENT OF UZBEKISTAN TRAINING

Another illustration of terrorist training comes from the region containing Uzbekistan, a central Asian country that was once within the Soviet Union (Olcott and Babajanov, 2003). When the Soviet Union disintegrated, fragile new governments were established in former Soviet Republics as their economies, social welfare systems, and military forces struggled to survive. The once powerful Red Army saw its personnel selling weaponry in exchange for basic human needs. In Uzbekistan, during the late 1980s and 1990s, a power vacuum enabled Muslim activists to gain recruits and form the Islamic Renaissance Party that rejected the secular state. To avoid a civil war, the Uzbek government purged Islamic groups through arrests and disappearances. Those who escaped fled to nearby Tajikistan and Afghanistan and formed the Islamic Movement of Uzbekistan whose members attended terrorist training camps in the region. Here is a summary from student notebooks from these camps that predate the expansion of al-Qaida.

- The training emphasizes hatred in the name of religious purification. People are either followers of the true faith or they are not.
- Although the students were not very educated and they made many mistakes when writing in their notebooks in Arabic, Russian, and their native Uzbek, they knew how to make deadly weapons and they learned through actual practice.
- Topics of training included cartography (i.e., making maps), small arms, including several types of the Kalashnikov rifle, the RPG, targeting and using sighting instruments, mines, and improvised explosive devices (IEDs).
- The student notebooks contained detailed drawings of the best locations for the placement of explosives at bridges, buildings, and water sources. Diagrams of the placement of mines showed how to camouflage them to avoid detection by approaching soldiers.
- Poisons were also studied and how to make poisons from common substances. One poisonous substance was made from corn flour, beef, yak dung, alcohol, and water. The students were also taught how to conceal odors so as not to alert victims. Safety was another topic and when to wear gloves and a mask.
- The final portion of the training covered when and how to make jihad and hatred for Jews, Christians, Americans, and Russians.

TERRORIST METHODS OF OPERATION

Martin (2003: 252) writes about the **new terrorism** of the 21st century and defines it as follows: "A typology of terrorism characterized by a loose cell-based organization structure, asymmetrical tactics, the threatened use of weapons of mass destruction, potentially high casualty rates, and usually a religious or mystical motivation." He adds that advances in technology, information, and transnational interconnectivity today influence terrorism. Terrorists have easy access to cell phones, computers, and the opportunity to locate almost anything (e.g., weapons of mass destruction, target information) on the Web. They travel the globe, often use false documents, and establish small, decentralized cells.

As discussed in the previous chapter, asymmetrical warfare offers terrorists (who are not a match against a powerful enemy in a conventional war) unorthodox methods to strike unexpectedly at symbolic targets and cause high casualties for maximum propaganda. In the Israeli–Palestinian conflict of recent years, Palestinian suicidal martyrs, with bombs strapped to their bodies, reached Israel and boarded buses or entered restaurants and detonated their explosives. The carnage immediately became global news.

A **modus operandi** (MO) or method of operation may characterize a terrorist group or individual terrorist. Also known as "signature crimes," these terms refer to the characteristic way in which an act is committed. As examples, some terrorist groups commit suicide bombings to inflict mass casualties, whereas others target diplomats and military and police officials for assassination. During the 1970s and 1980s, the Red Brigades of Italy used "kneecapping" to cripple their enemies; essentially, firearms were aimed low to destroy a victim's knee joints and kneecaps. Terrorists and criminals may use multiple MOs, or vary their MOs, to mislead authorities.

Risk Management Solutions, Inc. (2004b: 38) refers to the evolving MO of al-Qaida attacks as "multiple, synchronized detonations of large scale bombs, carefully planned, rehearsed, and resourced over many months of preparation." Also, as al-Qaida switches from **"hardened" targets** (i.e., locations with increased security, such as military bases and government buildings) to **"soft" targets** (i.e., locations with minimal security, such as schools, housing complexes, and houses of worship) (Figure 2-2), a developing MO is a preemptive armed assault (while using disguises) on security officers at access points to clear the way for the bomb run.

Terrorists follow a sequence of steps in an attack. Here is a generalization:

- *Step 1, significant event:* An enormous number of possible events can prompt a terrorist attack. Examples include an anniversary date, government action or inaction, violence against the terrorist group, and the availability of a particular target.

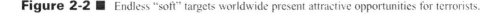

Figure 2-2 ■ Endless "soft" targets worldwide present attractive opportunities for terrorists.

- *Step 2, purpose:* This step has two parts: it delineates the message to be conveyed to the world once the attack is executed and media attention has focused on the attack; and the intended impact of the attack. The intended impact may force a government or corporation to change policies, but this may not occur.
- *Step 3, target selection, research, and surveillance:* Numerous targets are available to terrorists. The purpose of the attack influences the target. For instance, if terrorists in a particular country maintain a hatred for foreigners, tourists and international corporations may be subject to attack. Research and surveillance is an ongoing process because it serves as a foundation for a change in plans or subsequent attacks.
- *Step 4, planning the attack:* Terrorists have tremendous advantages in timing an attack and methods of attack. Questions in planning include those that relate to financing, intelligence, security, communications, cover stories, documents, equipment, vehicles, weapons, safe houses, ploys, assignments, and escape (if needed).
- *Step 5, attack:* At this point, following careful planning, the attack is executed. The results will vary depending on numerous factors.
- *Step 6, evaluation of immediate and long-term impact:* Terrorists assess the immediate impact of their attack, including casualties (victims and terrorists), property damage, media attention, and government and public reaction. The long-term impact can also include media attention and government and public reaction. Over a period of time, the policies of authorities may or may not change.

The list that follows contains terrorist strategies and tactics to illustrate the range of methods they employ and their cunning and creativity. A **strategy** means to plan and command forces to meet an enemy under advantageous conditions, whereas a **tactic** applies the most promising techniques of employing forces, weapons, and resources.

- Terrorists, such as al-Qaida, are often meticulous in their surveillance of potential targets and use disguises (Sauter *et al.*, 2004: 94).
- They may communicate an anonymous threat to a potential target to monitor response and procedures.
- Terrorists often emulate military methods as they plan, train, and execute their attacks. They have a high level of concern for security of operations and they are in need of intelligence, weapons, communications equipment, and vehicles.
- They may use the identification, uniforms, or vehicles of delivery, utility, emergency, or other type of service to access a target or dress as females to lower the perceived threat.
- Terrorists research the Web, libraries, and other sources for target intelligence. According to the al-Qaida training manual (discussed earlier), 80% of information about an enemy can be obtained legally through the Web.
- A terrorist may be planted in an organization as an employee to obtain information. The terrorist may work for a service or consulting firm to access many locations.
- Terrorists may attempt to detect surveillance by conducting dry runs of planned activities, using secondary roads and public transportation, employing neighborhood lookouts and tail vehicles, and establishing prearranged signals (Nason, 2004: 5).
- Terrorists are keenly aware that counterterrorism analysts study terrorist groups, seek intelligence, and piece together information to anticipate terrorist plans and attacks. Studies of terrorist groups and their methods are available from many sources. Terrorists study these resources and, in a "cat and mouse game," seek to mislead analysts by releasing bogus information to disrupt the intelligence process. Terrorists maintain an advantage over analysts because terrorists plot and analysts must seek to uncover the plot.
- Terrorists may employ economic warfare or target symbols of capitalism to harm an enemy. The airline industry and other businesses suffered economic hardship following the

9/11 attacks that included the World Trade Center. During 1997, the killing of several foreign tourists devastated the Egyptian tourist industry.

- Domestic right-wing terrorists are less organized than terrorists with links to the Middle East. The Christian Identify movement, with connections to the KKK, and World Church of the Creator members are noted for limited planning and random violence by lone wolves. They justify their rage through twisted religious teachings (Baker, 2005: 386).

- The Animal Liberation Front (ALF) and the Earth Liberation Front (ELF) commit arson through the use of improvised incendiary devices equipped with crude timing components. Members develop intelligence through surveillance of targets and reviews of industry publications. They may post details of their bombing devices and targets on their Web sites. ELF advocates "monkey wrenching," a euphemism for arson, tree spiking, and sabotage against industries perceived to be harming the environment (FBI, 2002).

- ALF and ELF, like al-Qaida, have a decentralized structure and operate in cells. ALF and ELF carry out direct action according to Web-posted guidelines. Each cell is autonomous and anonymous. Such a structure helps maintain security and evade law enforcement (Earth Liberation Front, 2004).

- The extremist animal rights group, **People for the Ethical Treatment of Animals** (PETA), has threatened researchers and calls for the violent destruction of animal industries. Their "Kids Campaign" includes distributing "unhappy meals" (boxes containing a toy bloody animal) at McDonald's restaurants and promoting "animals are your friends, not your food" (Speth, 2004: 6A).

- Various terrorist groups publish manuals on tactics as a tool to advance their cause. Antiabortionists have written a manual to close down abortion clinics by squirting Superglue into key holes so clinics cannot open, drilling holes into the low points of flat roofs, and placing garden hoses into mail slots and other openings to cause flooding ("Pro-Life Terrorism: A How-To," 1995).

METHODS OF VIOLENCE

Terrorists favor certain types of violent acts. These include bombings, suicide bombings, assassinations, assaults, kidnappings, and hijacking. They have tremendous advantages over authorities as they secretly plan their surprise attacks with discretion and flexibility over target location, victims, time of attack, weapons, and creative methods.

BOMBINGS

Bombings are a favored method of violence chosen by terrorists because of the potential for high casualties and severe property damage. The terrorist can remain at a distance from a detonated bomb and avoid injury and initial capture. Resourcefulness and creativity are hallmarks of terrorist bombings. Bombs can be constructed from so many items that are readily available and bombs can be hidden in almost anything.

Just one lone bomber can cause fear and loss of confidence in government by citizens. Eric Rudolph baffled police for years as he disappeared in the mountains of North Carolina. He was arrested in 2003 for four bombings: the 1996 Olympic Centennial Park bombing in Atlanta that killed 1 and injured 111, two abortion clinic bombings (one killed a police officer), and a bombing of a gay nightclub that injured 110.

In 2004, the U.S. Department of Justice released information on Jose Padilla, a U.S. citizen from Chicago, held indefinitely as an "enemy combatant." Padilla, trained by al-Qaida in Afghanistan, was alleged to have been planning to locate, on the Internet, multiple high-rise apartment buildings supplied by natural gas, rent apartments in each, seal all the openings, turn on the gas, and use timers to detonate each building simultaneously.

Devious planning by terrorists can intensify the impact of bombings on people and assets. The **secondary explosion** is a horrible terrorist ploy: an initial explosion draws first responders, assets, bystanders, and the media and then a second, larger bomb is detonated for more devastating losses. In the **safe area bombing**, terrorists call in a bomb threat at a facility and observe the evacuation and, more importantly, the assembly area. With such intelligence, a bomb is planted in the "safe area" to kill and injure more people than if the bomb exploded in the building where people are scattered.

The U.S. Department of Homeland Security periodically issues warnings of terrorist bomb-making techniques. It has warned that al-Qaida has been training its operatives to create a cotton-like explosive that can be placed inside clothes, toys, and pillows. The explosive is made by mixing nitric acid with cotton and then adding nitroglycerine. The end product is called nitrocellulose that can be lit to cause an explosion. Although X-ray machines cannot detect this explosive, trace-detection machines can detect the substance. Another warning focused on pressure cookers packed with explosives that can be initiated using simple electronic components, including digital watches, garage door openers, and cell phones.

SUICIDE BOMBINGS

Suicide attacks have a long history. The Assassins of the Mideast, during the 11th and 12th centuries, were early suicide attackers who inspired later generations (see Chapter 1). The Japanese **kamikaze** of World War II, in a desperate attempt to defend Japan against U.S. forces, crashed their bomb-filled planes into enemy ships. The 9/11 attackers were very successful in their suicide mission. Coupled with weapons of mass destruction, suicide attacks are a very serious threat to global security. Hoffman (2004: 103) notes that suicide bombings are inexpensive, effective, guarantee media coverage, are the ultimate "smart bomb," and "tear at the fabric of trust that holds societies together." Hoffman traveled to Israel to study the problem, as Israel has been deeply affected by suicide bombings. During 2002, Israel suffered an average of five suicide bombings per month. Hoffman begins his story of Israel's experience with suicide bombings by visiting a hospital and looking at X-rays with a doctor. A young girl was on her way to school when a suicide terrorist detonated a bomb on her bus. Eleven were killed and 50 others wounded. The explosion was so powerful that the hands to the bomber's watch turned into projectiles, lodging in the girl's neck and ripping an artery. The doctor explains other similar cases involving a nail in the neck, nuts and bolts in a thigh, and a ball bearing in a skull. Here are other points made by Hoffman in his research.

- The attacks cost about $150 and no escape plan was needed.
- Early on, the attackers carried their bombs in backpacks or duffel bags rather than under their clothes as they do now.
- Early on, the attackers were male, aged 17 to 23, and unmarried. Israeli authorities denied work permits to Palestinians fitting that description. Later, no clear profile was useful. They dressed as Israel soldiers, Orthodox Jews, and donned wigs to look like hip Israelis.
- Buses were preferred targets. Winter and summer were the best seasons for attacks because closed windows (for heat or AC) maximized the explosion and killing potential. As shrapnel pierced flesh and broke bones, the shock wave destroyed lungs and internal organs. When the fuel tank exploded, it caused a fireball that burned the victims.
- Only 2 or 3 kilograms of explosive on a bus can kill as many people as a 20- to 30-kilogram bomb left on a sidewalk or in a restaurant.
- The suicide bomber is flexible and can change plans at the last second to respond to security or to increase lethality. In one case, a female bomber was deterred from an open-air market because of a strong police presence so she walked down the street to a busy bus stop to detonate her bomb.
- Terrorist groups such as Hamas, the Palestine Islamic Jihad, and the al-Aqsa Martyrs Brigade recruit suicide bombers, conduct reconnaissance, prepare the bomb, and identify the target.

- Prior to the attack, the bomber is sequestered in a safe house, away from family and friends, for final preparations for martyrdom and psychological reinforcement. A film crew does a video recording for propaganda and recruitment.
- A handler assists the bomber by guiding him or her to the target while avoiding checkpoints and security. The handler may use a cell phone or other device to trigger the blast from a distance.
- Suicide bombings in Israel have terrorized Israeli society. They have changed people's daily life and their routines. People choose a taxi rather than a bus and avoid crowds such as at restaurants and markets.

In addition to men, women maintain a role as suicide bombers in various regions of the world. The al-Aqsa Martyrs Brigade believes that suicide bombing is more effective against Israel's occupation of Palestinian land and other injustices than guerrilla warfare. According to this group, the old stereotypical suicide bomber of male, unmarried, immature, undereducated, between 17 and 23 years old, and fanatically religious has changed to female, mature, intelligent, and between 18 and 25 years old (Tierney, 2002). In Chechnya, where the Chechens have been seeking independence from Russia for over 150 years, women play a dominant role in suicide bombings. Russians call the female attackers "black widows" because many are relatives of Chechens killed in the war for independence (Zakaria, 2003: 57).

Bunker (2005) explains suicide bomber advantages. He writes that the suicide bomber can precisely deliver the bomb to the target (even hardened targets). There are limited opportunities for authorities to find the bomb and safely remove it from the target area. There is no planned escape. The offender is unlikely to be a medical burden to comrades because of wounds, nor is an interrogation by authorities likely. Suicide bombers can create a hazardous materials incident if they are infected by a disease or if they apply poison to the bomb components.

THE EFFICIENCY OF SUICIDE BOMBING TECHNIQUES

In early 2001, Dahmane Abd al-Sattar, a Tunisian al-Qaida member based in Belgium, received the most important mission of his life. He and an accomplice had been ordered to execute a suicide bomb attack on Ahmed Shah Massoud, leader of the Northern Alliance in Afghanistan. With the help of several European-based coconspirators, Sattar and his accomplice departed on a long journey, posing as journalists and using forged passports. Their first stop was in England to obtain a letter of introduction from a prominent Islamic religious leader to gain access to Massoud. Next, they traveled to Pakistan where, with the letter in hand, they received visas at the Afghanistan embassy. Then to Kabul (controlled by the Taliban at the time), the capital of Afghanistan, where they obtained permission to enter the Panjshir Valley to meet their target. Following negotiations, the assassins got approval to interview Massoud. One placed a rigged camera on a table facing Massoud. Sattar asked Massoud what he would do with Osama bin Laden if he (Massoud) returned to power. Massoud reportedly laughed and then the camera-bomb exploded, killing him and one assassin. The other assassin was shot dead by bodyguards. This attack helped al-Qaida by killing the most capable leader of the Northern Alliance and also showed the efficiency of suicide bombing techniques (Smith, 2002).

ASSASSINATIONS

To begin with, not all assassins are terrorists. Assassins may be angered at a prominent person or mentally disturbed. President James Garfield was assassinated in 1881 by a disappointed office seeker. In 1981, John Hinckley, who was trying to impress actress Jody Foster, wounded President Ronald Reagan in a failed assassination attempt.

Assassinations have been a popular terrorist method for centuries. The killing of just one prominent individual can have a profound impact on society and politics. This is why terrorists look to assassinations as a powerful weapon. One of the causes of World War I was the assassination of Archduke Ferdinand of Austria in 1914. The assassination of President John F. Kennedy in 1963 is still shrouded in debate over who was behind the killing. The former Prime Minister of Israel, Yitzhak Rabin, was gunned down in 1995 by an Israeli student-extremist because of Rabin's peace efforts with the Palestinians. Although Rabin had received threats, he refused a bullet-resistant vest and other safety precautions. His assassin dressed as a chauffeur and waited near Rabin's vehicle.

"TARGETED KILLING" OR ASSASSINATION?

Because of appalling attacks on its civilian population by Palestinians, primarily suicide bombers, Israel retaliated with what the Israeli government has called **"targeted killing"** (Stein, 2003). Between September 2000 and December 2002, Palestinians killed 443 Israeli civilians, including 83 minors. Many more were injured. The "targeted killing" has resulted in the deaths of 86 terrorists and 40 Palestinian bystanders. The methods used by Israeli authorities include threats, extortion, or payments to collaborators for information; use of disguises (e.g., women, Arabs) to reach the target; and helicopter gun ships to fire missiles at target vehicles.

"Targeted killing" is controversial. Opponents argue that it is illegal according to international and Israeli law and that "targeted killing" is a euphemism for assassination. Amnesty International and Human Rights Watch see this Israeli action as assassination and the term "targeted killing" is unknown in international law. Supporters claim it is not assassination because Israel is at war with terrorists and those targeted are combatants or part of a military chain of command.

The United States has had internal debate over the topic of assassination (Lowry, 2002). In 1975, Senator Church's Congressional committee criticized the CIA as a "dirty tricks" operation and focused on shadowy U.S. involvement in the killings of politicians in the Congo, the Dominican Republic, and Vietnam. Questions surfaced about whether the CIA was operating with the necessary democratic accountability. These killings resulted from "peacetime political preferences," although peacetime was difficult to define during the Cold War, according to Lowry. Senator Church said "We have gained little, and lost a great deal, by our part policy of compulsive interventionism." International law recognizes heads of state and diplomats as off limits to assassination in peacetime, but war changes the rules.

Hanley (2006) reported on research by Jenna Jordan, of the University of Chicago, who studied 72 cases of targeted killings during the last century. She found that if the group was religious based, like al-Qaida, in 4 out of 5 cases, the group carried on, despite the killing of its leader. Jenna argued that such killings fuel the movement. In January of 2006, when a U.S. missile strike on a home in Pakistan targeted an al-Qaida deputy, 13 villagers were killed and possibly a few al-Qaida operatives, but the deputy was not present. Following the attack, demonstrators filled streets in Pakistan and chanted "death to America" in support of Jihad.

CRITICAL THINKING:

Is the Israeli policy of "targeted killing" actually assassination? Should the United States use assassination in the war against terrorism? Support your answers.

ASSAULTS

Assaults include various types of violent attacks against an endless number of hard and soft targets (Figure 2-3). An armed group of terrorists may storm a military base, police station, government building, airport, school, house of worship, or other location to inflict as many casualties as possible before withdrawing. The assault may lead to a hostage situation, assassination, bombing, or other violent events. Infrastructure, such as a power-generating station or oil pipeline, is another target. Terrorists can also assault a location from a distance through mortars and rockets.

KIDNAPPING AND HOSTAGE TAKING

Poland (1988: 137) differentiates **kidnapping** and hostage taking by defining the former as [seizing and] confining the victim to a *secret location* and making demands or the victim will be killed. Terrorists, and criminals without political motivations, have used kidnapping with success. **Hostage taking** involves a *direct confrontation with authorities at a known location* while victims are held. Terrorists usually seek media attention for their cause and make other demands. Criminals without political motivations may take a hostage because of, for example, a botched robbery. These definitions have problems and Poland admits "the distinction is often blurred."

Offenders who kidnap and hold hostages can be quite creative and crafty, causing problems for victims and authorities. Schiller (1985: 59) offers the following case: In 1976, the descendant of a wealthy German businessman was kidnapped after leaving a university building in Bavaria. Richard Oetker, 25, was forced into a small wooden box measuring $60 \times 70 \times 120$ centimeters.

Figure 2-3 ■ Armed fighters. Source: www.hamasonline.com

He had to assume an unnaturally bent and cramped position and was connected to an electrical device that would kill him if he tried to escape. Two days later the family delivered a huge ransom and then Oetker was found in a forest, crippled for life. Electrical shocks had cracked two breastbones and both thighbones, his heart rhythm was irregular, and a lung had collapsed from shallow, cramped breathing for 47 hours. Two years later an unemployed, mechanically inclined economist was arrested after a banknote from the ransom was traced to him. Most of the ransom remains lost and no accomplices were arrested.

The massacre at the **Munich olympics** in 1972 had a profound impact on the world and future police operations against terrorists (Simonsen and Spindlove, 2004: 184–185; Poland, 2005: 156–157). As shown in Chapter 1, **Black September Palestinian terrorists** disguised themselves as athletes to enter the Olympic games with AK-47s and hand grenades. Once inside, they shot dead two Israeli athletes and then held other Israeli athletes hostage. The terrorists demanded the release of 234 Palestinians held in Israeli jails and freedom for other terrorists. The Israeli government refused to negotiate. However, German authorities agreed to take the terrorists and the remaining hostages to an airport for a flight to Cairo. When the group arrived, German police sharpshooters opened fire and the terrorists threw hand grenades into the helicopter holding the bound Israelis. In the end, 11 Israeli athletes, 1 police officer, and 5 terrorists were killed. The German police were subject to much criticism for their failed rescue. Police agencies worldwide saw the need for special, elite units with expertise in hostage negotiation. The Israeli response was to hunt down major terrorist participants and eliminate them through assassination.

During 2004, following the second war in Iraq involving the United States, al-Qaida terrorists began a campaign of beheading their enemies as a terrorist tactic and to force foreigners out of Iraq (Associated Press, June 19, 2004). In Saudi Arabia, al-Qaida applied this tactic to drive foreign workers away and undermine the royal family. In one case, Paul Johnson, a U.S. citizen working on helicopters in Saudi Arabia, was kidnapped. Thousands of Saudi police searched several Riyadh neighborhoods going door to door as helicopters flew overhead. At the same time, a videotape appeared on a Web site demanding the release, within 72 hours, of all militants held by the Saudi government, otherwise al-Qaida would kill Johnson. Interestingly, people living in fundamentalist districts of Riyadh stated that the kidnappers enjoyed popular support because of U.S. policy in Iraq and America's support of Israel. One resident, while eating at a restaurant called "Jihad," referred to U.S. armed forces abuse of Iraqi prisoners and Israeli military action against Palestinians. Although an FBI team specializing in hostage rescue and profiling was dispatched to help Saudi authorities, and despite the massive search for Johnson, a Web site showed a man's head, face forward, being held by a hand, a beheaded body lying on a bed, and a knife. An al-Qaida statement threatened enemies of Islam with the same fate and emphasized that Johnson got a taste of what Muslims have experienced from Apache helicopter fire and missiles. Soon after the beheading, Saudi security forces tracked down and killed the leader of the terror cell responsible for the crime. One month later, Johnson's head was found in a home freezer in an al-Qaida hideout during a raid by Saudi security forces. Also found were a SAM-7 missile, explosives, video cameras, and cash.

HIJACKING

Hijacking means that a vehicle has been seized through unlawful action. Terrorists have applied this method for many years for reasons such as shock value and media attention, to hold hostages in exchange for demands, to use the vehicle as a weapon, or for transportation. Vehicles are varied and, thus, terrorists may target aircrafts, buses, autos, ships, trains, or whatever vehicle their creative minds focus on.

Skyjacking is a term used to describe the hijacking of an aircraft. Skyjacking creates global media attention, and as events unfold, this terrorist method can be deadly. In 1986, Pan Am Flight 73 was being loaded with passengers at Karachi International Airport when four Arab-speaking terrorists seized the plane. They held 375 passengers and 15 crew members for 16 hours.

When electricity on the plane began to fail and the lights dimmed, the terrorists panicked and began firing wildly at the cowering passengers. Then, Pakistani commandos took back the plane, but 21 hostages were killed and 60 were wounded. The 9/11 attacks against the United States illustrate the dangers and complications resulting from planes being seized by terrorists. In this case the planes became weapons of mass destruction.

In 1985, Palestinian terrorists disguised as tourists hijacked an Italian cruise ship named the Archille Lauro. The terrorists threatened to kill passengers unless Israel released Palestinian prisoners. They also said they would blow up the ship if a rescue was initiated. During the hijacking, an American Jew named Leon Klinghoffer, who had been confined to a wheelchair, argued with the terrorists, and when their demands were not met, he was shot and tossed overboard. Egypt was able to negotiate the release of the passengers in exchange for safe passage out of the country. As the terrorists were being flown to a safe haven, U.S. jet fighters were able to intercept the plane because of excellent intelligence. The plane was forced down in Italy and the terrorists were seized by Italian authorities and tried in an Italian court.

CYBERTERRORISM

Cyberterrorism refers to the exploitation and attack of cyberspace targets by terrorists as a method to cause harm to reach terrorist goals. Because of our widespread dependence on information technology, telecommunications, and the Internet, cyberspace is a tempting target for terrorists. The targets for attack are endless—disruption of electrical power grids, international financial transactions, air traffic controls, drinking water systems, and so forth. Our infrastructure, businesses, and institutions are already battling viruses and worms from hackers. If terrorists expand the assault, then creativity, boldness, and lethality are likely to take on new meanings. Although there have been few cyberterrorism attacks (Denning, 2001: 281), terrorists are notorious for locating target weaknesses to exploit for spectacular losses.

If **cyberwarfare** is an indication of what will occur in the future, the threat of cyberterrorism appears more ominous. The military of many countries has expanded operations to cyberspace and "cold cyberspace battles" have been fought. Israeli and Palestinian hackers have attacked each other's Internet infrastructures (Kabay and Walsh, 2000: 34). As a world power, U.S. government sites are attacked repeatedly. In 2001, following the loss of a Chinese fighter jet in a collision with a U.S. reconnaissance aircraft, pro-Chinese hackers defaced or crashed 100 U.S. government and commercial Web sites. American hackers retaliated by damaging 300 Chinese Web sites (National Infrastructure Protection Center, 2001).

Like hackers, cyberterrorists have the advantage of attacking from almost anywhere, by themselves, at minimal expense, without risk of harm, and with limited risk of detection. Furthermore, cyberterrorists can cover their tracks and, with the use of encryption programs that are almost unbreakable, make the attack appear as if it originated from another source. These encryption programs also provide more secure communications among terrorists (Denning, 2001).

MEDIA SUPPORT FOR TERRORISTS

A high priority of terrorists is to seek media coverage for their cause. They can send a statement of grievances and demands to the media, however, the impact will likely be less than if they commit a violent act. Unfortunately, the more outrageous, violent, and lethal the terrorist act, the more publicity terrorists will reap from the media. It can be argued that the media is a tool of terrorists. At the same time, the media may sensationalize attacks to boost ratings that can transfer into greater profits. *Is this a symbiotic relationship whereby each feeds off the other for mutual benefit? Is the media the reason why terrorism is receiving so much attention and why it seems to be growing? Should government censor the media to reduce terrorism?* These questions can generate much debate.

A free society abhors censorship (i.e., government control over what the media can release to the public). The First Amendment of the Bill of Rights of the U.S. Constitution states: "Congress shall make no law ... abridging the freedom of speech, or the press...." The media argues for the right to have access to news on terrorist events, crimes, and disasters, and to report such news.

From the law enforcement perspective, police caution that in hostage situations, for example, media reporting can cause harm to victims. When crimes occur and police collect evidence, they withhold information on evidence from the media because a case can be lost. For instance, a murder would likely destroy shoes that had been worn to the crime scene if the media reported that police possessed a cast of a shoe print found at the crime scene.

Combs (2003: 148) writes: "But media is clearly not responsible for terrorist acts occurring." However, she adds: "It is possible to infer from a variety of studies on this issue that the media can impact terrorists by what Schmid [1982] terms **built-in escalation imperative** that requires that terrorists must commit more and more bizarre and cruel acts to gain media attention." Combs offers examples, such as between 1985 and 1989, when shooting a single American stopped generating many articles, bombings resulting in multiple deaths grew.

In reference to news stories on terrorism, here is a summary of the goals of terrorists, the media, and democratic government (Combs, 2003: 149–153):

TERRORISTS
- Welcome free publicity to a global audience concerning their cause and how to correct grievances.
- Strive for a favorable understanding by the audience as to why the violence occurred.
- Seek legitimacy and identity to recruit members and to generate funding.
- Try to destabilize the enemy through fear that the government is weak.

MEDIA
- Is in competition to report the news first.
- Strives for dramatic presentations.
- Seeks to protect the public's right to know about news.
- Wants to protect themselves from violence.

GOVERNMENT
- Seeks help from the media to end terrorist incidents and to save lives.
- Prefers to portray attacks as criminal and against innocent victims.
- Aims to deny terrorists a platform to express their views and seek support.
- Prefers that the media share information with government and act in a discreet manner.

CRITICAL THINKING:
Does the media play a role in causing terrorism? Should government control the media during terrorist incidents? Explain.

The Internet has become a helpful avenue of communications for terrorist groups. Free discussion boards and e-mail accounts enable sympathizers to chat worldwide and messages may be encrypted. This free flow of communications, including Web sites, aids in seeking support, recruitment, and fund raising. The Web has proven useful to terrorists in releasing video of taped speeches and even gruesome images of beheadings, as was done by al-Qaida in Iraq during 2004. Countermeasures lag as Web hosting companies try to close such sites. And, as sites are closed, others appear as replacements. Police and the military focus on the Internet to collect intelligence, as an avenue to infiltrate terrorist groups, and to gather evidence for prosecution.

Using digital technology, terrorists and sympathizers have employed common authoring software to mass produce and sell globally CDs and DVDs to portray their perspective on current events. Amateur digital video from digital cameras is bringing violence to the Internet and competing with traditional media outlets. The professionalism, standards, and objectivity of journalists (although the meaning of these terms is subject to debate) are in competition with amateurs who have access to technology that brings manipulation to new heights.

The news media is subjective and biased. To illustrate, newspaper editors decide each day what story will make front page headlines, what stories will be placed in subsequent pages, and what stories will not be printed at all. Globally, people receive subjective and biased news about the Mideast. The reasons for this are numerous and debatable. Governments of any nation, including their military, as well as political and other groups, are likely to offer press releases and supply information to the media that favor their policies and agendas. Naturally, the U.S. government releases information to the media that supports U.S. policy in the Mideast. Media consumers in the Mideast and elsewhere seek alternative viewpoints on current events. One alternative source to Western news sources is the Arab-based *Al-Jazeera*. It has been described by the Bush administration as a "mouthpiece for Osama bin Laden" and by Mideast politicians as a source of American propaganda. *Al-Jazeera* is described as the Mideast's only independent news station; its headquarters is in Qatar. For people who have lived in the United States and the Mideast, they are amazed at how differently the media covers the same events (Ali, 2004: 12). The Aljazeera.net Web site claims that it goes behind the scenes to provide every visitor with "the news they don't see" (Aljazeera.Net, 2004a). For example, *Al-Jazeera* reported that Iran accused the United States of supporting terrorism. The story began when Iran announced that it had developed a ballistic missile capable of reaching Israel. The next day, President Bush countered by stating that Iran was continuing to harbor and assist terrorists. To counter Bush's statements, the Iranian foreign minister accused U.S. armed forces of allowing an armed Iranian terrorist group to operate from Iraq even though it was a registered terrorist organization (Aljazeera.Net, 2004b).

FINANCIAL SUPPORT FOR TERRORISTS

Although individual terrorist attacks are not necessarily expensive, the support of terrorist networks, training camps, command and control, and infrastructure requires either a large reserve of cash or the ability to raise cash continually. Unlike organized crime, such as the illegal drug trade or human trafficking, terrorist groups generally need financing to continue their operations. Terrorists raise, move, and use money that may leave a trail for investigators (Buckley and Meese, 2004: 51).

White (2003: 40–42) refers to the research of Adams (1986) concerning the financing of terrorist groups. Here are major points from Adams' work.

- Terrorism changed between the 1960s and the 1980s and many Western countries did not modify their policies.
- While terrorism was changing, the United States and other Western nations' antiterrorism policies focused primarily on state-sponsored terrorism. However, major terrorist groups became independent of states and created their own financial support network to survive.
- The best strategy to control terrorism is to focus on the financial networks that support independent terrorist groups.
- Adams supports his contentions by providing examples: The Palestinian Liberation Organization (PLO) formed an economic wing named the Samed in 1970. It is a business group designed to support the PLO. The Provisional IRA operated an organized crime network in Northern Ireland and secured funds by intimidating retailers into paying protection money. Also, it has established front businesses and used terrorism to drive the competition out of business.

Terrorist financing involves many types of illegal and legal businesses. A variety of terrorist groups use commodities (e.g., diamonds, gold) and money laundering as part of their financing network. **Money laundering** involves transforming the profits from illegal activities into usable forms and hiding the origins of the profits. The opening of this chapter provides an example of terrorist financing and money laundering by Hizballah.

The al-Qaida global network has a history of operating a variety of business enterprises that support its activities. For example, in 2004, a United Nations–Sierra Leone court (West Africa) stated that al-Qaida suspects converted "terror cash" into untraceable "blood diamonds." The National Commission on Terrorist Attacks Upon the United States (2004) (also known as the "9/11 Commission") stated that al-Qaida and Usama bin Ladin obtained money from a variety of sources. The commission declared: "No persuasive evidence exists that al-Qaida relied on the drug trade as an important source of revenue, had any substantial involvement with conflict diamonds, or was financially sponsored by any foreign government."

Another source of funding for terrorists is charities. Although many legitimate charities exist and provide assistance to the needy, charities have also been used as fronts to collect money for terrorist activities.

The National Commission on Terrorist Attacks Upon the United States (2004) claimed that, contrary to myth, Usama bin Ladin did not have access to significant wealth from an inheritance or businesses and did not personally fund al-Qaida. He was born into a wealthy Saudi family, but his family severed ties to him. Al-Qaida was funded by diversions of money (about $30 million annually) from Islamic charities collected from witting and unwitting donors.

The commission reported that the 9/11 attacks cost between $400,000 and $500,000, and most of the money passed through the hijackers' bank accounts in the United States. The money was moved by wire transfers from overseas, physical transport of cash or traveler's checks, and accessing foreign accounts by debit or credit cards. While in the United States, the hijackers spent the money on flight training, travel, and living expenses (e.g., housing, food, cars, and auto insurance). Although they blended into the global financial system, they also left a paper trail.

In 2004, top executives of the Dallas-based Holy Land Foundation for Relief and Development, which claimed to be the largest Muslin charity in the United States, were indicted by a Federal grand jury for funneling millions of dollars to Hamas to support and encourage families involved in violence (e.g., suicide bombers) against Israel. The charges included supporting a foreign terrorist organization, conspiracy, money laundering, and filing false tax returns.

The 9/11 attacks led to the freezing of al-Qaida assets and those of other terrorist groups and suspect charities. At the same time, al-Qaida and various terrorist groups use the **hawala system**, an old Islamic method of transferring funds globally through brokers who acknowledge transactions based on trust. The informal nature of this system, without government oversight, leaves a limited "paper trail," an advantage to terrorist financing. The commission admits that al-Qaida financing remains a difficult target for intelligence gathering.

In addition to the crime of terrorism, terrorists are involved in a variety of other crimes, many of which are perpetrated to support themselves and their operations. They have a flagrant disregard for international, national, and local laws and justify their behavior as part of the struggle for their cause.

NARCOTERRORISM

The U.S. Drug Enforcement Administration (DEA) defines **narcoterrorism** as a "subset of terrorism in which terrorist groups or individuals participate directly or indirectly in the cultivation, manufacture, transportation or distribution of controlled substances and the monies derived from these activities" (Barnard, 2003). Terrorists and drug traffickers cooperate with each other for a variety of reasons. A terrorist group may offer training and weapons to traffickers in exchange for cash as both groups unite to keep police and military forces at bay. Terrorists and drug traffickers engage in what legitimate organizations refer to as cross training. Each group learns the others' skills and methods. When terrorists assist drug traffickers, they can learn more about protecting areas under cultivation and during the manufacturing process; the distribution system; money laundering; and how to influence government officials. Drug traffickers can learn about the following from terrorists: explosives, bombing, weapons, false documents, kidnapping, and exploitation of the media. The enormously profitable illegal drug business has a corrupting influence over government officials that enhances the operations of these criminals while undermining legitimate government. The revenue stream from the illegal drug trade is attractive to terrorists.

Latin America has been a hotbed of narcoterrorism, especially in Columbia. The **M-19** organization has battled the Columbian government and U.S. interests in Columbia since 1974. This group has occupied towns, attacked army garrisons, assassinated officials, kidnapped wealthy people, and hijacked airlines. M-19 is well known for seizing Bogota's Palace of Justice where 500 people were held hostage and 50 were killed, including 11 Supreme Court Justices. Funds are obtained by extorting money from coca leaf and marijuana growers. Another Columbian terrorist group is the **Revolutionary Armed Forces of Columbia** (FARC). Like M-19, it is a classic narcoterrorist group that maintains a close link to drug traffickers, especially by protecting the processing of coca (Lyman and Potter, 2004: 408–409).

Peru is another South American nation plagued by the problem of narcoterrorism. The group **Shining Path** has allied itself with coca growers and drug traffickers to subvert and battle the Peruvian government (Garamone, 2003).

In the Mideast, Afghanistan, Syria, and Lebanon have been involved with the illegal drug trade and terrorism for many years. In fact, it has been argued that nearly every documented terrorist group has had, or currently has, ties to drug trafficking (Barnard, 2003). The White House's Office of Drug Control Policy notes that the security situation in certain countries, such as Afghanistan, complicates the task of fighting the war against terrorism and the war against drugs at the same time. Consequently, in the last few years, opium production has increased in Afghanistan and a portion of profits is going to terrorists. Additionally, other types of drugs and sources are open to terrorists. In 2003, the U.S.S. Decatur, a guided missile destroyer, intercepted a 40-foot boat in the Persian Gulf and found it to be carrying nearly 2 tons of hashish worth about $8 million and men with ties to al-Qaida. In 2002, U.S. authorities discovered a group of men of Mideast descent who were involved in the manufacturing of methamphetamine in several large U.S. cities. The men were linked to Hezbollah and other terrorist groups in Lebanon and Yemen (Barnard, 2003). Historically, authorities confiscate a very small percentage of illegal drugs. Thus, narcoterrorism is probably much worse than reported.

CRITICAL THINKING:

What impact do you think narcoterrorism is having on governments today and what are your predictions for its impact on governments in the future? How can it be controlled?

TERRORIST WEAPONS
CONVENTIONAL WEAPONS

The United Nations, Office on Drugs and Crime (2004) provides a listing and explanation of conventional terrorist weapons as covered next. First, some basic terms and definitions from the United Nations. **Manufactured firearms** refer to those arms made professionally by arms factories, whereas **improvised firearms** are made by nonprofessional arms factories or by illicit workshops. Firearms are also called **bored weapons**, referring to the barrel from which a bullet or projectile is fired, or the tube used to launch a projectile.

Manufactured firearms can be divided into three categories.

- Small arms are under the level of medium machine guns or, using a loose rule, not belt-fed machine guns. These small arms include auto-pistols, revolvers, rifles, submachine guns, assault rifles, and light machine guns.
- Medium-size infantry weapons refer to medium-sized machine guns (many belt fed), small mortars, rocket-propelled grenades, and small caliber wire-guided missiles.
- Heavy infantry weapons include heavy caliber machine guns, heavy caliber mortars, large caliber wire-guided missiles, shoulder-held antitank missile launchers, and some rockets not in the category of artillery.

Four examples of weapons possessed by terrorists are explained next.

1. *AK-47 (Soviet rifle).* This weapon, invented by Mikhail Kalashnikov, became the standard rifle for the Soviet Army in 1949 until it was succeeded by the AKM. During the Cold War, the AK-47 was supplied by the former Soviet Union to anti-Western armed forces and insurgent terrorists. It became a symbol of left-wing revolution and is still in the arsenal of armies, guerrillas, and terrorists. Between 30 and 50 million copies and variations of the AK-47 were distributed globally to make it the most widely used rife in the world (Figure 2-4).
2. *RPG-7.* Issued by the former Soviet Union, China, and North Korea, this simple weapon is effective against a variety of targets within a range of about 500 meters for a fixed target (e.g., building) and about 300 meters when fired at a moving target (Figure 2-5). The RPG-7 is a shoulder-fired, muzzle-loaded, antitank and antipersonnel grenade launcher. It can also bring down a helicopter. The RPG-7 fires a fin-stabilized, oversized grenade from a tube. The launcher weighs 15.9 pounds and has an optical sight. Upon firing, it leaves a telltale blue-gray smoke and flash signature that helps identify the firer. U.S. forces in Vietnam used sandbags and chicken wire on vehicles to cause the RPG-7 grenade to explode before meeting the skin of vehicles. This technique continues to be applied, as in Iraq. Additional protection methods include avoiding the same route, pushing through ambush positions to avoid setting up a target, smoke grenades, and aerial surveillance (Mordica, 2003). The RPG is widely available in illegal international arms markets and is in the arsenal of many terrorists groups, such as those in the Middle East and Latin America.

Figure 2-4 ■ AK-47, Soviet assault rifle.

Figure 2-5 ■ Rocket-propelled grenade. Source: www.hamasonline.com

3. *Stinger*. The U.S.-made stinger is a single person, portable, heat-seeking, shoulder-fired surface-to-air missile (SAM). It proved its value when the Afghan Mujahedeen forced the Soviets out of Afghanistan during the late 1980s. The Stinger has targeted jets, helicopters, and commercial airliners.
4. *SA-7*. When the Soviet Union collapsed, thousands of SAMs were sold and found their way into the arsenals of several terrorist and guerrilla groups. The SA-7, also called the Grail, uses an optical sight and tracking system with an infrared (i.e., heat-seeking) device to reach aircraft.

THE DANGER OF SAM

SAM is the initials for surface-to-air missile. Of the many types of SAMs, one variation is the portable, heat-seeking, shoulder-fired missile. Generally, the portable SAM weighs about 35 to 70 pounds, is about the size of a golf bag, and can be set up and fired in a matter of seconds with limited training. The SA-7, for example, produced in Russia, works as follows: working something like a point-and-shoot camera, the shooter aims at an aircraft while giving the missile a moment to lock onto the heat of the aircraft engines. When the trigger is pulled, a launch motor forces the missile out of the launch tube, the missile engine then ignites, and the missile races toward the target at more than 1000 mph. A navigational system corrects the course until impact. If the missile misses its target, it self-destructs after 14 to 17 seconds of flight. The SA-7 missile weighs 10.4 pounds, the system weighs 32.3 pounds, it has a range of about 3.4 miles, it takes 6–10 seconds to reload, and it can be purchased on the black market for as low as $5000.

It is estimated that 700,000 portable SAMs have been produced over the last three decades, and 27 terrorist groups, including al-Qaida, have the weapon. Globally, in the last 30 years, 35 attempts have been made to destroy civilian aircraft with the weapon. The results: 24 planes were shot down, more than 500 killed, and all but one of the aircraft was a propeller airplane. In 1998, 40 people were killed when rebels shot down a Congo Airlines Boeing 727.

Continued

THE DANGER OF SAM—Cont'd

Portable SAMs are difficult to defend against because of the small size and the capability of firing these weapons from a rooftop, truck, or boat, among other locations. Defensive systems exist on military aircraft and some commercial jets (e.g., Israel's El Al jetliners). These defensive systems include decoy flares and laser pulses to confuse SAM heat-seeking capabilities. Security patrols in an around airports offer another defensive option that requires careful planning.

Unfortunately, black market smuggling of SAMs is a problem. International cooperation has worked to combat the problem. In 2003, the United States, Russian, and British authorities conducted a sting operation: Russian agents working undercover sold a disabled SAM to a British arms dealer, and FBI agents, posing as terrorists, purchased it. The British man was arrested in New Jersey for smuggling the SAM into the United States (Bayles and Locy, 2003).

BOMBS AND OTHER EXPLOSIVES

Terrorists are creative and resourceful in their bomb-making activities. A bomb can be placed in almost anything—a pipe, letter, book, package, cell phone, radio, vehicle, bicycle, podium, pillow, and so forth. Terrorist bombs are mostly improvised. In other words, they construct bombs from available materials gathered through theft or the misappropriation of military or commercial blasting supplies. Fertilizer and household ingredients are other sources. The Web or terrorist training and manuals provide instructions. **Improvised explosive device** (IED) is the name for such assembled bombs that kill or maim (Figure 2-6). Unfortunately for terrorists, their lack of quality training, and use of bomb components that are substandard, has periodically caused IEDs to detonate prematurely.

In an IED, the trigger activates the fuse that ignites the explosive. These three components are integrated in various ways in IEDs. Nails and other materials may be added to the IED to increase lethality. An IED may contain an antihandling device that causes it to detonate when it is handled or moved. Coalition personnel in Iraq have been killed repeatedly when IEDs—hidden along roads in trash containers, light poles, dead people and animals, and other locations—were detonated

Figure 2-6 ■ Improvised explosive device. Pressure-release firing device. Source: Federal Emergency Management Agency (2000).

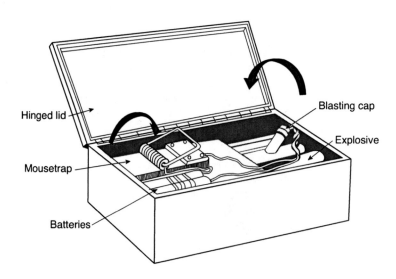

while convoys and patrols passed nearby. Among numerous ploys of terrorists, one involves authorities discovering a bomb (really a decoy) and as responders are drawn to the location to cordon off the area and dismantle it, another bomb explodes.

Explosive charges favored by terrorists include Semtex, RDX (Cyclonite or Hexogen), PETN (raw RDX), C4 (plastic explosive), TNT, fertilizer, and dynamite. Plastic explosives, such as Semtex, RDX, and C4, are like puddy and can be molded to fit into many harmless looking objects (e.g., toy, camera). Manufacturers of plastic explosives often include a chemical marker so unauthorized use can be traced back to the source.

The methods or triggers used to detonate IEDs are pressure (i.e., physical, water, or atmospheric); electronic signal (i.e., remote control or radio frequency); electronic pulse (i.e., detonator box); photoelectric cell (at dawn); motion, heat, or radiation detector; circuit connection (antihandling device); time switch (electronic or acid activated); and fuse wire.

There are several types of IEDs. The most common is the pipe bomb, which is made easily from a metal pipe crammed with explosives and tightly sealed. Nails may be wrapped around the pipe to increase deaths and injuries. The Molotov cocktail is even easier to make; the process involves filling a glass bottle with fuel, such as gasoline, and stuffing the top with a rag to be lit before throwing it. When the bottle hits the target, the glass typically breaks, covering the target in flames. The term incendiary refers to bombs that are designed to cause fire. The vehicle bomb may be a truck, car, boat, airplane, or other types of vehicle containing an IED. Vehicle bombs are popular with terrorists because vehicles are mobile and commonly left unattended and contain electrical power to trigger the bomb and a fuel source to intensify the explosion. The fertilizer truck bomb contains ammonium nitrate and hundreds of pounds of this substance are required to cause major damage, as illustrated by the truck bomb that destroyed the Murrah Federal Building in Oklahoma City in 1995.

WEAPONS OF MASS DESTRUCTION

DEFINITION

A **weapon of mass destruction** (WMD) is something capable of inflicting mass casualties and/or destroying or rendering high-value assets as useless. Although chemical, biological, nuclear, and radiological weapons often serve as examples of WMD, many things can be used as a WMD. This became painfully true from the 9/11 attacks when airliners, loaded with fuel, became missiles, killed thousands of people, leveled the 110-story Twin Towers of the World Trade Center, and hit the Pentagon. These attacks and how they were conducted were a surprise and very successful.

The term **weapon of mass effect** (WME) describes the human reactions and events surrounding the use of a WMD that may result in limited or no casualties or physical damage. The mass effect may be sensationalized media reporting, panic, and social and political change.

The range of potential WMD attacks depends on the creativity of the enemy. Examples include blowing up a train filled with toxic chemicals as it travels near a town while the wind is blowing toward the town; driving a fuel truck loaded with explosives into a high school gymnasium during a championship basketball game; detonating multiple speed boat bombs on the same side of a cruise ship that is in deep water, far from land, at night, when the passengers are asleep; introducing chemical or biological agents into free beverages at a popular concert during the summer; placing a radiological device, disguised as HVAC equipment, near the intake vents of a crowded building during its peak business hours; and attacking key electrical substations and high-voltage transmission lines to cause a cascade of power failures that disrupt almost all aspects of life and then exploit the crisis by attacking other targets. The number of "soft" targets capable of being targeted is astounding. The MO of terrorists is long-term planning and attacking multiple targets simultaneously, possibly employing a novel weapon and approach. Following the attack, authorities may recognize vulnerabilities and the need for countermeasures to "harden" targets. In response, terrorists will likely seek a "soft" target for the next attack.

CRITICAL THINKING:

If you were a terrorist, what creative plan would you employ to use a WMD?

BIOLOGICAL WEAPONS

The use of biological weapons has a long history. During the 14th century, a plague that killed about a third of the population of Europe was alleged to have begun when Mongol forces, in their siege of Caffa in the Crimea, catapulted infected corpses into the city (Rotfeld, 2001: 2). British commanders in the French and Indian War (1754–1767) transferred disease-infected blankets to enemy warriors (Barkan and Bryjak, 2004). The Japanese invasion of China, in 1937, included fleas infected with diseases and placed in wheat dropped from planes over Chinese towns (Combs, 2003: 259). The United States, England, the former Soviet Union, and many other countries have developed biological weapons over many decades. Treaties attempt to eliminate production of such weapons and destroy current inventories.

Like chemical weapons, biological weapons may be perceived as a "poor man's atomic bomb" and developing countries may look to these WMD as an avenue to deter enemies. Because certain biological weapons carry the potential of uncontrollable spread of disease, unanticipated victim-ization (e.g., one's own group) may cause terrorists and "rogue" states to select other WMD such as chemical or radiological. A biological weapons program is easy to disguise because the same biotechnology equipment is used in pharmaceutical manufacturing. This fact also provides cover for the procurement of equipment.

Biological weapons cause flu-like symptoms and then death. Detection and containment are difficult because the onset of symptoms and then the identification of the agent are delayed.

The Central Intelligence Agency (2003) warns that advances in biotechnology have the poten-tial to create a more dangerous biological warfare threat than what exists today and that engineered biological agents could be worse than any disease known. The UN (United Nations, Office on Drugs and Crime, n.d.) sees advances in genetic biotechnology as increasing the potential for **ethnic targeting**, meaning a single race is impacted by a biological weapon. In the near future, such weapons may be able to target genetic or cellular differences among ethnic groups. This would reduce one of the obstacles to using biological weapons—the risk of infecting one's own group. Europeans decimated the American Indian population during westward expansion because the Indians had no resistance to diseases from Europe.

The delivery methods for biological agents vary and include sprayer, artillery shell, and missile. The strategy for respiratory infections is to create a cloud of suspended microscopic droplets containing bacterial or virus particles. Terrorists may employ biological agents to contaminate water or food sources, especially because detection is difficult.

The Centers for Disease Control Web site (www.bt.cdc.gov) offers extensive information on WMD. Five common types of biological agents are explained next. They are bacteria, rickettsiae, viruses, fungi, and toxins.

Bacteria are single-celled organisms that multiply by cell division. They can cause disease in humans, animals, and plants. Examples include plague, anthrax, and cholera.

Plague is caused by the bacterium *Yersinia pestis* and it is found in rodents and fleas worldwide. It attacks the respiratory and gastrointestinal systems. Pneumonic plague infects the lungs, causing headache, fever, cough, and weakness. Transmission between people can occur from respiratory droplets. Treatment with antibiotics is essential during the early stages of infection.

Anthrax is emphasized here because it was used to attack the United States in 2001. It is a deadly infectious disease caused by the bacterium called *Bacillus anthracis*. The bacterium is commonly found in soil and, although it can infect humans, occurs most frequently in plant-eating animals. Its occurrence is rare in the United States, it is not contagious, and the victims must be directly exposed to it. The inflection occurs in three forms: cutaneous (i.e., from a cut on the skin), inhalation, and intestinal (i.e., eating tainted meat). Symptoms: for cutaneous anthrax, a skin ulcer; for inhalation anthrax, respiratory failure; and for intestinal anthrax, nausea, vomiting, and diarrhea. Treatment includes antibiotics administered early on and a vaccine exists.

The development of anthrax as a WMD has a history throughout the 20th century. Today, at least a dozen countries have the capability of using anthrax as a WMD. A Congressional study found that a Scud missile loaded with anthrax could kill 10,000 people in an urban area (United Nations, Office on Drugs and Crime, n.d.).

During the fall of 2001, following the 9/11 attacks, letters containing anthrax spores were mailed to news media personnel and congressional officials, leading to the first case of intentional release of anthrax in the United States (U.S. General Accounting Office, 2003). Several states and Washington, DC, were affected. Eleven people were victimized by the cutaneous form and 11 from the inhalation form. Five people died, all from inhalation anthrax. The anthrax was in the form of white powder and placed in envelopes. During mail processing at post offices, other government offices, and businesses, it was released and it contaminated air, equipment, buildings, and people who touched and inhaled the spores. In addition to the unfortunate casualties, the attacks caused enormous disruptions and expenses to organizations. At about the same time, other countries reported similar attacks.

Rickettsiae resemble bacteria, but are parasites that live inside individual host cells. Examples are typhus, Rocky Mountain spotted fever, and Q fever.

Viruses are much smaller than bacteria and depend upon living cells to multiply. They will not live long outside of a host. Examples include smallpox, Ebola, and foot-and-mouth disease (an antianimal agent).

Smallpox is a highly contagious virus. Wild smallpox was eradicated worldwide in 1977, but samples continue to exist and it can be used as a weapon. In the United States, routine vaccination ended in 1972. In most cases, the disease is spread by infected saliva droplets that a victim encounters during face-to-face contact with an ill person. An aerosol release or a group of infected suicide terrorists traveling around a city would cause a major health emergency. Initial symptoms include high fever, fatigue, aches, a rash, pus-filled lesions, and scabs. There is no proven treatment, but the U.S. government has accelerated production of a new vaccine. Patients must be isolated to prevent spreading the virus.

Fungi can cause serious disease to humans and destroy crops. When used to attack vital crops of a nation, starvation and economic disaster can result.

Toxins are poisonous substances produced naturally by animal, plant, or microbe. Many types exist from bacteria, fungi, insects, and other animals. They are not manufactured by humans as with chemical agents, and several types are easy to obtain. Al-Qaida documents from Afghanistan referred to the toxins nicotine and solanine to be used to poison food and water supplies. Nicotine is from tobacco plants and solanine is contained in old potatoes. Other toxins are botulism and ricin.

Botulism is a very poisonous substance caused by a toxin made by a bacterium known as *Clostridium botulinum*. This poison is usually foodborne and symptoms may begin within 6 hours to 2 weeks. The symptoms include vision problems, slurred speech, difficulty breathing and swallowing, and muscle weakness. This nerve toxin can be made into an aerosol weapon and lead to death from respiratory failure. The Aum Shinrikyo group in Japan sprayed this toxin over Tokyo from airplanes, but their efforts to harm people were unsuccessful. The CDC stores a supply of antitoxin against botulism that can reduce the severity of symptoms. Most patients recover if treatment occurs early on.

Ricin is a poison from the beans of the castor oil plant and is easy to make. It was prepared as a WMD during World War II and is more deadly than nerve gas. Ricin has been used in assassinations because it is difficult to detect. In 2003, a vial of ricin was found with a threatening note at a mail facility in Greenville, South Carolina. No one was harmed, but the incident showed the need for training personnel and coordination among agencies.

Severe poisoning by ingesting ricin causes nausea, vomiting, diarrhea, and death by the third day. Severe poisoning by inhalation causes cough, fever, weakness, cardiovascular collapse, and death within 36 to 48 hours. There is no known antidote for ricin poisoning.

CHEMICAL WEAPONS

Chemical weapons evolved more recently in history than biological weapons. World War I became the first battleground noted for massive casualties from chemical weapons. One million casualties, including 90,000 killed, occurred when German and Allied troops gassed each other with chlorine gas and mustard gas (United Nations, Office on Drugs and Crime, n.d.). The results were so devastating that World War II leaders on both sides, remembering the effects of poison gases from about 20 years earlier, limited their use of these weapons. Zykon-B gas was used by the Nazis against Jews, Gypsies, Soviet prisoners, and others. The war between Iran and Iraq, during the 1980s, became another conflict where poison gas was used with success. During 1987 and 1988, Saddam Hussein, leader of Iraq at the time, became the first world leader in modern times to use chemical WMD on his own people when about 5000 civilians were killed as Hussein's forces quashed a Kurdish revolt.

Compared to other major WMD, chemical agents such as pulmonary, blood, and blister are relatively easy to manufacture. Nerve agents are more difficult to produce. These substances are also available commercially, examples being cleaning fluids and insecticides.

Chemical agents may work immediately or cause delayed reactions. Some are difficult to detect because of being odorless and tasteless.

Most chemical agents are in a liquid form that must be aerosolized into droplets to be inhaled to be effective. Chemical agents can be delivered to targets through modified conventional munitions such as artillery shells and bombs. As with other WMD, dual-use equipment and technology help terrorists disguise their intentions. As examples, spray systems to broadcast agricultural chemicals and aerosol generate to disperse pesticides can also be used to release chemical WMD. Imagine the casualties from a chemical attack by a crop duster over a sports stadium, by use of the global positioning system to guide planes (manned or unmanned drones) to a target, or by backing up a truck to a building's HVAC system.

Five types of chemical agents follow.

Pulmonary agents are the oldest type that was first used in World War I. These agents stress the respiratory system, cause the lungs to fill with water, and choke the victim. Characterized as heavy gases, these agents stay at ground level and dissipate quickly in wind. Examples are chlorine and phosgene that are common industrial chemicals and are stored in cylinders or bottles.

Blood agents enter the body by breathing and disrupt the use of oxygen by the cells causing damage to body tissues. These agents are liquid or gas. Examples are cyanide and cyanogen chloride.

Blister agents, also known as mustard agents because of their odor, attack the skin, lungs, eyes, and digestive system. These agents are released by aerosol or vaporization and are rapidly absorbed by victims unless they are wearing protective clothing and a mask. Examples of these agents, which are simple to produce, include sulfur mustard, nitrogen mustard, and lewisite.

Nerve agents are similar to pesticides but are much more toxic. The aerosol form is the best method of release for these agents, which have no odor and have a likeness to water. Victims who have been exposed to nerve agents will experience a variety of harmful symptoms to eyes, skin, muscles, and other body parts, as they salivate, urinate, and defecate uncontrollably. Examples are VX, sarin, Soman, and tabun.

VX is a human-made chemical warfare agent that is the most potent of all nerve agents. It is odorless and tasteless, amber in color, very slow to evaporate, very persistent in the environment, and deadly. When it is released into the air, exposure can occur through skin contact, eye contact, and inhalation. It can also be used to contaminate food and water supplies. Symptoms are many and include runny nose, cough, chest tightness, diarrhea, nausea, and convulsions. Antidotes are available, but they must be used quickly. People exposed to VX should remove their clothes quickly and use soap and water to remove VX from their skin.

Irritating agents aim to incapacitate and are unlikely to result in death. Symptoms include irritation of both the eyes and respiratory system. Examples are tear gas (CS), MACE (CN), and capsicum/pepper spray.

AUM SHINRIKYO CULT

The **Aum Shinrikyo cult** was established in 1987 by guru Shoko Asahara, whose real name is Chizuo Matsumoto. Asahara recruited followers in Japan as he claimed to be the messiah. The cult aimed to take over Japan and then the world to purify everyone. Asahara predicted Armageddon, that it would begin by the United States starting World War III, and that only cult members would survive. Members, totaling 9000 in Japan and 40,000 worldwide at the time of the Tokyo subway attack, were alleged to have engaged in odd rituals, such as drinking the guru's blood and wearing electrical caps to keep their brain waves in tune with their master. The cult maintained a covert WMD program conducted by cult scientists while the cult was under police surveillance.

On March 20, 1995, Aum members pierced bags of the chemical nerve agent sarin on five separate subway trains as they converged on central Tokyo. The attack killed 12 passengers and injured up to 6000 as they fled while sickened and bleeding. The cult had tried previously, but failed, to use biological agents. Interestingly, Japanese police were scheduled to raid Asahara's headquarters in Tokyo on March 22nd to seize WMD. However, the cult had infiltrated the Japanese police, were tipped off about the impending raid, and they hastily launched the attack. The casualties would have been worse, but the sarin was not pure and the method of release was primitive.

In 2001, Russian police arrested Aum followers in Russia when they planned to set off bombs in Tokyo to free Asahara, who had been arrested. In 2002, in Japan, the cult changed its name to Aleph and claimed to have rejected the violence of its founder. It continues to engage in businesses and acquire property. Membership is less than 1000.

In 2004, Asahara, among others, was sentenced to death for the attacks. The 8-year trial, due to delays, was headed by a four-judge panel. There are no jury trials in Japan. In a separate court, the cult was ordered to pay 3.8 billion yen (U.S. $35 million) in damages to victims who still suffer from headaches, dizziness, and respiratory problems (U.S. Department of State, 2004; Associated Press, February 27, 2004).

CRITICAL THINKING:

In reference to the Aum Shinrikyo Cult, do you think the Japanese police should have been more aggressive in their investigation to prevent the sarin attack? Should police in the United States investigate religious terrorists with less intensity than political terrorists?

NUCLEAR WEAPONS

To end World War II in the Pacific against the Japanese and to avoid massive U.S. casualties from an invasion of the Japanese mainland, President Harry Truman approved the dropping of atomic bombs on Hiroshima and Nagasaki in 1945. Both cities were obliterated and sustained massive casualties. Then, an arms race began that continues today. The "nuclear club" has expanded from the United States to the United Kingdom, France, Russia, the People's Republic of China, India, Pakistan, Israel, South Africa, and other countries that possess covert development programs.

According to the United Nations, Office on Drugs and Crime (n.d.), when the Cold War ended, a black market in Soviet-era weapons began to flourish. Former Soviet citizens participated in smuggling nuclear materials from poorly secured facilities to unknown buyers and transnational criminal organizations. The market for nuclear materials includes "rogue states," desperate national liberation movements, and suppressed ethnic groups. What makes matters worse is that there are 280-armed conflicts of varying intensity occurring in the world.

Nuclear weapons are based on nuclear fission, fusion, or a combination of both. Fission weapons are uranium or plutonium based. A conventional explosive or laser beam triggers a chain reaction and energy is released. Fatalities can be over 100,000. Fusion weapons are hydrogen based, whereby atoms "melt" into each other rather than split to release energy. These weapons are triggered by fission causing a powerful thermonuclear explosion. Fatalities can be in the millions (United Nations, Office on Drugs and Crime, n.d.).

The explosion of a nuclear weapon creates a large fireball. Everything in the fireball vaporizes, including soil and water, and the fireball goes upward, creating a large mushroom cloud. Radioactive material from the weapon mixes with the particles in the cloud and then the mixture falls to earth in what is called fallout. Because fallout is composed of particles, it may be carried by wind for long distances. Because the fallout is radioactive, it can contaminate anything it lands on, such as water resources and crops (Centers for Disease Control, n.d.).

RADIOLOGICAL WEAPONS

Radiological weapons contain radioactive material that, although not exploding itself, is scattered by a conventional explosive. These weapons are often called "dirty bombs" and consist of radioactive material attached to a conventional bomb. The technical name for "dirty bomb" is a **radiological dispersion device** (RDD). It may contain radioactive material that is sealed in metal to prevent dispersal when handling it. Upon explosion, initial fatalities may be low, but climb over time due to cancer. However, the actual harm will depend on the grade of the radioactive material and the amount released. This weapon can make buildings and land unusable for many years. Its use is likely to cause fear, panic, and sensationalized media coverage.

Because terrorists are known to be creative, we can only surmise as to how they would construct a RDD and where it would be applied. It may become part of a vehicle bomb, detonated in a school, or introduced into food or water supplies. Another possibility is an attack of a nuclear facility to release radioactive material through a meltdown, explosion, or crashing a jet into the facility.

The Democratic Members of the House Select Committee on Homeland Security (2004) released a report entitled *America at Risk: Closing the Security Gap*. This report is from Democrats during a Republican presidential administration and it identified security gaps and proposes ways to close them. Although it can be argued that this report is a biased publication attacking the "other" political party, it does offer numerous items of interest. Here are items from this report pertaining to radiological weapons.

- Sources of radiological materials that can be used for "dirty bombs" are not secure. Commercially available radiological materials are used in many industries to, as examples, sterilize food, detect flaws in metal, and treat cancer.
- A "dirty bomb" has the potential to contaminate the site and nearby areas causing economic loss and clean-up costs. Such an attack could equal or exceed the $41 billion cost of the 9/11 attacks in New York City and at the Pentagon.
- Since 1999, in the United States, federal investigators have documented 1300 cases of lost, stolen, or abandoned radiological material.
- The most likely route of terrorist acquisition of radioactive material is through open and legal purchase from legitimate suppliers. The number of sources is unknown because no entity maintains records. The Nuclear Regulatory Commission estimates that there are about

two million sealed sources in the United States and they have contracted with a private investigative firm to locate the owners.

- The International Atomic Energy Agency lists 110 countries without adequate control of sealed sources.

The detonation of a RDD is a serious possibility in the future. In November of 1995, Chechen rebels placed a RDD, using dynamite and cesium 137, in Moscow's Izmailovo Park. It was not detonated. In 2002, suspected al-Qaida member Jose Padilla, trained in terrorist camps in Afghanistan, was arrested in Chicago for his role in a plot to explode a RDD in the United States.

DISCUSSION QUESTIONS

1. What aspects of our modern world do terrorists exploit to improve their success?
2. What are the organizational characteristics of al-Qaida?
3. How do you think terrorist training has changed since September 11, 2001?
4. Why should the police and military study terrorist modus operandi?
5. Which method of violence by terrorists do you think is the most successful? Explain.
6. Why is cyberterrorism a serious threat?
7. Does the media help terrorists? Explain.
8. How do terrorists finance their operations?
9. Why do more terrorists use conventional weapons rather than WMD?

APPLICATIONS

A note of caution is in order. A major purpose of the applications is to assist the reader in understanding the mind-set of terrorists and their thought processes when they plan and prepare for attacks. We are seeking to "think like a terrorist" because knowing one's enemy is a vital prerequisite to investigating terrorists, interrupting their plans, designing countermeasures, and taking other action. The reader is cautioned to not violate any laws or policies/procedures of any organization or to become involved in any unethical activity while engaged in the chapter applications or in the use of the educational and training materials contained in this book.

2A YOU BE THE TERRORIST CELL LEADER

As an experienced and well-educated terrorist cell leader, you are patiently planning and preparing for an attack. Now you must deal with the following items. Prioritize the items and explain your reasoning for the placement of each item in the order you selected.

- Item A: A female cell member has befriended a soldier from a nearby military base and this Saturday night, on a date, she will seek vital information. She needs a drug to secretly give the soldier to elicit as much information as possible.
- Item B: An elderly lady living in a nearby apartment, who is fascinated by police television programs, seems overly curious and asks you a lot of questions.
- Item C: You need to call a meeting of cell members to discuss how the next attack will generate the best possible media coverage for the cause. Your initial thought is to attack on an anniversary date.
- Item D: You need to assign cell members to more time conducting countersurveillance. In the last 2 weeks, two events have raised your suspicion that your cell may be under police surveillance, but you need more information.
- Item E: A new cell member traveling to join your cell was stopped at the border and has been in police custody since yesterday.
- Item F: A weapons supplier who was paid a large deposit has not delivered necessary weapons and explosives by the due date of 3 weeks ago. You will not telephone or e-mail him. He lives in the same city and a visit to him is overdue.

- Item G: A cell member is becoming impatient over the length of time it is taking to plan and prepare for the next attack. He wants to strap on explosives, go to the target, create a diversion, and penetrate security to detonate the explosives.

2B YOU BE THE SENIOR TERRORIST

As a senior terrorist, based in the Mideast, you are responsible for training and operations. You presently have two tasks to complete.

Task #1: A new recruit who has been trained made some poor decisions when traveling to Egypt to become part of sleeper cell. He obtained a bogus Egyptian passport, used a photo of himself with a beard and traditional Moslem dress for the passport, and rented a second floor apartment in an established area of Cairo, Egypt. You recalled the recruit and he is in front of you right now. What do you state to the recruit? Explain his errors, the rule related to each error, and the reasoning supporting each rule.

Task #2: Reports from the field have pinpointed deficiencies in training in the following areas and you must prepare new training materials.

When traveling through airports and border checkpoints, recruits are encountering difficulties when answering questions, such as the purpose of the visit, the source of money for traveling, and occupation. Prepare plausible answers for these questions, suggest guidelines for nonverbal behavior to prevent the detection of deception, and offer other helpful tips.

How can a recruit find out if someone is following him/her? Prepare three suggestions.

What type of information should be collected on a military base and how should the information be collected?

What type of information should be collected on a "soft target," such as a school or house of worship, and how should the information be collected?

2C YOU BE THE TERRORIST TRAINER

You are a terrorist in charge of designing a training program for new recruits. The training facility is at a private residential compound located in a suburb of a major Mideast city, with additional locations in rural areas for weapons training. The host country's intelligence agency covertly sanctions the training. Classes will be small so as not to attract attention. Design a curriculum for new recruits. What subjects will you offer and how many hours will be assigned to each subject?

Although the recruits were screened carefully, what methods will you use to ensure both the loyalty of each trainee and that no one has infiltrated the class of trainees?

2D YOU BE THE TERRORIST PLANNER

We have seen creativity, resourcefulness, and patience on the part of terrorists. We also understand the importance of knowing the enemy. In this application, the community in which you live will serve as the setting so you can think about vulnerabilities of local, potential targets.

You are the leader of a terrorist cell that is planning and preparing for an attack. Cell members were born in the Mideast, but live and work in the United States. What are your plans for a local attack? Answer the following questions.

1. How will the operation be financed?
2. How many cell members are required for the operation and what are their roles and assignments?
3. What are the means of transportation and communication?
4. What types of false documents are needed?
5. How many safe houses are required?
6. What are the objectives and anticipated outcomes of the attack?
7. What types of weapons, equipment, and vehicles are required for the attack and what is the method of acquisition?
8. What is the method of violence (e.g., bombing, assassination, kidnapping, WMD)?
9. How will you facilitate media attention?
10. What is the primary target and why was it selected?
11. Who are the likely victims?
12. What is the secondary target and why was it selected?
13. When will the primary target be attacked? Season, date, day, time?

14. If multiple attacks occur simultaneously, explain.
15. What unique ploys have you designed into the plan to enhance its effectiveness and success?
16. What is the time line of the operation? How long will it take to plan, prepare, train, gather intelligence and resources, and execute the attack?
17. Is this a suicide mission? If not, what is the escape plan?
18. What type of intelligence is required and how will it be collected and stored?
19. What is the plan to prevent discovery of the cell and its plans? What are the methods for counter intelligence?
20. What plan will be implemented if cell members are arrested?
21. How will cell members remain cohesive?

2E   YOU BE THE DOMESTIC TERRORIST

The debate rages over what specifically drove you to seek revenge against state and federal agencies and your mortgage banker. It all started over the wetlands near your home where beavers dammed up the swamp and caused a flood that threatened to destroy your home while blocking an access road. For several years you sought help. The Environmental Protection Agency, the Army Corps of Engineers, and the State Highway Department visited your home and the area to study the problem. Following 5 years of dealing with bureaucrats, finger pointing, delay, and spending your savings on attorneys and consultants, you decide that since the water has reached the foundation of your home and you are tired of driving through water on the road, you will destroy the beaver dams.

During the last 2 years you have been attending meetings of the United Brotherhood Against Government Oppression (UBAGO) and agree with the group's opposition to excessive government taxation and regulations. Several members have had serious conflicts with state and federal agencies, and they harbor such intense hate for the government that they would like to see it destroyed. One of the members owns a rock quarry, has access to dynamite, and offers to help you blow up the beaver dams. You are overjoyed when the beaver dams are destroyed and the water recedes, but you are sick about being arrested with your buddy on a variety of criminal charges. You make bail and the stress of being arrested causes a heart attack. To make matters worse, the beavers have rebuilt dams and the flooding has returned. Unable to work and pay the mortgage on your property, two deputies show up at your door one day with eviction papers. Your anger has reached the boiling point, you refuse to leave, and you do not care much about anything, except revenge against those people who have made your life miserable. You turn to UBAGO for help. What is your plan of revenge?

WEB SITES

Al Jazeera: www.aljazeera.net
In a search engine, enter **Anarchist's Cookbook: Terrorist's Handbook**
Army of God: www.armyofgod.com
Center for Defense Information: www.cdi.org
Centers for Disease Control: www.bt.cdc.gov/
CNN: www.cnn.com
Popular Front for the Liberation of Palestine: http://members.tripod.com/~freepalestine
Project for the Research of Islamist Movements: http://www.e-prism.org/pages/1/
Risk Management Solutions, Inc.: www.rms.com
Socialist International: www.socialistinternational.org
Stormfront: www.stormfront.org
Terror Attack Database: www.ic.org.il
White Aryan Resistance: www.resist.com

NOTES

Adams, J. (1986). *The Financing of Terror.* New York: Simon & Schuster.
Ali, Lorraine (2004). "Al-Jazeera From Inside." *Newsweek*, CXLIII (June 14).
Aljazeera.Net (2004a). "About Al-Jazeera." http://english.aljazeera.net, retrieved June 23, 2004.
Aljazeera.Net (2004b). "Iran accuses US of supporting terrorism." http://english.aljazeera.net, retrieved July 21, 2004.

Associated Press (June 19, 2004). "Al Qaida cell beheads American hostage; Saudis kill group's leader."

Associated Press (February 27, 2004). "Cult leader gets death for 1995 Tokyo gas attack."

Baker, T. (2005). *Introducing Criminal Analysis: Crime Prevention and Intervention Strategies.* Upper Saddle River, NJ: Pearson Prentice Hall.

Barkan, S., and Bryjak, G. (2004). *Fundamentals of Criminal Justice.* Boston, MA: Allyn and Bacon.

Barnard, D. (2003). "Narco-Terrorism Realities: The Connection between Drugs and Terror." *Journal of Counterterrorism & Homeland Security International,* 9 (Winter).

Bauer, L. (2004). "Emerging Lessons from al-Qa'ida: Preventing Targeted Terrorist Violence." Anti-Terrorism Training, U.S. Department of Justice. August 18.

Bayles, F., and Locy, T. (2003). "Missile Intended to Shoot Down Jet." *USA Today* (August 13).

Bell, K. (2004). "Identifying, Investigating and Prosecuting Terrorist Financing Organizations." Anti-Terrorism Training, U.S. Department of Justice, April 2.

Broyles, D., and Rubio, M. (2004). "A Smokescreen for Terrorism." *United States Attorneys' Bulletin,* 52 (January).

Buckley, P., and Meese, M. (2004). "The Financial Front in the Global War on Terrorism." In R. Howard and R. Sawyer (Eds.). *Defeating Terrorism: Shaping the New Security Environment.* Guilford, CT: McGraw-Hill.

Bunker, R. (2005). *Suicide (Homicide) Bombers: Part I, Training Key #581.* Alexandria, VA: International Association of Chief's of Police, Inc.

Caruso, J. (2002). Acting Assistant Director, Counter Terrorism, FBI, US Senate Committee on Foreign Relations (September).

Centers for Disease Control (n.d.). *Frequently asked Questions about a Nuclear Blast.* www.bt.cdc.gov/radiation, retrieved August 5, 2004.

Central Intelligence Agency (2003). "The Darker Bioweapons Future." www.securitymanagement.com/, retrieved January 16, 2004.

Combs, C. (2003). *Terrorism in the Twenty-First Century,* 3rd ed. Upper Saddle River, NJ: Prentice-Hall.

Democratic Members of the House Select Committee on Homeland Security (2004). *America at Risk: Closing the Security Gap* (February). www.house.gov/hsc/democrats/, retrieved July 27, 2004.

Denning, D. (2001). "Activism, hacktivism, and cyberterrorism: The Internet as a tool for influencing foreign policy." In J. Arquilla and D. Ronfeldt (Eds.), *Networks and Netwars: The Future of Terror, Crime, and Militancy.* Santa Monica, CA: RAND.

Earth Liberation Front (2004). "Meet the ELF." http://earthliberationfront.com, retrieved May 3, 2004.

FBI (2002). "The Threat of Ecoterrorism." http://www.fbi.gov/congress/congress02/jarboe021202.htm, retrieved May 3, 2004.

Federal Emergency Management Agency (2000). *Emergency Response to Terrorism: Tactical Considerations: Company Officer* (March).

Fraser, J., and Fulton, I. (1984). "Terrorism Counteraction. FC 100-37." Fort Leavenworth, KS: U.S. Army Command and General Staff College.

Garamone, J. (2003). "US Working to Shore up Allies, Take on Narcoterror." *American Forces Press Service* (October 7).

Gueli, R. (2003). "Bin Laden and al Quaida: Challenging the assumptions of transnational terrorism." *Strategic Review for Southern Africa,* 25 (November).

Hanley, C. (2006). "Targeting Terror Leaders Might Not Stop Violence." Associated Press (January 22).

Hoffman, B. (2003). "The Logic of Suicide Terrorism." In R. Howard and R. Sawyer (Eds.), *Defeating Terrorism: Shaping the New Security Environment.* Guilford, CT: McGraw-Hill.

Intelligence Digest (2003). "Al-Qaida Influence Spreads" (December 4). www.janes.com/security international, retrieved January 5, 2004.

Kabay, M., and Walsh, L. (2002). "The Year in Computer Crime." *Information Security,* 3 (December).

Lowry, R. (2002). "A View to a Kill: Assassinations in War and Peace." *National Review,* 54 (March 11).

Lyman, M. and Potter, G. (2004). *Organized Crime,* 3rd ed. Upper Saddle River, NJ: Pearson Prentice Hall.

Martin, G. (2003). *Understanding Terrorism: Challenges, Perspectives, and Issues.* Thousand Oaks, CA: Sage.

Mordica, G. (2003). "Phase Four Operations in Iraq and the RPG-7." *News from the Front.* (November–December).

Nason, J. (2004). "Conducting Surveillance Operations: How to Get the Most Out of Them." *FBI Law Enforcement Bulletin,* 73 (May).

National Commission on Terrorist Attacks Upon the United States (2004). *Monograph on Terrorist Financing.* www.9-11commission.gov, retrieved August 25, 2004.

National Infrastructure Protection Center (2001). *The Threat to the US Information Infrastructure* (October).

Olcott, M., and Babajanov, B. (2003). "The Terrorist Notebooks." *Foreign Policy* (March/April).

Poland, J. (1988). *Understanding Terrorism: Groups, Strategies, and Responses.* Englewood Cliffs, NJ: Prentice Hall.

Poland, J. (2005). *Understanding Terrorism: Groups, Strategies, and Responses*, 2nd ed. Englewood Cliffs, NJ: Prentice Hall.

"Pro-Life Terrorism: A How-To" (1995). *Harper's Magazine* (January).

Risk Management Solutions, Inc. (2004a). *Managing Terrorism Risk in 2004.* www.rms.com, retrieved August 13, 2004.

Risk Management Solutions, Inc. (2004b). *Catastrophe, Injury, and Insurance: The Impact of Catastrophes on Workers Compensation, Life, and Health Insurance.* www.rms.com, retrieved August 13, 2004.

Rotfeld, A. (2001). *Biotechnology and the Future of the Biological and Toxin Weapons Convention.* Solna, Sweden: Stockholm International Peace Research Institute.

Sauter, M., Holshouser, K., and Doane, J. (2004). "A Pound of Prevention." *Security Management*, 48 (March).

Schiller, D. (1985). "The European Experience." In B. Jenkins (Ed.), *Terrorism and Personal Protection.* Boston, MA: Butterworth.

Schmid, A., and de Graff, J. (1982). *Violence as Communication: Insurgent Terrorism and the Western News Media.* Beverly Hills, CA: Sage. In C. Combs (2003). *Terrorism in the Twenty-First Century*, 3rd ed.

Simonsen, C., and Spindlove, J. (2004). *Terrorism Today*, 2nd ed. Upper Saddle River, NJ: Prentice-Hall.

Smith, P. (2002). "Transnational Terrorism and the al Qaida Model: Confronting New Realities." *Parameters* (Summer).

Speth, R. (2004). "Animal Rights Could Trample Those of Public." *The Clarion-Ledger* (July 3).

Stein, Y. (2003). "By Any Name Illegal and Immoral." *Ethics & International Affairs*, 17 (April).

Tierney, M. (2002). "Young, Gifted and Ready to Kill." *The Herald* (Glasgow, OK) (August 3).

United Nations, Office on Drugs and Crime (2004). *Conventional Terrorist Weapons.* www.unodc.org/unodc/terrorism _weapons_conventional.html, retrieved April 21, 2004.

United Nations, Office on Drugs and Crime (n.d.). *Terrorism and Weapons of Mass Destruction.* www.unodc.org/unodc/terrorism_weapons_mass_destruction, retrieved April 21, 2004.

U.S. Department of Justice (n.d.). *Al-Qaida Training Manual.* www.usdoj.gov./ag/trainingmanual.htm, retrieved January 6, 2004.

U.S. Department of State (2004). *Patterns of Global Terrorism 2003.* www.state.gov, retrieved April 30, 2004.

U.S. General Accounting Office (2003). "Public Health Response to Anthrax Incidents of 2001." www.gao.gov, retrieved January 16, 2004.

U.S. Government (2003). *National Strategy for Combating Terrorism.* www. Whitehouse.gov/, retrieved March 5, 2004.

White, J. (2003). *Terrorism: An Introduction*, 4th ed. Belmont, CA: Wadsworth/Thomson Learning.

Zakaria, F. (2003). "Suicide Bombers Can Be Stopped." *Newsweek* (August 25).

PART II

ACTION AGAINST TERRORISM

3

GOVERNMENT ACTION

OBJECTIVES

The study of this chapter will enable you to:
1. Discuss the challenges of measuring terrorism.
2. Describe the terrorist threats facing the United States, its citizens, and interests.
3. Detail the wealth and power of the United States.
4. Discuss the Cold War.
5. Outline the initial U.S. response to the September 11, 2001 terrorist attacks.
6. List and explain the four fronts in the *National Strategy for Combating Terrorism*.
7. List and explain the five tools and at least two programs applied by the U.S. Department of State to combat terrorism.
8. Name and describe four major Acts of Congress to combat terrorism.
9. Discuss the United Nations, international law, and international courts.
10. Evaluate war and U.S. foreign policy.
11. Discuss and detail government and terrorist options as each side confronts the other.
12. List and explain the results of the *9/11 Commission Report*.

KEY TERMS

fatwa
cultural generator
hot war
cold war
surrogate war
Soviet's Vietnam War
Cuban Missile Crisis
unipolar system
National Security Council
Homeland Security Council
National Security Act of 1947
National Strategy for Homeland Security
counterterrorism
antiterrorism
diplomacy
North Atlantic Treaty Organization

U.S.S. Cole
The Defense Against Weapons of Mass
   Destruction Act of 1996
Antiterrorism and Effective Death Penalty
   Act of 1996
U.S.A. Patriot Act of 2001
U.S.A. Patriot Improvement and Reauthorization
   Act of 2005
Homeland Security Act of 2002
Department of Homeland Security
Carl von Clausewitz
Sun Tzu
Department of State
Department of Defense
Central Intelligence Agency
intelligence community

KEY TERMS

Bush doctrine
preemptive force
just war doctrine
blowback
political democratization through military
    occupation

continuum of government options in response
    to terrorism
continuum of terrorist options in response to
    government action or inaction
terrorism continuum of minor effect to major
    effect

A DECLARATION OF WAR

In February 1998, the 40-year-old Saudi exile Usama bin Ladin and a fugitive Egyptian physician, Ayman al Zawahiri, arranged from their Afghan headquarters for an Arabic newspaper in London to publish what they termed a fatwa issued in the name of a "World Islamic Front." A **fatwa** is normally an interpretation of Islamic law by a respected Islamic authority, but bin Ladin, Zawahiri, and the three others who signed this statement were not scholars of Islamic law. Claiming that America had declared war against God and his messenger, they called for the murder of any American, anywhere on earth, as the "individual duty for every Muslim who can do it in any country in which it is possible to do it."

Three months later, when interviewed in Afghanistan by ABC-TV, bin Ladin enlarged on these themes. He claimed it was more important for Muslims to kill Americans than to kill other infidels. "It is far better for anyone to kill a single American soldier than to squander his efforts on other activities," he said. Asked whether he approved of terrorism and of attacks on civilians, he replied: "We believe that the worst thieves in the world today and the worst terrorists are the Americans. Nothing could stop you except perhaps retaliation in kind. We do not have to differentiate between military or civilian. As far as we are concerned, they are all targets."

Although novel for its open endorsement of indiscriminate killing, bin Ladin's 1998 declaration was only the latest in a long series of public and private calls since 1992 that singled out the United States for attack. In August 1996, bin Ladin had issued his own self-styled fatwa calling on Muslims to drive American soldiers out of Saudi Arabia. The long, disjointed document condemned the Saudi monarchy for allowing the presence of an army of infidels in a land with the sites most sacred to Islam and celebrated recent suicide bombings of American military facilities in the Kingdom. It praised the 1983 suicide bombing in Beirut that killed 241 U.S. Marines, the 1992 bombing in Aden, and especially the 1993 firefight in Somalia after which the United States "left the area carrying disappointment, humiliation, defeat and your dead with you."

bin Ladin said in his ABC interview that he and his followers had been preparing in Somalia for another long struggle, like that against the Soviets in Afghanistan, but "the United States rushed out of Somalia in shame and disgrace." Citing the Soviet army's withdrawal from Afghanistan as proof that a ragged army of dedicated Muslims could overcome a superpower, he told the interviewer: "We are certain that we shall—with the grace of Allah—prevail over the Americans." He went on to warn that "If the present injustice continues, it will inevitably move the battle to American soil."

Plans to attack the United States were developed with unwavering single mindedness throughout the 1990s. bin Ladin saw himself as called "to follow in the footsteps of the Messenger and to communicate his message to all nations," and to serve as the rallying point and organizer of a new kind of war to destroy America and bring the world to Islam. It is the story of eccentric and violent ideas sprouting in the fertile ground of political and social turmoil. It is the story of an organization poised to seize its historical moment. How did bin Ladin, with his call for the indiscriminate killing of Americans, win thousands of followers and some degree of approval from millions more?

The history, culture, and body of beliefs from which bin Ladin has shaped and spread his message are largely unknown to many Americans. Seizing on symbols of Islam's past greatness,

A DECLARATION OF WAR—Cont'd

he promises to restore pride to people who consider themselves the victims of successive foreign masters. He uses cultural and religious allusions to the holy Qur'an and some of its interpreters. He appeals to people disoriented by cyclonic change as they confront modernity and globalization. His rhetoric selectively draws from multiple sources—Islam, history, and the region's political and economic malaise.

Bin Ladin's Worldview

Despite his claims to universal leadership, Bin Ladin offers an extreme view of Islamic history designed to appeal mainly to Arabs and Sunnis. He draws on fundamentalists who blame the eventual destruction of the Caliphate on leaders who abandoned the pure path of religious devotion. He repeatedly calls on his followers to embrace martyrdom, as "the walls of oppression and humiliation cannot be demolished except in a rain of bullets." For those yearning for a lost sense of order in an older, more tranquil world, he offers his "Caliphate" as an imagined alternative to today's uncertainty. For others, he offers simplistic conspiracies to explain their world.

bin Ladin also relies heavily on the Egyptian writer Sayyid Qutb. A member of the Muslim Brotherhood executed in 1966 on charges of attempting to overthrow the government, Qutb mixed Islamic scholarship with a very superficial acquaintance with Western history and thought. Sent by the Egyptian government to study in the United States in the late 1940s, Qutb returned with an enormous loathing of Western society and history. He dismissed Western achievements as entirely material, arguing that Western society possesses "nothing that will satisfy its own conscience and justify its existence." Three basic themes emerge from Qutb's writings. First, he claimed that the world was beset with barbarism, licentiousness, and unbelief (a condition he called *jahiliyya*, the religious term for the period of ignorance prior to the revelations given to the Prophet Mohammed). Qutb argued that humans can choose only between Islam and jahiliyya. Second, he warned that more people, including Muslims, were attracted to jahiliyya and its material comforts than to his view of Islam; jahiliyya could therefore triumph over Islam. Third, no middle ground exists in what Qutb conceived as a struggle between God and Satan. All Muslims—as he defined them—therefore must take up arms in this fight. Any Muslim who rejects his ideas is just one more nonbeliever worthy of destruction.

bin Ladin shares Qutb's stark view, permitting him and his followers to rationalize even unprovoked mass murder as righteous defense of an embattled faith. Many Americans have wondered, "Why do 'they' hate us?" Some also ask, "What can we do to stop these attacks?"

bin Ladin and al-Qaida have given answers to both these questions. To the first, they say that America had attacked Islam; America is responsible for all conflicts involving Muslims. Thus, Americans are blamed when Israelis fight with Palestinians, when Russians fight with Chechens, when Indians fight with Kashmiri Muslims, and when the Philippine government fights ethnic Muslims in its southern islands. America is also held responsible for the governments of Muslim countries, derided by al-Qaida as "your agents." bin Ladin has stated flatly, "Our fight against these governments is not separate from our fight against you." These charges found a ready audience among millions of Arabs and Muslims angry at the United States because of issues ranging from Iraq to Palestine to America's support for their countries' repressive rulers. bin Ladin's grievance with the United States may have started in reaction to specific U.S. policies, but it quickly became far deeper.

To the second question, what America could do, al-Qaida's answer was that America should abandon the Middle East, convert to Islam, and end the immorality and godlessness of its society and culture: "It is saddening to tell you that you are the worst civilization witnessed by the history of mankind." If the United States did not comply, it would be at war with the Islamic nation, a nation that al-Qaida's leaders said "desires death more than you desire life."

Continued

A DECLARATION OF WAR—Cont'd

Most Muslims prefer a peaceful and inclusive vision of their faith, not the violent sectarianism of bin Ladin. Among Arabs, bin Ladin's followers are commonly nicknamed *takfiri*, or "those who define other Muslims as unbelievers," because of their readiness to demonize and murder those with whom they disagree. Beyond the theology lies the simple human fact that most Muslims, like most other human beings, are repelled by mass murder and barbarism whatever their justification (National Commission on Terrorist Attacks Upon the United States, 2004).

THE MEASUREMENT OF TERRORISM

The measurement of terrorism is problematic, as is the measurement of other social and political phenomena. To begin with, *why* is it important to measure terrorism? Measurements of terrorism help us to understand causative theories as we anticipate, prevent, and respond to terrorism. Data collected on terrorism influence not only government action against it, such as laws, plans, policies, budgets, and strategies, but also evaluations of government action. Measurements of terrorism also impact the business of counterterrorism (see Chapter 6), decisions on the geographic locations of business investment, and tourism.

Another question of importance is *how* do we measure terrorism? Disagreement exists over the methodology applied to the measurement of terrorism, and methodological differences influence both conclusions on terrorism and policy. Ideally, measurements of terrorism should be value free, providing an objective foundation for government policy. This leads us to another question: *who* in our society measures terrorism? Official government data have been a major source of information on terrorism. How objective are the government measurements? What are the methodological problems of data collection? *Do measurements of terrorism really reflect the administration of counterterrorism (e.g., how terrorism is defined; number of intelligence analysts and enforcement officers; number of investigations and arrests; and data collection and software) rather than actual terrorism?*

Although the emphasis here is on government measurements of terrorism, other sources of research on terrorism are universities and the private sector. The topics of research on terrorism that influence policy are varied and include surveys of citizens' perceptions of terrorism and their fear of terrorism and the role of the media in influencing perceptions of terrorism and terrorism itself.

The methodological problems of measuring terrorism include the following.

- Disagreement over the definition of terrorism. Multiple definitions.
- Inconsistency in the use of terminology.
- Varied criteria of what acts to include in data and what acts to exclude.
- Not all terrorism is reported and not all terrorism that is reported is recorded in official data.
- Comparisons are difficult among different sources of data.
- Measurement of the actual amount of terrorism is impossible.
- Researcher bias.
- Political interference in the methodology and reporting process.
- Excessive delay in publishing data.
- Frequent exclusion of the physical and psychological harm of terrorism and its direct and indirect costs to society and businesses.

A major official source of the measurement of terrorism has been the U.S. Department of State (DOS) through the annual publication entitled *Patterns of Global Terrorism*. Krueger and Laitin

(2004: 8–13) write that this source has limited credibility because there are no safeguards to ensure that data are accurate and not influenced by politics. The 2003 *Patterns of Global Terrorism* report had to be corrected and rereleased following criticism. Krueger and Laitin (2004) criticize the DOS statistics for inconsistent application of definitions, insufficient review, and partisan release of reports. They see no explanation of how the DOS distinguishes significant from nonsignificant terrorist incidents and no consistency when identifying domestic and international terrorist incidents from one year to the next. Several cross-border attacks on civilians in Africa have not been included in reports, although similar attacks in other regions are reported. In the 2002 report, a suicide attack by Chechen *shaheeds* against Russians are counted, but in the following report, Chechen "black widows" (suicide bombers) are omitted.

Historically, economic, crime, and other government data have been subject to manipulation. To improve the precision of DOS terrorism data, Krueger and Laitin (2004) recommend similar protections that are applied to government economic data, such as Congressional hearings where data can be explained. Also, they suggest improvements in data collection and analysis, insulation from partisan manipulation, and assigning the research to a neutral agency, perhaps the Government Accountability Office.

The U.S. Department of State, Office of Inspector General (OIG) (2005), reported that in April of 2005, less than 1 month before the DOS was to issue its 2004 mandated annual report, *Patterns of Global Terrorism*, the DOS ceased publishing it and instead published the first of its *Country Reports on Terrorism* (CRT). This new report excluded statistical data on significant international terrorist incidents that were found in the *Patterns* reports. Simultaneously, the National Counterterrorism Center (NCTC) published a separate report entitled *A Chronology of Significant International Terrorism 2004* that included statistical data that previously had been in the *Patterns* reports. The NCTC's 2004 report showed an increase in the number of reported significant international terrorist incidents between 2003 and 2004. The NCTC stated that the increase was "primarily the result of a modified reporting methodology as well as an increase in staff devoted to identifying terrorist incidents." Perl (2006: 4) writes "*International incidents* are those involving citizens of more than one country; *significant* involves bodily injury or death or property damage greater than $10,000." The OIG noted that although the CRT complies with relevant law pertaining to reporting to Congress, the publication changes led to allegations of political considerations in DOS decision making. Congress requested further review and reporting by the OIG.

The aforementioned issues illustrate the difficulty of measuring terrorism. For years, dedicated DOS personnel have compiled reports on terrorism as numerous variables influenced the process. Next, we continue to focus on terrorism data from the NCTC and the DOS. We also cover data from the National Memorial Institute for the Prevention of Terrorism.

NATIONAL COUNTERTERRORISM CENTER

The NCTC was established by The Intelligence Reform and Terrorism Prevention Act of 2004 (see Chapter 4). The director of the center is appointed by the President with advice and consent of the Senate. The purpose of the center is detection, prevention, disruption, preemption, and mitigation of transnational terrorism against the people and interests of the United States. The center analyzes and integrates global intelligence, excluding purely domestic information, and facilitates the exchange of information among government agencies. It conducts strategic operational planning for counterterrorism activities, including diplomatic, financial, military, homeland security, and law enforcement. The center does not direct the execution of operations. The center works with the CIA to prepare an annual report to the President.

The NCTC's 2004 report indicated about 9300 individuals wounded or killed in significant international terrorist incidents as compared to 4271 a year earlier. Of those, 1907 were killed in 2004 in comparison to 625 deaths in 2003. Of the 68 Americans killed in 2004, all but 8 were killed in Iraq and Afghanistan. The overwhelming number of victims were non-U.S. citizens, and many were Muslims. In 2004, there were 651 significant attacks compared to 208 in 2003, about a threefold increase. Ten percent of the total (64 attacks) were against U.S. interests, down from over one-third from the previous year. The NCTC contends that terrorist attacks are becoming more deadly. The top five attacks in 2004 resulted in over 4000 wounded and dead. Also, terrorism is becoming less United States focused and more global in scope (Perl, 2006: 4).

UNITED STATES DEPARTMENT OF STATE

The following information is from the U.S. Department of State (2004) and reflects revised 2003 statistics resulting from criticism of DOS methodology. DOS and NCTC data show similarities.

There were 208 acts of international terrorism in 2003, a slight increase from the published figure of 198 attacks in 2002, and a 42% drop from the level in 2001 of 355 attacks. Most of the attacks that have occurred during Operation Iraqi Freedom and Operation Enduring Freedom do not meet the long-standing U.S. definition of international terrorism because they were directed at combatants, i.e., United States and coalition forces on duty. Attacks against noncombatants, i.e., civilians and military personnel who at the time of the incident were unarmed and/or not on duty, are judged to be terrorist attacks.

A total of 625 persons were killed in the attacks of 2003, fewer than the 725 killed during 2002. A total of 3646 persons were wounded in the attacks that occurred in 2003, a sharp increase from 2013 persons wounded the year before. This increase reflects the numerous indiscriminate attacks during 2003 on "soft targets," such as places of worship, hotels, and commercial districts, intended to produce mass casualties.

Thirty-five U.S. citizens died in international terrorist attacks in 2003.

- Michael Rene Pouliot was killed on January 21 in Kuwait when a gunman fired at his vehicle that had halted at a stoplight.
- Thomas Janis was murdered by Revolutionary Armed Forces of Colombia (FARC) terrorists on February 13 in Colombia. Mr. Janis was the pilot of a plane that crashed in the jungle. He and a Colombian service member were wounded in the crash; the terrorists shot them when they were discovered. Three U.S. citizen passengers on the plane—Keith Stansell, Marc D. Gonsalves, and Thomas R. Howes—were kidnapped and are still being held hostage as of June 2004 by the FARC.
- William Hyde was killed on March 4 in Davao, Philippines, when a bomb hidden in a backpack exploded in a crowded airline terminal. Twenty other persons died, and 149 were wounded. The Moro Islamic Liberation Front (MILF) denies any connection to the suspected bomber, who claimed he was a MILF member.
- Abigail Elizabeth Litle was killed on March 5 when a suicide bomber boarded a bus in Haifa, Israel, and detonated an explosive device.
- Rabbi Elnatan Eli Horowitz and his wife, Debra Ruth Horowitz, were killed on March 7 when a Palestinian gunman opened fire on them as they were eating dinner in the settlement of Kiryat Arba.
- The deadliest anti-U.S. attack occurred in Riyadh, Saudi Arabia, on May 12 when suicide bombers in booby-trapped cars filled with explosives drove into the Vinnell, Jadewel, and Al-Hamra housing compounds, killing nine U.S. citizens. Killed at the Vinnell compound were Obaidah Yusuf Abdullah, Todd Michael Blair, Jason Eric Bentley, James Lee Carpenter II, Herman Diaz, Alex Jackson, Quincy Lee Knox, and Clifford J. Lawson. Mohammed Atef Al Kayyaly was killed at the Al-Hamra compound.
- Alan Beer and Bertin Joseph Tita were killed on June 11 in a bus bombing near Klal Center on Jaffa Road near Jerusalem.
- Howard Craig Goldstein was killed in a shooting attack near the West Bank settlement of Ofra on June 20.
- Fred Bryant, a civilian contractor, was killed on August 5 in Tikrit, Iraq, when his car ran over an improvised explosive device.

- Three U.S. citizens were among the victims of a deadly truck bombing of the U.N. headquarters in Baghdad's Canal Hotel on August 19. They were Arthur Helton, Richard Hooper, and Martha Teas. U.N. Special Representative Sergio Vieira de Mello was also among the 23 fatalities.
- Five U.S. citizens were killed in Jerusalem on August 19 when a suicide bomber riding on a bus detonated explosives attached to his body. They were Goldy Zarkowsky, Eli Zarkowsky, Mordechai Reinitz, Yessucher Dov Reinitz, and Tehilla Nathansen. Fifteen other persons were killed and 140 wounded in the attack.
- Dr. David Applebaum and his daughter, Naava Applebaum, were killed on September 9 in a bombing at the Cafe Hillel in Jerusalem.

Continued

From: U.S.Department of State Travel Warnings
Sent: Thursday, March 09, 2006 12:33 PM
To: DOSTRAVEL@LISTS.STATE.GOV
Subject: Worldwide Caution Public Announcement

The Department of State remains concerned about the continued threat of terrorist attacks, demonstrations, and other violent actions against U.S. citizens and interests overseas. Ongoing events in Iraq have resulted in demonstrations and associated violence in several countries. Americans are reminded that demonstrations and rioting can occur with little or no warning.

Current information suggests that al-Qa'ida and affiliated organizations continue to plan terrorist attacks against U.S. interests in multiple regions, including Europe, Asia, Africa, and the Middle East. These attacks may employ a wide variety of tactics to include assassinations, kidnappings, hijackings, and bombings.

Extremists may elect to use conventional or nonconventional weapons, and target both official and private interests. The hotel bombings in Jordan in early November illustrate how terrorists exploit vulnerabilities associated with soft targets. Additional examples of such targets include residential areas, business offices, clubs, restaurants, places of worship, schools, public areas, and locales where Americans gather in large numbers, including during holidays.

In the wake of the July 2005 London bombings and the March 2004 train attacks in Madrid, Americans are reminded of the potential for terrorists to attack public transportation systems. In addition, extremists may also select aviation and maritime services as possible targets.

U.S. citizens are strongly encouraged to maintain a high level of vigilance, be aware of local events, and take the appropriate steps to bolster their personal security. For additional information, please refer to "A Safe Trip Abroad </travel/tips/safety/safety_1747.html>" found at http://travel.state.gov </index.html>.

U.S. Government facilities worldwide remain at a heightened state of alert. These facilities may temporarily close or periodically suspend public services to assess their security posture. In those instances, U.S. embassies and consulates will make every effort to provide emergency services to U.S. citizens. Americans abroad are urged to monitor the local news and maintain contact with the nearest U.S. embassy or consulate.

As the department continues to develop information on any potential security threats to U.S. citizens overseas, it shares credible threat information through its Consular Information Program documents, available on the Internet at http://travel.state.gov </index.html>. In addition to information on the Internet, travelers may obtain up-to-date information on security conditions by calling 1-888-407-4747 toll-free in the United States or outside the United States and Canada on a regular toll line at 1-202-501-4444.

- Three U.S. citizens were killed on October 15 in the Gaza Strip as their U.S. Embassy Tel Aviv motorcade was struck by a roadside bomb. They were John Branchizio, Mark T. Parson, and John Martin Linde, Jr. All three were security contractors to the U.S. Embassy.
- Lt. Col. Charles H. Buehring was killed on October 26 in Baghdad during a rocket-propelled grenade attack on the Al-Rasheed Hotel. Deputy Secretary of Defense Paul D. Wolfowitz was staying at the hotel at the time of the attack.
- Two U.S. citizens, William Carlson and Christopher Glenn Mueller, were killed in an ambush by armed militants in Shkin, Afghanistan, on October 27. Both were U.S. Government contract workers.

NATIONAL MEMORIAL INSTITUTE FOR THE PREVENTION OF TERRORISM (MIPT)

The National Memorial Institute for the Prevention of Terrorism is a nonprofit institution focused on deterring and preventing terrorism on U.S. soil and mitigating its consequences. It was formed following the 1995 bombing of the Murrah federal building in Oklahoma City and is funded through the Department of Homeland Security. The MIPT sponsors research on procedures, training, and equipment relevant to emergency responders.

The MIPT Terrorism Knowledge Base (TKB) is a team effort of the MIPT, DFI International, the Rand Corporation, and university professors. This user-friendly Web resource provides information on domestic and international terrorism, terrorist incidents, and terrorist groups. It contains research, interactive maps, data, and links to other resources.

The TKB methodologies include data that are integrated from multiple terrorism incident resources, including both RAND and NCTC incident tracking systems. Terrorism group and leader profiles are from DFI International. An indictment database is also contained in the TKB.

The following TKB data are from the National Memorial Institute for the Prevention of Terrorism (2006). For *domestic terrorism* (i.e., defined as incidents by local nationals against a purely domestic target), between January 1, 2003 and December 31, 2005, the TKB reported 33 attacks in North America, primarily by ALF and ELF (see Chapter 1), with most labeled as "attacked business target," "attacked private citizens and property target," and "attacked government target." No injuries or fatalities were reported. For domestic terrorism during the same period, the TKB reported that the Middle East/Persian Gulf region had the highest numbers in three categories at 1882 incidents, 6671 injuries, and 3313 fatalities. The regions of North America and east and central Asia showed the lowest numbers among other regions for domestic terrorism.

For *international terrorism* (i.e., defined as incidents when terrorists go abroad to attack or choose a domestic target with links to other countries or attack an aircraft), between January 1, 2003 and December 31, 2005, the TKB reported that the Middle East/Persian Gulf region had the highest numbers in the three categories at 458 incidents, 2029 injuries, and 774 fatalities.

MIPT data comparing 2004 with 2005 show the following: Global incidents overall increased about 50%. Whereas the Middle East and south Asia (i.e., includes Pakistan, Afghanistan, and India) account for this increase, terrorist incidents in other regions of the world decreased by an average of almost 40%. Domestic incidents increased more than international incidents, pointing to an increase in internal conflicts among nations. There was also a 35% increase in fatalities and a 15% increase in injuries.

Here is a comparison of 2003 data made in 2006 from the DOS, the NCTC, and the TKB. As the measurement of terrorism is being refined, we are seeing a sharing of the same data among organizations. The Web home page of the NCTC provides a link to the TKB. For 2003, the DOS and the NCTC both reported the same number (625) killed in "significant international terrorist incidents" and the same number (208) of "significant attacks" (Perl, 2006: 4; U.S. Department of State, 2004).

For 2003, the TKB reported 470 killed in international terrorism and 1877 killed in domestic terrorism, for a total of 2347. The TKB reported 276 incidents of international terrorism and 1622 incidents of domestic terrorism, for a total of 1898.

THE UNITED STATES: WEALTHY AND POWERFUL

Prior to explaining the actions of the United States in response to terrorism, let us first study the position of the United States among other nations. The United States is a wealthy, powerful, world leader. Americans, on average, enjoy better food, water, housing, and services than most people of the world.

Brooks and Wohlforth (2002) offer standard components of national power to show just how dominant the United States is among other nations. The United States has the largest and most powerful military on earth (Figures 3-1 and 3-2). It spends more on defense than the next 15–20 biggest spenders combined. Its nuclear superiority, air force, navy, technical capabilities on the battlefield, and military research and development (R&D) are unmatched. The U.S. economy is twice as large as its closest rival, Japan, and California's economy is the fifth largest in the world, ahead of France. U.S. financial agencies (e.g., Export Import Bank) offer loans to other countries to facilitate business with the United States. Technologically, U.S. expenditures for R&D are nearly equaled to the next seven richest countries combined. The United States is projected to maintain dominance in these areas for decades. National strength can be gained by bringing super-power challengers, such as China, into the international political and economic system as thoroughly as possible. According to Nye (2002), the United States will probably remain the sole superpower well into this century, barring catastrophic events or the United States using its coercive power in an overbearing, unilateral manner, forcing a coalition to counter the United States.

The wealth and superpower status of the United States is dependent on many other nations of the world. Although the United States has an abundance of natural resources, the supply of raw materials in America is not infinite and the United States is becoming increasingly dependent on the raw materials of other countries. The price and uninterrupted flow of oil from several countries to the United States are major global issues. Additionally, many U.S. corporations have moved their operations overseas for inexpensive labor and to escape government regulations and labor unions. Because U.S. corporate investments overseas are substantial, the stability of governments overseas is vital. Trade (i.e., exports and imports) among the nations of the world adds to the

Figure 3-1 ■ On December 18, 2001, an F/A-18 "Hornet" lands on the flight deck of the U.S.S. Theodore Roosevelt in support of Operation Enduring Freedom (Afghanistan). U.S. Navy photo by Photographer's Mate 3rd Class Luke Williams. http://www.news.navy.mil/view_single.asp?id=255

Figure 3-2 ■ U.S. troops in security posture after being infiltrated by Black Hawk helicopter in Iraq during June 2004. DOD photo by Tech. Sgt. Scott Reed, U.S. Air Force. http://www.defenselink.mil/photos/Jun2004/040619-F-4884R-013.html

intricate and complex nature of the global economy. U.S. wealth and superpower status depends on a foreign policy that supports U.S. economic interests.

There are serious inequalities within the United States and between Americans and citizens of many other countries. This has been termed the "haves and the have nots." The United States is also a powerful **cultural generator**, meaning that American values, beliefs, ideologies, religions, products, and services maintain a constant global impact on the societies of other nations. This is part of the process of globalization (see Chapter 1). The global influence of American culture clashes with other, more conservative, cultures and is a major reason why many people of the world hate America and its citizens. Even though the United States has a heterogeneous society, is a land of numerous freedoms, and a destination of many people of the world escaping from religious and ethnic persecution, there are many nations that are conservative, lack the freedoms found in the United States, have a history of intolerance, and seek to maintain a homogeneous society.

Military action is one of several options available to the United States to control terrorism. Such action must be carefully considered in light of advantages and disadvantages.

THE COLD WAR

During the early part of the 20th century, the declining power of Britain created a power vacuum and the need for a powerful nation to continue to strive for global political and economic stability.

The United States filled this void as a way to ensure U.S. economic growth (Callahan, 1994). During this period, the Soviet Union opposed U.S. policies of (1) creating a worldwide capitalist economy and (2) supporting U.S. allies politically, militarily, and economically. The Soviets countered U.S. policies by providing support for its pro-communist allies. By the mid-20th century, two superpowers were locked in global competition, each side fearing the other and building an enormous arsenal of nuclear weapons.

Although the United States and Soviet Union were allies against the Nazis during World War II, distrust grew between these superpowers following this war that ended in 1945. Because the Soviets were invaded from the West two times within one generation, they maintained a strong influence over eastern Europe by ensuring pro-Soviet leadership, maintaining a large military presence, and quashing any opposition. These policies remained until the collapse of the Soviet Union in 1991. The United States has maintained military forces in western Europe from World War II to the present time.

Rather than engaging in a **hot war** of direct combat, both superpowers fought a **cold war** of ideologies, propaganda, and surrogate wars between the end of World War II and the collapse of the Soviet Union. The conflicting ideologies consisted of capitalism versus communism (see Chapter 1). A **surrogate war** means that a host country seeks to gain something by providing military and other support to another country to fight a hot war without the direct involvement of the host country. Some hot wars did occur between superpowers, but these wars were fought on the soil of smaller countries and the wars included few superpower military personnel. The U.S. military was directly involved in the Korean War (1950–1953) and the Vietnam War (1957–1975), while the Soviets and Chinese provided supplies to communist forces in both wars. In the Korean War, the Chinese military participated in the fighting. In 1979, the Soviet Union invaded Afghanistan to support a communist regime; however, they were forced to withdraw 10 years later by anti-Communist mujahidin forces, including Osama bin Laden, supplied and trained by the United States and other countries. This 10-year struggle has often been referred to as the **Soviet's Vietnam War**. Although these hot wars never escalated to nuclear conflict, the threat of such a war between two heavily armed nuclear giants created global fear, especially during the **Cuban missile crisis** of 1963. In this standoff, with the world waiting for possible nuclear war, the Soviets agreed to remove missiles from Cuba in exchange for the United States agreeing not to invade Cuba, an ally of the Soviet Union.

The demise of the Soviet Union created a power vacuum filled by the United States as the sole superpower. This position of power has enabled the United States to exercise its influence globally. Mayer (2003: 2) notes that scholars of international relations have labeled the modern world as a **unipolar system**, meaning that the United States is largely unchallenged.

Throughout the cold war, both superpowers sought to check the influence and power of each other. Numerous armed struggles and regime changes worldwide often pitted a Western-supported side against a communist-supported side. Each superpower worked to maintain a long list of friendly regimes through various economic and military aid packages.

When the Soviet Union collapsed, communism became less important as a ideology or revolutionary struggle in many countries, former Soviet republics experienced political turmoil, Soviet military and secret police power waned, and the United States became more influential. Fingar (2005) notes that the erosion of Soviet power was followed by "a reemergence of long repressed political aspirations, and the rise of ethnic and religious hatreds." These circumstances created a ripe climate for terrorists to expand their operations and seek power in former Soviet republics, countries bordering the former Soviet Union (e.g., Afghanistan), and countries formerly aided by the Soviets. As terrorism increased to seek ideological and religious goals, terrorist groups employed asymmetrical warfare to try to block the influence of the remaining superpower and other Western nations.

The declining power of Britain during the early part of the 20th century and the collapse of the Soviet Union in 1991 both created power vacuums filled by the United States, the sole superpower today.

Although the United States is wealthy, powerful, and the sole superpower, it has been subject to much criticism globally. As a world leader that impacts so many nations politically, economically, and culturally and as a "police agency" for many global conflicts, U.S. policies and actions rarely produce consensus among nations and the diversity of groups in the world. Unfortunately, among the options available to settle differences in the world is violence.

INITIAL UNITED STATES RESPONSE TO THE 9/11 ATTACKS

To begin with, the federal government contains three branches of government: the *executive branch* enforces laws, the *legislative branch* enacts laws, and the *judicial branch* interprets law. To prevent any one branch from becoming too powerful, a "system of checks and balances" characterizes our government. For example, as the executive branch enforces laws enacted by Congress to control terrorism, the judicial branch may rule in a court decision that the executive branch exceeded its authority under a particular law.

During crises, Congress and the judiciary defer to the President, who is commander-in-chief of the armed forces, as stated in Article II, Section 2 of the U.S. Constitution. This centralized power is especially important because of complex and quickly changing events. It is not practical to wait for congressional action when there is a need for immediate action. However, as discussed in this book, Congress and the judiciary, in addition to the executive branch, are involved in terrorism and homeland security issues.

The president relies on the **National Security Council** (NSC) and the **Homeland Security Council** (HSC) to formulate policy for the protection of the United States. The NSC was established through the **National Security Act of 1947** and consists of advisors who assist the president with domestic and foreign security issues. Major members include the vice president and the secretaries of state and defense. Others may serve as advisors, such as the chairman of the Joint Chiefs of Staff (i.e., the military advisor) and the director of the Central Intelligence Agency (CIA). The HSC, first established by executive order from President George W. Bush and then by the Homeland Security Act of 2002, consists of the president, the vice president, the secretary of homeland security, the attorney general, and the secretary of defense. Like the NSC, the president may request others to serve on the HSC. Both the NSC and the HSC use committees to develop policies and direct strategies. When the activities of both councils overlap, they meet for coordination purposes. The NSC has a history since the cold war, whereas the HSC is relatively new and is involved in many new initiatives. Through the HSC, the president issues homeland security presidential directives (HSPD) to initiate policies and programs that enhance homeland security.

On September 11, 2001, when the commercial jets crashed into the World Trade Center, President George W. Bush was promoting his education agenda in an elementary school in Florida. Upon learning that a second jet hit the towers, Bush immediately left for Air Force One. Because of the possibility of further attacks, he flew west and then eventually to Washington, DC, to give a speech to the nation from the White House. Citizens from across the country were waiting for leadership to respond to the surprise attacks. Not since the Japanese sneak attack against Pearl Harbor in 1941 had Americans experienced such devastation and deaths. Americans wanted government action and answers to numerous questions about the attacks. How could the wealthiest and most powerful nation on earth be subjected to such attacks?

Initial orders from President Bush following the 9/11 attacks included air patrols over New York City and Washington, DC; placing the military on a heightened state of alert; calling military reservists to active duty; securing U.S. borders; and prompting U.S. investigative and intelligence services to apply their resources to the attacks. Many issues began to accumulate soon after the attack, such as federal emergency assistance to the locations and victims of the attack, restoring civil aviation, and reopening the financial markets (National Commission on Terrorist Attacks Upon the United States, 2004: 326–327).

Following the attacks, Congress and the president appropriated $40 billion in emergency funds to compensate victims, assist with reconstruction in New York and Virginia, and strengthen counterterrorism. Private companies and charitable organizations raised money and donated supplies for victims. The private sector also worked with government to improve security of, for example, the food supply and critical infrastructure. Many locations received intense security, including nuclear power plants, airports, bridges, seaports, and special events. Cities reviewed emergency plans to improve responses to incidents. Congress appropriated $650 million for federal grant assistance to states and localities to enhance first responder terrorism preparedness, training, and equipment. Citizen volunteers also played a role in helping to protect their communities (Office of Homeland Security, 2002: A-1 to A-4).

Soon after the attacks, President Bush and his advisors formulated a plan for enhanced homeland security. Through executive order, the president created the Office of Homeland Security and appointed Pennsylvania governor Tom Ridge to lead the new office. This appointment resulted in criticism from both Democrats and Republicans because of concern over whether anyone could be effective in coordinating dozens of federal agencies involved in counterterrorism. To make matters worse during this appointment and controversy, the anthrax attacks were occurring and causing enormous problems (see Chapter 2).

U.S. GOVERNMENT ACTION AGAINST TERRORISM

Government action against terrorism focuses on a variety of fronts to reduce the problem. This section presents the fronts emphasized by the United States government and then provides a list of a broad array of options for government action.

> We must take the battle to the enemy, disrupt his plans and confront the worst threats before they emerge. In the world we have entered, the only path to safety is the path of action. And this nation will act.
>
> President George W. Bush, June 1, 2002

The U.S. Government, White House (2003), under President George W. Bush, issued a *National Strategy for Combating Terrorism* that focused on four fronts as explained next.

1. *Defeat.* This goal of the 4D strategy aims to defeat terrorist organizations of global reach through diplomatic, economic, information, law enforcement, military, financial, intelligence, and other instruments of power. The United States cannot wait for terrorists to attack and then respond. Thus, the United States will attack terrorist sanctuaries, leadership, command, communications, material support, and finances. This approach will disrupt terrorist activities and force them to disperse along regional lines. Then, the United States will work with regional partners to squeeze and isolate terrorists. When the regional campaign has localized the threat, the United States will further assist nations in reducing the threat (Figure 3-3), even though terrorist cells that are small and decentralized present challenges for the United States and its allies. Terrorists who seek WMD will be high-priority targets. This war is not a "clash of civilizations," it is a clash between civilization and those who would destroy it.

2. *Deny.* All nations must accept responsibility for taking action against terrorists within their borders. This means denying terrorists sanctuary and the opportunity to exist, train, plan, and execute attacks. Nations will be held accountable for the actions of their "guests." The United States will work with weak nations to assist them in meeting their international obligations and offer incentives for nations ending state sponsorship of terrorists.

Figure 3-3 ■ Operationalizing the strategy to reduce the scope and capability of terrorist groups.
Source: U.S. Government, White House (2003).

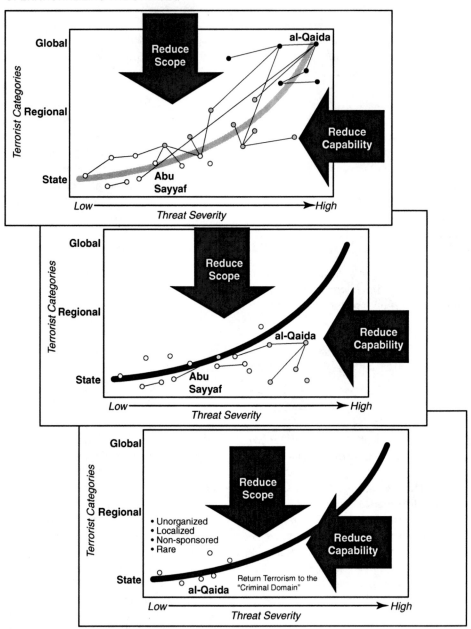

3. *Diminish.* This goal seeks to reduce political, social, and economic conditions that terrorists exploit. "While we recognize that there are many countries and people living with poverty, deprivation, social disenfranchisement, and unresolved political and regional disputes, those conditions do not justify the use of terror." The United States works with other nations to reduce unfortunate conditions and to win the "war of ideas" in support of democratic values and to promote economic freedom.

The United States will seek to support moderate and modern governments and those in the Muslim world. Muslims in Kuwait, Bosnia, and Kosovo, among other Muslims, have been assisted by the United States. Furthermore, finding a solution to the Israeli–Palestinian conflict is vital.

4. *Defend*. Terrorists are an adaptive enemy who are empowered by modern technology and emboldened by success, while avoiding the strengths of the United States and exploiting its vulnerabilities. The United States will defend its people, territory, national interests, and democratic principles. Within this strategy is the adage that the best defense is a good offense. The plan includes a focused effort from the entire U.S. society—federal, state, and local governments, the private sector, and the American people. A major component of defense is the **National Strategy for Homeland Security** (see Chapter 4).

In September of 2006, the executive branch of government released an updated National Strategy for Combating Terrorism (U.S. Government, White House, 2006a). Although the strategy remains primarily the same, the update noted successes in degrading the al-Qaida network, eliminating safe havens, and disrupting lines of support. The executive branch emphasized that in response to government efforts at counterterrorism, terrorists have adjusted, so the strategy must be refined to meet the evolving threat. At the same time, challenges remain, as summarized here from the updated strategy: terrorist networks are more dispersed; governments are not able to prevent all attacks; the use of WMD is a serious threat; some states, such as Syria and Iran, continue to harbor and support terrorists; and modern technology (e.g., the Internet) has been helpful to terrorists.

CRITICAL THINKING:

What are your views of the U.S. 4D strategy? Is it successful? Why or why not?

WHAT IS THE DIFFERENCE BETWEEN "COUNTERTERRORISM" AND "ANTITERRORISM?"

The terms "counterterrorism" and "antiterrorism" have varied definitions and writers may use these terms interchangeably within the same publication. **Counterterrorism** (U.S. Department of Defense, 2003) is defined as "offensive measures taken to prevent, deter, and respond to terrorism." This broad definition can include diplomatic options, policies, strategies, methods, and actions that aim to reduce or eliminate terrorism. **Antiterrorism** (U.S. Department of Defense, 1998) is defined as "defensive measures used to reduce the vulnerability of individuals and property to terrorist acts." This narrower term stresses target hardening, security, and training to prevent and mitigate terrorist attacks.

Differentiating counterterrorism and antiterrorism may be difficult in certain instances. For example, homeland security includes both counterterrorism (e.g., proactive investigations of suspects, collecting intelligence) and antiterrorism (e.g., increasing security at airports).

International terrorism can impact both domestic terrorism and counterterrorism, and domestic terrorism can impact both international terrorism and counterterrorism. Consequently, both international and domestic counterterrorism efforts should be characterized by collaboration and integration of resources and strategies to enhance success.

U.S. DEPARTMENT OF STATE ACTION AGAINST TERRORISM

The U.S. Department of State (2004) reiterates the *National Strategy for Combating Terrorism* and also emphasizes five "tools."

Diplomacy. Through **diplomacy** (i.e., negotiations between nations with the aim of producing the best possible agreement), the U.S. Department of State promotes international counterterrorism cooperation. *A major goal is to enhance the capabilities of allies for mutual benefit.* The **North Atlantic Treaty Organization** (NATO) (an alliance of countries from North America and Europe committed to safeguarding the security of its members through political and military means) has worked to transform its military capabilities to make this alliance more expeditionary and deployable against terrorist threats. NATO has also made counterterrorism contributions in the areas of WMD, maritime terrorism, and intelligence sharing. Groups of other nations have cooperated on many issues, such as terrorist financing, immigration controls, illegal arms trafficking, and seaport and aviation security.

[The United Nations (U.N.) and the European Union (E.U.) are additional organizations the United States works with to counter terrorism. Because terrorism has impacted many countries, counterterrorism has become a global effort, and cooperation among nations is essential on issues such as sharing information, prevention, investigation, and response. In Chapter 1, the problem of producing a universally agreeable definition of terrorism by U.N. member states was explained. Although the United Nations provides a foundation for international cooperation against terrorism, disagreement over terrorism is also reflected in the large number of U.N. members who have not ratified U.N. conventions and protocols on counterterrorism. At the same time, the United States works to enhance diplomacy to reduce the problem of terrorism. The E.U. consists of European countries whose activities cover a wide spectrum of public policies, such as economic, defense, and health. The E.U. works to establish a common legal framework and strategy against terrorism, while cooperating with the United Nations.]

Law Enforcement. International law enforcement cooperation increased following the 9/11 attacks and it continues to expand. Al-Qaida capabilities have been degraded and more than 3400 suspects have been arrested. For example, in 2003, a naturalized American citizen, Iyman Faris, pled guilty to surveilling a New York City bridge for al-Qaida and was sentenced to 20 years. In the same year, the U.S. Department of Justice unsealed a 50-count indictment against two Yemeni nationals for their role in the bombing in October 2000 of the **U.S.S. Cole** that killed 17 U.S. sailors and injured 39.

Intelligence. Quality intelligence shared among nations helps to track down terrorists and expose their plans. In 2003, the Terrorist Threat Integration Center was created to analyze threat-related information collected domestically and abroad and to ensure sharing of the information. Also in 2003, the Terrorist Screening Center was created to consolidate terrorist watch lists and provide 24/7 operational support to federal screeners around the world.

Financial. Countries throughout the world are waging a campaign to investigate, identify, and interdict the flow of money to terrorists groups. Nations have blocked over $100 million in terrorist assets. The United States offers training and assistance to other countries to improve their antimoney laundering strategies. Recommendations have been developed among nations to protect their financial systems from terrorist financiers.

Military. In Iraq, Afghanistan, and other countries military forces are combating terrorists. In Afghanistan, al-Qaida was denied a safe haven.

U.S. DEPARTMENT OF STATE (2005), REWARDS FOR JUSTICE PROGRAM

The Rewards for Justice Program is one of the most valuable U.S. Government assets in the fight against international terrorism. Established by the 1984 Act To Combat International Terrorism—Public Law 98-533—the program is administered by the U.S. Department of State's Bureau of Diplomatic Security.

Under the program, the secretary of state may offer rewards of up to $5 million for information that prevents or favorably resolves acts of international terrorism against U.S. persons or property worldwide. Rewards may also be paid for information leading to the arrest or conviction of terrorists attempting, committing, and conspiring to commit—or aiding and abetting in the commission of—such acts.

U.S. DEPARTMENT OF STATE (2005), REWARDS FOR JUSTICE PROGRAM—Cont'd

The USA Patriot Act of 2001 authorizes the secretary to offer or pay rewards of greater that $5 million if he determines that a greater amount is necessary to combat terrorism or to defend the United States against terrorist acts. In November 2002, the state and treasury departments announced a $5 million rewards program that will pay for information leading to the disruption of any terrorism financing operation.

Diplomatic security has fully supported the efforts of the private business sector and citizens to establish a Rewards for Justice Fund, a nongovernmental, nonprofit 501 C (3) charitable organization administered by a group of private U.S. citizens. One hundred percent of all donated funds will be used to supplement reward payments only. Diplomatic security has forged a strong relationship with the private business and U.S. citizen representatives of the Rewards for Justice Fund.

U.S. DEPARTMENT OF STATE (2004), INTERNATIONAL TERRORISM: U.S. HOSTAGES AND U.S. GOVERNMENT POLICY

The U.S. Government will make no concessions to individuals or groups holding official or private U.S. citizens hostage. The United States will use every appropriate resource to gain the safe return of U.S. citizens who are held hostage. At the same time, it is U.S. Government policy to deny hostage takers the benefits of ransom, prisoner releases, policy changes, or other acts of concession.

Basic Premises

It is internationally accepted that governments are responsible for the safety and welfare of persons within the borders of their nations. Aware of both the hostage threat and public security shortcomings in many parts of the world, the United States has developed enhanced physical and personal security programs for U.S. personnel and established cooperative arrangements with the U.S. private sector. It has also established bilateral assistance programs and close intelligence and law enforcement relationships with many nations to prevent hostage-taking incidents or resolve them in a manner that will deny the perpetrators benefits from their actions. The United States also seeks effective judicial prosecution and punishment for hostage takers victimizing the U.S. Government or its citizens and will use all legal methods to these ends, including extradition. U.S. policy and goals are clear, and the U.S. Government actively pursues them alone and in cooperation with other governments.

U.S. Government Responsibilities When Private U.S. Citizens are Taken Hostage

On the basis of past experience, the U.S. Government concluded that making concessions that benefit hostage takers in exchange for the release of hostages increased the danger that others will be taken hostage. U.S. Government policy is, therefore, to deny hostage takers the benefits of ransom, prisoner releases, policy changes, or other acts of concession. At the same time, the U.S. Government will make every effort, including contact with representatives of the captors, to obtain the release of hostages without making concessions to the hostage takers.

Consequently, the United States strongly urges U.S. companies and private citizens not to accede to hostage-taker demands. It believes that good security practices, relatively modest security expenditures, and continual close cooperation with embassy and local authorities can lower the risk to U.S. citizens living in high-threat environments.

Continued

U.S. DEPARTMENT OF STATE (2004), INTERNATIONAL TERRORISM: U.S. HOSTAGES AND U.S. GOVERNMENT POLICY—Cont'd

The U.S. Government is concerned for the welfare of its citizens but cannot support requests that host governments violate their own laws or abdicate their normal enforcement responsibilities.

If the employing organization or company works closely with local authorities and follows U.S. policy, U.S. Foreign Service posts can be involved actively in efforts to bring the incident to a safe conclusion. This includes providing reasonable administrative services and, if desired by local authorities and the U.S. entity, full participation in strategy sessions. Requests for U.S. Government technical assistance or expertise will be considered on a case-by-case basis. The full extent of U.S. Government participation must await an analysis of each specific set of circumstances.

The host government and the U.S. private organizations or citizen must understand that if they wish to follow a hostage-resolution path different from that of U.S. Government policy, they do so without U.S. Government approval. In the event a hostage-taking incident is resolved through concessions, U.S. policy remains steadfastly to pursue investigation leading to the apprehension and prosecution of hostage takers who victimize U.S. citizens.

Legal Caution

Under current U.S. law, 18 USC 1203 (Act for the Prevention and Punishment of the Crime of Hostage-Taking, enacted October 1984 in implementation of the U.N. convention on hostage taking), seizure of a U.S. citizen as a hostage anywhere in the world is a crime, as is any hostage-taking action in which the U.S. Government is a target or the hostage taker is a U.S. national. Such acts are, therefore, subject to investigation by the Federal Bureau of Investigation and to prosecution by U.S. authorities. Actions by private persons or entities that have the effect of aiding or abetting the hostage taking, concealing knowledge of it from the authorities, or obstructing its investigation may themselves be in violation of U.S. law.

CRITICAL THINKING:

Do you think U.S. policies on hostages are cruel? Why or why not?

ANTITERRORISM ASSISTANCE PROGRAM

Congress authorized the Antiterrorism Assistance (ATA) Program in 1983 as part of a major initiative of the U.S. Department of State against international terrorism. Since that time, ATA has provided training for more than 36,000 students from 142 countries. The ATA program provides training and related assistance to law enforcement and security services of selected friendly foreign governments. Assistance to the qualified countries focuses on the following objectives.

- Enhancing the antiterrorism skills of friendly countries by providing training and equipment to deter and counter the threats of terrorism.
- Strengthening the bilateral ties of the United States with friendly, foreign governments by offering concrete assistance in areas of mutual concern.
- Increasing respect for human rights by sharing with civilian authorities modern, humane, and effective antiterrorism techniques.

ANTITERRORISM ASSISTANCE PROGRAM—Cont'd

ATA courses are developed and customized in response to terrorism trends and patterns. The training can be categorized into four functional areas: crisis prevention, crisis management, crisis resolution, and investigation. Countries needing assistance are identified on the basis of the threat or actual level of terrorist activity they face.

Antiterrorism assistance and training may be conducted either in-country or within the United States. This arrangement provides flexibility to maximize the effectiveness of the program for countries of strategic importance in the global war on terrorism.

ATA programs may take the form of advisory assistance, such as police administration and management of police departments, how to train police instructors or develop a police academy, and modern interview and investigative techniques. This approach enables the program to provide a narrow focus to solutions for country-specific problems that are not resolved in the classroom-training environment. Equipment or explosive-detection trained dogs may also be included in the assistance package.

The ability of the United States to assist friendly governments to master the detection and prevention of terrorist activities will clearly enhance the mutual security of all the participating nations. Detecting and eliminating terrorist cells at the root before their violence can cross borders and oceans will ensure a safer world for all nations.

ATA continues its efforts to familiarize ambassadors, regional security officers, and other U.S. officials with the program offerings. The success of these efforts is evidenced by the fact that every frontline nation has requested antiterrorist assistance in some form. U.S. diplomats report that the ability of the United States to offer immediate, specific, and intensive training, along with technical tools and equipment, has succeeded in breaking down barriers and building trust. ATA is responding to the growing demand for training and services not only by expanding course selection, but also by pursuing development of the Center for Antiterrorism and Security Training.

Building Counterterrorism Capacity

Employing policy guidance from the Coordinator for Counterterrorism, the Bureau of Diplomatic Security's Office of Antiterrorism Assistance implements and manages the ATA program operations.

In Indonesia, throughout 2003, experienced Indonesian police officers received training in both investigative and response techniques to enhance their capabilities to combat terrorism. In July, 30 Indonesian National Police (INP) officers completed an intense 15-week counterterrorism investigation course sponsored by ATA. In October, 24 officers graduated from the Crisis Response (SWAT) course and 15 from the Explosive Incident Countermeasures course.

During the investigative course, instructors honed the analytical skills of the Indonesian police, emphasizing the importance of forensic evidence in finding and stopping terrorists. The Indonesian officers enrolled in the three classes attended a state-of-the-art training school approximately 30 miles south of Jakarta, which is equipped with an ATA-funded "shoot house" for simulating hostage situations, a number of ranges, and other facilities.

Graduates of these courses become the core members of the first national-level Indonesian National Police (INP) counterterrorism special detachment. This group was designated as "Special Detachment 88 Anti-Terror." The number "88," culturally a double lucky number in Indonesia, also represents a phonetic approximation of "ATA."

Equipped with these skills and working with other Indonesian police officials, Special Detachment 88 members have relentlessly investigated Jemaah Islamiya (JI) cells, conducted successful raids, and arrested key JI operatives.

Continued

ANTITERRORISM ASSISTANCE PROGRAM—Cont'd

Immediately after their graduation from the investigative course, the Indonesian police officers were called to investigate a bombing at the Indonesian Parliament. Due to their effective investigation, Special Detachment 88 members, along with others, were able to arrest two key bombing suspects a month later.

Special Detachment 88 members were also the first investigative responders to the scene of the Jakarta J.W. Marriott Hotel bombing on August 5th. Indonesian police, including Special Detachment members, nabbed key bombing suspects and alleged JI members in a resort town in Indonesia on October 28th. The suspects included Tohir, purported JI field commander and Ismail, the alleged buyer of the vehicle used in the bombing.

Also, in Colombia, United States and Colombian officials inaugurated an antikidnapping program in Facatativa, Colombia, in conjunction with ATA-sponsored antikidnapping training.

Colombia has the world's highest kidnapping rate. The country's three terrorist organizations (the FARC, ELN, and the AUC) are responsible for more than half of the 12,000 kidnappings since 1996. The GAULAs were created to combat the growing threat of terrorist-related kidnappings. The three-pronged U.S.-sponsored antikidnapping assistance program was designed to strengthen Colombia's capability to deal with this threat by training and equipping the GAULA units; assisting in the formation of an interagency antikidnapping joint task force; and creating an integrated data automation system to consolidate, track, and analyze relevant information.

On November 20th, GAULA units rescued Manuel Tequia Gonzales, a 61-year-old owner of a transport company in Colombia, after 41 days in captivity. The hostage takers, one 54-year-old male and one 32-year-old female, were also captured during the rescue operation. The kidnappers, armed with a 38 revolver and two hand grenades at the time of their capture, were attached to the 53rd FARC front. With the skills acquired through ATA training, the GAULA units completed the entire rescue operation in 45 seconds with no injuries.

The same evening another GAULA unit rescued Grace Fener de Giraldo, a 61-year-old housewife who had been in captivity for 12 days. Two females, each 23 years old, and one male, 20, all connected to the 51st FARC front, were holding Giraldo. The forces successfully rescued her, without any injury, in 12 seconds.

Despite the early success of the GAULAs, terrorists continue to abduct civilians on a regular basis in Colombia. Currently, 1468 Colombians and three Americans continue to be held by terrorist groups. Training and assistance, like that provided by ATA, will make the Colombian police forces better equipped, more efficient, and ultimately more successful in locating and rescuing hostages and capturing terrorists.

Reproduced courtesy of the U.S. Department of State, www.state.gov

LEGISLATIVE AND OTHER EXECUTIVE ACTION AGAINST TERRORISM

Although terrorism is a serious challenge to any society, it is particularly troublesome to democratic nations in comparison to totalitarian nations. In the United States, the Bill of Rights of the U.S. Constitution restricts police powers and provides a foundation for criticism of government methods of curtailing terrorism. When a democracy faces the threat of terrorism, government leaders and the legal system seek to balance public safety and civil liberties. In other words, to protect a population of a nation, what powers will be placed in the hands of the police at the expense of constitutional rights? For instance, should police be permitted to search homes without a warrant to eliminate a terrorist threat? Controversy surrounds legislative action to combat terrorism in a democratic system.

By outlawing terrorism and making it a criminal act, governments send a message that such behavior is wrong and offenders will be brought to justice. Governments can leverage such laws to build strength in the fight against terrorism. At the same time, repressive laws, or an overreaction by a government, can lead to disapproval of the government by the citizenry—a goal of terrorists. Consequently, legislative action against terrorism has its pitfalls. Here, an emphasis is placed on explaining major legislation, whereas in Chapter 5, the controversy over the legislation, including constitutional issues, is covered.

Laws, executive orders, and presidential directives provided the legal foundation for the war against terrorism prior to and following the 9/11 attacks (Bullock *et al.*, 2005: 29–59). Congress enacted **The Defense Against Weapons of Mass Destruction Act of 1996**, also called Nunn-Lugar. This legislation was influenced by three major terrorist attacks: the World Trade Center bombing in 1993, the Oklahoma City bombing in 1995, and the Tokyo subway sarin gas attack in 1995. This act provided the impetus for increased federal government preparedness activities and funding for training and equipment for first responders to respond to terrorism and WMD. Executive Order 13010 (July 15, 1996), Critical Infrastructure, established the President's Commission on Critical Infrastructure Protection and the related working group to facilitate government and private sector cooperation in protecting vital sectors of our nation, such as water supply systems, transportation, telecommunications, emergency services, and government. Presidential Decision Directives 62 "Combating Terrorism" and 63 "Critical Infrastructure Protection" were signed by President Clinton on May 22, 1998 to designate a national coordinator for security, infrastructure protection, and counterterrorism. The coordinator was not to direct agencies' activities, but to integrate policies and programs on unconventional threats against the homeland and Americans abroad.

These examples of legislative (including the Antiterrorism Act of 1996) and executive action show that the federal government was taking steps to improve protection against terrorism prior to September 11, 2001. However, it was the 9/11 attacks that exposed serious deficiencies in our defenses and the need for monumental changes.

ANTITERRORISM ACT OF 1996

The **Antiterrorism and Effective Death Penalty Act of 1996** was designed to prevent terrorist acts, enhance counterterrorism methods, and increase punishments. Provisions of the act include the following.

- Federal death penalty when a death results from a terrorist act.
- Federal crime to use the United States as a base for planning terrorist attacks overseas.
- Federal prosecution (rather than state prosecution) of crimes against on-duty federal personnel.
- Enhanced procedural controls over entry into the country and deportation. Denies visas to foreigners who are members of terrorist groups.
- Provides funding for antiterrorism measures by federal and state authorities.
- Bans fund raising and financial support within the United States for international terrorist groups.
- Authorizes the Secretary of State to establish a formal list of foreign terrorist organizations (FTOs).
- Requires identifying chemical markers to be added to plastic explosives during the manufacturing process.

Critics of the Antiterrorism Act of 1996 claimed that it infringed upon constitutional protections of due process. It was claimed that the act's death penalty provision would alienate nations that opposed the death penalty and they would be reluctant to extradite terrorists to the United States.

USA PATRIOT ACT OF 2001

On September 16, 2001, following the 9/11 attacks, U.S. Attorney General John Ashcroft sought help from congressional leaders to expand police powers in America to investigate and apprehend terrorist suspects. On October 26, 2001, President George W. Bush signed the **USA Patriot Act of 2001** into law. This law has been dubbed the Uniting and Strengthening America by Providing Appropriate Tools Required to Intercept and Obstruct Terrorism Act. The act contains 10 titles, portions of which are listed next.

TITLE I. ENHANCING DOMESTIC SECURITY AGAINST TERRORISM
- Sec. 101. Counterterrorism fund.
- Sec. 102. Sense of Congress condemning discrimination against Arab and Muslim Americans.
- Sec. 103. Increased funding for the technical support center at the Federal Bureau of Investigation.
- Sec. 104. Requests for military assistance to enforce prohibition in certain emergencies.

TITLE II. ENHANCED SURVEILLANCE PROCEDURES
- Sec. 201. Authority to intercept wire, oral, and electronic communications relating to terrorism.
- Sec. 202. Authority to intercept wire, oral, and electronic communications relating to computer fraud and abuse offenses.
- Sec. 203. Authority to share criminal investigative information.
- Sec. 206. Roving surveillance authority under the Foreign Intelligence Surveillance Act of 1978.
- Sec. 209. Seizure of voice-mail messages pursuant to warrants.
- Sec. 220. Nationwide service of search warrants for electronic evidence.

TITLE III. INTERNATIONAL MONEY LAUNDERING ABATEMENT AND ANTI-TERRORIST FINANCING ACT OF 2001
- Sec. 314. Cooperative efforts to deter money laundering.
- Sec. 330. International cooperation in investigations of money laundering, financial crimes, and the finances of terrorist groups.
- Sec. 351. Amendments relating to reporting of suspicious activities.
- Sec. 352. Anti-money laundering programs.
- Sec. 372. Forfeiture in currency reporting cases.

TITLE IV. PROTECTING THE BORDER
- Sec. 401. Ensuring adequate personnel on the northern border.
- Sec. 403. Access by the Department of State and the INS to certain identifying information in the criminal history records of visa applicants and applicants for admission to the United States.
- Sec. 412. Mandatory detention of suspected terrorists; habeas corpus; judicial review.
- Sec. 416. Foreign student monitoring program.
- Sec. 417. Machine readable passports.
- Sec. 418. Prevention of consulate shopping.

TITLE V. REMOVING OBSTACLES TO INVESTIGATING TERRORISM
- Sec. 501. Attorney General's authority to pay rewards to combat terrorism.
- Sec. 502. Secretary of State's authority to pay rewards.
- Sec. 503. DNA identification of terrorists and other violent offenders.

TITLE VI. PROVIDING FOR VICTIMS OF TERRORISM, PUBLIC SAFETY OFFICERS, AND THEIR FAMILIES

- Sec. 611. Expedited payment for public safety officers involved in the prevention, investigation, rescue, or recovery efforts related to a terrorist attack.
- Sec. 622. Crime victim compensation.
- Sec. 624. Victims of terrorism.

TITLE VII. INCREASED INFORMATION SHARING FOR CRITICAL INFRASTRUCTURE PROTECTION

- Sec. 711. Expansion of regional information sharing system to facilitate federal–state–local law enforcement response related to terrorist attacks.

TITLE VIII. STRENGTHENING THE CRIMINAL LAWS AGAINST TERRORISM

- Sec. 801. Terrorist attacks and other acts of violence against mass transportation systems.
- Sec. 803. Prohibition against harboring terrorists.
- Sec. 809. No statute of limitation for certain terrorism offenses.
- Sec. 812. Postrelease supervision of terrorists.
- Sec. 813. Inclusion of acts of terrorism as racketeering activity.
- Sec. 814. Deterrence and prevention of cyberterrorism.

TITLE IX. IMPROVED INTELLIGENCE

- Sec. 901. Responsibilities of director of Central Intelligence regarding foreign intelligence collected under Foreign Intelligence Surveillance Act of 1978.
- Sec. 907. National Virtual Translation Center.
- Sec. 908. Training of government officials regarding identification and use of foreign intelligence.

TITLE X. MISCELLANEOUS

- Sec. 1001. Review of the department of justice.
- Sec. 1005. First responders assistance act.
- Sec. 1006. Inadmissibility of aliens engaged in money laundering.
- Sec. 1011. Crimes against charitable Americans.
- Sec. 1014. Grant program for state and local domestic preparedness support.
- Sec. 1016. Critical infrastructures protection.

Among the enhanced police powers of the Patriot Act, it authorizes roving wiretaps. This means that police can obtain a warrant for a wiretap on *any* telephone used by a suspected terrorist. Prior to the act, judicial authorization was required for each telephone. Also, federal law enforcement officers can obtain search warrants that can be used nationwide and their subpoena powers were increased to obtain e-mail records of terrorists.

The act relaxed restriction on sharing information among U.S. law enforcement agencies and the intelligence community. The Treasury Department was provided with greater authority to force foreign banks dealing with U.S. banks to release information on large accounts suspected of money laundering.

Under the act, immigrant terrorist suspects can be held up to 7 days for questioning without specific charges. Criminal penalties were enhanced for terrorist acts, financing and harboring terrorists, and possession of WMD.

Among personnel increases and an infusion of new technology, the act tripled federal law enforcement officers involved in protection at the U.S. northern border. One hundred million dollars was also earmarked to improve technology and equipment at this border.

As with the Antiterrorism Act of 1996, an erosion of civil liberties became a major concern of those critical of the Patriot Act. To allay some of these fears, lawmakers included sunset provisions in this law so that expanded police powers would expire in 4 years. Still, the controversy continued. Chapter 5 includes a variety of viewpoints on this controversy.

USA PATRIOT IMPROVEMENT AND REAUTHORIZATION ACT OF 2005

On March 9, 2006, President George W. Bush signed the **USA Patriot Improvement and Reauthorization Act of 2005**. This legislation extended the Patriot Act, although it will face debate in 4 years on certain provisions. According to the White House, since the Patriot Act was first enacted, it has been vital to the war against terrorism and protecting the American people, while breaking up terror cells and prosecuting terrorist operatives in several states. The new act (U.S. Government, White House, 2006b) includes the following.

- It continues to authorize information sharing between intelligence and law enforcement officials and helps break down legal and bureaucratic walls separating intelligence officers and criminal investigators.
- It creates a new assistant attorney general for national security to allow the U.S. Department of Justice to better coordinate criminal cases against suspected terrorists.
- For those involved in terrorist financing, the act enhances penalties.
- It improves protection for mass transportation through standards and tough penalties.
- The new act includes The Combat Methamphetamine Epidemic Act of 2005 that makes the ingredients used in methamphetamine manufacturing more difficult to obtain and easier for police to track, while increasing penalties for smuggling and selling this substance.

Because of controversy in Congress over civil liberties protections and delays in extending the Patriot Act due to debate, the president was forced to negotiate new restrictions on the police powers of the act. These restrictions include the following.

- Recipients of a court-approved subpoena seeking information in terrorism investigations have the right to challenge a requirement that they not tell anyone.
- The new act drops the requirement that a person provide the FBI with the name of an attorney consulted on a National Security Letter (i.e., a demand for records).
- Clarifies that most libraries are not subject to National Security Letters demanding information on suspected terrorists. Only libraries that are Internet service providers are subject to this provision.

HOMELAND SECURITY ACT OF 2002

*The **Homeland Security Act of 2002** began the largest single reorganization of the federal government since 1947 when President Truman created the Department of Defense.* President George W. Bush signed it into law on November 25, 2002. The next chapter focuses on homeland security. Here, a brief overview of this legislation is presented. The act

- Established the **Department of Homeland Security** (DHS) as an agency of the executive branch of government, with a DHS secretary who reports to the president.
- Established within the office of the president the Homeland Security Council to advise the president.
- Detailed an organization chart and management structure for the DHS.
- Listed agencies and programs to be transferred to the DHS.
- Stated the responsibilities of the five directorates of the DHS: information analysis and infrastructure protection; science and technology; border and transportation security; emergency preparedness and response; and management. (The next chapter explains the reorganization of the DHS in 2005.)

UNITED NATIONS, INTERNATIONAL LAW, AND
INTERNATIONAL COURTS

The United Nations was formed in 1945 following World War II to promote world peace and human rights and to seek solutions to a variety of problems pertaining to politics, economics, poverty, and crime, among other areas. Its membership numbers 189 nations and its headquarters is in New York City.

The United States has been the largest financial contributor to the United Nations since 1945. The United States contributed about $3 billion in 2002. Most of this money goes to humanitarian/human rights (39%), followed by peacekeeping (31%). The remainder is spent on health, development, the environment, control of WMD, and other programs. In 2002, the United States funded 51% of the World Food Program to help feed 72 million people in 82 countries, 22% of the World Health Organization to control epidemics, and 25% of the budget to assist and protect refugees (U.S. Department of State, 2003).

As shown in Chapter 1, the United Nations has limited power to act on terrorism because it has no universally acceptable definition of terrorism. One nation may see violence as terrorism, while another may view it as a rebellion for independence and grant political asylum to a political offender. At the same time, the U.N. General Assembly (GA) has passed resolutions, with no enforcement powers, that condemn terrorism, while requesting that nations prevent and combat it through international cooperation, deny safe havens, and prosecute and extradite offenders. U.N. conventions and protocols to reduce terrorism have been adopted by the GA to become international law.

International law is unique in that it is supported primarily by formal, cooperative agreements (i.e., treaties) between and among nations. Custom is another source of international law. There is no formal international law enforcement agency that enforces international law. Nations agree voluntarily to international law through treaties to create stability and harmony. Treaties essentially result in the law being codified, or written down. For example, to deal with the problem of aircraft being hijacked, the first airline crimes' treaty was enacted in 1963 and called the Tokyo Convention on Offences and Certain Other Acts Committed on Board Aircraft. It aimed to restore control of hijacked aircraft to the captain and to return the aircraft and its passengers, crew, and cargo. Extradition treaties serve as another example; members hold and transfer custody of terrorists and other offenders among themselves.

The United Nations maintains international courts to deal with disputes among nations, terrorism, genocide, and other international crimes. The purpose is to bring offenders to justice.

The International Court of Justice, also called the World Court, sits in The Hague, The Netherlands, and is the main U.N. court. It is composed of 15 judges who are elected by U.N. members and sit for a term of 9 years. This court presides over disagreements between nations. Not all nations recognize the authority of international courts at all times. In Nicaragua v. U.S. (1984), the former filed a case with the World Court charging the United States with violating international law by supporting the Contra rebels and mining Nicaragua's harbors. The U.S. position was that the charges were political and that the court had no jurisdiction. The court ruled against the United States, as did world opinion, and the mining was halted.

The U.N. International Criminal Court (ICC) hears cases on crimes against humanity (e.g., genocide) and war criminals. Furthermore, the United Nations establishes special courts to hear horrific cases of genocide, as was the case with the violence in the former Yugoslavia and in Rwanda. Because the United States is a global military power, it offers little support for the ICC, fearing that U.S. leaders and military personnel might be prosecuted politically.

Rourke (2005: 296) explains some points of consideration when applying international law and morality.

- Most current international law and many concepts of mortality are based on Western ideas; this causes tension with non-Western countries on select issues.
- Certain issues are increasing in importance, such as the legality and conduct of war, human rights, and governing the biosphere.
- International law has traditionally focused on states. Now it includes individuals, their treatment, and the actions of individuals.

WAR AND FOREIGN POLICY

With so much violence, war, and terrorism in the world, we often ask, "why?" The issues are complex and there are no easy answers. Chapter 1 covered causes of terrorism. It also explained Barber's "Jihad" versus "McWorld" and Huntington's "clash of civilizations." This section spends time on the subjects of war (Figure 3-4) and foreign policy.

Rourke (2005: 298–336) offers the following points on war.

- War has existed since the beginning of humanity.
- There were almost 1000 wars during the last 1000 years. Over 147 million people perished during wars since the year 1000. Of the dead, 75% were killed in the 20th century and 89% since 1800. An increasing number of civilians are being killed per armed forces member.
- In 1961, President John F. Kennedy warned that "mankind must put an end to war, or war will put an end to mankind."
- War is a complex phenomenon that appears to have many causes.
- Military power has drawbacks: it creates the temptation to use it; it makes other countries insecure and it can cause an arms race; and it is costly, draining a nation's budget and siphoning funds from domestic programs.
- Military power serves as a psychological tool that strengthens diplomacy.
- Warfare can be classified into three categories: conventional warfare (e.g., great armies in huge battles); unconventional warfare (e.g., arms transfers to other countries to assist allies and to assist one's own domestic economy; special operations; and terrorism); and WMD.
- The lethality of weapons has sparked increased interest in arms control. Many treaties have been signed among nations to limit arms and testing of WMD. [Although nonproliferation treaties have attempted to slow the spread of WMD among nations, in 2004, the United Nations declared that 40 nations could create nuclear weapons.]

The philosophy behind traditional methods of warfare has been influenced greatly by the Prussian general and intellectual **Carl von Clausewitz** (1780–1831). His book, *On War*, published after his death under the guidance of his wife, has been translated into almost every major language. The book has been controversial and interpreted differently among a long list of writers (Bassford, 1994; Ingrao, 1989). The observations of von Clausewitz include the following.

Figure 3-4 ■ The United States has participated in many wars. An American World War II cemetery in the Philippines, site of many battles with the Japanese.

- Diplomacy is designed to impose a nation's will on the enemy.
- War is merely the pursuit of diplomacy by other means.
- Armies of citizens fighting for their country show greater determination than professional soldiers fighting for territory.
- A nation at war must take risks and act boldly to be victorious.
- An aggressor is always peace loving, preferring to take over a country unopposed.

Clausewitz emphasized the importance of uniting the will, citizens, and resources of a nation in a massive campaign to defeat an enemy in decisive battles. This has been a traditional approach to war. However, the strategy of terrorism is to avoid a massive confrontation because terrorists are no match against conventional armies. Terrorists apply asymmetrical warfare (i.e., unconventional methods, such as suicide attacks) to cause psychological harm to a nation and weaken its government and policies.

Another influential writer about war was **Sun Tzu**, a Chinese philosopher, who wrote *The Art of War*. The book focused on philosophy, logistics, espionage, and strategies and tactics during a time of feudal conflicts in China about 453–221 BC. This work influenced Chinese, Vietnamese, and Japanese military thinking, and it is popular in the business world. Sun Tzu noted the futility of seeking hard and fast rules of war and the subtle paradoxes of success in war. Points made by Sun Tzu include the following (Giles, 1910).

- All warfare is based on deception.
- The skillful leader subdues the enemy's troops without any fighting.
- If the enemy is in superior strength, evade him.
- Attack him where he is unprepared, appear where you are not expected.
- There is no instance of a country having benefited from prolonged warfare.

TRANSFORMING THE U.S. MILITARY

U.S. military doctrine needs to be less rooted in Cold War mindsets to guide U.S. forces against new challenges, particularly global terrorism, according to Brigadier General David Fastabend. He noted that under Cold War assumptions, the adversary was relatively steady and predictable. This is not so with the people who are violently opposed to Western culture. This enemy lacks structure and is able to adapt quickly to suit the circumstances. "Its weakness is actually its strength," and as "the enemy constantly adapts, so too must US military doctrine," he said (Miles, 2004).

According to Air Force General Richard B. Meyers, "transforming the US armed forces while still fighting a global war on terrorism is the biggest challenge facing military leaders today." He adds that the war on terrorism is unlike any war the United States has fought before. It demands new thinking, new tactics, and new capabilities. The transformation is more than buying new equipment or technology; it requires a change of culture in the military.

Meyers offered an example of new technology that does not have to be expensive. He refers to the Marine Corps' Dragon Eye, an unmanned aerial vehicle that looks like a radio-controlled airplane that you can purchase in a kit. "Add some sensors to it and it becomes an invaluable reconnaissance tool for a platoon trying to find out what's on the other side of the hill or on the next city street" (Garamone, 2003).

U.S. foreign policy is administered by the executive branch of government with approval and funding from Congress (Janda *et al.*, 1995: 715–720). As the United States became more powerful in world affairs following World War II, Congress passed the National Security Act of 1947 (see earlier discussion) to bolster foreign policy capabilities. The act established three federal organizations to work with the main executive branch foreign policy department—the **Department of State**. The **Department of Defense** (DOD) manages the U.S. military. The **National Security Council** (NSC) is a group of advisors who assist the president with foreign policy, as covered earlier. The **Central Intelligence Agency** gathers intelligence on foreign countries, but the DOD and the departments of state and energy and other government units also gather intelligence and are collectively referred to as the **intelligence community**. The Intelligence Reform and Terrorism Prevention Act of 2004 is discussed in the next chapter.

THE "BUSH DOCTRINE"

Rourke (2005: 49) explains opposing viewpoints on the **Bush doctrine**. This refers to the administration of President George W. Bush and its national security strategy for the United States (U.S. Government, White House, 2002). Bush proclaimed that the strength of the United States is in its military power and economic and political influence. He proposed using **preemptive force** (i.e., first strike at an enemy) to fight terrorism and tyrants. The reasoning supporting this doctrine is that counterterrorism is not successful in controlling global terrorism and that the Cold War strategy of nuclear deterrence is inadequate. Two problems with this controversial doctrine are the difficulty in defining terrorism and pinpointing the enemies and supporters. Another problem is the U.S. government placing too much emphasis on the military, which is prepared primarily for a conventional war, when law enforcement agencies play an important role in counterterrorism. Opponents claim that it is neoimperialism and it hurts the U.S. economy, hastens the decline of the United States as a superpower, and causes an arms race for WMD. An alternative to the Bush doctrine is to have the international community use preemptive force for worldwide benefit and not for the exclusive benefit of the United States. Proponents claim that the Bush doctrine is a positive response to unpredictable states such as Iraq and North Korea.

An example of the application of the Bush doctrine occurred 1 month following the 9/11 attacks when U.S. and coalition forces attacked Afghanistan to destroy both al-Qaida training camps and the Taliban regime that had supported al-Qaida. Several leaders of both groups escaped to the mountains between Afghanistan and Pakistan while being pursued by coalition forces. The 2003 invasion of Iraq is another example of the application of the Bush doctrine.

Shultz and Vogt (2003: 26) note that, morally, preemptive force is anchored in the **just war doctrine**. It places great importance on the state as a natural institution essential for citizen security and development. This viewpoint is so strong that it does not limit action to defensive measures and includes offensive action to protect vital rights and interests unjustly threatened by other states or nonstate actors (e.g., terrorists).

The just war doctrine has stirred much debate. Through history, nations and groups have relied on this philosophy in believing that their cause was just, while the enemy was unjust.

Falk (2002: 5) adds to the debate: "To think that military power and its methods can restore security to the American people is a dangerous delusion. Only an engagement with the root causes of terrorism can bring hope to the peoples of the Islamic world, and end their receptivity to un-Islamic appeals based on political extremism and terrorist methods." Furthermore, Gueli (2003) reminds us of the uncomfortable reality that the United States and its allies unknowingly have had (and most likely still do) terrorist cells in the homeland.

Stepanova (2003: 12) argues against combining counterterrorism with the war on terrorism. Her reasoning is that excessive reliance on the military has not worked well for the U.S.-led war on terrorism, nor helped to curb terrorist violence in Chechnya or between the Israelis and the Palestinians. Military force tends to be event driven, reactive, and short-term. She points out that armed forces, and special forces in particular, can play a role in counterterrorism, but the military is not designed for counterterrorism and should not assume a primary role.

Another relevant aspect of foreign policy is **blowback**. This refers to unanticipated negative results from foreign policy. An example is U.S. covert aid and training to the mujahidin in Afghanistan that played a role in defeating the Soviets and leading to the collapse of the Soviet Union.

Following the Soviet withdrawal, Afghanistan continued to be mired in a civil war that lasted for 10 years and led to rule by the Taliban who hosted al-Qaida. Many leaders of both groups were covertly supported and trained by the CIA in the struggle against the Soviets (Lowenthal, 2003).

IRAQ

Although the U.S.-led attack of Iraq in 2003 applied the Bush doctrine, the justification for the invasion will be debated for many years. The pretext (i.e., WMD) for invading Iraq and toppling Saddam Hussein's regime was not realized. Faulty intelligence was blamed for not finding WMD in Iraq and the focus shifted to Hussein's regime having the capability of producing WMD.

As President George W. Bush has stated, the United States is taking the war against terrorism to the enemy. On the downside, global opinion of the United States has dropped, especially in the Middle East (Figure 3-5), and the war in Iraq is serving to attract recruits against U.S. and coalition forces (similar to what occurred in Afghanistan when it was occupied by the Soviets). These recruits are not only involved in the insurgency, but are also being trained in terrorist methods.

Figure 3-5 ■ Map of the Middle East. Source: www.cia.gov. http://www.odci.gov/cia/publications/factbook/docs/refmaps.html. http://www.cia.gov/cia/publications/factbook/reference_maps/middle_east.html

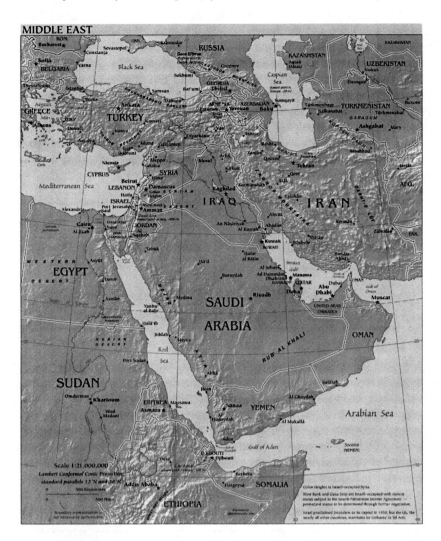

In addition to many civilian and military deaths and injuries from the war, it is costing the U.S. hundreds of billions of dollars.

A related issue concerning the violence in Iraq is **political democratization through military occupation**. This refers to the presence of a foreign military force in a country, possibly formerly ruled by an authoritarian regime, while free elections are promoted. The democratization of Iraq has become an effort at "ballots through bullets" and it is a major U.S. strategy to end the violence. Its success is difficult to predict because of numerous variables, such as political history, culture, and social conditions. The United States has had successes (e.g., West Germany and Japan) and failures (e.g., South Vietnam and Cuba) with this approach.

Paz (2005) writes that the fall of Saddam Hussein and the collapse of his regime created a vacuum in Iraq that attracted a steady flow of terrorists to that country. He also notes that the weak security situation in Iraq triggered the emergence of old conflicts among ethnic, tribal, and religious groups. Paz sees the insurgency in Iraq as presenting a golden opportunity for terrorists to consolidate and reinforce the insurgency and reinvigorate militant Islam worldwide by promoting a new ideology that combines the following elements: anti-Americanism and anti-Westernism; animosity toward Arab regimes deemed to have forsaken Islam (i.e., Iraq, Jordan, and Saudi Arabia); a "return home" and staging point for a larger offensive for holy Muslim fighters from places such as Afghanistan, Bosnia, Kosovo, and central Asia; and promoting the idea of the "ummah," not only as a global community of faithful Muslims, but as a political and strategic unit to generate solidarity and uniformity among Muslims. Paz views this new ideology as producing support and sympathy for the Iraqi insurgency and having a significant impact on the activities and mind-set of terrorists and the political culture of the global jihad.

Paz (2005) also explains the writings of the late Sheikh Yousef al-Ayiri, who, according to Paz, should be regarded as the leading architect of the jihad in Iraq and in other countries. Sheikh Yousef al-Ayiri saw the most dangerous enemy of Islam as the heretical and corrupting ideology of democracy because God Almighty has stated that there is no governing but by God. Sheikh Yousef al-Ayiri wrote that the ideology of democracy is rising in the Muslim world because many Muslims have forsaken the obligation of jihad. He argued for total and violent holy war against the forces of democracy.

CRITICAL THINKING:

What are your views of the "Bush doctrine" and political democratization through military occupation?

U.S. DEPARTMENT OF STATE (2004). SUMMARY OF THE U.S. MILITARY COUNTERTERRORISM CAMPAIGN IN 2003

Operation Iraqi Freedom

On March 19, 2003, the United States and coalition forces launched Operation Iraqi Freedom (OIF). Along with freeing the Iraqi people of a vicious dictator, OIF also shut down the Salman Pak training camp, where members of al-Qaida had trained, and disrupted the Abu Musab al-Zarqawi network, which had established a poison and explosives training camp in northeastern Iraq. OIF removed the prospective threat to the international community posed by the combination of an aggressive Iraqi regime, weapons of mass destruction capabilities, and terrorists. Iraq is now the central front for the global war on terrorism.

Since the end of major combat operations, coalition forces from 33 nations have been engaged in stability operations in Iraq, primarily against regime loyalists, remnants of Ansar al-Islam, and a number of foreign terrorists. This resistance has been responsible for such acts as the bombing of the United Nations headquarters in Baghdad on August 19, the attack of November 12 on the Italian military police

U.S. DEPARTMENT OF STATE (2004). SUMMARY OF THE U.S. MILITARY COUNTERTERRORISM CAMPAIGN IN 2003 – Cont'd

at Nasiriyah, and the coordinated attack on Bulgarian and Thai troops at Karbala on December 27. Former regime loyalists and foreign terrorists have proved adept at adjusting their tactics to maintain attacks on coalition forces, particularly with the use of vehicle-borne, improvised explosive devices. Coalition forces continued offensive action against these forces and, on December 13, captured the former Iraqi dictator Saddam Hussein in Operation Red Dawn. By the end of 2003, coalition forces had killed, captured, or taken into custody 42 of the 55 most-wanted members of the former regime of Saddam Hussein.

Coalition forces in Iraq also are training and equipping the new components of Iraq's security services, which include police, the Iraqi Civil Defense Corps, border police, the Iraqi Facility Protection Service, and a new Iraqi army. The coalition's goal is to build the Iraqi security services to approximately 225,000 members. With the transfer of governing authority from the Coalition Provisional Authority to the Iraqi Transitional National Assembly in 2004, Iraqi security services will play an increasing role in creating a stable and united Iraq, as well as preventing foreign terrorists from establishing operations in Iraq.

Operation Enduring Freedom

U.S. military forces continued to operate in the mountains of southern Afghanistan against al-Qaida terrorists, anticoalition militias, and Taliban insurgents throughout 2003. Antigovernment activity targeting Afghan security forces, civic leaders, and international aid workers continues to destabilize the southern regions of the country. These attacks resulted in the United Nations suspending operations in the southern provinces of Helmand, Oruzgan, Khandahar, and Zabol in 2003. The frequency of attacks rose steadily throughout the year, reaching peaks in September and early November and tapering off with the onset of winter.

Nevertheless, Afghanistan continued to make slow but steady progress back from 25 years of civil war and Taliban misrule. President Hamid Karzai worked throughout the year to replace unresponsive provincial governors and security chiefs and to centralize the collection of customs revenues and taxes. Aid continued to flow into Afghanistan from around the world in 2003, funding the completion of hundreds of clinics and schools and hundreds of kilometers of irrigation projects. The United States probably provided more than $2 billion in aid in fiscal year 2004, the largest single pledge by any government.

NATO formally assumed command of the International Security Assistance Force in August 2003, and the number of provincial reconstruction teams (PRTs) planned or fielded rose to 13, including new teams to begin work in early 2004. A large German PRT took over operations in Konduz, and Great Britain and New Zealand led PRTs in Mazar-i-Sharif and Bamian, respectively. PRTs are effective catalysts for reconstruction activity and regional security. Afghan police training is picking up speed, but efforts to build a new Afghan National Army have been hampered by problems with recruiting and retention. Approximately 5600 men were ready for duty in the Afghan National Army at the end of 2003, including a battalion of T-62 tanks.

Afghanistan remains a security challenge. Relying on the Pashtun-dominated and largely autonomous Federally Administered Tribal Area in Pakistan as a refuge, the Taliban regrouped in 2003 and conducted a classic insurgency in the remote rural areas of the southern Pashtun tribes using clan and family ties, propaganda, violence, and intimidation to maintain a foothold in several districts of Zabol and Oruzgan Provinces. Militant Islamic political parties openly supportive of the Taliban won landslide victories in legislative elections in 2003 in Pakistan's Baluchistan and Northwest Frontier provinces bordering Afghanistan, signaling a protracted counterinsurgency to eliminate the Taliban and other antigovernment elements.

CRITICAL THINKING:

Compare the U.S. State Department's account of the conflicts in Iraq and Afghanistan with the situation today. What are your viewpoints and suggestions?

UNITED STATES GOVERNMENT POLICY

Consider the following directions for U.S. government policy. Do you favor other directions not listed here? What is your opinion?

- Protect the homeland.
- Aggressively attack terrorists with a coalition of allies.
- Work more closely with the United Nations to establish larger multinational security forces for peacekeeping and security.
- Increase efforts to work with the United Nations to pursue peaceful solutions to global conflict, such as the crisis in the Mideast.
- Ameliorate events and circumstances that result in a cycle of hate and violence.
- Seek improved solutions for these issues: civil liberties, human rights, adverse effects of globalization, inequality, and WMD (Sidel and Levy, 2003).
- Search for allies in the moderate sectors and movements of the Muslim world to counter radical Islamic extremism.
- According to Stern (2001: 355–357), the United States should listen more. "We have a stake in the welfare of other peoples and need to devote a much higher priority to health, education, and economic development, or new Osamas will continue to arise."
- Do not forget the domestic front: invest more in the areas of health care, education, and jobs.

GOVERNMENT OPTIONS IN RESPONSE TO TERRORISM

Although the **continuum of government options in response to terrorism** (Figure 3-6), provides a view of the range of government actions, it is a generalization with exceptions. Furthermore, there is no exact science of predictability of success of specific government responses to terrorism. Government responses are complex and dependent on numerous variables, such as the nature of the tension and conflict, the methods and weapons used by terrorists, the power and resources of the government, and the level of popular support for the government and the terrorists. The following list offers an elaboration of the continuum.

- A soft-line response meets terrorist demands by addressing grievances, making reforms, releasing prisoners, or paying ransoms.
- Diplomacy can seek compromise through negotiation with terrorists. A peace process may produce results. However, diplomacy can also seek cooperation among allies to wage war against terrorists, as the United States has done with intensity since 9/11.

Figure 3-6 ■ Continuum of government options in response to terrorism.

SOFT-LINE RESPONSE					HARD-LINE RESPONSE
Releasing Prisoners Paying Ransoms Reforms	Diplomacy Negotiation Compromise Peace Process	Economic Sanctions Financial Strategies Assistance from Allies	Homeland Security Legalistic Response International Law National Laws to Increase Police Powers Imprisonment of Terrorists	Special Operations Covert Action Cyberwar	Military Force Preemptive Strikes Regime Change Imprisonment of Enemy Combatants

- Economic sanctions include trade restrictions on a regime to pressure it to end support of terrorism. This means that important items to support a nation's infrastructure, and also consumer items, are barred from legitimate paths to the targeted country. The United States has applied economic sanctions to several countries, including Cuba, Libya, and North Korea (Figure 3-7). Other countries and the United Nations have also participated in economic sanctions against select countries.
- Financial strategies block and freeze funds supporting terrorists.
- Homeland security and laws to increase police powers.
- Legalistic responses include the use of international law and treaties as an avenue for cooperation among nations. Examples include the extradition of terrorists and the use of international courts to prosecute and imprison terrorists. Criminal laws and law enforcement agencies among nations play a major role in combating terrorism.
- Special operations forces are highly trained, well-equipped, elite military and police units that are employed for counterterrorism and specialized missions. The United States has the Delta Force, Sea Air Land Forces (SEALs), and Green Berets, among other elite forces. England has the Special Air Service (SAS).
- Covert actions include kidnappings, torture, assassinations, and other secretive methods to eliminate terrorist groups.
- Paramilitary actions refer to irregular armed units supported and equipped by a government and based in local areas. Death squads, acting outside of the formal legal system with covert government support, may be a part of these units to covertly kidnap and kill enemies of the state.
- Preemptive military strikes are proactive and aim to destroy terrorist capabilities prior to attacks.
- Punitive military strikes are reprisals against terrorists. The killing of civilians and collateral damage are problems with military attacks. Israel, the United States, and other countries have applied these options.
- Conventional military attacks are used to defeat state sponsors of terrorism and terrorist bases and safe houses. This may result in long-term imprisonment of enemy combatants. An example is the U.S.-led coalition campaign against the Taliban in Afghanistan following the 9/11 attacks.

Figure 3-7 ■ Seoul, the capital of South Korea, is less than 30 miles from North Korea, labeled by President George W. Bush as part of the "axis of evil."

Figure 3-8 ■ Continuum of terrorist options in response to government action or inaction.

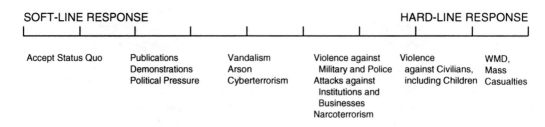

| SOFT-LINE RESPONSE | | | | | | | | HARD-LINE RESPONSE |

| Accept Status Quo | Publications
Demonstrations
Political Pressure | Vandalism
Arson
Cyberterrorism | Violence against
Military and Police
Attacks against
Institutions and
Businesses
Narcoterrorism | Violence
against Civilians,
including Children | WMD,
Mass
Casualties |

TERRORIST OPTIONS IN RESPONSE TO GOVERNMENT ACTION OR INACTION

We saw in Chapters 1 and 2 the history, characteristics, mind-set, methods, and weapons of terrorists. Figure 3-8 provides a **continuum of terrorist options in response to government action or inaction**. This continuum is a generalization with exceptions. The success of specific terrorist options depends on many variables. As with government options in response to terrorism, the success of terrorist options is difficult to predict. For example, General Pervez Musharraf, President of Pakistan, was initially hesitant to aggressively pursue Islamic militants because of their ties to the ethnic Pashtun population that straddles the Afghan border. However, once the militants twice tried to kill Musharraf by blowing up his convoy in late 2003, he ordered an aggressive series of raids and military operations.

THE 9/11 COMMISSION REPORT

The 9/11 Commission Report was prepared by the National Commission on Terrorist Attacks Upon the United States (2004). This commission was an independent, bipartisan group created by congressional legislation and President George W. Bush in late 2002 to prepare an account of the 9/11 attacks, the U.S. response, and recommendations to guard against future attacks. This document of over 400 pages is summarized next from the *Executive Summary*.

FINDINGS

- U.S. air defense on 9-11-01 depended on close interaction between the Federal Aviation Administration (FAA) and the North American Aerospace Defense Command (NORAD). At the time of the attacks, protocols were unsuited for hijacked planes being used as WMD. NORAD planning focused on hijacked planes coming from overseas. Senior military and FAA leaders had no effective communication with each other. Even the president could not reach some senior officials.
- None of the measures adopted by the U.S. government from 1998 to 2001 disturbed or even delayed the progress of the al-Qaida 9/11 plot. The terrorists located and exploited a broad array of weaknesses in security. They studied publicly available materials on aviation security and used weapons with less metal content than a handgun. Airline personnel were trained to be nonconfrontational in the event of a hijacking.
- Operational failures included not sharing information linking individuals in the U.S.S. Cole attack to the 9/11 terrorists, not discovering fraud on visa applications and passports, and not expanding no fly lists to include names from terrorist watch lists.
- "The most important failure was one of imagination." Leaders did not understand the gravity of the threat from al-Qaida.

- Terrorism was not the overriding national security concern under the Clinton or pre-9/11 Bush administrations. The attention Congress gave terrorism was "episodic and splintered across several committees."
- The FBI was not able to link intelligence from agents in the field to national priorities.
- The U.S. government failed at pooling and efficiently using intelligence from the CIA, FBI, state department, and military.
- U.S. diplomatic efforts were unsuccessful at persuading the Taliban regime in Afghanistan to stop offering sanctuary to al-Qaida and to expel bin Ladin to a country where he could face justice.
- "Protecting borders was not a national security issue before 9/11."
- U.S. authorities have yet to determine the origin of the money used for the 9/11 attacks.
- Following the attacks, first responders performed well and saved many lives. In New York, decision making was hampered by problems in command and control. Radios were unable to assist multiple commands in responding in a unified fashion.

RECOMMENDATIONS

Because of action by our government, we are safer today than on September 11, 2001. "But we are not safe." Therefore, we make the following recommendations.

- "The enemy is not just 'terrorism.' It is the threat posed specifically by Islamist terrorism, bin Ladin, and others who draw on a long tradition of extreme intolerance within a minority strain of Islam that does not distinguish politics from religion, and distorts both. The enemy is not Islam, the great world faith, but a perversion of Islam."
- Post-9/11 efforts rightly included military action to topple the Taliban and pursue al-Qaida. A broad array of methods must be continued for success: diplomacy, intelligence, covert action, law enforcement, economic policy, foreign aid, and homeland defense.
- A strategy of three dimensions is proposed: attack terrorists and their organizations; prevent the continued growth of Islamist terrorism through coalition efforts, a vision for a better future, and support for public education and economic openness; and protect against and prepare for terrorist attacks by applying biometric identifiers, improving transportation security, sharing information, improving federal funding to high-risk cities, enhancing first responder capabilities and communications, and cooperating with the private sector that controls 85% of the nation's infrastructure.
- Establish a National Counterterrorism Center (NCTC) to build unity of effort across the U.S. government, including the CIA, FBI, DOD, and Homeland Security. The NCTC would not make policy, that would be the work of the president and the National Security Council.
- Appoint a national intelligence director (NID) to oversee the NCTC. The NID should report to the president, yet be confirmed by the Senate. The system of "need to know" should be replaced by a system of "need to share."

The 9/11 Commission officially ended in August of 2004 after issuing its recommendations. However, it continued operating with private funds as the 9/11 Public Discourse Project to monitor federal government progress on the recommendations. In December 2005, the commission met for the last time to provide a "report card" on government action. The commission gave the government several "Fs" and "Ds" and one "A." It characterized the failures as "shocking" and "scandalous" because of a lack of urgency by the government. The government received an "F" on such issues as allocating funds to cities based on risk, improving radio communications for first responders, and prescreening airline passengers. The only "A" was for controlling terrorist financing.

There is no universal agreement on the commission's recommendations and many diverse viewpoints exist on the best strategies to control terrorism. Harris and Wodele (2006) studied several commission recommendations to examine roadblocks to implementation. They view the causes of the poor grades on the part of the federal government as falling within six categories and provide examples from *The 9/11 Commission Report*.

- *Congress is resistant to institutional change.* Example: Congressional changes are needed to improve legislative oversight of the executive branch's intelligence community. Example: The funding formula for homeland security needs refining so high-risk areas receive more assistance and pork-barrel spending can be reduced.
- *The bureaucracy resists new ideas.* Example: Information sharing among agencies requires presidential backing, policies that compel sharing, and related performance evaluations. Example: Effective prescreening of airline passengers requires control over turf battles and improved integration of the various terrorist watch lists.
- *Lack of funding.* Example: The screening of all airline passenger luggage occurs, but the screening of all airline cargo will cost tens of billions of dollars. Example: Congress has not provided enough funds for the development of new technologies to improve passenger, luggage, and cargo screening.
- *Lack of leadership.* Example: More needs to be done for protection against WMD. Example: Privacy and civil liberties require strengthening.
- *Special interests influence Congress and the White House.* Example: The TV broadcasting industry is blocking access to a portion of public airwaves for first responders to help them communicate more efficiently. Example: Although Saudi Arabia is a major source of oil for the United States, and an ally, the United States has not pressured the Saudi government enough to act against terrorists and their funding sources.
- *Inability to accurately gauge how the United States is perceived abroad.* Example: The U.S. treatment of terrorist detainees has resulted in global criticism; standards of cooperation with allies are needed. Example: The war against terrorism has harmed U.S. academic exchange with other countries.

CRITICAL THINKING:

What are your opinions of the 9/11 commission findings, recommendations, and "report card" of federal government action?

IS TERRORISM EFFECTIVE?

Prior to answering whether terrorism is effective, a prerequisite question is: What criteria can be applied to gauge the effectiveness of terrorism? Terrorists and others can argue that terrorism is effective when:

- Media attention focuses on a particular cause.
- People change their behavior and habits because of fear.
- Government overreacts through repressive measures that reflect negatively on the government.
- Support grows for a terrorist cause.
- Political and economic changes occur.
- Terrorist demands are met.
- Terrorists take control of a government and become legitimate leaders.

By applying the aforementioned criteria, which is also a **terrorism continuum of minor effect to major effect**, we can see that certain terrorist incidents have been, at a minimum, partially successful. Many terrorist events have received media attention. Following the 9/11 attacks, many people refrained from air travel, resulting in a downturn in the travel industry. Terrorism creates pressure on government to

IS TERRORISM EFFECTIVE?—Cont'd

take action. This may entail increased police powers and a reduction in civil liberties. A citizenry may abhor such action, while terrorists view it as proof of a repressive government and an opportunity to generate converts. Terrorist acts may increase the polarization between those who support a particular terrorist cause and those who are against the cause. This has been seen with the violence between Palestinians and Israelis. Governments are unlikely to openly meet terrorist demands; it would show a government being weak and it could lead to more terrorism. However, a government under pressure may work "behind the scenes" to rectify injustice. Another possibility is that the ideology and goals of a terrorist group may be so contrary to a government that both sides continue a lengthy cycle of violence. If we include terrorism in guerilla and revolutionary warfare, then we could say that terrorists have taken control of governments repeatedly through history and became legitimate leaders.

Singer (2004: 141) cites Secretary of Defense Donald Rumsfeld who wrote:

> Today we lack metrics to know if we are winning or losing the global war on terror. Are we capturing, killing, or deterring and dissuading more terrorists every day than the madrassas and the radical clerics are recruiting, training, and deploying against us?
> Does the US need to fashion a broad, integrated plan to stop the next generation of terrorists? The US is putting relatively little effort into a long-range plan, but we are putting a great deal of effort into trying to stop terrorists. The cost-benefit ratio is against us! Our cost is billions against the terrorists' costs of millions...Is our current situation such that "the harder we work, the behinder we get"?

CRITICAL THINKING:

Do you think terrorism is effective? If you answered "yes," what can be done to limit its effectiveness? If you answered "no," why do terrorist groups continue their attacks?

CONSIDER A CAREER AS AN FBI INTELLIGENCE ANALYST

Here's What It's Like: Up Close and Personal FBI (2004)

Catherine G. joined the FBI on a critical skills scholarship when she was just starting college. She worked at HQ during summer vacation, then reported for full time duty in 2001 after graduation. Catherine started in the foreign counterintelligence field on espionage matters. After the 9/11 attacks, she transferred to counterterrorism. Recently she has been working in the FBI's Indianapolis office with its Joint Terrorism Task Force (JTTF).

Q: Catherine, what's a typical working day like for you?

A: It's always interesting, that's for sure. Generally, I spend my time analyzing new intelligence from FBI and other sources, assessing its reliability, seeing how it fits into the bigger picture of what's going on in the world. As a strategic analyst for HQ, I'm responsible for a particular area in the terrorism arena, and I monitor it all day, every day, to identify trends in activity, methods, etc., as well as to look for things that DON'T fit the trend, to try to put these in context and identify what they mean. My assessments and recommendations go to national policymakers and also to agents in the field. Working with the JTTF in Indianapolis is more tactical in nature. I may help an agent put his or her case into a national or international context—supplying intelligence information or expertise on an issue or group, making connections between individuals or particular groups, or going on a source interview. I also

Continued

CONSIDER A CAREER AS AN FBI INTELLIGENCE ANALYST—Cont'd

make suggestions for case strategies and identify the knowns and unknowns in a given case so that investigations can be targeted and streamlined more effectively. It's fascinating. I wake up in the morning and can't wait to get to work.

Q: Have you ever traveled overseas or in the United States on a case?

A: I sure have. After 9/11, I worked on an interagency task force that, among other things, focused on how to make the visa issuance process in U.S. embassies and consulates more secure. I took a month-long trip to London, Abu Dhabi, Dubai, Riyadh, Jeddah, and Jakarta to study the process, talk to the people on the front lines, and come up with solutions that would enhance security without complicating the process. I learned a lot, and I got to see my recommendations implemented as the programs developed.

Q: What do you like best about the job?

A: For me, it's knowing that what I'm doing is really making a difference in national security. It's neat to work with top secret information and it's fun to know things that most people don't, but at the end of the day the best thing about working here is the fact that in some small way everything I do helps to protect America.

Q: Any advice to prospective FBI recruits?

A: Yes—jump in with both feet, be enthusiastic, and don't be afraid to ask questions! You'll be surprised at how quickly others will start coming to YOU for answers!

Link: Interested in applying? Go straight to www.fbijobs.com

DISCUSSION QUESTIONS

1. How serious is the terrorist threat facing the United States today?
2. How long do you think the United States will maintain its sole superpower status and what could cause this power to decline?
3. Do you think the U.S. government did enough in its initial response to the 9/11 attacks? Explain.
4. How can the National Strategy for Combating Terrorism be improved?
5. Of the five "tools" against terrorism applied by the U.S. Department of State, which one do you think is the most effective and which one do you think is the least effective? Justify your answers.
6. What are your views of the USA Patriot Act of 2001 and the USA Patriot Improvement and Reauthorization Act of 2005?
7. What are your views of the Homeland Security Act of 2002?
8. What impact do the United Nations, international law, and international courts have on terrorism?
9. What are your views of war?
10. What are the advantages and disadvantages of preemptive force?
11. Is the United States winning the global war on terrorism? Have U.S. government policies decreased or increased terrorist threats against American interests? Explain.
12. Of the options available to governments and terrorists, which do you view as most successful and least successful for each group and why?
13. What do you think are the two most significant recommendations of *The 9/11 Commission Report*?

APPLICATIONS

3A   YOU BE THE PRESIDENT OF THE UNITED STATES
You are the newly elected president of the United States. You won the election on a platform aimed at dealing more effectively with foreign affairs, war, terrorism, and domestic issues. Advisors on your staff and the Cabinet will be providing you with guidance and information for important decisions. The plan is to spend $200 billion, with the cooperation of Congress, to improve foreign and domestic problems. As president, how do you apportion the money among the following challenges? Explain to Congressional leaders your reasoning for your three highest allocations.

Amounts	Challenges
_____	In about 5 years, two additional nations will possess nuclear capabilities. One of the nations covertly supports terrorism. A plan and action must curb proliferation.
_____	During the last 5 years, global terrorism has been increasing against U.S. citizens and interests. Homeland security and counterterrorism must become more effective.
_____	Recently, a major plot of terrorists planning to use WMD was uncovered and stopped.
_____	Government officials predict that eventually such a plot will succeed. The Middle East remains a violent region and solutions must be found.
_____	A specific nation has been positively identified as supporting terrorists by offering them a safe haven, training facilities, and conventional weapons and explosives. Action must be taken immediately.
_____	Incentives are needed to recruit allies in the war against terrorism.
_____	Domestic problems of health care, education, training, jobs, poverty, and crime must be improved.
_____	Global problems of hunger, disease, and economic development must be improved.
_____	The United Nations is seeking additional funds to reduce hunger, disease, unemployment, violence, war, and human rights violations and to improve economic development and education.
_____	Incentives are needed to attract businesses and researchers to develop alternative fuels.

3B   YOU BE THE PRESIDENT OF THE UNITED STATES
As president of the United States, the FBI informs you that it has top secret, reliable intelligence that two suicide bombers are planning to detonate explosives simultaneously in New York City on two commuter buses. This intelligence is from a valuable undercover agent who has penetrated an al-Qaida cell in New York City. For years the U.S. intelligence community has been striving to penetrate al-Qaida cells.

The intelligence also states that cells in Chicago and Los Angeles are planning to detonate radiological dispersion devices (RDDs), or "dirty bombs," in these cities about 1 month following the bus attacks. An unknown supplier, possibly an intelligence service of a foreign nation, is due to deliver the RDDs to the cells about the time of the bus attacks. Authorities are very interested in collecting evidence and apprehending not only the cell members in all three cities, but also the network supplying the RDDs. If a foreign nation were involved, evidence would be vital for national security purposes.

As president, decide whether the FBI should arrest all cell members now or, at the expense of deaths and injuries on the two buses, when the RDDs are delivered. Explain your reasoning.

3C   YOU BE THE PRESIDENT OF THE UNITED STATES
As president of the United States, the CIA has informed you and the Cabinet that it has multiple sources of intelligence (e.g., human, satellite) showing that North Korea is training and supplying Middle East terrorists

to attack multiple U.S. targets worldwide with chemical and radiological WMD. Two training bases have been pinpointed in North Korea and your military advisors are recommending a preemptive strike. Do you follow their recommendations? What are your decisions, plans, and justifications?

3D   YOU BE THE MIDDLE EAST YOUTH

Ever since you were very young you have seen your family struggle to survive in a country dominated by a majority group of a different religion and ethnic background than your own. You have vivid memories of being 8 years old when government soldiers took your father away from home to never return. The soldiers wrecked the inside of your home, slapped your mother and sisters, and kicked you in the behind. Since then, your family has lived in squalor with barely enough to eat.

Each day your friends urge you to join their group that steals from members of the majority group. Some of your friends had brothers and fathers who were killed or disappeared because of conflicts with the majority group. You have a cousin who joined a group opposed to the government and you have not seen him in years. Every day you see older, unemployed men huddled around old televisions watching one violent news report after another. The whole world seems to be at war and you wonder if you should be fighting for your religious and ethnic group. Your aunt tells you to study hard and stay in school so you can get into college and secure a good job, but your uncle tells you "very few of our kind make it to college and get a decent job." If you were this teen, what direction would you pursue in your life and why?

WEB SITES

Center for Defense Information: www.cdi.org
CIA World Factbook: www.odci.gov/cia/publications/factbook
Islamic Resistance Movement-HAMAS: www.hamasonline.com
MIPT Terrorism Knowledge Base: www.tkb.org
National Commission on Terrorist Attacks Upon the United States: www.9-11commission.gov
National Counterterrorism Center: www.nctc.gov
Office of the President: www.whitehouse.gov
Stockholm International Peace Research Institute: web.sipri.org
United Nations: www.un.org
U.N. International Court of Justice: www.icj-cij.org
U.S. Department of Defense: www.defenselink.mil
U.S. Department of State: www.state.gov

NOTES

Bassford, C. (1994). *Clausewitz in English: The Reception of Clausewitz in Britian and America, 1815–1945.* Oxford, UK: Oxford University Press.

Brooks, S., and Wohlforth, W. (2002). "American Primacy in Perspective." *Foreign Affairs* (July/August).

Bullock, J., et al. (2005). *Introduction to Homeland Security.* Boston, MA: Elsevier.

Callahan, D. (1994). *Between Two Worlds: Realism, Idealism, and American Foreign Policy After the Cold War.* New York: HarperCollins.

Falk, R. (2002). "World Order After September 11: An Unmapped Minefield." *Turkish Daily News* (January 5).

FBI (2004). "Headline Archives, Consider a Career as an FBI Intelligence Analyst?" October 8. www.fbi.gov, retrieved November 4, 2004.

Fingar, T. (2005). "Security Threats to the United States." Statement before the Senate Select Committee on Intelligence (February 16).

Garamone, J. (2003). "Transformation Part of War on Terror, Meyer says." American Forces Press Service (December 3).

Giles, L. (1910). *Sun Tzu on the Art of War: The Oldest Military Treatise in the World.* Digireads.com (2005).

Gueli, R. (2003). "Bin Laden and Al-Qaida: Challenging the Assumptions of Transnational Terrorism." *Strategic Review for Southern Africa*, 25 (November).

Harris, S., and Wodele, G. (2006). "Bureaucracy hinders 9/11 commission recommendations." GOVEXEC.com. www.govexec.com/dailyfed/0106/011306njl.htm, retrieved, January 19, 2006.

Ingrao, C. (1989). "Clausewitz, Karl von" *World Book*, Vol. 4. Chicago: World Book, Inc.

Janda, K., Berry, J., and Goldman, J. (1995). *The Challenge of Democracy: Government in America*, 4th ed. Boston, MA: Houghton Mifflin.

Krueger, A., and Laitin, D. (2004). "Misunderestimating Terrorism." *Foreign Affairs* (September/October).

Lowenthal, M. (2003). *Intelligence: From Secrets to Policy*, 2nd ed. Washington, DC: CQ Press.

Mayer, J. (2003). *9-11: The Giant Awakens*. Belmont, CA: Wadsworth/Thomson Learning.

Miles, D. (2004). "Sweeping Changes Ahead in Military Doctrine to Meet Current Threat." American Forces Press Service (June 4).

National Commission on Terrorist Attacks Upon the United States (2004). *The 9/11 Commission Report.* www.9-11commission.gov/, retrieved July 26, 2004.

National Memorial Institute for the Prevention of Terrorism (2006). "MIPT Terrorism Knowledge Base." www.tkb.org, retrieved March 18, 2006.

Nye, J. (2002). "The New Rome Meets the New Barbarians." *The Economist* (March).

Office of Homeland Security (2002). *National Strategy for Homeland Security* (July). www.whitehouse.gov, retrieved September 14, 2004.

Paz, R. (2005). "The Impact of the War in Iraq on the Global Jihad." In H. Fradkin, *et al.* (Eds.), *Current Trends in Islamist Ideology*. Washington, DC: Hudson Institute.

Perl, R. (2006). "Terrorism and National Security: Issues and Trends." *CRS Issue Brief for Congress* (February 21). www.hsdl.org/homesec/docs/crs/nps21-022806-05.pdf, retrieved March 13, 2006.

Rourke, J. (2005). *International Politics on the World Stage*, 10th ed. New York: McGraw-Hill.

Shultz, R., and Vogt, A. (2003). "It's War! Fighting Post-11 September Global Terrorism through a Doctrine of Preemption." *Terrorism and Political Violence*, 15 (Spring).

Sidel, V., and Levy, B. (2003). "War, Terrorism, and Public Health." *Journal of Law, Medicine & Ethics*, 31 (Winter).

Singer, P. (2004). "The War on Terrorism: The Big Picture." *Parameters* (Summer).

Stepanova, E. (2003). *Anti-terrorism and Peace-building During and After Conflict*. Stockholm International Peace Research Institute (June).

Stern, J. (2001). "Preparing for a War on Terrorism." *Current History* (November).

U.S. Department of Defense (1998). *Joint Tactics, Techniques, and Procedures for Antiterrorism*. Joint Chiefs of Staff: Washington, DC.

U.S. Department of Defense (2003). *Dictionary of Military and Associated Terms*. Joint Chiefs of Staff: Washington, DC.

U.S. Department of State (2003). *US Participation in the United Nations: US Financial Contributions*. www.state.gov, retrieved September 22, 2003.

U.S. Department of State (2004). *Patterns of Global Terrorism 2003*. www.state.gov, retrieved April 30, 2004.

U.S. Department of State (2005). *Country Reports on Terrorism 2004*. www.hsdl.org, retrieved March 13, 2006.

U.S. Department of State, Office of Inspector General (2005). "Review of the Department of State's *Country Reports on Terrorism-2005*." http://oig.state.gov/documents/organization/58021.pdf, retrieved March 15, 2006.

U.S. Government, White House (2002). *The National Security Strategy of the United States of America*. www.whitehouse.gov/, retrieved September 27, 2004.

U.S. Government, White House (2003). *National Strategy for Combatting Terrorism*. www.whitehouse.gov/, retrieved March 5, 2004.

U.S. Government, White House (2006a). *National Strategy for Combating Terrorism*. www.whitehouse.gov/ncs/nsct/2006/nsct2006.pdf, retrieved September 5, 2006.

U.S. Government, White House (2006b). "Fact Sheet: Safeguarding America: President Bush Signs Patriot Act Reauthorization." www.whitehouse.gov/, retrieved March 11, 2006.

HOMELAND SECURITY

OBJECTIVES

The study of this chapter will enable you to:

1. Understand the difficulty of defining homeland security.
2. Trace the development of the Department of Homeland Security.
3. Explain the organizational structure of the Department of Homeland Security and the reorganization in 2005.
4. Recognize the multiple organizations that play a role in homeland security.
5. Understand the importance of state and local government homeland security missions.
6. Outline the National Strategy for Homeland Security.
7. Define and explain intelligence and intelligence community.
8. Describe how to counter terrorist financing.
9. Discuss multiple perspectives on homeland security.
10. Examine accountability and evaluation of national strategies against terrorism.

KEY TERMS

homeland security
Posse Comitatus Act
federalism
tenth amendment
first responders
National Strategy for Homeland Security
National Security Strategy of the United States
National Military Strategy for Combating
   Weapons of Mass Destruction
U.S. Northern Command
threat-vulnerability integration

"red team" techniques
stovepiping
connecting the dots
intelligence
intelligence community
The Intelligence Reform and Terrorism
   Prevention Act of 2004
Homeland Security Advisory System
data mining
Government Accountability Office

THE HIJACKING OF UNITED AIRLINES FLIGHT 175 ON SEPTEMBER 11, 2001

United Airlines Flight 175 was scheduled to depart for Los Angeles at 8:00. Captain Victor Saracini and First Officer Michael Horrocks piloted the Boeing 767, which had seven flight attendants. Fifty-six passengers boarded the flight. United 175 pushed back from its gate at 7:58 and departed Logan Airport at 8:14. By 8:33, it had reached its assigned cruising altitude of 31,000 feet. The flight attendants would have begun their cabin service.

The flight had taken off just as American 11 was being hijacked, and at 8:42 the United 175 flight crew completed their report on a "suspicious transmission" overheard from another plane (which turned out to have been Flight 11) just after takeoff. This was United 175's last communication with the ground. The hijackers attacked sometime between 8:42 and 8:46. They used knives (as reported by two passengers and a flight attendant), Mace (reported by one passenger), and the threat of a bomb (reported by the same passenger). They stabbed members of the flight crew (reported by a flight attendant and one passenger). Both pilots had been killed (reported by one flight attendant). The eyewitness accounts came from calls made from the rear of the plane, from passengers originally seated further forward in the cabin, a sign that passengers and perhaps crew had been moved to the back of the aircraft. Given similarities to American 11 in hijacker seating and in eyewitness reports of tactics and weapons, as well as the contact between the presumed team leaders, Atta and Shehhi, we believe the tactics were similar on both flights.

The first operational evidence that something was abnormal on United 175 came at 8:47 when the aircraft changed beacon codes twice within a minute. At 8:51, the flight deviated from its assigned altitude, and a minute later New York air traffic controllers began repeatedly and unsuccessfully trying to contact it.

At 8:52, in Easton, Connecticut, a man named Lee Hanson received a phone call from his son Peter, a passenger on United 175. His son told him: "I think they've taken over the cockpit—An attendant has been stabbed—and someone else up front may have been killed. The plane is making strange moves. Call United Airlines—Tell them it's Flight 175, Boston to LA." Lee Hanson then called the Easton Police Department and relayed what he had heard.

Also at 8:52, a male flight attendant called a United office in San Francisco, reaching Marc Policastro. The flight attendant reported that the flight had been hijacked, both pilots had been killed, a flight attendant had been stabbed, and the hijackers were probably flying the plane. The call lasted about 2 minutes, after which Policastro and a colleague tried unsuccessfully to contact the flight.

At 8:58, the flight took a heading toward New York City. At 8:59, Flight 175 passenger Brian David Sweeney tried to call his wife, Julie. He left a message on their home answering machine that the plane had been hijacked. He then called his mother, Louise Sweeney, told her the flight had been hijacked and added that the passengers were thinking about storming the cockpit to take control of the plane away from the hijackers.

At 9:00, Lee Hanson received a second call from his son Peter: It's getting bad, Dad—A stewardess was stabbed—They seem to have knives and Mace—They said they have a bomb—It's getting very bad on the plane—Passengers are throwing up and getting sick—The plane is making jerky movements—I don't think the pilot is flying the plane—I think we are going down—I think they intend to go to Chicago or someplace and fly into a building—Don't worry, Dad—If it happens, it'll be very fast—My God, my God. The call ended abruptly. Lee Hanson had heard a woman scream just before it cut off. He turned on a television, and in her home so did Louise Sweeney. Both then saw the second aircraft hit the World Trade Center. At 9:03, United Airlines Flight 175 struck the south tower of the World Trade Center. All on board, along with an unknown number of people in the tower, were killed instantly.

THE BATTLE FOR UNITED AIRLINES FLIGHT 93 ON SEPTEMBER 11, 2001

At 8:42, United Airlines Flight 93 took off from Newark (New Jersey) Liberty International Airport bound for San Francisco. The aircraft was piloted by Captain Jason Dahl and First Officer Leroy Homer, and there were five flight attendants. Thirty-seven passengers, including the hijackers, boarded the plane. Scheduled to depart the gate at 8:00, the Boeing 757's takeoff was delayed because of the airport's typically heavy morning traffic.

The hijackers had planned to take flights scheduled to depart at 7:45 (American 11), 8:00 (United 175 and United 93), and 8:10 (American 77). Three of the flights had actually taken off within 10 to 15 minutes of their planned departure times. United 93 would ordinarily have taken off about 15 minutes after pulling away from the gate. When it left the ground at 8:42, the flight was running more than 25 minutes late.

As United 93 left Newark, the flight's crew members were unaware of the hijacking of American 11. Around 9:00, the FAA, American, and United were facing the staggering realization of apparent multiple hijackings. At 9:03, they would see another aircraft strike the World Trade Center. Crisis managers at the FAA and the airlines did not yet act to warn other aircraft. At the same time, Boston Center realized that a message transmitted just before 8:25 by the hijacker pilot of American 11 included the phrase, "We have some planes." No one at the FAA or the airlines that day had ever dealt with multiple hijackings. Such a plot had not been carried out anywhere in the world in more than 30 years, and never in the United States. As news of the hijackings filtered through the FAA and the airlines, it does not seem to have occurred to their leadership that they needed to alert other aircraft in the air that they too might be at risk.

United 175 was hijacked between 8:42 and 8:46, and awareness of that hijacking began to spread after 8:51. American 77 was hijacked between 8:51 and 8:54. By 9:00, FAA and airline officials began to comprehend that attackers were going after multiple aircraft. American Airlines' nationwide ground stop between 9:05 and 9:10 was followed by a United Airlines ground stop. FAA controllers at Boston Center, which had tracked the first two hijackings, requested at 9:07 that Herndon Command Center "get messages to airborne aircraft to increase security for the cockpit." There is no evidence that Herndon took such action. Boston Center immediately began speculating about other aircraft that might be in danger, leading them to worry about a transcontinental flight—Delta 1989—that in fact was not hijacked. At 9:19, the FAA's New England regional office called Herndon and asked that Cleveland Center advise Delta 1989 to use extra cockpit security. United's first decisive action to notify its airborne aircraft to take defensive action did not come until 9:19, when a United flight dispatcher, Ed Ballinger, took the initiative to begin transmitting warnings to his 16 transcontinental flights: "Beware any cockpit intrusion—Two a/c [aircraft] hit World Trade Center." One of the flights that received the warning was United 93. Because Ballinger was still responsible for his other flights as well as Flight 175, his warning message was not transmitted to Flight 93 until 9:23.

By all accounts, the first 46 minutes of Flight 93's cross-country trip proceeded routinely. Radio communications from the plane were normal. Heading, speed, and altitude ran according to plan. At 9:24, Ballinger's warning to United 93 was received in the cockpit. Within 2 minutes, at 9:26, the pilot, Jason Dahl, responded with a note of puzzlement: "Ed, confirm latest mssg plz—Jason."

The hijackers attacked at 9:28. While traveling 35,000 feet above eastern Ohio, United 93 suddenly dropped 700 feet. Eleven seconds into the descent, the FAA's air traffic control center in Cleveland received the first of two radio transmissions from the aircraft. During the first broadcast, the captain or first officer could be heard declaring "Mayday" amid the sounds of a physical struggle in the cockpit. The second radio transmission, 35 seconds later, indicated that the fight was continuing. The captain or first officer could be heard shouting: "Hey get out of here—get out of here—get out of here."

The terrorists who hijacked three other commercial flights on 9/11 operated in five-man teams. They initiated their cockpit takeover within 30 minutes of takeoff. On Flight 93, however, the takeover took place 46 minutes after takeoff and there were only four hijackers. The operative likely intended to round out the team for this flight, Mohamed al Kahtani, had been refused entry by a suspicious immigration inspector at Florida's Orlando International Airport in August.

Continued

THE BATTLE FOR UNITED AIRLINES FLIGHT 93 ON SEPTEMBER 11, 2001—Cont'd

Because several passengers on United 93 described three hijackers on the plane, not four, some have wondered whether one of the hijackers had been able to use the cockpit jump seat from the outset of the flight. FAA rules allow use of this seat by documented and approved individuals, usually air carrier or FAA personnel. We have found no evidence indicating that one of the hijackers, or anyone else, sat there on this flight. All the hijackers had assigned seats in first class, and they seem to have used them. We believe it is more likely that Jarrah, the crucial pilot-trained member of their team, remained seated and inconspicuous until after the cockpit was seized; once inside, he would not have been visible to the passengers.

At 9:32, a hijacker, probably Jarrah, made or attempted to make the following announcement to the passengers of Flight 93: "Ladies and Gentlemen: Here the captain, please sit down keep remaining sitting. We have a bomb on board. So, sit." The flight data recorder (also recovered) indicates that Jarrah then instructed the plane's autopilot to turn the aircraft around and head east. The cockpit voice recorder data indicate that a woman, most likely a flight attendant, was being held captive in the cockpit. She struggled with one of the hijackers who killed or otherwise silenced her.

Shortly thereafter, the passengers and flight crew began a series of calls from GTE airphones and cellular phones. These calls between family, friends, and colleagues took place until the end of the flight and provided those on the ground with firsthand accounts. They enabled the passengers to gain critical information, including the news that two aircraft had slammed into the World Trade Center.

At 9:39, the FAA's Cleveland Air Route Traffic Control Center overheard a second announcement indicating that there was a bomb on board, that the plane was returning to the airport, and that they should remain seated. While it apparently was not heard by the passengers, this announcement, like those on Flight 11 and Flight 77, was intended to deceive them. Jarrah, like Atta earlier, may have inadvertently broadcast the message because he did not know how to operate the radio and the intercom. To our knowledge none of them had ever flown an actual airliner before.

At least 10 passengers and two crew members shared vital information with family, friends, colleagues, or others on the ground. All understood the plane had been hijacked. They said the hijackers wielded knives and claimed to have a bomb. The hijackers were wearing red bandanas, and they forced the passengers to the back of the aircraft. Callers reported that a passenger had been stabbed and that two people were lying on the floor of the cabin, injured or dead, possibly the captain and first officer. One caller reported that a flight attendant had been killed. One of the callers from United 93 also reported that he thought the hijackers might possess a gun, but none of the other callers reported the presence of a firearm. One recipient of a call from the aircraft recounted specifically asking her caller whether the hijackers had guns. The passenger replied that he did not see one. No evidence of firearms or of their identifiable remains was found at the aircraft's crash site, and the cockpit voice recorder gives no indication of a gun being fired or mentioned at any time. We believe that if the hijackers had possessed a gun, they would have used it in the flight's last minutes as the passengers fought back.

Passengers on three flights reported the hijackers' claim of having a bomb. The FBI told us they found no trace of explosives at the crash sites. One of the passengers who mentioned a bomb expressed his belief that it was not real. Lacking any evidence that the hijackers attempted to smuggle such illegal items past the security screening checkpoints, we believe the bombs were probably fake.

During at least five of the passengers' phone calls, information was shared about the attacks that had occurred earlier that morning at the World Trade Center. Five calls described the intent of passengers and surviving crew members to revolt against the hijackers. According to one call, they voted on whether to rush the terrorists in an attempt to retake the plane. They decided, and acted.

At 9:57, the passenger assault began. Several passengers had terminated phone calls with loved ones in order to join the revolt. One of the callers ended her message as follows: "Everyone's running up to first class. I've got to go. Bye."

THE BATTLE FOR UNITED AIRLINES FLIGHT 93 ON SEPTEMBER 11, 2001—Cont'd

The cockpit voice recorder captured the sounds of the passenger assault muffled by the intervening cockpit door. Some family members who listened to the recording report that they can hear the voice of a loved one among the din. We cannot identify whose voices can be heard, but the assault was sustained. In response, Jarrah immediately began to roll the airplane to the left and right, attempting to knock the passengers off balance. At 9:58, Jarrah told another hijacker in the cockpit to block the door. Jarrah continued to roll the airplane sharply left and right, but the assault continued. At 9:59, Jarrah changed tactics and pitched the nose of the airplane up and down to disrupt the assault. The recorder captured the sounds of loud thumps, crashes, shouts, and breaking glasses and plates. At 10:00, Jarrah stabilized the airplane. Five seconds later, Jarrah asked, "Is that it? Shall we finish it off?" A hijacker responded, "No. Not yet. When they all come, we finish it off." The sounds of fighting continued outside the cockpit. Again, Jarrah pitched the nose of the aircraft up and down. At 10:00, a passenger in the background said, "In the cockpit. If we don't we'll die!" Sixteen seconds later, a passenger yelled, "Roll it!" Jarrah stopped the violent maneuvers at about 10:01 and said, "Allah is the greatest! Allah is the greatest!" He then asked another hijacker in the cockpit, "Is that it? I mean, shall we put it down?" to which the other replied, "Yes, put it in it, and pull it down." The passengers continued their assault and at 10:02, a hijacker said, "Pull it down! Pull it down!" The hijackers remained at the controls but must have judged that the passengers were only seconds from overcoming them. The airplane headed down; the control wheel was turned hard to the right. The airplane rolled onto its back, and one of the hijackers began shouting "Allah is the greatest. Allah is the greatest." With the sounds of the passenger counterattack continuing, the aircraft plowed into an empty field in Shanksville, Pennsylvania, at 580 miles per hour, about 20 minutes' flying time from Washington, DC. Jarrah's objective was to crash his airliner into symbols of the American Republic, the Capitol or the White House. He was defeated by the alerted, unarmed passengers of United 93 (National Commission on Terrorist Attacks Upon the United States: 2004b).

HOMELAND SECURITY

Homeland security is an evolving concept. The Department of Homeland Security (DHS) is continuously developing its mission under changing circumstances and events. Numerous variables influence the DHS, such as terrorist incidents, natural disasters, public opinion, and politics. Educators who seek to develop a discipline of homeland security and academic programs are faced with a concept that is difficult to define. Its meaning varies depending on the background of the individual defining it (see Chapter 12).

The Office of Homeland Security (2002) provides the following definition: "**Homeland security** is a concerted national effort to prevent terrorist attacks within the United States, reduce America's vulnerability to terrorism, and minimize the damage and recover from attacks that do occur." How this definition evolves is subject to debate. Will HS become more responsive to "all hazards," such as hurricanes and pandemics? Will it increase its emphasis on emergency management? HS is in its infancy and its evolution remains to be seen.

The previous chapter provided a brief overview of the Homeland Security Act of 2002. This act created the Department of Homeland Security in January of 2003 and it became the nation's 15th and newest Cabinet department. The DHS consolidated 22 agencies, with about 170,000 employees, under one unified organization with the aim of improving defenses against terrorism, coordinating intelligence, and minimizing the damage from attacks and natural disasters.

The DHS was created primarily because of criticism that the 9/11 attacks could have been prevented if federal agencies had an improved system of cooperating with each other and sharing intelligence. Soon after the 9/11 attacks, President George W. Bush issued an executive order creating the Office of Homeland Security, to be directed by former Pennsylvania Governor Tom Ridge. However, Ridge encountered resistance to restructuring from the massive federal bureaucracy. This initial approach for reorganization was criticized by Congress and others who claimed it would be ineffective without Ridge having budgetary authority over the agencies he was seeking to change (Brookings Institution, 2003). Consequently, Congress acted to strengthen the goal the president was seeking. Congress became involved in protracted negotiations over various homeland security bills. A major issue dealt with the rights of employees who would fall under the DHS. Such employees retained federal civil service coverage. Finally, Congress put together a bill that would pass, be effective, and provide Ridge with the power to improve the cooperation and coordination among agencies.

President Bush's attempt to include major intelligence and law enforcement agencies—the FBI, the CIA, and the National Security Agency—into the final bill was not successful. However, the intelligence division of the DHS reviews reports developed from the intelligence community and makes decisions on credibility, whether to issue warnings, and what preventive strategies are most appropriate (Council on Foreign Relations, 2004a).

For fiscal year 2007, the president requested $42.7 billion for HS, an increase of 6% over the previous year. Five themes of this budget are increase preparedness and strengthen the Federal Emergency Management Agency (FEMA); enhance border security; enhance transportation security; improve information sharing; and improve the department's organization to maximize performance (U.S. Department of Homeland Security, 2006).

DEPARTMENT OF HOMELAND SECURITY ORGANIZATION (2003)

In January of 2003, former Pennsylvania Governor Tom Ridge became the first secretary of Homeland Security, a cabinet-level position within the executive branch of government. His first task was to organize the DHS. Figure 4-1 shows the original organization chart. The primary functions were divided among five directorates, each headed by an undersecretary, as explained next (Bullock *et al.*, 2005: 62–71). Following the explanation here of the original organization, modifications in the organization made during 2005 are discussed.

MANAGEMENT DIRECTORATE

This office was established to operate several administrative functions in support of the DHS. These include the budget, appropriations, accounting, procurement, human resources, information technology, property, equipment, facilities, and performance evaluations.

BORDER AND TRANSPORTATION SECURITY DIRECTORATE

This became the largest directorate, coordinating the functions of the following federal agencies: U.S. Customs Service, Immigration and Naturalization Service Enforcement Division, Animal and Plant Health Inspection Service, Transportation Security Administration, Office for Domestic Preparedness, and Federal Protective Service. The major goal includes security of air, land, and sea borders and transportation systems.

Border and transportation security tasks include:

- Secure access points and prevent the entry of terrorists and contraband into the United States.
- Administration and enforcement of rules governing entry into the United States and immigration.
- Enforce the customs laws of the United States.
- Administer the functions of the Animal and Plant Health Inspection Service.

Domestic preparedness tasks include:

- Coordinate federal preparedness activities in conjunction with state, local, and private sector emergency response efforts.
- Improve homeland security communications systems.
- Administer federal grants for protection against terrorism. Conduct training for personnel at all levels of government and international agencies.
- Work closely with the Emergency Preparedness and Response (EPR) directorate in preparation for a variety of disasters.
- Conduct risk management and risk analysis activities.

Figure 4-1 ■ Department of Homeland Security (original organization chart). Source: http://www.dhs.gov/interweb/assetlibrary/DHS_Org_Chart_2005.pdf

Department of Homeland Security

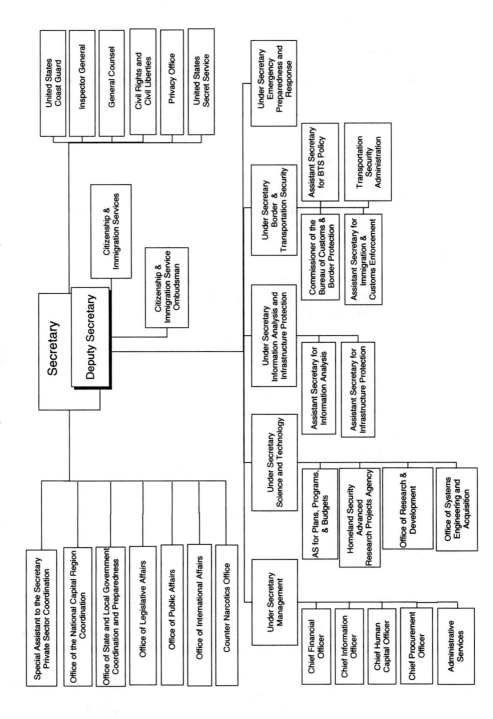

EMERGENCY PREPAREDNESS AND RESPONSE DIRECTORATE

This directorate was designed to include the Federal Emergency Management Agency, with the goals of preparing for and responding to natural and technological disasters and terrorism.

Tasks include the following.

- Manage disasters in coordination with local and state first responders.
- Administer the disaster relief fund.
- Emphasize risk management to include preparedness, prevention, response, and recovery.
- Promote public education and volunteerism to assist communities in preventing victimization rather than citizens relying solely on response.
- Train and evaluate local, state, and federal emergency responders.
- Administer the National Flood Insurance Program.
- Administer mitigation grant programs.
- Administer Citizen Corps programs such as the Community Emergency Response Teams (CERT).

INFORMATION ANALYSIS AND INFRASTRUCTURE PROTECTION (IAIP) DIRECTORATE

This directorate focused on the anticipation of terrorist threats, protection of critical infrastructure and cyberspace, and sharing threat information.

Information analysis tasks include the following.

- Identify and assess the nature and scope of terrorist threats.
- Administer the five-color-coded Homeland Security Advisory System.
- Ensure the efficient collection and sharing of information within the DHS and with external partners.
- Establish and utilize a secure and fully compatible National Security and Emergency Preparedness communications system for the federal government, including a secure information technology infrastructure.
- Conduct training on information analysis and sharing for all levels of government.

Infrastructure protection tasks include the following.

- Assess the risks of the critical infrastructure of the United States.
- Plan the protection of critical infrastructure.
- Provide technical assistance and crisis management support to the public and private sectors.
- Provide specific warning information to the public and private sectors.

SCIENCE AND TECHNOLOGY DIRECTORATE

This directorate was established to facilitate research and development aimed at preventing and mitigating WMD and other threats. The DHS seeks to use research to prevent catastrophic losses of life and major economic impact.

Tasks include the following.

- Develop new vaccines, antidotes, diagnostics, and therapies to combat biological and chemical weapons.
- Facilitate the development, testing, evaluation, and deployment of homeland security technologies.
- Award competitive grants to the public and private sectors to conduct research.

ADDITIONAL COMPONENTS OF HOMELAND SECURITY

The DHS absorbed several federal agencies, including the Coast Guard, Secret Service, Border Patrol, Immigration and Naturalization Service, Customs Service, and Transportation Security Administration.

The U.S. Coast Guard, for instance, was transferred to the DHS intact in 2003. Because the 9/11 attacks hit the U.S. mainland, the Coast Guard has had its missions expanded and its capabilities strained. Homeland security missions of the Coast Guard are ports, waterways, and coastal security; drug interdiction; migrant interdiction; and defense readiness to assist the U.S. Navy.

Nonhomeland security missions include marine safety; search and rescue; aids to navigation (e.g., buoys); marine resources (e.g., fishing treaties); environmental protection; and ice operations (Office of Inspector General, 2004a). Critics argue that increased security tasks by the Coast Guard hinders their traditional duties such as boating safety and rescue.

The U.S. Secret Service was also transferred to the DHS intact in 2003. Its traditional functions will continue protecting the president and other government officials, investigating counterfeiting of currency, protecting the nation's financial system, and providing security expertise for major events (e.g., economic summits, Super Bowls).

The Office of the Inspector General serves the DHS through audits and investigations. The goal of this unit is to reinforce the most efficient and effective use of resources and to prevent waste, abuse, and fraud. For example, this office released a report critical of the Transportation Security Administration for not adequately monitoring, measuring, and evaluating the performance of private screeners versus federalized screeners at airports. Recommendations were made to correct relevant problems (Office of Inspector General, 2004b).

The Homeland Security Act of 2002 not only made organizational changes in the federal government, it also enhanced existing programs and created new programs. Furthermore, government units outside the DHS initiated HS efforts. Examples of a variety of changes and efforts are listed here (Bullock *et al.*, 2005: 71–83).

- A National Homeland Security Council was established within the executive office of the president to assess risks and strategies and make recommendations to the president.
- Transfer the Bureau of Alcohol, Tobacco, and Firearms from the Department of the Treasury to the Department of Justice.
- The Arming Pilots Against Terrorism Act was incorporated into the HS act. It provides antiterrorism training for flight crews and permits pilots to defend aircraft cockpits with carefully selected weapons.
- The Critical Infrastructure Information Act, also incorporated into the HS act, exempts specific components of critical infrastructure from Freedom of Information Act regulations and, thus, hinders access to sensitive information by terrorists.
- The Corporation for National and Community Service, a federal agency outside the DHS, awards grants to communities, government agencies, and voluntary organizations to fund volunteer activities in homeland security at the community level.
- The U.S. Department of Agriculture (USDA) formed a Homeland Security Council to develop HS plans and efforts. Examples of USDA activities are increased personnel at borders to prevent agricultural pests and diseases from entering the United States; guidance documents to farmers, ranchers, and food processors to help them protect their operations; tracking system for disaster reporting; coordination with state and local authorities; and training. The Department of Agriculture's Food Safety Inspection and Agricultural Research Services work to prevent agroterrorism.
- The U.S. Department of Education formed the Office of Safe and Drug-Free Schools that will take a leadership role in promoting HS initiatives in the nation's education system, such as developing plans to deal with a variety of threats.

Many other federal departments and agencies support HS. The Department of Defense (DOD) is charged with protecting the United States from attack and it seeks to improve homeland security through global military operations and support to civil authorities. There are three circumstances under which the DOD would improve security domestically: (1) in extraordinary circumstances, conduct missions such as combat air patrols or maritime defense operations; (2) during emergencies involving attack, forest fires, floods, or other serious events; and (3) for "limited scope" missions where other agencies have the lead (e.g., Olympics). The DOD is implementing a *Strategy for Homeland Defense and Civil Support* (U.S. Department of Defense, 2005: 4) that aims to "integrate strategy, planning, and operational capabilities for homeland defense and civil support more fully into DOD processes."

Poland (2005: 248) notes that many legal issues arise from using the military for homeland security and several laws prohibit such action. Federal law prohibits the military from enforcing the law within the United States except as authorized by the Constitution or an Act of Congress. The **Posse Comitatus Act of 1878** bars the military from engaging in domestic law enforcement activities such as surveillance, arrest, search and seizure, and pursuit of offenders. However, confusion exists over the laws pertaining to the role of the military in HS. The NSHS favors a review of these laws since the military may improve HS, as it has done, for instance, with the Olympics. Chapter 7 also covers these issues.

The attorney general, as America's chief law enforcement officer, leads the nation in investigating and prosecuting terrorists. The FBI and CIA play a significant role in counterterrorism intelligence responsibilities. The Centers for Disease Control and Prevention and the National Institutes of Health provide vital expertise and resources to deal with the threat of bioterrorism.

> DHS does not have overarching authority for directing all aspects of the homeland security mission. As examples, the Department of Justice, the Department of Health and Human Services, and the Department of Defense are still major players in homeland security.
>
> Gilmore Commission, 2003

DEPARTMENT OF HOMELAND SECURITY REORGANIZATION (2005)

In December of 2004, the Heritage Foundation released a report entitled *DHS 2.0: Rethinking the Department of Homeland Security* (Carafano and Heyman, 2004). This report presented the conclusions of a task force that studied the organization and operations of the DHS. The task force consisted of representatives from both public and private sectors and they developed over 40 major recommendations. The report stated:

> Putting it bluntly, the current organization of DHS must be reformed because it hampers the Secretary of Homeland Security's ability to lead our nation's homeland security efforts. The organization is weighed down with bureaucratic layers, is rife with turf warfare, and lacks a structure for strategic thinking and policymaking. Additionally, since its creation, whether one looks at the department's capacity to organize and mobilize a response...the department has been slow to overcome the obstacles to becoming an effective 21st century national security instrument.

In July of 2005, following a DHS internal review process, the second Homeland Security Secretary, Michael Chertoff (Figure 4-2), announced plans for the first reorganization of the DHS (Figure 4-3). A summary of these changes are listed here (U.S. Department of Homeland Security, 2005).

- *Centralize and improve policy development and coordination.* A new directorate of policy will serve as the primary department-wide coordinator for policies, regulations, and other initiatives. This directorate will ensure the consistency of policy and regulatory development across various parts of the department, as well as perform long-range strategic policy planning. It will assume the policy coordination functions previously performed by the Border and Transportation Security (BTS) directorate. It will also create a single point of contact for internal and external stakeholders by consolidating or colocating similar activities from across the department. This new directorate will include Office of International Affairs; Office of Private Sector Liaison; Homeland Security Advisory Council; Office of Immigration Statistics; and Senior Asylum Officer.
- *Strengthen intelligence functions and information sharing.* A new Office of Intelligence and Analysis will ensure that information is gathered from all relevant field operations and other parts of the intelligence community; analyzed with a mission-oriented focus; informative to senior decision-makers; and disseminated to the appropriate federal, state, local, and private sector partners. Led by a chief intelligence officer who reports directly to the secretary, this office will be composed of analysts within the former information analysis directorate and draw on expertise of other DHS components with intelligence collection and analysis operations.

Figure 4-2 ■ On September 4, 2005, in New Orleans, Louisiana, Secretary of Homeland Security Michael Chertoff speaks with an urban search and rescue task force member involved in the response to the devastation from Hurricane Katrina. *Source: Jocelyn Augustino, FEMA.* http://www.photolibrary.fema.gov/photolibrary/photo_details.do?id=14608

- *Improve coordination and efficiency of operations.* A new director of operations coordination will enable DHS to more effectively conduct joint operations across all organizational elements; coordinate incident management activities; and utilize all resources within the department to translate intelligence and policy into immediate action. The Homeland Security Operations Center, which serves as the nation's nerve center for information sharing and domestic incident management on a 24/7/365 basis, will be a critical part of this new office.
- *Enhance coordination and deployment of preparedness assets.* The information analysis and infrastructure protection directorate will be renamed the directorate for preparedness and consolidate preparedness assets from across the department. The directorate for preparedness will facilitate grants and oversee nationwide preparedness efforts supporting first responder training, citizen awareness, public health, infrastructure and cyber security and ensure that proper steps are taken to protect high-risk targets. The directorate will be managed by an undersecretary and will include the following: a new assistant secretary for cyber security and telecommunications, responsible for identifying and assessing the vulnerability of critical telecommunications infrastructure and assets, providing timely, actionable, and valuable threat information, and leading the national response to cyber and telecommunications attacks; a new chief medical officer, responsible for carrying out the department's responsibilities to coordinate the response to biological attacks and to serve as a principal liaison between DHS and the Department of Health and Human Services, the Centers for Disease Control, the National Institutes of Health, and other key parts of the biomedical and public health communities; an assistant secretary for infrastructure protection; assets of the office of state and local government coordination and preparedness—responsible for grants, training, and exercises; the U.S. Fire Administration; and the Office of National Capitol Region Coordination.

OTHER DEPARTMENT REALIGNMENTS

- *Improve national response and recovery efforts by focusing FEMA on its core functions.* FEMA will report directly to the secretary of Homeland Security. In order to strengthen and enhance our nation's ability to respond to and recover from manmade or natural disasters, FEMA will now focus on its historic and vital mission of response and recovery.
- *Integrate Federal Air Marshal Service (FAMS) into broader aviation security efforts.* The FAMS will be moved from the Immigration and Customs Enforcement bureau to the

Figure 4-3 ■ Department of Homeland Security (reorganization chart). Source: http://www.dhs.gov/interweb/assetlibrary/DHSOrgCharts0705.pdf

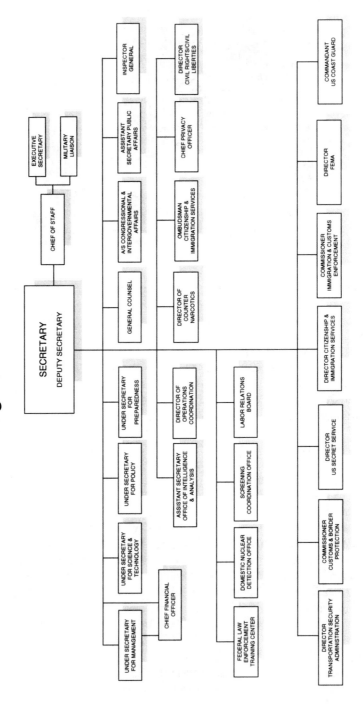

Department of Homeland Security
Organization Chart

Transportation Security Administration to increase operational coordination and strengthen efforts to meet this common goal of aviation security.

* *Merge legislative and intergovernmental affairs.* This new office of legislative and intergovernmental affairs will merge certain functions among the office of legislative affairs and the office of state and local government coordination in order to streamline intergovernmental relations efforts and better share homeland security information with members of Congress as well as state and local officials.
* *Assign office of security to management directorate.* The office of security will be moved to return oversight of that office to the undersecretary for management in order to better manage information systems, contractual activities, security accreditation, training and resources.

Reality Check: The Importance of State and Local Government Homeland Security Missions

The United States is a system rooted in **federalism**, whereby state governments share power with the federal government. In contrast to a totalitarian system of centralization, the American system is decentralized to promote greater freedoms. The **tenth amendment** of the U.S. Constitution reserves to the states and to the people all power not specifically delegated to the federal government. The United States has over 87,000 jurisdictions of overlapping federal, state, and local governments. This system presents challenges as HS is increased through enhanced coordination and communications, law enforcement and prevention, emergency response, and policy development and implementation. All states and many local jurisdictions have established a homeland security office in the executive branch to deal with terrorist attacks and a variety of other risks. Coordination is vital to avoid duplication and to produce the best possible multiagency emergency response to serious events.

Every day, minor or major disasters strike in America and it is the local agencies that respond. Fire fighters, police, and emergency medical technicians are the **first responders** *who rush to the scene to preserve life and to reduce property damage. Consequently, a terrorist attack or natural disaster becomes a local event, and the FBI, DHS, and FEMA do not arrive until later.* A U.S. conference of mayors report noted in 2003, "When you dial 9-1-1, the phone doesn't ring in the White House...those calls come in to your city's police, fire, and emergency medical personnel... our domestic troops." The conference of mayors estimated that cities have spent billions on HS needs and $70 million per week while the nation was at a heightened state of alert.

In its fifth and final annual report to the president and Congress, the *Gilmore Commission* released several critical statements pertaining to the federal role in leading state and local jurisdictions to improve HS. The full name of the commission is Advisory Panel to Assess Domestic Response Capabilities for Terrorism Involving Weapons of Mass Destruction (2003). A major question asked by the commission was: *"If local responders are in fact our first line of defense, have we succeeded in effectively empowering and enhancing state and local capabilities?"* The commission's extensive research showed the following.

* States feel the federal government is giving them some support, although areas for improvement still exist. This may reflect state governments' experience with federal grants and understanding the wide gap between "an announcement" and the time frame for actual funding.
* Local agencies show a similar theme, which may reveal a need for states to do a better job of managing expectations and educating locales on the grant process.
* There is a need for improved strategic guidance from the federal level about how states and localities will be evaluated on preparedness.
* The deficit in intelligence and information sharing requires continued improvements.
* Because local responders are closer to WMD threats and often know their own needs better than federal and state agencies, the federal government should have a goal to increase local flexibility and innovation (e.g., with the use of grants).

Continued

Reality Check: The Importance of State and Local Government Homeland Security Missions—Cont'd

Donald Plusquellic, a member of the U.S. conference of mayors, argues that grants from the federal government help with HS, but rules require cities to spend their own money first and then wait for reimbursement from the U.S. Treasury. He acknowledges that fronting the money for multimillion-dollar equipment is difficult. He adds that the process of obtaining federal funds is frustratingly slow. Research by U.S. Rep. Christopher Cox's committee on HS found that although billions of dollars are set aside for preparedness grants for state and local governments, much of it gets stuck in the funding pipeline (i.e., DHS and state governments). The problem appears to be antiquated grant processes and purchasing procedures at all levels of government that hinder speed. Inequality in funding is another problem. For example, one rural Wyoming county with a population of 11,500 received $546,000 in grants, while Jefferson, Kentucky (Louisville), with a population of nearly 700,000 and designated by the DHS as a high-threat urban area, received $783,000. Reform is gaining momentum and all levels of government are seeking solutions. States have streamlined the flow of funds and procurement systems (Logan, 2004).

In 2005, when Hurricane Katrina devastated Gulf Coast states and flooded New Orleans, the importance of disaster preparedness and response for "all hazards" (e.g., terrorism, natural disasters, and accidents) was echoed again, along with the challenges of immediate assistance; mutual aid agreements; common command and control standards among all levels of government; and equipment interoperability (e.g., the ability for different emergency responders to communicate on the same radio equipment). As the magnitude of the Katrina disaster unfolded, no level of government was prepared and "finger pointing" among politicians ensued. *One major lesson learned by state and local leaders again was not to expect immediate federal emergency assistance.*

NATIONAL STRATEGY FOR HOMELAND SECURITY

According to the White House under President George W. Bush, the Office of Homeland Security (2002) released the **National Strategy for Homeland Security** (NSHS) as a comprehensive and shared vision of how best to protect America from terrorist attacks. This strategy was compiled with the assistance of many people in a variety of occupations in the public and private sectors. A major goal was to facilitate shared responsibility and cooperation. The strategy focused on the following four questions.

- What are "homeland security" and its missions?
- What is to be accomplished and what are the most important goals?
- What is the federal executive branch doing now and what should it do in the future?
- What should nonfederal governments, the private sector, and citizens do to secure the homeland?

Publication of the NSHS preceded congressional approval of the DHS. The intent of the executive branch of government in publishing the NSHS was to provide a strategic vision for the proposed DHS that was eventually supported by Congress through the Homeland Security Act of 2002.

The NSHS concentrates on the following six critical mission areas.

- Intelligence and warning
- Border and transportation security
- Domestic counterterrorism
- Protecting critical infrastructure and key assets
- Defending against catastrophic threats
- Emergency preparedness and response

The NSHS relies on specific foundations, namely law, science and technology, information sharing and systems, and international cooperation. Furthermore, budgetary support for the NSHS will entail balancing benefits and costs.

Subsequent pages of this chapter cover topics contained in the NSHS, namely intelligence and warning, information sharing, domestic counterterrorism, and countering terrorist financing. NSHS topics are also covered later in this book, including emergency management, protecting critical infrastructure, and border and transportation security.

National Security and Homeland Security

The Office of Homeland Security (2002) discussed the link between the **National Security Strategy of the United States** (NSSUS) and the National Strategy for Homeland Security. The preamble to the U.S. Constitution defines the federal government's basic purpose as "...to form a more perfect Union, establish justice, insure domestic Tranquility, provide for the common defense, promote the general Welfare, and secure the Blessings of Liberty to ourselves and our Posterity." The NSSUS aims to ensure the sovereignty and independence of the United States, with our values and institutions intact. Both the NSSUS and the NSHS complement each other by addressing the challenge of terrorism. This link between both major strategies is important because "America has sought to protect its own sovereignty and independence through a strategy of global presence and engagement. In so doing, America has helped many other countries and peoples advance along the path of democracy, open markets, individual liberty, and peace with their neighbors." At the same time, there are enemies who disagree with America's role in the world and use violence to express their views. Because the United States is a great power, terrorists must use unconventional methods and weapons. They also take advantage of America's free society and openness to covertly insert terrorists into the United States.

In addition to the NSSUS and the NSHS, which together take precedence over all other national strategies, there are other, more specific, strategies of the United States that are subsumed within the twin concepts of national security and homeland security. They are as follow.

- National defense strategy
- National strategy for combating terrorism
- National strategy to combat weapons of mass destruction
- National strategy to secure cyberspace
- National drug control strategy
- National money laundering strategy

The link between the NSSUS and the NSHS can be seen with the **National Military Strategy for Combating Weapons of Mass Destruction.** This document outlines the role of the DOD in countering the threat of WMD and in fulfilling the president's national strategy to combat weapons of mass destruction. It focuses on "the greatest risk" confronting the United States and other countries. The document serves to build on efforts already under way in the DOD; provide a foundation for assigning specific tasks and responsibilities within the DOD; and work to ensure that military members operate as one team with one unified plan. The objectives are to keep WMD out of enemy hands, prevent proliferation, deter use, and if they are used, reduce their impact and respond (Miles, 2006; Chairman of the Joint Chiefs of Staff, DOD, 2006).

Another point regarding homeland security and national security is that they are intertwined because of the global scope of terrorism and the interdependencies of the United States with other countries. Whether we are referring to aviation security, border security, security of containerized cargo entering

Continued

National Security and Homeland Security—Cont'd

ports, intelligence, or other aspects of security, international cooperation is essential to integrate domestic and international security strategies to avoid gaps that could be exploited by terrorists.

The Rand Corporation (Larson and Peters, 2001) provides additional insight into the relationship between national security and homeland security. When the prevention of terrorist attacks fail, the government must respond through five missions.

- *Assist civilians.* First responders and local agencies and resources are the backbone of this effort.
- *Ensure continuity of government.* The 9/11 attacks illustrated the need for the protection of government leaders.
- *Ensure continuity of military operations.* Terrorist attacks could require domestic assistance from the military in addition to an armed response to terrorists. Defense planners must protect military personnel and resources. The 9/11 attack on the Pentagon serves as an example.
- *Border and coastal defense.* The border of the United States includes thousands of miles along the Canadian border, the Mexican border, and the east and west coasts. Access controls and inspections are necessary for people, vehicles, and goods reaching the United States. This overwhelming workload falls on a variety of federal, state, and local agencies.
- *National air defense.* For many years, the Air Force operated the North American Air Defense Command (NORAD) to detect and provide warning of missile or bomber attacks, especially during the Cold War. Following the 9/11 attacks, the Department of Defense formed the **U.S. Northern Command** (NORTH-COM) to provide air and other types of defense for the United States.

CRITICAL THINKING:

Should civilian airliners be shot out of the sky if they are controlled by terrorists who are flying toward a target?

INTELLIGENCE AND WARNING

The NSHS states the following.

- The United States must take action to avoid being surprised by another terrorist attack.
- Early warning of an impending terrorist attack is far more complicated than early warning of a nuclear attack.
- An intelligence and warning system must be established that is capable of detecting terrorist activity prior to an attack so that preemptive, preventive, and protective action can be taken.
- Agencies of government have not always fully shared information due to legal or cultural barriers and limitations of information systems.
- The U.S. intelligence community must do a better job of utilizing information from foreign-language documents and identifying, collecting, and analyzing information.

The NSHS recognizes four interrelated but distinct categories of intelligence and information analysis.

- *Tactical threat analysis* is actionable intelligence vital for preventing terrorist acts. Government analysis of current and potential terrorist activities helps disrupt and prevent terrorism and provides intelligence to specific targets, security and public safety personnel, or the general population.

- *Strategic analysis of the enemy* is in-depth intelligence on terrorist organizations, their supporters, motivations, goals, capabilities, and weaknesses. This intelligence supports short-term and long-term strategies to defeat terrorism.
- *Vulnerability assessments* are an integral part of intelligence and enable planners to project the consequence of possible terrorist attacks against specific facilities or different sectors of the economy or government. These projections, compiled with computer modeling and analysis tools, provide information to design and strengthen defenses against various threats.
- *Threat-vulnerability integration* entails mapping terrorist threats and capabilities, both current and future, against specific facility and sectoral vulnerabilities to permit authorities to determine which organizations pose the greatest threats. It provides input for planners developing thresholds for preemptive or protective action.

The NSHS describes three broad categories of action that can result from intelligence and information analysis.

- *Tactical preventive action* thwarts terrorists from executing their plots. The United States has at its disposal numerous tools (e.g., arrests, military action) to disrupt terrorist acts.
- *Warning and protective action* includes activating emergency plans, dispatching law enforcement patrols, increasing citizen awareness, and increasing security and protection.
- *Strategic response (policy)* sees the enemy of today as far different from those of the past. The United States is developing and creating new capabilities specifically designed to defeat the enemy of today and the enemy of the future. Strategic capability will be shaped through budgetary allocations and will be informed by intelligence and information. Policies will build international coalitions and reduce sources of support for terrorists.

The NSHS sees the following as major initiatives to improve intelligence and warning.

- *Enhance the analytic capabilities of the FBI.* The attorney general and the director of the FBI have placed preventing terrorist attacks as the FBI's top priority. FBI changes include increasing the number of staff analyzing intelligence and hiring applicants with specialized expertise, including foreign language capacity, computer skills, and science and engineering backgrounds. The CIA will send analysts to the FBI not only to enhance FBI capabilities, but also to improve the relationship between these two agencies.
- *Build new capabilities through the information analysis and infrastructure protection division of the DHS.* This involves a comprehensive vulnerability assessment of the nation's critical infrastructure and key assets to aid planning, evaluating potential effects of an attack on a given facility or sector, and investments in protection. Because intelligence and law enforcement agencies focus on detection and disruption of threats, there is a need for a key homeland security function known as **threat-vulnerability integration**: analyzing terrorist threats, mapping the threats against vulnerabilities, and improving protection. This approach would include prioritizing critical infrastructure protection and "target hardening."
- *Homeland security advisory system.* This system, managed by the DHS, disseminates information on the risk of terrorist acts to federal, state, and local authorities, the private sector, and the American people. It provides for public announcements of threat advisories and alerts, appropriate levels of vigilance, preparedness, and readiness in a series of graduated threat conditions. Each threat condition signifies corresponding suggested measures of response, such as increased surveillance, preparation for contingency procedures, and closing of facilities.
- *Utilize dual-use analysis to prevent attacks.* Terrorists use a variety of materials and equipment, often in a creative way, in their attacks. Examples include fertilizer, aerosol

generators, protective gear, antibiotics, and disease-causing agents. Many of these items are "dual-use" items, having both legitimate and illegitimate applications, and they are often purchased on the open market. If suspect buyers are identified and cross-referenced with intelligence and law enforcement databases and mapped against threat analyses, authorities' ability to detect terrorist activities at the preparation stage will be enhanced.

- *Employ "red team" techniques*. The DHS will work with the intelligence community to use "red team" techniques to improve the nation's defenses. In essence, certain DHS employees view the United States from the perspectives of terrorists, seeking to discern and predict the methods, means, and targets of terrorists. This process includes learning how terrorists think and plan, conducting government-sponsored exercises to uncover weaknesses in the nation's security, and improving protection.

Reality Check: Intelligence

Since the 9/11 attacks, the terms "intelligence" and "intelligence community" have been subject to attention and controversy. Most experts agree that there was a massive U.S. intelligence failure before the attacks. In the criticism over government incompetence, words echoed repeatedly were "stovepiping" and "connecting the dots." **Stovepiping** refers to organizations that operate in isolation from one another, closely protect internal information, avoid partnering with other organizations to improve overall efficiency and effectiveness, and do not recognize how their action or inaction impacts other organizations. **Connecting the dots** refers to clues that surfaced, prior to September 11, 2001, that were not pursued and shared by the CIA and the FBI to possibly prevent the attacks. Links between al-Qaida's previous plans and specific operatives pointed to indicators of an impending attack. Shultz and Vogt (2003) write that an FBI agent in Phoenix warned the agency in July 2001 that some Middle Eastern men training in American flight schools might be bin Laden agents. In addition the CIA possessed information about two of the hijackers dating back to an al-Qaida meeting in Malaysia in January 2000.

Lowenthal (2003: 8) defines **intelligence** as follows: "Intelligence is the process by which specific types of information important to national security are requested, collected, analyzed, and provided to policymakers; the products of that process; the safeguarding of these processes and this information by counterintelligence activities; and the carrying out of operations as requested by lawful authorities." Examples of intelligence are the plans for a terrorist attack development of a new weapon by another country, and ulterior motives of a rogue state.

Lowenthal (2003: 41–53) describes a seven-step intelligence process: (1) identifying needs and priorities (e.g., rogue states, terrorists, weapons proliferation); (2) collecting intelligence (e.g., human intelligence such as espionage; satellites); (3) processing and exploiting collected information to produce intelligence (e.g., processing imagery; decoding); (4) analysis and production (e.g., analysts, who are experts in their field, study information and prepare intelligence reports); (5) dissemination to policy makers (e.g., president's daily briefing presented by the CIA); (6) consumption (e.g., needs and preferences of policy makers); and (7) feedback (e.g., what intelligence has been useful and what intelligence requires increased emphasis).

The **intelligence community** of the United States consists of several government organizations that collect information. Since 1947, the CIA has brought together foreign intelligence for the president and the National Security Council (see Chapter 3). The Department of Defense has enormous resources, beyond the CIA, to collect intelligence. DOD organizations that collect intelligence include the National Security Agency, Defense Intelligence Agency, National Imagery and Mapping Agency, Defense Airborne Reconnaissance Programs, and the armed service intelligence units. The Departments of State, Treasury, and Energy also have intelligence units, although small. The FBI focuses on domestic intelligence, but it has expanded its work globally in recent years.

Since the 9/11 attacks, there have been many calls for reform of the intelligence community (Figure 4-4). The 9/11 Commission report proposed a restructuring of the US intelligence community

Reality Check: Intelligence—Cont'd

Figure 4-4 ■ Following the 9/11 attacks, serious deficiencies again surfaced concerning cooperation and sharing intelligence information among agencies of government. Source: U.S. Department of Homeland Security (2004b: 12). http://www.dhs.gov/interweb/assetlibrary/DHS_StratPlan_FINAL_spread.pdf

and the creation of an intelligence "czar" for better coordination and sharing of intelligence. President George W. Bush signed **The Intelligence Reform and Terrorism Prevention Act of 2004** to improve intelligence gathering and transform a system designed for the Cold War to a system more effective against terrorism. Although traditional intelligence gathering has focused on foreign countries and such topics as their policies, strategies, economies, technology, and military capabilities, the problem of terrorism requires an augmentation of intelligence gathering to include the methods, behaviors, strategies, tactics, and weapons of terrorists. The aim of the act is to make the intelligence community more unified, coordinated, and effective.

Highlights of The Intelligence Reform and Terrorism Prevention Act of 2004 are as follows.

- Establishes a director of national intelligence with authority over both the intelligence budget and personnel to improve the coordination of intelligence. The director is to oversee the nation's 15 separate intelligence agencies, including the CIA, which has been harshly criticized for its failures prior to the 9/11 attacks.
- Establishes the National Counterterrorism Center (NCTC) to coordinate counterterrorism planning, except operations, and share intelligence (see Chapter 3).
- Establishes an independent privacy and civil liberties board to review policies and practices, advise the executive branch, and provide to Congress an annual report that is unclassified to the greatest extent possible.
- Mandates an information-sharing environment for counterterrorism among all levels of government.
- Establishes a National Counter Proliferation Center.
- Restructures the FBI's intelligence capabilities through the creation of an intelligence directorate and requires enhanced intelligence skills of agents.
- The act also contains several nonintelligence provisions, including the following: requires the DHS to develop a national strategy for transportation security; upgrades to transportation and border security, and additional border patrol agents; additional immigration and customs investigators and detention beds; requirement that federal agencies establish minimum standards

Continued

Reality Check: Intelligence—Cont'd

for drivers licenses and identification necessary to board domestic commercial aircraft and gain access to federal facilities; creates new crimes and penalties to combat terrorism; and strengthens U.S. foreign policy against terrorism through a variety of initiatives, including the reporting of terrorist sanctuaries, impeding travel by terrorists, counternarcotics enforcement, and improving economic development and public education in the Middle East.

The impact of the act to improve the intelligence community will be an evolutionary process that will confront traditional resistance to changes, the protection of turf, and competition for resources. Success depends on several factors, such as the budgetary authority over intelligence of the director of national intelligence, leadership, and congressional oversight.

CRITICAL THINKING:

Why do you think the intelligence community failed to anticipate the 9/11 attacks?

Reality Check: Homeland Security Advisory System

The DHS established the **Homeland Security Advisory System** (HSAS) to assist the nation in remaining vigilant, prepared, and ready to deter terrorist attacks. The following threat conditions each represent an increasing risk of attack, and some suggested protective measures are listed for federal departments and agencies.

- *Low condition (green)* is declared when there is a low risk of attack. Protective measures should include training, assessment of vulnerabilities, and mitigation of vulnerabilities.
- *Guarded condition (blue)* results when there is a general risk of attack. In addition to the measures taken in the previous level, the following measures should be considered: checking communications with designated emergency response or command locations, reviewing and updating emergency response procedures, and providing the public with protective information.
- *Elevated condition (yellow)* is declared when there is significant risk of terrorist attacks. This level builds upon measures taken in lower threat conditions and adds increasing surveillance of critical locations, coordinating emergency plans among jurisdictions, refining protective measures according to the threat, and implementing appropriate contingency and emergency response plans.
- *High condition (orange)* reflects a high risk of attack. In addition to protective measures in the previous threat conditions, the following measures should be considered: coordinating security efforts with federal, state, and local law enforcement agencies or any National Guard or other armed forces organizations; enhancing protection at public events and considering alternative venues or even cancellation; preparing to execute contingency procedures, such as dispersing a workforce; and restricting threatened facility access to essential personnel only.
- *Severe condition (red)* is declared when there is a severe risk of attack. Under most circumstances, during this condition, the intense protective measures are not intended to be sustained for substantial periods of time. In addition to the protective measures in previous threat conditions, the following measures should be considered: increasing and directing personnel to address critical emergency needs; assigning emergency response personnel and prepositioning and mobilizing specially trained teams or resources; monitoring, redirecting, or constraining transportation systems; and closing public and government facilities.

Since the HSAS was implemented following 9/11, it has been subjected to much criticism and even ignored by the governments and citizens it was supposed to assist. It has been labeled a "damned if you do, damned if you don't" system. When a heightened level of alert is declared and an attack does not occur, complaints surface about the waste of resources and unnecessarily frightening the public and desensitizing them to alerts. Too many alerts can cause "alert fatigue" and a nonchalant attitude during subsequent alerts. If a warning is not issued when intelligence indicates a possible attack, and an attack does occur, authorities face serious repercussions (Bannon, 2004).

Elevated risks cost a lot of money. Cities spend millions of dollars on overtime for police, firefighters, and other employees. Also, promises from the federal government for funding for such expenses have not met local expectations. States and localities actually do not have to follow the HSAS. However, facilities under federal jurisdiction, such as nuclear power plants and airports, must follow specific procedures. Also, no standards are set for each alert level for state and local governments. Heightened security varies. In Tulsa, for example, when an orange alert is declared, the city's emergency management director contacts the National Guard and first responders to ensure that communication lines are clear. Specific posts are assigned around the city and physical security is enhanced in cooperation with the private sector. Charlotte, North Carolina, has an opposite view of alerts than Tulsa. Charlotte chose not to participate in most of the code oranges. The only one they reacted to was the one during the initial U.S. attack of Iraq in 2003. The concern was demonstrations by war protestors, not terrorism (Sostek, 2003).

The effectiveness of the HSAS is difficult to ascertain. An elevated risk may cause terrorists to abort an attack or the intense vigilance of authorities and citizens may uncover and disrupt terrorist plans.

A major criticism of the HSAS is that it is too broad, covering the whole United States. Many claim that it should be more specific to geographic areas and industries and be based on good intelligence. Research by the *Gilmore Commission* showed that state and local agencies want information on the type of incident likely to occur, where the threat is likely to occur, and during what time period to help them respond. Also suggested was a regional alert system and training for emergency responders on protective actions at different threat levels. During the summer of 2004, a specific alert on possible car or truck bombs was issued to financial institutions in three cities in the northeast based on seized al-Qaida documents. No attacks occurred.

Despite the criticism of the HSAS, it is an important system to provide warning of the possibility of attack and it serves to help us to remain vigilant, prepared, and ready. A major difficulty surrounding the HSAS is *when* to declare a heightened level of alert.

CRITICAL THINKING:

Do you think the DHS can supply the specific alert information to state and local governments as described by the *Gilmore Commission*? Explain.

INFORMATION SHARING AND SYSTEMS

The NSHS states that everyone involved in homeland security is heavily dependent on information and information systems. Although U.S. information technology is the most advanced in the world, it has not adequately supported HS. No single system integrates all HS information. What we have are disparate databases among federal, state, and local agencies. Information is often not shared "horizontally" (across the same level of government) or "vertically" (between federal, state, and local levels). Government agencies must continue to work to link, for example, personnel at border checkpoints and police officers on patrol with useful information to protect the homeland.

The NSHS notes that although the federal government spends about $50 billion a year on information technology, two major problems exist. First, the acquisition of information systems has not been routinely coordinated and new systems are often acquired to address specific agency needs. Second, legal and cultural barriers frequently block agencies from sharing information. Similar problems exist on the state and local levels. For example, many states operate terrorism, gang, and drug databases that other states cannot access. To remedy these problems, the NSHS seeks to integrate information sharing across federal, state, and local governments, and private industry and citizens.

Figure 4-5 ■ U.S. law enforcement agencies (and the military) conduct ongoing training and prepare to counter terrorism. *Source:* U.S. Department of Homeland Security. Photo by James Tourtellotte. http://www.customs.gov/xp/cgov/newsroom/photo_gallery/afc/bp/07.xml

Realistically, system integration and widespread access to databases will be a slow, but sure, process, as more information is made available to those who protect the homeland.

DOMESTIC COUNTERTERRORISM

As we know from the previous chapter, counterterrorism is a broad term encompassing many activities seeking to reduce or eliminate terrorism. The NSHS emphasizes that while law enforcement agencies continue to investigate and prosecute criminal activity, they will also assign priority to preventing and interdicting terrorist activity (Figure 4-5). Here is a list of additional points from the NSHS pertaining to the law enforcement role in domestic counterterrorism.

- Not only are federal law enforcement agencies and the U.S. intelligence community making improvements in sharing information, so are international, state, and local agencies.
- The FBI-led joint terrorism task forces (JTTFs), which have primary operational responsibility for terrorism investigations not related to ongoing prosecutions, will continue to draw on state and local partners and their capabilities to enhance intergovernmental coordination.
- The Department of Justice will continue to expand data in the FBI's National Crime Information Center (NCIC) which is accessible by about 650,000 state and local police officers. In addition to the data that have been included in this system for many years, such as wanted persons and stolen items, additions include information on subjects of domestic and foreign terrorism investigations and fugitive aliens in violation of final orders of deportation.
- The FBI is refining a consolidated terrorism watch list that serves as a central access point for information about individuals of investigative interest.
- Commercially available computer databases are increasingly being utilized in counterterrorism investigations to help in the search for patterns of criminal behavior.
- The Department of Justice is engaged in **data-mining** projects that utilize computer technology to analyze information to reveal patterns of behavior consistent with terrorist activities.
- A restructured FBI emphasizes prevention of terrorist attacks by, for example, shifting hundreds of field agents from criminal investigations to counterterrorism investigations.

COUNTERING TERRORIST FINANCING

We learned from Chapter 2 that one method of controlling terrorists is to disrupt the financial networks that support them. This includes targeting illegal and legal businesses and charities and money laundering. The NSHS emphasizes that the FBI should lead the federal government law enforcement effort against terrorist financing, with support from the DHS. The FBI's financial review group is a multiagency effort that investigates suspicious financial transactions to uncover and prosecute terrorist fund-raisers and develop predictive models to identify future illegal financing.

Terrorist financing specialists at the FBI note that internal auditors play a significant role in identifying and stopping financial support of terrorists. Terrorists and their supporters continue to devise new methods to hide their transactions. They may fake identities to open accounts with financial institutions or establish business relationships with commercial organizations; this has become easier because of E-banking and internet commerce. Indicators of possible terrorist financing include a customer changes address frequently, an account receives many deposits from varied and unknown sources, and a dormant account suddenly receives a large deposit followed by numerous small withdrawals that completely drain the account (Lim, 2004).

Financial institutions are increasingly improving their efforts to detect terrorist financing. Multiple types of "intelligent" software are available commercially that help identify out-of-pattern activity by conducting analyses of transactions, account profiles, patterns, and contexts. Security personnel in financial institutions use such software to check for not only terrorist financing, but also for money laundering, check fraud, identify theft, and other crimes. Various types of software can prepare lists of suspect accounts that are prioritized by risk scores and perform peer group comparisons (Beaulieu, 2004).

The Council on Foreign Relations (2004b) reports on the following recommendations from the United Nations and U.S. officials.

- Encourage other countries to target terrorist groups, better monitor suspect charities, and block channels of funding. (Note: As covered in Chapter 1, some countries and groups label "terrorists" as "freedom fighters.")
- Try to regulate hawala dealers and other informal payment systems.
- Continue to adapt to newer financing methods of supporters and terrorists.

Members of the 9/11 commission stated that the international community has choked off some terrorist financing, but that stopping the flow of funds is impossible. Creating profiles of terrorist fund-raisers and the ability of financial institutions to detect terrorist financing remain difficult. There are no unique "red flags" among millions of daily transactions, according to the committee members (Drees, 2004).

The National Commission on Terrorist Attacks Upon the United States (2004a), *Monograph on Terrorist Financing*, states that U.S. authorities have a much better understanding of terrorist financing today than prior to the 9/11 attacks. The FBI, CIA, and other agencies have developed extensive expertise in the clandestine movement of money. Still, the challenges persist because of the commingling of terrorist money with legitimate funds, unwitting donors, the complicated and secretive money trail, and dependence on foreign government reporting that is important because most terrorist assets and funding are overseas.

The Center for Defense Information (2002) lists U.S. and international laws and groups seeking to counter terrorist financing.

- *U.S. Executive Order 13224, signed September 24, 2001* calls for a list of all those "associated with" terrorist groups and the list includes fund-raisers, donors, charities, and banks. This executive order provides the treasury department with authority to freeze assets and block transactions.
- *Operation Green Quest* is an interagency task force of agents from the U.S. Customs Service, IRS, FBI, and Secret Service who employ undercover operations, electronic surveillance, and other methods to target underground financial systems, illicit charities, and corrupt financial institutions. Such efforts have led to arrests and asset seizures.

- *USA Patriot Act of 2001* asks financial businesses to enhance transaction transparency, to search for a common customer ID system, to prevent money laundering and terrorist financing, and to promote private–public sector cooperation.
- *U.N. Security Council Resolutions 1373 and 1390* require U.N. members to freeze funds and assets associated with the Taliban or al-Qaida, block U.N.-named terrorists from using their territories as a base and, under 1390, provides grounds for making it illegal to deal arms or train U.N.-named terrorists.
- *Financial Action Task Force* is a 31-nation intergovernmental organization originally established to control money laundering and now also targeting terrorist financing. It issues recommendations to members, such as enacting laws against terrorist financing and regulating informal remittance systems.
- *International Monetary Fund and the World Bank* work together against money laundering and terrorist financing and provide technical assistance to weaker states.
- *G7 and G20.* The G7 is made up of the world's seven richest industrial countries (United States, Japan, Germany, France, Britain, Italy, and Canada) to discuss the global economy. The G20 was created by the G7 to foster international financial stability. Both groups work to uphold U.N. measures against terrorist financing, create financial intelligence units (FIUs), increase information sharing, and assist weaker states.
- *Egmont Group* is an informal organization of FIUs among many countries dedicated to information sharing, training, and promoting FIUs.
- *Wolfsberg Group* is composed of the 12 leading financial institutions in the world. It stresses information sharing (especially concerning suspicious activity reports), unity of action, "know your customer" policies and procedures, and restrictions on transactions with informal remittance systems such as hawalas.

Controversy has developed over terrorist financing and countermeasures. Chapter 2 showed that Osama bin Laden's assets were previously overstated and that his financial support of al-Qaida is difficult to gauge. Also covered was the hawala system of transferring funds globally through an informal system of brokers with no "paper trail." Despite efforts of the global community in battling money laundering and terrorist financing, barriers include corrupt financial institutions, some controlled by organized criminals, and countries with weak regulatory systems for their financial industries.

According to the United Nations sanctions-monitoring committee, al-Qaida is able to finance its operations in less detectable ways and no longer needs large sums of money to execute attacks. The committee noted that in earlier years it was easy to freeze bank accounts of individuals and organizations linked to al-Qaida. Now, supporters are more flexible, decentralized, and staying ahead of sanctions. Among the challenges are investigating crime proceeds, especially from the drug trade; diverted charitable donations; counterfeit currency; credit card fraud; and the hawala system. The committee stated that al-Qaida no longer has to pay $10 to $20 million a year to the Taliban in Afghanistan and that its post-9/11 attacks cost less than $50,000 each. As examples, the bombings of the Madrid trains in March of 2004 that killed 191 passengers cost only $10,000, while the suicide truck bombing in Istanbul in November of 2003 that caused 62 deaths cost less than $40,000. The 9/11 attacks cost between $400,000 and $500,000 (Hoge, 2004).

CRITICAL THINKING:
How successful do you think governments can be in curtailing terrorist financing?

CONSIDER A CAREER AS AN FBI FINANCIAL ANALYST

Here's What It's Like: Up Close and Personal—FBI (2004)

Chris Poulos (Figure 4-6) works in our Terrorist Financing Operations Section in the Washington, DC, area. He came to the FBI just over a year ago following a 25-year career as a certified public accountant and certified fraud examiner, and did he ever bring a lot to the table. Strong educational background, with a B.S. and M.S. in accounting and auditing. Wide experience, to include working in national and regional firms and his own local firm...and also interesting experience, building up 10 years of civil and criminal case forensic accounting and litigation work. It was in this latter work that he rubbed elbows with retired FBI agents and was encouraged to apply for a fascinating career as an FBI financial analyst. Here is what he says about it.

Q: Chris, can you tell me what you like most about the job?

A: You know, I don't view what I do as a job; I view it as a career path choice. A job is something you do for money; a career is something you do because you want your life to have purpose and meaning, you want to make a difference. That's why I'm here, and that's how I feel about my work. It directly helps agents and professional support employees detect, prevent, disrupt, and dismantle terrorist organizations and the people that operate and support them. What could be more meaningful than that?

Q: What's a typical working day like?

A: Case work on a daily basis involves close financial analysis for alleged terrorist financing cases to determine where suspects get their money and how they spend it. In addition, you can be sent on "special assignments" to specific field offices to examine accounting, auditing, and tax records of a subject organization and offer investigative analysis and strategies. Investigations are always a team effort, which is very satisfying to me.

Q: Any advice for prospective FBI recruits?

A: This is a great job for anyone who has accounting skills, and a desire to make a difference in the safety of our communities, America as a whole, as well as the safety of our Allies. Your work will

Figure 4-6 ■ Chris Poulos, FBI Financial Analyst.

Continued

CONSIDER A CAREER AS AN FBI FINANCIAL ANALYST—Cont'd

directly help the FBI solve cases, and it will also strengthen cooperative ventures—sharing crucial information—with federal, state, local, and international law enforcement that will help prevent terrorist attacks. Once you become part of the FBI, you can find the area that gives you the most personal satisfaction, whether it be counterterrorism cases, intelligence work, counterintelligence, cyber, or criminal investigations. It's a great place—a place to grow personally and professionally.

Q: What about that growth? Any career development plans for your future?

A: In fact, yes. I discovered as a financial analyst that I have the skill and desire to work with intelligence, and I have just recently accepted an intelligence analyst position in my same terrorist financing operations section. I love it—I can't believe that I'm getting paid to do such fascinating work.

Link: Interested in applying? Go straight to www.fbijobs.gov

Source: http://www.fbi.gov/page2/oct04/finan101804.htm

U.S. DEPARTMENT OF HOMELAND SECURITY (2004a)

Fact Sheet: An Overview of America's Security since 9/11

The country has made great strides toward improving the security of our homeland since September 11th. The following is snapshot of the ways we are safer today.

Curb to Cockpit

Air travel is safer now than ever before due to the layered security DHS has put in place—hardened cockpit doors on 100% of large passenger aircraft, vulnerability assessments at over 75 of the nation's largest airports, 100% of all checked baggage is screened, deployment of thousands of federal air marshals, and a professionally trained screener workforce, which has intercepted more than 12.4 million prohibited items since their inception. In addition, a robust screening system is in place for all international flights into the United States, and all passenger names for domestic flights are checked against an expanded terrorist watch list.

Port to Port

New security measures specifically tailored to the individual port are now in place at every port in America. These layered measures begin overseas by screening cargo before it is loaded on ships in foreign ports. Homeland security screens 100% of high-risk cargo by targeting suspect cargo using a set of specific indicators. Every port in America has submitted a security plan, which includes security measures such as surveillance cameras and background checks on port workers. The department is also moving forward to implement "smart" technologies for cargo containers.

Secure Borders and Open Doors

The Department of Homeland Security has launched the US-VISIT system, which links databases to provide valuable information to port of entry officials and consular officials overseas and creates a database of pictures and finger scans of everyone entering the United States with a nonimmigrant visa (and soon to include visa waiver travelers). This new tool means that we have a much better idea of who is entering our country. If a traveler's finger scan hits a match on the terrorist watch list, the department is able to stop them from entering the country at the border. Over 200 people have already been turned away from our borders using this new system.

U.S. DEPARTMENT OF HOMELAND SECURITY (2004a)—Cont'd

Increased Information Sharing

Several information-sharing vehicles exist today that did not exist before September 11, 2001. The Homeland Security Information Network (HSIN), which is available in all 50 states, makes threat-related information available to law enforcement and emergency managers on a daily basis through a web-based system. Members of the private sector now receive threat-related information through the HSIN system. In addition, members of 35 different federal agencies are now all colocated together in DHS's new 24-hour Homeland Security Operations Center, which allows information coming from various sources to be synthesized together and then shared with other federal partners, such as the FBI and the Department of Defense. In addition, nearly 100 bulletins and other threat-related communiqués have been sent to homeland security professionals across the country.

Citizen Preparedness

September is national preparedness month. More than 80 partners and all 56 states and territories are making individual and family preparedness a priority across the nation by hosting events, offering training sessions, and distributing information. In addition, the public education campaign Ready and its Spanish language version Listo educates and empowers American citizens to prepare for and respond to potential terrorist attacks and other emergencies. Ready, the most successful public service campaign launched in Ad Council history, delivers its messages through the www.Ready.gov and www.Listo.gov web sites, radio, television, print and outdoor PSAs, brochures, and a variety of partnerships with private sector organizations. Ready Business will be launched to encourage small- to medium-sized businesses to take steps to safeguard their employees and assets while preparing for business continuity in the event of a disaster. Also, more than 1300 communities around the country, encompassing 50% of the U.S. population, have established Citizen Corps Councils to engage citizens in preparing, training and volunteer service, including delivering the important messages of the Ready campaign.

Interoperability

DHS's Safecom program provides long-term technical assistance to federal, state, tribal, and local programs that build and operate radio systems, and the RapidCom program focuses on the immediate development of incident-response interoperable emergency communications in high-threat urban areas. RapidCom will ensure that high-threat urban areas have incident-level, interoperable emergency communications equipment by September 30, 2004. The program will establish communications interoperability in these urban areas for an incident area approximately the size of the attacks on the World Trade Center towers on September 11th. At the incident area, all emergency personnel from various regional jurisdictions will be able to communicate using existing equipment that is made interoperable by a patch-panel device, interconnecting various models of equipment that would otherwise not be compatible.

Emerging Technologies

Homeland Security's Advanced Research Projects Agency (HSARPA) invests in the private sector, funding revolutionary new technological advances to make America safer. HSARPA has already delivered significant advances in radiological and nuclear detection and in biological and chemical countermeasures; ongoing projects include waterway vessel-tracking technology and new cargo security technologies for advanced container security. There have also been great strides made in harnessing scientific advances in biometrics to strengthen travel security and to help detect and counter identity theft. Through the Homeland Security Centers of Excellence program, the department is creating university-based partnerships to research issues essential to our security.

Continued

BioWatch/BioShield

An environmental monitoring system, BioWatch, monitors air samples on a frequent basis in major urban cities nationwide, providing early warning of a potential bio attack that would allow treatment before people get sick. Homeland security is also deploying and evaluating mobile automatic air-testing kits that house biological and chemical sensors for even quicker reporting. This program links the earliest detection possible with efforts to develop medical countermeasures and a program called BioShield that ensures vaccines, drugs, and medical supplies are ready for rapid distribution.

Integrated Planning

The Department of Homeland Security has led the development of the National Response Plan (NRP), which consolidates and reconciles multiple national-level incident response plans into a single, focused, universally understood strategy.

CRITICAL THINKING:

In what ways has homeland security been successful? In what ways has it failed?

PERSPECTIVES ON HOMELAND SECURITY

Donald Kettl (2004: 7), a political scientist, offers interesting perspectives on homeland security. He writes that the words "homeland security" disturbed some Americans who claimed it sounded like it was derived from Hitler's Third Reich. Historically, "homeland" was used by Zionists working to establish a Jewish homeland in Palestine. Fascists in Germany and Austria used the term to refer to "homeland defense." The term "homeland security" caught on in the United States prior to 9/11 as conservatives and think tanks explored preparing the nation for the possibility of terrorist attacks. (The "civil defense" connection to homeland security is explored in Chapter 7.)

Kettl (2004: 28) notes that we can spend enormous sums of money and still a smart terrorist may find a crack in security as an avenue for attack. At the same time, well-planned security can frustrate many terrorist plots. A key defensive strategy is *strong coordination* among the many players involved in prevention and response.

Kettl (2004: 82) also writes that the more time goes by without an attack, the greater the pressure to reduce investments in homeland security and shift spending to other needs and the greater the complaints to reduce inconvenience and increase civil liberties and civil rights. Such backsliding could increase the risk of attack.

Harlan Ullman (2003), an international studies expert, justifies the need for a DHS that coordinates efforts among many agencies of government by comparing it to the era of the National Security Act of 1947, during the Cold War. Remnants of this act are still with us today. Ullman writes:

> The old structure is *vertical*, with responsibilities neatly divided among diplomacy (State Department), military force (Defense Department), intelligence (CIA), and other agencies. This was fine when there was a seemingly monolithic, single threat such as the Soviet Union. Today, the dangers of terror and extremism are *horizontal*, cutting across many government agencies and branches.

For example, law enforcement and intelligence must work closer together to improve results in the war against terrorism. Consular services, which grant visas to foreign nationals, are as much a part of the first line of defense as are U.S. forces stationed overseas. These are the realities of today.

Crank and Gregor (2005: 103–136) offer a criminal justice perspective and see the DHS in a state of continual development influenced by politics and practical concerns in the face of terrorism. They note that the form and function of the DHS will change following another significant attack, and they link counterterrorism laws with crime-fighting efforts.

Crank and Gregor also write of the military component of domestic security. They refer to Northern Command. Its purpose is to defend North America, but the controversy is whether such activity violates the Posee Comitatus Act of 1878, which prohibits military intervention in domestic civil affairs. The act ended the use of federal troops to oversee elections in the former Confederacy and it ended military law enforcement duties in the West. Although exceptions to the act have been enacted (e.g., National Guard under state authority or federalized under the president; drug war duties), issues include limited training of the military on citizen rights and domestic security missions.

CRITICAL THINKING:
What are your perspectives on homeland security?

ACCOUNTABILITY AND EVALUATION OF NATIONAL STRATEGIES AGAINST TERRORISM

Citizens and government leaders expect efficiency and effectiveness from the efforts of government agencies and programs. The National Commission on Terrorist Attacks Upon the United States (2004b) concluded that the failure of government agencies to prevent the 9/11 attacks resulted from problems of accountability, responsibility, and coordination. The commission emphasized the need for measures of performance to gauge the success of strategies against terrorism. Many questions can be formulated from the conclusions of the commission. Examples are as follow. *What is homeland security? Who is to be accountable for homeland security? What is successful homeland security? How do we measure the success of homeland security?* Answers to these questions are difficult to resolve. Also, it is important to note that many government departments and agencies (e.g., DHS, DOD, CIA, and FBI) are involved in homeland security, and questions of accountability and success should focus on all government bodies receiving funding and implementing programs of counterterrorism and all-hazard response.

Prior to the 9/11 attacks, government efforts against terrorism were highly fragmented and decentralized. There was no centralized coordination point from which to direct a homeland security strategy. Many agencies countered terrorism, and priorities and objectives differed and cooperation and sharing information was inefficient. Now the United States has a DHS and several national strategies to combat terrorism. Still, questions and problems persist. Was the DHS implemented too quickly because of political pressure to respond to the 9/11 attacks? Are government agencies doing a better job of cooperating and sharing information? What can be done to improve the efficiency and effectiveness of the DHS, other departments and agencies involved in homeland security, and national strategies against terrorism? These difficult questions and others will be the subject of debate and publications for many years.

The **Government Accountability Office** (GAO), formerly named the General Accounting Office, is one source of evaluation for national strategies against terrorism. The GAO works for Congress to study programs and expenditures of the federal government. It is independent, nonpartisan, and often referred to as "Congress's watchdog." In addition to evaluating federal programs, the GAO conducts federal government audits, issues legal opinions, and makes recommendations. Its work leads to new laws, government improvements, and savings of tax dollars.

A General Accounting Office (2004a) report entitled *Combating Terrorism: Evaluation of Selected Characteristics in National Strategies Related to Terrorism* was released on February 3, 2004.

It identified and defined six desirable characteristics of an effective national terrorism and homeland security strategy and evaluated whether national strategies addressed those characteristics. The characteristics are as follow.

1. Purpose, scope, and methodology: addresses why the strategy was produced, the scope of coverage, the process by which it was developed, mission areas, and principles or theories guiding its development.
2. Problem definition and risk management: pinpoints the problems the strategy addresses, their causes, and operating environment. It also entails threats, vulnerabilities, and how to manage risks.
3. Goals, subordinate objectives, activities, and performance measures: includes the steps to produce results, priorities, and performance measures to gauge results.
4. Resources, investments, and risk management: covers costs, resources and investments, and where they will be targeted. Additionally, mechanisms are used to allocate resources, such as grants and loans. Guidance on managing resources is important for implementing parties.
5. Organizational roles, responsibilities, and coordination: this characteristic focuses on which groups will implement the strategy, their activities, coordinating efforts, and who is in charge prior to, during, and following a crisis.
6. Integration and implementation: addresses how national strategy relates to other national strategies and various levels of government.

The GAO identified the aforementioned characteristics by consulting statutory requirements of the strategies, as well as reviewing legislative and executive branch guidance for other national strategies. Also, the GAO studied the Government Performance and Results Act of 1993, which requires federal agencies to prepare a strategic plan and performance measures; guidance from the office of management and budget; recommendations of national commissions; and other sources.

National strategies are not required by executive or legislative mandate to address a consistent set of characteristics. The GAO found no commonly accepted set of characteristics.

The GAO listed the following national strategies that relate to combating terrorism and homeland security, in part or in whole.

- National Security Strategy of the United States of America (NSSUS)
- National Strategy for Homeland Security (NSHS)
- National Strategy for Combating Terrorism (NSCT)
- National Strategy to Combat Weapons of Mass Destruction (NSCWMD)
- National Strategy for the Physical Protection of Critical Infrastructure and Key Assets (NSPPCIKA)
- National Strategy to Secure Cyberspace (NSSC)
- 2002 National Money Laundering Strategy (NMLS)

Earlier in the chapter, a box listed several national strategies (several of which were just listed) and the dominance of the NSSUS and the NSHS. The GAO reported separately on the classified national military strategic plan for the war on terrorism.

The GAO found considerable variation in the way in which the seven national strategies address the desirable characteristics. Most of the strategies partially addressed the six characteristics. None of the strategies addressed all of the elements of resources, investments, and risk management or integration and implementation. The GAO noted that improvements could be made. While the strategies identify goals, subordinate objectives, and specific activities, weaknesses included establishing priorities, milestones, and performance measures—elements important for evaluating progress and ensuring effective oversight. On the whole, the NSHS and the NSPPCIKA addressed the greatest number of characteristics, whereas the NSSUS and the NSCWMD addressed the fewest.

Figure 4-7 ■ Hierarchy of national strategies for combating terrorism and improving homeland security. Source: General Accounting Office (2004a: 8). www.gao.gov/new.items/d04408t.pdf

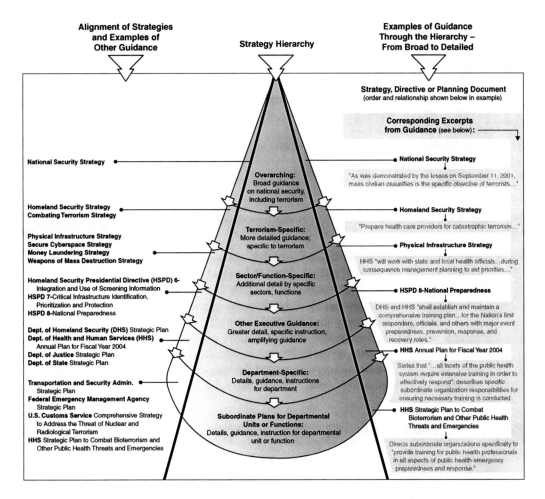

The GAO found that the strategies are organized in a rough hierarchy (Figure 4-7), with the NSSUS providing an overarching strategy for national security as a whole. The other strategies provide more detail. Executive branch guidance is further provided through executive orders and directives that elaborate on the national strategies. Further down the hierarchy are agency-specific strategic and performance plans and other details and guidance to implementing parties.

Following the GAO report, the GAO began a series of reports to assess and baseline the progress and effectiveness of federal agency efforts to improve HS mission performance. One related General Accounting Office (2004b) report is entitled *Status of Key Recommendations GAO Has Made to DHS and Its Legacy Agencies*. This report responded to the request by Congress to ascertain the status of key recommendations the GAO made to the DHS and its legacy agencies (i.e., merged into the DHS), time frames for implementation, and challenges the DHS faces. The GAO reviewed 325 recommendations in unclassified reports issued to the DHS and its 22 legacy agencies. The GAO consulted with subject matter experts who made the recommendations to prioritize them according to the greatest risk. One hundred and four key recommendations were identified and GAO personnel met with DHS personnel to obtain documents on actions taken, time frames, and challenges. As of June 28, 2004, the DHS implemented 40 of the 104 recommendations and 63 were being addressed by the DHS. The GAO closed 1 recommendation due to the closing of one legacy agency. As examples, the 27 recommendations fully implemented by the DHS's BTS directorate have resulted in a reduction in weaknesses and inefficiencies of the land ports of entry inspection process. The BTS has also benefited with more timely and accurate information on the smuggling of aliens and the legal status of immigrants. In the EPR directorate, the implementation of 3 of 6 key recommendations has resulted in improved emergency response and planning.

CRITICAL THINKING:

Do you think the GAO serves a useful purpose or does it meddle in the important affairs of government agencies?

DISCUSSION QUESTIONS

1. How would you define homeland security? Do you think the federal government has clearly defined the concept and mission of homeland security? Explain your answers.
2. What are your views of the reorganization of the Department of Homeland Security?
3. What are the roles of state and local governments in homeland security?
4. What is the national strategy for homeland security?
5. What is the relationship between national security and homeland security?
6. How can the effectiveness of the intelligence community be improved?
7. What are your views on countering terrorist financing?
8. What are your views on evaluating national strategies against terrorism?

APPLICATIONS

4A YOU BE THE SECRETARY OF HOMELAND SECURITY

As secretary of homeland security you are given the authority with other major federal agencies to coordinate a response to the following crisis: The FBI has positively confirmed the presence of a cell of terrorists preparing multiple RDDs ("dirty bombs") in a warehouse in Chicago. The terrorists are planning to detonate the bombs in Chicago in 3 days. What can you do to protect the citizens of Chicago? How will you integrate your plans with law enforcement authorities, and possibly the military? Who should be informed of the crisis? Should the public be informed? Why or why not? Should part of the city be evacuated? Why or why not? Explain your answers and the justification supporting each.

4B YOU BE THE HEAD OF A FEDERAL LAW ENFORCEMENT TASK FORCE

Refer back to your work in Application 2D, "You Be the Terrorist Planner." As head of a federal law enforcement task force, you have this terrorist plan in your hands, collected from human and electronic intelligence. The attack date is 4 months away. You inform your superior and the DHS is notified. What are your short-term and long-term plans to capitalize on this intelligence bonanza?

4C YOU BE THE GAO MANAGING DIRECTOR

You are a managing director in the GAO who is leading a team evaluating the present state of the NSHS. The foundation for the evaluation will be the six desirable characteristics of an effective national terrorism and homeland security strategy. You will be meeting with your staff next week to begin the evaluation. Right now you want general, preliminary information on the NSHS so you conduct Web research and compare what you find to the desirable characteristics. What parts of the desirable characteristics do you find in the NSHS? What are your preliminary findings and conclusions?

4D   YOU BE THE TERRORIST FUNDRAISER

As a global traveling salesperson who was raised in the Middle East, you have a strong hate for the United States, Israel, Christianity, and Western values. With links to a terrorist group, you are charged with raising funds for the group. At the same time, you prefer to avoid leaving a paper or electronic trail through financial institutions. What are your innovative plans and methods to make money, and how will you get the money into the hands of the terrorists?

WEB SITES

Central Intelligence Agency: www.odci.gov
Federal Bureau of Investigation: www.fbi.gov
Federal Emergency Management Agency: www.fema.gov
Government Accountability Office: www.gao.gov
International Policy Institute for Counterterrorism: www.ict.org.il/
National Counterintelligence Center: www.nacic.gov
National League of Cities: www.nlc.org
United Kingdom Security Service (MI5): www.mi5.gov.uk
U.S. Conference of Mayors: www.usmayors.org
U.S. Department of Homeland Security: www.dhs.gov

NOTES

Advisory Panel to Assess Domestic Response Capabilities for Terrorism Involving Weapons of Mass Destruction (2003). *Forging America's New Normalcy: Securing Our Homeland, Preserving Our Liberty*, www.rand.org, retrieved March 5, 2004.

Bannon, A. (2004). "Color-coding—or just color-confusing?" *Homeland Protection Professional*, 3 (September).

Beaulieu, E. (2004). "Finding a needle in a haystack: Banks harness software to detect money laundering, terrorist financing." *Security Director News*, 1 (November).

Brookings Institution (2003). "Protecting the American Homeland: One Year On." Washington, DC. January.

Bullock, J., *et al.* (2005). *Introduction to Homeland Security*. Boston, MA: Elsevier.

Carafano, J., and Heyman, D. (2004). *DHS 2.0: Rethinking the Department of Homeland Security*. Washington, DC: The Heritage Foundation.

Center for Defense Information (2002). "CDI Fact Sheet: Anti-Terrorist Finance Measures." www.cdi.org/terrorism/finance.cfm, retrieved October 25, 2004.

Chairman of the Joint Chiefs of Staff, DOD (2006). *National Military Strategy for Combating Weapons of Mass Destruction*. (February 13). www.defenselink.mil/pdf/NMS-CWMD2006.pdf, retrieved March 28, 2006.

Council on Foreign Relations (2004a). "Department of Homeland Security." www.terrorismanswers.org, retrieved October 6, 2004.

Council on Foreign Relations (2004b). "The Money: Drying Up the Funds for Terror." www.terrorismanswers.org, retrieved October 6, 2004.

Crank, J., and Gregor, P. (2005). *Counter-Terrorism After 9/11: Justice, Security and Ethics Reconsidered*. Cincinnati, OH: Anderson Pub.

Drees, C. (2004). "US Struggles to Understand Al Qaida Finances." http://abcnews.go.com, retrieved October 1, 2004.

FBI (2004). "Headline Archives, Consider a Career as an FBI Financial Analyst?" October 15. www.fbi.gov, retrieved November 4, 2004.

General Accounting Office (2004a). *Combating Terrorism: Evaluation of Selected Characteristics in National Strategies Related to Terrorism*. www.gao.gov, retrieved October 28, 2004.

General Accounting Office (2004b). *Status of Key Recommendations GAO Has Made to DHS and Its Legacy Agencies*. www.gao.gov, retrieved October 28, 2004.

Hoge, W. (2004). "UN Seeks Tighter Sanctions as Qaeda Skirts Money Controls." www.nytimes.com, retrieved August 31, 2004.

Kettl, D. (2004). *System Under Stress: Homeland Security and American Politics*. Washington, DC: CQ Press.

Larson, E., and Peters, J. (2001). *Preparing the US Army for Homeland Security: Concepts, Issues, and Options*. Santa Monica, CA: RAND. In Kettl, D. (2004). *System Under Stress: Homeland Security and American Politics*.

Lim, F. (2004). "Internal auditors can play vital role to stop terror financing: FBI." www.channelnewsasia.com, retrieved November 23, 2004.

Logan, C. (2004). "Politics and Promises." *CQ/Governing* (October).

Lowenthal, M. (2003). *Intelligence: From Secrets to Policy*, 2nd ed. Washington, DC: CQ Press.

Miles, D. (2006). "Report Provides Strategic Vision for Countering WMD" (March 24). www.defenselink.mil/news/mar2006/20060324_4592.html, retrieved March 28, 2006.

National Commission on Terrorist Attacks Upon the United States (2004a). *Monograph on Terrorist Financing*. www.9-11commission.gov, retrieved August 25, 2004.

National Commission on Terrorist Attacks Upon the United States (2004b). *The 9/11 Commission Report*. www.9-11commission.gov, retrieved July 26, 2004.

Office of Homeland Security (2002). *National Strategy for Homeland Security*. Washington, DC: The White House (July).

Office of Inspector General (2004a). *FY 2003 Mission Performance United States Coast Guard*. Washington, DC: DHS (September).

Office of Inspector General (2004b). *Transportation Security Administration Review of the TSA Passenger and Baggage Screening Pilot Program*. Washington, DC: DHS (September).

Poland, J. (2005). *Understanding Terrorism: Groups, Strategies, and Responses*. Englewood Cliffs, NJ: Prentice Hall.

Shultz, R., and Vogt, A. (2003). "It's War! Fighting Post-11 September Global Terrorism through a Doctrine of Preemption." *Terrorism and Political Violence*, 15 (Spring).

Sostek, A. (2003). "Orange Crush." *Governing*, 16 (August).

Ullman, H. (2003). "Defusing Danger to US Security." *The World & I* (January).

U.S. Department of Defense (2005). *Strategy for Homeland Defense and Civil Support* (June). www.defenselink.nil/news/jun2005/d20050630homeland.pdf, retrieved July 12, 2005.

U.S. Department of Homeland Security (2004a). *Fact Sheet: An Overview of America's Security Since 9/11* (September 7). www.dhs.gov, retrieved September 9, 2004.

U.S. Department of Homeland Security (2004b). *Securing Our Homeland: US Department of Homeland Security Strategic Plan*. www.dhs.gov, retrieved October 1, 2004.

U.S. Department of Homeland Security (2005). "Homeland Security Secretary Michael Chertoff Announces Six-Point Agenda for Department of Homeland Security" (July 13 press release). www.dhs.gov, retrieved July 15, 2005.

U.S. Department of Homeland Security (2006). *Fact Sheet: U.S. Department of Homeland Security Announces Six Percent Increase in Fiscal Year 2007 Budget Request* (February 6). www.dhs.gov, retrieved February 8, 2006.

LEGAL ISSUES

OBJECTIVES

The study of this chapter will enable you to:
1. Describe the pendulums of justice.
2. List and detail constitutional rights.
3. Discuss the controversy and legal action among the three branches of the federal government as legal guidelines are developed for government investigations.
4. Discuss the debate over the rights of noncitizens.
5. Differentiate "racial profiling" and "legal profiling."
6. Explain the role of civilian courts in the processing of suspected terrorists.
7. Define and explain the terms "enemy combatants" and "military tribunals" and summarize relevant court decisions.

KEY TERMS

crime control model
due process model
criminal justice system
consensus model
conflict model
exclusionary rule
reasonable suspicion
probable cause
criminal justice versus victim justice models
victimology
posttraumatic stress
Stockholm syndrome
homeland security and national security model
writ of habeas corpus
closed-circuit television
unmanned aerial vehicles
radio frequency identification

data mining
Omnibus Crime Control and Safe Streets Act of 1968
Foreign Intelligence Surveillance Act
roving wiretaps
delayed notice
sneak-and-peak
National Security Letter
American Civil Liberties Union
attorney–client privilege
racial profiling
legal profiling
Geneva conventions
enemy combatant
military tribunal
court-martial

THE 9/11 COMMISSION REPORT

The following excerpts from the *9/11 Commission Report* (National Commission on Terrorist Attacks Upon the United States, 2004) illustrate characteristics of terrorist conspirators, such as long-term relationships with each other, similar religious and cultural views, strong hate for U.S. foreign policies, global reach, secrecy, technical skills, creativity, and long-term and patient planning. Consequently, law enforcement and military investigations and intelligence gathering of terrorists are very challenging. Penetrations of such groups through undercover investigations are extremely difficult and dangerous. In addition to other nations, the U.S government has emphasized the need for extraordinary investigative and confinement methods to control terrorism, as illustrated through the issues covered in this chapter.

Khalid Sheikh Mohammed

No one exemplifies the model of the terrorist entrepreneur more clearly than Khalid Sheikh Mohammed (KSM) (Figure 5-1), *the principal architect of the 9/11 attacks.* KSM followed a rather tortuous path to his eventual membership in al-Qaida. Highly educated and equally comfortable in a government office or a terrorist safehouse, KSM applied his imagination, technical aptitude, and managerial skills to hatching and planning an extraordinary array of terrorist schemes. These ideas included conventional car bombing, political assassination, aircraft bombing, hijacking, reservoir poisoning, and, ultimately, the use of aircraft as missiles guided by suicide operatives.

Like his nephew Ramzi Yousef (3 years KSM's junior), KSM grew up in Kuwait but traces his ethnic lineage to the Baluchistan region straddling Iran and Pakistan. Raised in a religious family, KSM claims to have joined the Muslim brotherhood at age 16 and to have become enamored of violent jihad at youth camps in the desert. In 1983, following his graduation from secondary school, KSM left Kuwait to enroll at Chowan College, a small Baptist school in Murfreesboro, North Carolina. After a semester at Chowan, KSM transferred to North Carolina Agricultural and Technical State University in Greensboro, which he attended with Yousef's brother, another future al-Qaida member. KSM earned a degree in mechanical engineering in December 1986.

Although he apparently did not attract attention for extreme Islamist beliefs or activities while in the United States, KSM plunged into the anti-Soviet Afghan jihad soon after graduating from college. Visiting Pakistan for the first time in early 1987, he traveled to Peshawar, where his brother Zahid introduced him to the famous Afghan *mujahid* Abdul Rasul Sayyaf, head of the Hizbul-Ittihad

Figure 5-1 ■ Khalid Sheikh Mohammed, mastermind of the 9/11 plot, at the time of his capture in 2003. Source: National Commission on Terrorist Attacks Upon the United States (2004).

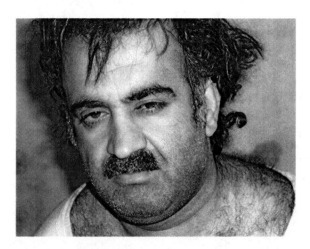

THE 9/11 COMMISSION REPORT—Cont'd

El-Islami (Islamic Union Party). Sayyaf became KSM's mentor and provided KSM with military training at Sayyaf's Sada camp. KSM claims he then fought the Soviets and remained at the front for 3 months before being summoned to perform administrative duties for Abdullah Azzam. KSM next took a job working for an electronics firm that catered to the communications needs of Afghan groups, where he learned about drills used to excavate caves in Afghanistan. Between 1988 and 1992, KSM helped run a nongovernmental organization.

Detainee Interrogation Reports

Chapters 5 and 7 (National Commission on Terrorist Attacks Upon the United States, 2004) rely heavily on information obtained from captured al-Qaida members. A number of these "detainees" have firsthand knowledge of the 9/11 plot. Assessing the truth of statements by these witnesses—sworn enemies of the United States—is challenging. Our access to them has been limited to the review of intelligence reports based on communications received from the locations where the actual interrogations took place. We submitted questions for use in the interrogations, but had no control over whether, when, or how questions of particular interest would be asked. Nor were we allowed to talk to the interrogators so that we could better judge the credibility of the detainees and clarify ambiguities in the reporting. We were told that our requests might disrupt the sensitive interrogation process.

We have nonetheless decided to include information from captured 9/11 conspirators and al-Qaida members in our report. We have evaluated their statements carefully and have attempted to corroborate them with documents and statements of others. In this report, we indicate where such statements provide the foundation for our narrative. We have been authorized to identify by name only 10 detainees whose custody has been confirmed officially by the U.S. government.

In 1992, KSM spent some time fighting alongside the mujahideen in Bosnia and supporting that effort with financial donations. After returning briefly to Pakistan, he moved his family to Qatar at the suggestion of the former minister of Islamic affairs of Qatar, Sheikh Abdallah bin Khalid bin Hamad al Thani. KSM took a position in Qatar as project engineer with the Qatari ministry of electricity and water. Although he engaged in extensive international travel during his tenure at the ministry, much of it in furtherance of terrorist activity, KSM would hold his position there until early 1996, when he fled to Pakistan to avoid capture by U.S. authorities.

KSM first came to the attention of U.S. law enforcement as a result of his cameo role in the first World Trade Center bombing. According to KSM, he learned of Ramzi Yousef's intention to launch an attack inside the United States in 1991 or 1992, when Yousef was receiving explosives training in Afghanistan. During the fall of 1992, while Yousef was building the bomb he would use in that attack, KSM and Yousef had numerous telephone conversations during which Yousef discussed his progress and sought additional funding. On November 3, 1992, KSM wired $660 from Qatar to the bank account of Yousef's coconspirator, Mohammed Salameh. KSM does not appear to have contributed any more substantially to this operation.

Yousef's instant notoriety as the mastermind of the 1993 World Trade Center bombing inspired KSM to become involved in planning attacks against the United States. By his own account, KSM's animus toward the United States evolved, not from his experiences in the United States as a student, but rather from his violent disagreement with U.S. foreign policy favoring Israel. In 1994, KSM accompanied Yousef to the Philippines, and the two of them began planning what is now known as the Manila air or "Bojinka" plot—the intended bombing of 12 U.S. commercial jumbo jets over the Pacific during a 2-day span. This marked the first time KSM took part in the actual planning of a terrorist operation. While sharing an apartment in Manila during the summer of 1994, he and Yousef acquired chemicals and other materials necessary to construct bombs and timers. They also cased target flights to Hong Kong and Seoul that would have onward legs to the United States. During this same period, KSM and Yousef also developed plans to assassinate President Clinton during his November 1994 trip to Manila and to bomb U.S.-bound cargo carriers by smuggling jackets containing nitrocellulose on board.

Continued

THE 9/11 COMMISSION REPORT—Cont'd

KSM left the Philippines in September 1994 and met up with Yousef in Karachi following their casing flights. There they enlisted Wali Khan Amin Shah, also known as Usama Asmurai, in the Manila air plot. During the fall of 1994, Yousef returned to Manila and successfully tested the digital watch timer he had invented, bombing a movie theater and a Philippine Airlines flight en route to Tokyo. The plot unraveled after the Philippine authorities discovered Yousef's bomb-making operation in Manila; but by that time, KSM was safely back at his government job in Qatar. Yousef attempted to follow through on the cargo carriers plan, but he was arrested in Islamabad by Pakistani authorities on February 7, 1995, after an accomplice turned him in.

KSM continued to travel among the worldwide jihadist community after Yousef's arrest, visiting Sudan, Yemen, Malaysia, and Brazil in 1995. No clear evidence connected him to terrorist activities in those locations. While in Sudan, he reportedly failed in his attempt to meet with bin Ladin. However, KSM did see Atef, who gave him a contact in Brazil. In January 1996, well aware that U.S. authorities were chasing him, he left Qatar for good and fled to Afghanistan, where he renewed his relationship with Rasul Sayyaf. Just as KSM was reestablishing himself in Afghanistan in mid-1996, bin Ladin and his colleagues were also completing their migration from Sudan. Through Atef, KSM arranged a meeting with bin Ladin in Tora Bora, a mountainous redoubt from the Afghan war days. At the meeting, KSM presented the al-Qaida leader with a menu of ideas for terrorist operations. According to KSM, this meeting was the first time he had seen bin Ladin since 1989. Although they had fought together in 1987, bin Ladin and KSM did not yet enjoy an especially close working relationship. Indeed, KSM has acknowledged that bin Ladin likely agreed to meet with him because of the renown of his nephew, Yousef.

At the meeting, KSM briefed bin Ladin and Atef on the first World Trade Center bombing, the Manila air plot, the cargo carriers plan, and other activities pursued by KSM and his colleagues in the Philippines. KSM also presented a proposal for an operation that would involve training pilots who would crash planes into buildings in the United States. This proposal eventually would become the 9/11 operation.

KSM knew that the successful staging of such an attack would require personnel, money, and logistical support that only an extensive and well-funded organization like al-Qaida could provide. He thought the operation might appeal to bin Ladin, who had a long record of denouncing the United States. From KSM's perspective, bin Ladin was in the process of consolidating his new position in Afghanistan while hearing out others' ideas, and had not yet settled on an agenda for future anti-U.S. operations. At the meeting, bin Ladin listened to KSM's ideas without much comment, but did ask KSM formally to join al-Qaida and move his family to Afghanistan. KSM declined. He preferred to remain independent and retain the option of working with other mujahideen groups still operating in Afghanistan, including the group led by his old mentor, Sayyaf. Sayyaf was close to Ahmed Shah Massoud, the leader of the northern alliance. Therefore working with him might be a problem for KSM because bin Ladin was building ties to the rival Taliban.

After meeting with bin Ladin, KSM says he journeyed onward to India, Indonesia, and Malaysia, where he met with Jemaah Islamiah's Hambali. Hambali was an Indonesian veteran of the Afghan war looking to expand the jihad into southeast Asia. In Iran, KSM rejoined his family and arranged to move them to Karachi; he claims to have relocated by January 1997.

After settling his family in Karachi, KSM tried to join the mujahid leader Ibn al Khattab in Chechnya. Unable to travel through Azerbaijan, KSM returned to Karachi and then to Afghanistan to renew contacts with bin Ladin and his colleagues. Although KSM may not have been a member of al-Qaida at this time, he admits traveling frequently between Pakistan and Afghanistan in 1997 and the first half of 1998, visiting bin Ladin and cultivating relationships with his lieutenants, Atef and Sayf al Adl, by assisting them with computer and media projects.

According to KSM, the 1998 bombings of the U.S. embassies in Nairobi and Dar es Salaam marked a watershed in the evolution of the 9/11 plot. KSM claimed these bombings convinced him that bin Ladin was truly committed to attacking the United States. He continued to make himself useful,

THE 9/11 COMMISSION REPORT—Cont'd

collecting news articles and helping other al-Qaida members with their outdated computer equipment. Bin Ladin, apparently at Atef's urging, finally decided to give KSM the green light for the 9/11 operation sometime in late 1988 or early 1999.

Al-Qaida Aims at the American Homeland

KSM accepted bin Ladin's standing invitation to move to Kandahar and work directly with al-Qaida. In addition to supervising the planning and preparations for the 9/11 operation, KSM worked with and eventually led al-Qaida's media committee. However, KSM states he refused to swear a formal oath of allegiance to bin Ladin, thereby retaining a last vestige of his cherished autonomy.

At this point, late 1998 to early 1999, planning for the 9/11 operation began in earnest. Yet while the 9/11 project occupied the bulk of KSM's attention, he continued to consider other possibilities for terrorist attacks. For example, he sent al-Qaida operative Issa al Britani to Kuala Lumpur, Malaysia, to learn about the jihad in southeast Asia from Hambali. Thereafter, KSM claims, at bin Ladin's direction in early 2001, he sent Britani to the United States to case potential economic and "Jewish" targets in New York City. Furthermore, during the summer of 2001, KSM approached bin Ladin with the idea of recruiting a Saudi Arabian air force pilot to commandeer a Saudi fighter jet and attack the Israeli city of Eilat. Bin Ladin reportedly liked this proposal, but he instructed KSM to concentrate on the 9/11 operation first. Similarly, KSM's proposals to Atef around this same time for attacks in Thailand, Singapore, Indonesia, and the Maldives were never executed, although Hambali's Jemaah Islamiah operatives did some casing of possible targets.

KSM appears to have been popular among the al-Qaida rank and file. He was reportedly regarded as an effective leader, especially after the 9/11 attacks. Co-workers describe him as an intelligent, efficient, and even-tempered manager who approached his projects with a single-minded dedication that he expected his colleagues to share. Al-Qaida associate Abu Zubaydah has expressed more qualified admiration for KSM's innate creativity, emphasizing instead his ability to incorporate the improvements suggested by others. Nashiri has been similarly measured, observing that although KSM floated many general ideas for attacks, he rarely conceived a specific operation himself. Perhaps these estimates reflect a touch of jealousy; in any case, KSM was plainly a capable coordinator, having had years to hone his skills and build relationships.

INTRODUCTION

The problem of terrorism and the strategies to counter it result in a variety of legal issues. We begin with the basic concept of balancing "crime control and due process" to help us to understand the concept of balancing "homeland security and national security with due process." Knowledge of this "balancing process" provides a foundation for subsequent topics, namely legislation and court decisions that guide government investigations, rights of citizens and noncitizens, profiling, civilian courts, enemy combatants, and military justice.

The topics of this chapter are controversial and they have become both national and international issues. At the same time, America has been under a great strain since the 9/11 attacks as it recovers, responds, and seeks to protect itself under the U.S. Constitution.

THE PENDULUMS OF JUSTICE

CRIME CONTROL VERSUS DUE PROCESS MODELS

One perspective for understanding justice is to view it as a multitude of pendulums, each over a separate continuum containing opposite ends. A pendulum moves along its continuum depending on factors such as court decisions, legislation, executive orders, public opinion, politics, and the media.

Figure 5-2 ■ Crime control versus due process.

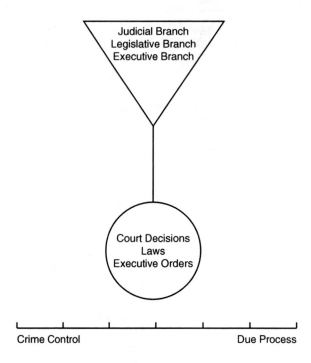

The well-known crime control versus due process models serve as an example (**Figure 5-2**). Herbert Packer (1968) characterizes the **crime control model** by swift and efficient justice, whereas the **due process model** slows the administration of justice because of constitutional and procedural safeguards that protect defendants.

Crime control is maintained within our society through a **criminal justice system** of police, courts, and corrections agencies, that when viewed as operating harmoniously, have been referred to as the **consensus model**. However, some would argue that the criminal justice system is actually a nonsystem of criminal justice (American Bar Association, 1972). Also named the **conflict model**, these agencies do not always cooperate, coordinate, and share information. Friction may develop among agencies over power, politics, jurisdiction, workload, funding, and accountability. Cultural differences among agencies, petty jealousies, and mutual distrust add to the conflict. Criminal justice agencies that fall within the conflict model are not optimizing tax dollars and are less efficient and effective. A famous example of the conflict model is the infamous Charles Manson murders, in 1969, when the Los Angeles Police Department and the Los Angeles Sheriff's Department took one-and-a half years to make arrests because information was not shared. This type of problem persists today. (We can draw an analogy to the intelligence community that has characteristics of the conflict model. This was the case prior to the 9/11 attacks, and the problems persist today even though efforts are continuing to correct problems of cooperation and sharing intelligence information.)

Even though police agencies may have characteristics of the conflict model, they protect society by maintaining order, enforcing laws, and pursuing offenders. When arrests occur, arrestees are processed through courts and corrections agencies. At the same time, actions against citizens by the criminal justice system and its practitioners are controlled by the Bill of Rights of the U.S. Constitution. In other words, the Bill of Rights protects citizens against government police powers. Amendments of the Bill of Rights relevant to criminal justice and homeland security are listed next.

FIRST AMENDMENT

"Congress shall make no law respecting an establishment of religion, or prohibiting the free exercise thereof; or abridging the freedom of speech, or of the press; or the right of the people peaceably to assemble, and to petition the government for a redress of grievances."

SECOND AMENDMENT

"A well-regulated militia being necessary to the security of a free state, the right of the people to keep and bear arms, shall not be infringed."

FOURTH AMENDMENT

"The right of the people to be secure in their persons, houses, papers, and effects, against unreasonable searches and seizures, shall not be violated, and no warrants shall issue, but upon probable cause, supported by oath or affirmation, and particularly describing the place to be searched, and the persons or things to be seized."

FIFTH AMENDMENT

"No person shall be held to answer for a capital, or otherwise infamous crime, unless on a presentment or indictment of a grand jury, except in cases arising in the land or naval forces, or in the militia, when in actual service in time of war or public danger; nor shall any person be subject for the same offense to be twice put in jeopardy of life or limb; nor shall be compelled in any criminal case to be a witness against himself, nor be deprived of life, liberty, or property, without due process of law; nor shall private property be taken for public use, without just compensation."

SIXTH AMENDMENT

"In all criminal prosecutions, the accused shall enjoy the right to a speedy and public trail, by an impartial jury of the state and district wherein the crime shall have been committed, which district shall have been previously ascertained by law, and to be informed of the nature and cause of the accusation; to be confronted with the witness against him; to have compulsory process for obtaining witnesses in his favor, and to have the assistance of counsel for his defense."

EIGHTH AMENDMENT

" Excessive bail shall not be required, nor excessive fines imposed, nor cruel and unusual punishment inflicted."

FOURTEENTH AMENDMENT

Section 1. "All persons born or naturalized in the United States, and subject to the jurisdiction thereof, are citizens of the United States and the state wherein they reside. No state shall make or enforce any law which shall abridge the privileges or immunities of citizens of the United States; nor shall any state deprive any person of life, liberty, or property, without due process of law; nor deny to any person within its jurisdiction the equal protection of the laws."

Let us examine three landmark U.S. Supreme Court cases to illustrate the pendulum swings involving the crime control versus due process models. Then, with this foundation, we can shift to the homeland security and national security versus due process models.

Mapp v. Ohio, 367 US 643, 644 (1961): In 1957, Mrs. Dollree Mapp refused to let police into her home to search for gambling paraphernalia and a suspect in a recent bombing. As police forced their way into her home, she demanded a search warrant. An officer held up a piece of paper, supposedly a valid search warrant, and Mapp grabbed it and placed it in her bra. Police retrieved the paper and handcuffed Mapp. The only evidence found was pornographic material. Mapp was arrested, jailed, and subsequently convicted in an Ohio court for possession of pornography. No search warrant was produced at trial. When the case finally reached the U.S. Supreme Court, it called into question the legality of the arrest, search, and seizure, and the actions of the police. The court's decision restricted state and local police by ruling that the exclusionary rule applies to all courts, besides federal courts. The **exclusionary rule** prohibits law enforcement officers from using illegally seized evidence at a criminal trial. Although police and prosecutors were outraged over the U.S. Supreme Court's decision, claiming that they would be hindered in controlling crime, the Mapp decision actually increased the professionalism of police and prosecutors as they adhered to the fourth amendment, rather than violating citizen rights.

Miranda v. Arizona, 384 US 436 (1966): Ernesto Miranda was arrested by Phoenix, Arizona, police for kidnapping and rape. He was then interrogated for 2 hours by detectives without being advised of his right to counsel. Miranda signed a confession and was subsequently convicted. When the case reached the U.S. Supreme Court, its decision emphasized suspect rights and ruled that the fifth amendment privilege against self-incrimination requires police to inform *suspects in custody* of their constitutional rights *prior to questioning*. Otherwise, evidence provided by the suspect will not be admissible in court. Miranda rights are not required if a suspect is not in custody. If a suspect is in custody, Miranda rights are required only if police are about to question the suspect.

MIRANDA WARNINGS

1. You have the right to remain silent.
2. If you give up the right to remain silent, anything you say can and will be used against you in a court of law.
3. You have the right to speak with an attorney and to have the attorney present during questioning.
4. If you so desire and cannot afford one, an attorney will be appointed for you without charge before questioning.

Waiver

1. Do you understand each of these rights I have read to you?
2. Having these rights in mind, do you wish to give up your rights as I have explained them to you and talk to me now?

Terry v. Ohio, 393 US 1 (1968): In 1963, a Cleveland, Ohio, police detective standing across the street from a liquor store observed three men who appeared to be "casing" the store. The detective confronted the men and identified himself as a police officer. He frisked the men and found .38 caliber revolvers on two of them. Both men were arrested and charged with carrying concealed weapons. The U.S. Supreme Court ruled that this police action did not violate the fourth amendment. **Reasonable suspicion** is legal justification based on facts or inference from facts to cause a person of reasonable caution to conclude that criminal activity has occurred or is occurring. In *Terry*, the court provided six rules for police to conduct a "stop and frisk": (1) reasonable suspicion of criminal activity exists; (2) reasonable suspicion that the subject may be armed and dangerous; (3) police identify themselves to the subject(s); (4) police question the subject(s); (5) nothing in the confrontation dispels the officer's fear; and (6) police pat-down outer clothing for weapons.

Reasonable suspicion is less evidence than *probable cause*. Probable cause is evidence required for an arrest or to obtain an arrest or search warrant as stated in the fourth amendment. **Probable cause** is evidence of facts and circumstances to cause a person of reasonable caution to conclude that a particular person has committed or is committing a specific crime. For example, a police officer observes a suspect in a liquor store with a gun pointed at a clerk. The clerk gives money to the suspect who then flees. The officer has probable cause to make an arrest of the suspect for armed robbery.

In reference to the crime control versus due process models (Figure 5-2) and the *Mapp, Miranda, and Terry* cases, in which direction did the pendulum swing upon the decision in each case?

Since these major cases were decided, numerous other related cases followed that modified legal guidelines for police and even threatened to overturn these landmark decisions. For example, several U.S. Supreme Court cases resulted in exceptions to the exclusionary rule and, under certain conditions, permit police to conduct "warrantless searches." Court cases have also established exceptions to the *Miranda* requirements. Consult criminal justice sources for case precedents impacting the *Mapp, Miranda*, and *Terry* cases.

Several other pendulums help us to understand our system of justice. The **criminal justice versus victim justice models** show offenders and victims against each other, striving for justice and rights. Traditionally, the criminal justice system stressed fairness and justice for offenders, while victims received limited attention. However, the last quarter of the 20th century was marked by states enacting laws providing for a victim bill of rights, victim compensation, victim impact statements, and other victim rights. The federal system has also promoted victim rights. It has been argued that as the pendulum moved toward victim rights, offender rights were reduced. For instance, the use of victim impact statements during offender sentencing may cause an increase in punishment and offenders claimed that this violated the eighth amendment prohibition against cruel and unusual punishment. *A major point here is that the pendulums provide a pictorial view of the direction of our justice system as it responds to court decisions, legislation, and other factors* (Purpura, 2001: 53–54).

Reality Check: Research on the Victims of Terrorism and Other Disasters

The criminal justice versus victim justice models expose the rights and needs of both terrorists and victims of terrorism. Many publications on the rights of apprehended terrorists rarely cover victim issues; this has been the tradition of the *criminal* justice system. Social scientists finally began studying victims and their plight in the mid-20th century. Research on typologies of victims by Hans von Hentig and Benjamin Mendelsohn, in 1948 and 1956, respectively, established the science of **victimology** (i.e., the study of victims and their interactions with offenders and the criminal justice system). Their typologies focused on the conditions leading to victimization and the possible degree of responsibility by the victim.

In reference to victims of terrorism and other disasters, new research directions are needed beyond the study of such topics as posttraumatic stress and the Stockholm syndrome. **Posttraumatic stress** refers to psychological symptoms resulting from a major stressful event. Symptoms include anxiety, fear, and sleeping difficulties. Professional assistance may be required. The **Stockholm syndrome** involves hostages who sympathize with their captors and become emotionally attached to them. The term came from a hostage situation in Stockholm, Sweden, in 1973, when four Swedes who were held in a bank vault for 6 days with robbers became emotionally attached to their captors.

When we look to the victims of the 9/11 attacks and other disasters (e.g., Hurricane Katrina), including the deceased and their families, the injured, the displaced, first responders and other recovery workers, government, and businesses, the issues are enormous and research is needed. Studies are beginning to focus on relevant issues. For example, the U.S. Department of Justice, Office of Victims of Crime (n.d.) studied state victim assistance services and offered lessons learned to state, federal, and private decision makers for organizing effective responses to future mass criminal victimization. Many of these lessons learned are applicable to "all hazards" and require research and the development of career paths. Examples of lessons learned involve the following: training on the physical and psychological effects of disasters; toll-free hotlines; centralized victim resources; counseling on mental health issues, and legal and financial services; stress management; and public events for healing. (Chapter 7, under "Terrorism Insurance," covers the victim compensation fund established by Congress following the 9/11 attacks.)

HOMELAND SECURITY AND NATIONAL SECURITY VERSUS DUE PROCESS MODELS

With the aforementioned basic knowledge of the justice system, we can now shift to the homeland security and national security versus due process models (Figure 5-3). The **homeland security and national security model** emphasizes the protection of the United States and its people, assets, and interests from not only terrorism, but other potential risks, whether from human or natural causes. (National security emphasizes the protection of the United States globally, besides domestically. Homeland security emphasizes protection domestically, but its reach is global.) In this model, government takes action through laws passed by Congress, executive orders from the president, and court decisions. Although government action seeks to preserve and strengthen the nation, it may reduce citizen and human rights. The due process model emphasizes constitutional and procedural safeguards for citizens, rights of noncitizens, and human rights. The due process model is evolving and becomes more pronounced following government action in response to subsequent attacks or disasters. Rights may involve invasions of privacy; discrimination against certain groups; immigration law; freedoms of speech, religion, press, and assembly; safeguards against law enforcement and military investigative and detention powers at home and overseas; due process for enemy combatants; the opportunity to be inoculated and the right to refuse inoculation in cases of WMD; property owner access and compensation pertaining to WMD and other disaster sites; and forced evacuation. Following Hurricane Katrina in 2005, the police and military forced remaining residents of New Orleans to evacuate the flooded city because of health concerns and a destroyed infrastructure.

CRITICAL THINKING:

Do you think the U.S. government is balancing homeland security and national security with constitutional protections and human rights? Explain your answer.

Figure 5-3 ■ Homeland security and national security versus due process.

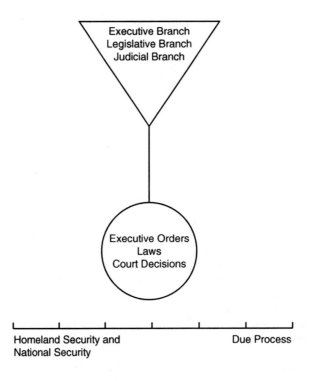

CRISES AND PENDULUM SWINGS AWAY FROM CONSTITUTIONAL AND HUMAN RIGHTS

The history of the United States contains periods when serious events created a climate of uncertainty and fear that caused government leaders at the time to curtail constitutional and human rights. Here we look at five examples.

ALIEN AND SEDITION ACTS

During President John Adam's term in office (1797–1801), Congress passed laws to silence opposition to an expected war with France. The Federalist Party, of which Adams was a member, controlled Congress, supported Great Britain, and passed the alien and sedition acts. The Democratic–Republican party favored France and received support from immigrants, especially those from France. The alien and sedition acts were passed in 1798 and consisted of four laws. The alien enemies act empowered the president to imprison or deport citizens of enemy nations. The sedition act imprisoned those who criticized the government. The alien friends act permitted citizens of friendly nations to be deported if they were considered dangerous. The naturalization act required a person born in another country to live in the United States for 14 years before becoming a citizen. Many people opposed the acts as an infringement of the first amendment and the controversy was debated during the 1800 presidential election. The Democratic–Republicans defeated the Federalists, and after President Thomas Jefferson took office in 1801, the acts either expired or were repealed or amended (Combs, 1988).

THE CIVIL WAR

During the Civil War, President Abraham Lincoln ordered the suspension of the right to habeas corpus. A **writ of habeas corpus** is a judicial order directing a person holding a prisoner to bring the prisoner before a judicial officer to determine the lawfulness of the imprisonment. In other words, the constitutional protection that government will not hold citizens without bringing them to trial. The U.S. Constitution, Article III, Section 9 reads: " The privilege of the writ of habeas corpus shall not be suspended, unless when in a case of rebellion or invasion the public safety may require it."

Lincoln ordered the military detention of hundreds of suspected Confederate sympathizers, 31 Maryland legislators, and an Ohio congressman. These actions were ruled unconstitutional by Chief Justice Roger Taney, but Lincoln ignored the order. Lincoln also closed newspapers that criticized the war (Mayer, 2003).

THE COMMUNIST THREAT

Following World War I, the United States suffered from economic problems and rioting. At the same time, the Communist Party was growing as people looked to this party for solutions. President Woodrow Wilson's attorney general, A. Mitchell Palmer, became part of a "Red Scare," recruited J. Edgar Hoover (who later became first director of the FBI), and they began a law enforcement effort against left wing groups by using the Espionage Act of 1917 and the Sedition Act of 1918.

During 1919, bombs exploded in eight cities and Palmer's home was hit. The communists were blamed and Palmer argued that they were seeking to control the government. The "Palmer raids" began following the bombings and federal authorities, without search warrants, focused on left-wing groups and labor unions. Thousands of people were arrested, and most were eventually released without being charged with a crime.

When the communists failed to take over the government, Palmer was criticized for violating the Bill of Rights. He was convicted of misappropriating government funds. One theory is that the "Red Scare" was a ploy for his political aspirations (Feuerlicht, 1971).

JAPANESE INTERNMENT IN THE UNITED STATES

The Japanese surprise air attack on Pearl Harbor in 1941 shocked Americans, brought the United States into World War II, and intensified prejudice against Asians. Fearing a Japanese invasion of the West Coast and sabotage, the War Relocation Authority was created under the administration of President Franklin D. Roosevelt. The army moved over 100,000 people of Japanese ancestry, who were mostly U.S. citizens, to internment camps in western states. *This action was upheld by the U.S. Supreme Court on the reasoning that, during war, the executive branch must make quick, decisive decisions and the other two branches must trust the executive branch.* Ironically, German Americans were not confined.

In Korematsu v. United States, 323 US 214 (1944), the U.S. Supreme Court upheld the internment of people of Japanese ancestry following the Japanese attack on Pearl Harbor. Fred Korematsu was of Japanese ancestry and a U.S. citizen living in California. Following the attack, he tried to join the U.S. Army, but was rejected for health reasons. He then began a career as a welder for a defense industry. In 1942 he had a good job and a Caucasian girlfriend who was not affected by the relocation of the Japanese. Korematsu sought to avoid relocation by claiming to be of Mexican ancestry. His ploy did not succeed and he was arrested for violating the exclusion orders.

This case is important because Justice Hugo Black asserted that "racial restrictions" are "immediately suspect" and should be given "the most rigid scrutiny." "This is the only case in which the Supreme Court applied the 'rigid scrutiny' test to a racial restriction and upheld the challenged law" (Hall *et al.*, 2005: 437).

By 1945, the last internment camp was closed, but these citizens had lost their property and businesses. Finally, the Civil Liberties Act of 1988 acknowledged the injustice, payments were made to surviving internees, and the government issued an apology (Myer, 1971).

McCARTHYISM AND THE COMMUNIST THREAT

The Cold War, fear that Communists were seeking to take over the government, and spying by the Soviet Union and China created substantial concern about an internal threat. Senator Joseph McCarthy became the voice and driving force of allegations of a communist conspiracy in the United States. He became chairman of a Senate investigations subcommittee in 1953 and this committee interrogated citizens as outlandish accusations were made during televised hearings. Unidentified informers provided weak evidence to support the committee whose actions ruined several people's careers. Some were imprisoned, even after exercising their right to remain silent. The press and his colleagues eventually criticized McCarthy's methods. He is remembered as a demagogue, although others see his efforts as important for enlightening Americans about the threat of communism (Herman, 2000).

CRITICAL THINKING:

Which of the events just described do you view as the worst infringement on constitutional or human rights? Explain your decisions.

GOVERNMENT INVESTIGATIONS

THE FOURTH AMENDMENT AND GOVERNMENT INVESTIGATIONS

The fourth amendment prohibits government officials from conducting unreasonable searches and seizures and requires officials to obtain a search warrant prior to conducting searches, with exceptions. A law enforcement officer obtains a search warrant from a judge by showing probable cause and describing the place to be searched and the persons or things to be seized. Exceptions to search warrants are known as "warrantless searches." Examples supported by case law include a search of a person being arrested; emergency searches where there is a danger to life, the possibility of escape, or the destruction of evidence; search of a vehicle; and consent to search when a subject provides permission to search.

Electronic surveillance and wiretapping have also been subject to court supervision, with exceptions. The former refers to electronic devices that are used to covertly listen to conversations, whereas the latter refers to the interception of telephone communications. Advances in technology have expanded investigators' options in intercepting communications, beyond planting a "bug" or tapping into a telephone line. Examples include cellular phones, e-mails, and faxes. Because telephone traffic travels over space radio in several modes (e.g., cellular, microwave, and satellite), the investigator's (or spy's) job is made much easier and safer because no on-premises tap is required. As investigators take advantage of new technology to control crime and terrorism, court rulings seek to uphold constitutional rights (Purpura, 2002: 443–444). In Katz v. United States, 389 U.S. 347 (1967), the U.S. Supreme Court ruled that when police monitored a subject's telephone calls from a public phone, using an electronic device, when the person sought privacy, even in a public place, the police violated the fourth amendment and a warrant based on probable cause is required. The court also *acknowledged that the president had authority for warrantless surveillance for national security*.

In Berger v. New York, 388 U.S. 41, 50 (1967), the U.S. Supreme Court ruled that eavesdropping involves a serious intrusion on privacy and that indiscriminate use by police raises grave constitutional questions. The court provided guidelines for law enforcement authorities, including a showing of probable cause, a description of the conversations to be intercepted, and surveillance for a limited time.

IS "BIG BROTHER" WATCHING YOU?

In his classic novel, *1984*, George Orwell portrayed a totalitarian society in which the government, referred to as the "Party," had almost complete control over the people. The omnipresent "Big Brother" led the party. While posters reminded everyone that "Big Brother is Watching You," telescreens, which could not be turned off, broadcast brainwashing propaganda about the greatness of the government. Through coins, stamps, books, and films, the government emphasized the three slogans of the Party: "War is Peace," "Freedom is Slavery," and "Ignorance is Strength."

This police state included helicopters that hovered over communities to spy on residents and peer into their windows. Moreover, the "Thought Police" produced even more fear. The telescreens not only transmitted propaganda, they also transmitted back to the "Thought Police" both audio and video from inside the homes. People were taught to hate their enemies through thought control from the telescreens. Neighbors were recruited by the "Thought Police" to spy on each other to root out dissidents.

People lived by rigid schedules dictated by the "Thought Police." Loud alarms were transmitted through the telescreens to order people to do duties specified by the party.

Although Orwell's *1984* is fictitious, many people have been arguing for decades that government and other sectors of our society are abridging privacy and violating the U.S. Constitution and its Bill of Rights. In the war against terrorism, the arguments have grown stronger.

Let us review some technological capabilities existing today so we can think critically about the message of Orwell's novel and how it relates to the challenge of balancing homeland security and national security with due process. One of the most sensitive, yet pervasive types of surveillance technology within our society is **closed-circuit television** (CCTV) (Figure 5-4). This technology is located on public streets and in buildings throughout the world. From a security perspective, it assists in deterrence, surveillance, apprehension, and prosecution. However, it also serves many other purposes, such as an aid to traffic control and to observe a business manufacturing process. Retail businesses are finding CCTV to be helpful to management through real-time video (and less often, audio) transmitted via the Internet or wireless to almost all points on earth. A businessperson on one continent can watch multiple businesses on another continent. Features of CCTV systems include miniaturized pinhole lenses that are capable of being hidden in almost anything, such as in clothes,

Continued

IS "BIG BROTHER" WATCHING YOU?—Cont'd

Figure 5-4 ■ CCTV camera.

pocketbooks, clocks, and air vents. The extensive use of hidden surveillance cameras is difficult to measure. Increasing "intelligence" is being built into CCTV systems, including video motion detection, the identification and monitoring of people and vehicles, and digital storage to hard drive (Purpura, 2002: 175–178).

Police are increasingly employing video and audio systems in their everyday duties. Such equipment is installed on public streets, in police vehicles, and on the officers themselves to be transmitted wirelessly to other officers who are mobile or at police facilities.

Chicago serves as an example of how local authorities are monitoring activities within their jurisdiction (Meincke, 2004). This city established an operations command center set up to work "like the bridge of a battleship" to respond to terrorism, crowd control, bad weather, and other emergencies. Police, the fire department, the transit authority, schools, the airport, and other agencies feed thousands of cameras into the command center for real-time images and recording. Some cameras are equipped with audio equipment that detects gunshots and automatically alerts the command center, provides the location, and points the camera in the direction of the gunshot. Also, the emergency 911 system identifies the closest cameras to the location of the caller. Because personnel cannot monitor all the cameras, software alerts personnel to movement at sensitive locations. For instance, if a boat appeared at the water treatment plant, the image would appear on a monitor with an alert. Because the

IS "BIG BROTHER" WATCHING YOU?—Cont'd

cameras can be controlled from the operations center, abuse is a possibility. Training and strict protocols emphasize that cameras are to be focused on public areas and not used to zoom in on private windows.

The use of **unmanned aerial vehicles** (UAVs) for surveillance is growing. UAVs help protect borders and other vital locations. From thousands of feet in the air, these drones carry CCTV and other surveillance equipment to track people and vehicles, read license plates, and collect a variety of information. The military uses them for surveillance and search-and-destroy missions.

Radio frequency identification (RFID) is receiving a lot of attention from proponents and privacy advocates. This technology uses a tiny computer chip (i.e., tag) to identify and track almost anything from a distance by a reader. RFID chips use radio waves, similar to those used to broadcast FM radio programs, to communicate the location and status of the tagged item. RFID has broad applications. Business executives see this technology as helpful to save money, track merchandise, and improve product availability. RFID can track young children, patients, and pets. It is used in access control systems and to monitor assets vulnerable to theft. RFID is contained in the digital human implant, a syringe-injectable microchip that sits under the skin, and provides instant access to an individual's medical records and personal information. In the future, we may see such an implant enabling people to pass a "reader" that will recognize their identity, conduct sales transactions, open secured doors, etc. A global positioning satellite (GPS) technology implant is an available innovation that tracks an individual, along with vital signs, and relays the information wirelessly to the Internet, to be stored in a database for future reference.

Critics of RFID claim that because the radio waves travel through solid objects, the tags can be read through items people usually rely on for privacy (e.g., walls, purses). Consumer privacy and purchasing anonymity are also in jeopardy, with items such as medications and birth-control pills. Direct marketing efforts could benefit from this technology at the expense of people's privacy (Worldnetdaily, 2004).

New passports will contain chips using RFID technology. This will enable "readers" at borders to obtain, from the chips, a person's name, address, and digital photo, among other information. Critics argue that this technology will help identity thieves and other criminals because, with a proper reader, they can download the same information as the authorities.

Data mining is another advancing technology whereby large amounts of seemingly unconnected information is examined by using highly specialized software to find hidden patterns and relationships and to make predictions. "The Departments of Education, Defense, Homeland Security, Veterans Affairs, Health and Human Services, Interior, Labor, Justice and Treasury are among those that use this new technology to detect criminal or terrorist activity, manage human resources, do scientific research, detect fraud, reduce waste, and monitor law compliance" (Philpott, 2004: 24). Government agencies are using numerous data-mining programs to analyze personal information bought from the private sector, including assorted credit transactions, student loan information, bank account numbers, housing information, car rentals, and airline ticket purchases. Additionally, government records are included in data mining, with examples being passport applications, visas, work permits, driver's licenses, and justice system records, among other sources. These data-mining projects are known as evidence extraction and link discovery and focus on people, organizations, and events. A major problem with such reviews of millions of transactions is that it could place innocent people under suspicion (SiliconValley.com, 2004).

Democratic Members of the House Select Committee on Homeland Security (2004: 125–130) voiced their concerns over government use of information held by the private sector for data-mining projects, without notification to those customers. One example cited was in September 2003 when JetBlue admitted it had given five million passenger itineraries to a defense contractor to study ways to identify high-risk customers. New DHS initiatives have been derailed because of privacy and civil liberties issues.

Continued

IS "BIG BROTHER" WATCHING YOU?—Cont'd

The committee argues that there is no framework in the government for evaluating the security and privacy of new technologies. They recommend the following.

- A commission on privacy should be established to evaluate new technologies and design safeguards for government access to commercial databases.
- Private sector entities that share personal information of their customers with the government should be required to notify their customers of that fact, unless that disclosure impacts an ongoing investigation.
- The government should consider creating offices similar to the DHS privacy office in other agencies that handle sensitive information.

Various government agencies have departments that seek to preserve privacy and civil liberties. The Department of Homeland Security contains a privacy office and an office for civil rights and civil liberties. These offices provide input to DHS initiatives and serve as a communication channel with the public. However, the debate over security versus privacy and due proves will continue.

CRITICAL THINKING:

Do you think American society contains any of the characteristics described in Orwell's *1984*? Explain your answer.

CONTROVERSY AND LEGAL GUIDELINES OF GOVERNMENT INVESTIGATIONS

The following paragraphs explain the controversy and legal action among the three branches of the federal government as legal guidelines are developed for government investigations. This is an ongoing process and part of the "checks and balances" among the three branches of government (see Chapter 3).

During an era of street demonstrations and unrest over civil rights and the war in Vietnam, Congress enacted the **Omnibus Crime Control and Safe Streets Act of 1968**. The act aimed to improve the criminal justice system, especially the police. Title III of the act countered such court decisions as *Katz* and *Berger* by providing specific authorization procedures and rules for police when collecting evidence of violations of criminal law. Still, the *probable cause* requirement remained. However, *the act did not answer the question as to guidelines for investigations of threats to national security*. This question faced the U.S. Supreme Court in United States v. United States District Court, 407 US 297 (1972). A group of war protesters tried to blow up a CIA recruiting office in Ann Arbor, Michigan. The CIA held evidence from a potentially illegal wiretap, and the defendants, charged with conspiracy to destroy government property, wanted a determination as to whether, at trial, the prosecution had relied on tainted evidence. The attorney general admitted that a warrantless wiretap occurred for *domestic national security*. The court held that the government does not have the power to conduct national security wiretaps for domestic security matters without prior judicial authorization. The court suggested that Congress prepare guidelines differentiating wiretaps for *national security* and those for *ordinary criminal cases*. Congress answered this call through legislation known as **Foreign Intelligence Surveillance Act** (FISA) (Bulzomi, 2003; Tien, 2001).

Prior to the Patriot Act, there were exceptions to the *probable cause* requirement for surveillance under federal law. The exceptions included pen register or pen/trap orders. The former refers to recording all numbers entered into a specific telephone, whereas the latter identifies the telephone numbers of incoming calls to the specific telephone. These orders enabled investigators to contact a telephone company to obtain the telephone numbers of outgoing and incoming calls for a specific telephone. An investigator obtained such an order from a judge, not by showing probable cause, but by certifying that the information was needed for an ongoing criminal investigation. This lesser weight of evidence is permitted because obtaining telephone numbers is less intrusive than searches or wiretaps.

Another situation under which the *probable cause* requirement for surveillance under federal law was weakened falls under surveillance requests from the Foreign Intelligence Surveillance Court (FISC). This court was created in 1978 by Congress through the FISA to establish a legal regime for *foreign intelligence surveillance* separate from *ordinary police surveillance for criminal investigations*. It also provided for oversight of U.S. intelligence agencies (executive branch) that had spied on American citizens and abused surveillance powers, according to the 1975–1976 Church Committee hearings held by Congress. Congressional leaders saw the need for judicial scrutiny of the National Security Agency (a top secret agency that monitors international communications and performs other intelligence tasks), the CIA, and the FBI.

The FISC became a compromise between those who favored no restrictions on U.S. intelligence agencies and those who aimed to require intelligence agencies to apply for search warrants like police do. Congress required U.S. intelligence agencies to apply for warrants for wiretaps, other surveillance, and break-ins on suspected foreign agents, foreign governments, and terrorists. However, because domestic crime is not involved, *probable cause* is required only to show that the *target* of the intercept or search is a foreign agent, foreign government, or terrorist. A lesser standard is required for the warrant: certify that the *purpose* is to investigate foreign agents, foreign governments, or terrorists. The "certification" is from a high-ranking executive branch official who deems the information being sought is foreign intelligence information that cannot be obtained by normal investigative techniques.

The FISC is a secret court of federal district court judges, appointed by the chief justice of the U.S. Supreme Court, who individually review applications from the CIA and other agencies for electronic surveillance targeting foreign intelligence. Applications must first be approved by the U.S. attorney general before going to the FISC. The proceedings are nonadversarial. The court authorizes electronic eavesdropping, wiretapping, covert physical entries, pen/trap orders, and obtaining certain business records. It does not regulate the use of electronic surveillance outside the United States. An example is an e-mail sent by an individual in the United States to an individual in another country and it is intercepted outside the United States. The records and files of this court are sealed, with some exceptions. There are no requirements for the return, to the court, of executed warrants or an inventory of items confiscated. During 2003, the attorney general made 1727 applications to this court and 1724 were approved (Moschella, 2004). If an application is denied, it can be referred to the FISA court of review and its decision can be appealed directly to the U.S. Supreme Court.

Courts have permitted FISA-obtained information to be used in criminal cases. However, intelligence must be the primary objective of the surveillance.

Concerned that authorities would obtain an FISA order in a criminal investigation, rather than a Title III order that requires a greater weight of evidence, the courts developed a "primary purpose" test through several cases. In a case that began prior to the FISA, US v. Truong Dinh Hung, 629 F.2d 908 (4th Cir. 1980), the attorney general approved electronic surveillance under the foreign intelligence exception to the fourth amendment. The defendant moved to suppress evidence under the fourth amendment. The court agreed because the "primary purpose" of the investigation shifted from securing intelligence to collecting evidence of a crime, and the requirements of Title III were not included in the procedures.

The "primary purpose" test led the FISC and the U.S. Department of Justice (DOJ) to build a "wall" of policies between intelligence investigators and criminal investigators to avoid tainting FISC-ordered evidence gathering. Intelligence investigators were not to discuss foreign intelligence or counterintelligence investigations with criminal investigators. Such policies led to problems of coordination and sharing information between both types of investigators, even though international terrorism cases have both intelligence and criminal aspects (Bulzomi, 2003).

Following the 9/11 attacks, problems of coordination and sharing information became major criticisms of the government. *Congress rejected the "wall," and related case law, through the Patriotic Act.* It amended the FISA and changed the certification demanded of federal officials for a FISC order for electronic surveillance—from requiring that the "primary purpose" of the surveillance is to obtain foreign intelligence to requiring "a significant purpose." The Patriotic Act amends the FISA to enable coordination of investigations and sharing of information between intelligence officials (e.g., CIA) and law enforcement officials (e.g., FBI) without undermining the "significant purpose" of FISA surveillance. This shift of increased coordination and sharing of information resulted in new policies by the U.S. Attorney General that were rejected by the FISC. However, the attorney general, in the first ever appeal to the FISA court of review, received a favorable decision: the FISA does not bar the government's use of foreign intelligence information, including evidence of crimes, in certain types of criminal cases, and that the Patriot Act amendments to FISA do not violate the fourth amendment. This court added that the FISA applications require "significant purpose" and the FISA could be used to obtain evidence in criminal prosecution if it is related to a foreign intelligence threat. Examples include an ordinary crime such as robbery to finance terrorism or credit card fraud to hide the identity of a spy (Bulzomi, 2003).

Other changes under the Patriot Act are as follows.

- **Roving wiretaps** have been permitted since 1986, but the Patriot Act makes them easier to obtain. These taps mean that authorities can respond to time-sensitive criminal or terrorist activities by conducting electronic surveillance when the subject quickly switches cell phones, Internet accounts, or meeting locations. Section 206 permits targeting of a particular suspect, rather than a particular device.
- Section 219 expands the reach of search warrants in domestic and international terrorism cases from the jurisdiction where the warrant is issued to outside the jurisdiction. Federal authorities go to one U.S. magistrate rather than one in each jurisdiction.
- Section 213 of the Act authorizes **delayed notice** or **sneak-and-peak** searches in investigations. When seeking a search warrant, officers may show that if immediate notification is provided to the target of the search, it may have an adverse result. Thus, a home or business may be searched, items seized, and "bugs" planted, in secret, to prevent the destruction of evidence or to prevent the disclosure of a secret investigation. Cole and Dempsey (2006: 209–210) write that this provision applies to any federal crime, besides terrorism. Also, even before the Patriot Act, courts permitted "sneak-and-peek" in extraordinary circumstances, such as danger to life or the destruction of evidence.
- Because Section 216 extends pen register and pen/trap orders to technology beyond telephones, such as computer networks, Web browsing, and e-mail, this enables law enforcement authorities to obtain, from Internet service providers, the log of the Web sites a person visits and the addresses of that person's e-mail traffic.
- *The Patriotic Act authorizes the FISC to issue search orders against not only suspect foreign agents and terrorists, but also suspect U.S. citizens.* Section 215 of the act enables federal law enforcement authorities to apply to the FISC for an order to search for "any tangible things" connected to a suspected terrorist. As covered earlier, these officials would have to certify that the search is to protect against terrorism or spying. A probable cause standard is not required.
- Terrorism is a predicate offense (i.e., an offense linked to other offenses and penalties), permitting a wiretap under Title III and, thus, providing investigators with a choice of securing an FISC or Title III order for surveillance.

Another legal controversy is the federal government's use of **National Security Letters**. Although authorized by Congress since 1986, the Patriot Act expanded the letters' reach by permitting local FBI officials to certify that the requested information is relevant to a case of terrorism or spying. These letters are served on entities to retrieve such items as Internet, telephone, and financial records.

Reality Check: Why Is the Executive Branch Circumventing the Foreign Intelligence Surveillance Court?

In late 2005 and early 2006, prior to the Patriot Act reauthorization, controversy erupted in Congress over President Bush permitting the National Security Agency and other agencies to circumvent the FISC and, without warrants, spy on U.S. citizens. The administration's legal arguments included the implied authority in the president's constitutional role as commander in chief and the power Congress provided to the president when it passed the authorization for use of military force, following the 9/11 attacks. The Bush administration also pointed to frustrations over the speed and flexibility of the FISC. Questions remain for the three branches of government, such as the following: Why is the executive branch circumventing the FISC? What is the extent of secret surveillance and can this question be answered accurately? Who exactly decides on the authorization for surveillance and what criteria do they use? Is the FISC outdated due to new communication technology? How can government balance homeland security and national security with constitutional protections?

OPERATION G-STRING

In one criminal case, FBI agents in Las Vegas used the Patriot Act to prosecute the city's "strip-club baron" who was bribing local officials to halt efforts to promote an ordinance to limit physical contact during lap dances. In "Operation G-String," agents applied the Patriot Act, which permits them to obtain financial records of suspected terrorists or money launderers. The act's money laundering language is so broad that it can be used for more than 200 federal crimes, and there may be no connection to terrorism. Federal agencies that use this approach include the Internal Revenue Service (IRS), Postal Service, Secret Service, and Agriculture Department. "Operation G-String" was the first time the FBI used the act to prosecute local politicians (Isikoff, 2003).

Patriot Act: "Assault on the Bill of Rights?"

The Patriot Act has been labeled by many as an "assault on the Bill of Rights." Soon after the 9/11 attacks, Attorney General John Ashcroft began a campaign for congressional passage of the act to increase government investigative powers to control terrorism. In October of 2001, during the nation's first biological-weapons attack (letters containing anthrax sent through the U.S. mail and to two senators), the Patriot Act was passed overwhelmingly.

Even before the act passed, criticism began. Opponents claimed that in the haste for government action following the 9/11 attacks the White House and Congress panicked and the act went too far in passing a law that increased police powers.

Over 140 local governments and three states have passed resolutions condemning the act as a violation of civil liberties. Some of the resolutions prohibit local and state law enforcement officials from assisting federal officials using Patriot Act investigative procedures, such as "sneak and peek."

Critics have argued that the act is used to investigate nonterrorist crimes and that interest groups, such as those on either side of the abortion issue, could be targeted as domestic terrorists.

The **American Civil Liberties Union** (ACLU) has been a major critic of the Patriot Act. The ACLU is a public interest, "watchdog" group often referred to as a "champion of the Bill of Rights." It maintains a strong voice in justice issues, it has been involved in numerous landmark cases including the *Mapp* and *Miranda* decisions, and it is behind cases involving the Patriot Act.

The National League of Cities (2003) criticized a number of provisions of the Patriot Act for reducing civil liberties. These include Section 213, which allows law enforcement authorities to search homes without the presence of the owner and delaying notification to the owner; Section 218, which amends the probable cause requirement for secret searches or surveillance; and Sections 411 and 412, which provide the secretary of state with broad powers to designate domestic groups as "terrorist organizations" and the attorney general with the power to confine immigrants to indefinite detention or to deportation, without proving that a crime was committed.

Continued

OPERATION G-STRING—Cont'd

Both sides of the Patriot Act issue have played on the public's fear. Proponents claim that those against the Patriot Act would hinder important investigations and leave America vulnerable to terrorism. Opponents, such as the ACLU, argue that the FBI will target innocent people. A *USA TODAY* survey in early 2004 found that 71% of adults disapprove of "sneak-and-peak" searches. About half of adults were uneasy about federal authorities having the power, through the act, of obtaining personal records from a variety of sources. However, the survey suggested that Americans trust the attorney general more than the ACLU to balance national security and citizen rights (Locy, 2004). According to one spokesperson from the attorney general's office, once you get past the interest groups (e.g., ACLU), the rest of the country is saying, "just keep us safe" (Isikoff and Klaidman, 2003).

In the fall of 2004, U.S. District Judge Victor Marrero, in New York, became the first judge to rule a provision of the Patriot Act as unconstitutional. The civil case was filed by the ACLU on behalf of an Internet provider who received a National Security Letter. Marrero ruled that the compulsory, secret, and unreviewable (i.e., in court) demand for information violates the fourth amendment's protection against unreasonable search and seizure and the unlimited ban on disclosure by the recipient of the letter violates the first amendment right to free speech. Chapter 3 lists restrictions on police powers on the issues of this case under the USA Patriot Improvement and Reauthorization Act of 2005.

With so much controversy over the Patriot Act, one may ask: "In which direction will the pendulum swing in the coming years—security or due process?" The answer likely depends on how successful the government is in preventing terrorist attacks. Conversely, one major attack could strengthen the government's argument to enhance provisions of the act.

CRITICAL THINKING:

Do you think the Patriot Act is "an assault on the Bill of Rights?" Explain your answer.

It is important to note that state and local law enforcement officers must look to their individual states for legal guidance. Laws and procedures applicable in federal cases may be prohibited in state and local cases.

NONCITIZENS

ARRESTS OF NONCITIZENS FOLLOWING THE 9/11 ATTACKS

Following the 9/11 attacks, federal law enforcement agencies, led by Attorney General John Ashcroft, began an extensive and intense investigation that included detaining over 1000 noncitizens in the United States. Most were arrested for immigration violations and minor criminal charges having no relationship to terrorism. More serious charges included holding bogus licenses for hazardous materials. Some were held as material witnesses to the 9/11 attacks.

Because the 9/11 terrorists were noncitizens, Ashcroft increased the time that these arrestees could be held without charge and many did not know why they were being held (due process issues under the fifth amendment). Many did not have access to an attorney (right to counsel issue under the sixth amendment).

The **attorney–client privilege** was also in jeopardy because federal prisoners were having their conversations with attorneys monitored (right to counsel issue under the sixth amendment) whenever the attorney general found "reasonable suspicion" that the communications might support acts of terrorism. Under the laws of evidence, confidential communications between an attorney and a client are not to be disclosed; otherwise a client would not freely share information with their attorney in an effort to help in their defense.

Ashcroft was reluctant to release the number of people in custody and their names. In certain cases, federal authorities refused to release information on the location of arrestees to family members. Public safety and privacy were the justifications for withholding the information. For example, if al-Qaida knew which members of their organization were not available and which members were available, such information could assist in planning attacks. Eventually, most of the arrestees were released, many without being formally charged. However, there was great fear of more attacks following September 11, 2001. The American citizenry supported Ashcroft and the federal actions against noncitizens. A *Newsweek* poll found that 86% of citizens viewed the government's actions as appropriate (Mayer, 2003: 41–42).

In reference to the Patriot Act, Cole and Dempsey (2006: 202–203) write that under Section 412 the attorney general has the power to confine, without a hearing, any foreign national suspected of being a terrorist. Initially, the detention is for 7 days, but it can last indefinitely. Also, the definition of "terrorist activity" in the law is very broad. They note that preventive detention without a hearing to show that the detainee requires confinement violates due process and that the evidentiary threshold for detention—"reasonable grounds to believe"—is too low. They argue that the only legal recourse for aliens is to sue the government in federal court. Cole and Dempsey concede that the government has not applied this provision of the act, instead relying on other laws for confinement.

RIGHTS OF NONCITIZENS

Throughout the history of the United States, the rights of noncitizens have been debated inside and outside of courts and issues remain unsettled today. We can view part of this area of law, often called immigration law, as a pendulum of homeland security and national security versus noncitizen rights.

In Reno v. American-Arab Anti-Discrimination Committee, 525 US 471 (1999), the case began in 1987 when the Immigration and Naturalization Service arrested seven Palestinians and a Kenyan and charged them with being deportable because of membership in an organization that advocated communism and Palestinian causes. The plaintiffs filed suit challenging the constitutionality of the charges. Interestingly, the FBI director testified before Congress that if the plaintiffs had been citizens, there would have been no grounds for an arrest and that they had been arrested because of their association with a Communist organization. The U.S. Supreme Court ruled that even though they were to be deported because of their association with a terrorist group, as immigrants they had no right to challenge their deportation based on the first amendment. In essence, the court was saying that noncitizens do not possess the same rights held by U.S. citizens.

According to Crank and Gregor (2005: 140), foreigners, *legally* in the United States, have rights under the 14th amendment, Section 1 and the due process rights that apply to citizens also apply to noncitizens. Illegal immigrants also have rights when subject to deportation. Guttentag (2001), an ACLU advocate of noncitizen rights, states that under the constitution, noncitizens are entitled to due process and they are not to be discriminated against based on race or ethnicity. Also, he states that if noncitizens are in violation of immigration laws, they are subject to deportation based on legal procedures contained in the law.

In Yamataya v. Fischer, 189 US 86 (1903), the court ruled that deportation proceedings must meet due process standards: a hearing before an immigration judge, representation by a lawyer, reasonable notice of the hearing time, an opportunity to study evidence, an interpreter, and clear and convincing proof that grounds for the deportation are valid. In Zadvydas v. Davis, 121 S. Ct 2491 (2001), the court reaffirmed that due process rights apply to all persons within the United States, including aliens, whether their presence here is lawful, unlawful, temporary, or permanent. The court recognized that, from prior precedent, full constitutional protections might not apply to an alien who had not entered the United States (e.g., stopped at the border). The court also struck down indefinite detention of those ordered deported or removed after having entered the United States, but whom the government is unable to deport or remove. The court stated that

6 months is a reasonable time to effect a removal from the country; beyond this time the person would have to be released. Those stopped at the border before entry could also challenge their indefinite detention under *Zadvydas* (Vargas, 2002).

PROFILING

Profiling can be studied from two major perspectives: (1) local police and how they use profiling as a proactive method to control a variety of street crimes and help to identify terrorists in communities and (2) federal police and how they use profiling as a proactive method to not only control crime, but to protect our borders and identify terrorists both nationally and internationally. We begin with basic definitions and then the perspective from the local level.

Racial profiling is "any police-initiated action that relies on the race, ethnicity, or national origin rather than the behavior of an individual or information that leads the police to a particular individual who has been identified as being, or having been, engaged in criminal activity" (Shusta *et al.*, 2005: 527). **Legal profiling** includes a variety of factors, such as behavioral, situational, motivational, and background, that attract the attention of authorities. (Chapter 8 provides additional information on legal profiling.)

The Police Execution Research Forum (PERF) prepared a model policy on legal profiling for police agencies. It emphasizes that under the fourth amendment, "officers shall not consider race/ethnicity to establish reasonable suspicion or probable cause except when based on trustworthy, locally relevant information that links a person or persons of a specific race/ethnicity to a particular unlawful incident(s)" (Shusta *et al.*, 2005: 426). The policy disallows the use of race as an indicator of criminal behavior, disallows use of stereotypes/biases, and relies on specific descriptions of suspects, rather than predictions.

Ellmann (2002–2003: 675–730) maintains that domestic racial profiling is indeed unacceptable, except for acts of terrorism. He argues that to prevent terrorism, in an actual war against terrorism or related emergency, everyone must endure some intrusion on his or her rights. He goes on to write that profiling will produce many false positives, resulting in stigma, humiliation, and resentment. However, Ellmann sees profiling during a terrorist emergency balanced under the constitution by "strict scrutiny" whereby profiling is targeted carefully and conducted with restraint.

Police have used profiles globally for many years as a proactive crime and terrorism prevention method. In Israel, for example, profiles help identify Palestinian terrorists. Since the 9/11 attacks, profiling has been used globally to identify al-Qaida members. In the United States, a profile used by airport or border authorities may include (1) a man in his 20s or 30s who traveled from Saudi Arabia or Pakistan; (2) possibly living in New York, New Jersey, California, Michigan, or Florida; and (3) engaged in suspicious activity, such as being linked to explosives or WMD.

In November of 2001, Attorney General John Ashcroft ordered federal law enforcement authorities to interview almost 5000 men between the ages of 18 and 33, mostly from the Middle East, who entered the United States on student, business, or tourist visas after January 1, 2000. Ashcroft viewed these men as fitting the criteria of persons who might have information on terrorists. Authorities asked questions on why they were in the United States, their foreign travel, and if they had any knowledge of terrorist activities. Known as the "Responsible Cooperators Program," federal authorities offered the possibility of U.S. citizenship for significantly helpful information. Very few of the men were arrested and none on terrorist-related crimes. The initial interviews were followed by others. Although authorities cannot force individuals to answer questions, critics view the possibility of immigration charges as a form of coercion.

A memo from Ashcroft to federal prosecutors in November of 2001 stated that the interviewees "were not selected in order to single out a particular ethnic or religious group." However, Muslim- and Arab-American groups claimed that the interviews were racial profiling. Furthermore, some local police agencies refused to cooperate with the interviews because of constitutional issues, internal policies, or concern over police–community relations (Council on Foreign Relations, n.d.).

In 2003, President George W. Bush restricted racial profiling by federal law enforcement agencies, but allowed exceptions by permitting use of race and ethnicity to prevent potential terrorist attacks. The policy prohibits "generalized stereotypes" based on race or ethnicity, but permits authorities to include them as part of a specific description or tip from a reliable source ("Bush bans racial profiling," 2003: A14).

SAUDI ARABIAN GOVERNMENT PAYS LEGAL BILLS FOR ITS CITIZENS DETAINED IN THE UNITED STATES

Soon after the 9/11 attacks, U.S. law enforcement authorities focused heavily on Saudis living in the United States because 16 of the 19 9/11 terrorists were from Saudi Arabia. Hundreds of Saudis were detained and questioned. Most of the cases involved students charged with violations of immigration laws, but some were held on more serious charges.

The Saudi government acknowledged spending over $1 million for American lawyers and also paid for bonds so their citizens could be released. Realizing that their citizens were unfamiliar with the American legal system, the Saudi government saw the need for lawyers so their citizens could defend themselves. A U.S. lawyer, hired by the Saudi Embassy to coordinate the legal assistance, was surprised by the FBI criticism of the assistance effort and emphasized the importance of the right to counsel in the American criminal justice system.

The FBI saw the legal assistance effort as tantamount to buying off witnesses. The Saudi actions to pay legal bills and bonds of those being questioned could influence what the subjects say when they are being interviewed, according to the FBI. The United States does not provide its citizens with attorneys and bail funds in other countries; however, U.S. embassies do take action to seek fair treatment for U.S. citizens. Two years following the crackdown, a U.S. Department of Justice investigation concluded that many immigrants detained after the 9/11 attacks were improperly held for lengthy periods of time and some were subject to psychological and physical abuse (Solomon, 2003).

THE ENEMY

CIVILIAN COURTS

Civilian courts (i.e., federal and state courts) have been used to prosecute suspected terrorists who are alleged to have violated local, state, and federal laws. Such cases in civilian courts enable defendants to receive constitutional protections under the Bill of Rights.

Richard Reid, for example, a British citizen trained as a terrorist in Afghanistan, was tried and sentenced to life in prison in a federal court in Boston in January 2003 for trying to blow up an airliner traveling from Paris to Miami in December 2001. An airline attendant caught him trying to light a fuse for a bomb hidden in his shoe. Examples of others who have been prosecuted for terrorism in U.S. courts include four al-Qaida members involved in the bombings of U.S. embassies in Kenya and Tanzania who were captured, convicted, and sentenced to life without parole; and Ramzi Yousef, a prime suspect in the 1993 bombing of the World Trade Center, who was transferred to U.S. authorities by the Pakistani government, was tried and sentenced to 240 years in prison (others involved in the crime were also prosecuted and sentenced to 240 years).

U.S. citizens involved in terrorism or hostilities have also been prosecuted, convicted, and sentenced in U.S. civilian courts. Timothy McVeigh was convicted in federal court, and subsequently executed, for the 1995 bombing of the Alfred P. Murrah federal building in Oklahoma City.

Terry Nichols, an accomplice in the bombing, was convicted and sentenced to life in prison. John Walker Lindh (aka the "American Taliban") was captured during hostilities in Afghanistan carrying an AK-47 and grenades. He accepted a plea bargain in court and is serving a 20-year prison sentence.

Two problems associated with using civilian courts for terrorism-related cases are (1) the danger of victimization to anyone (e.g., judges, prosecutors, and witnesses) involved in the proceedings and (2) the revelation of information that may compromise national security.

THE RIGHTS OF THE ENEMY

Following the 9/11 attacks, when the United States attacked Afghanistan and its Taliban regime for supporting al-Qaida, hundreds of enemy soldiers and terrorists were captured. Many legal questions evolved from the capture of the enemy: What status should be applied to the captives? What rights should they possess? Should enemy/U.S. citizens possess different rights than enemy/non-U.S. citizens? How should the enemy be treated? Where would they be confined and for how long?

If the captives were to be classified as prisoners of war (POWs), interrogations would not be permitted; captives would only have to state their name, rank, and serial number. This situation would seriously hinder the U.S. government from gathering information on terrorist plans and activities. Also, the types of indictments against them would be limited. If their status were to be that of a suspected criminal, then they would receive a variety of due process rights (e.g., attorney and civilian courts).

President George W. Bush stated that the war on terrorism would be a new kind of war. This view is reflected in the status the U.S. government has given the captives: they are enemy combatants (also known as "unlawful combatants") because they do not meet the definition of "lawful combatants" handled under the **Geneva conventions** (i.e., treaties that are accepted by countries to provide for the humane treatment of POWs, the wounded, and civilians). According to the Department of Defense (n.d.), "the Third Geneva Convention of 1949 accords POW status only to enemy forces who follow certain rules: wear uniforms; do not deliberately target civilians; and otherwise fight in accordance with the laws and customs of war." The DOD views enemy forces in Afghanistan as not following these rules. Even though captives may not be classified as POWs, they are still entitled to humane treatment under the Geneva conventions. The Department of Defense (n.d.) defines an **enemy combatant** as an "individual who was part of or supporting Taliban or al-Qaida forces, or associated forces that are engaged in hostilities against the United States or its coalition partners. This includes any person who has committed a belligerent act or has directly supported hostilities in aid of enemy armed forces."

The DOD views the detention of enemy combatants (Figure 5-5) in wartime as "a matter of security and military necessity. It prevents enemy combatants from continuing the fight against the United States and its partners in the war on terror. Releasing enemy combatants before the end of the hostilities and allowing them to rejoin the fight would only prolong the conflict and endanger coalition forces and innocent civilians" (Department of Defense, n.d.).

The U.S. government authority to designate a person an enemy combatant rests with the president's war powers and the U.S. Supreme Court case Ex Parte Quirin, 317 US 1 (1942). This case dealt with eight Nazis who were not lawful combatants because they worked for the German army but were not enlisted in its ranks. They landed by submarine on beaches on Long Island and in Florida with a mission to sabotage military production facilities. All were apprehended and turned over to the military. One claimed to be an American citizen. The U.S. Supreme Court ruled that persons (including American citizens) being tried for offenses against the law of war were constitutionally tried by a military tribunal and they had no constitutional protections, such as the right to a jury trial. Six of the eight were executed (Reichel, 2005: 99–100). Ironically, the U.S. State Department has condemned other countries in the use of military tribunals for terrorists in their countries, according to Human Rights Watch.

Figure 5-5 ■ On January 10, 2002, at a security facility in Guantanamo Bay, Cuba, a Marine security team conducts a rehearsal for handling incoming Taliban and Al-Qaida detainees. U.S. Navy photo by Photographer's Mate 1st Class Michael W. Pendergrass. http://www.news.navy.mil/view_single.asp?id=541

CRITICAL THINKING:

Because enemies captured in Afghanistan have been designated "enemy combatants" rather than POWs, do you think U.S. armed forces personnel captured in future wars could be subject to a similar status? Why or why not?

Reichel (2005: 100–101) offers two implications for procedural criminal law from the designation of "enemy combatant." It can have a negative impact on the civilian criminal court process because of the power of the executive branch to designate U.S. citizens as enemy combatants and hold them without access to an attorney or the courts. Second, Reichel cites the case of six men from the Yemeni community in Lackawanna, New York, who were charged with aiding al-Qaida, attending a training camp, and belonging to a "sleeper cell." In July 2003, all six men pled guilty to terror charges and accepted prison terms between 6 and 9 years. Prosecutors used the powerful leverage of possibly designating them as "enemy combatants" if they did not plead guilty to the terror charges. The defendants sought to avoid indefinite detention.

IS THE UNITED STATES HIDING DETAINEES?

This question has provoked much speculation, media attention, and questioning of U.S. government officials by international organizations. Despite access to thousands of detainees in Iraq and elsewhere, the International Committee of the Red Cross (ICRC) suspects that the United States is holding detainees in secret facilities around the globe. The ICRC claims that captured terrorists, reported by the FBI, have not turned up in detention centers, and the United States has not been forthcoming with complete lists of detainees (Koppel, 2004).

A May 16, 2004 ABC-TV "Nightline" program entitled "The Disappeared" covered the secret CIA detention facilities overseas. Naturally, investigative reporters found that so much of these operations are secret: the name of detainees, locations of the facilities, rules, treatment, and the future of the detainees. It was reported in the media that one of the prisoners is Khalid Sheikh Mohammed, mastermind of the 9/11 plot. The news program reported that the detention facilities operate outside of the U.S. judicial system and the executive branch views the Geneva conventions as not applying to terrorists and their questioning. Arguments have been made that the United States is not adhering to international treaties it has signed and that congressional oversights are needed (Hentoff, 2004).

On September 6, 2006, President Bush, in a speech on terrorism, acknowledged (under global pressure) the existence of previously secret CIA prisons outside the United States. The administration stated that fewer than 100 people were detained by the CIA and the remaining people would be transferred to Guantanamo (Pickler, 2006).

CRITICAL THINKING:

What are your views of secret prisons operated by the U.S. government? Should torture be used to extract information from terrorists? Justify your answers.

MILITARY TRIBUNALS

Following the 9/11 attacks, on November 15, 2001, President George W. Bush signed an executive order for international terrorists to be tried in U.S. **military tribunals**, also called military commissions (Figure 5-6). This special military court is not controlled by procedures and constitutional protections found in civilian courts.

Tribunals were applied to captives from the war in Afghanistan, after 9/11, who were detained at the American naval base at Guantanamo, Cuba (Figures 5-7 and 5-8). This base originated from a 1903 lease to establish a base for the U.S. Navy. Cole and Dempsey (2006: 183–184) write:

> The administration chose to hold prisoners at Guantanamo precisely to avoid the limits of law. The administration claimed that it could warehouse there any person it labeled an "enemy combatant," or as President Bush put it, "a bad guy." It maintained that it could hold them until the war on terrorism ends, or as U.S. Defense Secretary Donald Rumsfeld elaborated, until there are no more terrorist organizations of global reach left in the world.

Early on, the rights of those confined were limited. Later, the prisoners were afforded more rights.

A military tribunal should not be confused with a **court-martial**. The latter uses evidence law similar to civilian courts, is frequently open to civilian observers, and permits appeals.

Figure 5-6 ■ Commissions building courtroom at Guantanamo Bay, Cuba. U.S. Navy photo by Photographer's Mate 1st Class Christopher Mobley. http://www.news.navy.mil/view_single.asp?id=17154

Initially, tribunals required a two-thirds majority of military officers to sentence a captive to death. Also, a defendant had the right to an attorney, but not the right to choose their own attorney. Following global and domestic criticism that the United States was not living up to the human rights it had espoused through its history, due process was expanded for the captives. Tribunal guidelines include the following:

- juries of three to seven military panelists
- unanimous vote for death penalty
- two-thirds vote for guilty verdict and sentencing
- proof beyond a reasonable doubt required to establish guilt
- hearsay evidence admissible
- opportunity for defendants to review evidence against them
- access to military lawyers and lawyers of their own choosing at their own expense
- no appeals to federal court, but a petition can be filed to a panel of military officers and civilians

Controversy over tribunals continues, despite historical precedents. During the Civil War, President Lincoln approved of military tribunals for rendering justice to Confederate saboteurs and thousands of others for a variety of charges. Also, as covered earlier, the U.S. Supreme Court approved of a military tribunal for the eight Nazis who landed by submarine on U.S. shores during World War II.

For the government, military tribunals offer the following advantages over civilian trials: speed and efficiency not hindered by as many due process protections, motions, and other delays; increased security for all parties; protection of classified information; and avoidance of publicity from both a public trial and an appeal that can result in a global, media event providing the enemy with an opportunity to publicize their cause.

Figure 5-7 ■ Detainee being escorted at security facility at Guantanamo Bay, Cuba. DOD photo by Seaman David P. Coleman, U.S. Navy. http://www.defenselink.mil/photos/May2003/030228-N-4936C-096.html

THE ENEMY AND COURT DECISIONS

In Hamdi v. Rumsfeld (03-6696), decided on June 28, 2004, the U.S. Supreme Court (Figure 5-9) ruled that a detained enemy combatant must be given the opportunity to contest his detention before a neutral fact-finder. The court held that the Authorization for Use of Military Force, passed after the 9/11 attacks, is an act of Congress that allows for detention of enemy combatants. Petitioner Hamdi, a U.S. citizen born in Louisiana, had been classified as an enemy combatant for fighting with the Taliban in Afghanistan, was captured in that conflict, and was detained at the naval brig in Charleston, South Carolina. His father filed a habeas petition for him under 28 USC 2241, alleging that the U.S. government held his son in violation of the 5th and 14th amendments. His father asserted that his son was doing "relief work" in Afghanistan before 9/11 and could not have received military training. Department of Defense records showed that Hamdi was captured with a Taliban unit and surrendered an AK-47 assault rifle (Legal Information Institute, 2004).

In another case, Jose Padilla (aka Abdullah al-Muhajir), a U.S. citizen, was arrested in 2002 at Chicago's O'Hare airport. He had been trained by al-Qaida in Afghanistan and he was to be questioned on al-Qaida's plans to detonate a "dirty bomb." He was brought to New York for detention in federal custody under a material witness warrant. Padilla was appointed an attorney and a

Figure 5-8 ■ A detention unit at Camp Delta, Guantanamo Bay, Cuba, on December 3, 2002, showing bed, comfort items, toilet on floor, and sink. DOD photo by Staff Sgt. Stephen Lewald, U.S. Army. http://www.defenselink.mil/photos/Dec2002/021203-A-7236L-010.html

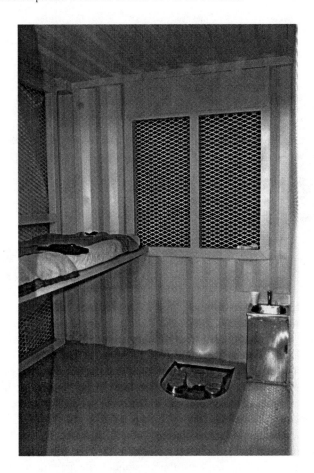

hearing was set; however, while being held, the executive branch designated him as an "enemy combatant." He was confined to the naval brig in Charleston, South Carolina, without access to counsel. In Rumsfeld v. Padilla (03-1027), decided June 28, 2004, the court ruled that the District Court for the Southern District of New York did not have jurisdiction to hear Padilla's habeas corpus petition.

Although Hamdi and Padilla are U.S. citizens, the former was captured in combat, while the latter was initially arrested and began to receive due process rights before being classified as an enemy combatant by the executive branch. Rather than charge Hamdi, the U.S. government sent him back to Saudi Arabia and set him free.

In Rasul *et al.* v. Bush *et al.* (03-334), decided on June 28, 2004, the court held that foreign nationals captured abroad and detained at Guantanamo may challenge the legality of their detention in federal courts. In other words, U.S. courts have jurisdiction over the Guantanamo detainees. The petitioners in this case, 2 Australians and 12 Kuwaitis, were captured during the war in Afghanistan and are being held in Guantanamo. They filed suit under federal law challenging the legality of their detention, alleging that they were not combatants against the United States or engaged in terrorism and that they had not been charged with an offense, received no counsel,

Figure 5-9 ■ The United States Supreme Court, one of the three powerful branches of the federal government, ruled that detainees at Guantanamo may have access to federal courts.

nor provided access to a court or tribunal. The District Court had earlier denied their habeas petitions (Legal Information Institute, 2004).

In reference to the legal controversy over military tribunals, Cole and Dempsey (2006: 189) refer to the decision in Hamdan v. Rumsfeld, 344 F. Supp. 2d 152 (D.D.C. 2004), in November 2004, when U.S. District Judge James Robertson ruled that the tribunals were illegal because they were being applied to persons not properly determined to be "enemy combatants" under the Geneva conventions and because the defendants were unable to confront secret evidence. This case was followed by Hamdan v. Rumsfeld, 2005 U.S. App. LEXIS 114–315 (D.C. Cir. July 15, 2005), in which a unanimous panel of judges, including John G. Roberts, Jr., now Chief Justice of the U.S. Supreme Court, reversed Judge Robertson and permitted the tribunals to proceed, emphasizing that the Geneva conventions do not limit the president in his treatment of al-Qaida prisoners. In June 2006, the U.S. Supreme Court ruled, in the case of Hamdan v. Rumsfeld, that the tribunals violated the Constitution and that the Geneva Conventions did apply to captives in the war on terrorism. Although the decision checked the president's power, his administration responded by working with Congress in an attempt to restore the tribunals through a new law. This occurred in October through the Military Commissions Act of 2006 that authorizes terror prosecutions before

COMBAT STATUS REVIEW TRIBUNALS (CSRT)

According to the DOD, in 2004 nearly 600 enemy combatants being held at the U.S. detention facility at Guantanamo had an opportunity to petition for their release (Rhem, 2004). The DOD designed a process to determine if detainees should continue to be held as a threat to the United States. The CSRT are administrative hearings and, thus, do not have to meet the standards of regular criminal proceedings. The process applies only to combatants captured in the Afghan theater and held at Guantanamo. The CSRT guidelines include the following:

- each detainee will present his case before a panel of three military officers
- an officer will be appointed as a representative to explain the proceedings, but not serve as a defense attorney

COMBAT STATUS REVIEW TRIBUNALS (CSRT)—Cont'd

- a translator will be supplied
- detainee family and home country can provide input
- Departments of State, Justice, and Homeland Security, and the CIA will provide input
- detainees are not permitted to see most of the evidence because it is classified
- the panel will decide to either continue to hold the detainee, release, or transfer him to his home country for continued detention

The *New York Times* provided a description of the CSRT (Lewis, 2004). Each day, shackled prisoners are led to a special doublewide trailer inside the Guantanamo detention facility to state their case before the panel. One 27-year-old Yemeni argued for an hour, denying he ever fought against the United States. The scraggly-bearded man, bound hand and foot, sat in a low chair, while his shackles were secured to a floor bolt. He appeared frustrated and angry. The Yemeni was unable to gesture with his hands and he spoke Arabic to a translator. He showed his contempt for the panel 10 feet away by ridiculing their questions.

According to the *New York Times*, these hearings are the executive branch's answer to the U.S. Supreme Court decision in *Rasul*, a ruling that detainees have a right to challenge their confinement through a writ of habeas corpus in federal court, even though the base is outside the United States. The Bush administration, seeking to retain control over the detainees, repeatedly argues its case in federal court and claims that the CSRT satisfies the rulings of the U.S. Supreme Court. Others claim that the executive branch is bypassing the court. Many detainees have been released.

Many of the detainees were unconvincing in their explanation of what they were doing when captured with AK-47s at battle sites. One Afghan, who served as a police chief under the Taliban, argued that he was an unwilling member of the Taliban. He admitted that he supervised a ritual stoning to death of three people charged with adultery, but claimed that he had not chosen the people or the sentences.

War-crimes trials at Guantanamo are also facing controversy. Problems include language translations and defense needs for information from the CSRT and other sources (Lewis, 2004).

CRITICAL THINKING:

What are your views of the way in which the executive branch handled the captives from the war in Afghanistan? What suggestions can you offer and why?

THE CASE OF THE YACHTED TERRORIST (FBI, 2004)

It was a bright, clear September day in the international waters of the eastern Mediterranean. A motorboat carrying a suspected terrorist, who was distinctly hung over from too much partying the night before, approached an 80-foot sailing yacht. From the yacht's deck, two women in shorts and halter tops beckoned him to come aboard. He eyed them appreciatively, thinking ahead to his imminent meeting with Joseph, an international drug dealer, who was promising him an opportunity to begin a lucrative new career. Was he ever about to be surprised.

The women and Joseph were undercover FBI agents. Once on deck, he was arrested and taken aboard a U.S. Navy munitions ship, the U.S.S. Butte, where he was read his rights and interrogated. As the Butte steamed toward a rendezvous with the aircraft carrier U.S.S. Saratoga, the suspect confessed to his involvement in several acts of terrorism. From the Saratoga, he was flown for a record-breaking 13 hours in a Navy Viking S-3 jet to be arraigned in Washington, DC, and ultimately was tried, convicted, and sentenced in a U.S. court. Case closed.

Continued

THE CASE OF THE YACHTED TERRORIST (FBI, 2004)—Cont'd

What's the significance of this remarkable operation? This was the first international terrorist to be apprehended overseas and brought back to the United States to stand trial.

When did it happen? On September 13, 1987.

Who was the terrorist? Fawaz Younis, one of the individuals implicated in the 1985 hijacking of a Royal Jordanian airliner. After taking the passengers hostage, including two Americans, and making several demands that were not met, the hijackers ordered the airplane's crew to land first in Cyprus, then Sicily, and finally Beirut. There they released the hostages, held a press conference, blew up the plane on the tarmac, and fled.

What Younis did not know was that his actions triggered a law passed by Congress just the year before—the Comprehensive Crime Control Act of 1984—that gave the FBI jurisdiction over terrorist acts in which Americans were taken hostage—no matter where the acts occurred; that authority was expanded in 1986 with the passage of the Omnibus Diplomatic Security and Antiterrorism Act.

Thus "Operation Goldenrod"—the first time those new authorities were used, sending a message to terrorists that we would pursue them no matter where they tried to hide.

What was the outcome? Younis was convicted of conspiracy, aircraft piracy, and hostage taking. In October 1989, he was sentenced to 30 years in prison.

military commissions and provides the president with the power to interpret international standards for prisoner treatment and interrogations.

The courts will continue to play a role in deciding whether the executive branch exceeded its power and in determining how certain aspects of the war on terrorism are managed.

DISCUSSION QUESTIONS

1. What are the pendulums of justice?
2. Should government increase police powers and curtail due process rights during serious crises?
3. What is the fourth amendment's relevance to government investigations?
4. What action did federal law enforcement agencies take toward noncitizens in the United States following the 9/11 attacks? What is your opinion of this action?
5. What is the difference between "racial profiling" and "legal profiling?"
6. Why did the U.S. government apply the status of "enemy combatants" to captives following the 9/11 attacks?

APPLICATIONS

5A YOU BE THE U.S. GOVERNMENT LEGAL SPECIALIST
You are a legal specialist working for a U.S. government agency. Your supervisor has requested that you provide a summary of the latest laws and court decisions pertaining to these topics: U.S. government investigations of suspected terrorists; the rights of citizens and noncitizens subject to investigations for alleged terrorist activity; and the rights of the enemy captured in the war against terrorism.

5B YOU BE THE LAW ENFORCEMENT OFFICER
You are a police lieutenant in a city police department. Since the 9/11 attacks, tension has developed between the local Arab-American/Muslim-American (AA/MA) communities and others. Immediately following the 9/11 attacks, several AA and MA men in the city and surrounding suburbs were detained, questioned, and released. Some were charged with immigration violations by federal authorities. Since 9/11, local

AAs and MAs have been victimized by various crimes such as assaults and vandalism. Two local mosques were defaced. Local AAs and MAs are bitter about their victimizations and how police treat them. Your assignment is to work with the local FBI to formulate a plan to build ties to these groups and seek their cooperation in the struggle against terrorism and other crimes. Prepare a plan and strategies. Also, study the following list, prioritize the items according to your opinion of the importance of each, and explain why you placed each in the order you listed (FBI, 2002: 40–43).

- Because humans have what is called negativity bias (i.e., humans are more affected by bad things happening than by good things happening), the good things done by police agencies will not be remembered as well as what is done poorly. Thus, reiterate successes as often as possible, both when they occur and when failures occur.
- Information provided by police should be as accurate as possible and the manner of presentation should be consistent. Erroneous information should be admitted and corrected as soon as possible. A response of "no comment" to an inquiry should be avoided because it creates the impression that information is being hidden; tell the audience when you cannot answer the question.
- To discourage individuals from joining extremist groups, police agencies can conduct information campaigns supported by AA and MA leaders; remind others of the backlash from the larger communities; emphasize the greater probability of political success from nonviolent strategies; and remind people of the victims from terrorist attacks.
- Establish good relationships with AA and MA groups before protection is needed against hate crimes and before the groups become a focal point of investigations. The "model of the beat cop" and community policing both offer avenues to develop positive relations. Police agencies find it difficult to obtain a second chance once a misunderstanding or problem occurs.
- To interact with AA and MA communities, police should have a basic understanding of world affairs, including world religions; the Arab–Israeli conflict; other global conflicts; and terrorism. This knowledge helps police become more sensitive to others in our multicultural environment.
- Contact the AA and MA communities via local organizations, including schools.
- Because the FBI is often not active on the community level, their presence is often interpreted as "bad news" rather than helpful. Thus, the FBI should work with local police to develop positive relations with AA and MA communities.
- Police agencies should nurture relationships with and recruit from AAs and MAs who view police in a positive light.

5C   YOU BE THE FBI AGENT
You are an FBI agent assigned to domestic counterterrorism investigations. A reliable informant has provided information about a U.S. citizen who is alleged to be operating businesses and charities that fund terrorist activities. How will you investigate and collect evidence for this case? What laws will you rely on in your investigation?

5D   YOU BE THE TERRORIST DETAINEE
You are an al-Qaida detainee captured in the Middle East and about to be interrogated by U.S. military personnel at a site outside the United States. For many years you have worked to eliminate the Western influence in the Middle East. You have been a member of al-Qaida for 5 years and have training and experience. As a devout Muslim believing in jihad, you are willing to die defending Islam and you will be rewarded in heaven. As part of an al-Qaida cell heading to the United States, you had planned to either detonate dirty bombs or plant explosives on passenger trains. What is your plan to withhold information when interrogated? What strategies do you think will be used against you? If you are at a point where you are forced to release information, what do you say? How do you convince interrogators that you are telling the truth?

5E   YOU BE THE MILITARY INTERROGATOR
You are part of a team of U.S. military personnel who are preparing to interrogate al-Qaida detainees captured in the Middle East and being held at a site outside the United States. What are your strategies of interrogation? Prioritize a list of 10 questions you would ask these detainees. What incentives do you

offer the detainees to facilitate cooperation? How do you deal with detainees who are uncooperative? How do you verify the truthfulness of the detainee statements?

5F YOU BE THE TERRORIST LEADER

As the leader of a terrorist cell in a Central American country, your cover involves being a chemistry instructor at a medical school. Other cell members hold skilled positions in the same country. As you have known for the last 2 years, the long-term target is the U.S. Naval Base at Guantanamo Bay, Cuba. Your spiritual leader has emphasized that it represents injustice, evil, and a major symbol of the U.S. war effort against Islam. You believe that the harsh treatment and torture experienced by your religious brothers at the base drew you to this mission.

The cell is working on two options. One option is to attack the stockade, even though fewer brothers are being held there than in the past. Brothers are unlikely to be freed in an attack, but an attack on this symbolic target will give brothers a chance for hope and an opportunity for the world to rejoice. The other option, in case the stockade is too formidable or closed due to global pressure, is to attack the Guantanamo community housing military personnel and their families.

A cell member has made inroads in the import/export business, has connections in the United States, and is seeking an opportunity to supply an item needed at either the military base or in the Guantanamo community. Another cell member is in the fishing business and has access to speedboats and other watercraft. A third cell member, a pilot, flies small planes for a delivery company and volunteers his services to charitable groups, including those linked to Cuba.

Collect information in the public domain on the military base, the stockade, and the community where military personnel and their families reside. Focus on public DOD Web sites, Guantanamo Bay newspapers and newsletters, and sites of special groups and events.

Based on the information you collect, choose whether you will target the stockade or the residential community, and justify your decision. What are your needs and plans of attack?

WEB SITES

American–Arab Anti-Discrimination Committee (ADC): www.adc.org

American Civil Liberties Union (ACLU): www.aclu.org

Amnesty International: www.amnesty.org

Department of Defense: www.dodmil

Duke University School of Law: www.law.duke.edu

Human Rights Watch: www.hrw.org

Legal Information Institute, Cornell University: www.law.cornell.edu

U.S. Naval Base Guantanamo Bay: www.nsgtmo.navy.mil

NOTES

American Bar Association (1972). *New Perspective on Urban Crime*. Washington, DC: ABA.

Bulzomi, M. (2003). "Foreign Intelligence Surveillance Act: Before and after the USA Patriot Act." *FBI Law Enforcement Bulletin*, 72 (June).

"Bush bans racial profiling" (2003). *Washington Post* (June 18). In R. Shusta *et al.* (2005). *Multicultural Law Enforcement: Strategies for Peacekeeping in a Diverse Society*, 3rd ed. Upper Saddle River, NJ: Pearson Prentice Hall.

Cole, D., and Dempsey, J. (2006). *Terrorism and the Constitution*. New York: The New Press.

Combs, J. (1988). "Alien and Sedition Acts." *World Book*, Vol. 1. Chicago: World Book, Inc.

Council on Foreign Relations (n.d.). "Balancing Security and Civil Liberties." www.terrorismanswers.org, retrieved October 6, 2004.

Crank, J. and Gregor, P. (2005). *Counter-Terrorism After 9/11: Justice, Security and Ethics Reconsidered*. Cincinnati, OH: Anderson Pub.

Democratic Members of the House Select Committee on Homeland Security (2004). *America at Risk: Closing the Security Gap* (February). www.house.gov/hsc/democrats/, retrieved July 27, 2004.

Department of Defense (n.d.). "Guantanamo Detainee Processes." www.dodmil/news/detainees.html, retrieved August 18, 2004.

Ellmann, S. (2002–2003). "Radical Profiling and Terrorism." *New York Law School Law Review*, 46.

FBI (2002). *Countering Terrorism: Integration of Practice and Theory* (February 28). Quantico, VA: FBI. Application list prepared with the assistance of this publication.

FBI (2004). "Headline Archives, the Case of the Yachted Terrorist" (September 15). www.fbi.gov, retrieved November 5, 2004.

Feuerlicht, R. (1971). *America's Reign of Terror: World War I, the Red Scare, and the Palmer Raids*. New York: Random House.

Guttentag, L. (2001). "ACLU's Lucas Guttentag: Immigrants and Civil Liberties." October 17. www.cnn.com/2001/COMMUNITY/10/17/guttentag. In J. Crank and P. Gregor (2005). *Counter-Terrorism after 9/11: Justice, Security and Ethics Reconsidered*.

Hall, K., Finkelman, P., and Ely, J. (2005). *American Legal History: Cases and Materials*, 3rd ed. New York: Oxford University Press.

Hentoff, N. (2004). "Rumors vanished in secret CIA prisons." Syndicated columnist, June 28.

Herman, A. (2000). *Joseph McCarthy: Reexamining the life and legacy of America's most hated senator*. New York: Free Press.

Isikoff, M. (2003). "Show-Me the Money." *Newsweek* (December 1).

Isikoff, M., and Klaidman, D. (2003). "Ashcroft's Campaign to Shore up the Patriot Act." *Newsweek* (August 25).

Koppel, N. (2004). "Red Cross believes US hiding detainees." Associated Press release, July 14.

Legal Information Institute (2004). "Supreme Court Collection." www.law.cornell.edu, retrieved December 6, 2004.

Lewis, N. (2004). "Guantanamo Prisoners Getting Their Day, but Hardly in Court." November 8. www.nytimes.com, retrieved November 8, 2004.

Locy, T. (2004). "Patriot Act blurred in the public mind." February 25. www.usatoday.com, retrieved February 26, 2004.

Mayer, J. (2003). *9-11: The Giant Awakens*. Belmont, CA: Wadsworth/Thomson.

Meincke, P. (2004). "Chicago officials present massive security network." November 16. www.ABC7Chicago.com, retrieved November 22, 2004.

Moschella, W. (2004), Assistant Attorney General, in letter to Mecham, L., Administrative Office of the United States Courts (April 30).

Myer, D. (1971). *Uprooted Americans: The Japanese Americans and the War Relocation Authority during World War II*. Tucson, AZ: University of Arizona Press.

National Commission on Terrorist Attacks Upon the United States (2004). *The 9/11 Commission Report*. www.9-11commission.gov/, retrieved July 26, 2004.

National League of Cities (2003). "Resolution #2004-37: Resolution Affirming the Principles of Federalism and Civil Liberties" (December).

Packer, H. (1968). *The Limits of the Criminal Sanction*. Stanford, CA: Stanford University Press.

Philpott, D. (2004). "Legal Issues: Defending the Homeland and Personal Freedoms." *Homeland Security Journal*, 2 (October).

Pickler, N. (2006). "Bush: secret prisons exist." Associated Press release, September 7.

Purpura, P. (2001). *Police and Community: Concepts and Cases*. Boston, MA: Allyn and Bacon.

Purpura, P. (2002). *Security & Loss Prevention: An Introduction*, 4th ed. Boston, MA: Butterworth-Heinemann.

Reichel, P. (2005). *Comparative Criminal Justice Systems*. Upper Saddle River, NJ: Pearson Prentice Hall.

Rhem, K. (2004). "Officials Set up Review Procedures for Guantanamo Detainees." May 19. www.defenselink.mil, retrieved May 19, 2004.

Shusta, R., *et al*. (2005). *Multicultural Law Enforcement: Strategies for Peacekeeping in a Diverse Society*, 3rd ed. Upper Saddle River, NJ: Pearson Prentice Hall.

SiliconValley.com (2004). "Controversial government data-mining research lives on." February 23. www.siliconvalley.com, retrieved June 2, 2004.

Solomon, J. (2003). "Saudis pay for bills of citizens detained in US." Associated Press release, October 18.

Tien, L. (2001). *Foreign Intelligence Surveillance Act: Frequently Asked Questions (and Answers)*. www.eff.org, retrieved November 17, 2004.

U.S. Department of Justice, Office of Victims of Crime (n.d.). *Responding to September 11 Victims: Lessons Learned From the States*. Washington, DC: U.S. Department of Justice. www.ovc.gov, retrieved April 18, 2005.

Vargas, M. (2002). *Removal Defense Checklist in Criminal Charge Cases*. October 15. NY State Defenders Association. www.nysda.org, retrieved December 2, 2004.

Worldnetdaily (2004). "Life with Big Brother: Tiny Tracking Chips Will Be 'Everywhere.'" October 2. www.worldnetdaily.com, retrieved November 22, 2004.

CHAPTER 6

PRIVATE SECTOR ACTION

OBJECTIVES

The study of this chapter will enable you to:

1. understand the losses, costs, and economic impact of the 9/11 attacks.
2. explain the business of homeland security and the interaction of government and business.
3. define privatization and explore its meaning in the global war on terrorism.
4. detail the private security industry and its role in homeland security.
5. list and describe at least five professional associations or industry groups and identify how each plays a role in homeland security.
6. discuss public–private partnerships and provide at least two examples.
7. discuss public police–private security cooperation.
8. explain the importance of citizen volunteers and volunteer organizations for homeland security.

KEY TERMS

business interruption
lobbyists
Support Anti-Terrorism by Fostering Effective
   Technologies Act of 2002
privatization
private military and private security companies
mercenary
transnational criminal organizations
social costs of terrorism
moral hazard
ASIS International
International Association of Security and
   Investigative Regulators

National Association of Security Companies
International Foundation for Protection Officers
National Fire Protection Association
American Society of Safety Engineers
American Chemistry Council
Food Products Association
Business Executives for National Security
American Red Cross
Salvation Army
National Volunteer Organizations Against
   Disasters
Citizen Corps
USA Freedom Corps

CAN AL-QAIDA DESTROY THE U.S. ECONOMY?

In an audiotape posted on an Islamic Web site in 2004, al-Qaida leader, Osama bin Laden, called on militants to attack the oil industry in the Middle East to destroy the U.S. economy. Bin Laden castigated Westerners for their intrusion into the Middle East to drain its oil supply. He also praised attacks against the United States in Saudi Arabia and in Iraq.

Bin Laden has used the economic threat repeatedly as a propaganda strategy to rally Islamic militants. He claims that militants have been successful on the economic front against superpowers. Although multiple factors led to the collapse of the Soviet Union, bin Laden claims that is was the mujahidin forces, including bin Laden, who fought against Soviet forces in Afghanistan for 10 years, in the 1980s, while draining the Soviet economy until the Soviet Union went bankrupt.

Bin Laden would also have others think that the 9/11 attacks caused a recession in the United States. A recession actually began earlier in 2001, although the attacks did adversely affect the travel and other industries. Bin Laden has taunted the U.S. government over its budget deficit of hundreds of billions of dollars—made worse by the wars in Iraq and Afghanistan, tax cuts, and an aging baby boom generation.

The economy of the former Soviet Union was different from the U.S. economy. The Soviets had an economy that was centralized, bureaucratic, and government owned and operated. The U.S. capitalist system is flexible and market driven, with less government controls.

Experts dispute the claims of bin Laden. Retired General William Odom, a specialist on the Soviet collapse, claims that terrorists "have never brought down a liberal democracy." ... "Terrorists like bin Laden can cause trouble but they're not a strategic problem, they're a tactical nuisance." Alan Krueger, a Princeton University economist, notes "the US economy is too large and diverse to be sunk by terrorism" (McHugh, 2004).

CRITICAL THINKING:

Do you think al-Qaida can destroy or harm the U.S. economy? Explain.

INTRODUCTION

In addition to government action against terrorism, there is a vast community of private sector businesses, organizations, associations, and volunteers that also play a major role in homeland security and the protection of American interests. Furthermore, joint-public/private sector initiatives exist. This chapter explores the private sector as an integral component of homeland security and shows how the public and private sectors interact.

LOSSES AND COSTS FROM THE 9/11 ATTACKS

Although the U.S. economy was in a recession beginning in March 2001, the 9/11 attacks did cause a temporary disruption of the nation's economy (Figure 6-1). Specifically, airlines suffered, consumer spending and business investment fell, and hundreds of thousands of layoffs occurred, mainly in the travel and leisure sectors. The attacks also cost the United States about $21 billion in property and insurance costs. Budget deficits followed the attacks because of the recession, tax cuts, the cost of combating terrorism, and the wars in Afghanistan and Iraq (Nyatepe-Coo, 2004: 87–88).

Quinley and Schmidt (2002: 30), risk specialists, estimate the *total direct cost of the 9/11 attacks on the World Trade Center (WTC) exceed $50 billion. About 3000 persons were killed*

Figure 6-1 ■ Terrorist attacks can cause not only loss of lives and injuries, but also tremendous economic losses.

in the attacks, including those at the Pentagon. Many of the victims at the WTC were born abroad, including many from Muslim countries. The deaths included people from about 80 nations. Thousands were injured, and others, including rescue workers, were affected by respiratory problems from the lingering smoke and dust at the WTC site. Direct costs from casualties included medical expenses, workers compensation payments, accidental death and dismemberment claims, and life insurance payments. Disability claims even came from individuals far from ground zero. Thousands of people needed counseling to deal with personal losses. Employees were assisted by Employee Assistance Programs (EAPs) and employers reported heavy demands on EAPs from employees far from the attack sites. (EAPs are used in the public and private sectors to help employees with a variety of problems, such as depression, substance abuse, and marital and financial problems. EAPs offer counseling and referral services to employees.) The psychological impact of the attacks became global. Media reports provided constant reminders of the carnage. Many people experienced fear and anxiety.

Quinley and Schmidt (2002: 31) note that when a terrorist attack occurs, some losses may be insurable, whereas others may not. Also, the impact on profits can be significant. Major corporations with operations in the WTC had charges in the tens of millions of dollars for uninsured losses. These charges paid life insurance benefits, extended medical coverage for surviving family members, counseling support services, relocation, and noncash items such as prepaid rent and leases.

Property damage near the WTC resulted from several causes. Firefighting efforts focused on life safety, and evacuated buildings were left to burn. Other causes were falling debris containing steel and concrete; a pressure wave, similar to a strong wind, from the collapsing towers; ground deformation from a sudden transfer of load that impacted buildings, roads, and underground infrastructure; and dust carried miles from ground zero (Risk Management Solutions, 2001).

Business interruption is another source of loss from the 9/11 attacks, although it can result from many other risks (e.g., natural disaster, accident) in addition to terrorism. It is defined as "the loss of profits of a business that suffers an indemnified loss when it is unable to manufacture its product(s) or provide its service" (Quinley and Schmidt, 2002: 33). Interdependencies within a business's operations or between separate businesses (e.g., a supplier to another business) can broaden the interruption.

Indirect costs from a terrorist incident are many. When infrastructure is destroyed, the impact can even reach those locations that sustained no property damage. Without utilities and passable roads, for example, businesses are unable to operate. Damaged subway stations beneath the WTC affected commuting patterns of many people. Businesses faced relocation costs and the expense of hiring replacement employees.

By the third month following the 9/11 attacks on the WTC, recovery costs amounted to about $700 million, primarily from the Federal Emergency Management Agency (FEMA), the U.S. Small Business Administration (SBA), and the state of New York. The federal government, as in other disasters, plays the largest role in providing financial and technical support for recovery. Specifically, about $344 million in public assistance was provided to New York City to repair infrastructure, restore critical services, and remove, transport, and sort debris. About $196 million in individual assistance, in the form of grants and loans, was spent on housing, mortgage, and rental needs; food stamps; and SBA low-interest loans to homeowners and businesses. About $151 million was provided through the U.S. Army Corps of Engineers, disaster medical assistance teams from the Department of Health and Human Services, and FEMA's Urban Search-and-Rescue Task Force (Haddow and Bullock, 2003: 96). Consequently, the enormous losses and costs from the 9/11 attacks illustrate the importance of the private sector, in addition to the public sector, taking action to prevent, mitigate, and recover from a variety of losses.

Long-term costs of the 9/11 attacks are far-reaching. Expenditures include enhanced national security, homeland security, and business security; war; higher insurance premiums; increased shipping costs; and costs resulting from immigration restrictions. The long-term impact of the 9/11 attacks also includes increased surveillance and access controls in society and enhanced police powers.

The *National Strategy for Homeland Security* (Office of Homeland Security, 2002: 65–66) includes economic response and recovery efforts under four central activities.

- *Local economic recovery.* The plan aims to improve federal support to state and local governments for enhanced economic recovery and private sector assistance.
- *Restoration of financial markets.* Following an attack, the Department of Homeland Security, the Department of the Treasury, and the White House would monitor financial markets and the impacts of attacks; develop responses; and work with state, local, and private sector entities.
- *National economic recovery.* Because a major attack can have an economic impact beyond the local area, the Departments of Homeland Security, Treasury, and State, the White House, and private sector participants would assess economic consequences and work to restore critical infrastructure and services to minimize economic disruptions.

- *Economic impact data.* Sound information about the nature and extent of the economic impact from an attack is vital for an effective response. The Department of Commerce's Economics and Statistics Administration and other federal agencies are preparing an economic monitoring, assessment, and reporting protocol to gather information on the economic status of an area before an incident and following an incident. The purpose is to help prepare an appropriate response.

Another concern following the 9/11 attacks was the movement toward globalization. We have seen an increase in controls over immigration, air travel, and the movement of goods and information. Although the attacks may have stalled the movement toward globalization, future trends suggest closer economic ties among the nations of the world (Nyatepe-Coo, 2004: 88).

> The 9/11 attacks were immensely successful and cost effective for the terrorists. With the loss of 19 terrorists and costs between $400,000 and $500,000, the attackers were able to kill about 3000 people, cause hundreds of billions of dollars in economic damage and spending on counterterrorism, and significantly impact global history. With such a huge kill ratio and investment payoff, governments and the private sector must succeed in controlling terrorism.

THE BUSINESS OF HOMELAND SECURITY

The homeland security market is a multibillion dollar industry of products and services. *Security Letter* reports on news from security businesses and provided results from two surveys on the size of the homeland security market and its growth.

Research by Homeland Security Research Corporation (HSRC) predicted that spending on homeland security would reach $50 billion in 2005, $125 billion in 2010, and $158 billion in 2015. For the rest of the decade, about 1.5% of gross domestic product (GDP) will be allocated to homeland security. HSRC reports the homeland security market breakdown, in 2005, as follows: 30% from DHS, 24% from the DOD and the intelligence community, 20% from other federal agencies, 20% from the private sector, and 6% from state and county homeland security. A decade later, HSRC predicts 22%, 33%, 18%, 22%, and 5%, respectively. HSRC notes that "a new industry was born on 9/11, and this industry is going to be a major player over the coming years" (Security Business, 2004a).

Civitas Group, another market research firm, points marketers with broad-use products and systems to concentrate on federal opportunities. This firm also sees plenty of opportunities for local security installers, integrators, and service businesses. They view the private sector as a large market because it controls 85% of the nation's critical infrastructure. Federal spending for security is huge, especially for aviation security in these areas: baggage screening, air cargo, information technology, and employee ID cards. The projection is $8.4 billion over 5 years. Maritime and port security is the next largest spending need for new Coast Guard vessels; port surveillance and monitoring; cargo screening, tracking, and locking systems; and seacoast surveillance technologies. Other major federal spending targets over the next 5 years are ground transportation security, border security, cybersecurity, emergency preparedness and response, prevention of terrorist use of WMD, intelligence systems, and related law enforcement spending (Security Business, 2004b).

In an article on government funding for homeland security and national defense, Paddock (2004: 6) writes: "the difference between the proposed budget and the emerging appropriation for homeland security reads like a textbook on the separation of powers." He adds: "... since the judicial branch focuses primarily on adjudicating disputes on how funding has been distributed, and equality is its primary goal, the real wrangling happens in the executive and legislative branches." With broad input from inside and outside of government, the office of the president prepares and delivers a proposed budget to Congress early in the year. The president's budget contains his vision and priorities. Upon receiving the budget, Congress sees it as a beginning point from which it will make modifications. The politics of Washington, DC, is illustrated through the budget process as politicians, interest groups, lobbyists, and others influence the budget. The closed-door conference process enables members of both the House of Representatives and the Senate to settle their differences and finalize the budget for the President's review and signature.

LOBBYISTS

The day after the 9/11 attacks, Washington **lobbyists**, who represent special interest groups, inundated congressional offices with calls that promoted their respective industries. The energized lobbyists represented a broad array of industries, such as defense, travel, insurance, computer, and others. Interestingly, they had redesigned their "sales pitch" to fit the new era of the war against terrorism. Congressman Edward Markey, a Democrat from Massachusetts, explained that no self-respecting lobbyist has not repackaged his position as a patriotic response to the tragedy. Although the insurance and airline industries had strong cases for assistance from the federal government because of huge losses, many other industries sought help. Farm lobbyists pushed for more farm subsidies to avert wartime disruption in the food supply, the oil industry aimed for drilling in the arctic wildlife refuge, and Boeing Aircraft and the U.S. Marines argued for a revival of the V-22 Osprey, a new aircraft grounded because of deadly crashes. The pressure on the federal system from lobbyists was vast. For instance, the American Traffic Safety Services Association, which represents manufacturers of traffic signs, requested more federal money for road signs to prevent traffic jams caused by people escaping from terrorist attacks. Date growers in California called for the addition of dates in food packages for Afghans during Ramadan, the Islamic holy month.

Lobbyists were not alone in their push for specific interests and agendas. The Bush administration and politicians from both parties saw the 9/11 attacks as additional justification for pre-9/11 proposals to protect America. In essence, politics thrive, even during national emergencies (Kernell and Jacobson, 2003: 488; Rosenbaum, 2001).

CRITICAL THINKING:

What are your views of lobbyists redesigning their "sales pitch" to fit the era of the war against terrorism?

BUSINESS OPPORTUNITIES

Many companies have made handsome profits and have seen their stock prices rise considerably because of the problem of terrorism. Invision Technologies, for example, maker of luggage scanning systems, has seen its stock soar 1367% from 2001 to 2004. The stock of RAE Systems, involved in chemical and radiation detection, climbed 730% during the same period. Other companies have had impressive performance. Successful companies often make products that have been sanctioned by homeland security law. For example, government mandates to improve aviation security have been a bonanza for Invision Technologies, a leader in X-ray machines and bomb detectors that check luggage.

Not all companies are successful. Many companies are struggling to market their products and services, but face frustration. Since 9/11, the government has given preference to those companies that have done business with the government prior to 9/11 and have proven to be trustworthy. The government is also fearful of investing in unproven technology. Other issues involve pressure on the Department of Homeland Security by the Office of Management and Budget to resolve security and integration problems before funds are awarded for contracts on new systems. Companies are concerned that government spending on homeland security may slow down because of increasing complacency the further we get from the 9/11 attacks, the costs of the conflict in Iraq; and the mounting federal deficit (Lemos, 2004).

Housman and Anikeeff (2004: 64–70) offer advice to companies seeking to contract with the Department of Homeland Security. Since 9/11, Congress has enacted many homeland security laws that impact numerous industries. Thus, markets are driven by federal laws, mandates, and regulations. For instance, the technology requirements mandated by the federal government for maritime facilities provide the direction companies must take to be successful in supplying security technology to ports and vessel owners. Likewise, federal statutes delegate mandates to states and localities for responding to WMD and companies should aim to fill such needs to remain profitable. Business people seeking contracts with the government should also understand the issues dominating homeland security procurement. These include proof that the product really works, how the product will increase security and safety and reduce vulnerabilities, and whether the product conforms to government regulations. Housman and Anikeeff note the importance of reaching the right people to make the best possible statements in the limited time available and to be convincing that the product or service is worth the interest of the government. They present similar advice for contracting on state and local levels. Additionally, contractors need to know state and local procurement regulations, and possibly who is the adjunct general for the National Guard or who is director of emergency management in each state. The Web offers a lot of information.

Another important issue for businesses is protection against liability. Companies that supply antiterrorism products, services, and software could be subject to litigation following a terrorist attack. Because no product is foolproof, each one has an error or failure rate. To illustrate, if a company does a superior job at researching, testing, and manufacturing a bomb screening system and it fails to detect one bomb that causes an airliner to crash, the company can face expensive liability. To encourage research and deployment of antiterrorism technologies, Congress passed the **Support Anti-Terrorism by Fostering Effective Technologies Act of 2002**, also known as the "SAFETY Act." As part of the Homeland Security Act, this law provides manufacturers or sellers with limited liability risks. Companies must submit plans for their technology to the Department of Homeland Security for review and to be eligible for protection. This requirement has raised concerns over the protection of intellectual property and trade secrets, and who would have access to this information and under what circumstances (Anderson, 2003: 140).

PRIVATIZING COUNTERTERRORISM

The challenges of combating terrorism require creative and innovative solutions. Governments struggle to collect information on terrorist groups whose members have similar cultural and religious ties and have a strong hate for Western society. Successful undercover penetrations or bribes are very difficult to achieve with terrorist groups. Their secretive and elusive methods and surprise, asymmetrical attacks make them a formidable opponent. They do not operate by the traditional rules of war. As President George W. Bush explained in a speech at the U.S. Military Academy in 2002, the 9/11 attacks represented "a new kind of war fought by a new kind of enemy," and the threats require "new thinking." Here we look at two avenues to supplement government efforts to combat terrorism: (1) private military and private security companies (PMPSCs) and (2) transnational criminal organizations (TCOs) (Mandel, 2004: 62–73).

PRIVATE MILITARY AND PRIVATE SECURITY COMPANIES

Privatization refers to private businesses performing tasks that have been accomplished historically by governments. Businesses sell their services to governments for a profit by claiming that they are more cost-effective and efficient than government agencies.

Private military and private security companies provide a wide variety of military and security services for a profit. These firms are growing rapidly worldwide. Governments, corporations, organizations, and individuals are relying on these companies for many reasons. A national government, for example, may need additional personnel because human resources and expertise are stretched to the limit and a rebel group is gaining strength. A corporation, organization (e.g., nonprofit aid group), or individual may require protection for operations in a foreign country containing an insurgency or a weak police or military. Also, a country may be dangerous because of a hodgepodge of self-defense forces, mercenary units, militias, and vigilante squads that maintain their own agendas. The uncontrolled proliferation of conventional arms has hastened the growth of armed groups.

Zarate (1998: 75–156) conducted extensive research on PMPSCs. He writes that the era when great states dominated the world, and often intervened in local and regional conflicts, no longer exists. This power vacuum has been filled by experienced military professionals who created PMPSCs that offer military and security services. Zarate notes that these companies originated in militarily advanced countries and rely on excess military expertise and a network of retired military officers.

Historically, governments have saved money by privatizing armed forces, also termed "mercenary armies." Advantages of mercenaries include greater flexibility in engaging in extra-legal activities such as covert assassination, kidnapping, or sabotage; the government escape route of "plausible deniability" (i.e., government deflecting responsibility for mercenary actions); speed of action because bureaucracy is limited; and less impact on the public from casualties when compared to casualties of government personnel. Mercenaries can also create problems for governments. For example, they can assist liberation movements to depose established regimes.

Zarate writes that the term mercenary is difficult to define and United Nations members disagree on its definition. He refers to a **mercenary** as "a soldier-for-hire, primarily motivated by pecuniary interests, who has no national or territorial stake in a conflict and is paid a salary above the average for others of his rank." Zarate sees the legal issues involving mercenaries as unclear, but views the legal status of companies that provide military and security services, such as training, security, and other noncombat activities, as outside the mercenary concerns of the international community.

Zarate offers two concerns: (1) PMPSCs could be hired by insurgents or foreign governments to destabilize an established regime or a government could hire a PMPSC to suppress a national liberation movement (e.g., group fighting colonialism or racism) and (2) PMPSCs that assist multinational corporations will act solely for the benefit of the corporation in foreign countries and create semisovereign entities supported by the contracting government. He adds that PMPSCs are regulated in most countries. In the United States, regulations are stringent and registration with the U.S. government is required.

In Iraq, companies helping to rebuild the country with multibillion dollar U.S. government appropriations initially relied on U.S. forces for protection. However, the growing insurgency forced U.S. forces to be redirected, and contractors quickly sought assistance from PMPSCs (Flores and Earl, 2004).

The hostilities in Iraq and Afghanistan provide excellent opportunities for PMPSCs, especially those companies with employees possessing military backgrounds who can provide support to the U.S. military and train the armies of weak countries. As the United States pursues a global war on terrorism, with limited armed forces, private contractors are in demand.

Reality Check: Private Companies in the War Zone

Krane (2003) reported that U.S. government outsourcing to private companies plays a major role in support of U.S. military operations worldwide. This is especially important because the United States has reduced its military. Private contractors support troops by handling a broad array of tasks, such as security, food preparation, mail, driving trucks, and bug control. Also, they may be attacked and forced to defend themselves. Because of the risks, salaries can range between $80,000 to over $100,00 per year, and tax free to $120,000. Experienced personnel, often with a military background, can earn $1000 a day. The number of private sector employees that support the U.S. military in Iraq is difficult to ascertain; estimates are between 10,000 and 20,000, making this group the largest coalition partner. There is about one contractor for every 10 military employees. Globally, private military companies earn about $100 billion annually from the government. Ninety companies were listed on the Web site for the Center for Public Integrity. U.S. legislators and others complain of the limited oversight of contractors hired by the executive branch of government and the connection between companies and politicians that fosters an aggressive foreign policy that creates profit from war.

Although accurate records are maintained of U.S. military casualties, the number of private workers killed is difficult to ascertain. Barstow (2004) reported on the gruesome deaths of four private security contractors killed, burned, mutilated, and hung from a bridge in Fallujah, Iraq, as a crowd celebrated under the charred, swinging corpses. Apparently, the contractors were lured into an ambush by men dressed in uniforms of the Iraqi Civil Defense Corps, who promised them safe passage through the dangerous city. However, the convoy encountered a classic ambush—it was blocked from the front and rear on a road, preventing escape.

CRITICAL THINKING:

If you could not find employment, would you seek employment in a war zone for 1 year to assist the U.S. military for a salary of $100,000, tax free? Why or why not?

TRANSNATIONAL CRIMINAL ORGANIZATIONS

Transnational criminal organizations generate profits through illegal enterprises that cross national boundaries. Examples of illegal enterprises include drugs, arms, stolen items, human trafficking, fraud, and extortion. Various groups make up TCOs, such as the Russian mobs, Italian mafia, Chinese triads, Japanese yakuza, and Columbia cartels.

Government partnering with TCOs can produce both positive and negative results, and the interaction is complex. Government involvement with TCOs to obtain intelligence has a long history and, today, government intelligence services rely on TCOs that have direct knowledge of terrorist groups. A government may have leverage (e.g., prosecution) over a TCO that can be applied to obtain valuable intelligence. A TCO may use means (e.g., torture) to obtain information that a government may avoid. TCOs may have cultural ties to terrorist groups that could aid in government undercover operations and action to disrupt terrorist financial resources and weapons acquisition. At the same time, if TCOs are assisting terrorists, they are also a serious threat and in violation of criminal laws beyond those resulting from their transnational crimes. TCOs may even use terrorist methods to protect their markets from government interference. Differentiating TCOs and terrorists, and the business and political agendas of each, are additional challenges for government as illustrated with narcoterrorism (see Chapter 2).

In 2005, President Bush signed the instrument of ratification for the UN Convention Against Transnational Organized Crime and its protocols on trafficking in persons and smuggling of migrants. According to the U.S. Department of State, widespread ratification among

U.N. members represents global efforts to combat transnational organized crime as a serious worldwide threat. This legally binding multilateral instrument is the first of its kind requiring parties that have not done so to adopt legislation criminalizing organized crime and cooperating with member states in investigating and prosecuting offenders.

ISSUES

Government use of PMPSCs and TCOs present complicated issues.

- How can governments best utilize PMPSCs?
- Is it ethical and legal for a government to partner with a TCO for intelligence or other assistance against terrorism?
- How can PMPSCs and TCOs be controlled?
- Will TCOs respond to the highest bidder—government or terrorists?
- How can governments be controlled when dealing with PMPSCs and TCOs?

CRITICAL THINKING:

What are your views of government contracting with private military and private security companies, and involvement with transnational criminal organizations?

PRIVATE SECURITY INDUSTRY

Studies of the private security industry suggest there may be as many as 90,000 private security organizations employing about two million security officers and other practitioners in the United States. There are about 17,784 state and local law enforcement agencies in the United States, employing 708,000 full-time sworn officers. Plus, there are about 88,500 federal law enforcement officers, bringing the total to about 797,000 officers (U.S. Department of Justice, Office of Community Oriented Policing Services, 2004: 1–2).

The *National Strategy for Homeland Security* (Office of Homeland Security, 2002: 65) states that private businesses and individuals reduce liability and contribute to homeland security when they protect their property (Figure 6-2). Protective measures include employee education and training, security services, and enhancements in technology. The *National Strategy* notes that insurers should provide the private sector with economic incentives to mitigate risks.

The costs of homeland security in the private sector are incurred by both the owners of businesses in the form of lower income and by the customers through higher prices. According to The Council of Economic Advisors, private businesses spent about $55 billion annually on private security prior to the 9/11 attacks and 50 to 100% more following the attacks. The percentage increase is subject to debate. *Security Letter* (Security Business, 2004a) reported that large corporations increased security spending only 4% since the 9/11 attacks, but this figure did not include security spending for information technology (IT) and human resources (HR).

According to Ewing (2004: 6), "even though the private sector owns 85 percent of the nation's critical infrastructure, it has done alarmingly little to protect it [from terrorism]." Ewing offers three reasons why the private sector has not participated in explosive spending to counter terrorism, similar to the federal government: (1) executives cannot justify security investments when they must improve financial performance and they must wait for tax incentives or government regulations; (2) spending could be wasteful prior to the setting of national standards; and (3) many executives see their companies as unlikely targets.

Figure 6-2 ■ Businesses implement security programs to protect people and property and to reduce liability. Private sector security also contributes to homeland security.

The Congressional Budget Office (2004: 2) provides an explanation as to "why the private sector might spend too little on security." "Businesses would be inclined to spend less on security than might be appropriate for the nation as a whole if they faced losses from an attack that would be less than the overall losses for society." Additionally, "there is a gap between the private and public costs of a terrorism event." "When terrorists target a business, they put others at risk, too." Others may not be able to hold the targeted business liable for damages they incur. "The **social costs of terrorism** would be the sum of those costs incurred by others and the private costs incurred by the targeted business."

According to the Congressional Budget Office, incomplete information about vulnerabilities, potential losses, or the costs of options for security can lead to minimal spending on security. Also, a business or the government may know of a specific target exposed to attack, but others may not know.

The term **moral hazard** refers to the reluctance of a business or individual from taking helpful protective measures because they see another party as likely to pay the costs of damages incurred. Insurers seek to reduce this problem by requiring the insured to take loss prevention measures and to pay a deductible and copayment. "In the case of homeland security, the prospect of moral hazard can create a gap between social and private costs if, for example, businesses expect the government to compensate them for major losses from an attack" (Congressional Budget Office, 2004: 3).

Although the private sector (i.e., businesses, institutions, and other entities) has been criticized for not doing enough to protect itself, at the same time, for hundreds of years, it has initiated its own methods of protecting its people and assets from a host of risks that have increased over time (Table 6-1). Historically, businesses simply could not depend on public sector (i.e., government) protection and the same holds true today. Consequently, many types of locations initiate security and loss prevention programs (Table 6-2). Large corporations and other entities may even maintain their own fully equipped and trained fire departments and emergency medical personnel to respond immediately to incidents while waiting for public emergency assistance.

Police, fire, and other public first responders are supported by tax dollars and, thus, funds, personnel, and resources are limited. Public police *serve the public* and concentrate on street crimes, traffic, and other public safety issues. They may patrol occasionally around businesses and they do respond to crimes against businesses. The fiscal limitations of public police cause companies, institutions, and a variety of organizations to establish their own proprietary (i.e., in-house) security force or contract the work to a service company, often called a "guard company." Private security officers patrol perimeters at private sector locations, maintain access controls, and perform other protection functions. With thousands of entities employing security officers, the qualifications, pay, training, equipment, and duties vary.

Large entities may have proprietary investigators, whereas smaller entities are likely to contract investigative work to an outside investigative firm. Private sector investigators perform many types of investigations, such as internal fraud, employee theft and embezzlement, applicant background check, computer crime, and due diligence (i.e., many types of investigations

---

Table 6-1 Risks[a]

Criminal acts	Natural disasters	Miscellaneous
Larceny/theft	Floods/excessive rain	Ethical misconduct
Burglary	Excessive snow/ice	Error
Robbery	Lightning	Waste
Embezzlement	Pestilence	Bad investment
Fraud	Earthquake	Accident
Shoplifting	Landslide	Equipment failure
Murder	Tornado	Fire
Terrorism	Hurricane	Explosion
Computer crime	Volcanic eruption	Pollution
Product tampering	Tidal wave	Power outage
Counterfeiting		Strike
Arson		Mine disaster
Vandalism		Chemical spill
Riot		Sonic boom
Extortion		Nuclear accident
Kidnapping		Proximity to risks
Hostage		War
Espionage		
Sabotage		
Mail crimes		
Bombing		
WMD		

[a]From Purpura (2002: 24).

Table 6-2 Locations Requiring Security and Loss Prevention Programs[a]	
Industrial	Hospital
Retail	Campus
Wholesale/warehouse	School
Railroad	Government
Airport/airline	Museum
Financial institution	Library
Office building	Park and recreation
Nuclear plant	Hotel/motel/restaurant
Utility	Sports/entertainment
Port	Others
Housing/residential	

[a]From Purpura (2002: 29).

legally expected to determine the accuracy of information, omissions, and financial status). Private sector investigations are either overt (i.e., open) or undercover (i.e., secret). The undercover private sector investigator may be hired as a regular employee, infiltrate employee groups, and collect information on a host of problems, such as theft and illegal drugs in the workplace. Public police may be involved in a private sector investigation in a partnership against crime. This would be mandatory if the private sector entity was to seek prosecution (Purpura, 2002: 240–242).

In addition to security officers and investigators, the private security field employs a wide variety of managers, supervisors, and specialists who perform duties as part of a proprietary security organization or as employees of a contract security service to client businesses or other entities. Security specialists may perform security surveys to identify vulnerabilities and design improved protection, prepare emergency plans, help coordinate physical security with IT security, or work with a team to protect people and assets from a variety of risks.

PROFESSIONALISM

For many years, business and government leaders have realized the importance of private security in helping to protect businesses, institutions, and other entities from crime, fire, accidents, and other risks. Today, we have extended this protection function to homeland security.

In 1976, the *Report of the Task Force on Private Security* of the National Advisory Committee on Criminal Justice Standards and Goals represented the first national effort to set standards and goals to maximize the professionalism, competency, and effectiveness of the private security industry. This report emphasized that all businesses that sell security services should be licensed and all personnel involved in such work should be registered. Additional recommendations included improved hiring criteria, higher salaries, better training, and state-level regulation (U.S. Department of Justice, 1976).

The U.S. Department of Justice also funded two other research reports on the private security industry, known as the *Hallcrest Reports. Private Security and Police in America: The Hallcrest Report* contained the contributions of both public police and private security to control crime, and problems and solutions of the security industry (Cunningham and Taylor, 1985). *Private Security Trends: 1970–2000, The Hallcrest Report II* provided security trends to the 21st century. It stated that private security is the nation's primary protective resource, outspending public law enforcement by 73% and employing 2.5 times the workforce (Cunningham *et al.*, 1990).

Common themes of the *Task Force Report* and the *Hallcrest Reports* were regulation of the security industry by all states; improved recruitment, selection, pay, and training of security personnel; and closer cooperation between public police and private security.

The American Society for Industrial Security, known as **ASIS International** (ASIS), is a major organization of security professionals who are at the forefront of improving the security industry through education and training, certifications, research, security guidelines, and global collaborative initiatives. The ASIS foundation funded research by Eastern Kentucky University, with support from the National Institute of Justice, to focus on three primary areas: (1) the size and economic strength of the various security sectors, including security services and providers of security technology; (2) changes in security trends pre- and post-9/11; and (3) the nature of the relationship between private security and law enforcement. Preliminary findings included the following (ASIS Foundation, 2004).

- Company security budgets in the United States increased 14% from 2001 to 2002, decreased slightly in 2003, and increased 10% in 2004.
- More companies are purchasing computer/network security systems (40%), burglar alarms (26%), and CCTV (24%) than any other types of security systems or products.
- Ninety percent of companies stated that security-related contacts with law enforcement had remained the same.

In 2005, the final report was released and it contained results of four different nationwide surveys: (1) all U.S. companies, (2) ASIS companies (ASIS members identified as security managers for companies), (3) ASIS security services (ASIS members identified as managers of companies that provide security services), and (4) local law enforcement agencies. A sample of the findings are listed next (Collins *et al.*, 2005).

- In the next fiscal year, all three types of companies expected increases in security budget/revenue.
- ASIS companies were about 20% more likely than all U.S. companies to report increased investments in security as a result of the 9/11 attacks.
- Over one-half of ASIS companies indicated an increased emphasis on information security following the 9/11 attacks compared to 31% of all U.S. companies.
- Of all U.S. companies, finance–insurance–real estate continue to be most impacted by 9/11, in comparison to transportation–communication–utilities, agriculture–mining–construction, manufacturing, and wholesale–retail.
- For all U.S. companies, the top three concerns were computer/network security, liability insurance, and employee theft. For ASIS companies, the top three were access control, property crime, and a tie between workplace violence and terrorism.
- One-half of ASIS companies reported increased contact with police agencies since 9/11, whereas only 10% of all U.S. companies reported increased contact. The researchers concluded that larger companies and those with professional security personnel have been much more likely to develop public–private partnerships than smaller companies.
- The least common type of contact with police agencies among ASIS companies and U.S. companies was on cyber crimes. The researchers surmise that the reason could be attributed to limited knowledge of cyber crime by police or inadequate response.

REGULATION OF THE PRIVATE SECURITY INDUSTRY

As with other industries, the private security field has its share of charlatans who tarnish the industry and create problems for consumers of security services and products (Table 6-3).

Table 6-3 Security Services and Products from the Private Sector[a]

Services	Products
Security officer protection	Access control systems
Investigation	Locks and keys
Undercover investigation	Intrusion detection systems
Central alarm station	Closed-circuit television
Armored truck	Fire alarm systems
Security survey	Barriers
Guard dog (canine)	Glazing
Deception detection	Doors
Honesty shopping service	Lighting
Terrorism countermeasures	Safes and vaults
Bodyguard/executive protection	Security vehicles
Information protection	Weapons
Information technology (IT) protection	Hardware and software to protect IT
Training	
Others	Others

[a]From Purpura (2002: 29).

The 9/11 attacks and associated fear have made this problem worse. In this multibillion dollar industry, sales personnel may exaggerate the capabilities of security services and systems, investigations and risk analyses may be exaggerated, and clients may be overbilled or billed for work not done. To protect consumers, and as national reports have recommended, states typically regulate, through licensing and registration, contract security officer services, private investigators, polygraph and other detection of deception specialists, and security alarm businesses. (Security consultants are generally not regulated, but consumers should verify professional memberships and certifications.) States vary widely on how they regulate this industry. Attempts, although unsuccessful, have been made through Congress to pass a national law to regulate this industry. To open a security business, state regulation may consist of these requirements: an application, a criminal records check, experience in the field, insurance, training, and an annual fee. Each state has its own requirements. States are seeking to improve both their regulation of the industry and the professionalism of security personnel, but problems remain.

One problem that has persisted for many years is the thoroughness of criminal records checks of security applicants. Historically, states would conduct criminal record checks of applicants only in the state of application. However, applicants may have a criminal record listed in other states and/or the federal system. Terrorists can exploit such a vulnerability by applying for security positions at critical infrastructure locations in states with weak regulatory controls. Following several years of effort by the security industry to reduce this problem, Congress passed the Private Security Officer Employment Authorization Act of 2004, which enables security service businesses and proprietary security organizations to check if applicants have a criminal history record with the FBI, which may emanate from one or more states. This act was included in the National Intelligence Reform Act of 2004.

Another serious issue is training for security officers. Proper training is essential *before* officers are assigned to duty. Training topics of importance include customer service, ethics, criminal law and procedure, constitutional protections, interviewing, surveillance, arrest techniques, post assignments and patrols, report writing, safety, fire protection, and specialized topics for client needs.

Efforts in Congress and in the legislatures of many states have been aimed at increasing training. However, there has been no success in Congress for a national training mandate and state training requirements vary. Because quality training means increases in costs in the competitive contract security business, such legislation has often been controversial.

Security Letter (McCurie, 2005: 2) reported that the United States lags behind other countries on security training. The Province of Ontario, Canada, requires 40 hours of training. Training hours required in Europe are as follow: Hungary, 350; Spain, 260; Sweden, 120; United Kingdom, 38; France, 32; and Germany, 24. In the United States, the required hours are AK, 48; CA, FL, and OK, 40; ND, 32; NY, 24; IL, 20; LA and VA, 16; MN and OR, 12; AZ, CT, GA, and UT, 8; AR, 6; NC, NV, SC, TN, and WA, 4; TX, 1; and 29 other states and DC, 0.

ASIS International, in its effort to increase professionalism and develop guidelines for the security industry, published *Private Security Selection and Training* (ASIS International, 2004). This guideline was written for proprietary and contract security and regulatory bodies. Its employment screening criteria includes 18 years of age for unarmed and 21 years of age for armed security officers; high school diploma, GED, or equivalent; fingerprints; criminal history check; drug screening; and other background checks. The training requirements include 48 hours of training within the first 100 days of employment.

The **International Association of Security and Investigative Regulators** (IASIR) consists of state licensing regulators who share information and seek to promote the professionalism of the security industry. Among the group's goals are to enhance the security applicant process, keep abreast of new technology, assist with education and training standards, and formulate model laws and regulations.

Whereas the IASIR consists of government regulators of the security industry, the **National Association of Security Companies** (NASCO) represents the interests of the multibillion dollar security officer service business. NASCO seeks to upgrade standards and improve professionalism in the industry, participate in the formulation of relevant legislation, promote uniformity of regulation throughout the Unites States, and increase public awareness of the important role of private security in conjunction with public police.

Reality Check: Do Business Security Executives View Terrorism as Their Number One Concern?

Business security executives have many concerns, in addition to terrorism. Here is a sample of responses from security executives who shared their priorities with the editors of *Corporate Security* (Security Executive Forum, 2003). A vice president of corporate security at a broadcasting company saw violence in the workplace as a major threat. This executive saw a greater chance of violence on the premises from an employee or outsider than from al-Qaida. A loss prevention manager also viewed violence in the workplace as a serious threat, especially as employees, former employees, and spouses of employees have made threats. Directors of security for an oil and gas company and a bank viewed the risks to information technology as the greatest threat. They agreed with the trend of traditional, physical security linking up with IT security. A director of surveillance for a resort saw the greatest threat to business coming from employees, specifically employee theft, fraud, and workplace violence. However, other security executives saw terrorism at the top of the list of threats. A director of security for a medical center saw a major threat to the nation's infrastructure, especially power stations, water supplies, and key transportation modes. A food company security director saw the next threats coming from bioterrorism or from an attack on the food industry (Security Executive Forum, 2003).

BASIC DIFFERENCES BETWEEN PUBLIC POLICE AND PRIVATE SECURITY

Primary differences pertain to the *employer*, the *interests served, basic strategies*, and *legal authority*. Public police are employed by governments and serve the general public. Tax dollars support public police activities. However, private security personnel are employed by and serve private concerns (e.g., businesses) that provide the funds for this type of protection. There are exceptions to these general statements. For instance, government agencies sometimes contract protection needs to private security agencies to cut costs. Also, public police often are involved in efforts to assist business owners in preventing crimes through security surveys and public education.

Another difference involves basic strategies. Public police devote considerable resources to *reacting* to crimes. This entails rapid response to serious crimes, investigation, and apprehension of offenders. Law enforcement is a key objective. In contrast, private security personnel stress the *prevention* of crimes; arrests are often deemphasized. These generalizations contain exceptions. For instance, public police have introduced *proactive strategies* to reduce crime through aggressive patrol methods and enhanced information systems that assist police officers on the street in identifying suspects they encounter.

The legal authority of public police and private security personnel is another distinguishing characteristic. Public police derive their authority from statutes and ordinances, whereas private security personnel function commonly as private citizens. Public police have greater arrest, search, and interrogation powers. Depending on the jurisdiction and state laws, private security personnel may be deputized or given special commissions that increase powers (Purpura, 2002: 31).

PROFESSIONAL ASSOCIATIONS AND INDUSTRY GROUPS

The private sector includes numerous professional associations dedicated to improving the world in which we live and in promoting safety and security. These missions are accomplished by enhancing the knowledge, skills, and capabilities of members through training and education; offering certifications to demonstrate competence; conducting research; producing "best practices" and standards; disseminating information; communicating the group's goals; forming partnerships to reach common objectives; participating in community service; and advocating positions on key issues.

Professional associations typically require annual dues that pay for administrative and other expenses that are beneficial to members. Membership benefits include opportunities to network among peers; subscriptions to the group's periodicals and informative e-mails; members-only Web site privileges; discounts on national and regional educational programs and seminars; opportunities to serve on specialized committees; and career guidance and placement services.

The reader is urged to join one or more professional associations for a truly enriching experience as one develops his or her career. What is invested in membership activities impacts what is received in return. This section provides a summary of some associations, whose Web addresses are at the end of the chapter, to show how each plays a role in homeland security. Subsequent chapters also provide insights into professional associations. The reader should look to associations to decide which ones fit their vocation and interests for a more professional career.

ASIS International, formed in 1955, is the leading general organization of protection executives and specialists with more than 33,000 members worldwide. This organization includes all of the aforementioned characteristics of professional associations. It offers three certifications: certified protection professional, physical security professional, and professional certified investigator. For each certification, the candidate must pay a fee for administration, meet eligibility requirements, and successfully pass an examination. At this group's headquarters in Alexandria, Virginia, is the O.P. Norton Information Resource Center (IRC) that contains a clearinghouse of security industry knowledge. The professional librarians at the IRC are superb sources of information and members can borrow items on site or through the U.S. mail. ASIS International publishes *Security Management* and addresses specific security industry issues through guidelines that increase the effectiveness and productivity of security practices and solutions.

Whereas ASIS International is the leading professional association of security executives and specialists, the **International Foundation for Protection Officers** (IFPO), founded in 1988, is the leading professional association of security officers who are on the front lines of protecting businesses, institutions, other entities, and our infrastructure. The IFPO has global reach and serves to help professionalize officers through training and certification. It has developed several distance delivery courses and programs: the entry level protection officer, the basic protection officer, the certified protection officer program, the security supervisor program, and the certified security supervisor program. All programs are designed for self-paced home study and some are available on-line. Many corporations and institutions have included these programs into their professional development programs for security personnel. The IFPO publishes *Protection News*, a quarterly newsletter of valuable information, trends, and commentary.

The **National Fire Protection Association** (NFPA), established in 1896, is a potent voice in fire protection and public safety, with over 75,000 members representing nearly 100 nations. It publishes fire standards and codes that are often incorporated into state and local fire laws. One of its popular codes is the NFPA 101 Life Safety Code, which establishes minimum require-ments for new and existing buildings to protect occupants from fire, smoke, and other hazards. Another popular code is the NFPA 1 Fire Prevention Code, which provides the requirements to establish a reasonable level of fire safety and property protection in new and existing buildings. The NFPA has many ongoing committee projects developing publications on a wide variety of safety issues, such as aircraft rescue and fire fighting, emergency medical services, explosion protection systems, protective clothing and equipment, fire doors and windows, fire investigations, training, loss prevention, and firefighter professional qualifications.

The NFPA is heavily involved in public safety education for people of all ages and professional development through seminars, conferences, and publications. Its certification programs include certified fire protection specialist, certified fire inspector, and certified fire plans examiner. The NFPA is a major source of fire data analysis and research. It publishes several periodicals, including the *NFPA Journal*.

The **American Society of Safety Engineers** (ASSE), founded in 1911, is the oldest and largest professional safety organization dedicated to advancing the safety profession and enhancing the knowledge of safety practitioners who focus on the protection of people, property, and the environment. With 30,000 individual members, the ASSE is involved in national programs, standards, education, training, publications, and certification. The society's standards development committee participates globally in standards development to expand the body of knowledge on safety. Members have served on federal committees and supported safety and health legislation. The society maintains a strong commitment to proactive government affairs, having impacted regulations promulgated by the Occupational Safety and Health Administration (OSHA), the Environmental Protection Agency (EPA), and the Army Corps of Engineers.

The **National Association of County and City Health Officials** (NACCHO) provides us with an illustration of the wide variety of associations that play important roles in homeland security and public safety in general. The NACCHO, which acts as an advocacy group, provides education, information, research, and technical assistance to local health departments and it facilitates partnerships among all levels of government to improve public health. This association has been active in the area of emergency response to bioterrorism; however, it maintains the belief that the preparedness for bioterrorism permits the development of a multiuse infrastructure to respond to *all hazards*. It partners with the Centers for Disease Control (CDC), a federal agency, on several programs to improve responses to not only bioterrorism, but also communicable diseases and environmental health threats.

Another example among the many organizations that improve homeland security is the **American Chemistry Council** (ACC). The ACC is an industry advocate group that represents the leading companies involved in the business of chemistry. It sponsors research on the potential impacts that chemicals may have on the health of human and wildlife populations and the environment. The ACC offers publications, sponsors science meetings, and partners with the U.S. EPA, among other groups. The ACC promotes its "Responsible Care Security Code" that addresses plant site, transportation, and cyber security. It supports meaningful federal security legislation for the chemical industry.

The **Food Products Association** (FPA) is a global industry group representing the multibillion dollar food processing business on scientific and public policy issues involving food safety and security, nutrition, technical and regulatory matters, and consumer affairs. FPA members produce processed and packaged food and drinks or provide supplies and services to food manufactures. The benefits of membership include education, publications, Web site access, networking, testing and evaluation, consultation, legislative advocacy, and crisis management assistance. The FPA maintains a Center for Food Security and Emergency Preparedness. This office offers a wide array of support, training, and response programs. Assistance is available for risk analysis, security plans in conjunction with federal regulations and guidelines, and protection against workplace violence, terrorism, and fraud.

The next chapter provides information on risk management and emergency management groups, and in other chapters, a variety of specialized groups are discussed. In addition to professional associations and industry groups, let us not forget the many federal and state agencies that offer a wealth of information on homeland security, terrorism, and public and life safety. Examples are the Department of Homeland Security (DHS), FEMA, EPA, and OSHA, among many others. As we know, the Web is a superb source of information.

CRITICAL THINKING:

While developing your career, would you join a professional association? Why or why not?

PUBLIC–PRIVATE SECTOR PARTNERSHIPS

Reimer (2004: 10–12) sees the national system of preparedness for terrorism as a work in progress requiring a series of partnerships among the various levels of government, the public and private sectors, and the military. He notes that the strength of these partnerships will determine our level of preparedness. With the private sector owning 85% of U.S. critical infrastructure, Reimer emphasizes that private sector cooperation is essential. However, Reimer writes of the need for a common definition of "critical infrastructure" and the importance of defining the responsibilities of the public and private sectors.

Weidenbaum (2004: 189) argues that "the multifaceted national response to the September 11 terrorist attacks are altering the balance between the public and private sectors in the US." He describes the federal government effort against terrorism as a "mega priority" of programs and activities. This includes increased spending on the military and homeland security, special assistance and funding to companies heavily affected, and an expansion of government regulation of private activity, especially business. Weidenbaum notes that terrorism results in a hidden tax on businesses in the United States and overseas in the form of added costs of operation. In a business, security is an expense that raises the cost of production. Security expenses include security officers, security systems, and personnel investigations. Other costs are higher insurance premiums, larger inventories to protect against delays, and teleconferencing equipment to replace travel.

The U.S. Treasury Department, for example, has directed companies in not only the finance business, but also brokerage firms, casinos, and other businesses to reduce terrorist financing by taking specific steps at their own expense, such as establishing or expanding antimoney-laundering programs. The U.S. Department of Transportation has greatly increased security of all modes of transportation, beyond the airline industry. The U.S. Food and Drug Administration provides guidelines to the food industry to prevent terrorist attacks on the nation's food supply. The Nuclear Regulatory Commission ensures that nuclear power plants maintain an optimum level of security. The chapter on infrastructure expands on this interaction between government and industry that results in expensive upgrades of security and protection.

Although the federal government regulates certain aspects of private industries to protect against terrorism and other risks, it does listen to industry concerns about the impact of regulations, but this does not necessarily mean that the government will change its position.

SHARING INFORMATION

To facilitate communications and to share information on homeland security with private industry, the federal government hosts conferences and training sessions. Federal initiatives include disaster-preparedness grants from FEMA involving coordination efforts of local governments and businesses. Another initiative is the Information Sharing and Analysis Centers (ISACs). These are generally private sector networks of organizations that the federal government has helped create to share information on threats to critical industries and coordinate efforts to identify and reduce vulnerabilities. For example, the North American Electric Reliability Council shares threat indications and analyses to help participants in the electricity sector take protective action. Chemical, petroleum, and other industries participate in ISACs (Congressional Budget Office, 2004: 6–7).

A variety of other public–private sector information-sharing programs are operating. For example, the Homeland Security Information Network-Critical Infrastructure (HSIN-CI) enables key executives in the public and private sectors to receive alerts and notifications from the DHS via phone (landline and wireless), e-mail, fax, or pager. It is set up on a regional basis with regional Web sites and not every region receives the same alerts.

Another example is the terrorism early warning (TEW) concept that originated with the Los Angeles County Sheriff's Department in 1996. It involves gathering intelligence from a variety of sources, analyzing it, and distributing it to first responders and to private industry within a given region. The idea has spread to other states, TEWs exchange information, and the DHS supports the concept.

SHARING ASSETS

Another way in which public and private sectors can partner is by sharing assets. Businesses in the United States, for example, own many trucks, aircraft, buildings, heavy equipment, communications systems, etc. In the event of an emergency, these assets could be helpful to governments at all levels. Businesses also employ all types of specialists who could volunteer their time during an emergency. A bioterrorism attack, for instance, could require the need for mass inoculations and the need for volunteers from the private sector medical community. But how can these partnerships be coordinated? One avenue is the **Business Executives for National Security** (BENS). This organization is nationwide, nonpartisan, and works to help improve the safety and security of America. It created a business force initiative to plan for the utilization of both business personnel and physical assets in the event of a terrorist attack. Since 1982, BENS members have been applying their business experience to find practical solutions to national security challenges. Noting that no business could survive under the weight of 70% overhead and support versus only 30% for operations (the Department of Defense's situation), BENS's Tail-to-Tooth Commission (a panel of CEOs, former defense secretaries, members of Congress, and the military) pinpointed practices the Pentagon can discontinue and replace with world-class business methods to improve efficiency and save billions of dollars annually. Additionally, BENS members have partnered with government leaders to work on solutions to stop the proliferation of WMD, track terrorist financing, improve intelligence capabilities, and prepare communities for bioterrorism.

CRITICAL THINKING:

What are your views of what Business Executives for National Security is trying to accomplish?

PUBLIC POLICE–PRIVATE SECURITY COOPERATION

According to a 2004 national policy summit on public police and private security cooperation, only 5–10% of law enforcement chief executives participate in partnerships with private security (U.S. Department of Justice, Office of Community Oriented Policing Services, 2004: 2). Although both groups have much to offer each other, they are not always comfortable working together. Police criticize security over their lower standards for screening and training and they may see security as a threat to their domain. Police often fall short of understanding the important role of private security. At the same time, some security personnel see police as elitists and claim that police are not concerned about security until they seek a position in the security field.

Cooperation between both groups takes many forms and occurs at many levels of government. To varying degrees, both groups share information with each other, attend each other's conferences, and plan together for protection and emergencies. They even work side by side at certain sites, such as downtown districts, government buildings, and special events. Plus, many off-duty police officers work part-time in security and retire to assume a security position.

An improved partnership between both groups can be beneficial to our nation by improving planning and emergency response and by sharing information, expertise, and training. In 2004, at a national policy summit, public police and private security leaders recommended that both groups should make a formal commitment to cooperate. Also, the DHS and/or the DOJ should fund relevant research and training; create an advisory council to oversee partnerships to address tactical issues and intelligence sharing, improve selection and training for private security personnel, and create a national partnership center; and organize periodic summits on relevant issues. On the local level, immediate action should be taken to improve joint response to critical incidents; coordinate infrastructure protection; improve communications and data interoperability; bolster information sharing; prevent and investigate high-tech crime; and plan responses to workplace crime (U.S. Department of Justice, Office of Community Oriented Policing Services, 2004: 3–4).

CITIZEN VOLUNTEERS

The *National Strategy for Homeland Security* (Office of Homeland Security 2002: 12) makes the following statements concerning the importance of citizens becoming involved in homeland security.

> All of us have a key role to play in America's war on terrorism. Terrorists may live and travel among us and attack our homes and our places of business, governance, and recreation. In order to defeat an enemy who uses our very way of life as a weapon—who takes advantage of our freedoms and liberties—every American must be willing to do his or her part to protect our homeland.

Brian Jenkins, a noted authority on terrorism, points out that although public and private sectors maintain contingency plans to put into effect during heightened states of alert and emergencies, citizens must "learn to take care of themselves, to be mentally tough and self-reliant. Those who expect the government to protect them from everything are in for a lot of disappointments." He writes that for homeland security to succeed, citizens must be involved in the defense of their communities, and with quality training, "the entire United States can be turned into a vast neighborhood watch—a difficult environment for terrorists." Jenkins goes on to note that there will never be enough police and firefighters to protect all citizens. Also, the first people at the scene of an attack are the unfortunate people who are there at the time of the attack. They need to learn how to protect themselves and others until first responders arrive. Jenkins (2003) offers the following recommendations.

- More "news you can use" stories in the media.
- Schools, employers, and private organizations can provide practical instruction on how to respond to various emergencies.
- More trained volunteers.
- Because there are about two million people involved in the private security industry, special training can be mandated for these people.

VOLUNTEER ORGANIZATIONS

Volunteer organizations play a vital role of assistance when disasters strike (Figure 6-3). Two noteworthy, national groups are the **American Red Cross** and the **Salvation Army**. Red Cross chapters have been involved in a variety of community-based programs for many years. These include services for seniors, volunteers for hospitals and nursing homes, food pantry and hot lunch programs, homeless shelters, and youth programs. The Salvation Army also has a long

Figure 6-3 ■ Hurricane disaster victims in Florida obtain assistance from a relief center staffed by volunteers. Courtesy: FEMA. http://www.photolibrary.fema.gov/photolibrary/photodetails.do?id=10738

history of helping people. It is an evangelical organization dedicated to helping needy people through free temporary shelter and meals. The Salvation Army's thrift stores receive donated clothes and household goods that are sold to generate revenue. This group is also known for its adult substance abuse rehabilitation centers. Both the Red Cross and the Salvation Army partner with all levels of government to support the immediate, critical needs of disaster victims. These needs include food, shelter, and clothing.

Many other volunteer groups assist disaster victims. The **National Volunteer Organizations Against Disasters** (NVOAD) consists of several national groups that rely on NVOAD to coordinate disaster response for increased efficiency.

CITIZEN CORPS

In January of 2002, President George W. Bush launched **Citizen Corps** to coordinate and channel citizen volunteers to help with homeland security and disaster preparedness efforts. Citizen Corps is a part of **USA Freedom Corps**—a federal government program that facilitates a partnership of nonprofit, business, educational, faith-based, and other sectors to increase citizen involvement in their communities. USA Freedom Corps seeks to create a culture of service, citizenship, and responsibility, while increasing civic awareness and community involvement. In addition to Citizen Corps, USA Freedom Corps includes four other federal service programs.

1. *The Peace Corps* is a volunteer program whereby members work with people in developing countries to improve their living conditions and promote understanding between nations.
2. *AmeriCorps* consists of members who are selected by and serve with local and national nonprofit organizations such as the American Red Cross, Habitat of Humanity, and Boys and Girls Clubs of America. Members earn a living allowance and an educational award that can pay for college. Most of the grant funding for this program is allocated to state service commissions that award grants to groups that focus on local needs.
3. *Learn and Serve America* offers grants to educational institutions and nonprofit groups to facilitate community service and good citizenship by students.
4. *Senior Corps* utilizes the experience and skills of older citizens for a wide variety of volunteer community activities, including educational services for children and adults, safety patrols, and assistance following disasters.

Citizen Corps is coordinated by the Federal Emergency Management Agency within the Department of Homeland Security. Citizen Corps funds organizing and training activities of local Citizen Corps Councils, which aim to increase community involvement in the Citizen Corps, facilitate community action plans, and identify local resources. Programs and partners of the Citizen Corps follow (U.S. Department of Homeland Security, 2005).

COMMUNITY EMERGENCY RESPONSE TEAM (CERT)

The CERT Program, administered by the DHS, educates citizens about disaster preparedness and they receive training in basic disaster response skills, light search and rescue, and disaster medical operations. If a disaster occurs that overwhelms first responders or if victims are waiting for assistance, CERT members, in their neighborhood or workplace, can provide support until help arrives. At one fire emergency, CERT members assisted with evacuation, handled donations, and prepared food for firefighters. These trained volunteers are also beneficial for nonemergency projects that improve public safety, such as distributing disaster education material, providing services at special events, and providing smoke alarms to residents.

To become a CERT member, a citizen completes training from a sponsoring agency, such as an emergency management agency, fire department, or police department. These agencies receive support from Citizen Corps Program funds allocated to each state.

FIRE CORPS

The Fire Corps aims to support fire departments across the country by enabling citizen volunteers to participate in nonemergency activities. This assistance permits firefighters to spend more time with critical tasks. Fire Corps volunteers perform routine administrative tasks and expand educational outreach to community residents to help them protect themselves from fire hazards. The Fire Corps is a partnership of the DHS and numerous fire service organizations.

MEDICAL RESERVE CORPS (MRC)

The MRC consists of practicing and retired physicians, nurses, and other health professionals who volunteer their services to address public health issues and assist their communities during large-scale emergencies. How a MRC is utilized is decided locally. For example, a MRC can volunteer at local health centers and hospitals to assist with ongoing public health needs, such as immunizations, screenings, and nutrition. During an emergency, a MRC can assist response teams with patients and provide direct care. The MRC is administered by the U.S. Department of Health and Human Services.

NEIGHBORHOOD WATCH PROGRAM (NWP)

The NWP has been in existence for over 30 years as a popular way to unite local officials, police, and citizens to protect communities. It is funded by the U.S. Department of Justice and administered by the National Sheriffs' Association. The program consists of neighborhood residents who watch for suspicious activity and report such activity to police and other residents. The major goals of the NWP are to get citizens involved in local crime prevention, improve community safety and security, make people feel more secure, and reclaim high-crime areas. Neighborhoods that participate in this program are recognized by the familiar "crime watch" street sign (Figure 6-4). Following the 9/11 attacks, the need to secure our communities has become more important and the NWP has taken on an expanded role. The NWP can serve as a foundation for terrorism awareness, disaster preparedness, and the CERT program.

Figure 6-4 ■ The Neighborhood Watch Program has taken on greater significance since the 9/11 attacks.

VOLUNTEERS IN POLICE SERVICE (VIPS)

Because the 9/11 attacks resulted in increased demands on public police, innovation has been a way to better utilize limited budgets and resources. One avenue to allow police to spend more time on essential duties is to seek the assistance of citizen volunteers. VIPS utilizes the time and skills of civilian volunteers to supplement police tasks. This program recruits, screens, trains, and integrates citizens into the activities of police agencies. VIPS is funded by the U.S. Department of Justice and administered by the International Association of Chiefs of Police (IACP).

ARE SPONTANEOUS VOLUNTEERS DANGEROUS?

Disasters often draw spontaneous volunteers who are eager to help by offering their time, expertise, and equipment. These individuals can range from volunteers who show up with a pair of gloves and a shovel, ready to dig through debris, to medical doctors. Spontaneous volunteers can provide valuable assistance at a disaster site, but they can also create problems and hinder recovery efforts. Wagman (2005: 34–38) writes about issues involving spontaneous volunteers and what can be done to prepare for them.

Wagman refers to research by Kendra and Wachtendorf (2002), from the Disaster Research Center, University of Delaware, who identified six motivations for people to converge on a disaster site.

1. People evacuated return to seek information or retrieve possessions from their home or workplace.
2. Outsiders travel to the site to gather information on family and friends.
3. Volunteers arrive to help.
4. People are curious about the disaster.
5. Some are motivated by greed. Vendors may arrive to sell items for a profit that is supposed to benefit victims.
6. Fans of emergency workers may arrive to wave flags, display banners, and show appreciation.

Wagman notes the danger to spontaneous volunteers, such as hazards customary to disasters (e.g., fire and falling debris) and exposure to hazardous substances and WMD. Spontaneous volunteers typically do not possess the training, expertise, protective gear, and equipment of emergency professionals.

Other issues include liability and workers compensation. What if a volunteer is injured or injures someone else? Emergency managers should determine who is and who is not a designated volunteer.

What can government do about spontaneous volunteers? Wagman writes that emergency management agencies and volunteer organizations across the country are working on ways to manage the problem. Ideally, all volunteers should be affiliated with an established organization. In reality, this is not so and turning away volunteers can result in adverse publicity and bad feelings. Solutions include (1) planning in the preparedness phase for coordination of unaffiliated volunteers when a disaster strikes; (2) establishing a volunteer coordinator position in government and training the individual; (3) planning for a processing center for volunteers, near a disaster site, so volunteers can be interviewed on expertise and equipment, be registered and issued identification, and receive an assignment with a supervisor; and (4) look to Citizens Corps as an avenue to channel volunteers, before disasters strike. Wagman writes that Florida's system of using a hotline for volunteers in 2004, during multiple hurricanes, handled about 100,000 calls and was a critical tool to manage spontaneous volunteers.

CRITICAL THINKING:

Do you think spontaneous volunteers are more helpful or harmful following a disaster? Explain your answer.

GET READY NOW

The U.S. Department of Homeland Security publishes a concise brochure entitled "Get Ready Now" to help individuals and families prepare for terrorist attacks or other emergencies (Figure 6-5). The brochure describes what to include in an emergency supply kit, a family communications plan, and emergency plans.

Figure 6-5 ■ "Get Ready Now" brochure helps families prepare for terrorist attacks and other emergencies. Source: U.S. Department of Homeland Security. http://www.ready.gov/readygov_trifold_brochure.pdf

Recommended Supplies to Include in a Basic Kit:

- **Water** one gallon per person per day, for drinking and sanitation
- **Food** at least a three-day supply of non-perishable food
- **Battery-powered radio** and **extra batteries**
- **Flashlight** and **extra batteries**
- **First Aid kit**
- **Whistle** to signal for help
- **Filter mask** or cotton t-shirt, to help filter the air
- **Moist towelettes** for sanitation
- **Wrench or pliers** to turn off utilities
- **Manual can opener** for food (if kit contains canned food)
- **Plastic sheeting and duct tape** to shelter-in-place
- **Garbage bags and plastic ties** for personal sanitation
- **Unique family needs**, such as daily prescription medications, infant formula or diapers, and important family documents

This common sense framework is designed to launch a process of learning about citizen preparedness. For the most current information and recommendations, go online to www.ready.gov.

Distributed in partnership with:

citizen ★corps

Preparing Makes Sense. Get Ready Now.

Homeland Security
www.ready.gov

US Department of Homeland Security, Washington, DC 20528

Preparing Makes Sense.

The likelihood that you and your family will survive a house fire depends as much on having a working smoke detector and an exit strategy as on a well-trained fire department. The same is true for surviving a terrorist attack or other emergency. We must have the tools and plans in place to make it on our own, at least for a period of time, no matter where we are when disaster strikes. Just like having a working smoke detector, preparing for the unexpected makes sense.

Get ready now.

1 Get a Kit
of Emergency Supplies.

Be prepared to improvise and use what you have on hand to make it on your own for at least three days, maybe longer. While there are many things that might make you more comfortable, think first about fresh water, food and clean air.

Consider two kits. In one, put everything you will need to stay where you are and make it on your own. The other should be a lightweight, smaller version you can take with you if you care to get away.

You'll need a gallon of water per person per day for drinking and sanitation. Include in the kit a three-day supply of non-perishable foods that are easy to store and prepare such as protein bars, dried fruit or canned foods. If you live in a cold weather climate, include warm clothes and a sleeping bag for each member of the family.

Some potential terrorist attacks can only hurt you if they get into your body, so think about creating a barrier between yourself and any contamination. It's smart to have something to cover each member of the family that covers their mouth and nose, such as two to three layers of a cotton t-shirt, handkerchief or towel or filter masks, readily available in hardware stores. It is very important that most of the air you breathe comes through the mask, not around it. Do whatever you can to make the best fit possible for children.

Also, include **duct tape and heavyweight garbage bags or plastic sheeting** that can be used to seal windows and doors if you need to create a barrier between yourself and any potential contamination outside.

2 Make a Plan
For What You Will Do in an Emergency.

Plan in advance what you will do in an emergency. Be prepared to assess the situation. Use common sense and whatever you have on hand to take care of yourself and your loved ones.

Develop a Family Communications Plan. Your family may not be together when disaster strikes, so plan how you will contact one another and review what you will do in different situations. **Consider a plan where each family member calls, or e-mails, the same friend or relative in the event of an emergency.** It may be easier to make a long-distance phone call than to call across town, so an **out-of-town contact** may be in a better position to communicate among separated family members. Be sure each person knows the phone number and has coins or a prepaid phone card to call the emergency contact. You may have trouble getting through, or the phone system may be down altogether, but be patient.

Depending on your circumstances and the nature of the attack, the first important decision is whether you stay put or get away. You should understand and plan for both possibilities. Use common sense and the information you are learning here to determine if there is immediate danger. **Watch television and listen to the radio for official instructions as they become available.**

Create a Plan to Shelter-in-Place. There are circumstances when staying put and creating a barrier between yourself and potentially contaminated air outside, a process known as sheltering-in-place and sealing the room, can be a matter of survival. **If you see large amounts of debris in the air, or if local authorities say the air is badly contaminated, you may want to shelter-in-place and seal the room. Consider precutting plastic sheeting to seal windows, doors and air vents.** Each piece should be several inches larger than the space you want to cover so that you can duct tape it flat against the wall. Label each piece with the location of where it fits.

Use all available information to assess the situation. If you see large amounts of debris in the air, or if local authorities say the air is badly contaminated, you may want to shelter-in-place. Quickly bring your family and pets inside, lock doors, and close windows, air vents and fireplace dampers. Immediately turn off air conditioning, forced-air heating systems, exhaust fans and clothes dryers. Take your emergency supplies and go into the room you have designated. Seal all windows, doors and vents. Understand that sealing the room is a temporary measure to create a barrier between you and contaminated air. Listen to the radio or check the Internet for instructions.

Create a Plan to Get Away. Plan in advance how you will assemble your family and anticipate where you will go. **Choose several destinations in different directions so you have**

options in an emergency. If you have a car, keep at least a half tank of gas in it at all times. **Become familiar with alternate routes as well as other means of transportation out of your area.** If you do not have a car, plan how you will leave if you have to. **Take your emergency supply kit,** unless you have reason to believe it is contaminated, and lock the door behind you. Take pets with you if you are told to evacuate. However, if you are going to a public shelter, keep in mind they may not be allowed inside. If you believe the air may be contaminated, drive with your windows and vents closed and keep the air conditioning and heater turned off. Listen to the radio for instructions.

Know Emergency Plans at School and Work. Think about the places where your family spends time: school, work and other places you visit. Talk to your children's schools **and your employer about emergency plans.** Find out how they will communicate with families during an emergency. If you are an employer, be sure you have an emergency preparedness plan. Review and practice it with your employees. A community working together during an emergency also makes sense. **Talk to your neighbors about how you can work together.**

3 Be Informed
About What Might Happen.

Some of the things you can do to prepare for the unexpected, such as assembling a supply kit and developing a family communications plan, are the same for both a natural or man-made emergency. However there are significant differences among potential terrorist threats, such as biological, chemical, explosive, nuclear and radiological, which will impact the decisions you make and the actions you take. By beginning a process of learning about these specific threats, you are **preparing yourself** to react in an emergency. Go to **www.ready.gov** to learn more about potential terrorist threats and other emergencies or call 1-800-BE-READY (1-800-237-5239) for a free brochure.

Be prepared to adapt this information to your personal circumstances and make every effort to follow instructions received from authorities on the scene. With these simple preparations, you can be ready for the unexpected.

Get ready now.

4 Get Involved
in Preparing Your Community.

After preparing yourself and your family for possible emergencies, take the next step and get involved in preparing your community. Join **Citizen Corps** which actively involves citizens in making our communities and our nation safer, stronger and better prepared. We all have a role to play in keeping our hometowns secure from emergencies of all kinds. Citizen Corps work hard to help people prepare, train and volunteer in their communities. Go to www.citizencorps.gov for more information and to get involved.

ARE YOU READY?

The Federal Emergency Management Agency publishes *Are You Ready? An In-depth Guide to Citizen Preparedness* (Figure 6-6). This publication presents disaster survival techniques and how to prepare for and respond to both natural and man-made disasters. It is a comprehensive guide to personal emergency preparedness that includes information on how to prepare a disaster supply kit, how to locate and evacuate to a shelter, emergency planning for people with disabilities, and care for pets during an emergency. The guide covers natural hazards (e.g., hurricanes and earthquakes), technological hazards (e.g., hazardous materials), and terrorism.

Figure 6-6 ■ *Are You Ready? An In-depth Guide to Citizen Preparedness.* Source: Federal Emergency Management Agency, www.fema.gov/pdf/areyouready/cover.pdf

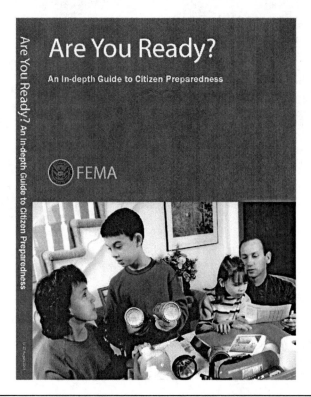

DISCUSSION QUESTIONS

1. How costly was the 9/11 attack on New York City?
2. Is it immoral to profit from the problem of terrorism? Explain.
3. Should government continue to privatize counterterrorism? Explain.
4. What is the role of transnational criminal organizations in the war on terrorism? What are the advantages and disadvantages of governments relying on these groups to combat terrorism?
5. What are the problems of the private security industry and how can it become more professional?
6. What are the benefits of joining professional associations?

7. What are the benefits of public–private sector partnerships?
8. How are citizen volunteers helpful to homeland security?
9. Should citizens do more to take care of themselves and prepare for disasters? Explain.

APPLICATIONS

6A YOU BE THE INVESTOR

As a private citizen you have some cash available to invest in stocks and you are thinking about investing in at least two companies that support efforts against terrorism. You collect and study information on companies from the Web, brokers, or other sources. What two companies do you select for investment and why?

6B YOU BE THE TERRORIST

As the leader of a terrorist cell in the United States, you and your brothers have narrowed potential targets to one specific type of entity located in every state. Part of your intelligence gathering is to study security at these facilities. Your surveillance and research show that this type of entity is typically protected by contract private security officers who are regulated differently in each state with respect to security officer applicant screening, training, and government inspections of these contract security businesses. Your preliminary attack plans include planting one of your brothers at the target as a security officer or obtaining security uniforms for some type of ruse to gain access. You and your brothers are now searching the Web and other sources for states with the weakest laws, regulations, and professional standards (e.g., applicant screening and training) for security officers. What are the three worst states that would become top targets?

6C YOU BE THE VOLUNTEER

You would like to perform volunteer service in your community to assist emergency workers if a disaster strikes. You view volunteer work as a way to give to your community while at the same time learning about a variety of hazards and how to prepare and respond to them. Also, this is a way to network and build your resume as you develop your career. Following your research, which volunteer group do you join and why?

WEB SITES

American Chemistry Council: www.americanchemistry.com
American Society of Safety Engineers: www.asse.org
ASIS International: www.asisonline.org
Business Executives for National Security: www.bens.org
Citizen Corps: www.citizencorps.gov
citizen preparation for terrorism: www.ready.gov
Department of Defense: www.dod.mil
federal budget: www.whitehouse.gov and www.congress.gov
International Association of Security and Investigative Regulators: www.iasir.org
International Foundation for Protection Officers: www.ifpo.org
National Association of County and City Health Officials: www.naccho.org
National Association of Security Companies: www.nasco.org
National Fire Protection Association: www.nfpa.org
Neighborhood Watch: www.usaonwatch.org

NOTES

ASIS Foundation (2004). *The ASIS Foundation Security Report: Scope and Emerging Trends*, Preliminary Findings. www.asisonline.org, retrieved January 6, 2005.

ASIS International (2004). *Private Security Officer Selection and Training*. www.asisonline.org, retrieved January 3, 2005.

Anderson, T. (2003). "Legal Reporter." *Security Management*, 47 (November).

Barstow, D. (2004). "Security Firm Says Its Workers Were Lured Into Iraqi Ambush." *NY Times* (April 9).

Collins, P., *et al.* (2005). "The ASIS Foundation Security Report: Scope and Emerging Trends." Alexandria, VA: ASIS, International.

Congressional Budget Office (2004). *Homeland Security and the Private Sector.* Washington, DC: Congress of the United States.

Cunningham, W., and Taylor, T. (1985). *Private Security and Police in America: The Hallcrest Report.* Portland, OR: Chancellor Press.

Cunningham, W., *et al.* (1990). *Private Security Trends: 1970–2000, The Hallcrest Report II.* Boston, MA: Butterworth-Heinemann.

Ewing, L. (2004). "The Missing Link in the Partnership." *Homeland Security,* 1 (September).

Flores, T., and Earl, J. (2004). "What Are Security's Lessons in Iraq?" *Security Management,* 48 (November).

Haddow, G., and Bullock, J. (2003). *Introduction to Emergency Management.* Boston, MA: Butterworth-Heinemann.

Housman, R., and Anikeeff, T. (2004). "How Companies Can Compete for Contracts." *Security Management,* 48 (January).

Jenkins, B. (2003). "All Citizens Now First Responders." *USA Today* (March 23).

Kendra, J., and Wachtendorf, T. (2002). "Rebel Food ... Renegade Supplies: Convergence after the World Trade Center Attack." Research paper from Disaster Research Center, University of Delaware. www.udel.edu/DRC/.

Kernell, S., and Jacobson, G. (2003). *The Logic of American Politics.* Washington, DC: C Q Press.

Krane, J. (2003). "Private army grows around US mission in Iraq, world." Associated press release, October 30.

Lemos, R. (2004). "Companies profiting from fear." *Homeland Security Digital Agenda.* www.news.com, retrieved October 19, 2004.

Mandel, R. (2004). "Fighting Fire with Fire: Privatizing Counterterrorism." In R. Howard and R. Sawyer (Eds.), *Defeating Terrorism: Shaping the New Security Environment.* Guilford, CT: McGraw-Hill.

McCrie, R. (2005). "Training: Ontario Introduces a Bill Requiring 40 Hrs. Pre-Assignment." *Security Letter,* XXXV (January 3).

McHugh, D. (2004). "Bin Laden says he can destroy US economy." Associated Press release, December 19.

Nyatepe-Coo, A. (2004). "Economic Implications of Terrorism." In A. Nyatepe-Coo and D. Zeisler-Vralsted (Eds.), *Understanding Terrorism: Threats in an Uncertain World.* Upper Saddle River, NJ: Pearson Prentice Hall.

Office of Homeland Security (2002). *National Strategy for Homeland Security.* Washington, DC: The White House (July).

Paddock, M. (2004). "Many Hands Shape the Funding Picture for 2005." *Homeland Defense Journal,* 2 (September).

Purpura, P. (2002). Security and Loss Prevention, 4th ed. Boston, MA: Butterworth-Heinemann.

Quinley, K., and Schmidt, D. (2002). *Business At Risk: How to Assess, Mitigate, and Respond to Terrorist Threats.* Cincinnati, OH: The National Underwriter Co.

Reimer, D. (2004). "The Private Sector Must Be a Partner in Homeland Security." *Homeland Security,* 1 (September).

Risk Management Solutions (2001). *World Trade Center Disaster: RMS Special Report* (September 18).

Rosenbaum, D. (2001). "Since Sept. 11, Lobbyists Use New Pitches for Old Pleas." *New York Times on the Web.* www.nytimes.com, retrieved December 3, 2001. In S. Kernell and G. Jacobson (2003). *The Logic of American Politics.*

Security Business (2004a). "Show Me The Money! US Homeland Security Market to Hit $50B In '05." *Security Letter,* XXXIV (August).

Security Business (2004b). "Homeland Security Market To Reach $42.4B Next Year, Study Estimates." *Security Letter,* XXXIV (September).

Security Executive Forum (2003). "Not Everyone Sees Preventing Terrorist Attacks as Job 1 for Corporate Security." *Corporate Security,* 29 (November 30).

U.S. Department of Homeland Security (2005). *Citizen Corps: Programs and Partners.* www.citizencorps.gov/prograns, retrieved January 3, 2005.

U.S. Department of Justice (1976). Abstract for the *Report of the Task Force on Private Security.* Washington, DC: National Criminal Justice Reference Service.

U.S. Department of Justice, Office of Community Oriented Policing Services (2004). *National Policy Summit: Building Private Security/Public Policing Partnerships to Prevent and Respond to Terrorism and Public Disorder.* www.cops.usdoj.gov, retrieved January 4, 2005.

Wagman, D. (2005). "Well-intentioned, sometimes misguided." *Homeland Protection Professional*, 4 (January/February).

Weidenbaum, M. (2004). "Government, Business, and the Response to Terrorism." In T. Badey (Ed.), *Homeland Security*. Guilford, CT: McGraw-Hill/Dushkin.

Zarate, J. (1998). "The Emergence of a New Dog of War: Private International Security Companies, International Law, and the New World Order." *Stanford Journal of International Law*, 34 (January).

PART III

PROTECTION METHODS

CHAPTER 7

RISK MANAGEMENT AND EMERGENCY MANAGEMENT

OBJECTIVES

The study of this chapter will enable you to:

1. Define and explain both risk management and emergency management.
2. Explain how risk management and emergency management are linked.
3. List and explain the steps in the risk management process.
4. Name and explain six risk management tools.
5. Discuss enterprise risk management.
6. Describe risk management functions in business and government.
7. Discuss risk management in the federal government.
8. Trace the development of emergency management.
9. List and explain the emergency management disciplines.
10. Discuss business continuity.
11. Describe the national response plan, the national incident management system, and the national preparedness goal.
12. Explain the role of the military in emergency management.

KEY TERMS

risk management
emergency management
business continuity
enterprise risk management
Terrorism Risk Insurance Act of 2002
victim compensation fund
risk modeling
Delphi approach
game theory
heartland security approach
hazard modeling

Public Risk Management Association
Risk and Insurance Management Society
State Risk and Insurance Management
    Association
systems theory
chaos theory
decision theory
management theory
organizational behavior theory
risk perception and communication theory
social constructionist theory

KEY TERMS

Weberian theory
Marxist theory
civil defense programs
community-based mitigation
Federal Emergency Management Agency (FEMA)
all-hazards preparedness concept
generic emergency management
specialized emergency management
National Emergency Management Association
International Association of Emergency
    Managers
The International Emergency Management
    Society
mitigation
national response plan

national incident management system
national preparedness goal
response
incident command system
National Guard
recovery
preparedness
emergency operations plan
NFPA 1600 Standard on Disaster/Emergency
    Management and Business Continuity
    Programs
metrics
logistics
The Insurrection Act

TRAIN COLLISION AND CHLORINE RELEASE

The following information is from a U.S. Department of Homeland Security situation report, dated January 7, 2005, on the status of a South Carolina train collision and chlorine release.

On January 5, Norfolk Southern freight train #192 was assembled in Macon, Georgia, for its daily service trip to Columbia, South Carolina. Train #192 consisted of two SD60 diesel locomotives and 42 cars, 25 loaded and 17 empty. After stopping in Augusta, Georgia, for a crew change, it proceeded into South Carolina. The first 5 cars were hauling nonhazardous materials, as required by law; however, the 6th and 7th cars were chlorine tank cars, the 8th car carried sodium hydroxide, and the 9th car carried chlorine.

In Graniteville, South Carolina, at approximately 7:00 PM, a yard crew moved one locomotive and two freight cars onto a sideline, via a switch from the main track. After parking the small train next to the Avondale Mills Textile Plant, the crew left for the night.

On January 6, at 2:40 AM, NS train #192 was proceeding en route through Graniteville, South Carolina, and was abruptly directed off the mainline at 45 mph onto the sideline, colliding with the small-parked train. The resulting impact derailed both trains. The engineer was killed, chlorine fumes were released into the air, and sodium hydroxide spilled. Aerial photos indicated three locomotives and 15 cars were off track.

Chlorine is a potentially fatal gas that can damage the respiratory and central nervous systems, the throat, nose, and eyes. Chlorine is a strong oxidizing agent and poses a serious fire and explosion risk because it promotes combustion, like oxygen. Any resulting fire would form irritating and toxic gases. The sodium hydroxide was being carried in liquid form and, as such, is extremely corrosive on contact.

Local response included the Graniteville Fire Department, Aiken County Sheriff's Office, Aiken (SC) and Richmond (GA) county HAZMAT teams, and several area county emergency agencies. The South Carolina Emergency Operations Center elevated their activation to 24-hour operations. State of South Carolina agencies involved included Department of Health and Environmental Control, Department of Public Safety, State Law Enforcement Division, Department of Transportation, and Highway Patrol. Norfolk Southern response included a HAZMAT team, railroad police, and investigators.

TRAIN COLLISION AND CHLORINE RELEASE—Cont'd

Federal agencies on the scene included Federal Bureau of Investigation, Environmental Protection Agency, Federal Emergency Management Agency, National Transportation Safety Board, and Federal Railroad Administration. The U.S. Department of Energy, Savannah River Site, provided a HAZMAT team, stress managers, and several security officers. DOE also provided several chemical plume assessments. Fort Gordon provided a decontamination team, while the U.S. Coast Guard provided a HAZMAT team and a strike team to assist in monitoring air quality. The Federal Aviation Administration established a temporary flight restriction zone out to a 5-mile radius and up to 3000 feet from the derailment.

During the emergency, reports from the hot zone indicated that one chlorine tank car leaked approximately 70 to 80% of its 90 tons of material. The second chlorine car was believed to be leaking; however, confirmation was not initially possible due to the hazardous conditions at the scene. The condition of the third chlorine car was also unknown. An undetermined quantity of leaking sodium hydroxide from one car and diesel fuel from the locomotives were contributing to the incident.

Initially a 2-mile shelter-in-place order was issued, but at 6 PM an evacuation order was given for the 5400 people within a 1-mile radius of the site. At least 12 people refused to leave the evacuation area. Chlorine continued to leak and the gas settled near the ground as temperatures dropped. The South Carolina Emergency Management Division confirmed 8 fatalities and 234 people were taken to six area hospitals for treatment, with 53 admitted. Inhaling chlorine fumes, except for the engineer of the moving train who died in the crash, caused all the deaths.

Air monitoring was ongoing and the condition was considered stable. Crews pulled damaged cars and debris from the site and conducted further damage assessments throughout the night. The off-loading of chemical products was expected to be conducted in the morning by transferring the cargo to new rail cars. Crews were seeking to identify the owners of the chlorine tank cars. Once established, maintenance records could be obtained to assist investigators.

Local officials reported that four schools and over six textile plants in the area were closed because of the accident. Area hospitals reported resuming normal operations. One dead horse was reported, but no calls for sick animals were received and the livestock concentration in the area was minimal.

Preliminary investigations conducted by Norfolk Southern Police and the FBI confirmed that there was no tampering with the railroad lock on the switch. A thorough investigation will be conducted once the scene is deemed safe. Once the site has been released for repair, Norfolk Southern claims that the line can be repaired in 24 hours. This rail line is not a major thoroughfare and a detour is already in place.

The following, additional information on the Graniteville, South Carolina, train wreck is from the Associated Press (Holland, 1-8-05; Jordan, 1-8-05; Holland, 1-9-05). When the accident occurred, townspeople heard and felt a boom that was followed by a greenish-yellow fog that rolled into the community. The toxic cloud smelled like bleach, while irritating eyes and lungs and causing people to gasp. One volunteer firefighter, who ran to the scene without protective equipment, said he talked to God and said, "I am not dying here." Another volunteer firefighter drove to the scene and met two train crewmembers and spoke, but when one collapsed and the firefighter, without protective equipment, smelled the fumes, he fled.

A total of nine people died and the chlorine fumes sickened over 250. Six workers died at a nearby textile mill, another man was found in a truck, another in his home, and the train engineer died at a hospital. The wreck occurred near a textile mill where 400 workers were on the night shift making denim. Some of the mill workers acted like emergency responders, warning others to leave the area because of the greenish-yellow toxic fog engulfing the area. One employee piled co-workers in his truck and drove to a hospital as eyes burned and lungs hurt from the smell that was stronger than any cleaning solution.

Continued

TRAIN COLLISION AND CHLORINE RELEASE—Cont'd

In addition to the evacuation, a dusk-to-dawn curfew was imposed within 2 miles of the wreck. Rescue workers in protective suits searched buildings and homes for victims. One man, living three blocks from the wreck, watched from his home as men in HAZMAT suits rode through deserted streets on four-wheelers looking for victims. This resident claimed that the plastic on his windows to keep out the cold winter air and towels under his doors kept out the toxic fumes. During a telephone interview by Associated Press following the disaster, the resident stated that the outside air quality was improving because he saw some rescue workers without face masks.

Some residents evacuated from the town waited at a shelter set up at a local university. A church was used by Norfolk Southern Railroad to meet with residents who received payments for hotel rooms and other expenses, and $100 gift cards to Wal-Mart.

During the emergency, officials monitored the air. Environmental crews worked to stop the chlorine leak. The strategy was to work around the clock in two nine-member crews to apply a steel patch over a hole the size of a fist. Once the patch was applied, the chlorine was converted from a liquid into gas and offloaded. The leaking tank held 30 to 40% of the original contents, which can carry as much as 90 tons of liquid chlorine under pressure. The liquid turns to gas when released.

In February 1978, near Youngstown, Florida, a ruptured tank car involved in a train derailment sent a cloud of chlorine gas over a highway, killing eight people. In June 2004, near San Antonio, Texas, the collision of two freight trains caused a chlorine cloud that killed a conductor and two nearby residents.

According to the U.S. Environmental Protection Agency, chlorine gas is greenish-yellow in color. It is heavier than air, causing it to sink to low areas. Chlorine is used to disinfect water, swimming pools, and sewage. It is also used in food processing systems, paper mills, and water-cooling systems. It irritates the nose, throat, and lungs, and can lead to bronchitis, asthma, headaches, heart disease, and meningitis. Treatment consists of fresh air, flushing the eyes for 15 minutes, removal of contaminated clothes, and washing with plenty of soap and water.

RISK MANAGEMENT AND EMERGENCY MANAGEMENT

This section begins with definitions and the connection between risk management and emergency management. **Risk management**, originating from the private sector, makes the most efficient and cost-effective before-the-loss plans for an after-the-loss continuation of an entity. A business, for example, plans for possible disasters, and if one occurs, it seeks to recover and resume business as quickly as possible. **Emergency management**, originating from government, focuses on preparation for potential emergencies and disasters and the coordination of response and resources during such events. In other words, government has an obligation to protect citizens and communities by preparing for disasters, responding quickly when disasters strike, and helping communities to recover.

We often see risk management and emergency management separated; however, these tasks are linked. In the public sector, some small cities and counties combine these functions and a single employee is responsible for both. Larger government units separate these functions, although both units should work together and share expertise and resources. On the federal level, as discussed in subsequent pages, the Government Accountability Office (formally the General Accounting Office) is a strong proponent of risk management to guide homeland security preparedness (i.e., emergency management) efforts and favoring its applicability throughout government (Decker, 2001). In the private sector, businesses may choose to place **business continuity** (a term often used in the private sector for emergency management or disaster preparedness), insurance, safety, security, and other functions under the risk manager. What we have is the evolution of four disciplines: public sector (government) risk management and emergency management and private sector (business) risk management and business continuity.

Returning to the public sector, both risk management and emergency management contain the word "management." Thus, risks and emergencies need to be managed. This includes a host of activities, such as planning, marketing, budgeting, organizing, staffing, directing, and controlling

Both risk management and emergency management disciplines contain a body of knowledge, many publications, college degree programs, associations, certifications, and employment opportunities, among other characteristics of professions. Although interdisciplinary clashes are inevitable (and often healthy) over definitions of terms, theories, practices, turf, and so forth, both disciplines should cooperate and produce products (e.g., research, reports) beneficial to the broad, mutual challenges these disciplines face (e.g., homeland security, disasters).

Chapter 6 discussed the numerous risks facing the private sector that also impact the public sector. Examples are natural disasters, accidents, fires, and crimes such as terrorism. Furthermore, consideration of global risks is important because countries are becoming increasingly interdependent, our world is "shrinking," and risks penetrate borders. For instance, although terrorism, the proliferation of WMD, and war are serious issues, government and business leaders should understand and prepare for risks involving diseases, conflicts over natural resources, and human migration. With so many risks facing our world, government and business leaders manage them by studying and prioritizing them and then taking action. Risk management is a method of studying and prioritizing risks and it serves as a vital foundation for emergency management (or business continuity) programs. The U.S. Department of Homeland Security (2004b: 54) states: "We will guide our actions with sound risk management principles that take a global perspective and are forward-looking. Risks must be well understood, and risk management approaches developed, before solutions can be implemented."

Since the 9/11 attacks (Figures 7-1 and 7-2), all levels of government have placed a significant emphasis on the risk of terrorist attacks and emergency management to respond to such attacks.

Figure 7-1 ■ Urban search and rescue crew member searches rubble for survivors following 9/11 terrorist attack on World Trade Center. FEMA photo by Michael Rieger. http://www.photolibrary.fema.gov/ photolibrary/photo_details.do?id=3997

Figure 7-2 ■ Pentagon, Arlington, Virginia, following 9/11 Attack. U.S. Navy photo by Photographer's Mate 2nd Class Bob Houlihan. http://www.news.navy.mil/view_single.asp?id=122

Conversely, private sector action and spending against the risk of terrorism has varied widely, depending on the industry. (Return to Chapter 6 for explanations of the private sector taking less action and spending less than the federal government against the risk of terrorism.)

Since the 9/11 attacks, both public and private sectors have published an enormous amount of information on the attacks and the response. The federal government has been a leader in related publications. State and local governments have also provided valuable information. Private sector publications on terrorism and homeland security emanate from many sources, such as industry groups, professional associations, businesses, volunteer groups, publishing companies, and the media. *The private sector, specifically the insurance industry, plays a major role in influencing the body of knowledge of risk management and business continuity, whereas the federal government does the same with emergency management.*

Risk management is a method of studying and prioritizing risks and serves as a vital foundation for emergency management (or business continuity) programs that prepare for and respond to potential losses.

RISK AND HAZARD DEFINITIONS

The terms "risk" and "hazard" have several definitions and uses. Their definitions are influenced by various disciplines and the context of usage.

Risk

Quinley and Schmidt (2002: 4), from the insurance and risk management discipline, define risk as "a measure of the frequency or probability of a negative event and the severity or consequences of that negative event." Leimberg *et al.* (2002: 82), from the same discipline, define risk as "exposure to damages that arises from property damage or bodily injury."

Haddow and Bullock (2003: 15), from the emergency management discipline, use the definition of risk from the National Governors Association: "... susceptibility to death, injury, damage, destruction, disruption, stoppage and so forth."

Walter *et al.* (2004: 951), from the fire protection discipline, define risk as "the chance of injury, damage, or loss; hazard." Angle (2005: 313), from the same discipline, sees risk as "the resultant outcome of exposure to a hazard."

ASIS International (2003: 5), from the security discipline, defines risk as "the possibility of loss resulting from a threat, security incident, or event."

From these definitions of risk we see variations, but also common characteristics. Important concepts are measurement of the frequency, probability, and severity of losses from exposure to threats or hazards. The management and measurement of risk are important processes that are continually being developed.

Hazard

The insurance and risk management discipline uses the term "event or hazard risk," and Leimberg *et al.* (2002: 21) define hazard as "the risk of loss without possibility of gain; risks that traditionally have been insurable."

Haddow and Bullock (2003: 15) use the definition of hazard from the National Governors Association: "a source of danger that may or may not lead to an emergency or disaster and is named after the emergency/disaster that could be so precipitated."

The U.S. Department of Homeland Security (2004a: 66) defines hazard as "something that is potentially dangerous or harmful, often the root cause of an unwanted outcome."

The U.S. Department of Justice (2000: 37) defines hazard as "any circumstances, natural or manmade, that may adversely affect or attack the community's businesses or residences."

From these definitions of hazards we see variations, but also common characteristics. Important concepts are a source of danger that has the potential to cause unwanted outcomes such as injury, death, property damage, economic loss, and environmental damage that impact our society adversely.

RISK MANAGEMENT

Risk management has its origin in the insurance industry. Experts in the insurance industry differ as to the precise origin of risk management. Some trace its beginning to 1931, with the establishment of the insurance section of the American Management Association. Others refer to the 1960s when businesses, in increasing numbers, began to realize that insurance was too expensive to be used as the only tool against risks.

As written earlier, risk management makes the most efficient and cost-effective before-the-loss plans for an after-the-loss continuation of an entity. Leimberg *et al.* (2002: 6), from the insurance industry, define risk management as follows: "A preloss exercise that reflects an organization's postloss goals; a process to recognize and manage faulty and potentially dangerous operations, trends, and policies that could lead to loss and to minimize losses that do occur." The U.S. Government

Accountability Office offers this definition (Decker, 2001: 3): "Risk management is a systematic and analytical process to consider the likelihood that a threat will endanger an asset (e.g., a structure, individual, or function) and to identify actions that reduce the risk and mitigate the consequences of an attack."

Although risk management is often associated with business, its applicability is society-wide, including government, all types of organizations, the family, and individuals. The purpose of risk management is to protect people and assets.

Theories relevant to risk management and emergency management not only draw on numerous disciplines, but they also draw on some of the same disciplines (see the theories relevant to emergency management later in the chapter). Risk management theory draws on probability and statistics, mathematics, engineering, economics, business, and the social sciences, among other disciplines. The theories explained next, summarized from the work of Borodzicz (2005: 14–47), illustrate how the study of risk has changed from concentrating on measuring the probability of risk to also understanding the psychological, cultural, and social context of risk.

Risk perception theory focuses on how humans learn from their environment and react to it. Psychologists apply a cognitive research approach to understand how humans gain knowledge through perception and reasoning. For instance, risk can be researched by isolating a variable and simulating it in a laboratory with a group of subjects in an experiment involving risk decision making (e.g., gambling). The psychometric approach is another method of researching risk and involves a survey to measure individual views of risks. Research on risk perception shows that people find unusual risks to be more terrifying than familiar ones and, interestingly, the familiar risks claim the most lives; voluntary risk (e.g., smoking) is preferred over imposed risk (e.g., a hazardous industry moving near one's home); and people have limited trust in official data.

Risk communication theory concerns itself with communication perceptions of experts and lay citizens. Although experts work to simplify information for lay citizens, communication of simplified information, and behavior change, may not be successful. Research on this topic focuses on lay citizen perceptions of risk within the context of psychological, social, cultural, and political factors. Risk communication theory is important because it holds answers for educating and preparing citizens for emergencies.

THE RISK MANAGEMENT PROCESS

During the 1960s, the need developed for a systematic approach for evaluating risk. This void was filled by what became known as the risk management process, explained next from Leimberg *et al.* (2002: 2–3).

STEP 1, RISK IDENTIFICATION

This is an important step because unless risks can be identified, they cannot be managed. Risks are divided into various categories. First-party risks involve owned assets. Damage to a company truck is a first-party risk. Third-party risks pertain to liability resulting from business operations. If a company truck is involved in a traffic accident, the company may be liable for property damage and injury to others not connected to the company. Baseline risks refer to risks that must be covered through insurance because of state law. Examples are vehicle operation and workers compensation.

STEP 2, QUANTITATIVE ANALYSIS

Through a variety of tools and methods, risk quantification seeks to predict the maximum and expected financial loss from each identified risk. If a fire destroys a building costing $10 million to replace, the maximum loss is $10 million. However, loss prevention methods (e.g., fire-resistive construction and a sprinkler system) can reduce the loss significantly. Risk quantification for physical assets is usually easier than for public liability and worker safety. A major question for businesses is "How much loss can we absorb and still survive financially?" Insurance is one of several risk manage tools that businesses use to manage risks.

STEP 3, EVALUATE TREATMENT OPTIONS

Once risks have been identified and quantified, a study is undertaken of options to treat the loss exposures. This is done through two means: risk financing and risk control. Risk financing is very broad and can be categorized as "on-balance sheet" and "off-balance sheet." The former includes insurance policy deductibles and self-insured loss exposures. Basically, a company absorbs losses. The latter includes insurance policies and contractual transfers of risk. Risk control, also known as loss prevention, involves precautions to reduce risk as illustrated earlier. Other examples include using safety belts in vehicles and installing a guard on a machine to prevent injury. Transferring risks off-balance sheet is not free, and costs can increase. For example, workers operating a machine may be covered through workers compensation insurance, however, if workers are injured repeatedly at the machine, insurance premiums will increase.

STEP 4, IMPLEMENTATION

Once the treatment options are studied, the next step is to put the selected ones into practice.

STEP 5, MONITORING AND ADJUSTING

The risk management process concludes with program oversight. This step includes program reviews in conjunction with a risk management information system. Because nothing remains static, a successful organization must make changes to survive.

Leimberg *et al.* (2002: 4) provide the following points on risk management.

- The primary contribution of risk management is that it provides senior management with a variety of techniques and tools designed to manage risk and capital.
- Risk management has proven that an excessive reliance on insurance can be expensive and an inefficient use of capital.
- "In fact, in the most sophisticated risk management programs, insurance plays a relatively minor role."
- Large organizations usually employ risk managers who plan a management regimen according to the preloss and postloss goals of the organization.
- Risk management costs must be considered investments. In most cases, the benefits are realized long term.
- "It is extremely difficult to measure tangible benefits against a nonevent (i.e., the catastrophic loss did not occur due to our highly effective risk management program). Yet this is the challenge facing all risk managers. Ultimately, the metrics that senior management uses to gauge success—for example, earnings growth and return on invested capital—must also serve as the yardsticks used to measure the effectiveness of risk management."

RISK MANAGEMENT TOOLS

Risk management tools are as follows.

- *Risk transfer.* Risk is transferred to insurance. However, this approach can become expensive so other methods and tools should be considered in risk management.
- *Deductibles.* The insured party pays for small losses up to a specific amount. The insurer pays for losses above the specific amount, less the deductible. Higher deductibles lower insurance premiums.
- *Risk assumption.* A company may choose to assume a risk and insurance is not obtained. However, other risk management tools may be employed. For example, with self-insurance, rather than paying a premium, a company invests in a fund for availability in case of loss.
- *Risk avoidance.* In this approach, a business avoids a risk. For example, a company may decide not to open a branch office in a specific geographic area for numerous reasons, such as the likelihood of natural disasters, unfavorable government policies, or terrorism.

- *Risk spreading*. This tool seeks to reduce potential losses by spreading the risk among multiple locations. Since the 9/11 attacks, companies are rethinking their policies of concentrating all of their personnel and resources in one building in one urban area.
- *Risk abatement*. The goal with this tool is to decrease risk though loss prevention measures. Although the risk is not eliminated, it is reduced. Examples include establishing a security program at a company to prevent losses from crime or promoting a safety program at a manufacturing company to prevent accidents.

ENTERPRISE RISK MANAGEMENT

The functions of risk managers are becoming more complex as the world changes. They are playing an increasingly important role in planning for the survivability of businesses. A major trend today in the risk management field is **enterprise risk management** (ERM). Leimberg *et al.* (2002: 6) define it as "a management process that identifies, defines, quantifies, compares, prioritizes, and treats all of the material risks facing an organization, whether or not it is insurable." Leimberg and colleagues describe the trend of two separate and distinct forms of risk management. Event risk management focuses on traditional risks, such as theft and worker injury, that insurance covers. Financial risk management protects the financial assets of a business from risks that insurers do not cover. Examples are foreign currency exchange risk, credit risk, and interest rate movements. Various capital risk transfer tools are available to protect financial assets. A derivative, for instance, similar to insurance, protects against fluctuations in foreign currency rates. ERM seeks to combine event and financial risk for a comprehensive approach to business risks.

TERRORISM INSURANCE

The **Terrorism Risk Insurance Act of 2002** (TRIA) requires insurance companies to provide terrorism coverage to businesses willing to purchase it. Participating insurance companies pay out a claim (a deductible) before TRIA pays for the loss. TRIA losses are capped at $100 billion.

According to Ramani Ayer, chairman of Hartford Financial Services Group, Inc., the act has been a good temporary answer to calm the insurance industry that faced a huge disaster—the 9/11 attacks. Because of the scale of possible terrorist-related losses in the future, the federal government must have a role, according to Ayer. He refers to a risk model of a suitcase nuclear bomb explosion in New York City that could overwhelm the property/casualty insurance industry. The model of the scenario shows half a million deaths and insured losses of over $300 billion, approaching the insurance industry's capacity of about $370 billion. Ayer compares TRIA to the Federal Deposit Insurance Corp. (FDIC), a federal insurance program designed to insure bank deposits following the numerous bank failures due to the Great Depression. Ayer sees a TRIA-type program as vital to the U.S. economy and as an aid to help businesses recover through insurance (Pilla, 2004).

Opponents of TRIA see it as a government "bailout" of the insurance industry. The Consumer Federation of America suggests that the insurance industry can afford a 9/11 type of loss every 6 years and that the risk is low for most of the United States, except for New York, Washington, DC, and other major cities. GAO data suggest that only 10 to 30% of businesses have purchased terrorism insurance (Crowley, 2004).

Following the 9/11 attacks, major liability issues surfaced as victims' families contemplated lawsuits. Congress ameliorated the problem by creating a **victim compensation fund**, whereby the federal government offered to assume liability in lieu of litigation. The program was a success; over 98% of victims' families chose to file claims rather than sue. It is unknown if a subsequent attack will be handled in the same way.

TERRORISM INSURANCE—Cont'd

According to Crowley (2004), terrorism is far less predictable than natural disasters, as the latter have an abundance of historical data. This unpredictability makes assessing risk especially difficult. Starner (2003) notes that TRIA did not provide insurers with assistance when it came to underwriting or setting rates. Consequently, the insurance industry has sought help from insurance service companies that offer risk modeling for natural disasters and other risks. These service firms have shifted their skills to the risk of terrorism to assist insurers in deciding how to underwrite coverage and how to price it.

Although the TRIA was set to expire at the end of 2005, President Bush signed a 2-year extension on December 22, 2005. The extension raised industry deductibles and copayments to gradually reduce the federal government's involvement in the program, while increasing the private sector role (BOMA Files, 2006: 20).

CRITICAL THINKING:

What is your opinion of the Terrorism Risk Insurance Act?

RISK MODELING ATTEMPTS TO ESTIMATE THE RISK OF TERRORISM

Yates (2004: 42) offers the following "point/counterpoint" on risk modeling. First of all, no person, nor technology, can predict when and where terrorists will strike. However, **risk modeling** has evolved from the insurance industry to estimate a variety of risks. Modeling has become increasingly important because of the complex nature of the insurance industry, catastrophic losses from a variety of events, and the Terrorism Risk Insurance Act of 2002.

Various approaches are used in modeling. AIR Worldwide Corporation relies on the **Delphi approach**, which was developed by the Rand Corporation during World War II. It consists of sending a structured questionnaire to a group of experts and then conducting a statistical analysis to generate probabilistic forecasts, such as the numbers of attacks and where they might occur. The experts play the role of the decision makers in terrorist groups. (This approach has a link to red team techniques.) The AIR model contains hundreds of thousands of entries to represent a wide range of potential targets. Examples are buildings, bridges, and tourist attractions.

Risk Management Solutions, Inc. (RMS) uses **game theory**. Starner (2003: 32) states: "Game theory suggests that the likelihood—and targets—of a future terrorist attack can be modeled by understanding the operational and behavioral characteristics of the terrorist organization." It involves the concept that adversaries are rational and make choices based on their information and rules. Game theory is a method to get inside the minds of terrorists. The key is to know adversaries and their rules to anticipate their actions. RMS literature (Gunaratna, 2003: 7) states: "The logistical burden of each attack mode in the RMS model has been analyzed using red team techniques."

Game theory is applied at the DHS Center of Excellence at the University of Wisconsin–Madison (see Chapter 12). Referred to as the Center for Risk and Economic Analysis of Terrorism Events (CREATE), researchers are working on a computer model to identify the targets that terrorists are most likely to attack. This would assist authorities in prioritizing limited resources. The challenge is to think as terrorists do to anticipate where an attack may occur and which landmarks are famous enough to attract them. CREATE researchers believe that terrorists focus on targets representing symbols that are recognized globally because the media coverage following such an attack helps their cause. The researchers also view public fear as sometimes disproportionate to the threat, especially for small-scale threats. Traditional risk analyses focus on fatalities and costs of natural disasters. CREATE researchers apply

Continued

RISK MODELING ATTEMPTS TO ESTIMATE THE RISK OF TERRORISM—Cont'd

game theory because terrorists are "intelligent adversaries" who fine-tune their attack depending on how the target is protected (Associated Press, February 6, 2006).

EQECAT, Inc., claims that its model is the most comprehensive on the market because it contains over 10 million events and hundreds of thousands of "high probability" terrorist targets. Its model uses a **heartland security approach**, meaning that the model considers not only major cities and attractions, but also targets that may appear as unlikely targets. An attack directed at America's heartland, say Des Moines, Iowa, seems unlikely, but such an attack could have a major psychological impact on the United States (Starner, 2003: 36).

Risk modeling has its critics. One critic from the fire protection engineering field supports **hazard modeling** over risk modeling and argues that the former predicts the results of a certain type of bomb exploding in a certain type of building, whereas the latter deals with much more uncertainty—when and where the bomb will be detonated. Conversely, terrorist modeling experts argue that although there are uncertainties, there have been about 6000 terrorist events to study for patterns to help understand vulnerabilities that can be protected worldwide.

This paragraph contains paraphrased statements from the RMS marketing brochure on their U.S. Terrorism Risk Model (Gunaratna *et al.*, 2003). The brochure states that the model primarily serves insurance companies in setting premium rates, but its applicability is wider. RMS states that the model quantifies risk from both foreign and domestic terrorist organizations and supports multiline risk analysis for events impacting a variety of insurance policies: property, business interruption, workers compensation, life, personal accident, and accidental death and dismemberment. RMS adds that the model quantifies the impact of a range of potential terrorist attacks (e.g., conventional bombs, WMD) on specific types of insurance and analyzes key drivers of loss by city, location, and type of target. Insurers are interested in knowing their greatest multiline exposure concentrations. RMS touts its high-resolution terrorism risk maps of cities and maps showing attack footprints to insurance portfolio exposures that provide guidance to insurers. RMS sees increased terrorism risk at soft targets. RMS emphasizes that although managing the terrorism risk is important to the survival of a company, it is only one part of the catastrophe risk puzzle. RMS claims that its models allow the user to view total catastrophe losses on an enterprise-wide basis.

Insurers are searching for answers and models can provide direction. For example, Stoneman (2003: 18) writes that insurance underwriters are asking specific questions about the number of employees at individual buildings at specific geographic locations so they can compute the risk they are accepting. For instance, if 3000 employees are at one location, it represents a $3 billion workers compensation exposure in a state that puts a $1 million price tag on a life.

RISK MANAGEMENT IN GOVERNMENT

The private sector, especially the insurance industry, has played the lead role in advancing the discipline of risk management. Simply put, the public sector is "playing catch up." The **Public Risk Management Association** (PRIMA), the largest network of public risk management practitioners, states: "Risk management in the public sector finds itself at a challenging moment in time.... there is a very high level of interest in the subject, but a lack of clarity and consistency as to its meaning, form and purpose." The group sees pockets of advanced risk management practice in the United States; however, most small government entities do not have a formal risk management unit. PRIMA sees various segments of the discipline spread among departments in government (e.g., insurance, purchasing, and finance) and efforts to unify the function under the emerging concept of enterprise risk management have just begun in the public sector (Public Risk Management Association, 2003).

PRIMA offers compelling reasons why the public sector should continue to develop its risk management expertise.

- The cost of risk is increasing.
- Government agency revenues are diminishing.
- The insurance industry is in a crisis.
- The future of organizations is less predictable.
- Risk managers can bring value to government entities, especially when thinking beyond the traditional risk management concept.

PRIMA has published core competencies to promote consistency of practice; join together trends and forces that fall under the risk management umbrella; and reinforce risk management as a specific job and function within government. Sample competencies that illustrate the requirements and functions of the job are as follows.

- Specific knowledge of insurance markets and alternative risk financing programs.
- An understanding of government and politics.
- An awareness of the relationship of risk management to other fields, such as human resources, safety and health law, operations, budgeting, and auditing.
- Knowledge of guidelines and standards [e.g., International Organization for Standardization (ISO)] that influence the external evaluation of risk management practices.
- An understanding of risk identification, assessment, prevention, and control.
- Knowledge of catastrophe management and the rules and standards applicable to issues such as homeland security and emergency management.
- Knowledge of management principles, information technology, communications skills, and critical thinking.

RISK MANAGEMENT FUNCTIONS IN BUSINESS AND GOVERNMENT

This section describes what a risk manager does in a business and then describes the functions in government. There are many similarities in job functions of risk managers in the private and public sectors.

Traditionally, in business, risk managers develop specifications for insurance needs, meet with insurance company representatives or brokers, check on the financial health of insurance companies, and then choose the best insurance policies at the best possible premium rates. A delicate balance is sought between excessive protection (i.e., too much insurance) and excessive exposure (i.e., too much risk). A major question is: What amount of risk will be assumed by the business beyond that covered by insurance and other risk management tools? Risk managers must explain the program in financial terms to top executives. Is the program cost-effective? Does it provide the most efficient use of capital? The expectations of the programs and insurance coverage must be clearly understood. A risk manager's job could be in jeopardy if a serious loss is not covered, plus a business may not survive (Purpura, 2002: 334–335).

Government has become increasingly aware of the importance of risk management. Let us look at one unnamed local government risk management department to gain a perspective of what the job entails in the public sector. The risk manager plans, directs, administers, and coordinates the risk management program. The local government budget contains line items on insurance costs for property casualty, vehicle, and workers compensation insurance. Loss prevention, loss transfer (insurance), and risk issues are major activities of the risk management program. Duties include administration, coordination, and adjustment of all property/casualty, liability, and vehicle claims brought against the local government; management of the contract review system with the local government attorney; training of employees on risk and safety topics; and developing policies and procedures.

The risk management division of the state of Minnesota provides an illustration of the role and influence state government can have on risk management in state agencies. The division's mission is to promote proactive risk management techniques; provide methods to minimize adverse impacts of risks and losses; absorb risk while maintaining a stable financial profile; and ensuring the long-term financial security of the state. The division serves as the state's internal insurance agency and purchases: automobile liability insurance for all state owned and leased vehicles; collision and comprehensive insurance on vehicles for agencies that select the coverage; "all risk" property and business interruption insurance; and boiler and machinery, crime, and other specific coverage's depending on need. If risks are unique, coverage is purchased through the commercial insurance market. A variety of consulting services are offered to state agencies, including how to apply risk management tools. The division and state agency efforts to prevent and control losses have resulted in millions of dollars in dividends being returned to state agencies. When premiums are collected, the money is invested. The difference between premium and investment income, less losses and expenses paid out, equals the amount eligible for dividends (Minnesota, 2005).

In both public and private sectors, risk managers serve as coordinators to prevent and control losses. This means interaction with specialists in safety, health, environmental protection, fire protection, life safety, security, human resources, and other fields. A safety program, for instance, can prevent and control losses and save money. Such a program can include a policy requiring employees to use safety belts when operating employer vehicles, requiring completion of a defensive driving course, and implementing policies to reinforce the use of safety equipment (e.g., hard hats, safety glasses). Programs that promote employee health (e.g., diet, smoking cessation) are among many other types of programs that reduce risks and insurance costs.

Generally, in businesses, the risk manager is likely to have a business degree, possibly in risk management and insurance, and business experience. This practitioner is likely to be knowledgeable of business finance and investments, as the job entails the most profitable utilization of capital in conjunction with risk management options. In the public sector, the risk manager often has a background in government and possibly a degree in public administration, business, or risk management and insurance.

THE RISK MANAGEMENT PROFESSION

Several groups play a role in promoting the professionalism of risk management. Chapter 6 described the characteristics of professional associations and their many benefits.

The **Risk and Insurance Management Society, Inc.** (RIMS) is a preeminent group serving the needs of risk managers and enhancing their profile as a vital component of organizational success. It was founded in 1950, represents nearly 4800 private and public entities, and serves about 8900 risk management professionals. RIMS is characterized by chapters located in many geographic areas, conferences and other educational opportunities, periodicals, best practices, and advocacy of its viewpoints. The RIMS Fellow designation signifies professional competency.

The National Alliance for Insurance Education & Research offers the certified risk manager designation. It requires completion of five courses and examinations within 5 years.

The **Public Risk Management Association** (PRIMA) is the largest network of public risk managers. PRIMA offers numerous services to its members, similar to other professional associations.

The **State Risk and Insurance Management Association** (STRIMA) represents risk and insurance managers in state governments. The group promotes the advancement of risk management principles and practices in the public sector. The STRIMA offers training opportunities and it promotes member information exchange and high ethical standards.

RISK MANAGEMENT IN THE FEDERAL GOVERNMENT

The U.S. Government Accountability Office (GAO) is a strong proponent of risk management. Since 1996, the GAO has produced several reports recommending that the federal government use risk management as an important element in developing a national strategy to combat terrorism. In 1998, the GAO asked Congress to consider requiring that the domestic preparedness program use a risk management approach with state and local governments to prepare for terrorist use of WMD. In 1999, the GAO recommended that the FBI conduct threat and other assessments at the national level as part of a risk management approach. In 2001, the GAO made recommendations to the Department of Defense (DOD) to apply risk management to force protection. Both the FBI and the DOD have concurred with these GAO recommendations, although results have been inconclusive (Decker, 2001: 4).

During 2005, the GAO continued its positive position on risk management, emphasizing its importance to guide the allocation of resources and investments for improving homeland security. It also noted that the 9/11 and Gilmore commissions made recommendations on the need for risk management. In referring to the U.S. Office of Management and Budget (OMB), the GAO challenged this office to develop a framework and supporting tools for cost allocations in a risk management process. The U.S. Government Accountability Office (2005: 124–125) stated that "... a vacuum exists in which benefits of homeland security investments are often not quantified and are almost never valued in monetary terms. As OMB guidance is relatively silent on acceptable treatments of nonquantifiable benefits, there is a lack of criteria to guide agency analysts in developing information to inform management."

Obviously, the GAO is seeking improvements in the management and accountability of funds spent on homeland security. GAO recommendations and reports can expose important issues that result in improvements in government. The public sector should also look to business methods from the private sector to enhance efficiency, effectiveness, return on investment, and performance measures.

CRITICAL THINKING:

Why do you think risk management has been slower to develop in government in comparison to the business sector?

GAO RISK MANAGEMENT APPROACH

The GAO states that risk management principles acknowledge that although risks generally cannot be eliminated, enhanced protection from known or potential threats can reduce it. The risk management approach offers a method to study threats and risks as a foundation for planning protection. This method is applied by or endorsed by federal agencies, government commissions, and businesses. There are many variations of this method. This section discusses the perspective of the GAO. In Chapter 10, on protecting critical infrastructure, the focus is on the National Infrastructure Protection Plan. It takes the principles of the National Strategy for Homeland Security to the next level and applies a "risk management framework."

The GAO views a risk management approach as having three elements: threat assessment, vulnerability assessment, and criticality assessment (Figure 7-3). The following information is from the GAO publication, *A Risk Management Approach Can Guide Preparedness Efforts* (Decker, 2001: 8–12).

THREAT ASSESSMENT

A threat assessment is used to evaluate the likelihood of terrorist activity against a given asset. It is a decision support tool that helps establish and prioritize security-program requirements,

Figure 7-3 ■ Risk management approach. Source: Decker (2001). http://www.gao.gov/new.items/ d02208t.pdf

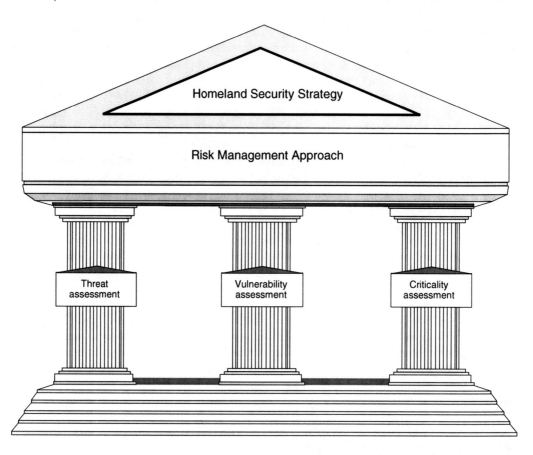

Homeland Security Strategy

Risk Management Approach

| Threat assessment | Vulnerability assessment | Criticality assessment |

planning, and resource allocations. A threat assessment identifies and evaluates each threat on the basis of various factors, including capability, intention, and impact of an attack. Intelligence and law enforcement agencies assess the foreign and domestic terrorist threats to the United States. Threat information gathered by both intelligence and law enforcement communities can produce threat assessments for use in national security strategy planning.

Several federal government organizations, as well as companies in the private sector, apply some formal threat assessment process in their programs, or such assessments have been recommended for implementation. For example, the DOD uses threat assessments for its antiterrorism program designed to protect military installations. The DOD evaluates threats on the basis of several factors, including a terrorist group's intentions, capabilities, and past activities. The assessments provide installation commanders with a list of credible threats that can be used in conjunction with other information (such as the state of the installation's preparedness) to prepare against attack, to recover from the effects of an attack, and to target resources adequately.

From the private sector, an unnamed leading multinational oil company attempts to identify threats in order to decide how to manage risk in a cost-effective manner. Because the company operates overseas, its facilities and operations are exposed to a multitude of threats, including terrorism, political instability, and religious or tribal conflict. In characterizing the threat, the company examines the historical record of security and safety breaches and obtains location-specific threat information from government organizations and other sources. It then evaluates these threats in terms of company assets that represent likely targets.

While threat assessments are key decision support tools, it should be recognized that, even if updated often, threat assessments might not adequately capture emerging threats posed by some terrorist groups. No matter how much we know about potential threats, we will never know that we have identified every threat or that we have complete information even about the threats of which we are aware. Consequently, a risk management approach to prepare for terrorism with its two additional assessments, discussed next, can provide better assurance of preparedness for a terrorist attack.

VULNERABILITY ASSESSMENT

A vulnerability assessment is a process that identifies weaknesses in physical structures, personnel protection systems, processes, or other areas that may be exploited by terrorists and may suggest options to eliminate or mitigate those weaknesses. For example, a vulnerability assessment might reveal weaknesses in an organization's security systems, financial management processes, computer networks, or unprotected key infrastructure, such as water supplies, bridges, and tunnels. In general, these assessments are conducted by teams of experts skilled in such areas as engineering, intelligence, security, information systems, and finance. For example, at many military bases, experts have identified security concerns including the distance from parking lots to important buildings as being so close that a car bomb detonation would damage or destroy the buildings and the people working in them. To mitigate this threat, experts have advised that the distance between parking lots and some buildings be increased. Another security enhancement might be to reinforce the windows in buildings to prevent glass from flying into the building if an explosion occurs.

Various tools and methods can be used to assess vulnerabilities to not only terrorism, but also all hazards. For example, geographic information systems can help identify adjacent hazards that could facilitate attacks or are potential targets themselves and, thus, present the potential for collateral damage (Figure 7-4). As covered earlier, modeling can be used to anticipate various scenarios (Figure 7-5).

Figure 7-4 ■ Using geographic information systems to identify adjacent hazards. Note the large fuel storage facilities (right) in the vicinity of the office buildings (center) being assessed. Source: U.S. Department of Homeland Security (2003). Reference Manual to Mitigate Potential Terrorist Attacks against Buildings. Washington, DC: FEMA.

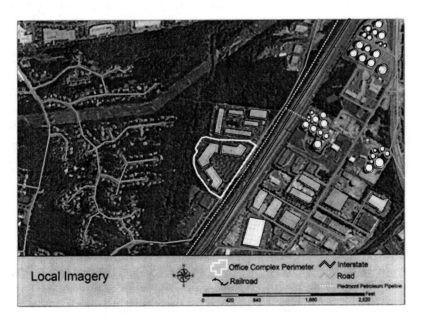

Figure 7-5 ■ Estimated plume from a 1-ton chlorine spill from a railroad car in Washington, DC. Source: U.S. Department of Homeland Security (2003). Reference Manual to Mitigate Potential Terrorist attacks against Buildings. Washington, DC: FEMA.

With information on both threats and vulnerabilities, planners and decision makers are in a better position to manage the risk of a terrorist attack by targeting resources more effectively. However, threat and vulnerability assessments need to be bolstered by a criticality assessment, which is the final major element of the risk management approach. Because we may not be able to afford the same level of protection for all vulnerable assets, it is necessary to prioritize which are most important and, thus, would receive the highest level of protection.

CRITICALITY ASSESSMENT

A criticality assessment is a process designed to systematically identify and evaluate important assets and infrastructure in terms of various factors, such as the mission and significance of a target. For example, nuclear power plants, key bridges, and major computer networks might be identified as "critical" in terms of their importance to national security, economic activity, and public safety. In addition, facilities might be critical at certain times, but not others. For example, large sports stadiums, shopping malls, or office towers, when in use by large numbers of people, may represent an important target, but are less important when they are empty. Criticality assessments are important because they provide a basis for identifying which assets and structures are relatively more important to protect from an attack. The assessments provide information to prioritize assets and allocate resources to special protective actions. These assessments have considered such factors as the importance of a structure to accomplish a mission, the ability to reconstitute this capability, and the potential cost to repair or replace the asset.

The multinational oil company mentioned earlier uses descriptive values to categorize the loss of a structure as catastrophic, critical, marginal, or negligible. It then assigns values to its key assets. This process results in a matrix that ranks as highest risk the most important assets with the threat scenarios it believes are most likely to occur.

Managers can make better decisions based on this risk management approach. After threat, vulnerability, and criticality assessments have been completed and evaluated, key actions can be taken to better prepare us against potential attacks or events.

CRITICAL THINKING:

Compare and contrast the risk management process of Leimberg *et al.* (2002) with the risk management approach of the GAO.

EMERGENCY MANAGEMENT

McEntire (2004: 14) writes that the profession of emergency management, as well as scholarship in this area, is undergoing a massive transformation. He notes several concerns over the development of emergency management theory. These include definitions of terms, what hazards to focus on, what variables to explore (e.g., location of buildings, building construction, politics, critical incident stress), and what disciplines should contribute to emergency management. McEntire writes that one way to foster theory is to change the name of the field of emergency management, and he offers these alternatives that are being circulated among his colleagues: "disaster management," "risk management," "sustainable hazards management," or "disaster vulnerability management." The transformation of emergency management is also reflected in academic programs as explained in Chapter 12.

McEntire writes that there is no single overarching theory of emergency management because it would be impossible to develop a theory that would contain every single variable and issue involving disasters. He sees systems or chaos theory as gaining recognition because they incorporate many causative variables. McEntire (2004: 15–18) also offers other theories and concepts, several of which are summarized here, that he views as relevant to emergency management. Notice the similarities in some of the following theories to those explained under risk management (i.e., risk perception theory; risk communication theory).

- **Systems theory** involves diverse systems that interact in complicated ways and impact vulnerability. These systems include natural, built, technological, social, political, economic, and cultural environments.
- **Chaos theory** has similarities to systems theory in that many variables interact and impact vulnerability. This theory points to the difficulty of detecting simple linear cause and effect relationships and it seeks to address multiple variables simultaneously to mitigate vulnerability.
- **Decision theory** views disasters as characterized by uncertainty and limited information that results in increased vulnerability to causalities, disruption, and other negative consequences. This theory focuses on perceptions, communications, bureaucracy, politics, and other variables that impact the aftermath of disasters.
- **Management theory** explains disasters as political and organizational problems. Vulnerability to disasters can be reduced through effective leadership and improved planning. Leaders have the responsibility to partner with a wide variety of players to reach objectives that reduce vulnerability.
- **Organizational behavior theory** sees agencies concerned about their own interests and turf, without understanding how their action or inaction impacts others. Cultural barriers, a lack of communications, and other variables limit partnering to increase efficiency and effectiveness. Improved communications during the 9/11 attacks in New York City would have saved some of the lives of firefighters, police, and others.

- **Risk perception and communication theory** focuses on the apathy of citizens prior to disasters. Vulnerability can increase if citizens do not understand the consequences of disasters and do not take action for self-protection (e.g., evacuation). Citizens may be more likely to reduce their vulnerability if authorities communicate risk accurately and convincingly.
- **Social constructionist theory** shifts from hazards, that we cannot control, to the role of humans in disasters, who determine, through decisions, the degree of vulnerability. For example, citizen decisions to reside in areas subject to mudslides.
- **Weberian theory** looks to culture, including values, attitudes, practices, and socialization, as contributing to increased vulnerability. Other factors under this theory resulting in greater vulnerability are weak emergency management institutions and a lack of professionalization among emergency managers.
- **Marxist theory** explains economic conditions and political powerlessness as playing roles in disaster vulnerability. The poor and minorities are more likely to reside in vulnerable areas and are often unable to act to protect themselves. The Hurricane Katrina disaster serves as an example; thousands of citizens were trapped in flooded New Orleans that was built below sea level.

THE DEVELOPMENT OF EMERGENCY MANAGEMENT

As written at the beginning of this chapter, emergency management focuses on preparation for potential emergencies and disasters and the coordination of response and resources during such events. Haddow and Bullock (2003: 1) describe emergency management as follows.

- The management of the effects of disasters.
- The discipline dealing with risk and risk avoidance.
- An essential role of government.

Haddock and Bullock (2003: 1–13) trace the development of emergency management. A summary of their research is described next.

The U.S. Constitution is at the foundation of the states' responsibility for public health and safety. However, when states and localities become overwhelmed, the federal government provides assistance. The first example of the federal government becoming involved in a disaster was when, in 1803, a Congressional act was passed to provide financial assistance to a New Hampshire town that was destroyed by fire. During the Great Depression (1930s), President Franklin D. Roosevelt spent enormous federal funds on projects to put people to work and to stimulate the economy. Such projects had relevance to emergency management. The Tennessee Valley Authority was created to not only produce hydroelectric power, but to also reduce flooding. The Flood Control Act of 1934 provided the U.S. Army Corps of Engineers with increased authority to build flood control projects.

During the 1950s, as the Cold War (see Chapter 3) brought with it the threat of nuclear war, **civil defense programs** grew. These programs were characterized by communities and families building bomb shelters as a defense against attack from the Soviet Union. Air raid drills became common at schools—children practiced going under their desks or kneeling down in the hall while covering their heads. Civil defense directors, often retired military personnel, were appointed at the local and state levels, and these individuals represent the beginning of emergency management in the United States. The Federal Civil Defense Administration (FCDA) provided technical assistance to local and state governments. Another agency, the Office of Defense Mobilization (ODM), was established in the DOD to quickly amass materials and production in the event of war. In 1958, both the FCDA and the ODM were merged into the Office of Civil and Defense Mobilization.

A series of destructive hurricanes in the 1950s resulted in ad hoc Congressional legislation to fund assistance to the affected states. The 1960s also saw its share of natural disasters that resulted in President John F. Kennedy's administration, in 1961, creating the Office of Emergency Preparedness to deal with natural disasters. Through the 1960s, natural disasters were followed by ad hoc legislation for funds. The absence of flood insurance on the standard homeowner policy prompted Congress to enact the National Flood Insurance Act of 1968, which created the National Flood Insurance Program (NFIP). This noteworthy act included the concept of **community-based mitigation**, whereby action was taken against the risk prior to the disaster. When a community joined the NFIP, the program offered federally subsidized, low-cost flood insurance to citizens in exchange for the community enacting an ordinance banning future development in its floodplains. As a voluntary program, the NFIP was not successful. The Flood Insurance Act of 1972 created an incentive for communities to join the NFIP. This act required mandatory purchase of flood insurance for homeowner loans backed by federal mortgages, and a significant number of mortgages were federally backed.

The 1970s brought to light the fragmentation of federal, state, and local agencies responsible for risk and disasters. Over 100 federal agencies added to the confusion and turf wars. Unfortunately, the problems were compounded during disasters. The administration of President Jimmy Carter sought reform and consolidation of federal emergency management. The **Federal Emergency Management Agency** (FEMA) was established by Executive Order 12127 on March 31, 1979. The goal of this effort was to consolidate emergency preparedness, mitigation, and response into one agency, with a director who would report directly to the president. John Macy, who was in the Carter cabinet, became the director of FEMA. He emphasized similarities between natural hazards preparedness and civil defense and developed an "all-hazards" approach containing direction, control, and warning as goals common to all emergencies, from minor events to major events (Figure 7-6). FEMA (2004) states: "The **all-hazards preparedness concept** is simple in that how you prepare for one disaster or emergency situation is the same for any other disaster."

"All hazards" include natural disasters (e.g., hurricane) and human-made events (e.g., inadvertent accidents, such as an aircraft crash, and deliberate events, such as the terrorist bombing of an aircraft). Another category is technological events. An example is an electric service blackout resulting from a variety of possible causes.

Figure 7-6 ■ The U.S. government is working to provide an all-hazards response capability. Source: U.S. Department of Homeland Security (2004b). http://www.dhs.gov/interweb/assetlibrary/DHS_StratPlan_FINAL_spread.pdf

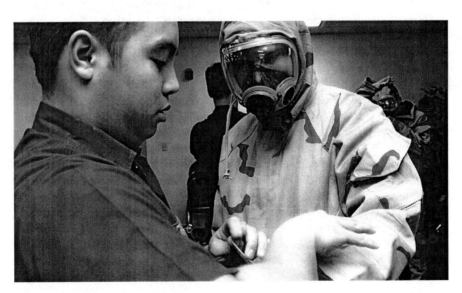

The author of this book argues that the all-hazards approach seeks to maximize the efficiency and cost effectiveness of emergency management efforts through a realization that different risks and disasters contain similarities that can benefit, to a certain degree, from generic approaches to emergency management. However, there is a point at which **generic emergency management** must divide into **specialized emergency management**. For example, the detonation of a "dirty bomb" or an approaching hurricane necessitates evacuation; however, the victims and the scene of these disasters require markedly different expertise, treatment, and equipment.

Through the 1980s, FEMA experienced numerous troubles and criticism. It continued to exist as a fragmented organization. In 1982, President Ronald Reagan appointed Louis Guiffrida as director of FEMA. He was a friend of Ed Meese, the attorney general and advisor to the president. The top priority of FEMA became preparation for nuclear attack, at the expense of other risks. Environmental cleanup (e.g., Love Canal) became another priority. States saw their funding for emergency management decline. An undercurrent of discontent grew nationally and within FEMA. Congressional hearings and a grand jury investigation of misuse of government funds led to the resignation of Guiffrida and his top aides. President Reagan then appointed General Julius Becton as the new director. He restored integrity to FEMA and continued the work of his predecessor. The FEMA list of priorities ranked earthquake, hurricane, and flood programs low on the list. Senator Al Gore of Tennessee concluded that FEMA needed to change its priorities and work closer with federal, state, and local partners to prepare for natural disasters.

By the end of the 1980s, FEMA was in need of serious reform. FEMA's problems included tension with its partners at the state and local level over priorities and funding, and difficulty in responding to natural disasters. In 1989, Hurricane Hugo became the worst hurricane in a decade and caused 85 deaths and damage of more than $15 billion as it slammed into South Carolina, North Carolina, and other locations. The FEMA response was so poor that Senator Ernest Hollings (D-SC) called the agency the "sorriest bunch of bureaucratic jackasses." The FEMA problems with Hurricane Andrew, in 1992, in Florida, further eroded confidence in the agency.

Reform in FEMA finally occurred in 1993 when President William Clinton nominated James L. Witt, of Arkansas, to be director. Witt was the first director with emergency management experience and was skilled at building partnerships and serving customers. Inside FEMA, Witt fostered ties to employees, reorganized the agency, and supported new technologies to deliver disaster services. Externally, he improved relationships with state and local governments, Congress, and the media. Subsequent disasters, such as the Midwest floods in 1993 that resulted in nine states being declared disaster areas and the Northridge, California, earthquake in 1994, tested the reforms FEMA had made. Witt was elevated to be a member of President Clinton's cabinet, illustrating the importance of emergency management. Witt then sought to influence the nation's governors in elevating state emergency management directors to cabinet posts.

The World Trade Center bombing in 1993 and the Oklahoma City bombing in 1995 brought the issue of terrorism to the forefront of emergency management. A major question surfaced: Which agency would be in charge following a terrorist attack? Prior to the 9/11 attacks, several federal agencies sought leadership against terrorism. Major agencies included FEMA, the Department of Justice (DOJ) (it contains the FBI), the DOD, the National Guard, and the Department of Health and Human Services (HHS). Coordination was poor as agencies pursued their own agendas. The DOD and the DOJ received the most funds. State and local governments felt unprepared and complained about their vulnerabilities and needs. As we know, the 9/11 attacks resulted in a massive reorganization of the federal government to better coordinate both actions against terrorism and homeland security.

In September of 2005, FEMA experienced another setback when its director, Michael Brown, was relieved as commander of Hurricane Katrina relief efforts along the Gulf Coast and was sent back to Washington, DC. Three days later he resigned. Critics argued that he was the former head of an Arabian horse association and that he had no background in disaster relief when his friend and then-FEMA director, Joe Allbaugh, hired him in 2001 to serve as FEMA's general counsel.

Although "finger pointing" occurred by politicians at all levels of government as the relief effort became overwhelmed, Michael Brown became the classic scapegoat.

CRITICAL THINKING:

We have seen in the development of emergency management that its leaders have placed an emphasis on different risks over the years. Today, do you think emergency management leaders are placing too much emphasis on the problem of terrorism, without enough emphasis on other risks?

THE EMERGENCY MANAGEMENT PROFESSION

As with risk management, undergraduate and graduate degrees are offered in emergency management, and this profession has evolved with the assistance of several organizations as described next.

The **National Emergency Management Association (NEMA)** began in 1974 when state directors of emergency services united to share information on common issues and problems. (The development of emergency management, as discussed earlier, shows that, during the 1970s, the profession faced serious challenges.) NEMA is dedicated to enhancing our nation's ability to prepare for, respond to, and recover from emergencies, disasters, and threats. State directors are the core membership, but others in related occupations in the public and private sectors may join. NEMA holds conferences, conducts training, and offers publications. In 1990, NEMA became an affiliate with the Council of State Governments (CSG) in a partnership to promote the role of the state in our federal system of government.

The **International Association of Emergency Managers (IAEM)** is an educational organization that promotes the goals of saving lives and protecting property during emergencies and disasters. The IAEM offers conferences, publications, employment information, scholarships, and certification and accreditation programs. The IAEM certified emergency manager designation is supported by FEMA, NEMA, and other organizations. The Emergency Management Accreditation Program (EMAP) is a credential for agencies that meet standards of professionalism and competence. It is a voluntary process based on a national standard (NFPA 1600). The process involves documentation, on-site assessment, committee review, and periodic review.

The International Emergency Management Society (TIEMS) seeks to bring the benefits of modern emergency management tools and techniques to society for a safer world. This group has membership chapters, supporters, and sponsors worldwide. TIEMS holds conferences and workshops and offers publications.

DRI International (DRII) promotes a base of common knowledge for the business continuity/disaster recovery industry through education, standards, and publications. It certifies qualified individuals. DRII, together with the Business Continuity Institute (BCI) from the United Kingdom, publishes the *Professional Practices for Business Continuity Planners* as the industry's international standard.

Individual states, such as Colorado, Florida, and Michigan, also certify emergency managers. A listing of state certification programs can be found in the *NFPA 1600 Standard on Disaster/Emergency Management and Business Continuity Programs*. This standard is covered later in this chapter under business continuity.

EMERGENCY MANAGEMENT DISCIPLINES

Haddow and Bullock (2003) divide emergency management into the disciplines of mitigation, response, recovery, preparedness, and communications. *Although they emphasize natural hazards, their writing provides a foundation for multiple risks, including terrorism.* A portion of the following pages is based on their work.

Natural disasters result in lost lives, injuries, and multibillion dollar costs. The causes are many, including global warming and other climatological changes. Societal behavior also contributes to risks, such as development and dense population along coastal areas and in cities, the filling in of floodplains, and deforestation.

MITIGATION

Haddow and Bullock (2003: 37) define mitigation as "a sustained action to reduce or eliminate risk to people and property from hazards and their effects." The U.S. Department of Homeland Security (2004c) defines **mitigation** as follows.

> The activities designed to reduce or eliminate risks to persons or property or to lessen the actual or potential effects or consequences of an incident. Mitigation measures may be implemented prior to, during, or after an incident. Mitigation measures are often informed by lessons learned from prior incidents. Mitigation involves ongoing actions to reduce exposure to, probability of, or potential loss from hazards. Measures may include zoning and building codes, floodplain buyouts, and analysis of hazard-related data to determine where it is safe to build or locate temporary facilities. Mitigation can include efforts to educate governments, businesses, and the public on measures they can take to reduce loss and injury.

Mitigation differs from other disciplines of emergency management in the following ways.

- It looks at long-term solutions to reduce risk, as opposed to preparedness for emergencies and disasters.
- Mitigation programs require partners outside of traditional emergency management. Examples are land-use planners, construction and building officials, and community leaders.
- The skills and tools for mitigation (e.g., marketing and public relations, consensus building) are different from the first-responder skills required in emergencies and disasters.
- Outside of fire protection professionals who promote mitigation through building codes and public education, emergency management practitioners have traditionally focused on preparedness, response, and recovery. However, mitigation is now receiving more attention because of leadership at the federal level, larger disasters, increases in funding, and greater value and professionalism in emergency management.

Mitigation tools that are widely accepted and applied to reduce risk are listed and explained next.

- *Hazard identification and mapping* shows the location of hazards. This tool serves as a foundation for mitigation. Government agencies and the private sector have programs that map hazards. FEMA's National Flood Insurance Program (NFIP) contains detailed flood maps and studies, and the U.S. Geological Survey has the same for earthquakes and landslides. Geographic information systems have become popular as a tool for planners. Software is evolving that enables the human and built environment to be superimposed onto the hazards to quantify risk.
- *Design and construction* for mitigation are dependent on building codes, design, and landscaping considerations. This is essentially a state and local responsibility. Examples are using fire-retardant building materials such as slate for roofing in wildfire areas.
- *Land-use planning* is most successful at the local level where most decisions on land-use occur. Strategies include storm water management, zoning, and environmental review. An example is the Alquist-Priola Act in California that limits building near earthquake faults.
- *Financial incentives* to promote mitigation take many forms. Examples include special tax assessments or bonds to pay for relocation assistance. Repetitive flooding led citizens of Napa, California, and Tulsa, Oklahoma, to pass a small tax increase to mitigate the problem; the investment reduced economic losses from subsequent flooding. Berkeley, California, passed several bond issues for seismic retrofit of public buildings, schools, and homes.

- *Insurance* is another mitigation tool. The NFIP serves as an example. (See the earlier discussion of this successful program.)
- *Structural controls* are controversial because they can protect one area and increase damage in another. The levee is a common form of structural control. The U.S. Army Corps of Engineers has built levees across the United States to control flooding. Levees can be breached and they give residents a false sense of safety that can stimulate increased building; this was the case with the 1993 Midwest floods. New Orleans, a city built below sea level, where relocation is not an option, has levees; they were no match for Hurricane Katrina in 2005 and the city flooded. Other structural controls are seawalls and jetties that stabilize the beach and reduce erosion, but they can save one area at the expense of another.

There are various reasons why mitigation is not more widely used. The reasons include denial of the risk, cost, lack of political will, and dependence on government assistance if disaster strikes. At the same time, mitigation has a history of successful programs.

NATIONAL RESPONSE PLAN (NRP), NATIONAL INCIDENT MANAGEMENT SYSTEM (NIMS), AND NATIONAL PREPAREDNESS GOAL

The 9/11 attacks changed dramatically emergency response plans in the United States. In addition to a host of manmade and natural hazards, such as accidents, earthquakes, hurricanes, and floods, the United States faces creative, asymmetrical attacks by terrorists who resort to WMD. This range of hazards and threats has resulted in the need for a unified and coordinated national approach to emergency management. This need is met through the **NRP** (U.S. Department of Homeland Security, 2004a), the **NIMS** (U.S. Department of Homeland Security, 2004c), and the **national preparedness goal** (the goal). Both the NRP and the NIMS are national, rather than federal plans, and aim to align the patchwork of federal emergency management plans into an effective and efficient structure, while coordinating the capabilities and resources of all levels of government and the private sector.

According to the Department of Homeland Security, the NRP is an all-hazards approach incorporating best practices and procedures from many incident management disciplines. It ties together emergency management activities to include prevention, mitigation, preparedness, response, and recovery.

The NRP is designed to coordinate structures, roles, and responsibilities among federal, state, and local levels of government. It requires cooperation, collaboration, and information sharing among jurisdictions, as well as between public and private sectors. It groups capabilities and resources that are most likely to be needed during an incident. Examples are firefighting, search and rescue, and mass care. It outlines core responsibilities and expertise for specific contingencies (e.g., radiological, biological, cyber). The NRP describes common processes and specific administrative requirements (e.g., fiscal, worker safety and health). It also includes a glossary, acronyms, and authorities.

The NRP priorities are to save lives, protect health and safety, secure the homeland, protect and restore critical infrastructure, conduct investigations to resolve incidents, protect property, and facilitate recovery.

The NRP multiagency coordination structure includes the responsibilities of the president and a flexible national capability that addresses local, regional, and national issues. It is a signed and binding agreement among 32 federal departments and agencies, the American Red Cross, and the National Voluntary Organizations Active in Disasters. The Department of Homeland Security maintains the NRP.

Continued

NATIONAL RESPONSE PLAN (NRP), NATIONAL INCIDENT MANAGEMENT SYSTEM (NIMS), AND NATIONAL PREPAREDNESS GOAL—Cont'd

The principal authorities that guide the structure and implementation of the NRP are numerous federal laws, executive orders, and presidential directives. The NRP lists 42 laws. An example is the Homeland Security Act of 2002 (see Chapter 3). Another example is the Robert T. Stafford Disaster Relief and Emergency Assistance Act of 1974. Amended in 2002, and known as the Stafford act, this federal law establishes the programs and processes for the federal government to provide disaster and emergency assistance to states, local governments, tribal nations, individuals, and nonprofit organizations. It covers all hazards, including terrorism. This act includes the process for governors to request federal assistance from the President (Figure 7-7).

Figure 7-7 ■ Overview of initial federal involvement under the Stafford act. Source: U.S. Department of Homeland Security (2004a). http://www.dhs.gov/interweb/assetlibrary/NRPbaseplan.pdf

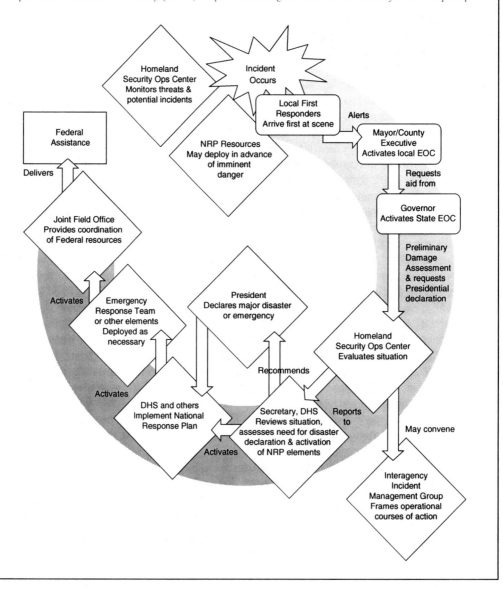

NATIONAL RESPONSE PLAN (NRP), NATIONAL INCIDENT MANAGEMENT SYSTEM (NIMS), AND NATIONAL PREPAREDNESS GOAL—Cont'd

The Homeland Security Presidential Directive (HSPD)-5, Management of Domestic Incidents, February 28, 2003, is intended to establish a single, comprehensive NRP and NIMS. This directive designates the secretary of homeland security to administer these programs.

The NIMS was developed with input from many groups in the public and private sectors. It represents best practices, strives for standardization, and contains a core set of doctrine, concepts, principles, terminology, and organizational processes. HSPD-5 requires all federal agencies and departments to adopt the NIMS and makes it a requirement for state and local organizations to receive federal preparedness assistance. The NIMS integration center publishes standards, guidelines, and compliance protocols. The DHS offers no-cost, on-line training for the NIMS and thousands have completed the training.

NIMS emphasizes standardization. Examples include standardization in incident command structure, planning, training, exercises, personnel qualifications and certification, equipment, resource management, forms, and information management. On December 17, 2003, the president issued Homeland Security Presidential Directive 8 *"National Preparedness"* (HSPD-8). The purpose of HSPD-8 is to

> establish policies to strengthen the preparedness of the United States to prevent and respond to threatened or actual domestic terrorist attacks, major disasters, and other emergencies by requiring a national domestic all-hazards preparedness goal, establishing mechanisms for improved delivery of Federal preparedness assistance to State and local governments, and outlining actions to strengthen preparedness capabilities of Federal, State, and local entities.

The *goal* will guide federal departments and agencies, state, territorial, local and tribal officials, the private sector, nongovernment organizations, and the public in determining how to most effectively and efficiently strengthen preparedness for terrorist attacks, major disasters, and other emergencies. The *goal* utilizes a capabilities-based planning approach: planning, under uncertainty, to provide capabilities suitable for a wide range of threats and hazards, within an economic framework that necessitates prioritization and choice. Capabilities-based planning addresses uncertainty by analyzing a wide range of possible scenarios (e.g., WMD, natural disasters, cyber, pandemic influenza) to identify required capabilities. The purpose of the *goal* is to develop readiness priorities, targets, and metrics. It focuses on three key questions: How prepared do we need to be? How prepared are we? How do we prioritize efforts to close the gap?

RESPONSE

The National Incident Management System (U.S. Department of Homeland Security, 2004c: 136) defines **response** as follows.

> Activities that address the short-term, direct effects of an incident. Response includes immediate actions to save lives, protect property, and meet basic human needs. Response also includes the execution of emergency operations plans and of mitigation activities designed to limit the loss of life, personal injury, property damage, and other unfavorable outcomes. As indicated by the situation, response activities include applying intelligence and other information to lessen the effects or consequences of an incident; increased security operations; continuing investigations into nature and source of the threat; ongoing public health and agricultural surveillance and testing processes; immunizations, isolation, or quarantine; and specific law enforcement operations aimed at preempting, interdicting, or disrupting illegal activity, and apprehending actual perpetrators and bringing them to justice.

First responders at emergencies and disasters are usually local police, fire, and emergency medical specialists, not state or federal personnel. Initial objectives of first responders are to save lives, tend to the injured, protect property, and secure the scene. Supporting first responders are local emergency management personnel and government officials that follow a chain of command that may reach the president of the United States (see the NRP and NIMS).

Through the 1990s, the emergency management system in the United States has responded to floods, earthquakes, hurricanes, tornadoes, and terrorist attacks. In addition to local, state, and federal responses, volunteer organizations and the business community have participated in recovery efforts.

The 9/11 attacks and the resultant loss of so many first responders have caused a reevaluation of response procedures. Government units from across the country have reworked their emergency plans to better protect first responders and communities from WMD.

Here is a list of what may be contained in a community emergency plan.

- Instruction for use
- Basic plan
- Glossary
- Acronyms and abbreviations
- Statutes and ordinances authorizing emergency operations
- How to seek a proclamation of an emergency
- Mutual aid agreements
- Operations plan
- Assignment of responsibilities (e.g., government leaders such as mayor, county manager, police chief, sheriff, fire chief, EMS coordinator, social services director, medical examiner, health director, public works director, and volunteer coordinators)
- Direction and control
- Communications
- Public information
- Evacuation and transportation
- Shelter and mass care
- Damage assessment/recovery
- Search and rescue
- Others

Among the responsibilities of a local emergency manager are

- Perform duties as specified in law.
- Plan according to local, state, and federal guidelines.
- Use the NIMS **incident command system** (ICS) to facilitate near-term and long-term operations for a wide variety of emergencies. It is used by all levels of government and the private sector and consists of five functional areas: command, operations, planning, logistics, and finance/administration (U.S. Department of Homeland Security, 2004c: 7).
- Prepare emergency operations plans.
- Maintain liaison with other jurisdictions and government agencies, the media, utility companies, and other infrastructure.
- Conduct training, drills, and exercises.
- Request funding and manage a budget.
- Maintain equipment and inventories of supplies.
- Test emergency systems.
- Identify population groups requiring special needs during an emergency.
- In an emergency, establish disaster assistance centers and shelters.

The NIMS stresses coordination in emergency management and response. The following terms from the NIMS (U.S. Department of Homeland Security, 2004c) are especially important in this regard.

1. *Area command (unified area command):* An organization established (1) to oversee the management of multiple incidents that are each being handled by an ICS organization or (2) to oversee the management of large or multiple incidents to which several incident management teams have been assigned. Area command has the responsibility to set overall strategy and priorities, allocate critical resources according to priorities, ensure that incidents are managed properly, and ensure that objectives are met and strategies followed. Area command becomes **unified area command** when incidents are multijurisdictional. Area command may be established at an emergency operations center facility or at some location other than an incident command post.

2. *Emergency operations centers (EOCs):* The physical location at which the coordination of information and resources to support domestic incident management activities normally takes place. An EOC may be a temporary facility or may be located in a more central or permanently established facility, perhaps at a higher level of organization within a jurisdiction. EOCs may be organized by major functional disciplines (e.g., fire, law enforcement, and medical services), by jurisdiction (e.g., Federal, State, regional, county, city, tribal), or some combination thereof.

3. *Incident command system:* A standardized on-scene emergency management construct specifically designed to provide for the adoption of an integrated organizational structure that reflects the complexity and demands of single or multiple incidents, without being hindered by jurisdictional boundaries. ICS is the combination of facilities, equipment, personnel, procedures, and communications operating within a common organizational structure, designed to aid in the management of resources during incidents. It is used for all kinds of emergencies and is applicable to small as well as large and complex incidents. ICS is used by various jurisdictions and functional agencies, both public and private, to organize field-level incident management operations.

4. *Incident commander (IC):* The individual responsible for all incident activities, including the development of strategies and tactics and the ordering and the release of resources. The IC has overall authority and responsibility for conducting incident operations and is responsible for the management of all incident operations at the incident site.

5. *Incident objectives:* Statements of guidance and direction necessary for selecting appropriate strategy(s) and the tactical direction of resources. Incident objectives are based on realistic expectations of what can be accomplished. Incident objectives must be achievable and measurable, yet flexible enough to allow strategic and tactical alternatives.

6. *Multiagency coordination systems:* These systems provide the architecture to support coordination for incident prioritization, critical resource allocation, communications systems integration, and information coordination. The components of multiagency coordination systems include facilities, equipment, EOCs, specific multiagency coordination entities, personnel, procedures, and communications. These systems assist agencies and organizations to fully integrate the subsystems of the NIMS.

All 50 states and six territories of the United States operate an office of emergency management. The names of these offices vary, as does the placement in the organizational structure of each jurisdiction. National Guard adjutant generals lead these offices in most states, followed by leadership by civilian employees. Governors rely primarily on their state **National Guard** for responding to disasters. National Guard resources include personnel, communications systems, air and road transport, heavy construction equipment, mass care and feeding equipment, and assorted supplies (e.g., tents, beds, blankets, medical). When a state is overwhelmed by a disaster, the governor may request federal assistance under a presidential disaster or emergency declaration.

The Homeland Security Act of 2002 established the DHS to reduce our nation's vulnerability to terrorism, natural disasters, and other emergencies and to assist in recovery. Pursuant to HSPD-5, the secretary of homeland security is responsible for coordinating federal operations in response to emergencies and disasters. Coordinating features in the NRP are as follow:

Homeland Security Operations Center (HSOC): The HSOC serves as the primary national level multiagency hub for domestic situational awareness and operational coordination. The HSOC also includes DHS components, such as the National Infrastructure Coordinating Center (NICC), which has primary responsibility for coordinating communications with the nation's critical infrastructure during an incident.

National Response Coordination Center (NRCC): The NRCC, a functional component of the HSOC, is a multiagency center that provides overall federal response coordination.

Regional Response Coordination Center (RRCC): At the regional level, the RRCC coordinates regional response efforts and implements local federal program support until a joint field office is established.

Interagency Incident Management Group (IIMG): A tailored group of senior federal interagency experts who provide strategic advice to the secretary of homeland security during an actual or potential incident of national significance.

Joint Field Office (JFO): A temporary federal facility established locally to provide a central point to coordinate resources in support of state, local, and tribal authorities.

Principal Federal Official (PFO): A PFO may be designated by the secretary of homeland security during a potential or actual incident of national significance. While individual federal officials retain their authorities pertaining to specific aspects of incident management, the PFO works in conjunction with these officials to coordinate overall federal incident management efforts.

CRITICAL THINKING:

What is your opinion of the federal, state, and local emergency response to the train collision and chlorine release described at the beginning of this chapter?

RECOVERY

Recovery involves actions to help individuals and communities return to normal. The NIMS (U.S. Department of Homeland Security, 2004c: 135) defines **recovery** as follows:

The development, coordination, and execution of service- and site-restoration plans; the reconstitution of government operations and services; individual, private-sector, nongovernmental, and public-assistance programs to provide housing and to promote restoration; long-term care and treatment of affected persons; additional measures for social, political, environmental, and economic restoration; evaluation of the incident to identify lessons learned; post incident reporting; and development of initiatives to mitigate the effects of future incidents.

The NRP describes the JFO as the central coordination point among all levels of government and voluntary groups for recovery assistance programs. The JFO operation section includes the following branches: the Human Services Branch (HSB), the Infrastructure Support Branch (ISB), and the Community Recovery and Mitigation Branch (CRMB). The HSB and the ISB assess state and local needs at the beginning of an incident and prepare a time frame for program delivery. The three branches seek to coordinate with one another to meet needs. Here is a description of the functions of each branch.

HSB: helps individuals, families, and businesses meet basic needs and return to self-sufficiency; coordinates volunteer groups and disaster recovery centers (DRCs) that are staffed by federal, state, local, tribal, and voluntary groups; and ensures that DRCs can provide program information, advice, counseling, and technical assistance.

ISB: coordinates assistance programs authorized by the Stafford act to aid state and local governments and nonprofit groups to repair or replace public facilities and associated environmental restoration.

CRMB: works with the other branches and other governmental officials to assess long-term impacts of an incident of national significance (i.e., based on criteria of HSPD-5—an actual or potential high-impact event requiring a response from all levels of government and the private sector); define available resources; and plan action, as well as reduce the impact of future disasters.

Haddow and Bullock (2003: 95) write: "There is often a theoretical debate over when the response function ends and the recovery function begins." They describe the response function as immediate action to save lives, protect property, and meet basic human needs, whereas the recovery function is not easy to classify because it often begins within hours of a disaster and can continue for years. Haddow and Bullock view *the goal of effective recovery as bringing all of the players together to plan, finance, and prepare a recovery strategy*. In addition to the roles of all levels of government, recovery includes the role of the insurance industry that provides financial support. However, the federal government plays the largest role in technical and financial support for recovery.

The range of programs that the federal government has been involved in over the years, especially through FEMA, has been enormous and costing tens of billions of dollars. Here are examples from Haddock and Bullock (2003: 98–108).

- FEMA's *national processing service centers*, since 1994, have processed over 2.5 million applications and received over 2.8 million telephone calls for more than 275 major disasters.
- FEMA's *disaster housing program* ensures that disaster victims have a safe place to live and it offers funds, not covered by insurance, for lodging expenses, repairs, and mortgage payments.
- FEMA's *individual and family grant program*, in cooperation with the states, provides $2,000 to $4,000 to an individual or family for housing, personal property, medical, funeral, and other expenses not covered by insurance or other assistance.
- FEMA, under the authority of the Stafford act, administers the *public assistance program* that provides federal assistance to state and local governments and to certain nonprofit groups. These grants enable them to recover from disasters and take action on mitigation. Examples of targets for these grants include debris removal from roads and repairs to roads, bridges, and utility systems.
- In addition to FEMA, many other federal (and state) agencies contribute to recovery. Examples are the U.S. Army Corps of Engineers, U.S. Small Business Administration, and the Departments of Housing and Urban Development, Agriculture, Health and Human Services, Transportation, Commerce, and Labor.

PREPAREDNESS

The NIMS (U.S. Department of Homeland Security, 2004c: 134) defines **preparedness** as follows.

The range of deliberate, critical tasks and activities necessary to build, sustain, and improve the operational capability to prevent, protect against, respond to, and recover from domestic incidents. Preparedness is a continuous process. Preparedness involves efforts at all levels of government and between government and the private sector and nongovernmental organizations to identify threats, determine vulnerabilities, and identify required resources. Within the NIMS, preparedness is operationally focused on establishing guidelines, protocols, and standards for planning, training and exercises, personnel qualification and certification, equipment certification, and publication management.

Under the NIMS, preparedness is based on the following core concepts and principles.

- *Levels of capability*: actions to establish and sustain prescribed levels of capability to execute a full range of incident management operations.
- *A unified approach*: ensures integration and interoperability among all jurisdictions and between public and private sectors.
- *NIMS publications*: provide guidelines; protocols; and standards for planning, training, qualifications and certification.
- *Mitigation*: composed of important elements of preparedness across the incident management spectrum from prevention through response and recovery.

All levels of government are responsible for implementing the preparedness cycle in advance of an incident and including the private sector and nonprofit groups. The NIMS provides a foundation to enhance preparedness and to implement the preparedness cycle: planning, training, equipping, exercising, evaluating, and taking action to mitigate.

Each jurisdiction develops an **emergency operations plan**. It describes organizational structures, roles and responsibilities, policies, procedures, and protocols.

Haddow and Bullock (2003: 115) see preparedness as a state of readiness to respond to emergencies and disasters. They look back in history and note that the predecessors of today's emergency managers placed a heavy emphasis on preparedness. One example is U.S. preparation for the possibility of nuclear attack by the Soviet Union during the Cold War.

Preparedness is the job of everyone and all sectors of our society. The federal government fosters this philosophy through its numerous programs and educational packages that aim to get people involved in preparedness. The DHS and FEMA Web sites offer such resources. Also, see the previous chapter.

FEMA is a leader in developing and teaching emergency management. It manages the Emergency Management Institute and the National Fire Academy, both located at Emmitsburg, Maryland. FEMA has trained over a million firefighters and emergency managers, it has helped to establish degree programs in colleges and universities, and it is expanding its distance and on-line programs.

Once a preparedness plan is developed, the next step is exercising the plan to evaluate its efficiency and effectiveness and to test systems, facilities, equipment, and personnel. Exercises are helpful to all levels of government and the private sector. They are usually scenario driven. A full-scale exercise evaluates most of a plan over an extended period of time under conditions as close as possible to actual emergency conditions. A partial-scale exercise is for limited duration and contains limited goals and personnel. A functional exercise is used to evaluate specific procedures that are similar, such as medical treatment or communications. Table-top exercises usually involve senior staff reacting to a specific scenario. Injected messages simulate an actual emergency and a facilitator keeps the group focused on the exercise objectives that may include emerging policies and procedures and plan revisions.

Exercises have been subject to criticism for not being realistic. Oppenheimer (2004: 1–2) writes that government exercises attract widespread media attention and that authorities attach considerable importance to them. He argues that it is difficult to duplicate real-life events and that some exercises simply do not represent anything close to a real terrorist attack, especially when the participants know where and when the attack will occur. Here are Oppenheimer's comments on different types of exercises.

- An exercise involving a mock chemical attack would require first responders to be well protected from a range of chemicals and be able to decontaminate victims within minutes.

- A fake radiological attack requires protection gear against radiation, plus detectors to identify the type of radioactive isotope used by terrorists. Decontamination would involve the victims and the entire affected area for an extended period of time.
- A mock biological attack is not feasible because it takes time before a deliberate release is suspected.
- At the same time, Oppenheimer admits, some exercises do show weaknesses that can be corrected.

From the business sector, Desouza (2004) writes that scenarios and drills are subject to complaints because of being too expensive, a disruption of the workplace, and they can instill unneeded fear in employees. He stresses that exercises must be realistic and serve as a method of learning about crises. Desouza sees a good exercise as focusing on roles and responsibilities, communication protocols, and protection of people and assets.

The U.S. Government Accountability Office (2005: 114–115) identified a number of challenges in emergency preparedness and response that must be overcome if the nation is to effectively minimize damage and successfully recover from future terrorist attacks. One challenge involves the adoption of an "all-hazards" approach. This would ensure improved preparation while simultaneously better preparing our nation for natural disasters. Another challenge involves improved governmental planning and coordination with regard to first responders. An example is the National Capital Region, where no coordinated region-wide plan exists for first responder priorities. Other concerns are better preparation for first responders encountering WMD; restructuring the federal grant system; improving public health communications and information sharing; better preparation for health care providers to respond to bioterrorism; and defining the role and responsibilities of the DOD in defending the homeland.

Pelfrey (2005) sees flaws in the preparedness process established by the federal government. He claims that "... a consensus strategic process of disaggregating preparedness into phases or elements to organize the preparedness process has not been articulated." Pelfrey writes that "preparedness" is complex; it should be divided into its component parts to strategically address the parts and to describe it as a timeline and "cycle." He also argues that the NRP and the NIMS focus on "the incident"; however, "prevention" is mentioned only superficially in the NRP and the NIMS, yet it should be the first priority. Pelfrey sees prevention as deterring, detecting, and eliminating the threat of terrorism.

BUSINESS CONTINUITY

Business continuity can be referred to as the private sector perspective on emergency management. There are many different opinions on the best way to approach business continuity. However, it usually begins with a plan to increase the survivability of a business when it faces an emergency. The plan focuses on such activities as risk management; employee safety; data backup systems; limited, if any, recovery time; and physical security.

Haddow and Bullock (2003: 132) write that external factors such as infrastructure and public safety authorities play a key role in whether business continuity is successful. Thus, especially since the 9/11 attacks, increased public–private sector cooperation has occurred.

Garris (2005: 28–32) notes that in our litigious society, organizations that fail to plan for emergencies could be held liable for injuries or deaths. Garris recommends learning about codes, regulations, and laws that need to be followed in developing a plan. These codes are from such sources as OSHA, NFPA, EPA, and ADA, as well as from city and state authorities. Garris writes that 44% of all businesses that suffer a disaster never reopen.

Continued

BUSINESS CONTINUITY—Cont'd

The **NFPA 1600 Standard on Disaster/Emergency Management and Business Continuity Programs** has been acknowledged by the U.S. Congress, American National Standards Institute (ANSI), and the 9/11 Commission. It has been endorsed by FEMA, DRII, NEMA, and IAEM. *This standard has been referred to as the "national preparedness standard" for all organizations, including government and business.* FEMA's Local Capability Assessment for Readiness (LCAR) Program, used as a benchmark for state and local governments, is based on NFPA 1600, as well as NEMA's Emergency Management Accreditation Program. NFPA 1600 serves as a benchmark of basic criteria for a comprehensive program and contains elements from *emergency management and business continuity.* There has been a convergence of these fields and a convergence of public and private sector efforts. Disasters (e.g., the 9/11 attacks) are showing the vital interdependencies of the public and private sectors.

The NFPA 1600 includes standards on program management, risk assessment, mitigation, training, and logistics, among other standards. It also contains definitions of terms and lists of resources and organizations.

The NFPA 1600 is not without its detractors (Davis, 2005). The Business Continuity Institute, located in the United Kingdom, claims that there is no business continuity document, and in NFPA 1600, business continuity is buried within emergency management. In addition, there are DRII and ANSI groups looking to the ISO for enhanced business continuity standards.

The *Business Continuity Guideline* (ASIS, International, 2004) offers interrelated processes and activities that help in creating, testing, and maintaining an organization-wide plan for emergencies. Here is a sample of questions from the appendix of the guideline.

- Has your organization planned for survival?
- Is the business continuity plan up to date?
- Has the internal audit, security, and insurance units reviewed the plan?
- Has a planning team been appointed?
- Has a risk assessment been conducted?
- Are people protected?
- Have critical business processes been identified and ranked?
- Is technology (i.e., data, systems) protected?
- Have resources required for recovery been identified?
- Have personnel been trained and exercises conducted?
- Has a crisis management center been identified?
- Have alternative worksites been identified?

Another source for business continuity planning, especially for small- and medium-sized businesses, is the DHS Web site www.ready.gov. It offers guidelines, sample emergency plans, tips for mail safety, and security suggestions and uses an all-hazards approach.

Croy (2005) writes that nearly all entities will be faced with unexpected emergencies from time to time and the focus is changing from avoidance of threat to "landing on your feet" in spite of it. Among the trends Croy sees is a convergence of risk management strategies in business—business continuity, disaster recovery, information security, and physical security. Executives are becoming more directly involved in this convergence because of government regulations that hold them personally and legally liable for financial controls, access to critical information, customer privacy, and physical security.

From the information technology (IT) perspective, Persson (2005) sees the need for increased effort to provide quantitative, accurate, and empirical reporting on how disaster recovery and business continuity are working. He refers to **metrics** and defines it as "relating to or pertaining to measurement." Persson offers these benefits of metrics.

BUSINESS CONTINUITY — Cont'd

- They present activities in objective terms.
- Metrics help focus on issues. For example, if the recovery time objective is 6 hours on paper, but testing shows it is 24 hours, this issue needs to be addressed.
- It can be included in personnel objectives (i.e., responsibilities) and measured.

Here is a sample of metrics applicable to continuity planning from Persson's IT perspective:

- Disaster recovery planning as a percentage of total IT budget. This may be between 2 and 8%.
- Percentage of mission critical applications covered. The goal should be to recover 100%.
- Anticipated recovery time.
- Total number of outages per year by category (e.g., power, network, virus).

Drawing on Persson's IT work, metrics can be applied more broadly. Examples include the business continuity budget as a percentage of assets or revenue; the number of full-time employees (may be less than 1.0) who work on business continuity per $10 million dollars of assets or revenue; and metrics can be compared within and among industries.

Rutkowski *et al.* (2005) researched perceptions of IT threats among IT and business managers. They found surprisingly different views on IT threats and their effects on business. The business managers had some knowledge of the cost of an IT service failure, but lacked an understanding of IT problems. The IT managers had grossly underestimated the impact on customers and business processes from an IT service failure. The lesson from this research is the importance of bringing multiple perspectives together for enhanced business continuity planning.

COMMUNICATIONS

The NIMS (U.S. Department of Homeland Security, 2004c: 49) emphasizes the importance of communications, information management, and information and intelligence sharing. Also important are a common operating picture and systems interoperability (see Chapter 8) to disseminate warnings, communicate operational decisions, prepare for requests, and maintain overall awareness across jurisdictions.

Under the NIMS, jurisdictional systems must be able to work together and not interfere with one another. Interoperability and compatibility can be achieved through communications and data standards, digital data formats, equipment standards, and design standards.

Another concern pertains to those who access the NIMS information system and contribute to it. They must be properly authenticated and certified for security purposes.

Haddow and Bullock (2003: 141–163) offer communications tips for emergency managers:

- Proactively communicate within the organization and externally.
- Officials should partner with the media and provide accurate and timely information.
- Officials should tell their story before it is done for them.
- Exercise care when communicating risk to citizens.
- Research shows that hazard awareness campaigns are most effective when they use a mix of techniques. Radio and television work best for initiating or maintaining awareness, whereas printed matter works best for detailed information.
- Use the Internet.

Additional, practical points when cooperating with the media include the following.

- Ensure that all employees and partners know that information released to the media must flow through a designated spokesperson, who may be called a public affairs officer.
- Employees and partners should realize that media representatives might be aggressive in seeking information. Like investigators, they want answers to basic questions: Who? What? Where? When? How? Why?
- When speaking with the media, avoid returning hostility, saying "no comment" or "off the record," guessing at answers, or offering personal opinions.
- If you do not know an answer, say so. Offer to provide additional information at a later time when facts are available.

MILITARY SUPPORT

Although the military is a "tool of last resort" in a disaster, it can provide significant resources to civilian authorities on a moment's notice. Federal troops can provide communications, transportation, food, water, shelter, and other assets under what is referred to as **logistics**. Specifically, U.S. Northern Command (NORTH-COM), in the Department of Defense, is charged with protecting the United States from foreign attacks and is responsible for supplying military resources to emergency responders. The DOD emphasizes that it understands its role in assisting civilian authorities—serve to support, not take the lead.

A state's governor is responsible for disaster response, with the option of requesting assistance from FEMA. Then, if necessary, FEMA can contact the DOD for assistance. Once the request arrives, DOD officials must determine whether the request is legal under the Posse Comitatus Act (PCA), a Civil War-era act that generally prohibits the military from engaging in civilian law enforcement. This act, under Section 1385 of Title 18, United States Code (USC), states:

> Whoever, except in cases and under circumstances expressly authorized by the Constitution or Act of Congress, willfully uses any part of the Army or Air Force as a posse comitatus or otherwise to execute the laws shall be fined under this title or imprisoned not more than two years, or both.

The PCA does not apply to the U.S. Coast Guard in peacetime or to the National Guard in Title 32 or State Active Duty status. The substantive prohibitions of the PCA were extended to all the services with the enactment of Title 10 USC, Section 375. As required by Title 10 USC, Section 375, the secretary of defense issued DOD Directive 5525.5, which precludes members of the Army, Navy, Air Force, or Marine Corps from direct participation in a search, seizure, arrest, or other similar activity unless participation in such activity by such member is otherwise authorized by law.

Prohibiting direct military involvement in civilian law enforcement is in keeping with long-standing U.S. law and policy limiting the military's role in domestic affairs. However, this law has been labeled as archaic because it limits the military from responding to disasters. Consequently, a modification of the law is an option to enable greater flexibility in the use of DOD resources to respond quickly to disasters (Burns, 2005).

Congress enacted a number of exceptions to the PCA that allow the military, in certain situations, to assist civilian law enforcement agencies in enforcing the laws of the United States. The most common example is counterdrug assistance (Title 10 USC, Sections 371–381). Other examples include the following.

- **The Insurrection Act** (Title 10 USC, Sections 331–335). This Civil War-era act allows the president to use U.S. military personnel at the request of a state legislature or governor to suppress insurrections. It also allows the president to use federal troops to enforce federal laws when rebellion against the authority of the United States makes it impracticable to enforce the laws of the United States. An example of when this law was invoked was in 1992 when California Governor Pete Wilson requested federal troops to quell race riots in Los Angeles. President George H.W. Bush dispatched 4000 active-duty troops.

- Assistance in the case of crimes involving nuclear materials (Title 18 USC, Section 831). This statute permits DOD personnel to assist the justice department in enforcing prohibitions regarding nuclear materials when the attorney general and the secretary of defense jointly determine that an "emergency situation" exists that poses a serious threat to U.S. interests and is beyond the capability of civilian law enforcement agencies.
- Emergency situations involving chemical or biological weapons of mass destruction (Title 10 USC, Section 382). When the attorney general and the secretary of defense jointly determine that an "emergency situation" exists that poses a serious threat to U.S. interests and is beyond the capability of civilian law enforcement agencies. DOD personnel may assist the justice department in enforcing prohibitions regarding biological or chemical weapons of mass destruction.

An example of the DOD assisting in past disasters includes Hurricane Katrina, in August of 2005, when New Orleans was flooded and city residents were forced to evacuate. Because Gulf-state and FEMA resources were overwhelmed, the DOD provided massive aid to assist victims, conduct search-and-rescue missions, maintain order, and deal with the flooding. President George Bush sent Army and Marine helicopters, Navy ships, and troops of the 82nd Airborne Division from Fort Bragg, North Carolina.

In August of 2004, Hurricane Charley cut a path of destruction across Florida. The DOD assisted victims by sending C-17 and C-130 cargo aircraft to airlift over 800,000 pounds of supplies to the disaster site. During October 2003, when southern California faced 11 wildfires, authorities realized that firefighters were overwhelmed. NORTH-COM responded by dispatching eight C-130 aircraft with airborne firefighting systems and six CH-53 helicopters with fire-suppression buckets (Wentworth, 2005: 28–33).

Reality Check: Hurricane Katrina

Despite the best intentions and efforts of the specialists who formulated the "all-hazards" national response plan, the national incident management system, and the national preparedness goal, Hurricane Katrina, in 2005, showed the difficulty of planning for disasters. The hurricane caused about 1300 deaths, the flooding of New Orleans, and enormous destruction along Gulf-coast states. The media, reporting from New Orleans, offered vivid coverage of looters, snipers, fires, bloated corpses, victims sitting on rooftops or swimming through toxic water, and the awful conditions at the Superdome where people sought shelter and help from the government. Today, many victims of Hurricane Katrina are living in cities across the United States and are unable or unwilling to return to their communities while rebuilding goes on.

One major lesson from the Hurricane Katrina disaster was the collapse of intergovernmental relations. The NRP calls for an immediate activation of a joint operations center to bring together all levels of government. Why did this NRP requirement occur so slowly? Why did each level of government appear inept with their authority? Why were the resources inadequate? Did the federal government place too much emphasis on the threat of terrorism at the expense of emergency management? Local, state, and federal officials blamed each other for the response failures, and the issues were politicized. Interestingly, officials received warning of the approaching hurricane. A WMD attack is unlikely to be preceded by a warning. If a warning preceded Hurricane Katrina and government reacted so inadequately, what type of government reaction can citizens expect from a surprise WMD attack?

Another major lesson was the chaos that can result from a serious disaster, whether from a WMD attack, pandemic, or other cause. Leaders should learn from the Katrina disaster and enhance planning at all levels of government.

Continued

Reality Check: Hurricane Katrina—Cont'd

In 2006, following congressional hearings that exposed the shortcomings of government response to Hurricane Katrina, a revised NRP was formulated to react more quickly with improved resources. U.S. Government Accountability Office (2006a) staff visited the affected areas, interviewed officials, and analyzed a variety of information. It found widespread dissatisfaction with the preparedness and response, and many of the lessons that emerged from Hurricane Katrina were similar to those the USGAO identified more than a decade ago with Hurricane Andrew. For example, the president should designate a senior official in the White House to oversee federal preparedness and response to major disasters. Again, in 2006, the USGAO recommended that, prior to disasters, the leadership roles, responsibilities, and lines of authority for all levels of government must be clearly defined prior to disasters. The USGAO also emphasized the need for strong advance planning among responding organizations, as well as robust training and exercises to test plans in advance of disasters. Changes are inevitable for all future plans because disasters are often unpredictable and public and private sector plans typically fall short of need during major disasters.

Following Hurricanes Katrina and Rita, as of mid-December 2005, FEMA had distributed nearly $5.4 billion in assistance to more than 1.4 million registrants under the Individuals and Households Program to meet necessary expenses and serious needs, such as temporary housing and property repair. Because of the devastation, FEMA also activated expedited assistance to provide fast track money to victims. USGAO investigators found rampant fraud with expedited assistance. FEMA made millions of dollars in payments to thousands of registrants who used social security numbers that were never issued or belonged to deceased or other individuals, and several hundred registrants used bogus damaged property addresses. FEMA made duplicate expedited assistance payments of $2000 to about 5000 of the 11,000 debit card recipients—once through the distribution of debit cards and again through a check or electronic funds transfer. Although most of the payments were applied to necessities, some funds were used for adult entertainment, bail bond services, to pay traffic tickets, and to purchase weapons. The USGAO recommended improvements by FEMA to automate the validation of identities and damaged properties (U.S. Government Accountability Office, 2006a).

DISCUSSION QUESTIONS

1. Refer to the story of the train collision and chlorine release at the beginning of the chapter. Compare and contrast the reporting by the Department of Homeland Security (beginning of the story) with the reporting by the Associated Press (toward the end of the story). What are your findings and views?
2. In what ways are risk management and emergency management linked together?
3. Of the risk management tools, which one do you view as most useful to business and government? Support your answer.
4. Risk management developed in the private sector. Does it have a useful role in government? Explain your answer.
5. If you had to choose between risk management and emergency management professions, which one would you choose and why?
6. Of the emergency management disciplines, which one do you view as most useful to business and government? Support your answer.
7. What are your views of the national response plan, the national incident management system, and the national preparedness goal?
8. What are your overall views of the way in which federal, state, and local governments handled Hurricane Katrina and its consequences? Do you think our nation is prepared to deal with a WMD attack by terrorists? Explain your answers.
9. How do you think risk management and emergency management will evolve in the future in business and in government?

APPLICATIONS

7A   YOU BE THE CORPORATE DIRECTOR OF RISK MANAGEMENT

You are a corporate risk management executive responsible for insurance, business continuity, and the corporate safety and security departments. You are challenged by the following list of tasks upon returning to your office. Prioritize these tasks and explain why you placed them in your particular order of importance.

Item A: E-mail message. At your request, an insurance company representative replies that she can meet with you at your convenience to explain why the corporate liability insurance premium will rise by 10% next year.

Item B: Telephone voice message. An accident on the premises between a truck and a forklift has resulted in two injured employees. The director of human resources wants to meet with you immediately.

Item C: E-mail message. As treasurer of a regional risk management association, you are assigned to arrange the next meeting, including location, meal, and speaker.

Item D: Your "to do list" states that you need to reevaluate the risks facing the corporation and implement an improved risk management plan that maximizes risk management tools and is more financially sound.

Item E: Telephone call. A security officer on the premises calls and states he cannot locate a security supervisor; there is a fire in the warehouse; he can extinguish it; and you do not have to call the fire department.

Item F: Telephone voice message. Your boss wants to meet with you immediately because insurance covered only 50% of losses from an accident at another corporate plant.

Item G: Telephone voice message. An attorney representing a plaintiff/employee in a sexual harassment suit against the corporation wants to speak with you.

Item H: Telephone voice message. The president of the corporation wants to know what you are doing about the recurring bomb threats that are forcing the main plant to evacuate, production to slow, and monetary losses to multiply.

Item I: E-mail message. The information technology director needs to meet with you as soon as possible. The corporate IT business continuity plan was rejected by one of the insurers of the corporation.

7B   YOU BE THE CHIEF SECURITY OFFICER

You are the chief security officer for a major manufacturing company based in the United States. You are responsible for protecting people and assets, including business continuity. You report to the director of risk management.

Your office is at a large plant located in a rural area, east of a large city. You are at this location and you have just been notified that a HAZMAT incident recently occurred at a school about 5 miles away, toward the city, and there are many fatalities. There is a strong possibility that terrorists released a chemical agent using bogus emergency rescue trucks. A toxic cloud is hanging over the school and the chemical has yet to be identified. An evacuation order was given to all those living within 3 miles of the school. Beyond that point the order was given to remain indoors and shelter-in-place. Depending on wind direction, people at your location may be in danger.

You contact both the state emergency management agency and the state police to verify the information you received. You learn that a major road running by the school is open to those evacuating, but closed to westbound traffic. Most employees, in their commute home to the nearby city, use this road and head toward the school. You also learn that the terrorists left the school and are heading east. The 250 employees at the plant are due to end their shift in 10 minutes and head home. What actions do you take to protect people and assets?

7C   YOU BE THE EMERGENCY MANAGEMENT DIRECTOR

You are the emergency management director for a county government and are challenged by the following list of tasks upon returning to your office. Prioritize these tasks and explain why you placed them in your particular order of importance.

Item A: Your "to do list" states that you need to coordinate another meeting with the public and private sectors to prepare for emergencies and disasters.

Item B: Telephone voice message. Your boss wants to know why there is no record of your NIMS training, a requirement the county grant writer said is vital for federal government funding.

Item C: Your "to do list" states that you need to update communication plans in the event of an emergency. You do not have an updated list of contacts to be used for public information dissemination.

Item D: Your "to do list" states that an updated inventory is needed of emergency food and water, medical supplies, protective suits, and equipment.

Item E: E-mail message. Your boss wants to meet with you as soon as possible about your taking on the additional responsibilities of risk management for the county.

Item F: E-mail message. An emergency management director in a nearby county wants to know when you can meet with local and regional first responders to work on emergency communication problems.

Item G: Telephone voice message. Your boss wants to know why you are 2 months overdue on updating, testing, and conducting exercises for the emergency operations plan within your jurisdiction.

Item H: Telephone call. You receive a telephone call about a tanker truck containing hazardous materials that overturned about 2 miles west of the county line outside of your jurisdiction.

Item I: E-mail message. Your plans and ideas for a new county emergency operations center are due today.

Item J: Your "to do list" states that you need to update your list of disaster assistance centers and shelters for emergencies.

7D   YOU BE THE DEPUTY EMERGENCY MANAGEMENT DIRECTOR

As the deputy emergency management director for a city along the coast, you are part of a team revising the city's emergency management plans. Your present assignments are to (1) revise the plans to ensure evacuation of the city in case a major hurricane or other disaster strikes the area and (2) if holdouts remain following the event, and if infrastructure is destroyed and safety and health concerns occur, ensure that the holdouts are removed from the city. Prepare a list of at least 10 questions to serve as a foundation for your plans. What resources and agencies would you rely on to enhance your plans?

7E   YOU BE THE INCIDENT COMMANDER

Two sensors on a main highway leading to a professional football stadium picked up radiation. The sensors were activated at 7:00 PM and the stadium is filling with fans for a major, nationally televised game due to begin at 8:00 PM. The time is now 7:30 PM. The activated sensors are 10 miles from the stadium and traffic is moving very slowly.

Although you are the local incident commander, state and federal agencies have been notified of the emergency; however, you are uncertain when they will arrive. For example, federal emergency plans place the elite U.S. commando unit, Delta Force, in charge of seizing nuclear materials, killing offenders, if necessary, and transferring the materials to government scientists to render the materials or device safe.

As incident commander, answer the following questions with justification for each.

1. Do you wait for Delta Force, the FBI, or other federal or state agencies before taking action?
2. Do you try to verify the findings of the sensors before taking action?
3. Do you dispatch police, fire, and EMS to the area?
4. Do you establish roadblocks and search all vehicles with proper equipment to detect radiation?
5. Do you request, from your superior, an order for the game to be cancelled and the fans sent home?
6. Do you request, from your superior, an order for the population in the area to be evacuated?
7. What other requests from your superior or orders do you have in mind?
8. Are you comfortable with all of your decisions and the possibility that terrorists may have planned for a quick detonation of the device upon being discovered?

WEB SITES

Business Continuity Institute: www.thebci.org
Centers for Disease Control: www.bt.cdc.gov
DRI International: www.drii.org
Emergency Management Accreditation Program: www.emaponline.org/index.cfm
Federal Emergency Management Agency: www.fema.org
International Association of Emergency Managers: www.iaem.com

National Alliance for Insurance Education & Research: www.TheNationalAlliance.com
National Emergency Management Association: www.nemaweb.org
Office for Domestic Preparedness: www.ojp.usdoj.gov
Public Risk Management Association: www.primacentral.org
Risk and Insurance Management Society: www.rims.org
Risk World: www.riskworld.com
Society for Risk Analysis: www.sr.org
State Risk and Insurance Management Association: www.strima.org
The International Emergency Management Society: www.tiems.org
U.S. Department of Homeland Security: www.dhs.gov
U.S. Department of Homeland Security: www.ready.gov (site for business continuity planning)
U.S. Northern Command: http://www.northcom.mil

NOTES

ASIS International (2003). *General Security Risk Assessment Guideline*. www.asisonline.org, retrieved January 3, 2005.

ASIS International (2004). *Business Continuity Guideline*. www.asisonline.org, retrieved January 3, 2005.

Angle, J. (2005). *Occupational Safety and Health in the Emergency Services*, 2nd ed. Clifton Park, NY: Delmar Pub.

Associated Press (February 6, 2006). "Professor uses math, science to predict terrorist targets."

BOMA Files (2006). "Terrorism Insurance Program Extended in Final Days of Session." *Buildings*, 100 (February).

Borodzicz, E. (2005). *Risk, Crisis and Security Management*. West Sussex, England: Wiley.

Burns, R. (2005). Associated Press. "Bush's vision might lead to historic changes for military during disasters" (September 18).

Crowley, P. (2004). "Next Steps for Terrorism Insurance." *Homeland Security*, 1 (September).

Croy, M. (2005). "Landing on Your Feet: Being Prepared in the 21st Century." *Disaster Recovery Journal*, 18 (Winter). www.drj.com, retrieved January 28, 2005.

Davis, S. (2005). "NFPA 1600." www.davislogic.com, retrieved March 17, 2005.

Decker, R. (2001). *Homeland Security: A Risk Management Approach Can Guide Preparedness Efforts* (October 31). www.gao.gov, retrieved February 15, 2005.

Desouza, K. (2004). "Simulating Disaster Scenarios: A Missing Link in Crisis Management." *Disaster Recovery Journal*, 17 (Summer). www.drj.com, retrieved January 28, 2005.

FEMA (2004). "All-Hazards Preparedness." www.fema.gov/preparedness/hazards_prepare.shtm, retrieved March 1, 2005.

Garris, L. (2005). "Make-or-Break Steps for Disaster Preparation." *Buildings*, 99 (February).

Gunaratna, R., *et al.* (2003). *Managing Terrorism Risk*. Newark, CA: Risk Management Solutions, Inc.

Haddow, G., and Bullock, J. (2003). *Introduction to Emergency Management*. Boston, MA: Butterworth-Heinemann.

Holland, J. (2005). "Chemical spill in Graniteville claims ninth victim." Associated Press release, January 9.

Holland, J. (2005). "Residents recall train wreck." Associated Press release, January 8.

Jordan, J. (2005). "Cleanup crews work on tanker." Associated Press release, January 8.

Leimberg, S., *et al.* (2002). *The Tools and Techniques of Risk Management and Insurance*. Cincinnati, OH: The National Underwriter Co.

McEntire, D. (2004). "The Status of Emergency Management Theory: Issues, Barriers, and Recommendations for Improved Scholarship." Paper presented at the FEMA Higher Education Conference, Emmitsburg, MD, June 8. www.training.fema.gov/EMIWeb/edu/highpapers.asp, retrieved February 14, 2006.

Minnesota (2005). Risk Management Division. www.mainserver.state.mn.us/risk, retrieved February 18, 2005.

Oppenheimer, A. (2004). "Special Report—Making a mockery of terrorism." *Jane's Terrorism & Security Monitor* (April 15). www.janes.com

Pelfrey, W. (2005). "The Cycle of Preparedness: Establishing a Framework to Prepare for Terrorist Threats." *Journal of Homeland Security and Emergency Management*, 2.

Persson, J. (2005). "The Time Has Come for DRP Metrics." *Disaster Recovery Journal*, 18 (Winter). www.drj.com, retrieved January 28, 2005.

Pilla, D. (2004). "Terrorism Still Biggest Property/Casualty Threat, Hartford Chief Warns." Best Wire Services (November 18). www.bestweek.com, retrieved January 6, 2005.

Public Risk Management Association (2003). *Core Competency Statement: A Framework for Public Risk Management*. www.primacentral.org, retrieved February 18, 2005.

Purpura, P. (2002). *Security and Loss Prevention*, 4th ed. Boston, MA: Butterworth-Heinemann.

Quinley, K., and Schmidt, D. (2002). *Business at Risk: How to Assess, Mitigate, and Respond to Terrorist Threats*. Cincinnati, OH: The National Underwriter Co.

Rockett, J. (2001). "The U.S. View of Hazards and Sustainable Development: A Few Thoughts from Europe." *Risk Management: An International Journal*, 3.

Rutkowski, A., *et al.* (2005). "When Stakeholders Perceive Threats and Risks Differently: The Use of Group Support Systems to Develop a Common Understanding and a Shared Response." *Journal of Homeland Security and Emergency Management*, 2.

Starner, T. (2003). "Modeling for Terrorism." *Risk & Insurance* (April 1).

Stoneman, B. (2003). "An Aversion to Dispersion." *Risk & Insurance* (September 15).

U.S. Department of Homeland Security (2004a). *National Response Plan*. www.dhs.gov, retrieved January 12, 2005.

U.S. Department of Homeland Security (2004b). *Securing Our Homeland: U.S. Department of Homeland Security Strategic Plan*. www.dhs.gov, retrieved October 1, 2004.

U.S. Department of Homeland Security (2004c). *National Incident Management System*. www.dhs.gov, retrieved February 10, 2005.

U.S. Department of Justice (2000). *Critical Incident Protocol: A Public and Private Partnership*. www.ojp.usdoj.gov, retrieved November 18, 2003.

U.S. Government Accountability Office (2005). *Agency Plans, Implementation, and Challenges Regarding the National Strategy for Homeland Security* (January). www.gao.gov/cgi-bin/getrpt?GAO-05-33, retrieved February 15, 2005.

U.S. Government Accountability Office (2006a). "Statement by Comptroller General David M. Walker on GAO's Preliminary Observations Regarding Preparedness and Response to Hurricanes Katrina and Rita" (February 1). www.gao.gov/new.items/d06365r.pdf, retrieved February 3, 2006.

U.S. Government Accountability Office (2006b). "Expedited Assistance for Victims of Hurricanes Katrina and Rita, FEMA's Control Weaknesses Exposed the Government to Significant Fraud and Abuse" (February 13). www.gao.gov/new.items/d06403t.pdf, retrieved February 14, 2006.

Walter, A., *et al.* (2004). *Firefighter's Handbook*, 2nd ed. Clifton Park, NY: Delmar Pub.

Wentworth, S. (2005). "Help on the home front." *Homeland Protection Professional*, 4 (January/February).

Yates, R. (2004). "Does risk assessment work for terrorism?" *Homeland Protection Professional*, 3 (August).

CHAPTER 8

LIFE SAFETY AND PUBLIC SAFETY

OBJECTIVES

The study of this chapter will enable you to:

1. Define and explain both life safety and public safety.
2. Explain how life safety and public safety are linked.
3. Differentiate regulations and standards and provide examples of each.
4. Discuss building designs and building codes to improve life safety.
5. Describe the National Fire Protection Association 101 Life Safety Code.
6. List at least 10 strategies to promote life safety and fire protection in buildings.
7. Discuss the role of public police in public safety.
8. Discuss the role of the fire service in public safety.
9. Discuss the role of the emergency medical service in public safety.
10. Discuss the medical system response during a WMD attack or pandemic.
11. Discuss the role of second responders when an emergency occurs.
12. Explain government response to the four major types of WMD.

KEY TERMS

life safety
true first responders
public safety
interoperability
regulations
consensus standards
codes
recommended practices
Occupational Safety and Health
   Administration
code of federal regulations
standard of care
code war
delayed egress lock

NFPA 101 Life Safety Code
authority having jurisdiction
standpipes
International Facility Management Association
Building Owners & Managers Association
   International
proactive policing
reactive policing
community policing
SARA model
Homeland Security Standards Database
public safety assistance time line
triage
personal protective equipment

KEY TERMS

first receivers
Public Health Security and Bioterrorism
    Preparedness and Response Act of 2002
Centers for Disease Control and
    Prevention

strategic national stockpile
pandemic
zoonotic disease
quarantine enforcement
second responders

9/11 TRANSCRIPTS RELEASED

The following is from a *USA TODAY* (Cauchon *et al.*, 2003) news story on the radio transmissions and telephone calls during the 9/11 attacks. "A man on the 92nd floor called the police with what was—though he did not know it—the question of his life. 'We need to know if we need to get out of here, because we know there's an explosion,' said the caller, who was in the south tower of the World Trade Center. A jet had just crashed into the Trade Center's north tower. 'Should we stay or should we not?' The officer on the line asked whether there was smoke on the floor. Told no, he replied: 'I would wait 'til further notice.' 'All right,' the caller said. 'Don't evacuate.' He then hung up. Almost all the roughly 600 people in the top floors of the south tower died after a second hijacked airliner crashed into the 80th floor shortly after 9 AM. The failure to evacuate the building was one of the day's great tragedies. The exchange between the office worker and the policeman was one of many revealed when the Port Authority of New York and New Jersey, which owned and patrolled the office complex, released transcripts of 260 hours of radio transmissions and telephone calls on 9/11."

Morgan Stanley

The following is from the U.S. Department of Homeland Security, READYBusiness (n.d.). "In 1993, when terrorists attacked the World Trade Center for the first time, financial services company Morgan Stanley learned a life-saving lesson. It took the company 4 hours that day to evacuate its employees, some of whom had to walk down 60 or more flights of stairs to safety. While none of Morgan Stanley's employees were killed in the attack, the company's management decided its disaster plan just wasn't good enough. Morgan Stanley took a close look at its operation, analyzed the potential disaster risk and developed a multi-faceted disaster plan. Perhaps just as importantly, it practiced the plan frequently to provide for employee safety in the event of another disaster. On September 11, 2001, the planning and practice paid off. Immediately after the first hijacked plane struck One World Trade Center, Morgan Stanley security executives ordered the company's 3800 employees to evacuate from World Trade Center buildings Two and Five. This time, it took them just 45 minutes to get out to safety! The crisis management did not stop at that point, however. Morgan Stanley offered grief counseling to workers and increased its security presence. It also used effective communications strategies to provide timely, appropriate information to management and employees, investors and clients, and regulators and the media. Morgan Stanley still lost 13 people on September 11th, but many more could have died if the company had not had a solid disaster plan that was practiced over and over again. In making a commitment to prepare its most valuable asset, its people, Morgan Stanley ensured the firm's future."

LIFE SAFETY AND PUBLIC SAFETY

The previous chapter showed that risk management grew out of the insurance industry, spread through the business community, is being applied by government, and is promoted by the U.S. Government Accountability Office and the U.S. Department of Homeland Security. We also learned that risk management is at the foundation of emergency management because we need to learn about risks (i.e., threat, vulnerability, and criticality) to improve the focus of emergency management resources.

Life safety pertains to building construction design that increases safety, what organizations and employees can do in preparation for emergencies, and what they can do once an emergency occurs. *Citizens cannot depend on government during the initial stages of an emergency.* Steps must be taken by citizens—in their home, workplace, and in public—to protect themselves (see Chapter 6) for a duration that may last from a few minutes, to possibly days, until government first responders and assistance arrive. In other words, the **true first responders** are the victims of an unfortunate event.

Public safety involves primarily government employees who plan, train, and equip themselves for emergencies. They respond as quickly as possible to the scene of an emergency to save lives, care for the injured, protect people and property, and restore order.

During an emergency at a corporation or institution, when proprietary life safety specialists (e.g., security officers, floor wardens, and employees trained in firefighting and first aid) perform their duties, their work will *merge* with the duties of arriving first responders [e.g., police, firefighters, emergency medical service (EMS)]. Joint planning and training, prior to an emergency, can improve coordination, life safety, and public safety. Azoulay (2006: 20) emphasizes the importance of the private sector establishing relationships with first responders. His suggestions include designated rest stations for police and fire personnel at shopping malls and other private sector locations, inviting first responders to lunch on a monthly basis, and providing first responders with access to Web-based emergency response software to view floor plans, fire hydrants, sprinkler systems, and so forth.

Interestingly, the public safety community embraces a wide variety of strategies when responding to an emergency. Some responders rush into a scene no matter what the danger. Others exercise extreme caution. A related problem is that any one of the three major public safety responder groups (i.e., police, fire, EMS) can arrive first with their different strategies and different training. It is uncommon for the three groups to train together. Elliott (2004: 32) favors bringing all three together for training to teach one paradigm for emergency response. The private sector (i.e., life safety specialists and security) should be added to this approach.

Friction over strategies may develop among public safety first responders during planning or at the scene of an emergency. An illustration of disagreement occurred in May of 2005 when the New York City fire chief openly criticized the mayor in the city council chamber by stating that it "makes no sense" and risks danger to give the police initial control at hazardous materials emergencies. The fire chief said the mayor received "bad advice" and the fire chief suggested that the protocol was a power grab by the New York City Police Department (NYPD). The fire chief noted: "Instead of seeking to control each other, agencies having major roles at terrorist events must learn how to work together to command these incidents." The police commissioner supported the protocol so police can rule out criminal or terrorist involvement in the incident. The commissioner, annoyed at the council for their questioning of him, said to reporters, "it's fun to ask these questions on television—it gives everybody face time." The controversy exposed again the frustrations and rivalries among first responders and the confusion that occurs at emergency sites if agencies do not cooperate.

Cohen (2003: 72) writes that during the 9/11 attacks at the World Trade Center (WTC), an unforeseen enemy of first responders was their own communications systems. During the months following the attacks, a serious flaw was found in the police and fire radio systems: they were incompatible. When the first WTC tower collapsed, police were notified to evacuate the second tower, but firefighters (on a different system) did not hear the warning and hundreds of first responders died. This serious problem can be solved by what has been called **interoperability**— the ability of multiple agencies to communicate using technology. The technology for interoperability is available today; however, two challenges are funding and selecting the technology. The issue of interoperability has been discussed in many forums, including the National Strategy for Homeland Security (Office of Homeland Security, 2002: 43), which established the following goal: "Enable seamless communication among all responders."

Not only must first responders communicate with each other, but also interoperability should occur with neighboring responders, federal agencies, and local companies. The United States Conference of Mayors conducted a survey on percent interoperable and what can be done to improve the situation. They received responses from 190 small and large cities in 41 states. The results: 77% of the cities have interoperable communications across their police and fire departments and 74% with neighboring cities; 88% reported that they are not interoperable with homeland security agencies, such as FEMA, and 83% are not interoperable with the FBI; 97% of cities with a major chemical plant reported no interoperability between the plant and first responders; the same held true for cities with major rail (84%) and seaport (92%) facilities. Money was a major obstacle. Seventy-five percent of cities were hindered by the use of different radio frequencies (Tech Talk, 2004).

CRITICAL THINKING:

In addition to joint planning and training, what can be done to improve the coordination of life safety and public safety?

LIFE SAFETY

REGULATIONS AND STANDARDS

A knowledge and an understanding of regulations and standards are essential for life safety programs. **Regulations** are rules or laws enacted at the federal, state, or local levels with the requirement to comply. **Consensus standards** are accepted industry practices developed through a consensus process (i.e., open to review and modifications by experts who agree on how a specific task should be performed prior to the final standard). Consensus standards do not have the force of law unless a jurisdiction adopts them as law.

Angle (2005: 21) offers these definitions: "**Codes** are standards that cover broad subject areas, which can be adopted into law independently of other codes, or standards." "**Recommended practices** are standards, which are similar in content to standards and codes, but are nonmandatory in compliance." The National Fire Protection Association (NFPA) publishes standards, recommended practices, and codes.

It is important to note that the terms "regulations," "standards," "codes," and "recommended practices" are not uniformly applied in the literature or by the public and private sectors. The **Occupational Safety and Health Administration** (OSHA), for example, uses the term "standards" in the content of "regulations."

REGULATIONS

Federal regulations are contained in the **code of federal regulations** (CFR). A widely known example of federal regulations is found in Title 29 CFR, OSHA. OSHA is a federal agency, under the U.S. Department of Labor, established to administer the law on safety and health in the workplace resulting from the William Steiger Occupational Safety and Health Act of 1970. The act's jurisdiction is very broad and includes private and public employers and their employees in the 50 states and other U.S. possessions. Outside of workplaces covered by other federal agencies, OSHA impacts federal, state, and local government workplaces.

OSHA is a government law enforcement agency. The fourth amendment applies to OSHA inspections under the U.S. Supreme Court case, Marshall v. Barlow (1978). An OSHA inspector must obtain a search warrant for a workplace inspection, unless the employer consents. Usually, the employer consents. A violation of an OSHA regulation can result in legal action against an employer. Penalties of thousands of dollars can result.

Because OSHA regulations are constantly being updated, it is the employer's responsibility to keep up to date. Two sources of information are the OSHA Web site (www.osha.gov) and the Federal Register (http://fr.cos.com/). Access to the latter requires a fee. There are thousands of OSHA regulations that cover many issues such as personal protective equipment, prevention of electrical hazards, first aid, fire protection, and emergencies in the workplace.

An example of an OSHA regulation that promotes life safety is 1910.38 Emergency Action Plans. It includes these minimum elements.

- An emergency action plan must be in writing, kept in the workplace, and available to employees for review.
- Procedures for reporting a fire or other emergency.
- Procedures for emergency evacuation, including type of evacuation and exit route assignments.
- Procedures to account for all employees after evacuation.
- Procedures to be followed by employees performing rescue or medical duties.
- An employer must have and maintain an employee alarm system that uses a distinctive signal for each purpose.
- An employer must designate and train employees to assist in a safe and orderly evacuation of other employees.
- An employer must review the emergency action plan with each employee.

Another OSHA regulation oriented toward life safety is 1910.39 Fire Protection Plans. It includes these minimum elements.

- A fire protection plan must be in writing, kept in the workplace, and available to employees for review.
- A list of all major five hazards, proper handling and storage procedures for hazardous materials, potential ignition sources and their control, and the type of fire protection equipment necessary to control each major hazard.
- Procedures to control accumulations of flammable and combustible waste materials.
- Procedures for regular maintenance of safeguards installed on heat-producing equipment to prevent the accidental ignition of combustible materials.
- The name or job title of employees responsible for maintaining equipment to prevent or control sources of ignition or fires and for control of fuel source hazards.
- An employer must inform employees upon initial assignment to a job of the fire hazards to which they are exposed and review with each employee those parts of the fire protection plan necessary for self-protection.

Fried (2004a: 30), an attorney and expert witness, notes that at least 70% of OSHA fines are tied to employers failing to have a written OSHA safety plan, and plans vary depending on the type of workplace. Another frequent OSHA violation results from improper or lack of employee training. If OSHA investigates an injury, an employer should have a stronger defense with established policies and procedures concerning the hazard in question and proof that this information was communicated to employees. An employer should not only document education and training, but also provide refresher courses.

CRITICAL THINKING:

Opponents of OSHA claim that its regulations are expensive for businesses to implement. Proponents, such as labor groups, argue that OSHA reinforces a safe workplace and prevents deaths and injuries. Is it "regulatory overkill?" What do you think?

STANDARDS

Although standards may not be adopted as law by a jurisdiction, they may be used to establish a standard of care or used during litigation. Angle (2005: 22) defines **standard of care** as "the concept of what a reasonable person with similar training and equipment would do in a similar situation." In the emergency medical field, for example, a practitioner can prevent a claim of negligence if he/she performs in the same way as another reasonable person with the same training and equipment. In other words, everyone has certain expectations of performance.

An employer can face a claim of negligence by failing to adhere to policies and procedures, standards, or legal mandates (Fried, 2004b: 30). Suppose employees are injured during an emergency evacuation and sue. Experts may be hired by opposite sides of the civil case to provide expertise and testimony on whether the employer provided a safe workplace and properly planned for emergencies. Comparisons may be made of what reasonable prudent management would do. If the defense side can show that management did everything reasonable management would have done under the same circumstances, then the employer has a good chance of showing that he/she acted reasonably and should not be liable for injuries.

Fried makes interesting observations about standards and litigation. He notes that if industry experts seek to develop a standard to benefit themselves or others or to sell products or services, then the standard would not have significant weight in court. Another question sure to surface is how the standard was developed. Consensus standards often do not meet the scientific rigor of, say, how the medical profession uses multiple blind tests to determine if a drug works. Fried (2004b: 30) writes: "Thus, for any standard to pass legal muster under the Daubert challenge (requiring proof that a standard or conclusion is based on scientific or sound research), the standard needs to be tested and proven to be correct. Otherwise the standard is just a suggestion."

Although the NFPA, for example, outlines ideal actions and what an ideal manager should achieve based on industry experts, failure to meet standards does not mean law was violated or someone is negligent. A judge may declare a standard introduced in court as not applicable in that jurisdiction because no court or legal body authorized them, even though an expert witness might argue that an unofficial standard has become an industry standard of practice. Fried writes that if over 50% of employers follow a conduct —whether or not from a standard—that conduct could be considered the reasonable industry standard that should be followed.

The NFPA 1600 Standard on Disaster/Emergency Management and Business Continuity Programs was explained in the previous chapter. It was shown that this standard has received intense, widespread support from both the private sector and the government. As stated earlier, it has been referred to as the "National Preparedness Standard for all organizations, including government and business." At the same time, the NFPA has no enforcement authority; its standards are advisory. A government jurisdiction can adopt a standard as law and enforce it. This has been done by many jurisdictions with the NFPA 101 Life Safety Code.

BUILDING DESIGN AND BUILDING CODES

Changes in building design and building codes are a slow process and new codes often do not apply to existing buildings. Experts (e.g., structural engineers), industry groups (e.g., real estate), and government leaders frequently disagree over what changes, if any, should be made. The following information on trends in building design and building codes since the 9/11 attacks is from Gips (2005: 43–49), the National Institute of Standards and Technology (2005), and the International Code Council (2004).

- Guidance for local governments for building codes is found with the International Code Council (ICC) or the NFPA. The ICC's International Building Code (IBC) has been widely adopted in the United States. The NFPA writes the Life Safety Code (LSC) and the Building Construction and Safety Code (BCSC). The LSC has been adopted by far more jurisdictions than the BCSC.
- The IBC establishes minimum standards for the design and installation of building systems and it addresses issues of occupancy, safety, and technology. It plays a major role in transforming lessons from the 9/11 attacks into updated building codes and it relies on research from the U.S. Department of Commerce, National Institute of Standards and Technology (NIST). The NIST detailed reports on the collapse of the WTC towers and its reports also include the impact of natural hazards (e.g., hurricanes) on tall buildings.
- NIST research found the following factors in the collapse sequence of the WTC towers: each aircraft severed perimeter columns, damaged interior core columns, and knocked off fireproofing from steel; jet fuel initially fed the fires, followed by building contents, and air from destroyed walls and windows; and floor sagging and exposure to high temperatures caused the perimeter columns to bow inward and buckle.
- NIST recommendations that could have improved the WTC structural performance on 9/11 are fireproofing less susceptible to being dislodged; perimeter columns and floor framing with greater mass to enhance thermal and buckling performance; compartmentation to retard spread of fire; windows with improved thermal performance; fire-protected and hardened elevators; and redundant water supply for standpipes.
- One successful code change of the IBC is that buildings 420 feet and higher (about 42 floors) must have a minimum 3-hour structural fire-resistance rating, whether sprinklers are present or not. The earlier rating was for 2 hours, with sprinklers. The reasoning for the change is that fire departments are generally not capable of supplying adequate water pressure and flow to floors above 420 feet, and the building must be able to stand on its own.
- IBC proposals that were rejected: widen stairs from 44 inches to 72 inches in buildings 20 stories and higher and encasing stairwells in either concrete or masonry in buildings 25 stories and higher.
- Both the ICC and the NFPA have committees that focus on NIST research that may serve to support changes in their respective building codes. Issues drawing attention include evacuation procedures, fire resistance, collapse, redundant water supplies, and how to prevent metal-detection equipment from hindering emergency egress.
- Although the NFPA is hesitant about endorsing alternative escape systems, it does acknowledge the following that need further study: use of elevators during emergencies, platforms that move along the outside of a building, high-wire escape to nearby buildings, and parachutes.
- The new Seven World Trade Center building at "ground zero" has gone beyond building code requirements. It is protected against progressive collapse by, for example, spray-on fireproofing that is five times more adhesive than what is required by existing standards. Stairs and elevators are fully encased in reinforced concrete. (FEMA found that at the WTC, during the attacks, plasterboard that was designed to provide fire resistance to the stairways was knocked off by the impact of the jets.) In the new WTC, fire stairs are located at opposite ends of

the building. (FEMA noted that the jets were able to destroy two sets of emergency stairways because they were close together.) In the new WTC, stairs have triple redundancy for light: emergency lighting, battery power, and photoluminescent paint.

- Chicago is another city enhancing building safety following the 9/11 attacks. The emphasis is more on planning than building designs, and like other locales, it ties building height to safety requirements. For instance, buildings 540 feet or higher must file an emergency evacuation plan with the city's office of emergency communications. The plan includes evacuation procedures, posting of a floor plan, a list of occupants needing assistance, drills, marked stairwells to identify floor number, and the site of reentry locations.

- Innovations and changes in buildings for safety include sensors in HVAC systems to detect WMD, multiple HVAC systems to isolate fire and other hazards, HVAC "nanofilters" to capture harmful agents, stairway pressurization to reduce smoke, and wider stairs for evacuation and emergency response.

- ICC (2004) research of the building departments of the 15 most populated cities in the United States found that officials varied in their reporting of top concerns. The most often cited concern was inadequate resources during the building boom for permitting and plan inspection services.

- Eight of the 15 building departments in the ICC research stated that they were involved in some form of response program concerning the risk of terrorism.

- All 15 cities expressed concerns about weather and natural disasters, and emergency plans are in place, drills are conducted, and supplies (e.g., cots, water, and generators) are stockpiled.

- ICC areas of ongoing study include balanced fire protection, including active (i.e., fire sprinkler) versus passive (i.e., fire resistive construction) requirements; emergency evacuation with elevators; special evacuation needs of persons with disabilities; and carbon monoxide detectors.

- Dr. W. Gene Corley (2004), team leader of the WTC Building Performance Study, writes that NFPA data from a 10-year study of 8000 commercial fires showed that sprinklers do not operate about 16% of the time. He notes that despite this risk of failure, model codes increasingly rely on sprinklers, while reducing fire-resistant construction. Also, although many view fire barriers as costly excess, first responders see them as lifesavers and another method to prevent building collapse.

- Local governments have been slow to make changes in building or life safety codes since the 9/11 attacks. However, insurance companies can raise premiums on coverage for buildings not meeting recommended criteria. Such insurer action can lead to stricter building codes.

- Although terrorism may appear as a remote threat to building owners, an "all hazard" approach brings to light numerous risks. This broader perspective impacts building codes, the standard of care that courts might impose for building protection, and liability issues.

Reality Check: The Code War

Swope (2006: 20–23) writes about the **code war** that describes rival groups lobbying governments to accept their competing sets of standards. For many years, the business community has urged governments to standardize building codes among cities and states to reduce construction costs. On one side of the competition is the ICC, a group supported by government building and code enforcement officials, architects, and building owners and managers. The NFPA heads the other side. It is supported by fire chiefs and unions representing building specialists. Government and industry prefer one code and they are faced with a major question: "Which code to choose?"

Swope (2006: 22) notes that the code war also involves the ICC and NFPA acting as "two publishing houses engaged in a war for book sales." When a government adopts a model code or when codes change, officials, architects, engineers, construction specialists, and others must purchase up-to-date copies. Each code group earns tens of millions of dollars annually from publication sales.

Reality Check: The Code War—Cont'd

A major difference between the ICC and the NFPA is how they update their codebooks. The ICC only allows building officials to vote on changes. The ICC sees this as a way to prevent special interests (e.g., trade unions, manufactures) from influencing the codes. The NFPA permits all of its members to vote, although checks and balances are applied to prevent undue influence.

Other groups are also in competition. For instance, ASIS, International and the NFPA each have committees involved in the subject of security.

Reality Check: Security versus Safety

Each year, the workplace is subject to employees and outsiders causing both violent victimizations and billions of dollars in theft. To prevent these losses, management may decide to implement dangerous security methods that may reduce crime, but, at the same time, hinder escape in an emergency. The classic blunder that has resulted in numerous deaths is the use of a chain and lock on the inside to secure double doors together (Figure 8-1). This universal code violation can bring out the ire of a fire marshal or other government inspector.

In 1991, a fire occurred at the Imperial Chicken Processing Plant in Hamlet, North Carolina. The fire began at a ruptured hydraulic line near a 25-foot-long deep fryer vat. Because management wanted to prevent theft and vandalism, fire doors were locked from the outside. As the fire spread quickly, workers could be heard screaming, "let me out," and a subsequent investigation found shoeprint indentations on the inside of at least one door. Twenty-five people died and another 49 were injured from the fire. The 11-year-old plant had not been subjected to a state safety inspection because of a lack of inspectors in the state. Hamlet Fire Chief David Fuller said that he could not confirm nor deny that fire exits were locked or blocked. He did confirm that several bodies were found near exits and in a meat locker. A plant executive was found guilty of criminal charges and sentenced to prison (Emergency Response & Research Institute, 1991).

One option at a door for security and safety is to install an alarm on a door that is activated when the door is opened (Figure 8-2). Another option that must be carefully planned for a door to promote security and safety is the delayed egress lock. It can prevent theft and unauthorized passage, while providing time for a security response to the access point. A **delayed egress lock** is on the inside of a door and stays locked for a fixed time, say 15 seconds, after a bar on the door is pushed and an alarm is activated. Signage and Braille are required to alert people of the delay. In an emergency, these devices should be unlocked immediately through a connection to the building's fire protection system as specified in NFPA 101.

The Las Vegas MGM Grand Hotel fire in 1985 serves as another illustration of how security can hinder escape during an emergency. All the exit doors to the stairwell had a controlled exit device. When the occupants went in the stairwell, they faced smoke, but the doors were locked on the stairwell side to increase security for each floor. A person had to exit the building on the ground floor to regain access. As heavy smoke began to rise in the stairwell, and with no access back into the upper floors, several occupants were trapped and died (Moore, 1997: 69–70).

NFPA 101 LIFE SAFETY CODE

The **NFPA 101 Life Safety Code** is used in every state and adopted statewide in 38 states. It is also used by numerous federal agencies. The state fire marshal's office serves as a resource if one seeks to find out if the code has been adopted in a particular locale and which edition is being used. The code is published every 3 years.

The state fire marshal often serves as the **authority having jurisdiction** (AHJ), meaning the person or office charged with enforcing the code. In some jurisdictions, the AHJ is the fire department

Figure 8-1 ■ Code violation.

Figure 8-2 ■ How many life safety features can you spot in this photograph?

or building department. For some occupancies, there is more than one AHJ. A hospital may require approval for life safety from the state fire marshal, local building official, fire department, state health care licensing agency, Joint Commission on Accreditation of Healthcare Organizations, U.S. Department of Health and Human Services–Health Care Financing Administration, and the facility's insurance carrier.

The NFPA 101 Life Safety Code publication begins with a disclaimer of liability as paraphrased next. NFPA codes, standards, recommended practices, and guides are developed through a consensus standards development process approved by the American National Standards Institute. This process recruits volunteers with varied expertise and viewpoints to achieve consensus on fire and other safety issues. The NFPA does not independently test, evaluate or verify the accuracy of information contained in its codes and standards. It does not list, certify, test, or inspect products, designs, or installations. The NFPA disclaims liability for any personal injury or property damage resulting from the use of its documents. Its documents are not released to render professional or other services, and the NFPA has no enforcement powers.

The history of NFPA 101 began with a presentation by R. H. Newbern at the 1911 annual meeting of the NFPA. The following year, his presentation resulted in the Committee on Safety to Life publishing *Exit Drills in Factories, Schools, Department Stores and Theaters*. This committee studied notable fires and causes of loss of life and prepared standards for the construction of stairways, fire escapes, and egress routes. The publication of additional pamphlets, which were widely circulated and put into general use, provided the foundation for the NFPA 101 Life Safety Code. New material and revisions to the Code continued throughout the 20th century. National attention focused on the importance of adequate exits and fire safety following the Cocoanut Grove Night Club Fire in Boston in 1942, resulting in 492 deaths. The code was increasingly being used for regulatory purposes.

The 1991 edition contained numerous new requirements for mandatory sprinklers in a variety of facilities. The 1994 edition contained new requirements for egress, areas of refuge, and ramps to conform to the Americans with Disabilities Act Accessibility Guidelines.

In the 2003 edition, the first part consists of Chapters 1 through 11 (except Chapter 5) and is called the base chapters or fundamental chapters. Chapter 5 explains the performance-based option (i.e., building design features meeting specific life safety code performance objectives). Many of the provisions of the first part are mandatory for specific occupancies. Some provisions are mandated only when referenced by a specific occupancy, whereas other provisions are exempted for specific occupancy. The statement, "where permitted by Chapters 12 through 42," refers to provisions that can be used only where specifically permitted by an occupancy chapter (e.g., educational, health care, lodging, industrial). An example is, in Chapter 7, 7.2.1.6.1 on delayed egress locks that are allowed only when permitted by Chapters 12 through 42. If the permission is not found in an occupancy chapter, the delayed egress lock cannot be used in that type of facility. Other types of restricted permission are found for such features as double cylinder locks, security grills, and revolving doors.

Here are samples from the NFPA 101 Life Safety Code.

CHAPTER 1 ADMINISTRATION

1.1.2 Danger to Life from Fire. The *Code* addresses those construction, protection, and occupancy features necessary to minimize danger to life from fire, including smoke, fumes, or panic.

1.1.3 Egress Facilities. The *Code* establishes minimum criteria for the design of egress facilities so as to allow prompt escape of occupants from buildings or, where desirable, into safe areas within buildings.

CHAPTER 3 DEFINITIONS

3.2.4 Labeled. Equipment or materials to which has been attached a label, symbol, or other identifying mark of an organization that is acceptable to the authority having jurisdiction and concerned with product evaluation, that maintains periodic inspection of production of labeled equipment or materials, and by whose labeling the manufacturer indicates compliance with appropriate standards or performance in a specified manner.

3.2.5 Listed. Equipment, materials, or services included in a list published by an organization that is acceptable to the authority having jurisdiction and concerned with evaluation of products or services, that maintains periodic inspection of production of listed equipment or materials or periodic evaluation of services, and whose listing states that either the equipment, material, or service meets appropriate designated standards or has been tested and found suitable for a specified purpose.

CHAPTER 7 MEANS OF EGRESS

7.1.10 Means of Egress Reliability.

7.1.10.1 Means of egress shall be continuously maintained free of all obstructions or impediments to full instant use in the case of fire or other emergency.

7.2.1.5 Locks, Latches, and Alarm Devices.

7.2.1.5.1 Doors shall be arranged to be opened readily from the egress side whenever the building is occupied.

7.2.1.5.2 Locks, if provided, shall not require the use of a key, a tool, or special knowledge or effort for operation from the egress side.

7.2.1.6 Special Locking Arrangements.

7.2.1.6.1 Delayed-Egress Locks. Approved, listed, delayed egress locks shall be permitted to be installed on doors serving low and ordinary hazard contents in buildings protected throughout by an approved, supervised automatic fire detection system in accordance with Section 9.6 or an approved, supervised automatic sprinkler system in accordance with Section 9.7, and where permitted in Chapter 12 through Chapter 42, provided that the following criteria are met:

(1) The doors shall unlock upon actuation of one of the following:

    (a) An approved, supervised automatic sprinkler system in accordance with Section 9.7

    (b) Any heat detector

    (c) Not more than two smoke detectors of an approved, supervised automatic fire detection system in accordance with Section 9.6

(2) The doors shall unlock upon loss of power controlling the lock or locking mechanism.

(3) An irreversible process shall release the lock within 15 seconds, or 30 seconds where approved by the authority having jurisdiction, upon application of a force to the release device required in 7.2.1.5.9 under the following conditions:

    (a) The force shall not be required to exceed 67 N (15 lbf).

    (b) The force shall not be required to be continuously applied for more than 3 seconds.

(c) The initiation of the release process shall activate an audible signal in the vicinity of the door.

(d) Once the door lock has been released by the application of force to the releasing device, relocking shall be by manual means only.

(4) A readily visible, durable sign in letters not less than 25 mm (1 in.) high and not less than 3.2 mm (1/8 in.) in stroke width on a contrasting background that reads as follows shall be located on the door adjacent to the release device:

PUSH UNTIL ALARM SOUNDS

DOOR CAN BE OPENED IN 15 SECONDS

7.2.1.7 Panic Hardware and Fire Exit Hardware.

7.2.1.7.1 Where a door is required to be equipped with panic or fire exit hardware, such hardware shall meet the following criteria:

(1) It shall consist of a cross bar or a push pad, the actuating portion of which extends across not less than one-half of the width of the door leaf.

(2) It shall be mounted as follows:

(a) New installations shall be not less than 865 mm (34 in.), nor more than 1220 mm (48 in.), above the floor.

(b) Existing installations shall be not less than 760 mm (30 in.), nor more than 1220 mm (48 in.), above the floor.

(3) It shall be constructed so that a horizontal force not to exceed 66 N (15 lbf) actuates the cross bar or push pad and latches.

7.2.1.7.3 Required panic hardware and fire exit hardware, in other than detention and correctional occupancies as otherwise provided in Chapter 22 and Chapter 23, shall not be equipped with any locking device, set screw, or other arrangement that prevents the release of the latch when pressure is applied to the releasing device.

7.9 Emergency Lighting.

7.9.1.1 Emergency lighting facilities for means of egress shall be provided in accordance with Section 7.9 for the following:

(1) Buildings or structures where required in Chapter 11 through Chapter 42

(2) Underground and limited access structures as addressed in Section 11.7

(3) High-rise buildings as required by other sections of this *Code*

(4) Doors equipped with delayed-egress locks

(5) Stair shaft and vestibule of smokeproof enclosures, for which the following also apply:

(a) The stair shaft and vestibule shall be permitted to include a standby generator that is installed for the smokeproof enclosure mechanical ventilation equipment.

(b) The standby generator shall be permitted to be used for the stair shaft and vestibule emergency lighting power supply.

CHAPTER 9 BUILDING SERVICE AND FIRE PROTECTION EQUIPMENT

9.7.1 Automatic Sprinklers.

9.7.1.1 Each automatic sprinkler system required by another section of this *Code* shall be in accordance with one of the following:

(1) NFPA 13, *Standard for the Installation of Sprinkler Systems*

(2) NFPA 13R, *Standard for the Installation of Sprinkler Systems in Residential Occupancies up to and Including Four Stories in Height*

(3) NFPA 13D, *Standard for the Installation of Sprinkler Systems in One- and Two-Family Dwellings and Manufactured Homes*

9.7.1.2 Sprinkler piping serving not more than six sprinklers for any isolated hazardous area shall be permitted to be connected directly to a domestic water supply system having a capacity sufficient to provide 6.1 mm/min (0.15 gpm/ft^2) throughout the entire enclosed area. An indicating shutoff valve, supervised in accordance with 9.7.2 or NFPA 13, *Standard for the Installation of Sprinkler Systems*, shall be installed in an accessible, visible, location between the sprinklers and the connection to the domestic water supply.

CHAPTER 11 SPECIAL STRUCTURES AND HIGH-RISE BUILDINGS

11.8.2 Extinguishing Requirements.

11.8.2.1 High-rise buildings shall be protected throughout by an approved, supervised automatic sprinkler system in accordance with Section 9.7. A sprinkler control valve and a waterflow device shall be provided for each floor.

11.8.4 Emergency Lighting and Standby Power.

11.8.4.1 Emergency lighting in accordance with Section 7.9 shall be provided.

LIFE SAFETY, WORLD TRADE CENTER, SEPTEMBER 11, 2001

The NIST (2005) listed the following factors as enhancing life safety at the WTC on September 11, 2001.

- The towers were occupied by one-third of capacity of 25,000 occupants. The egress capacity (number and width of exits and stairways) was adequate.
- Functioning elevators in WTC 2 enabled nearly 3000 occupants to self-evacuate prior to aircraft impact.
- Two-thirds of surviving occupants participated in a fire drill in the prior 12 months, with 93% instructed on the nearest stairwell.
- Emergency responders provided evacuation assistance.
- As a result of the aforementioned factors, about 87% of WTC tower occupants, including over 99% below the floors of impact, were able to evacuate successfully.

NIST (2005) recommendations that could have improved life safety at the WTC towers on September 11, 2001 include the following.

- Improved structural performance to delay or prevent collapse.
- Improved stairwell integrity via increased remoteness of stairwells and/or enhanced structural integrity of stairwell enclosures.

LIFE SAFETY, WORLD TRADE CENTER, SEPTEMBER 11, 2001—Cont'd

- Better communications to occupants and among first responders via improved systems.
- Better command and control for large-scale incident management.
- Better evacuation training.
- Fire-protected and hardened elevators.
- Better smoke and fire control systems.

SAFETY AND FIRE PROTECTION IN BUILDINGS

Here is a list of suggestions to promote safety and fire protection in buildings (U.S. Fire Administration, 2004; Carter *et al.*, 2004; Azano and Gilbertie, 2003; Quinley and Schmidt, 2002; Purpura, 2002). Although evacuation is emphasized in the following list, an "all hazards" approach requires various emergency procedures depending on the hazards.

- A committee should be formed to plan life safety.
- Life safety plans should be coordinated with public safety agencies and a variety of groups on the premises (e.g., management, employees in general, safety and security officers, and others).
- All employees should understand emergency notification systems, evacuation procedures, and where to assemble outside. OSHA requires that all employees be trained in the building's emergency action plan (EAP), and the NFPA 101 Life Safety Code requires periodic drills based on the type of occupancy.
- Training, education, drills, and exercises are an investment in life safety. Records should be maintained of such activities for regulators, insurers, and others. The records should be secured in multiple locations.
- A chain of command and hierarchy of life safety volunteers should be maintained. For example, a building executive can choose floor wardens who can choose assistant floor wardens and searchers. Floor wardens and assistants are trained and then they train occupants and lead drills. Searchers ensure no one is left behind.
- Training for floor wardens and assistants should include these topics: the variety of risks (e.g., fire, workplace violence), the evacuation plan, escape routes, safety, means of communication, what to do if someone is injured, where to assemble outside the building, and counts.
- Wardens can be supplied with evacuation kits containing a flashlight, reflective vest, clipboard for recording employees outside the building, and flag to mark the rendezvous point.
- Depending on the type of emergency, occupants may have to shelter in place or seek protection in a public building.
- Training and proper equipment are essential for fire brigades and HAZMAT teams.
- Employees with responsibilities during emergencies should be trained in the use of fire alarms, fire extinguishes, standpipes and hose systems, communication systems, ventilation systems, and how and when to turn off utilities. First-aid training is also important.
- A portable fire extinguisher enables an individual to extinguish a small fire. However, training and proper usage are important. Knowledge of classes of fires is a good beginning point: Class A fires consist of ordinary combustible materials, such as paper and wood. Class B fires are fueled by flammable liquids, such as gasoline. Class C fires occur in electrical components. Class D fires are rare and are fueled by combustible metals, such as magnesium.
- The proper selection of a portable fire extinguisher is vital during a fire. For example, water must not be used on a Class B fire because, for instance, gasoline will float on water and spread. Water applied to a Class C fire might cause electrocution of a person. To reduce confusion, most locations use multipurpose dry chemical extinguishers that are applied to A, B, or C fires.

- Standpipes and hose systems enable people to fight a fire in multistory buildings. **Standpipes** are vertical pipes in a building that enable a water supply to reach an outlet on each floor of a building; a wall cabinet is used to house a folded or rolled hose, a control valve, and possibly a fire extinguisher (Figure 8-3). The hose should be removed prior to turning the water on and the nozzle should be held tightly so it does not whip from the water pressure and cause injury. There are multiple types of standpipe systems; planning and training are a necessity.
- Evacuation plans should be developed and evacuation routes should be posted on every floor.
- Evacuation plans should include occupants with special needs and employees should be assigned to assist them.
- Never lock fire exits.
- Emergency first responders must be contacted as soon as possible during a serious event. Also, do not assume someone else called 911.
- Evacuation of high-rise buildings is complicated because of the number of occupants and the time needed to evacuate, especially those in upper floors. A minor fire may require evacuation of the floor containing the fire and two floors both above and below the fire. A serious fire would require a total evacuation.
- Evacuation plans should include areas of refuge (e.g., oversized landing at a stairwell or sealed smoke or fire compartments on a floor) and how they will be used. A method of communication should be installed at the area of refuge.
- Before opening a door during a fire emergency, feel the door with the back of your hand to gauge temperature. If it is warm, opening it may cause smoke and fire to enter. This means you may be forced to stay in your office or apartment. Stuff the cracks around the door with towels. Telephone the fire department to inform them about your location and go to the window with a flashlight or wave a sheet.
- If the door is not warm, brace your body against it, stay low, and open it slowly. If there is no smoke or fire, evacuate.
- If smoke is around you, stay low because smoke rises. Place a cloth over your mouth and nose.
- Employee information is crucial during an emergency and it should be up to date. Also important is a contact list of public safety agencies, medical services, regulators, government officials, critical suppliers, and others.
- Building and site maps are important to indicate such features as utility shutoffs, water lines, electrical and other utilities, floor plans, exits, stairways, hazards, and high-value assets.
- Integrated fire protection systems in "smart buildings" perform numerous functions automatically. Detectors measure smoke and increases in temperature and sound an alarm. Sprinklers automatically extinguish a fire. A computer system shows the fire pinpointed on a monitor, the fire department is notified, a public address system provides safety messages, specific utilities are turned off, and elevators are returned to ground level to encourage the use of stairs.
- Practitioners responsible for safety and fire protection programs should seek feedback to improve performance. Feedback can be gathered from training, drills, and exercises. Also, audits can expose deficiencies in the expertise of personnel, equipment, systems, communications, and coordination with others.
- It is essential that fire protection equipment be inspected, tested, and maintained so it is ready and operable during an emergency. An inspection form can be designed for a facility to check on things such as sprinkler control valves and portable fire extinguishers. Sprinkler control valves should be locked in the open position. Portable fire extinguishers should be checked to ensure that each is charged and ready to use.
- For an emergency in a community, such as a HAZMAT or WMD incident, preplanning for an entity should identify what type of public warning system(s) is utilized. An example is outdoor sirens. Once notified of an emergency, radio and television can be a source of official information.

Figure 8-3 ■ Wall cabinet containing standpipe system, hose, and fire extinguisher.

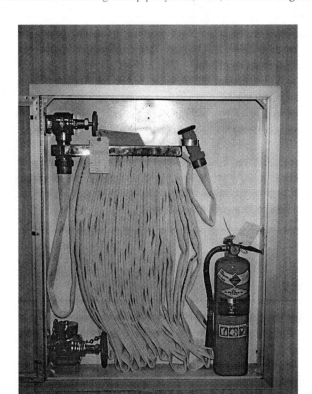

• An airborne hazard (e.g., WMD) outside of a building may necessitate sheltering-in place. For example, a plume of hazardous material may be approaching a high-rise building with no time to evacuate and traffic would block escape. Ideal rooms to shelter in place would be on the opposite side of the approaching plume, above the first floor, windowless, and with a minimum number of vents and doors. Duct tape or other materials can be used to seal the room and the HVAC system should be turned off. Because many hazardous agents are heavier than air, occupants should shelter in place in upper floors.

CLASSIFICATIONS OF VULNERABILITIES OF BUILDINGS

Archibald *et al.* (2002), authors of the RAND publication, *Security and Safety in Los Angeles High-Rise Buildings after 9/11*, describe three classifications of vulnerabilities facing buildings.

Structural vulnerabilities include building features that may be exploited by terrorists and other adversaries. Examples include limitations of the fire suppression system (e.g., sprinklers), building design features that increase the impact of an explosion, and air ducts vulnerable to the introduction of a hazardous substance.

Operational vulnerabilities refer to characteristics and behavior of tenants that may serve to increase the likelihood of victimization or be exploited by offenders. A tenant may be perceived as a symbol of economic wealth, a capitalist, or the cause of globalization.

Continued

CLASSIFICATIONS OF VULNERABILITIES OF BUILDINGS—Cont'd

Contextual vulnerabilities involve a building's proximity to nearby, potential targets. Examples are chemical plant, government building, and seaport. Risk management is a beginning point to deal with these three classifications of vulnerabilities.

To add to the work of Archibald *et al.* (2002), here are two other vulnerabilities.

Geographic vulnerabilities are another classification that can impact buildings. Certain geographic regions are more prone to specific types of natural disasters. Examples are earthquakes, hurricanes, flooding, tornadoes, and winter storms. Terrorists may exploit the circumstances surrounding a natural disaster.

Technological vulnerabilities can lead to another type of emergency impacting buildings. It refers to an interruption or loss of a utility service (e.g., electrical power, gas, or water), information system, communication system, and transportation system, among other types of services. Terrorists may cause such an interruption of service or exploit the problem.

BUILDINGS AND FACILITIES PROFESSION

Two major associations are described here that promote professionalism and safety in buildings and facilities. These groups hold characteristics of professional associations and offer benefits to members as described in Chapter 6.

The **International Facility Management Association** (IFMA) is a global professional association that certifies facility managers, conducts research, provides educational programs, publishes reports and periodicals, and has a code of ethics. The IFMA offers the certified facility manager (CFM) credential, requiring work experience, education, and the ability to pass a comprehensive examination.

The **Building Owners & Managers Association International** (BOMA) is a global professional association that serves the needs of building owners and managers. It is involved in issues and advocacy, research, publications, and education and training. The group provides security alerts. BOMA offers various designations through its institute and all designations require the study of health and safety issues. One designation is the facilities management administrator for those who manage a manufacturing facility or service business.

PUBLIC SAFETY

Up to this point, in this chapter, we have learned that the design of buildings plays an important role in life safety, and employers and employees can do a lot to prepare and respond to emergencies while waiting for government first responders. *Life safety and public safety efforts are not separate and distinct from each other. They have been integrated for many years.* For example, when government promulgates building codes and life safety codes as law, government inspectors from various agencies visit businesses and institutions to conduct inspections and enforce regulations and codes. When a new building or construction is planned, government building inspectors, fire department personnel, and other government specialists typically review plans for approval. Firefighters often conduct prefire planning of buildings. An on-site survey, with the aid of a checklist, pinpoints life safety and fire protection characteristics of buildings and occupants. This would include exits, sprinklers, training, and drills. In communities, prefire planning may even include the keys to major buildings being stored in fire trucks to reduce damage to access points when firefighters respond to alarms at buildings and must enter quickly.

Public police are also involved in the integration of life safety and public safety prior to emergencies. They may meet with private security management to coordinate efforts at protecting people and assets. Police often maintain floor plans of banks and other high-risk locations to assist them when responding to crimes, such as a robberies and hostage incidents. Violence in the workplace has caused public police to plan, train, and drill with institutions (e.g., schools) and businesses.

PUBLIC POLICE

In the United States, there are 13,524 municipal police agencies, 3070 sheriff's departments, plus state police agencies and dozens of federal law enforcement agencies. Employees of these agencies, divided into sworn/not sworn, are as follows: local police, 440,920/124,995; sheriff's departments, 164,711/129,112; state, 56,384/30,680; and federal, 88,000/72,000 (Bureau of Justice Statistics, 2003).

In addition to their primary role in public safety, public police play an important role in combating terrorism and responding to "all hazard" emergencies. They are both proactive and reactive. **Proactive policing** means action is taken to prevent a problem before it occurs. **Reactive policing** means responding to an incident after it occurs. Traditionally, police have been reactive: they respond quickly to a crime scene, investigate, interview, collect evidence, and seek to arrest the offender. They also respond quickly to a variety of other emergencies, including accidents and fires.

PROACTIVE POLICING

According to the Council on Foreign Relations (2004a), public police agencies have made numerous changes since the 9/11 attacks. They have strengthened liaisons with other police agencies and other first responders, changed training to prepare for WMD, increased patrols and improved security in communities, created new counterterrorism units and reassigned officers to these units, and employed new technology (e.g., sensors to detect WMD, more CCTV) and equipment (e.g., protective suits).

The Police Executive Research Forum (2003–2004), with funding from the U.S. Department of Justice Office of Community Oriented Policing Services, organized a series of forums for law enforcement executives to produce practical advice for addressing problems related to terrorism. Forum results included these priorities: local–federal partnerships, security clearances and information sharing, reengineering intelligence, training and awareness, working with diverse communities, and WMD.

Because community policing has been a dominant policing philosophy since the 1990s, its relevance to the problem of terrorism has been debated. **Community policing** (CP) involves police seeking closer communications and partnering with diverse citizens and groups to control crime, reduce fear, solve community problems, and improve the quality of life (Purpura, 2001: 252). De Guzman (2002) argues that some tenets of CP appear to be inconsistent with the new roles of police in combating terrorism. He states that it is futile for police to try to win the hearts and minds of terrorists who must be incapacitated, and counterterrorism measures threaten trust between police and the public. Scheider and colleagues (n.d.) write that although the 9/11 attacks can cause police agencies to fall back on more traditional methods, CP is beneficial against terrorism. They note that officers assigned to a specific neighborhood can build trust and relationships with residents that can lead to vital intelligence. Also, they write that the problem-solving model within CP is well suited to prevent terrorism. They cite the **SARA model**: scanning identifies potential targets in a locale. Analysis involves a study of the likelihood of an attack and its impact. Response produces prevention plans and crisis response. Assessment refines the plans.

Weiss (2004: 27–28) sees four key concerns related to proactive policing following his study of *The 9/11 Commission Report* (National Commission on Terrorist Attacks Upon the United States, 2004). He acknowledges that although local police do not generally have the capacity to engage in *intelligence analysis*, especially related to national security, they do have enormous capacity to *gather intelligence.* Weiss points to a bureau of justice statistics study revealing that 21% of citizens have contact annually with police and half of those contacts occur during traffic stops. He argues that this contact is an underused source of information.

Sweeney (2005: 15) notes that the Highway Safety Committee of the International Association of Chiefs of Police (IACP) and the National Highway Traffic Safety Administration has worked on numerous projects to increase law enforcement officer interest in proactive traffic patrol. Publications from the IACP have included information on the possibility of officers interdicting and preventing terrorism through traffic patrol.

Another area of crucial concern, according to Weiss, is *information sharing.* The FBI has promoted efforts to reduce related problems, but Weiss sees frustration by local police who want *any* information that suggests a threat on the local level.

A third point of Weiss concerns *cooperation and communications between disparate agencies,* including police, fire, EMS, and emergency management. Although the public safety community has invested heavily to enhance closer ties among these groups through planning, procedures, and communications networks, Weiss argues that these relationships may be challenged during a disaster because these groups may revert to isolated, independent actions.

The fourth concern of Weiss is harm to local *police community relations* because of certain law enforcement methods. He cites the use of immigration laws as leverage to gather information. This approach causes suspicion and distrust in the community and results in long-term damage to police community relations and information flow.

Shusta *et al.* (2005: 31) offer tips for improving police community relations in multicultural communities: allow the public to see police in nonenforcement roles; treat all groups objectively; be personable and friendly to minority-group members; do not appear uncomfortable about discussing racial issues; educate citizens about the police; and do not be afraid to be a change agent in your department to improve relations.

OPERATION ATLAS

Since Operation Iraqi Freedom in March 2003, the New York City Police Department has initiated Operation Atlas, a comprehensive antiterrorism and security program for the city (New York City Police Department, 2003). Depending on security concerns and world events, the program can be fully deployed or scaled back. Operation Atlas received high marks from former Secretary of Homeland Security, Tom Ridge, who called it "a model for other communities to follow."

Core elements of Operation Atlas are increased personnel deployment, transit system security, patrol operations/increased coverage, and intelligence. Key strategies are flexible staffing and assignments and unpredictable deployment. Because police commanders seek not to be "creatures of habit" in their deployment of specialized units throughout the city, terrorists and other offenders are more likely to be surprised and their operations disrupted when police appear unexpectedly.

Examples of Operation Atlas strategies are as follows.

- Heavily armed HERCULES teams are deployed randomly.
- Counter assault teams in unmarked armored vehicles ("CAT CARS") with heavily armed officers are deployed.
- Additional police are deployed for patrolling high-density transit locations.
- Undercover teams ride the subways.
- Vehicles parked in front of sensitive locations are towed.
- COBRA teams are deployed to deal with WMD.

OPERATION ATLAS—Cont'd

- HAMMER teams, police and fire department experts in hazardous materials, are deployed jointly.
- Systematic citywide searches are conducted for radioactive material or devices.
- Daily assessments are made to determine which houses of worship, hotels, landmarks, and other attractions merit additional protection.
- Fuel depots in the region are under surveillance.
- In cooperation with New Jersey authorities, sites in New Jersey are being inspected for the storage of radioactive material.
- Security at small airports in the region is assessed to prevent general aviation from being used as a weapon.

CRITICAL THINKING:

What does it mean to be a "creature of habit" and why is it dangerous?

BEING PROACTIVE WHEN PATROLLING AND ON POST ASSIGNMENTS

Law enforcement officers, as well as private security officers and members of the armed forces, are often assigned to patrol or stationary post duties. Proper training ensures that personnel are proactive to maximize their effectiveness. This includes the use of their five senses as they perform their duties. These senses include sight, hearing, smell, touch, and taste. To illustrate, a police officer stops a subject after *observing* suspicious behavior. At the scene of a fire, an officer *hears* a faint cry for help. In another incident, an officer enters a building and *smells* and *tastes* a strong chemical in the air. Upon spotting a stolen and abandoned vehicle, an officer *touches* the front hood and feels heat from a recently operating engine.

Experienced personnel may develop what has been called a sixth sense. Coleman (1986: 106) defines it as follows: "This sixth sense is not as obvious as the other five but the officer's perception or conclusion, based on his experience, knowledge, and the utilization of other senses, must be given consideration as a viable information gathering source."

Through training and experience, law enforcement officers develop skills in recognizing behaviors that *may* indicate criminal behavior is about to occur, is occurring, or has occurred. Such skills can be shifted to the problem of terrorism and have been called terrorist attack preincident indicators (TAPIs) (Nance, 2003). TAPIs include *legal profiling*, not *racial profiling* (see Chapter 5). Legal profiling includes a variety of factors—behavioral, situational, motivational, and background—that attract the attention of authorities. A profile is based on data and research that produce indicators and characteristics that authorities rely on as a foundation to stop individuals. *At the same time, authorities should avoid stereotypes based on race, religion, and ethnic background because terrorists may rely on police stereotypes to deceive them.*

Authorities are increasingly aware of the deceptive and creative methods used by terrorists. They may dress as first responders and show up in a police vehicle, ambulance, or fire truck. In addition to falsifying their identity, carrying forged documents to travel globally, and possessing counterfeit currency, they may pass themselves off as Christians and shave their beard to reduce suspicion (Figure 8-4) and even recruit women, children, and Caucasians.

Figure 8-4 ■ Terrorists falsify their identity, carry forged documents, and practice deception.

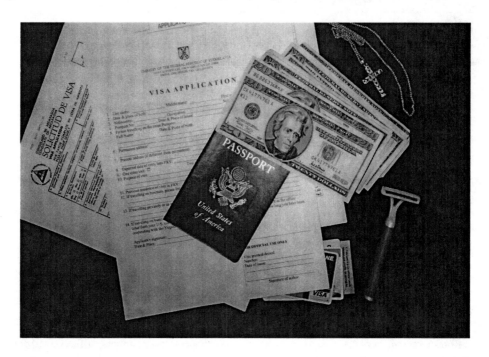

The following factors *may* indicate terrorist or other criminal activity (U.S. Department of Homeland Security, n.d.).

PREOPERATIONAL PLANNING AND SURVEILLANCE

- surveillance and using disguises (e.g., vendors, panhandlers)
- telephone, or e-mail threats to observe emergency procedures
- individual shows unusual or prolonged interest in security measures or personnel
- individual questions security or facility personnel and/or observes security drills and procedures
- unusual behavior such as staring or quickly looking away
- individual actively engages in "boundary probing," beginning with physical approaches to measure possible access restriction and/or law enforcement presence and response
- individual possesses multiple hotel receipts, car rental receipts, or other indications of frequent and erratic travel and/or is evasive when questioned concerning past and future plans and destinations
- discreet use of still cameras, video recorders, or note taking at nontourist type locations, e.g., government facilities, airports, bridges, chemical plants
- unusual items are observed within the vehicle, such as blueprints, maps, sketching materials, surveillance equipment, e.g., binoculars, video cameras, cameras with extensive adaptable lenses, car batteries, wires, household chemicals, etc.
- improper attempts to acquire, or suspicious possession of, official vehicles, uniforms, badges, or access cards

VEHICLE-BORNE IMPROVISED EXPLOSIVE DEVICES

- vehicle may exhibit signs of recent modification to handle heavier loads, create additional storage areas, or increase fuel capacity or vehicle speed

- vehicle has excessively darkened/tinted windows or may have temporary window coverings affixed to prevent viewing vehicle's interior
- vehicle shows signs of theft, e.g., damaged locks, missing windows, altered ignition, etc.
- vehicle bears temporary commercial placard affixed with tape or magnets or permanent commercial placard that is unusual, unrecognizable, or misspelled
- vehicle appears to be out of place with the environment, e.g., a tractor-trailer parked in a residential neighborhood, and may have out-of-state or temporary plates
- vehicle may contain batteries, wiring, timers, or other power supply or switching components in the passenger compartment
- vehicle may contain unmarked packages or unusual items such as PVC pipe, magnets, compressed gas cylinders, and fire extinguishers within the passenger compartment

SUICIDE BOMBERS

- individual wears inappropriate attire, such as loose or bulky clothing inconsistent with current weather conditions
- individual seems to be wearing an inordinate amount of perfumes, colognes, or other scents that may be used to mask "chemical" type odors
- the individual is carrying heavy luggage or a bag or is wearing a backpack
- the individual repeatedly pats upper body or appears to rearrange clothing excessively
- the individual is unresponsive to authoritative voice command
- individual may be sweating, mumbling, or may exhibit unusually calm and detached behavior
- individual may be wearing disguises appropriate to target areas to elude detection, e.g., military, medic, firefighter, or police uniforms, or may pose as a pregnant woman

REACTIVE POLICING

Once an emergency occurs, public police mobilize their resources and arrive at the scene as quickly as possible to perform specialized duties, as other first responders. Traditional police duties during an emergency include assisting victims, directing traffic (especially to facilitate access by firefighters, EMS, and other first responders), and approaching the emergency as a possible crime scene. As an earlier part of this chapter stated, citizens cannot depend on government during the initial stages of an emergency and, thus, life safety initiatives result in action such as evacuation, shelter in place, movement of the injured to safety, firefighting by employees, and sprinkler system activation. Of course, the arrival of first responders enhances both life safety and public safety.

Since the 9/11 attacks, when over 400 emergency responders were killed (Houser *et al.*, 2004: xv), first responders have been much more cautious during emergencies because of the possibility of a WMD, secondary explosions, and other hazards. Many changes have occurred in planning, training, equipment, policies, and procedures.

Houghton and Schachter (2005: 11–17) refer to coordinated terrorist attacks and describe them as occurring simultaneously or nearly so and conducted by a single terrorist group or jointly by sympathetic groups. They see the number of these types of attacks as increasing because of greater loss of life, injuries and property damage, and the impairment of first responders. Also, these sophisticated attacks increase both the credibility of terrorist groups and media attention. Houghton and Schachter classify coordinated terrorist attacks into three categories.

1. *Parallel device attacks* apply more than one device simultaneously or almost simultaneously at the same location. Rather than one large device (e.g., bomb), small devices and multiple devices are less likely to be detected. Also, multiple terrorists improve the chances that one or more will succeed. The triple-suicide bombing by Hamas in 1997 at a pedestrian mall

in Jerusalem killed 5 people and injured 181. Three males, one dressed as a woman, each detonated a 4- to 5-pound bomb made with nuts and bolts to cause puncture and blast injuries.

2. *Secondary attacks* involve one attack followed by one or more additional attacks in the same area, often to target first responders, but also victimizing the injured again, Good Samaritans, and onlookers. This terrorist method delays treatment of the injured and demonstrates the vulnerability of first responders. It is becoming a popular method globally.

3. *Multiple dispersed attacks* occur simultaneously or nearly simultaneously at different locations. This method can overwhelm first responders. Al-Qaida and the groups it has inspired use this method. An example is the 2004 Madrid train bombings, where several trains packed with commuters were blown apart.

Houghton and Schachter note that their categories are not mutually exclusive. Attacks can overlap all three categories. Their recommendations for first responders include not sending all personnel and assets to a site; establishing a secure perimeter far enough from the site to increase safety; sweeping for other devices; videotaping and interviewing bystanders who may be eyewitnesses or terrorist spotters; decentralizing personnel and equipment; and mutual aid agreements with other jurisdictions.

The reader is referred to the previous chapter for the national response plan (NRP) and how it seeks to coordinate all levels of government and the private sector. Although law enforcement plays a supportive role in this plan, a major duty of police agencies is to conduct investigations.

INVESTIGATING TERRORISM

Terrorists commit a variety of crimes. Besides the crime of terrorism, they may commit murder, kidnapping, conspiracy, bombing, arson, skyjacking, assault, extortion, and drug offenses. The motivation behind a portion of these crimes is to raise funds to support the cause and its objectives.

Proactive investigations of suspected terrorist activity include surveillance, use of informants, undercover operations, intelligence gathering, and use of the multiagency task force concept. The beginning chapters of this book provide a source of numerous questions about terrorists (e.g., motivations, affiliations, methods of operation, weapons) for intelligence gathering. Proactive investigative methods are also appropriate for the traditional *reactive investigations* that are emphasized next.

When emergencies and disasters occur, multiple police agencies respond to investigate whether the event is linked to criminal acts. The "Terrorism Incident Law Enforcement and Investigation Annex," within the NRP (U.S. Department of Homeland Security, 2004), states: "The law enforcement and investigative response to a terrorist threat or incident within the United States is a highly coordinated, multiagency state, local, tribal, and federal responsibility. In support of this mission, the following federal agencies have primary responsibility for certain aspects of the overall law enforcement and investigative response: Department of Defense (DOD), Department of Energy (DOE), Department of Health and Human Services (HHS), Department of Homeland Security (DHS), Department of Justice/FBI, and Environmental Protection Agency (EPA)." *The U.S. attorney general, head of the Department of Justice containing the FBI, has the lead responsibility for criminal investigations of terrorist acts or threats.* An FBI Joint Operations Center (JOC) is a command post that coordinates federal law enforcement assets and police agencies from all levels of government when an incident or threat develops. This process is part of the unified approach to domestic incident management as specified in the NRP and NIMS.

When police investigators respond to a suspected terrorist incident, they focus on specific priorities. Care for victims is a top priority. Safety at the scene is also very important, besides looking for suspects. Terrorists may "bait" first responders and onlookers to an incident and then attack with more lethal weapons (e.g., vehicle bomb). If a hazardous substance is at the scene, precautions, protective equipment, and access controls are vital. The scene must also be secured and protected to ensure that evidence is not disturbed.

CRITICAL THINKING:

Knowing that terrorists are creative and cunning, how can police protect the site of an emergency against a vehicle bomb or other types of attack?

In the early stages of a crime scene investigation, *recording the scene* is important. This is accomplished through various types of camera equipment, plus sketching and measuring. Still photos and video are shot from ground level and possibly from an aircraft. A video camera should be used to record the crowd, as witnesses and suspects may be nearby. Because video cameras are pervasive (i.e., inside and outside of buildings, on street poles, in vehicles, used by tourists and others, in cell phones), investigators should seek recordings of activities that occurred prior to, during, and following an incident.

Investigators at a crime scene use their expertise to search for evidence that links a person or persons to the crime. *Offenders typically leave items (e.g., fingerprints, DNA, tools) at a crime scene and take items (e.g., valuables, microscopic particles) with them.* Many terrorist crime scenes involve the detonation of a bomb. *Bomb scenes typically contain everything that was at the scene before the detonation, although it may be in a different form.* Investigators must carefully sift through debris to locate bomb components that may contain clues to the manufacturer, fingerprints, or match substances found on a suspect or in the suspect's home or vehicle. A WMD (e.g., "dirty bomb") requires extra precautions and protective gear by investigators.

Because offenders commit crimes in unique ways, investigators maintain databases on how each serious crime is committed. These methods of how crimes are committed, also known as modus operandi, can help identify suspects. For example, a terrorist may use the same type of explosive and timer in multiple bombings. An earlier bombing investigation and a more recent bombing investigation may both result in enough information to point to a particular suspect.

Dempsey and Forst (2005: 441) offer methods of investigating terrorism that are common to investigations in general. These methods include interviewing, canvassing (i.e., searching an area for witnesses), establishing tip lines, following up on tips, reinterviewing, and recanvassing. They also recommend the use of informants and offer the example of the arrest of Ranzi Ahmed Yousef, previously number one on the FBI's Most Wanted List for his role as the alleged main plotter behind the 1993 World Trade Center bombing in New York City. An informer, seeking $2 million in reward, walked into the American Embassy in Islamabad, Pakistan, and revealed Yousef's location. A team of Pakistani and American police went to his hotel room, broke down the door, and rushed in to find him in bed with a suitcase of explosives nearby. Dempsey and Forst also value numerous types of surveillance. Examples are following suspects, audio, and video.

William Dyson (2005: 55–68), a retired FBI agent and terrorism investigator, writes that every investigative technique applied to solve criminal cases can also be used for investigations into terrorism. He notes that a key distinction between ordinary criminals and terrorists is that the former often assume they know how police operate, but they lack the knowledge depth of terrorists who study police methods and alert group members about police techniques. Dyson adds that terrorists fear police and employ numerous security procedures that make surveillance, arrest, and prosecution difficult. Terrorist groups often provide members with manuals, guides, or verbal training on security, covert operations, target selection, and staging attacks. Dyson recommends that police learn from the same resources provided to terrorists for a better understanding of how terrorists protect themselves and operate.

Casey (2004:1–6) describes a major method in which local, state, and federal police [e.g., FBI, ATF, Bureau of Immigration and Customs Enforcement (ICE)] have worked together. It is through the joint terrorism task forces (JTTFs). Headed by the FBI, the goals are to establish proactive investigations and joint responses and investigations when terrorist incidents occur.

JTTFs maximize talent, resources, and technology, while having global reach. FBI-sponsored task forces have two common elements that make them unique: written memorandums of understanding between participating police agencies and FBI funding that pays expenses for state and local police for such items as overtime, vehicles, gas, cell phones, and laptop computers. The FBI maintains a JTTF in each of its 56 field offices. The FBI also maintains the National Joint Terrorism Task Force (NJTTF) in Washington, DC. It contains every federal law enforcement and intelligence agency (e.g., CIA) at one location. JTTF members, and any police officer in the United States, can contact the NJTTF for assistance.

WORLD TRADE CENTER CRIME SCENE, SEPTEMBER 11, 2001

The 9/11 attacks of the World Trade Center resulted in an enormous and complicated crime scene (Dempsey and Forst, 2005: 441; Becker, 2005: 69–70). The crime scene consisted of 16 acres and 140 million tons of debris. The evidence was varied and included human remains, building debris, and airliner parts. To collect evidence, sifting of all debris was required, as was done at the Oklahoma City bombing. Major priorities were to search for survivors and account for and identify victims and remains. To identify remains, a variety of disciplines were employed, including pathology, odontology, biology, and anthropology. DNA was used to establish identity. Personal items (e.g., jewelry, clothing) at the scene also helped identify victims.

The precise location of evidence helped reconstruct the event. Initially, handwritten notes described each item and the notes included rough measurements of its location, along with the date and time of discovery. A tracking number was assigned to each object recovered. The information was entered into a database. Problems included mismatched numbers and the danger of moving around the debris for measurements. The New York City Fire Department enlisted the assistance of a firm specializing in wireless data transmission systems that incorporate global positioning system (GPS) technology (i.e., a system that uses satellites to compute position). The equipment included handheld terminals that contained bar code scanners and radio transceivers for sending information to host computers. When recovery personnel found an item, they used the terminal to key in a brief description, a bar code was attached to the item, the item's bar code was scanned, and its location was recorded by a GPS link (accurate to within 3 feet). Later, the item could be rescanned to retrieve information from a database. As the information was collected, it was instantly uploaded into one of several laptops set up as host computers for the database.

One day following the attacks, the Fresh Kills Landfill on Staten Island was designated as a secondary crime scene. Trucks began hauling items from Ground Zero. Over the next 10 months, tons of material were examined for human remains, personal effects, and evidence. About 1.7 million hours were worked by numerous police agencies, resulting in the recovery of approximately 4257 human remains and the identification of 300 individuals; 4000 personal photographs; $78,000 in currency; 54,000 personal items (e.g., driver's licenses and identification cards); and 1358 vehicles, including 102 fire apparatus and 61 police vehicles.

FIRE SERVICE

Fire departments are local institutions. There are about 31,000 local fire departments in the United States and over one million firefighters, of which about 750,000 are volunteers. Over half of firefighters protect small, rural communities of fewer than 5000 residents, and these locales rely on volunteer departments with scarce resources. One of the best strategies for these locales, outside of major metropolitan areas, is to develop mutual aid agreements to share resources. This approach improves preparation and response to fires and emergencies, including WMD incidents (U.S. Department of Homeland Security, n.d.).

The "Firefighting Annex," within the NRP (U.S. Department of Homeland Security, 2004), states that the primary agency for coordination during a significant fire is the U.S. Department of Agriculture/Forest Service, with support from the Departments of Commerce, Defense, Homeland Security, Interior, and the Environmental Protection Agency. The function is to detect and suppress wildland, rural, and urban fires resulting from an incident of national significance, and to provide personnel and equipment to supplement all levels of government in firefighting.

Because of the firefighting limitations of small, rural communities, corporations in these locales often establish their own private fire department (on the premises) that rivals public fire departments in vehicles, equipment, and training. Major factors behind the decision to establish these private firefighting capabilities are risk management, life safety, insurance costs, and business continuity.

Public firefighter duties include proactive efforts at fire prevention through inspection of buildings, training and drills, public relations campaigns, and prefire planning with private sector life safety and building specialists. Once a fire call is received, firefighters respond as quickly as possible, suppress fire, rescue people, and, if trained, provide emergency care and handle hazardous materials.

Because 343 New York City firefighters died from the 9/11 attacks on the World Trade Center, there has been a reevaluation of emergency response. Firefighters have received additional training on WMD (Figure 8-5), secondary explosions, entering buildings, and coordinating with other first responders. Also, their equipment is changing. The **Homeland Security Standards Database** is a project coordinated by the American National Standards Institute, in cooperation with the DHS, to provide a one-stop access to homeland security standards on a host of topics such as protective equipment, communications equipment, and safety standards.

Today, first responders are less likely to rush into a building or area if a building is about to collapse or if victims are coughing and being overcome by a hazardous substance. The **public safety assistance time line** (PSATL) is the total time it takes for first responders to arrive on the scene (once they are notified of an emergency), plus the time it takes for first responders to plan their on-the-scene strategies, ensure conditions are safe so they do not become victims themselves,

Figure 8-5 ■ Firefighter testing hazardous substance. Source: Smiths Detection, Inc.

don protective equipment, and, finally, assist victims and protect property. Because each emergency is unique, the PSATL may be a few minutes or it may be longer.

$$\text{response time (RT)} + \text{on-the-scene planning and preparation (OSPP)}$$
$$= \text{public safety assistance time line (PSATL)}$$

PUBLIC SAFETY ASSISTANCE TIME LINE

The PSATL not only impacts the time it takes for first responders to assist victims and protect property, it also influences the planning relevant to protection ratings of construction materials and security methods. As examples, a fire door in a building that has a rating of 1 hour (i.e., it can withstand a fire for about 1 hour), or a fire safe with a similar rating. Examples of other important considerations are victims holding out in a safe room or trapped in a vault.

Analyses of how the New York City and Arlington County Fire Departments responded to the 9/11 attacks showed the need for better communications, better command-and-control facilities, and more equipment. Both departments had problems contacting off-duty first responders and supplying them with adequate protective clothing, self-contained breathing apparatus cylinders, and other equipment. Another problem was well-meaning first responders from neighboring jurisdictions who "self-dispatched" and decided on where they would work and what they would do in the emergency; this undermines the incident command system (Mathews, 2004: 14–18).

Reality Check: In an Emergency, if You Are an Occupant of a High-Rise Building, Do You Wait for First Responders or Depend on Your Life Safety Skills?

The National Institute of Standards and Technology (2005), in their study of how the World Trade Center towers collapsed, also researched the physiological impact on first responders as they climb stairs in a high-rise building. The NIST stated that from the time the first jet hit WTC 1 to the collapse of WTC 2, a period of about 1 hour and 12 minutes, responders inside WTC 1 were able to climb to floors in the 40s out of 110 stories. During part of their climb, elevators assisted responders who reached floors in the 50s to 70s. An outfitted firefighter wearing full protective clothing (e.g., helmet, boots) and self-contained breathing apparatus carries about 50 lbs. Other equipment (e.g., radio, lights, extra air bottle, ax, ropes, and hose) can add an additional 50 lbs. The rate of climb by firefighters with equipment was about 2.0 minutes per floor. For police, with less equipment, the rate of climb was about 1.4 minutes per floor. The NIST noted that responders had difficulty negotiating stairs and doorways and that stairways became plugged with traffic as occupants were coming down and as individuals with disabilities and obese occupants were being assisted. The NIST concluded: *"... emergency response time factors related to the rate of fire growth, the ability to rescue building occupants, and the ability to bring a fire under control become more critical with every additional floor in building height."* Alternative methods of transporting responders and equipment to upper floors should be pursued.

CRITICAL THINKING:

What are your views of the nearby box on the NIST research and what is your answer to the opening question?

EMERGENCY MEDICAL SERVICE

The U.S. Department of Homeland Security (n.d.) reports that there are over 155,000 nationally registered emergency medical technicians (EMT). Houser *et al.* (2004), researchers for the RAND Corporation, list 500,000 emergency medical service responders. Carter *et al.* (2004: 691) write that "Emergency medical responses constitute more than 50 percent of total emergency responses for many fire departments across the country. In some jurisdictions, emergency medical calls make up 70 to 80 percent of the fire department's total emergency responses per year." Swope (2004: 58) adds that in many cities, as the number of fires drop, fire departments have been taking over EMS duties. However, Swope notes that the effectiveness of this move is debatable.

Firefighters are increasingly improving their skills at emergency medical services and can deliver lifesaving techniques to stabilize patients while waiting for EMTs and paramedics. Some firefighters are also EMT qualified. In comparison to EMTs, paramedics receive more training and perform more procedures during a medical emergency. States vary on training and qualification for these positions.

Training is especially important to render the most appropriate care and for self-protection. During a medical emergency, numerous critical, time-sensitive decisions must be made (Angle, 2005: 118). Examples are the safest and quickest route to the scene, medical treatment techniques, drug dosages, and the most appropriate method of transporting the patient. **Triage** is a term relevant to sites of medical emergencies and is defined as follows: "A quick and systematic method of identifying which patients are in serious condition and which patients are not, so that the more seriously injured patients can be treated first" (Carter, 2004: 954).

Safety issues pertain to traffic accidents while responding to or leaving the scene, disease, emotionally upset family members, violent offenders, and hazardous materials. **Personal protective equipment** (PPE) is essential; it depends on the type of incident. At a minimum, PPE must include universal precautions (e.g., gloves, mask, protective eyewear) to prevent disease transmission, but it can range to a bullet-resistant vest for high-risk incidents or locations.

When EMS arrives at a business or institution, they may find victims under care as part of a proprietary life safety emergency plan. Security officers and other personnel at sites are often trained to administer first aid, and they may possess additional training. *This is an example of where life safety and public safety merge.* EMS responders should continue the medical care begun by the life safety personnel and transport patients to the hospital (Figure 8-6).

MEDICAL SYSTEM RESPONSE

How would U.S. hospitals and the public health system handle a WMD attack? Would hospitals be overwhelmed? Answers to these questions are debated frequently. Most of the terrorism preparedness activities for hospitals focus on large hospitals in urban areas and much more needs to be done. The Council on Foreign Relations (2004b) states that U.S. emergency room teams are not properly trained or equipped to deal with large numbers of victims from a WMD attack. Panicked citizens would likely flood emergency rooms. This occurred in the 1995 sarin gas attack of the Tokyo subway system. Interestingly, following the 9/11 attacks at the World Trade Center, hospitals were not as flooded as experts thought they would be because of the high number of fatalities.

Marghella (2004: 9) writes that medical planners are finding it very difficult to predict what type of resources will be needed following a WMD event. He offers these reasons: we have little historical data and the outcome of a WMD attack can vary depending on the type of agent and dose used, the dispersion method, weather, and the density of the population. (Medical planners can possibly benefit by integrating with risk management specialists and employing risk management tools as explained in the previous chapter.)

In 2005, a congressionally ordered exercise called TOPOFF 3, designed to expose flaws in the nation's ability to respond to a widespread biological disaster, produced many challenges.

Figure 8-6 ■ On September 11, 2001, medical personnel load wounded into an ambulance at the first medical triage area set up outside the Pentagon after a hijacked commercial airliner crashed into the southwest corner of the building. U.S. Navy Photo by Journalist 1st Class Mark D. Faram. http://www.news.navy.mil/view_single.asp?id=123

In New Jersey, for example, borders were closed to contain the "plague" and schools were closed so they could be used as antibiotic distribution sites. However, many employees of one hospital commuted from Pennsylvania. Also, because schools closed, hospital employees had to make arrangements to care for their children. As hospitals were overwhelmed with "infected patients," the hospitals had staffing shortages. Obviously, the exercise was a success in that it showed flaws in the emergency response that needed correction.

In a biological attack, a major difficulty is detection because symptoms are similar to what is usually found in emergency room patients. Once discovered, hospitals, other locations, and people exposed to the disease would be quarantined. Antibiotics would be used to treat anthrax. Victims of smallpox would receive a vaccine to reduce the severity of the illness.

In a chemical attack, victims would go through decontamination by firefighters and EMS. Care would include fluids and oxygen through ventilators. Victims exposed to nerve agents, such as sarin or VX, would need antidotes immediately. Those exposed to blister agents, such as mustard gas, would receive painkillers, antibiotics, and ointments for burns. Radiation exposure presents additional challenges. Obviously, medical system capabilities and the availability of staff, equipment, and medications will dictate how many victims can be treated. Mass casualties could easily overwhelm the medical system.

The Council on Foreign Relations (2004b) offers these suggestions from medical experts:

- improve cooperation and sharing information in the medical system
- conduct exercises based on various WMD attack scenarios
- train staff to recognize symptoms of various weapons, determine treatment, protect themselves, and isolate patients
- plan for "surge capacity"— massive treatment
- vaccinate staff

- stockpile drugs
- prepare showers, brushes, and detergents for decontamination
- establish surveillance to monitor disease

The overall goal of OSHA is to create a safe working environment for employees in numerous industries and occupations. OSHA has been involved in assisting hospitals in protecting their employees through information (Jensen, 2005: 6). In a WMD incident, hospital employees become **first receivers** who treat incoming victims. OSHA information assists hospitals in creating emergency plans for worst-case scenarios and training. It also offers suggestions for PPE for hospital employees (e.g., head-to-toes protective suit and respirator). First responders at a hazardous site are covered under OSHA's standard on hazardous waste operations and emergency response. First receivers also need standards of protection, including security officers at hospitals who help maintain order, and control traffic and access by victims who may be in a state of panic and need to be decontaminated and quarantined. *Without quality security plans and PPE, civil disturbance can cause a hospital to become a disaster site.*

The "Public Health and Medical Services Annex" within the NRP (U.S. Department of Homeland Security, 2004) states that the U.S. Department of Health and Human Services (HHS) coordinates federal assistance to supplement all levels of government in response to public health and medical care needs for potential or actual incidents of national significance. HHS may request assistance from other departments (Figure 8-7). For example, HHS may request the DHS and the

Figure 8-7 ■ During a medical emergency, the U.S. Department of Health and Human Services may request assistance from the U.S. Departments of Homeland Security and Defense. Source: U.S. Department of Homeland Security (2004). Securing Our Homeland: Strategic Plan. www.dhs.gov/interweb/assetlibrary/DHS_StratPlan_FINAL_spread.pd

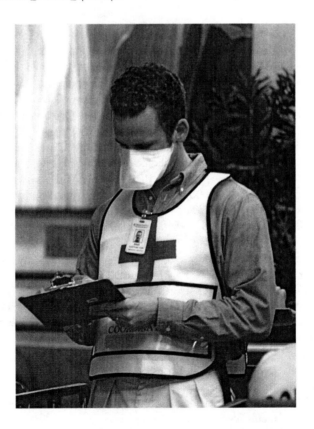

DOD to assist in providing victim identification and mortuary services. Among the many functions of HHS, it coordinates with state health agencies to enhance surveillance systems to monitor the health of the general population, carries out field studies, monitors injury and disease patterns, and provides technical expertise.

President Bush signed the **Public Health Security and Bioterrorism Preparedness and Response Act of 2002**. This legislation recognized emergency room workers as major responders to the problem of terrorism and promoted a national curriculum of training to respond to biological agents. It also provided for a real-time surveillance system among emergency rooms, state public health departments, and the **Centers for Disease Control and Prevention** (CDC)—the lead agency, in HHS, if a communicable disease outbreak occurs.

In 2004, the CDC led a coalition of federal agencies to help cities increase their capacity to deliver medicines and supplies during a major public health emergency. The goal is to distribute antidotes and vaccines from the **strategic national stockpile**. *The challenge being addressed is the delivery of these medicines to millions of people at the local level in a very short period of time.* Another challenge is the training of medical personnel and volunteers. According to Mason (2005: 19–25), more than 80% of the health care resources in the United States are controlled by the private sector. However, major health care plans are being made by government. Another challenge is coordination among multiple agencies at different levels of government, nongovernment agencies, and the private sector.

The medical system must also prepare for the psychological impact on victims of terrorism. Although a great deal has been accomplished to increase protection against terrorism, the mental health of victims is an issue in need of research to serve as a foundation for plans and action. A terrorist event can result in acute and long-term stress, anxiety, depression, anger, sleeping difficulties, and other problems. (See the Chapter 5 discussion of victims of terrorism, including posttraumatic stress.)

PANDEMICS

The medical system is at the forefront of defenses against not only bioterrorism, but also the spread of infectious diseases not caused by terrorists. A **pandemic** is an outbreak of an infectious disease that impacts humans over a large geographic area. Pandemics have occurred though history, with many from zoonotic diseases resulting from the domestication of animals. **Zoonotic diseases** are diseases transmitted from animals to humans. Examples are West Nile virus, which can cause encephalitis, avian influenza, and human monkeypox. One type of avian influenza is the "bird flu" strain that is causing a great deal of concern worldwide. Examples of pandemics occurring through history include the bubonic plague, also called the "Black Death," that killed about 20 million Europeans during the 1300s, seven cholera pandemics throughout the 1800s and 1900s, and numerous influenza pandemics. The 1918–1919 "Spanish flu" caused the highest number of known influenza deaths. Over 500,000 people died in the United States and up to 50 million may have died worldwide. Many people died within the first few days of infection, and nearly half of those who died were young, healthy adults (Centers for Disease Control and Prevention, Department of Health and Human Services, 2006).

Pandemic viruses develop when a sudden change occurs in influenza A viruses. New combinations of proteins on the surface of the virus cause the changes. To cause a pandemic, the new virus must have the capacity to spread easily from person to person.

The CDC and the World Health Organization (WHO) have extensive surveillance programs to monitor and detect influenza activity worldwide. The CDC is involved in preparedness activities through vaccine development and production, stockpiling of medications, research, risk communications, and unified initiatives with other organizations.

A vaccine is unlikely to be available in the early stages of a pandemic. Scientists must select the virus strain that will provide the best protection. Then, manufacturers use the strain to produce a vaccine. Antiviral medications are available, but they may not work because virus strains can become resistance to the medications.

According to the CDC, the severity of the next influenza pandemic cannot be predicted. Modeling studies suggest that the impact could be substantial. Between 15 and 35% of the U.S. population could be affected and the economic impact could range between $71 and $166 billion (Centers for Disease Control and Prevention, Department of Health and Human Services, 2006).

Pandemics present numerous issues relevant to homeland security and emergency management. A pandemic is likely to last longer than most emergencies and may include "waves" separated by months. The number of health-care workers and first responders available to work may be reduced because of exposure and the need to care for ill family members. Also, resources, vaccines, and medications in many locations could be limited (Centers for Disease Control and Prevention, Department of Health and Human Services, 2006).

During a pandemic, people who have had contact with symptomatic persons may be asked to voluntarily quarantine themselves. Those with and without symptoms may wear face masks to control the spread of disease. Government may decide to close schools and other locations of mass gatherings. If a pandemic is particularly lethal, health-care workers would implement corpse-management procedures to safely destroy infected human remains, and government would apply emergency powers to enforce measures such as rationing and curfews (Tucker, 2006).

A serious pandemic can result in **quarantine enforcement**. It is the use of government authorities, such as police, health-care specialists, or the military, to restrict the movement of people, by force, if necessary, for purposes of public health and safety. Quarantine enforcement can create controversy over protection of public health versus civil liberties.

SECOND RESPONDERS

At the site of an emergency, once first responders perform their duties, second responders may be contacted for assistance. **Second responders** restore normalcy and vital services to a community following first responder action and include a variety of government agencies, volunteer groups, and public works and utility specialists. Generally, second responders do not respond to emergencies as quickly as local police, fire, and EMS. Initially, the site of the emergency may be too dangerous for second responders. Later, when the site is less dangerous, first and second responders can coordinate their work.

Second responders, such as volunteer groups, including the American Red Cross and Salvation Army, provide basic needs (e.g., food, water) during an emergency. Government (e.g., state emergency management, FEMA) also provides aid as quickly as possible.

Serious disasters can destroy infrastructure within communities. This includes drinking water systems, utilities, roads, transportation systems, and government buildings. Citizens want normalcy. They want housing, food, water, electricity, and so forth. They want to see businesses reopen and their children going to school. Second responders play a major role in *recovery*.

Following a disaster, emergency management (Chapter 7) coordinates response and recovery and accesses need. Government public works and sanitation departments use heavy equipment and trucks to remove debris. Local water and wastewater treatment departments work to restore these services. The restoration of roads and transportation systems are also an important priority. Utility companies work to restore services (e.g., electricity, gas, telephone, and Internet service).

In the NRP (U.S. Department of Homeland Security, 2004), the Emergency Support Function, Public Works and Engineering Annex lists two primary agencies, the DOD/U.S. Army Corps of Engineers and the DHS/Emergency Preparedness and Response/FEMA, plus 10 U.S. departments, other agencies, and the American Red Cross. The major purposes of these organizations are to deliver technical and engineering expertise, construction management, and other support to prevent, prepare for, respond to, and recover from an incident of national significance. Additional action includes pre- and postincident assessments of infrastructure, executing emergency contracts for life-saving and life-sustaining services, and providing emergency repair of infrastructure. This annex states: *"State, local, and tribal governments are responsible for their own public works and infrastructures and have the primary responsibility for incident prevention, preparedness, response, and recovery." ..."The private sector is a partner and/or lead for the rapid restoration of infrastructure-related services."*

RESPONSE TO WEAPONS OF MASS DESTRUCTION

WMD are explained in Chapter 2 and earlier in this chapter. Here the emphasis is on action by first responders and the federal government.

RESPONDING TO A CHEMICAL ATTACK

The U.S. Department of Homeland Security, Office for Domestic Preparedness (2004) distributed a video on guidelines for first responders facing WMD incidents. A summary of this program, that emphasizes a chemical attack, follows.

A WMD attack has the potential to incapacitate first responders by direct or secondary contact (e.g., contaminated victims). The scene must be controlled and large numbers of victims may require decontamination. In the Tokyo sarin attack, some first responders and hospital staff were contaminated by victims' clothing, shoes, and skin. *It is important to remember that responders cannot help others if they become victims themselves.*

STEPS FOR FIRST RESPONDERS

Recognize the danger. Pay close attention to the dispatcher's report, e.g., multiple victims leaving a building, falling to the ground, coughing, and complaining of dizziness. Upon approaching the scene, be aware of wind direction, weather conditions, type of building, occupancy, and number of victims. The victims of a chemical attack may experience SLUDGE: salivation, lacrimation (tearing), urination, defecation, gastrointestinal distress, and emesis (vomiting).

Protect yourself. Do not rush into an area if you see multiple people down. You may become part of the problem. Warn others about the situation and report the facts and dangers. Be aware that a secondary explosion or sniper may be next. Emergency vehicles should be at least 300 feet away from the victims or dangerous area. Anyone entering the "hot zone" should wear the highest level of protection (i.e., vapor-tight, fully encapsulated suit with self-contained breathing apparatus).

Control the scene. Access controls should be maintained at 360° around the scene and only authorized, properly trained and equipped personnel should be admitted. When HAZMAT personnel arrive, they will identify the "hot zones" based on readings from detection equipment. Public address systems can keep victims informed on procedures while responders maintain safe distances. At the same time, remember to preserve evidence, as the incident location is also a crime scene.

Rescue and decontaminate the victims. As soon as possible, victims should be brought to a shower area that can be established with fire trucks and related equipment. The outer layer of clothing should be removed and the victims should be flushed and then covered. Up to 80% of contaminants can be removed by taking off the outer layer of clothing. Kits are available that permit privacy curtains for the decontamination corridor. Runoff of the water should be controlled. Further decontamination may be necessary prior to sending patients to hospitals and triage areas.

Call for additional help. Establish a command post 700 to 2000 feet away to coordinate operations. Ensure that space is available to expand the command post as other agencies respond. A variety of agencies may respond, such as more local units, state units, FEMA, the FBI, public health, and the DOD.

RESPONDING TO A BIOLOGICAL ATTACK

Bioterrorism is difficult to detect. Indications of an attack are likely to surface when victims visit hospitals and a trend is discovered through centralized reporting to local and state health agencies. The CDC, as covered earlier, is the agency that monitors public health threats. At hospitals, victims would be treated. The federal government has a "rapid response team" of medical personnel who have been vaccinated from a variety of biological threats and can enter infected locales. Vaccines do not exist for all biological threats. During an outbreak, an area (e.g., city) may require quarantine, backed by the military.

RESPONDING TO A RADIATION ATTACK

The Council on Foreign Relations (2004c) and the Central Intelligence Agency (1998) offer the following information on responding to radiation attacks.

- Specialized equipment is required to determine the size of the effected area and if the level of radioactivity presents long-term hazards. Radiological materials are not recognized by senses and are colorless and odorless.
- To reduce exposure to radiation, victims would need to be decontaminated by removing irradiated clothing, washing the body, and purging inhaled or ingested materials. These methods do not protect against "penetrating radiation" (e.g., gamma rays or neutrons).
- People endangered by "penetrating radiation" should go as far as possible from the source and maximize the amount of shielding between themselves and the source.
- Potassium iodide is recommended to prevent medical problems and cancer of the thyroid gland, but it offers no protection against other types of radiation problems.
- The onset of symptoms requires days to weeks.
- The incident area would require evacuation and decontamination to remove radioactive material and to keep radioactive dust from spreading. Contaminated buildings, roads, and soil may have to be removed.
- Many communities have neglected plans for a radiation attack since the Cold War ended. Since the 9/11 attacks, first responders have improved their response capabilities that vary.
- The federal response would come from several departments, namely the Departments of Homeland Security, Energy, and Defense. Federal agencies responding would include the FBI and EPA.

RESPONDING TO A NUCLEAR ATTACK

Although a nuclear weapon is difficult to construct, deliver, and detonate, worst-case scenarios must be considered. Depending on the type of bomb, casualties could be enormous, along with an awful impact on physical and mental health, the economy, and society. If a warning occurs, people should take shelter in basements and subways, unless time is available for an evacuation of the area to several miles away.

First responders must be properly trained and equipped to perform their duties following a nuclear explosion. Enormous numbers of victims would need treatment and hospitals may be destroyed. Medical problems would include thermal radiation burns, wounds, fractures, and infection. Potassium iodide is recommended. The radioactive fallout from the blast requires people to be decontaminated. Refer to the "radiation attack" discussion given earlier for additional information applicable to nuclear attack.

DISCUSSION QUESTIONS

1. Refer to the stories of the 9/11 attacks at the beginning of this chapter. What are your views on the ways in which the people in the stories responded to the emergency situation?
2. In what ways are life safety and public safety linked together?
3. What are the purposes of regulations and standards?
4. What do you think are the five most important building designs for life safety?
5. What do you think are the five most important steps occupants of a building can take to promote life safety?

6. How can public safety agencies enhance their effectiveness when preparing for and responding to WMD attacks or other all-hazard emergencies?
7. How can the medical system enhance its effectiveness when preparing for and responding to WMD attacks or other all-hazard emergencies?
8. Why are second responders important?
9. What do you think government, the private sector, and citizens need to do to improve preparation for and response to WMD attacks or other all-hazard emergencies?

APPLICATIONS

8A YOU BE THE DESIGNER OF LIFE SAFETY

You are the lead designer of life safety for a planned 100-story high-rise office building. It will house a variety of tenants, some of which may attract terrorists. Your aim is to prepare life safety for all hazards. Prioritize a list of 10 life safety strategies to protect occupants. Justify why you placed each of the top 3 at the beginning of your list.

8B YOU BE THE FIRE COMMANDER

Upon arriving at the scene of a fire at a multistory office building, you notice that the people escaping are coughing and some are falling to the ground and gasping for air. You smell an unusual odor, you begin coughing, and your eyes are burning. Other first responders are having similar problems as they assist the injured. What do you do?

8C YOU BE THE INCIDENT COMMANDER

As an incident commander at the site of a bombing, you have just been informed that a secondary device was located near where police, firefighters, and EMS personnel are struggling to care for about 200 injured victims. Many victims are crying or screaming for help and they are unable to move. Responders are overwhelmed and assistance from other jurisdictions will not arrive soon. What do you do?

8D YOU BE THE TERRORIST CELL LEADER

You are the leader of a terrorist cell of U.S. citizens in a large city in the United States. The city contains many symbolic targets, including many government and commercial buildings and tourist attractions. However, the city maintains an aggressive police force that has initiated numerous counterterrorism strategies. Two of your cell operatives are city police officers, but they are not yet assigned to counterterrorism units. Another operative is with the city fire service and another is working with EMS. Your cell has collected intelligence as specified in the subsequent list. With this intelligence in mind, what target do you select in this typical American city and what weapon of attack do you employ? Which five methods in the list influenced your planning decisions the most and why?

- City police coordinate emergency management with other city first responders, and all responders are trained and equipped to confront WMD.
- The city first responders coordinate emergency management with state and federal authorities.
- City police work with state and federal police on training, investigations, intelligence, and other law enforcement activities.
- City police maintain contact with a wide variety of infrastructure sectors (e.g., water, transportation, energy, and chemical) for investigations, intelligence, prevention, and emergency management.
- City police conduct counterterrorism training for a wide variety of public and private sector employees, including the following: private security officers; building employees; utility employees; bus, taxi, truck, and other transportation workers; school employees; and employees of houses of worship.
- The city maintains an extensive CCTV system on public streets.
- At unpredictable times, the city police deploy heavily armed antiterrorism units throughout the city at government and commercial buildings, tourist attractions, transportation hubs, ports, bridges, tunnels, cultural events, houses of worship, schools, and hospitals.
- City police maintain an intelligence division that performs several functions, including gathering intelligence, maintaining contact with other law enforcement agencies, and studying global events.

- Wiretapping and electronic surveillance are conducted by numerous police investigative units.
- Undercover operations are extensive, including the penetration of Mosques, bogus utility work, and use of bogus neighborhood retail stores (operated by undercover police of Middle East heritage) in Muslim communities and near Mosques.
- Interviewing and surveillance target businesses selling dual-use items.
- The informant system developed by city police is extensive and the budget for informants is large to pay for information and even informant bills. Also, certain crimes are ignored in exchange for information.
- A large budget is maintained for reward money for information from the public on crime and terrorism.

8E   YOU BE THE DIRECTOR OF THE STRATEGIC NATIONAL STOCKPILE

As director of the strategic national stockpile, the national repository of medicines and related supplies, you are faced with a difficult decision. Citizens of five cities have been exposed to anthrax by terrorists. The disease is spreading rapidly and the five cities have been quarantined. Antibiotics are available for only 2,000,000 people and each city has a population of about 1,000,000. What is your plan for distributing the antibiotics? What criteria do you use to make your decisions?

WEB SITES

American Hospital Association: www.hospitalconnect.com
Building Owners & Managers Association: www.boma.org
Centers for Disease Control and Prevention: www.cdc.gov
Center for State Homeland Security: www.cshs-us.org
Federal Emergency Management Agency: www.fema.gov
Homeland Security Standards Database: http://www.hssd.us/
International Association of Chiefs of Police: www.theiacp.org
International Association of Fire Chiefs: www.iafc.org
International Code Council: www.iccsafe.org
International Facility Management Association: www.ifma.org
National Association of Emergency Medical Technicians: www.naemt.org
National Fire Protection Association: www.nfpa.org
National Governors Association's Center for Best Practices: www.nga.org/center
National League of Cities: www.nlc.org
Occupational Safety and Health Administration: www.osha.gov
Police Executive Research Forum: www.policeforum.org
U.S. Conference of Mayors: www.usmayors.org
U.S. Department of Defense: www.defenselink.nil
U.S. Department of Health and Human Services: www.hhs.gov
U.S. Department of Homeland Security: www.dhs.gov
U.S. Department of Justice, Office of Community Oriented Policing Services:
   www.cops.usdoj.gov

NOTES

Angle, J. (2005). Occupational Safety and Health in the Emergency Services, 2nd ed. Clifton Park, NY: Thomas Delmar.
Archibald, R., *et al.* (2002). *Security and Safety in Los Angeles High-Rise Buildings After 9/11*. Santa Monica, CA: RAND Corp.
Azano, H., and Gilbertie, M. (2003). "Making Planning a Priority." *Security Management* (May).
Azoulay, O. (2006). "Proactive Security in the World of Terrorism." *Disaster Recovery Journal*, 19 (Winter).
Becker, R. (2005). *Criminal Investigation*, 2nd ed. Sudbury, MA: Jones and Bartlett.
Bureau of Justice Statistics (2003). *Law Enforcement Statistics*. www.ojp.usdoj.gov.
Carter, W., *et al.* (2004). *Firefighter's Handbook: Essentials of Firefighting and Emergency Response*, 2nd ed. Clifton Park, NY: Thomas Delmar.
Casey, J. (2004). "Managing Joint Terrorism Task Force Resources." *FBI Law Enforcement Bulletin*, 73 (November).
Cauchon, D., *et al.* (2003). "Just-released transcripts give voice to the horror." *USA TODAY* (August 28). www.usatoday.com, retrieved August 29, 2003.

Centers for Disease Control and Prevention, Department of Health and Human Services (2006). "Key Facts about Pandemic Influenza." www.cdc.gov/flu/pandemic/keyfacts.htm, retrieved January 24, 2006.

Central Intelligence Agency (1998). *Chemical/Biological/Radiological Incident Handbook* (October). www.fas.org, retrieved June 4, 2004.

Cohen, J. (2003). "Radio System Interoperability." *Security Products* (October).

Coleman, J. (1986). *Practical Knowledge for a Private Security Officer*. Springfield, IL: Charles C Thomas.

Corley, W. (2004). "A Call for Balanced Fire Protection." *Buildings*, 98 (June).

Council on Foreign Relations (2004a). "Police Departments." www.terrorismanswers.org, retrieved September 30, 2004.

Council on Foreign Relations (2004b). "Hospital Emergency Rooms." www.terrorismanswers.org, retrieved October 6, 2004.

Council on Foreign Relations (2004c). "Responding to Radiation Attacks." www.terrorismanswers.org, retrieved October 6, 2004.

De Guzman, M. (2002). "The Changing Roles and Strategies of the Police in a Time of Terror" (February 15). Speech at Indiana University South Bend. www.dushkin.com, retrieved December 17, 2003.

Dempsey, J., and Forst, L. (2005). *An Introduction to Policing*. Belmont, CA: Thomson Wadsworth.

Dyson, W. (2005). *Terrorism: An Investigator's Handbook*. www.lexisnexis.com/anderson

Elliott, T. (2004). "Practical Advice for Tactical Triage." *Homeland Protection Professional*, 3 (September).

Emergency Response & Research Institute (1991). "Fire Violations Kill Twenty-Five in Chicken Plant." www.emergency.com/nc-five.htm, retrieved April 8, 2005.

Fried, G. (2004a). "Ask the Expert." *Public Venue Security* (March/April).

Fried, G. (2004b). "Ask the Expert." *Public Venue Security* (May/June).

Gips, M. (2005). "The Challenge of Making Safer Structures." *Security Management* 49 (March).

Houghton, B., and Schachter, J. (2005). "Coordinated Terrorist Attacks: Implications for Local Responders." *FBI Law Enforcement Bulletin*, 74 (May).

Houser, A., *et al.* (2004). *Emergency Responder Injuries and Fatalities*. Santa Monica, CA: RAND Corp.

International Code Council (2004). "Resources Top Building Official Concerns." *Building Safety Bulletin*, II (July).

Jensen, R. (2005). "Welcome! OSHA Joins Security." *Security Products*, 9 (February).

Marghella, P. (2004). "Red Sky At Dawn ..." *Homeland Defense Journal*, 2 (October).

Mason, M. (2005). "No Cure In Sight." *Homeland Security* 2 (March/April).

Mathews, J. (2004). "A Tale of 2 Fire Departments." *Homeland Security* (March).

McIntire, M., and O'Donnell, M. (2005). "Fire Chief Challenges New York Emergency Plan." *The New York Times* (May 10). www.nytimes.com/2005/05/10/nyregion, retrieved May 10, 2005.

Moore, W. (1997). "Building Life Safety and Security Needs." *Security Technology and Design* (January–February).

Nance, M. (2003). *The Terrorist Recognition Handbook*. Guilford, CT: Lyons Press.

National Commission on Terrorist Attacks Upon the United States (2004). *The 9/11 Commission Report*. www.9-11commission.gov/, retrieved July 26, 2004.

National Institute of Standards and Technology (2005). "Latest Findings from NIST World Trade Center Investigation." www.nist.gov, retrieved April 8, 2005.

New York City Police Department (2003). "Operation Atlas." www.nyc.gov/html/nypd/html/atlas.html, retrieved April 18, 2005.

Office of Homeland Security (2002). *National Strategy for Homeland Security* (July). www.whitehouse.gov, retrieved September 14, 2004.

Police Executive Research Forum (2003–2004). *Protecting Your Community from Terrorism: Strategies for Local Law Enforcement Series*. Washington, DC: PERF.

Purpura, P. (2001). *Police and Community: Concepts and Cases*. Boston, MA: Allyn & Bacon.

Purpura, P. (2002). *Security and Loss Prevention: An Introduction*, 4th ed. Boston, MA: Butterworth-Heinemann.

Quinley, K., and Schmidt, D. (2002). *Businesses at Risk: How to Assess, Mitigate, and Respond to Terrorist Threats*. Cincinnati, OH: The National Underwritten Co.

Scheider, M., Chapman, E., and Seelman, M. (n.d.). "Connecting the Dots for a Proactive Approach." www.cops.usdoj.gov, retrieved February 2, 2004.

Shusta, R., *et al.* (2005). *Multicultural Law Enforcement: Strategies for Peacekeeping in a Diverse Society*, 3rd Ed. Upper Saddle River, NJ: Pearson Prentice Hall.

Sweeney, E. (2005). "The Patrol Officer: America's Intelligence on the Ground." *FBI Law Enforcement Bulletin*, 74 (September).

Swope, C. (2004). "Emergency Repair: Louisville to let EMS stand on its own." *Governing*, 18 (October).

Swope, C. (2006). "The Code War." *Governing*, 19 (January).

Tech Talk (2004). "Responders, Private Sector Incommunicado." *Security Management*, 48 (October).

Tucker, P. (2006). "Preparing for Pandemic." *The Futurist* (January–February).

U.S. Department of Homeland Security (n.d.). "About First Responders." www.dhs.gov/dhspublic, retrieved February 11, 2005.

U.S. Department of Homeland Security (2004). *National Response Plan.* www.dhs.gov, retrieved January 12, 2005.

U.S. Department of Homeland Security and FBI (n.d.). "Vigilance: Patrolling in the New Era of Terrorism." Brochure.

U.S. Department of Homeland Security, Office for Domestic Preparedness (2004). *Weapons of Mass Destruction and the First Responder* (video) (January).

U.S. Department of Homeland Security, READYBusiness (n.d.). Testimonials. www.ready.gov/business/testimonials.html, retrieved January 3, 2005.

U.S. Fire Administration (2004). "Danger Above: A Factsheet on High-Rise Safety" (November 23). http://usfa.fema.gov/safety/atrisk/high-rise/high-rise.shtm, retrieved April 4, 2005.

Weiss, A. (2004). "Four Key Concerns for Law Enforcement." *Homeland Protection Professional*, 3 (November/December).

9

SECURITY

OBJECTIVES

The study of this chapter will enable you to:

1. Explain the role of security in relation to the problem of terrorism.
2. Define security and loss prevention.
3. Describe how security programs meet organizational and customer needs.
4. Discuss how risk analysis, metrics, and critical thinking support security programs.
5. List and define the five "Ds" of security.
6. List and explain at least 10 methods to mitigate terrorist attacks against buildings.
7. List and explain at least 10 security strategies to protect people and assets.

KEY TERMS

security	lifestyle perspectives
loss prevention	hostile surveillance
state-mandated training	stand-off distance
site-specific training	keep out zones
value added	perimeter
marketing	barrier systems
risk analysis	blast and antiramming walls
risk assessment	crime displacement
target-rich environment	access controls
traffic calming strategies	contraband
crime prevention through environmental design	biometric security systems
situational crime prevention	The Americans with Disabilities Act of 1990
rational choice theory	intrusion detection system
routine activities theory	

INTERNAL THREATS

Although the present chapter emphasizes security strategies to protect against external threats, internal threats can be equally devastating to an organization. Security strategies and target hardening may become so formidable at a facility that an outside adversary may decide to seek another target or attack from within by, for example, seeking employment at the target or offering something of value to an employee.

The U.S. Department of Homeland Security, Science and Technology Directorate and the Executive Office of the President, Office of Science and Technology Policy (2004: 42) warned that the greatest threats to critical infrastructure (e.g., food, water, electricity) are from the insider who performs actions that could destroy or degrade systems and services. Insider threats develop from individuals who have authorization to access information and infrastructure resources. These threats are difficult to guard against because the offenders are on the inside and trusted. They exploit vulnerabilities and have advantages over outsiders in choosing the time, place, and method of attack.

Both public and private sectors are prone to insider threats. For instance, in 2001, Robert Hanssen, a 25-year FBI veteran who worked in counterintelligence, was charged with spying for the former Soviet Union, and then Russia, for 15 years in exchange for $1.4 million in cash and diamonds. He was convicted and sentenced to life in prison without parole. In 1994, CIA counterintelligence officer Aldrich Ames was also sentenced to life in prison without parole after he admitted selling secrets to the Soviets in exchange for $2.5 million.

The private sector (i.e., businesses) is plagued by corporate spying and internal theft and fraud. As with government, the private sector is also faced with internal and external threats to its information systems. In one example of an internal threat, a systems administrator in a hospital learned that she was about to be fired so she arranged for a "severance package" for herself by encrypting a critical patient database. Her supervisor feared the worst and loss of his job, so in exchange for the decryption key, the manager arranged for a termination "bonus" and an agreement that the hospital would not prosecute (Purpura, 2002: 142; Shaw et al., 2000: 62). Although several issues evolve from this case (e.g., isolating a soon-to-be terminated employee from information technology; not leaking that she was to be fired; prosecution), the point is that internal threats can be very harmful to organizations.

Numerous measures can be taken to protect an organization from internal threats. Examples are employment applicant screening, policy and procedural controls, access controls, physical security technology, auditing, investigations, and prosecution (Purpura, 2002: 143–185).

The U.S. Department of Homeland Security, Science and Technology Directorate and the Executive Office of the President, Office of Science and Technology Policy (2004: 42–44) offers research directions for protection against insider threats.

- *Intent detection:* This involves examining combinations of observations, actions, relationships, and past history to sense possible offending behavior. Various methods are used to support this approach, including surveillance, cataloging, pattern recognition, and computational analysis. These methods are applicable to the physical and cyber domains.
- *Detection and monitoring:* Detection should draw attention to early recognition of a pattern of action that is erratic or outside of the norm. Computer models are necessary to distinguish between random behavior and behavior indicative of a possible internal threat. Then, computer systems must monitor the possible problem.
- *Protection and prevention:* This includes security measures that are overt or covert. Examples are incremental access, job-specific access controls, and repetitive checking. These measures and others require research to build solutions to internal threats.

SECURITY AND TERRORISM

Security is not *the* answer to the problem of terrorism. The spectrum of government responses to terrorism (Chapter 3) shows that security (under homeland security) is one of many options available to government to thwart terrorism. Security programs are commonly in place at businesses, institutions, government buildings, and other entities to protect people and assets from a host of risks, besides terrorism. When the threat of terrorism surfaces or other hazards occurs, security programs are enhanced through greater vigilance, additional personnel, and tighter access controls, among other strategies.

In addition to the financial costs of security, it also costs in terms of restrictions on freedom of movement and privacy. Depending on the location, people may be required to park away from buildings and walk, wait in line at entrances to be searched along with their personal possessions, subject to surveillance, and be temporarily detained for questioning. Security practitioners are challenged to not only thwart terrorists and other criminals, but to do so while upholding democratic values (see Chapter 5).

The private security industry and its relationship to the *National Strategy for Homeland Security* were explained in Chapter 6. This chapter focuses on specific security strategies to protect people and assets. Three major types of security strategies are security personnel, policies and procedures, and physical security.

SECURITY DEFINED

Within our organized society, security is provided primarily by armed forces, public safety agencies, and private security. The methods of private security have increased in terms of specialization and diversification. Methods not previously associated with security have emerged and become important components of the total security effort. Security officers, fences, and alarms have been the hallmark of traditional security functions. Today, with society becoming increasingly complex and with numerous risks facing organizations, additional specializations have been added to the security function. Examples include investigations, risk analysis, information technology (IT) security, crisis management, executive protection, fraud auditing, terrorism countermeasures, and fire protection, among many other specializations. Entities differ on how they organize the security function, the personnel involved, their specializations, and to whom they report. Because of the increase in diverse specializations within the security function, many businesses and security practitioners favor a broader term for all of these functions, known as loss prevention. Another reason why organizations may shift their terminology from "security" to "loss prevention" involves the negative connotations that may be linked to security. The word "security" can suggest restrictions on people's movement, uniformed officers, badges, arrests, alarms, criminals, and other terms that may have negative connotations. "Loss prevention" presents a softer image and it is believed that it enhances cooperation from others. Although there has been a clamor for increased "security" since the 9/11 attacks, and what appears as a world filled with increasingly serious risks, many organizations continue to retain the term "loss prevention" because they face many risks other than terrorism (see Chapter 6 for business security executives who have many concerns, besides terrorism). Consequently, management in each organization selects the term that meets their needs.

Security is narrowly defined as traditional methods (security officers, fences, alarms) used to increase the likelihood of a crime-controlled, tranquil, and uninterrupted environment. **Loss prevention** is broadly defined as almost any method (e.g., security officers, fraud auditing, safety, fire protection) used to increase the likelihood of preventing and controlling loss (e.g., people, money, productivity, materials) resulting from a host of risks (e.g., crime, fire, accident, error, poor supervision or management, and bad investment). Loss prevention is interdisciplinary and looks to many fields of study (e.g., security, law, criminal justice, business, safety, fire science, emergency management, sociology, and psychology) for answers to protection problems. This broad definition provides a foundation for the loss prevention practitioner whose innovations are limited only by his or her imagination (Purpura, 2002: 7).

Security is narrowly defined; *loss prevention* is broadly defined.

Employment titles for those individuals who perform security and loss prevention duties vary widely among organizations. The titles include vice president, director, or manager of security, corporate security, loss prevention, or assets protection.

Another title receiving attention is the chief security officer (CSO). The *Chief Security Officer Guideline* (ASIS, International, 2004) is designed "… as a model for organizations to utilize in the development of a leadership function to provide a comprehensive, integrated security risk strategy to contribute to the viability and success of the organization." This guideline is a response to an increasingly serious threat environment and it recommends that the CSO report to the most senior level executive of the organization. The guideline lists specific risks, job duties and services, and skills required. The CSO designation and the guideline supporting it provide an excellent reference from which the security profession and senior management can draw on to improve the protection of people and assets and help organizations survive in a world filled with risks.

The U.S. Government Accountability Office (2005: 43–44), in highlighting the ASIS, International, *Chief Security Officer Guideline*, wrote: "Having a chief security officer position for physical assets is recognized in the security industry as essential in organizations with large numbers of mission-critical facilities."

CSO (2004) explains that the CSO title originated from those individuals whose employment duties focused on IT security. The title has also been applied to physical security and the safety of employees and assets, while being separated from IT security.

At the same time, security technology is increasingly database driven and network delivered, thereby producing a convergence of physical security and IT security. Thus, certain organizations combine these two functions under the title CSO.

Harowitz (2005: 42–51) notes that the CSO designation has not produced a rapid change in the titles of security practitioners. Among 4000 U.S. ASIS, International members who responded to a 2004 salary survey by that organization, only 6 were CSOs. However, research conducted by Eastern Kentucky University, with funding from ASIS, International and the National Institute of Justice, found that 25% of ASIS members and 5% of all U.S. companies used the CSO designation (Collins et al., 2005: 23). Research should be expanded to other related professional associations and vocations, such as information technology, especially in light of the merging of IT security and physical security in many organizations.

THE SECURITY PROFESSION

Several groups promote professionalism in the security field. Two noteworthy security groups covered earlier in this book follow.

ASIS, International is the leading general organization of protection executives and specialists. It serves members globally. Its monthly magazine, *Security Management*, is an excellent resource. This group offers numerous educational opportunities and three certification programs.

The International Foundation for Protection Officers (IFPO) is the leading organization working to professionalize security officers. It publishes *The Protection Officer* magazine and offers the certified protection officer program, among other certification programs.

SECURITY TO MEET ORGANIZATIONAL NEEDS

We read in Chapter 6 that 85% of the nation's critical infrastructure is owned by the private sector. Companies, institutions, and a variety of organizations establish security programs and these programs have similarities and differences.

Similarities include the goal of protecting people and assets; internal sources of risk (e.g., employee theft and substance abuse); external sources of risk (e.g., robbery, burglary, shoplifting, and computer virus); and the integration of security in programs (e.g., life safety) that protect against all hazards. A clear-cut division between internal and external sources of risk and countermeasures is not possible because certain risks may be from both internal and external sources, and certain security countermeasures may protect against both internal and external sources of risk. For instance, violence in the workplace can result from an internal source of risk (e.g., one employee assaulting another) or an external source of risk (e.g., robbery on the premises). Security officers and CCTV, for example, protect against both. Furthermore, an entity can face both internal and external sources of risk at the same time. An employee and an outsider may conspire to steal proprietary information from a company or commit a terrorist act. Despite the overlap, certain risks are primarily from internal sources (e.g., employee theft and substance abuse) or external sources (e.g., robbery, burglary, shoplifting, and computer virus).

Differences among security programs result from the unique needs of a particular organization. A nuclear plant faces risks different than a retail store, and security strategies differ. A major goal of the security practitioner is to meet the needs of the organization. This includes ensuring that security strategies are coordinated with business objectives. The strict access controls and redundant perimeter security of a nuclear plant would hinder business at a retail store that requires a steady flow of customers who feel comfortable walking in and making purchases. Training is a reflection of the differences among security programs. The U.S. Nuclear Regulatory Commission requires an armed response force at a nuclear plant. The security personnel must be trained and proficient in the use of a variety of firearms to counter an adversary and protect the facility. Security and loss prevention training in a retail environment concentrate on the problems of employee theft and shoplifting; firearms training is atypical.

Differences in security training are also seen when **state-mandated training** (i.e., required by law or regulations) ends and an organization begins **site-specific training**. Here again, the unique needs of the organization surface. A facility with a high risk of fire will likely incorporate fire prevention and fire suppression topics and competencies into training for security personnel to meet the specific needs of the site.

CUSTOMER SERVICE AND NEEDS

Another aspect of security programs in both private and public sectors is customer service. A security program will have problems surviving if it does not satisfy customer needs. The tolerance of an organization not receiving quality customer service from a security program will vary. In the contract security business, for example, these service companies usually place a high priority on customer service to increase the chances for contract renewal and to market themselves to potential clients. Security managers in either contract or proprietary (in-house) security programs should ascertain specific needs of customers. This can be done through interviews or surveys of customers. Examples of customer service are ensuring that security officers are on post as scheduled; officers are courteous; and as the organization changes, the security program is flexible to meet changing needs. Like well-managed companies, security programs should be customer driven through constant contact with customers who provide feedback and direction. Customers should be made aware that they are receiving value from the services provided. Corporations often use the term **value added**. It means that all corporate departments must prove their value to the business by translating expenditures into bottom-line impact. Security departments must go beyond preparing a report of security accomplishments. For example, include in the report that the hiring of a bad check specialist recovered several times his or her salary, that the expenditures for workers' compensation fraud investigations saved hundreds of thousands of dollars, or that an investment in security technology saved on personnel costs.

Marketing is a discipline that can enhance security programs. It consists of researching a target market and the needs of customers and developing products and services to secure a profit. The concepts of marketing can be applied to many types of organizations. Market segmentation divides a market into specific groups of consumers. Target marketing chooses a market segment for a specific product or service. To illustrate the applicability to security, suppose a security executive divides employees of a corporation into distinct groups based on their security needs. These groups are executives, women, production employees, sales representatives, and truck drivers. Once the market is segmented, security training can be implemented for each group. Research and a risk analysis can pinpoint needs. Executives can be trained on self-protection at home and abroad and receive information on security and safety from the U.S. Department of State (see the nearby box). The other groups can also receive training on self-protection, plus other needs they specify. Women may request special training on self-protection as a female head of household. Production employees may be concerned about how to protect their tools. Sales representatives may request self-protection information while traveling. Truck drivers may seek information on antihijacking methods. The key is to meet customer needs (Purpura, 2002: 94–95).

PROTECTING INTERESTS ABROAD

Although the 9/11 attacks showed the vulnerabilities of the United States in the homeland, people and facilities abroad are much more susceptible to terrorists. As homeland security increases, this differentiation increases (Radford, 2004: 68–72).

As covered earlier in this book, globalization and "U.S. imperialism" have been at the foundation of tensions worldwide. Radford notes that the bigger the brand name and the more closely the brand is connected to the United States, the more attractive the business is to terrorists. Strikes against symbolic U.S. targets abroad are in line with terrorist goals of driving foreign businesses away from indigenous cultures and religions. Also, the attacks are not only centered in the Middle East. For example, Reuters News Service (2005) reported that Buenos Aires police found bombs at outlets of three different U.S.-based companies—McDonald's, Blockbuster, and Citibank. Pamphlets at the sites, by the "Mariano Moreno National Liberation Commando," stated: "our aim is to liberate Argentina from imperialism."

In addition to hardening targets (the main thrust of this chapter), an all-hazards or holistic approach should be used to protect U.S. citizens abroad. Radford recommends pretravel training and preparation, support while deployed, and capability to respond to a crisis (e.g., security or medical). Prior to traveling, an analysis of risks of the destination is important, as well as supplying the traveler with comprehensive information on the destination (e.g., vaccinations, medical services, culture, crime rate, and terrorist threat). Once the traveler reaches the destination, various technologies can be used to track the traveler.

Radford emphasizes that a significant duty of care liability rests with corporations that send employees abroad. Thus, a comprehensive plan can promote safety and security, while reducing liability exposure.

THE U.S. DEPARTMENT OF STATE ISSUES INFORMATION SHEETS TO HELP PROTECT U.S. CITIZENS TRAVELING OVERSEAS

The U.S. Department of State Information Sheets cover entry/exit requirements, safety and security, information for victims of crime, medical facilities and health information, medical insurance, traffic safety and road conditions, aviation safety oversight, special circumstances, criminal penalties, children's issues, and registration/embassy location. The following information sheet is on Vietnam; however, several sources of information and suggestions apply to most countries.

From: U.S. Department of State Travel Warnings

Sent: Monday, May 09, 2005 2:39 PM

To: DOSTRAVEL@LISTS.STATE.GOV

Subject: Vietnam Consular Information Sheet

Vietnam Consular Information Sheet

May 09, 2005

Country Description

Vietnam is a developing, mainly agrarian country in the process of moving from a centrally planned to a market economy. Political control rests in the Communist Party. Tourist facilities are not well established, but are improving in certain areas, especially in Hanoi, Ho Chi Minh City, and some beach and mountain resorts. Read the Department of State Background Notes on Vietnam at http://www.state.gov/r/pa/ei/bgn/4130.htm for additional information.

Entry/Exit Requirements

A valid passport and Vietnamese visa are required. A visa must be obtained from a Vietnamese Embassy or Consulate before traveling to Vietnam; entry visas are not available upon arrival. Americans arriving without an appropriate Vietnamese visa will not be permitted to enter and will be subject to immediate deportation. Vietnamese visas are usually valid for only one entry. Persons planning to leave Vietnam and reenter from another country should be sure to obtain a visa allowing multiple entries. See our Foreign Entry Requirements brochure for more information on Vietnam and other countries. Visit the Embassy of Vietnam Web site at www.Vietnamembassy-usa.org for the most current visa information.

Even with a valid visa, some travelers have been refused entry to Vietnam. U.S. citizens are cautioned that Vietnamese immigration regulations require foreigners entering Vietnam to undertake only the activity for which their visas were issued. Change of purpose requires permission from the appropriate Vietnamese authority in advance. U.S. citizens whose stated purpose of travel was tourism but who engaged in religious proselytizing have had religious materials confiscated and have been expelled from Vietnam.

An American whose U.S. passport is lost or stolen in Vietnam must obtain both a replacement passport and a replacement visa. The U.S. Embassy and Consulate General can issue limited validity emergency replacement passports in as little as 1 day, but the Vietnamese government requires 3 working days, not to include the day of application, to issue a replacement visa. Neither the U.S. Embassy nor the Consulate General can expedite replacement Vietnamese visas.

Current information on visa and entry requirements may be obtained from the Vietnamese Embassy, 1233 20th Street NW, Suite 400, Washington, DC 20036, tel: 202-861-0737, fax: 202-861-0917, Internet: http://www.vietnamembassy-usa.org/; the Vietnamese Consulate General, 1700 California Street–Suite 430, San Francisco, CA 94109, tel: (415) 922-1707, fax: 415-922-1848, Internet: http://www.vietnamconsulate-sf.org/, or from the nearest Vietnamese Embassy or Consulate overseas.

Continued

THE U.S. DEPARTMENT OF STATE ISSUES INFORMATION SHEETS TO HELP PROTECT U.S. CITIZENS TRAVELING OVERSEAS — Cont'd

Read our information on dual nationality and the prevention of international child abduction at http://travel.state.gov/travel/cis_pa_tw/cis/cis_1469.html. For customs information see http://travel.state.gov/travel/cis_pa_tw/cis/cis_1468.html.

Safety and Security

In recent years, Vietnam's Central Highland provinces have been the scene of ethnic minority protests and clashes with security forces. Official U.S. personnel and tourists are sometimes not authorized to travel to the Central Highland areas without prior consent from the government of Vietnam. These travel limitations hinder the ability of the U.S. government to provide assistance to private U.S. citizens in those areas.

U.S. citizens have been detained after traveling in areas close to the Vietnamese borders with China, Cambodia, and Laos. These areas and other restricted areas are not always marked, and there are no warnings about prohibited travel. Travelers should avoid such areas unless written permission is obtained in advance from local authorities.

Large gatherings, such as those forming at the scene of traffic accidents, can become violent and should be avoided. For the latest security information, Americans traveling abroad should regularly monitor the Department's Internet Web site at http://travel.state.gov/ where the current Worldwide Caution Public Announcement, Travel Warnings, and Public Announcements can be found.

Up-to-date information on safety and security can also be obtained by calling 1-888-407-4747 toll free in the United States, or for callers outside the United States and Canada, a regular toll-line at 1-202-501-4444. These numbers are available from 8:00 AM to 8:00 PM eastern time, Monday through Friday (except U.S. federal holidays).

The Department of State urges American citizens to take responsibility for their own personal security while traveling overseas. For general information about appropriate measures travelers can take to protect themselves in an overseas environment, see the Department of State's pamphlet A Safe Trip Abroad at http://travel.state.gov/travel/tips/safety/safety_1747html.

Crime

Cities in Vietnam have the typical crime problems of many other large cities throughout the world. Pickpocketing and other petty crimes occur regularly. Although violent crimes such as armed robbery are still relatively rare in Vietnam, perpetrators have grown increasingly bold, and the U.S. Consulate General has received recent reports of knives and razors being used in attempted robberies in Ho Chi Minh City. Thieves congregate around hotels frequented by foreign tourists and business people, and assaults have been reported in outlying areas. The evolving nature of incidents warrants caution on the part of the U.S. traveler. Travelers are advised not to resist theft attempts and to report them both to police and to the U.S. Embassy in Hanoi or the U.S. Consulate in Ho Chi Minh City.

Motorcyclists, mostly carrying passengers, are known to grab bags, cameras, and other valuables from pedestrians or passengers riding in "cyclos" (pedicabs) or on the back of rented motorcycles. Serious injuries have resulted when thieves snatched purses or bags, which were strapped across their victims' bodies, leading to the victim being dragged along the ground by the thief's motorcycle. In November 2003, an American citizen victim of a drive-by purse snatching was dragged to the ground and seriously injured in this manner.

Passengers in cyclos (pedicabs) may be especially prone to thefts of personal possessions by snatch-and-grab thieves because they ride in a semireclining position that readily exposes their belongings and does not allow good visibility or movement. As some cyclo drivers have reportedly kidnapped passengers and extorted money, it may be risky to hire cyclos not associated with reputable hotels or restaurants.

THE U.S. DEPARTMENT OF STATE ISSUES INFORMATION SHEETS TO HELP PROTECT U.S. CITIZENS TRAVELING OVERSEAS — Cont'd

Travelers are strongly advised to keep passports and other important valuables in hotel safes or other secure locations. Travelers are advised to carry a photocopy of their passport with them when going out. The loss or theft abroad of a U.S. passport should be reported immediately to the local police and the U.S. Embassy or the U.S. Consulate General. U.S. citizens must obtain a police report from the local police office in order to apply for a replacement passport and a Vietnamese exit visa.

There have been occasional reports of incidents in which an unknown substance was used to taint drinks, leaving the victim susceptible to further criminal acts. Travelers are advised to avoid leaving drinks or food unattended and should avoid going to unfamiliar venues alone. Travelers should also avoid purchasing liquor from street vendors, as the quality of the contents cannot be assured.

Recreational drugs available in Vietnam can be extremely potent, and more than one American has died of an accidental overdose. Penalties for possession of drugs of any kind are severe (please refer to the Criminal Penalties section).

Some U.S. citizens have reported threats of death or physical injury related to personal business disputes. The U.S. Embassy and the U.S. Consulate General do not provide personal protection services. U.S. citizens who do not have confidence in the ability of the local police to protect them may wish to depart the country expeditiously.

Information for Victims of Crime

If you are the victim of a crime while overseas, in addition to reporting to local police, please contact the nearest U.S. Embassy or Consulate for assistance. The Embassy/Consulate staff can, for example, assist you to find appropriate medical care, contact family members or friends, and explain how funds could be transferred. Although the investigation and the prosecution of the crime are solely the responsibility of local authorities, consular officers can help you to understand the local criminal justice process and to find an attorney if needed. In Hanoi, the American Citizen Services (ACS) is located at Rose Garden Tower, #6 Ngoc Khanh, Hanoi. The telephone number is (84-4) 831-4590 Monday thru Friday and (84-4) 772-1500 after hours and weekends. In Ho Chi Minh City, ACS is located at U.S. Consular Section, 4 Le Duan St., Dist. 1, Ho Chi Minh City. Telephone number (84-8) 822-9433.

See our information on victims of crime at http://travel.state.gov/travel/tips/emergencies/emergencies_1748.html.

Medical Facilities and Health Information

Medical facilities in Vietnam do not meet international standards and frequently lack medicines and supplies. Medical personnel in Vietnam, particularly outside Hanoi and Ho Chi Minh City, may speak little or no English. Doctors and hospitals expect immediate cash payment for health services. International health clinics in Hanoi and Ho Chi Minh City can provide acceptable care for minor illnesses and injuries, but more serious problems will often require medical evacuation to Bangkok or Singapore. Although many medications can be purchased at pharmacies without prescriptions, many common U.S. medications are not available in Vietnam. Travelers may obtain lists of local English-speaking physicians from the U.S. Embassy in Hanoi or the U.S. Consulate General in Ho Chi Minh City. Travelers are reminded that neither office may recommend specific medical practitioners or hospitals. Emergency medical response services are generally unresponsive, unreliable, or completely unavailable.

Travelers should be cautious when drinking nonbottled water and in using ice cubes in drinks. Travelers may wish to drink only bottled or canned beverages, or beverages that have been boiled (such as hot tea and coffee).

Continued

THE U.S. DEPARTMENT OF STATE ISSUES INFORMATION SHEETS TO HELP PROTECT U.S. CITIZENS TRAVELING OVERSEAS—Cont'd

Travelers to Vietnam and other southeast Asian countries affected by avian influenza are cautioned to avoid poultry farms, contact with animals in live food markets, and any surfaces that appear to be contaminated with feces from poultry or other animals. See more information about avian flu at http://www.cdc.gov/flu/avian/index.htm.

Information on vaccinations and other health precautions, such as safe food and water precautions and insect bite protection, may be obtained from the Centers for Disease Control and Prevention's hot-line for international travelers at 1-877-FYI-TRIP (1-877-394-8747); fax 1-888-CDC-FAXX (1-888-232-3299), or via the CDC's Internet site at http://www.cdc.gov/travel. For information about outbreaks of infectious diseases abroad, consult the World Health Organization's (WHO) Web site at http://www.who.int/en. Further health information for travelers is available at http://www.who.int/ith.

Medical Insurance

The Department of State strongly urges Americans to consult with their medical insurance company prior to traveling abroad to confirm whether their policy applies overseas and whether it will cover emergency expenses such as a medical evacuation. Please see our information on medical insurance overseas at http://travel.state.gov/travel/cis_pa_tw/cis/cis_1470.html.

Traffic Safety and Road Conditions

While in a foreign country, U.S. citizens may encounter road conditions that differ significantly from those in the United States. The following information concerning Vietnam is provided for general reference only and may not be totally accurate in a particular location or circumstance.

Traffic in Vietnam is chaotic. Traffic accidents, mostly involving motorcycles and often resulting in traumatic head injury, are an increasingly serious hazard. At least 30 people die each day from transportation-related injuries. Traffic accident injuries are the leading cause of death and are the single greatest health risk that U.S. citizens will face in Vietnam.

Traffic moves on the right, although drivers frequently cross to the left to pass or turn, and motorcycles and bicycles often travel (illegally) against the flow of traffic. Horns are used constantly, often for no apparent reason. Streets in major cities are choked with motorcycles, cars, buses, trucks, bicycles, pedestrians, and cyclos. Outside the cities, livestock compete with vehicles for road space. Sudden stops by motorcycles and bicycles make driving a particular hazard. Nationwide, drivers do not follow basic traffic principles, vehicles do not yield right of way, and there is little adherence to traffic laws or enforcement by traffic police. The number of traffic lights in Hanoi and Ho Chi Minh City is increasing, but red lights are often not obeyed. Most Vietnamese ride motorcycles, and an entire family often rides on one motorcycle.

Road conditions are poor nationwide. Numerous tragic accidents have occurred due to poor road conditions that resulted in landslides, and American travelers have lost their lives in this way. Travelers should exercise extra caution in the countryside, as road conditions are particularly poor in rural areas.

Driving at night is especially dangerous and drivers should exercise extreme caution. Roads are poorly lit, and there are few road signs. Buses and trucks often travel at high speed with bright lights that are rarely dimmed. Some motor vehicles may not use lights at all, vehicles of all types often stop in the road without any illumination, and livestock are likely to be encountered.

Motorcyclists and bicyclists are strongly urged to wear helmets. Passengers in cars or taxis should use seatbelts when available, but should be aware that Vietnamese vehicles often are not equipped with working seatbelts. The Vietnamese government began mandating the use of motorcycle helmets on major roads leading to large urban centers in January 2001, but application and enforcement of this law have been slow and sporadic at best. New laws have been promulgated concerning the use of

THE U.S. DEPARTMENT OF STATE ISSUES INFORMATION SHEETS TO HELP PROTECT U.S. CITIZENS TRAVELING OVERSEAS—Cont'd

motorcycle helmets in urban areas as well, but have not been enforced. Child car seats are not available in Vietnam.

Penalties for driving under the influence of alcohol or causing an accident resulting in injury or death can include fines, confiscation of driving permits, or imprisonment. U.S. citizens involved in traffic accidents have been barred from leaving Vietnam before paying compensation (often determined arbitrarily) for property damage or injuries.

Emergency roadside help is theoretically available nationwide by dialing 113 for police, 114 for fire brigade, and 115 for an ambulance. Efficiency of these services is well below U.S. standards, however, and locating a public telephone is often difficult or impossible. Trauma care is not widely available.

The urban speed limit ranges from 30 to 40 km/h. The rural speed limit ranges from 40 to 60 km/h. Both speed limits are routinely ignored. Pedestrians should be careful, as sidewalks are extremely congested and uneven, and drivers of bicycles, motorcycles, and other vehicles routinely ignore traffic signals and traffic flows, and even drive on sidewalks. For safety, pedestrians should look carefully in both directions before crossing streets, even when using a marked crosswalk with a green "walk" light illuminated.

International driving permits and U.S. drivers' licenses are not valid in Vietnam. Foreigners renting vehicles risk prosecution and/or imprisonment for driving without a Vietnamese license endorsed for the appropriate vehicle. Americans who wish to drive in Vietnam should contact any office of the Provincial Public Transportation Service of the Vietnamese Department of Communications and Transport to obtain a Vietnamese driver's license. The U.S. Embassy in Hanoi and Consulate General in Ho Chi Minh City cannot assist U.S. citizens in obtaining Vietnamese driver's permits or notarize U.S. drivers' licenses for use in Vietnam.

Most Vietnamese travel within Vietnam by long-distance bus or train. Both are slow, and safety conditions do not approach U.S. standards. Local buses and taxis are available in some areas, particularly in the larger cities. Safety standards vary widely depending on the individual company operating the service, but are generally much lower than what would be found in the United States.

For additional information about road travel in Vietnam, see the U.S. Embassy Hanoi Web site at http://hanoi.usembassy.gov or the U.S. Consulate General in Ho Chi Minh City's Web site at http://hochiminh.usconsulate.gov.

Please refer to our road safety page for more information at http://travel.state.gov/travel/tips/safety/safety_1179html.

Aviation Safety Oversight

As no Vietnamese air carriers currently provide direct commercial air service between the United States and Vietnam, the U.S. Federal Aviation Administration (FAA) has not assessed the Vietnam Civil Aviation Authority for compliance with ICAO international aviation safety standards. For more information, travelers may visit the FAA's Internet Web site at http://www.faa.gov/avr/iasa/index.cfm.

Special Circumstances

Foreign currency (including cash and travelers cheques) in excess of U.S.$3000, cash exceeding Vietnamese Dong (VND) 5,000,000, and gold exceeding 300 grams must be declared at customs upon arrival and departure. There is no limitation on either the export or the import of U.S. dollars or other foreign currency by U.S. citizens, provided that all currency in excess of U.S.$3000 (or its equivalent in other foreign currencies) or in excess of VND 5,000,000 in cash is declared upon arrival and departure and is supported by appropriate documentation. If excess cash is not declared, it is confiscated at the port of entry/exit and the passenger may be arrested and/or fined.

Continued

THE U.S. DEPARTMENT OF STATE ISSUES INFORMATION SHEETS TO HELP PROTECT U.S. CITIZENS TRAVELING OVERSEAS—Cont'd

Vietnamese law prohibits the export of antiques, but the laws on the subject are vague and unevenly enforced. Antique objects are subject to inspection and seizure by customs authorities with no compensation made to owners/travelers. The determination of what is an "antique" can be arbitrary. Purchasers of nonantique items of value should retain receipts and confirmation from shop owners and/or the Ministry of Culture and the Customs Department to prevent seizure upon departure.

Vietnamese government authorities have seized documents, audio and video tapes, compact discs, literature, and personal letters they deem to be religious, pornographic, political in nature, or intended for religious or political proselytizing. The authorities are also increasingly detaining and expelling individuals believed to be engaged in such activities. Individuals arriving at airports with videotapes or materials considered to be pornographic have been detained and heavily fined (up to U.S.$2000 for one videotape). It is illegal to import weapons, ammunition, explosives, military equipment and tools, narcotics, drugs, toxic chemicals, pornographic and subversive materials, firecrackers, children's toys that have "negative effects on personality development, social order and security," or cigarettes in excess of the stipulated allowance.

Vietnamese security personnel may place foreign visitors under surveillance. Hotel rooms, telephone conversations, fax transmissions, and e-mail communications may be monitored, and personal possessions in hotel rooms may be searched.

Foreign visitors to Vietnam have been arbitrarily arrested, detained, or expelled for activities that would not be considered crimes in the United States. Visitors deemed suspicious by Vietnamese security personnel may be detained, along with their Vietnamese contacts, relatives, and friends. Local security officials have called in some U.S. citizens of Vietnamese origin for "discussions" not related to any suspected or alleged violation of law. These meetings normally do not result in any action against the traveler, but are nevertheless intimidating.

Foreign visitors are not permitted to invite Vietnamese nationals of the opposite sex to their hotel rooms, and police may raid hotels without notice or consent. Couples may be asked to present a marriage certificate to local authorities in order to stay together in a hotel or family residence. Involvement in politics, possession of political material, business activities that have not been licensed by appropriate authorities, or nonsanctioned religious activities (including proselytizing) can result in detention. Sponsors of small, informal religious gatherings such as bible-study groups in hotel rooms, as well as distributors of religious materials, have been detained, fined, and expelled.

The Vietnamese government has occasionally seized the passports and blocked the departure of foreigners involved in commercial disputes. The U.S. Embassy or Consulate General may issue a new passport to a U.S. citizen in such a situation, but the Vietnamese exit ban could remain in effect, preventing departure.

Taking photographs of anything that could be perceived as being of military or security interest may result in problems with authorities. Tourists should be cautious when traveling near military bases and avoid photographing in these areas.

A 1994 agreement between the United States and Vietnam provides for immediate notification of and reciprocal access within 96 hours to each other's detained citizens. Bearers of U.S. passports who enter Vietnam with a Vietnamese visa, including those of Vietnamese origin, are regarded as U.S. citizens by the U.S. government for purposes of notification and access. Therefore, U.S. citizens are encouraged to carry photocopies of passport data and photo pages with them at all times so that, if questioned by Vietnamese officials, proof of U.S. citizenship is readily available.

Despite the 1994 agreement, U.S. consular officers in Vietnam are rarely notified in a timely manner when a U.S. citizen is arrested or detained. There have also generally been very significant delays in obtaining access to incarcerated U.S. citizens. This has been particularly true when the U.S. citizen is

THE U.S. DEPARTMENT OF STATE ISSUES INFORMATION SHEETS TO HELP PROTECT U.S. CITIZENS TRAVELING OVERSEAS—Cont'd

being held during the investigatory stage that Vietnamese officials do not consider as covered by the bilateral agreement. The investigatory stage can last up to 1 year and often proceeds without the formal filing of any charges. Americans should note that the problem of access has been particularly evident when the U.S. citizen is considered by the Vietnamese government to be a citizen of Vietnam, irrespective of proof of U.S. citizenship. U.S. citizens, even dual citizens, have the right, according to the 1994 agreement, to consular access if they were admitted into Vietnam as a U.S. citizen with their U.S. passport and should insist upon contact with the U.S. Embassy or the U.S. Consulate General.

Civil procedures in Vietnam, such as marriage, divorce, documenting the birth of a child, and issuance of death certificates, are highly bureaucratic, painstakingly slow, and often require chain authentication. Please contact the Vietnamese Embassy in Washington, DC, or the Vietnamese Consulate General in San Francisco concerning documentary requirements for these services. Please see our information on customs regulations at http://travel.state.gov/travel/cis_pa_tw/cis/cis_1468.html.

Criminal Penalties

While in a foreign country, a U.S. citizen is subject to that country's laws and regulations, which sometimes differ significantly from those in the United States and may not afford the protections available to the individual under U.S. law. Penalties for breaking the law can be more severe than in the United States for similar offenses. Persons violating Vietnamese laws, even unknowingly, may be expelled, arrested, or imprisoned. Penalties for possession, use, or trafficking in illegal drugs in Vietnam are severe, and convicted offenders can expect long jail sentences and heavy fines. Engaging in illicit sexual conduct with children or using or disseminating child pornography in a foreign country is a crime, prosecutable in the United States. For more information visit http://travel.state.gov/travel/cis_pa_tw/cis/cis_1467.html.

Children's Issues

For information on international adoption of children and international parental child abduction, see the Office of Children's Issues Web site at http://travel.state.gov/family/family_1732.html.

Registration/Embassy Location

Americans living or traveling in Vietnam are encouraged to register with the nearest U.S. Embassy or Consulate through the state department's travel registration Web site, https://travelregistration.state.gov/, and to obtain updated information on travel and security within Vietnam. Americans without Internet access may register directly with the nearest U.S. Embassy or Consulate. By registering, American citizens make it easier for the Embassy or Consulate to contact them in case of emergency. The Consular Section of the U.S. Embassy in Hanoi is located at 6 Ngoc Khanh, Ba Dinh District, Hanoi, Socialist Republic of Vietnam, telephone: (84-4) 831-4590; after hours emergency telephone number: (84-4) 772-1500; fax: (84-4) 831-4578, Web site: http://hanoi.usembassy.gov/.

The U.S. Consulate General in Ho Chi Minh City is located at 4 Le Duan, District 1, Ho Chi Minh City, Socialist Republic of Vietnam, telephone: (84-8) 822-9433; fax: (84-8) 822-9434; Web site: http://hochiminh.usconsulate.gov/.

SECURITY STRATEGIES

Much of the remainder of this chapter is based on Purpura (2002). Several additional sources are used to update the information.

It is important to note that a trend in security is the convergence of information technology (IT) and physical security. Physical security is increasingly relying on IT systems and related software. Both specializations and related technologies are uniting for common objectives. To illustrate, IT systems and physical security systems have sensors that generate data that is managed. As examples, an IT system will have an anti-virus program and a physical security system will have motion detectors.

RISK ANALYSIS

Chapter 7 discussed the importance of risk management as a foundation for emergency management and homeland security. It serves as a tool to pinpoint specific, prioritized needs so scarce resources can be spent efficiently. Here we explain risk analysis, a term and process with roots in risk management. This link can be seen in the "risk management process" and the "GAO risk management approach" in Chapter 7. This section begins with definitions from the *General Security Risk Assessment Guideline* (ASIS, International, 2003).

> **Risk analysis** is defined as "a detailed examination including risk assessment, risk evaluation, and risk management alternatives, performed to understand the nature of unwanted, negative consequences to human life, health, property, or the environment; an analytical process to provide information regarding undesirable events; the process of quantification of the probabilities and expected consequences for identified risks."
>
> **Risk assessment** is "the process of assessing security-related risks from internal and external threats to an entity, its assets, or personnel."

The *General Security Risk Assessment Guideline* provides in-depth information. It recognizes that data available on certain risks facing organizations may be too limited to conduct quantitative risk analysis. Thus, this guideline offers both quantitative (i.e., capable of being measured and represented in numerical terms) and qualitative (i.e., characteristic of something) approaches.

A three-step risk analysis process (Purpura, 2002: 48–50) with qualitative and quantitative characteristics is explained next to provide the reader with a foundation from which to build.

THE LOSS PREVENTION SURVEY

The purpose of a loss prevention survey is to pinpoint risks and vulnerabilities (e.g., inadequate access controls, unsafe conditions) and develop a foundation for improved protection. The survey should tailor its questions to the unique needs of the premises to be surveyed. The merging of IT specialists into the risk analysis process is vital for comprehensive protection. The survey includes a day and night physical examination of the location requiring a loss prevention program. The list that follows, expanded from Crawford (1995: 85–90), is a beginning point for topics for the survey that can take several days.

1. Geography, climate (possible natural disaster), nearby hazards, or potential targets
2. Social, economic, and political climate surrounding the facility (possible high crime rate and unrest)
3. Past incidents, complaints, and civil action
4. Condition of physical security, fire protection, and safety measures
5. Hazardous substances and protection measures
6. Policies and procedures and enforcement
7. Quality of security personnel (e.g., applicant screening, training, and supervision; properly registered and licensed)
8. Protection of people and assets

9. Protection of IT systems and information
10. Protection of communications systems (e.g., telephones, fax machines, e-mail)
11. Protection of utilities
12. Protection of parking lots
13. Protection of product, service, and image

The survey document usually consists of a checklist in the form of questions that remind the loss prevention practitioner or committee of what to examine. A list attached to the survey can contain the targets, e.g., people, money, equipment, and IT systems, that must be protected and the present strategies, if any, used to protect them. Blueprints of the facility and a map of the surrounding area also are helpful to the survey. Computer software generating three-dimensional views of the facility and geographic information systems (Chapter 7) provide further assistance.

IDENTIFYING VULNERABILITIES

Once the survey is completed, vulnerabilities can be isolated. For example, perimeter security and access controls may be weak, certain policies and procedures may be ignored, and specific people and assets may require improved protection. Vulnerabilities may also show that security, fire, and life safety strategies are outdated and must be brought up to current codes and standards.

DETERMINING PROBABILITY, FREQUENCY, AND COST

The third step requires an analysis of the probability, frequency, and cost of each loss. Shoplifting and employee theft are common in retail stores, and numerous incidents can add up to serious losses. Fire and explosion are potential risks at a chemical facility; even one incident can be financially devastating. The frequency of shoplifting and employee theft incidents at a retail store will likely be greater than the frequency of fires and explosions at a chemical facility. However, it is impossible to pinpoint accurately when, where, and how many times losses will occur. When the questions of probability, frequency, and cost of losses arise, practitioners must rely on their own experience, records and statistics, communication with fellow practitioners, and information provided by trade publications. Also helpful is risk analysis software.

It is argued that security directors of large, complex organizations should use quantitative, rather than qualitative, risk analysis when exposures cannot be evaluated intuitively, especially for the protection of IT and e-business (Jacobson, 2000: 142–144). The process begins with a mathematical model that can be simple or complex. A simple formula is $ALE = I \times F$, where "ALE" is annual loss exposure, "I" is impact (i.e., dollar loss if the event occurs), and "F" is frequency (i.e., the number of times the event will occur each year). Software tools are available to organize and automate complex risk analyses. Debate continues over when to use quantitative risk analysis, its cost and value, how much guesswork goes into the process, and which formula and software are best. Two points are clear: (1) there are many opinions and styles of risk analysis and (2) what works for one organization may not work for another.

METRICS

As written in Chapter 7 under business continuity, **metrics** relates to or pertains to measurement. In that chapter, metrics was applied to business continuity planning.

Wailgum (2005) notes that security executives and chief executive officers want to know how security operations are working and how they can improve. Metrics can provide the numbers and context on performance of the security function. He adds that metrics vary by security executive, organization, and industry.

Wailgum offers examples of how metrics are used by various businesses. A utility company uses metrics to gauge its compliance with federal regulations. For example, it compares performance on "readiness reviews" among different facilities. Readiness reviews assess whether employees understand threat plans and what to do when the threat level is raised or lowered. It also covers physical security and emergency action plans, among other areas. Another example is penetration testing to breach security. How far can someone reach without a badge? Can someone talk his or her way around delivery procedures? These evaluations can be quantified and compared over time.

Wailgum also refers to a retail chain of thousands of stores. One metric used is the number of robberies per 1000 stores. This figure is compared to the rates of other similar retail chains. Another metric is cash loss as a percentage of sales for every retail unit. The retailer uses many other metrics.

CRITICAL THINKING

The date of September 11, 2001 marked a turning point in the history of security. Because of these devastating attacks, not only have homeland defense, security, safety, and military strategies changed, but also our way of thinking has changed. We cannot afford to have failures in our planning and imagination of what criminals can do. To improve security, we must seek new tools to assist us in our thinking processes. Critical thinking skills can counter business as usual. Critical thinking helps us to become an active learner to not only absorb information, but to probe and shape knowledge. The critical thinker cuts through "hype" and emotion and goes beyond collecting "facts" and memorizing information in an effort to understand causes, motives, and changes. Critical thinking skills provide a foundation for creative planning while helping us to anticipate future events. The critical thinker asks many questions and the questions are often easier to formulate than the answers. Critical thinking requires us to "jump out of our own skin" to see the world from the perspective of others. Although this is not an easy process, we are much better informed prior to our conclusions and decisions. Critical thinking is not to be used as a tool to open up the floodgates of criticism in the workplace. It is to be applied discreetly to understand the world and to meet challenges. A professional's success depends on his or her thinking process applied to everyday duties and long-range planning. Critical thinking adds an extra edge to the repertoire of tools available to security and loss prevention practitioners. Security challenges have become increasingly complex because as we plan for protection and face a multitude of threats in a rapidly changing environment, we must expect the unexpected, while staying within our budgets. The security practitioner should be creative, have an excellent imagination, apply critical thinking skills, and carefully prioritize security strategies to produce the best possible security program (Purpura, 2002: 3–4).

The critical thinking process should also include how terrorists and other criminals change their methods and/or switch targets in response to established and enhanced security. This relates to the classic "cat and mouse game" between adversaries who seek to outwit each other.

How can we think critically? As we think through complex challenges, we need a method of sorting conflicting claims, differentiating between fact and opinion, weighing "evidence" or "proof," being perceptive to our biases and those of others, and drawing logical conclusions. Ellis (1991: 184–185) suggests a four-step strategy for critical thinking.

1. *Understanding the point of view.*

   - Listen/read without early judgment.
   - Seek to understand the source's background (e.g., culture, education, experience, and values).
   - Try to "live in their shoes."
   - Summarize their viewpoint.

2. *Seek other views.*

   - Seek viewpoints, questions, answers, ideas, and solutions from others.

3. *Evaluate the various viewpoints.*

   - Look for assumptions (i.e., an opinion that something is true, without evidence), exceptions, gaps in logic, oversimplification, selective perception, either/or thinking, and personal attacks.

4. *Construct a reasonable view.*

  • Study multiple viewpoints, combine perspectives, and produce an original viewpoint that is a creative act and the essence of critical thinking.

SECURITY MAXIMS

A critical thinking approach can be applied to security maxims to improve security. Here are four maxims to ponder.

1. Security is never foolproof. The term "foolproof" is a misnomer. Instead of burglarproof, fireproof, or bulletproof, replace "proof" with "resistant."
2. State-of-the-art security has its vulnerabilities. History is filled with grand security strategies that failed.
3. Security often is as good as the time it takes to get through it. The longer the time delay facing the offender, the greater the protection and chances that he or she will abort the offense, be apprehended, or seek another victim.
4. Security must focus on not only what is leaving a facility (e.g., company assets) but also what is entering (e.g., weapons, explosives, illegal drugs, and anger).

Three Models of Security

Apply a critical thinking approach to the statement that all security strategies fall under one of the following three models.

1. It protects people and/or assets.
2. It accomplishes nothing.
3. It helps offenders.

  Illustrations of security protecting people or assets are seen when a hospital security officer escorts nurses to their vehicles at night or when a safe proves too formidable for a burglar, who leaves the scene. Security accomplishes nothing when security officers sleep on the job or fail to make their rounds or when alarm systems remain inoperable. Sometimes unknown to security practitioners and those they serve are the security strategies that actually help offenders. This can occur when security officers are poorly screened and they commit crimes. The ordinary padlock is an example of how physical security can assist offenders. An unlocked padlock hanging on an open gate can invite padlock substitution, whereby the offender replaces it with his or her own padlock, returns at night to gain access, and then secures the gate with the original padlock. Such cases are difficult to investigate because signs of forced entry may be absent. Fences, another example, often are built with a top rail and supports for barbed wire that are strong enough to assist and support people, rather than the fence and barbed wire. Also, attractive-looking picket fences have been knocked down by offenders and used as ladders.
  Security practitioners should identify and classify all security strategies under these models to expose useful, wasteful, and harmful methods. This endeavor should be a perpetual process within risk analysis, careful planning, critical thinking, testing, and research to facilitate cost-effective, results-oriented security. Although these challenging goals require time and effort, the net result is a superior security and loss prevention program (Purpura, 2002: 56–57).

CRITICAL THINKING:

Apply your critical thinking skills to the nearby box on "Security Maxims" and "Three Models of Security." Produce original viewpoints that are creative acts and the essence of critical thinking.

Purposes of Security

Security can be conceptualized around the five Ds (Purpura, 2002: 189–190).

Deter. The mere presence of physical security can dissuade offenders from committing criminal acts. The impact of physical security can be enhanced through an *aura of security.* An aura is a distinctive atmosphere surrounding something. Supportive management and security personnel should work to produce a professional security image. They should remain mum on such topics as the number and types of intrusion detection sensors on the premises and security system weaknesses. Security patrols should be unpredictable and never routine. Signs help to project an aura of security by stating, for example: PREMISES PROTECTED BY HIGH-TECH REDUNDANT SECURITY. Such signs can be placed along a perimeter and near openings to buildings. The aura of security strives to produce a strong psychological deterrent so offenders will consider the success of a crime to be unlikely. It is important to note that no guarantees come with deterrence. (Criminal justice policies are in serious trouble because deterrence is faulty; criminals continue to commit crimes even while facing long sentences.) In the security realm, deterrence must be backed up with the following four "Ds."

Detect. Offenders should be detected and their location pinpointed as soon as they step onto the premises or commit a violation on the premises. This can be accomplished through observation, CCTV, intrusion sensors, duress alarms, weapons screenings, protective dogs, and hotlines.

Delay. Security is often measured by the time it takes to get through it. *Redundant* (e.g., two fences; two types of intrusion sensors) and *layered* (e.g., perimeter fence, strong doors at buildings) security creates a time delay. Thus, the offender may become frustrated and decide to depart or the delay may provide time for a response force to arrive to make an apprehension.

Deny. Strong physical security, often called "target hardening," can deny access. A steel door and a safe are examples. Frequent bank deposits of cash and other valuables extend the opportunity to deny the offender success.

Destroy. When you believe your life or another's will be taken, you are legally permitted to use deadly force. An asset (e.g., proprietary information on a computer disk) may require destruction before it falls into the wrong hands.

CRITICAL THINKING:

Which "D" do you view as most important? Which "D" do you view as least important? Explain your answers.

Mitigating Terrorist Attacks against Buildings

In the *Reference Manual to Mitigate Potential Terrorist Attacks Against Buildings* (U.S. Department of Homeland Security, 2003: iii), here referred to as FEMA 426, it is written that building designs can serve to mitigate multiple hazards. For example, hurricane window design, especially against flying debris, and seismic standards for nonstructural building components apply also to bomb explosions. Ventilation system design against airborne WMD also protects against hazardous material release, whether intentional or accidental. Designs that mitigate multiple hazards are more cost effective and easier to justify than designs that serve one hazard.

Planners, architects, and landscape designers should pool their ideas at the early stages of design when mitigation is the least costly and implemented most easily. At the same time, asset protection objectives must be balanced with other objectives, including efficient use of land and resources, aesthetics, and fiscal constraints. FEMA 426 refers to site-level considerations for security that include land use controls, landscape architecture, site planning, and other strategies to mitigate risks of terrorism and other hazards.

Land use controls, including zoning and land development regulations, can impact security because they define urban configurations that can decrease or increase risks from crime and terrorism. For instance, managing stormwater on site can add security through water retention facilities that serve as a vehicle barrier and blast setback. This reduces the need for off-site pipes and manholes that can be used for access or to conceal weapons.

In Chapter 7, mitigating the threat of car bombs at buildings was covered within the vulnerability assessment portion of the GAO risk management approach. Also, Chapter 7 discussed mitigation within emergency management. Chapter 8 covered life safety in buildings. Here we concentrate on site mitigation measures against terrorists and other criminals (Figure 9-1).

FEMA 426 offers several building design suggestions to increase security. A **target-rich environment** is created when people, property, and operations are concentrated in a dense area. However, a dense cluster can maximize standoff (i.e., protection when a blast occurs) from the perimeter. Additional security benefits are a reduction in the number of access and surveillance points and a shorter perimeter to protect. A dense cluster of buildings can possibly save energy costs through, for instance, heat transfer from heat-producing areas to heat-consuming areas. Also, external lighting would not be dispersed over a large area, requiring more lights and energy. In contrast, dispersed buildings, people, and operations spread the risk. However, dispersal can increase the complexity of security (e.g., more access points) and may require more resources (e.g., security officers, CCTV, lighting perimeter protection).

FEMA 426 recommends that designers consolidate buildings that are functionally compatible and have similar threat levels. For instance, mailrooms, shipping and receiving docks, and visitor screening areas, where people and materials are often closely monitored prior to access, should be isolated and separated from concentrations of people, operations, and key assets.

The design of open space with protection in mind offers several benefits: easy to monitor and detect intruders, vehicles, and weapons; standoff value from a blast; previous open space permits stormwater to percolate back into the ground, reducing the need for pipes, manholes, and other covert access points and weapon concealment sites; and offers wetland or vegetated area to improve aesthetic value while hindering vehicle intrusion.

Here are other suggestions for buildings from FEMA 426.

- Provide redundant utility systems to continue life safety, security, and rescue functions in case of an emergency.
- Because hardened glazing may cause windows not to blow out in a blast, a system for smoke removal is essential.
- When possible, elevate fresh-air intakes to reduce the potential of hazardous materials entering a building from ground level. The intakes should be sloped down and have screens in case a device is thrown toward the opening.
- Manipulation of the HVAC system could minimize the spread of a hazardous agent. Filtration systems are another option, although expensive.

ROADS AND PARKING LOTS

The design of roads and parking lots influences security at buildings. A designer can propose minimizing vehicle velocity because, for example, a bollard (Figure 9-2) that can stop a 15,000-pound truck moving at 35 mph may not be able to stop the same truck moving at 55 mph (FEMA 426). *The road itself can become a security measure by avoiding a straight path to the building.* A straight road enables a vehicle to gather speed to ram a barrier, penetrate a building, and then detonate a bomb. Approaches should be parallel to the building and contain high curbs, trees, or berms to prevent vehicles from leaving the road. Curving roads with tight corners offer another strategy.

Traffic calming strategies are subtler and communicate appropriate speed. Examples are speed humps and raised crosswalks. A speed hump is not as rough as a speed bump. The latter is often used in parking lots. All these strategies reduce speed and liability while increasing safety.

Figure 9-1 ■ Summary of site mitigation measures. Source: U.S. Department of Homeland Security (2003).

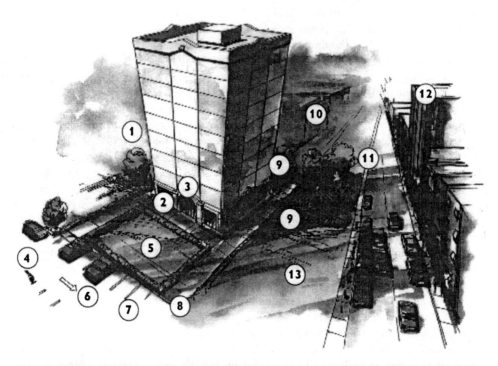

1. Locate assets stored on site, but outside the building within view of occupied rooms in the facility.	8. Minimize vehicle access points.
2. Eliminate parking beneath buildings.	9. Eliminate potential hiding places near the building; provide an unobstructed view around building.
3. Minimize exterior signage or other indications of asset locations.	10. Site building within view of other occupied buildings on the site.
4. Locate trash receptacles as far from the building as possible.	11. Maximize distance from the building to the site boundary.
5. Eliminate lines of approach perpendicular to the building.	12. Locate building away from natural or manmade vantage points.
6. Locate parking to obtain stand-off distance from the building.	13. Secure access to power/heat plants, gas mains, water supplies, and electrical service.
7. Illuminate building exteriors or sites where exposed assets are located.	

Drawbacks are that the response time of first responders increases and snow removal may become difficult.

Different types of parking lots present various security issues. Surface lots keep vehicles away from buildings, consume large amounts of land, and may add to stormwater runoff volume. On-street parking provides no setback. A garage may require blast resistance. If the garage is under a building, a serious vulnerability exists, as an underground bomb blast can be devastating. Security for parking lots is important to prevent crime and premise liability exposure, besides terrorism.

LANDSCAPE AND URBAN DESIGN

Landscape elements including landforms, water features, and vegetation are not only attractive, but they can enhance security and serve as a barrier. Trees, vegetative groupings, and earth berms offer some degree of blast shielding. The types of plants that create perimeter protection and deter offenders include firethorn, Spanish bayonet, holly, barberry, and multiflora rose bushes. The privet hedge grows almost anywhere and requires minimal care. Careful planning is important to avoid liability from injuries, the hindering of emergency response, and the use of landscape for concealment.

Figure 9-2 ■ Streetscape security elements. Source: U.S. Department of Homeland Security (2003).

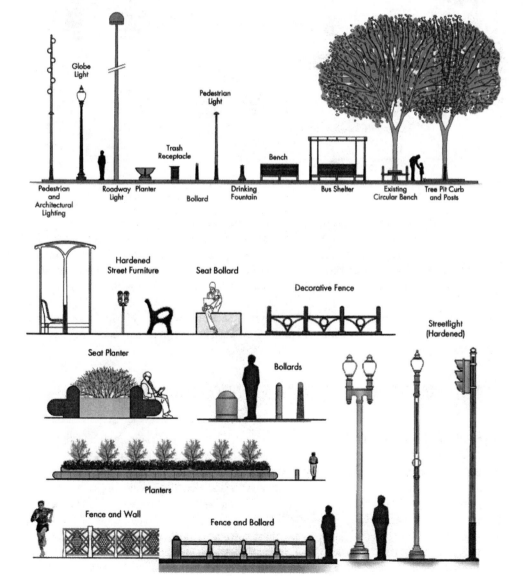

Continued

Figure 9-2 ■ **Cont'd**

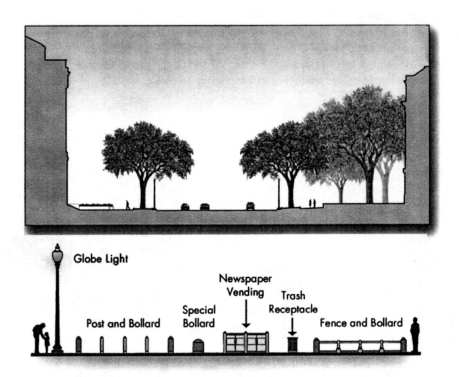

Urban design offers many opportunities to increase security. However, many needs enter into urban design, beside security. Examples include the efficient movement of people and vehicles, aesthetics, business needs, evacuation, and emergency response. Security should be integrated with a multitude of needs. Aesthetics can possibly be maintained through bollards, planters, or decorative boulders rather than walls and fences, but these decisions rest with the risks of the particular location.

The hardening of street furniture offers another security option. This includes light poles, planters, benches, and water fountains (Figure 9-2). These items can be hardened to serve as vehicle barriers.

CRIME PREVENTION THROUGH ENVIRONMENTAL DESIGN

Crime Prevention through Environmental Design (CPTED) is relevant to landscape and urban design. During the late 1960s and early 1970s, Oscar Newman (1972) conducted innovative research into the relationship between architectural design and crime prevention that developed into the concept of defensible space. He studied over 100 housing projects and identified design elements that inhibit crime. For instance, Newman favored the creation of surveillance opportunities through windows for residents and the recognition that the neighborhood surrounding the residential setting influences safety. An essential part of defensible space is to create designs that change residents' use of public places (e.g., increase pedestrian traffic at night), while reducing fear of crime; this is hoped to have a snowballing effect. Oscar Newman found that physical design features of public housing affect both

CRIME PREVENTION THROUGH ENVIRONMENTAL DESIGN—Cont'd

the rates of victimization of residents and their perception of security. CPTED evolved from Newman's concept of defensible space and is applicable not only to public housing but to businesses, industries, public buildings, transportation systems, and schools, among other locations. In the past, the U.S. Department of Justice funded CPTED programs in several cities (Purpura, 2002: 190–191).

An illustration of how CPTED is applied can be seen with the design of Marriott hotels (Murphy, 2000: 84–88). To make offenders as visible as possible, traffic is directed toward the front of hotels. Lobbies are designed so that people walking to guest rooms or elevators must pass the front desk. On the outside, hedges are emphasized to produce a psychological barrier that is more appealing than a fence. Pathways are well lit and guide guests away from isolated areas. Parking lots are characterized by lighting, clear lines of sight, and access controls. Walls of the garage are painted white to enhance lighting. On the inside of hotels, the swimming pool, exercise room, and vending and laundry areas have glass doors and walls to permit maximum witness potential. One application of CCTV is to aim cameras at persons standing at the lobby desk and to install the monitor in plain view. Because people can see themselves, robberies have declined. CPTED enhances traditional security methods such as patrolling officers and emergency call boxes.

SITUATIONAL CRIME PREVENTION

Situational Crime Prevention (SCP) is closely related to CPTED. "This approach encompasses many CPTED principles; however, it focuses on managerial and user behavior factors that affect opportunities for criminal behavior in a specific setting for a specific crime, whereas CPTED focuses on changing the physical design aspects of environments to deter criminal activity" (U.S. Department of Homeland Security, 2003: 2–19).

Lab (2004: 177) writes: "Instead of attempting to make sweeping changes in an entire community or neighborhood, situational prevention is aimed at specific problems, places, people, or times. The situational approach assumes that a greater degree of problem identification and planning will take place prior to program implementation and that the impact will be more focused and, perhaps, identifiable."

Lab (2004: 177) traces SCP to the crime prevention work of the British Home Office (Clark, 1983) in the late 1970s. The goal was to successfully address different crime problems.

Lab (2004: 178–179) sees the theoretical basis for SCP from the following perspectives.

- **Rational choice theory**: individuals make calculated decisions about crime based on many inputs, including the potential payoff, the risk, and needs. (See Chapter 1 where this theory is tied directly to terrorists.)
- **Routine activities theory**: day-to-day activities of people result in the convergence of motivated offenders with victims (e.g., multiple-income households leave more homes unoccupied and subject to burglary). Increased mobility in society brings victims and offenders together more so than in the past. (With multiple modes of modern transportation, potential terrorist targets are plentiful.)
- **Lifestyle perspectives**: this approach focuses on the activity of the victim as a contributing factor in criminal acts and victimization. Individual lifestyle and behavioral choices can lead to victimization (e.g., an individual who frequents bars where fights occur often increases the risk of assault). The famous Italian politician, Aldo Moro, who was a "creature of habit," became an easy target for the Red Brigades terrorist group (see Chapter 1).

Continued

SITUATIONAL CRIME PREVENTION—Cont'd

Both CPTED and SCP contain strategies to thwart terrorism, besides crime. CPTED provides "defensible space" that may inhibit terrorist planning and execution of an attack. The CPTED concept of "natural surveillance" through, for example, the strategic location of windows (e.g., overlooking a road or parking lot) enables many individuals to watch for suspicious activity. SCP has characteristics of risk analysis and risk management. As covered earlier, it seeks more precise problem identification and planning prior to program implementation and the impact will be more focused. SCP targets specific problems (e.g., terrorism), places (e.g., high-risk buildings), people (e.g., employees, executives, politicians), or times (e.g., anniversary dates observed by terrorists; elections).

HOSTILE SURVEILLANCE

Hostile surveillance refers to a variety of methods used by an adversary to collect intelligence. FEMA 426 offers strategies to counter hostile surveillance, including landforms, landscaping (e.g., trees), building orientation, and screening. Each can block line of sight. Careful planning is important because each strategy may contain advantages and disadvantages for security. Trees may provide line-of-sight protection for only part of the year if the leaves fall off. Buildings requiring a clear zone to monitor the surrounding area would have to forego blocking line of sight. Buildings should not be located near higher surrounding terrain, buildings owned by unfamiliar parties, or vegetation or ditches that can provide concealment.

STAND-OFF DISTANCE

Stand-off distance is the distance between an asset and a threat (Figure 9-3). FEMA 426 views *distance* as the most effective and desirable strategy against a blast because other methods may vary in effectiveness, be more costly, and result in unintended consequences. A blast wall can become a part of the fragmentation if a bomb is detonated close to it. Urban environments create challenges when designing stand-off distance because land is often expensive. There is no ideal stand-off distance; numerous variables enter into planning, including the type of threat or explosive, construction characteristics and target hardening, and desired level of protection.

Keep out zones help maintain a specific distance between vehicles or people and a building. This is accomplished by installing perimeter security (e.g., fences), access controls, bollards, and other security methods. If terrorists plan to attack a specific building, they will likely use

Figure 9-3 ■ Concept of standoff distance. Source: U.S. Department of Homeland Security (2003).

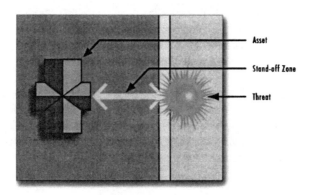

surveillance to study security features, look for vulnerabilities, and try to penetrate access controls and defenses through creative means.

MITIGATION FOR EXPLOSIVE BLASTS

Although numerous building design features can mitigate explosive blasts, many factors enter into the design of buildings, including cost, purpose, occupancy, and location. A high-risk building should incorporate more mitigation features than a low-risk building. Because significant changes to existing buildings may be too expensive, lower cost changes must be sought. Bollards and strong gates are less expensive than making major structural changes to a building. Examples of mitigation features from FEMA 426 are as follows.

- Avoid "U"- or "L"-shaped building designs that trap the shock waves of a blast. Circular buildings reduce a shock wave better than a rectangular building because of the angle of incidence of the shock wave.
- Avoid exposed structural elements (e.g., columns) on the exterior of a facility.
- Install as much glazing (i.e., windows) as possible away from the street side.
- Stagger doors located across from one another in interior hallways to limit the force of a blast through the building.
- High-security rooms should be blast and fragment resistant.
- Provide pitched roofs to permit deflection of launched explosives.

PERIMETER SECURITY

Perimeter means outer boundary, and it is often the property line and the first line of defense against unauthorized access (Purpura, 2002: 191–221). Building access points such as doors and windows are considered part of perimeter defenses at many locations. Typical perimeter security begins with a fence and gate and may include multiple security methods (e.g., card access, locks, sensors, lighting, CCTV, and patrols) to increase protection. The following variables assist in the design of perimeter security.

1. Whatever perimeter security methods are planned, they should interrelate with the total loss prevention program.
2. Perimeter security needs to be cost effective. When plans are presented to management, they are likely to ask: "What type of return will we have on the investment?"
3. Although the least number of entrances strengthens perimeter security, the plan must not interfere with normal business and emergency situations.
4. Perimeter security has a psychological impact on potential intruders. It signals a warning to outsiders that steps have been taken to block intrusions. Offenders actually "shop" for vulnerable businesses.
5. Even though a property line may be well protected, the possibility of unauthorized entry cannot be totally eliminated. For example, a fence can be breached by going over, under, or through it.
6. Penetration of a perimeter is possible from within. Merchandise may be thrown over a fence or out of a window. A variety of things are subject to smuggling by persons walking or using a vehicle while exiting through a perimeter.
7. The perimeter of a building, especially in urban areas, often is the building's walls. A thief may enter through a wall from an adjoining building.
8. To permit an unobstructed view, both sides of a perimeter should be kept clear of vehicles, equipment, and vegetation. This allows for what is known as clear zones.
9. Consider integrating perimeter intrusion sensors with landscape sprinkler systems. Trespassers, protesters, and other intruders will be discouraged, plus, when wet, they are easier to find and identify.

10. Perimeter security methods are exposed to a hostile outdoor environment not found indoors. Adequate clothing and shelter are necessary for personnel. The selection of proper security systems prevents false alarms from animals, vehicle vibrations, and adverse weather.
11. Perimeter security should be inspected periodically.

BARRIERS

Post and Kingsbury (1977: 502–503) state: "The physical security process utilizes a number of **barrier systems**, all of which serve specific needs. These systems include natural, structural, human, animals, and energy barriers." Natural barriers are rivers, hills, cliffs, mountains, foliage, and other features difficult to overcome. Fences, walls, planters, doors, and the architectural arrangement of buildings are structural barriers (Figure 9-4). Human barriers include security officers who scrutinize people, vehicles, and things entering and leaving a facility. The typical animal barrier is a dog. Energy barriers include protective lighting and intrusion sensors.

The most common type of barrier is a chain-link fence topped with barbed wire. A search of the Web shows many industry standards for fences from the American Society for Testing and Materials (ASTM), Underwriters Laboratory (UL), International Organization for Standardization (ISO), and other groups from the United States and overseas. An example of a fence standard is ASTM F1043-00, Standard Specification for Strength and Protective Coatings on Metal Industrial Chain Link Fence Framework. This standard covers fences up to 12 feet with post spacing not to exceed 10 feet.

One advantage of chain-link fencing is that it allows observation from both sides: a security officer looking out and a public police officer looking in. Foliage and decorative plastic woven through the fence can reduce visibility and aid offenders. Opposition to chain-link fencing sometimes develops because management wants to avoid an institutional-looking environment. Hedges are an alternative.

It is advisable that the chain-link fence be made of at least nine-gauge or heavier wire with $2'' \times 2''$ diamond-shaped mesh. It should be at least 7 feet high. Its posts should be set in concrete and spaced no more than 10 feet apart. The bottom should be within 2 inches of hard ground; if the ground is soft, the fence can become more secure if extended a few inches below the ground. Recommended at the top is a top guard: supporting arms about 1 or 2 feet long containing three or four strands of taut barbed wire 6 inches apart and facing outward at 45°.

To protect a fence against ramming by a vehicle, fences can be constructed with antiramming cables that run the length of the fence and act to prevent a vehicle from penetrating the fence. Sensors can also be applied to fences as discussed in subsequent pages.

Figure 9-4 ■ Application of perimeter barrier elements. Source: U.S. Department of Homeland Security (2003).

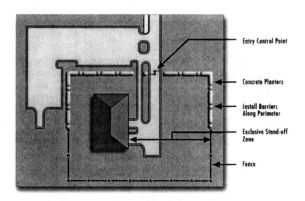

Barbed wire fences are less effective and used less frequently than chain-link fences. Each strand of barbed wire is constructed of two 12-gauge wires twisted and barbed every 4 inches. For adequate protection, vertical support posts are placed 6 feet apart, and the parallel strands of barbed wire are from 2 to 6 inches apart. A good height is 8 feet.

Concertina fences consist of coils of steel razor wire clipped together to form cylinders weighing about 55 pounds. Each cylinder is stretched to form a coil-type barrier 3 feet high and 50 feet long. The ends of each 50-foot coil need to be clipped to the next coil to obviate movement. Stakes also stabilize these fences. This fence was developed by the military to act as a quickly constructed barrier. When one coil is placed on another, they create a 6-foot-high barrier. One coil placed on two as a base provides a pyramid-like barrier difficult to penetrate. Concertina fences are especially helpful for quick temporary repairs to damaged fences.

Razor ribbon or coiled barbed tape are increasing in popularity. They are similar to concertina fencing in many ways. Every few inches along the coil are sharp spikes, looking something like a sharpened bow tie.

Gates are necessary for traffic through fences. The fewer gates, the better because, like windows and doors, they are weak points along a perimeter. Gates usually are secured with a chain and padlock. Uniformed officers stationed at each gate and fence opening increase security while enabling the observation of people and vehicles.

Vehicle barriers control traffic and stop vehicles from penetrating a perimeter. The problems of drive-by shootings and vehicle bombs have resulted in greater use of vehicle barriers. These barriers are assigned government-certified ratings by the Departments of State and Defense based on the level of protection (Kessinger, 2004: 57–66); however, rating systems vary among government agencies. One agency, for example, tests barriers against 15,000-pound trucks traveling up to 50 miles per hour, while another agency tests 10,000-pound trucks traveling the same speed. Passive vehicle barriers are fixed and include decorative bollards, large concrete planters, specially engineered and anchored park benches, hardened fencing, fence cabling, and trees. Active vehicle barriers (Figure 9-5) are used at entrances and include gates, barrier arms, and pop-up type systems that are set underground and, when activated, spring up to block a vehicle. As we know, no security method is foolproof, and careful security planning is vital. In 1997, to protest government policy, the environmental group Greenpeace penetrated government security in Washington, DC, and dumped 4 tons of coal outside the Capitol building. The driver of the truck drove the wrong way up a one-way drive leading to the building.

Walls are costly and a substitute for fences when management is against the use of a wire fence. Attractive walls can be designed to produce security equal to fences while blending into surrounding architecture. Walls are made from a variety of materials: bricks, concrete blocks, stones, and cement. Depending on design, the top of walls, say 8 to 10 feet high, may contain barbed wire, spikes, or broken glass set in cement. Offenders often avoid injury by throwing a blanket or jacket over the top of the wall (or fence) before scaling it. Many jurisdictions prohibit ominous features at the top of barriers. Check local ordinances. An advantage of a wall is that outsiders are hindered from observing inside. However, observation by public police during patrols also is hindered; this can benefit an intruder.

Blast and antiramming walls provide protection for buildings, especially in urban areas where standoff distance may be unavailable. Revel (2003: 40) wrote that a test of a blast wall conducted by the U.S. Government's Technical Support Working Group (TSWG) showed the effectiveness of this security method. The blast wall sustained an explosion more powerful than the one that destroyed the Murrah Federal Building and the effects on the test building behind the blast wall were reduced by about 90%. The blast wall was constructed by first inserting in the ground 18-foot blast posts, with 9 feet extending above the ground. Then steel-jacketed concrete and rebar-filled panels were lowered between the posts in an interlocking pattern. When the explosion occurred, the posts twisted and deflected the blast above and back from the panels, directing the force up and beyond the lower structural steel of the building and around

Figure 9-5 ■   Active vehicle barriers. Source: U.S. Army (2001).

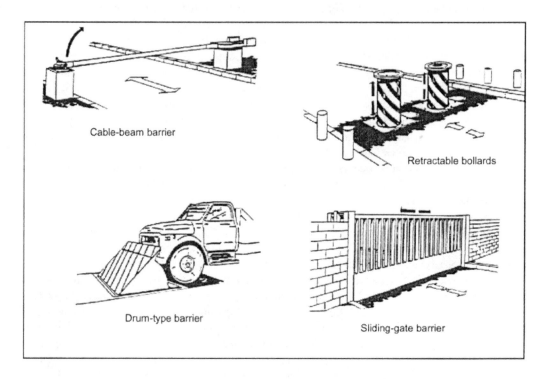

Cable-beam barrier

Retractable bollards

Drum-type barrier

Sliding-gate barrier

the ends of the wall. The blast wall is also capable of absorbing large vehicle impact at high speeds.

Hedges or shrubbery are useful as barriers as covered earlier. A combination of hedge and fence is useful. Hedges should be less than 3 feet high and placed on the inside to avoid injury to those passing by and to create an added obstacle for someone attempting to scale the fence.

Municipal codes restrict the heights of fences, walls, and hedges to maintain an attractive environment devoid of threatening-looking barriers. Certain kinds of barriers may be prohibited to ensure conformity. Planning should encompass research of local standards.

The following list can help eliminate weak points along a perimeter or barrier.

1. Utility poles, trees, boxes, pallets, forklifts, tools, and other objects outside of a building can be used to scale a barrier.
2. Ladders left outside help offenders. Stationary ladders are made less accessible via a steel cage with a locked door.
3. A common wall is shared by two separate entities. Offenders may break through a common wall.
4. A roof is easy to penetrate. A few tools, such as a drill and saw, enable offenders to actually cut through the roof. Because lighting, alarms, and patrols rarely involve the roof, this weakness is attractive to offenders. A rope ladder often is employed to descend from the roof, or a forklift might be used to lift items to the roof. Vehicle keys should be hidden and other precautions taken. Alarms, lights, patrols, and a roof fence to hinder access from an adjoining building deter offenders.
5. Roof hatches, skylights, basement windows, air-conditioning and other vent and duct systems, crawl spaces between floors and under buildings, fire escapes, and utility covers may need a combination of locks, alarms, steel bars, heavy mesh, fences, and inspections. A widely favored standard is that any opening greater than 96 square inches requires increased protection.

PERSPECTIVES ON SECURITY

Stinson (1984), a security and terrorism specialist, argues that the U.S. approach to counterterrorism is similar to its approach to crime prevention—physical security and target hardening are both applied to the problems of terrorism and crime. This may cause offenders to seek softer targets. Stinson's argument is akin to **crime displacement**, whereby criminals (or terrorists) seek another victim if they encounter too many obstacles at a potential target. Taking displacement a step further, it appears as if terrorists are "chasing targets," meaning that when potential targets are hardened (e.g., military bases, airports), softer targets are found (e.g., trains, buses, hotels, schools, or houses of worship). When softer targets are victimized, they are hardened and then terrorists seek other targets as the cycle continues.

Stinson's research showed that when no physical security was established at a target, terrorists had a 100% success rate. However, when a target was hardened, their success rate was 85%. Thus, it can be said that victimization may be reduced by 15% through target hardening. Stinson does not advocate eliminating target hardening, but rather enhancing a broad spectrum of efforts against terrorism, such as using behavioral models to predict likely targets and improving intelligence.

CRITICAL THINKING:

What is your opinion of Stinson's perspective on security? What is your opinion of terrorists "chasing targets?"

GLAZING

Annealed glass, also called plate glass, is commonly used in buildings. It has low strength and, upon failure, fractures into razor-sharp pieces. Fully thermally tempered glass (TTG) is four to five times stronger than annealed glass and, upon failure, will fracture into small cube-shaped fragments. Building codes generally require TTG anywhere the public can touch (e.g., entrance doors). Wire-reinforced glass is made of annealed glass with an embedded layer of wire mesh. It is applied as a fire-resistant and forced entry barrier. All three types of glass present a dangerous hazard from a blast (U.S. Department of Homeland Security, 2003).

Traditionally, window protection focused on hindering forced entry. Today, we are seeing increasing designs that mitigate the hazardous effects of flying glass from a variety of risks, besides explosion. A balanced design (i.e., type of glass, glass frame, frame to building) means that all the window components have compatible capacities and fail at the same pressure levels. The U.S. General Services Administration publishes glazing protection levels based on how far glass fragments would enter a space and cause injuries. (See the Web site at the end of the chapter.) It is important to note that the highest level of protection for glazing may not mitigate the effects from a large explosion (U.S. Department of Homeland Security, 2003).

Glass can be designed to block penetration of bullets, defeat attempted forced entry, remain intact following an explosion or other disaster, and protect against electronic eavesdropping. The Web shows many standards for glazing from the American Architectural Manufacturers Association (AAMA), UL, ASTM, ISO, the Consumer Product Safety Commission, and overseas groups. Security glazing should be evaluated on comparative testing to an established national consensus standard such as ASTM F1233(8), Standard Test Method for Security Glazing Materials and Systems. Important issues for glazing include product life cycle, durability, installation, maintenance, and framing (Saflex, Inc., 2005).

UL classifies bullet-resistant windows into eight protection levels, with levels one to three rated against handguns and four to eight rated against rifles. Level four or higher windows usually are applied by government agencies and the military. Protective windows are made of glass, plastic, or mixtures of each.

Laminated glass offers protection from bomb blasts and hurricanes and it absorbs a bullet as it passes through various glass layers. The advantage of glass is in its maintenance: easy to clean and less likely to scratch than plastic. It is less expensive per square foot than plastic, but heavier, which requires more workers and stronger frames. Glass has a tendency to spall (i.e., chip) when hit by a bullet. UL752-listed glass holds up to three shots, and then it begins to shatter from subsequent shots.

Two types of plastic used in windows are acrylic and polycarbonate. Both vary in thickness and are lighter and more easily scratched than glass. Acrylic windows are clear and monolithic, whereas glass and polycarbonate windows are laminates consisting of layers of material bonded one on top of the other. Acrylic will deflect bullets and hold together under sustained hits. Some spalling may occur. Polycarbonate windows are stronger than acrylics against high-powered weapons. Local codes may require glazing to pop out in an emergency.

In addition to protective windows, wall armor is important for certain environments because employees may duck below a window for protection. These steel or fiberglass plates also are rated.

Burglar-resistant windows are rated (UL 972, Burglary Resisting Glazing Material), available in acrylic and polycarbonate materials, and protect against hammers, flame, "smash and grab," and other attacks. Combined bullet- and burglar-resistant windows are available. Although window protection is an expense that may be difficult to justify, insurers may offer discounts on insurance premiums for such installations.

Following the Oklahoma City bombing, considerable interest focused on the vulnerability of flying glass due to not only explosions, but also accidents or natural disasters. Experts report that 75% of all damage and injury from bomb blasts results from flying and falling glass. Vendors sell shatter-resistant film, also called fragment retention film, that is applied to the glass surface to reduce this problem. Conversely, a report on the 1993 World Trade Center attack claimed that the destroyed windows permitted deadly gases to escape from the building, enabling occupants to survive.

Blast curtains are window draperies made of special fabrics designed to stop glass window shards that are caused by explosions and other hazards. Various designs serve to catch broken glass and let the gas and air pressure dissipate through the fabric mesh. The fibers of these curtains can be several times as strong as steel wire. The U.S. General Services Administration establishes criteria for these products (Owen, 2003: 143–144).

Electronic security glazing, containing metalized fabrics, can prevent electromagnetic signals inside a location from being intercepted from outside, while also protecting a facility from external electromagnetic radiation interference from outside sources. Standards for this type of glazing are from the National Security Agency, NSA 65-8.

Businesses and institutions often contain widows that do not open. For windows that do open, a latch or lock on the inside provides some protection. The double-hung window, often applied at residences, can be secured with a lock, but emergency escape must be a top priority.

By covering windows with grating or security screens, additional steps have been taken to protect windows and impede entrance by an intruder or items being thrown out by a dishonest employee. Window grating consists of metal bars constructed across windows. These bars run horizontally and vertically to produce an effective form of protection. Although these bars are not aesthetically pleasing, they can be purchased with attractive ornamental designs. Security screens are composed of steel or stainless steel wire (mesh) welded to a frame. Screens have some distinct advantages over window grating. Employees can pass pilfered items through window bars more easily than through a screen. Security screens look like ordinary screens, but they are much heavier in construction and can stop rocks and other objects.

When planning window protection, one must consider the need for emergency escape and ventilation. To ensure safety, certain windows can be targeted for the dismantling of window protection during business hours.

ELECTRONIC PROTECTION FOR WINDOWS

Four categories of electronic protection for windows are vibration, glass breakage, contact-switch sensors, and foil. Vibration sensors respond to vibration or shock. They are attached right on the glass or window frame. These sensors are noted for their low false alarm rate and are applicable to fences, walls, and valuable artwork, among other things. Glass-breakage sensors react to glass breaking. A sensor the size of a large coin is placed directly on the glass and can detect glass breakage several feet away. Some types operate via a tuning fork, which is tuned to the frequency produced by breaking glass. Others employ a microphone and electric amplifier. Contact switches, placed on a window and window frame, activate an alarm when the window is opened and the electrical circuit is interrupted. Window foil, which has lost much of its popularity, consists of lead foil tape less than 1 inch wide and paper thin that is applied right on the glass near the edges of a window. In the nonalarm state, electricity passes through the foil to form a closed circuit. When the foil is broken, an alarm is sounded. Window foil is inexpensive and easy to maintain. One disadvantage is that an offender may cut the glass without disturbing the foil.

Doors

Many standards apply to doors from the AAMA, ANSI, ASTM, UL, ISO, NFPA, the National Association of Architectural Metal Manufacturers, and the Steel Door Institute. Also, other countries have standards. Doors having fire ratings require certain frame and hardware requirements. Decisions on the type of lock and whether electronic access will be applied also impact hardware. Decisions on doors are especially crucial because of daily use, the importance of emergency escape, and the potential for satisfying or enraging users and management.

Businesses and institutions generally use aluminum doors. Composed of an aluminum frame, most of the door is covered by glass. Without adequate protection, the glass is vulnerable, and prying the weak aluminum is not difficult.

Hollow-core doors render complex locks useless because an offender can punch right through the door. Thin wood panels or glass on a door are additional weak points. More expensive, solid-core doors are stronger; they are made of solid wood (over an inch thick) without the use of weak fillers. To reinforce hollow-core or solid-core doors, one can attach 16-gauge steel sheets via one-way screws. An alternative is to install an all-metal door.

Whenever possible, door hinges should be placed on the inside. Door hinges that face outside enable easy entry. By using a screwdriver and hammer, one can raise the pins out of the hinges to enable the door to be lifted away.

ELECTRONIC PROTECTION FOR DOORS

Contact switches applied to doors offer electronic protection. Greater protection is provided when contact switches are recessed in the edges of the door and frame. Other kinds of electronic sensors applied at doors include vibration sensors, pressure mats, and various types of motion detectors aimed in the area of the door. These sensors are explained in subsequent pages.

Access Controls

Access controls regulate people, vehicles, and items during movement into, out of, and within a building or facility. With regulation, people and assets are easier to protect. If a person or vehicle can enter a facility easily, the location is vulnerable to a host of problems, but if a person or vehicle must stop at an access checkpoint where a uniformed officer follows access policies and procedure (e.g., records ID information; issues a pass), then losses can be prevented.

Access controls vary from simple to complex. A simple setup includes locks and keys, officers checking identification badges, and written logs of entries and exits. More complex systems use access cards that activate electronic locking devices while a CCTV system observes; records and video are stored in these systems. A prime factor influencing the kind of system employed is need.

A research laboratory developing a new product requires strict access controls, whereas a retail business would require minimal controls.

CONTROLLING EMPLOYEE AND VISITOR TRAFFIC

The fewest entrances and exits are best. This permits officers to observe people entering and departing. If possible, employees should be routed to the access point closest to the workplace away from valuable assets.

Visitors include customers, salespeople, vendors, service people, contractors, and government employees. A variety of techniques are applicable to visitor access control. An appointment system enables preparation for visitors. Whatever the reason for the visit, the shortest route to specific destinations should be chosen, away from valuable assets and dangerous conditions. A record or log of visits is wise. Relevant information would be name of the visitor, date of visit, time entering and leaving, purpose, specific location visited, name of employee escorting visitor, and temporary badge number. These records aid investigators. Whenever possible, procedures should minimize employee–visitor contact.

CONTROLLING THE MOVEMENT OF PACKAGES AND PROPERTY

The movement of packages and property also must be subject to access controls. Many locations require precautions against bombs and WMD. Policies and procedures are a necessity for incoming and outgoing items.

CONTRABAND DETECTION

Contraband is an item that is illegal to possess or prohibited from being brought into a specific area. Examples are weapons, illegal drugs, and explosives. *Security officers play a crucial role in spotting contraband* at businesses, schools, airports, courthouses, and many other locations. They use special devices to locate contraband and these expensive *devices are as good as the personnel behind them*. Here is an overview of these devices.

- *Metal detectors* transmit a magnetic field that is disturbed by a metallic object, which sets off a light or audio signal. Two types of metal detectors are handheld and walk through. False alarms are a common problem.
- *X-ray scanners* use pulsed energy to penetrate objects that are shown on a color monitor. Drugs, plastic explosives, and firearms with plastic parts are difficult to identify with this method of detection.
- *Dual-energy systems* use X-rays at different energy levels to classify objects as organic, inorganic, or mixed. Colors are assigned to each classification to help spot contraband. When color and shape are observed, these systems are good at detecting explosives, as most are organic.
- *Computed tomography scanners* are like CAT scanners used in hospitals. An X-ray source is spun around an object taking slice pictures that show on a computer. Although this device is expensive, detection of items is good.

EMPLOYEE IDENTIFICATION SYSTEM

The use of an employee identification (card or badge) system depends on the number of employees that must be accounted for and recognized by other employees. An ID system not only prevents unauthorized people from entering a facility, but also deters unauthorized employees from entering restricted areas. For the system to operate efficiently, clear policies should state the use of ID cards, where and when the cards are to be displayed on the person, who should collect cards from employees who quit or are fired, and the penalties for noncompliance. A lost or stolen card should be reported so that the proper information reaches all interested personnel. Sometimes ID systems become a joke, and employees refuse to wear them or they decorate them or wear them in odd locations on their person. To sustain an ID system, proper socialization is essential.

Simple ID cards contain employer and employee names. A more complex system could include an array of information: name, signature, employee number, physical characteristics (e.g., height, weight, hair and eye colors), validation date, authorized signature, location of work assignment, thumbprint, and color photo. ID cards are becoming increasingly sophisticated and combined with multiple technologies for multiple purposes (e.g., as access cards).

ID cards can contain various levels of security and storage within the card. Entities with low data storage needs can look to cards with magnetic stripes or bar codes. The former contain digital data, such as access privileges and employment history, while the latter permit organizations to collect data. Enhanced security is gained through hologram seals that leave a checkerboard pattern if they are removed. Holographic images can be added that change color and appearance when held at various angles. Unique two- or three-dimensional hologram images make the cards difficult to duplicate. Hidden features can be added to cards, such as laser-viewable images and nano or micro text requiring magnification to view it. Security is strengthened when ID card printers are protected by a lock and/or password (Stromberg, 2005: 30–32).

AUTOMATIC ACCESS CONTROL

Because keys are difficult to control and easy to duplicate, there are limitations to the lock-and-key method of access control. Because of these problems, the need for improved access control, and technological innovations, a huge market has been created for electronic card access control systems. These systems are flexible. Unauthorized duplication of cards can be difficult and personnel (i.e., an officer at each entrance) costs are saved. The card contains coded information "read" by the system for access or denial.

Standards for these systems were slow to develop. However, this is changing due to the convergence of physical security and IT security and to large customers (e.g., the federal government) requiring their many facilities to be interoperable.

Before an automatic access control system is implemented, several considerations are necessary. *Safety must be a prime factor to ensure quick exit in case of emergency.* Another consideration is the adaptability of the system to the type of door presently in use. Can the system accommodate all traffic requirements? How many entrances and exits must be controlled? Will there be an annoying waiting period for those who want to gain access? Are additions to the system possible? What if the system breaks down? Is a backup source of power available (e.g., generators)?

Tailgating is another concern. This is when an authorized user lets in an unauthorized user. To thwart this problem, a security officer can be assigned to each access point, but this approach is expensive when compared to applying CCTV, revolving doors, or turnstiles. Revolving doors can be expensive initially and they are not an approved fire exit. Optical turnstiles contain invisible infrared beams to count people entering to control tailgating.

A summary of cards used in card access systems follows.

- *Magnetic stripe cards* are plastic, laminated cards (like credit cards) that have a magnetic stripe along one edge onto which a code is printed. When the card is inserted, magnetically encoded data are compared to data stored in a computer and access is granted on verification.
- *Magnetic dot cards* contain magnetic material, often barium ferrite, laminated between plastic layers. The dots create a magnetic pattern that activates internal sensors in a card reader.
- *Weigand cards* employ a coded pattern on a magnetized wire within the card to generate a code number. To gain access, the card is passed through a sensing reader.
- *Bar-coded cards* contain an array of tiny vertical lines that can be visible and vulnerable to photocopying or invisible and read by an infrared reader.
- *Proximity cards* need not be inserted into a reader but placed in its "proximity." A code is sent via radio frequency, magnetic field, or microchip-tuned circuit.

- *Smart cards* contain an integrated circuit chip within the plastic that serves as a miniature computer as it records and stores information and personal identification codes in its memory. Security is increased because information is held in the card rather than the reader. These cards permit a host of activities from access control to making purchases, while almost eliminating the need for keys or cash.

Radio frequency identification (RFID) is a popular technology applicable to not only access controls, but also many other functions. It has been labeled as the next step beyond bar code—those thin black bars on items that can be read with a scanner to ring up sales, take inventory, and be used for many other accountability functions. RFID goes further by providing each item with its own unique ID number that is matched with information in a database, and instead of being read by a scanner, as with bar codes, RFID tags communicate with a stationary or handheld reader by using radio waves. Active tags send radio waves to a reader and are more expensive than passive tags that send back a radio wave beamed to them. In addition to the tags, system costs include readers, a computer system, and software.

Access controls can be enhanced with RFID because readers can keep track of a person, vehicle, or object holding a tag. *The implications of this technology are enormous, especially if the tags are placed in consumer goods.* The American Civil Liberties Union has expressed concern over privacy issues related to RFID. Another problem is offenders hacking into the technology. For example, researchers at John Hopkins University hacked into encoded vehicle keyless entry systems and a cashless payment system for gasoline. Although RFID systems have problems, there are many uses for homeland security. Airports are testing personal RFID tags to ensure that only authorized workers are within secure areas. Because the tags can be stolen, they are combined with smart cards that contain biometric information. RFID is also applicable to airport luggage. Other uses include tracking first responders, vehicles, and equipment at an emergency scene; combined with other technology, such as sensors, keeping track of cargo and detecting WMD; and tracking livestock and other foods (Ferris, 2005: 16).

Biometric security systems have been praised as a major advance in access control. These systems verify an individual's identity through fingerprint scan, hand scan (hand geometry), iris scan (the iris is the colored part around the pupil of the eye), retina scan (the retina is the sensory membrane lining the eye and receiving the image formed by the lense), voice patterns, physical action of writing, and facial scan. The biometric leaders are fingerprint, hand, iris, and face recognition (Piazza, 2005: 41–55). Research continues to improve biometrics. Voice and writing are being refined, and research is being conducted on gait, body odor, heartbeat, and inner ear bones. In the near term we will not see facial scan pick a known terrorist out of a crowd, but the technology is evolving. Digitized photos shot at angles or in poor light can be flawed. The challenge with facial scan is identifying a person on the move (Philpott: 2005: 16–21).

Basically, biometric systems operate by storing identifying information in a computer to be compared with information presented by a subject requesting access. The applications are endless: doors, computers, vehicles, and so on. Although biometric systems have been touted as being invincible, no security is foolproof, as illustrated by terrorists who cut off the thumb of a bank manager to gain entry through a fingerprint-based access control system.

The great advantage of biometrics is that it links the event to a particular individual, whereas a card, personal identification number (PIN), or password may be used by an unauthorized individual.

Video identification is another strategy to facilitate positive identification. Two forms are photo ID badges and image storage and retrieval systems. A security officer verifies the image with a host computer on a monitor or display terminal that also contains personal data.

Figure 9-6 ■ Three technology approaches to access control. Source: National Institute of Justice (1999).

Increasing Security

**What you
HAVE
(ID card or badge)**

**What you
KNOW
(Password or PIN number,
usually with card reader)**

**Who you
ARE
(Biometrics identifiers,
usually with a PIN number)**

Access controls often use multiple technologies, such as smart cards and biometrics. One location may require a card, another location may require a PIN and a card, and another may require biometric identifiers and a PIN (Figure 9-6). Many systems feature a distress code that can be entered if someone is being victimized. Another feature is an alarm that sounds during unauthorized attempted entry. Access systems can be programmed to allow select access according to time, day, and location. The logging capabilities are another feature to ascertain personnel location by time, date, and resources expended (e.g., computer time, parking space, cafeteria).

We are seeing an increasing merger of card access systems and biometric technology, and, thus, missing or stolen cards are less of a concern. We will see more point-of-sale readers that accept biometric samples for check cashing, credit cards, and other transactions. The use of biometric systems will become universal—banking, correctional facilities, welfare control programs, and so forth.

LOCKS AND KEYS

The basic purpose of a lock-and-key system is to hinder unauthorized entry. Attempts to enter a secure location usually are made at a window or door to a building or at a door somewhere within a building. Consequently, locks deter unauthorized access from outsiders and insiders. *Many see a lock as only a delaying device that is valued by the amount of time needed to defeat it* (Purpura, 2002: 161–170). Standards related to locks include those from ANSI, ASTM, and UL. Local ordinances may specify certain locks.

Almost all locking devices are operated by a key, numerical combination, card, or electricity. Most key-operated locks (except padlocks) use a bolt or latch. The bolt (or deadbolt) extends from a door lock into a bolt receptacle within the door frame. Authorized entry is made by using an appropriate key to manually move the bolt into the door lock. Latches are spring loaded and less secure than a bolt. They are cut on an angle to permit them to slide right into the strike when the door is closed. Unless the latch is equipped with a locking bar (deadlatch), a credit card or knife can be used to push the latch back to open the door.

The cylinder part of a lock contains the keyway, pins, and other mechanisms that permit the bolt or latch to be moved by a key for access. Double-cylinder locks, in which a cylinder is located on each side of a door, are a popular form of added security as compared to single-cylinder locks. Double-cylinder locks require a key for both sides. With a single-cylinder lock, a thief may be able to break glass or remove a wood panel and then reach inside to turn the knob to release the lock. For safety's sake, locations that use double-cylinder locks must prepare for emergency escape by having a key readily available.

Key-in-knob locks are used universally, but are being replaced by key-in-the-lever locks to be compliant with the Americans with Disabilities Act (ADA). As the name implies, the keyway is in the knob or lever. Most contain a keyway on the outside and a button on the insider for locking from within.

The Americans with Disabilities Act of 1990 prohibits discrimination against individuals with disabilities and increases their access to services and jobs. The law requires employers to make reasonable accommodations for employees with a disability if doing so would not create an undue hardship for the employer. Reasonable accommodations include making existing facilities accessible and modifying a workstation. The ADA has had a significant impact on the security and safety designs of buildings. Access controls, doorways, elevators, and emergency alarm systems are among the many physical features of a building that must accommodate disabled people. The Equal Employment Opportunity Commission enforces the act.

Volumes have been written about locks. Here is a summary of various types of locks.

- *Warded (or skeleton key tumbler) lock.* This older kind of lock is disengaged when a skeleton key makes direct contact with a bolt and slides it back into the door. It is an easy lock to pick. A strong piece of L-shaped wire can be inserted into the keyway to move the bolt. Warded locks are still in use in many older buildings and are recognized by a keyway that permits seeing through. *Locks on handcuffs are of the warded kind and can be defeated by a knowledgeable offender.*
- *Disc tumbler (or wafer tumbler) lock.* Originally designed for the automobile industry, its use has expanded to desks, cabinets, files, and padlocks. The operation of this lock entails spring-loaded flat metal discs, instead of pins, that align when the proper key is used. These locks are mass produced, inexpensive, and have a short life expectancy. More security is offered than a warded lock can provide, but disc tumbler locks are subject to defeat by improper keys or being jimmied.
- *Pin tumbler lock.* Invented by Linus Yale in 1844, the pin tumbler lock is used widely in industry and residences. Its security surpasses that of the warded and disc tumbler locks.
- *Lever lock.* Lever locks vary widely. Basically, these locks disengage when the proper key aligns tumblers. Those found in cabinets, chests, and desks often provide minimal security, whereas those found in bank safe deposit boxes are more complex and provide greater security. The better quality lever lock offers more security than the best pin tumbler lock.

- *Combination lock.* This lock requires manipulating a numbered dial(s) to gain access. Combination locks usually have three or four dials that must be aligned in the correct order for entrance. These locks provide greater security than key locks because a limited number of people probably will know the lock combination, keys are unnecessary, and lock picking is obviated. They are used for safes, bank vaults, and high-security filing cabinets. With older combination locks, skillful burglars are able actually to listen to the locking mechanism to open the lock; more advanced mechanisms have reduced this weakness. A serious vulnerability results when an offender watches the opening of a combination lock with either binoculars or a telescope. Retailers sometimes place combination safes near the front door for viewing by patrolling police; however, unless the retailer uses his or her body to block the dial from viewing, losses may result. This same weakness exists where access is permitted by typing a PIN into a keyboard for access to a parking lot, doorway, or secure area.
- *Combination padlock.* This lock is similar in operation to a combination lock. It is used on employee or student lockers and in conjunction with safety hasps or chains. Some of these locks have a keyway so they can be opened with a key.
- *Padlock.* Requiring a key, this lock is used on lockers or in conjunction with hasps or chains. Numerous kinds exist, each affording different levels of protection. Low-security padlocks contain warded locks, whereas more secure ones have disc tumbler, pin tumbler, or lever characteristics. Serial numbers on padlocks are a security hazard similar to combination padlocks.

Other kinds of locks include devices that have a bolt that locks vertically instead of horizontally. Emergency exit locks with alarms or "panic alarms" enable quick exit in emergencies while deterring unauthorized door use. Sequence-locking devices require locking the doors in a predetermined order; this ensures that all doors are locked because the outer doors will not lock until the inner doors are locked.

The use of interchangeable core locks is a quick method to deal with the theft, duplication, or loss of keys. Using a special control key, one core (that part containing the keyway) is simply replaced by another. A different key then is needed to operate the lock. This system, although more expensive initially, minimizes the need for a locksmith or the complete changing of locks.

Automatic locking and unlocking devices also are a part of the broad spectrum of methods to control access. Digital locking systems open doors when a particular numbered combination is typed. If the wrong number is typed, an alarm is sounded. Combinations can be changed when necessary. Electromagnetic locks use magnetism, electricity, and a metal plate around doors to hold doors closed. When the electricity is turned off, the door can be opened. Remote locks enable opening a door electronically from a remote location. Before releasing the door lock, an officer seated in front of a console identifies an individual at a door by use of CCTV and a two-way intercom.

Trends taking place with locks and keys include increasing use of electronics and microchip technology. For example, hybrids have been developed whereby a key can serve as a standard hardware key in one door and an electronic key in another door. Manufacturers also offer mechanical locks and keys with microchip technology to produce an intelligent system that can provide an audit trail. Such systems are self-contained on a door and use a common watch-type battery. A key collection device is used to retrieve data. As electronics get smaller, we will see more of it being merged with mechanical locks. Another trend is electronic locks on the perimeter and hardware locks on inner doors.

Both enormous expenditures and personnel efforts may be used to protect against external threats (e.g., terrorists, spies, robbers, and burglars) without enough consideration for internal threats (e.g., employee offenders who may be terrorists or spies).

INTRUSION DETECTION SYSTEMS

An **intrusion detection system** detects and reports an event or stimulus within its detection area. A response is essential.

The basic components of an intrusion detection system are sensor, control unit, and annunciator. Sensors detect intrusion by, for example, heat or movement. The control unit receives the alarm notification from the sensor and then activates a silent alarm or annunciator (e.g., a bell or siren), which usually produces a human response.

INTERIOR SENSORS

A variety of standards exist for intrusion detection systems from UL, ISO, the Institute of Electrical and Electronics Engineers, and other groups. Here is a list of interior sensors (Purpura, 2002: 171–174).

- *A balanced magnetic switch* consists of a switch mounted to a door (or window) frame and a magnet mounted to a moveable door or window. When the door is closed, the magnet holds the switch closed to complete a circuit. An alarm is triggered when the door is opened and the circuit is interrupted.
- *A mechanical contact switch* contains a push-button-actuated switch that is recessed into a surface. An item is placed on it that depresses the switch, completing the alarm circuit. Lifting the item interrupts the circuit and signals an alarm.
- *Pressure-sensitive mats* contain two layers of metal strips or screen wire separated by sections of foam rubber or other flexible material. When pressure is applied, as by a person walking on the mat, both layers meet and complete an electrical contact to signal an alarm. These mats are applied as internal traps at doors, windows, main traffic points, and near valuable assets. The cost is low and these mats are difficult to detect. If detected by an offender, he or she can walk around it.
- *Grid wire sensors* are made of fine insulated wire attached to protected surfaces in a grid pattern consisting of two circuits, one running vertical, the other horizontal, and each overlapping the other. An interruption in either circuit signals an alarm. This type of sensor is applied to grill work, screens, walls, floors, ceilings, doors, and other locations. Although these sensors are difficult for an offender to spot, they are expensive to install and an offender can jump the circuit.
- *Trip wire sensors* use a spring-loaded switch attached to a wire stretched across a protected area. An intruder "trips" the alarm (i.e., opens the circuit) when the wire is pulled loose from the switch. These sensors are often applied to ducts, but they can be applied to other locations. If spotted by an offender, he or she may be able to circumvent it.
- *Vibration sensors* detect low-frequency energy resulting from the force applied in an attack of a structure. They are applied to walls, floors, and ceilings. Various sensor models require proper selection.
- *Capacitance sensors* create an electrical field around metallic objects that, when disturbed, signal an alarm. These sensors are applied to safes, file cabinets, grills at openings (e.g., windows), and other metal objects. One sensor can protect many objects; however, it is subject to defeat by using insulation (e.g., heavy gloves).
- *Infrared photoelectric beam sensors* activate an alarm when an invisible infrared beam of light is interrupted. If the system is detected, an offender may jump over or crawl under the beam to defeat it.
- *Microwave motion detectors* operate on the Doppler frequency shift principle. An energy field is transmitted into an area and monitored for a change in the pattern and frequency, which results in an alarm. Because microwave energy penetrates a variety of construction materials, care is required for placement and aiming. However, this can be an advantage in protecting multiple rooms and large areas with one sensor. These sensors can be defeated by objects blocking the sensor or by fast or slow movement.

- *Passive infrared intrusion sensors (PIR)* are passive in that they do not transmit a signal for an intruder to disturb. Rather, moving infrared radiation (from a person) is detected against the radiation environment of a room. When an intruder enters the room, the level of infrared energy changes and an alarm is activated. Although the PIR is not subject to many nuisance alarms, it should not be aimed at sources of heat or surfaces that can reflect energy. The PIR can be defeated by blocking the sensor so it cannot pick up heat.
- *Passive audio detectors* listen for noise created by intruders. Various models filter out naturally occurring noises not indicating forced entry. They can use public address system speakers in buildings, which can act as microphones to listen to intruders. The actual conversation of intruders can be picked up and recorded by these systems. To enhance this system, CCTV can provide visual verification of an alarm condition, video in real time and still images digitally to security or police, and evidence. The audio also can be two way, enabling security to warn the intruders. *Such audiovisual systems must be applied with extreme care to protect privacy, confidentiality, and sensitive information and to avoid violating state and federal wiretapping laws.*
- *Fiber optics* technology is growing in popularity for intrusion detection. It involves the transportation of information via guided light waves in an optical fiber. This sensor can be attached to or inserted in many things requiring protection. When stress is applied to the fiber-optic cable, an infrared light pulsing through the cable reacts to the stress and signals an alarm.

Two types of sensor technologies often are applied to a location to reduce false alarms, prevent defeat techniques, or fulfill unique needs. The combination of microwave and passive infrared sensors is a popular example of applying dual technologies. Reporting can be designed so an alarm is signaled when both sensors detect an intrusion (to reduce false alarms) or when either sensor detects an intrusion. Sensors are also becoming "smarter" by sending sensor data to a control panel or computer, distinguishing between human and animals, and activating a trouble output if the sensor lense is blocked. Supervised wireless sensors have become a major advancement because sensors can be placed at the best location without the expense of running a wire; these sensors are monitored constantly for integrity of the radio frequency link between the sensor and panel, status of the battery, and if the sensor is functioning normally.

PERIMETER SENSORS
Here is a list of intrusion sensors for perimeters (Purpura, 2002: 204–209; Reddick, 2005: 36–42).

- *Ported coaxial cable*: creates an electromagnetic field around buried "leaky" cables. The field is above and below ground and senses mass, velocity, and conductivity of humans and vehicles.
- *Fence disturbance*: mounted on a fence, these sensors are varied and include motion sensing (vibration), acoustic, and fiber optic.
- *Bistatic microwave*: these sensors establish a zone through transmitting and receiving antennas. They operate via microwave frequencies and detect changes in the signal from movement between the antennas. Because of blind spots near each antenna, the microwave zones must be overlapped.
- *Electric field*: detection depends on penetration of a volumetric field and a change in capacitance created by field wires and sensor wires attached to a fence or posts. It is good for heavily contoured terrain.
- *Video motion*: processes changes in video signals from CCTV cameras aimed at specific zones.
- *Surface wave*: these sensors establish an electromagnetic field around a pair of parallel wires supported by poles. Disturbance of the field sets off an alarm. This technology is used primarily for rapid deployment.

- *Taut wire*: this system, attached to a fence or poles, consists of parallel wires connected to sensors that signal an alarm when the wire is stretched or cut.
- *Fiber optics*: this perimeter protection can take the form of a fiber-optic net installed on a fence. When an intruder applies stress, an infrared light source pulsing through the system notes the stress or break and activates an alarm. Optical fibers can be attached to or inserted within numerous items to signal an alarm, including razor ribbon, security grilles, windows, and doors.

No one technology is perfect. As with interior intrusion detection systems, perimeter intrusion detection systems rely on dual technology to strengthen intrusion detection and reduce false alarms. When selecting a system, it is wise to remember that manufacturers' claims often are based on perfect weather. Security decision makers must clearly understand the advantages and disadvantages of each type of system under a variety of conditions.

ALARM SIGNALING SYSTEMS

Alarm signaling systems transmit data from a protected area to an annunciation system. Local ordinances and codes may restrict certain systems, designate to whom the alarm may be transmitted, or limit the length of time the alarm is permitted to sound outside.

Local alarm systems notify, by sound or lights, people in the hearing or seeing range of the signal. This includes the intruder, who may flee.

A central station alarm system receives intrusion or fire signals or both at a computer console located and monitored a distance away from the protected location. When an alarm signal is received, central station personnel contact police, firefighters, or other responders. Resources for central station design are available from UL, NFPA, and the Security Industry Association.

A variety of data transmission systems are utilized to signal an alarm. Telephone lines have been used for many years. Radio frequency and microwave data transmission systems often are applied where telephone lines are not available or where hardwire lines are not practical. Fiber-optic data transmission systems are a popular option. It is more secure and less subject to interference than older methods of transmitting data. Fiber optics differs from the conventional transmission of electrical energy in copper wires. These cables are either underground or aboveground. Fiber-optic systems often support computer-based multiplex data communications systems. Alarm signals should be backed up by multiple technologies. Options for off-site transmission of activity include satellite, local area network, wide area network, cellular, and the Internet. Cellular is especially useful for backup since it is more likely to remain in operation in certain disasters. It can also be used as a primary transmission method (Zwirn, 2003: 74–83).

Among the advances in alarm monitoring is remote programming. By this method, a central station can perform a variety of functions without ever visiting the site. Capabilities include system arming and disarming, unlocking doors, diagnostics and corrections and, with access systems, adding or deleting cards.

Alarm systems also may be multiplexed or integrated. Multiplexing is a method of transmitting multiple information signals over a single communications channel. This single communications channel reduces line requirements by allowing signal transmission from many protected facilities. Two other advantages are that more detailed information can be transmitted, such as telling which detector is in an alarm state, and transmission line security is enhanced through the use of encoding. Integrated systems combine multiple systems (e.g., alarm monitoring, access controls, and CCTV).

CLOSED-CIRCUIT TELEVISION

Closed-circuit television assists in deterrence, surveillance, apprehension, and prosecution. Although it may be costly initially, CCTV reduces personnel costs because it allows the viewing of multiple locations by one person. Accessories include zoom lenses, remote pan (i.e., side-to-side movement), and tilt (i.e., up-and-down movement) mechanisms that enable viewing mobility and opportunities to obtain a close look at any suspicious activity. Additional features include tamperproof housings that impede those interested in disabling cameras. Different models are resistant to bullets, explosion, dust, and severe weather. Housings are manufactured with heaters, defrosters, windshield wipers, washers, and sun shields. Low-light-level cameras provide the means to view outside when very little light is available. When no visible light is available, an infrared illuminator creates light, invisible to the naked eye, but visible to infrared-sensitive cameras. Another option is thermal-imaging cameras that sense heat and are especially helpful to spot intruders in darkness, fog, smoke, and foliage. Standards for CCTV systems are available from several sources.

CCTV cameras are pervasive in our society. At businesses and institutions, cameras are commonly placed at parking lots, access points, shipping and receiving docks, merchandise storage areas, cashier locations, computer rooms, and overlooking files, safes, vaults.

Constant monitoring of a CCTV system ensures its loss prevention capabilities. Personnel that are not rotated periodically become fatigued from watching too much television. This is a serious problem that is often overlooked. Regular employees may "test" the monitoring of the system by placing a bag or rag over a camera or even spraying the lens with paint. If employees see that there is no response, CCTV becomes a hoax. The use of dummy cameras is not recommended because, when employees discover the dummy, loss prevention appears to be a deceitful farce.

Automated video surveillance provides an alternative to requiring an operator to watch CCTV monitors by programming cameras to recognize specific features and compare these to an identification database. These systems can be programmed to recognize biometric features (e.g., facial scan) and unusual patterns (e.g., a person, vehicle, or item in an odd location), while playing a role in automated intrusion detection and "following" people and vehicles.

The extent of the use of hidden surveillance cameras is difficult to measure. Pinhole lenses are a popular component of hidden surveillance cameras. They get their name from the outer opening of the lens, which is 1/8 to 1/4 inch in diameter and difficult to spot. Cameras are hidden in almost any location, such as clocks, file cabinets, computers, sprinkler heads, and mannequins.

Several methods can be applied to transmit the camera image to the monitor: coaxial cable, fiber optics, microwave, radio frequency, telephone lines, and the Internet. Furthermore, it is becoming increasingly common to see video images on personal digital assistants and cell phones (Merrifield, 2005: 52–54). What we have is the opportunity (as with other electronic security systems) for say, an executive in New York, to monitor inside his/her business in Hong Kong. Recording capabilities to hard drive provide a record for subsequent review and the record can serve as evidence.

With camera phones so prevalent in our world, these devices are a threat to privacy and proprietary information. Management must develop policies and procedures for camera phone use on the premises.

LIGHTING

From a security perspective, two major purposes of lighting are to *create a psychological deterrent to intrusion* and *to enable detection*. Good lighting is considered such an effective crime control method that the law, in many locales, requires buildings to maintain adequate lighting.

From a business marketing perspective, lighting contains bottom-line benefits that can help in budget justification. Examples include attracting customers looking for a safe location to shop, enhancing curbside appeal, and helping to focus customer attention on select merchandise.

One way to analyze security lighting deficiencies is to go to the building at night and study the possible methods of entry and areas where inadequate lighting will aid an offender. Before the visit, one should contact local police as a precaution against mistaken identity and to recruit their assistance in spotting weak points in lighting. Another option is to hire a professional service company to conduct a lighting study based on guidelines from the Illuminating Engineering Society of North America.

Lumens (of light output) per watt (of power input) are a measure of lamp efficiency. Initial lumens-per-watt data are based on the light output of lamps when new; however, light output declines with use. Illuminance is the intensity of light falling on a surface, measured in foot-candles (FC) (English units) or lux (metric units). The FC is the measure of how bright the light is when it reaches 1 foot from the source. One lux equals 0.0929 FC. The light provided by direct sunlight on a clear day is about 10,000 FC, an overcast day would yield about 100 FC, and a full moon about 0.01 FC. The following is a sample of outdoor lighting luminance recommended by the Illuminating Engineering Society of North America: self-parking area, 1 FC; attendant parking area, 2 FC; covered parking area, 5 FC; active pedestrian entrance, 5 FC; and building surroundings, 1 FC. It generally is recommended that gates and doors, where identification of persons and things takes place, should have at least 2 FC. An office should have a light level of about 50 FC.

The following lamps are applied outdoors.

- *Incandescent* lamps are commonly found at residences. Passing electrical current through a tungsten wire that becomes white hot produces light. These lamps produce 10 to 20 lumens per watt, are the least efficient and most expensive to operate, and have a short lifetime of from 1000 to 2000 hours.
- *Halogen* and *quartz halogen* lamps are incandescent bulbs filled with halogen gas (like sealed-beam auto headlights) and provide about 25% better efficiency and life than ordinary incandescent bulbs.
- *Fluorescent* lamps pass electricity through a gas enclosed in a glass tube to produce light, producing 40 to 80 lumens per watt. They create twice the light and less than half the heat of an incandescent bulb of equal wattage and cost 5 to 10 times as much. Fluorescent lamps do not provide high levels of light output. The lifetime is 10,000 to 15,000 hours. They are not used extensively outdoors, except for signage.
- *Mercury vapor* lamps also pass electricity through a gas. The yield is 30 to 60 lumens per watt and the life is about 20,000 hours.
- *Metal halide* lamps are also of the gaseous type. The yield is 80 to 100 lumens per watt, and the life is about 10,000 hours. They often are used at sports stadiums because they imitate daylight conditions and colors appear natural. Consequently, these lamps complement CCTV systems, but they are the most expensive light to install and maintain.
- *High-pressure sodium* lamps are gaseous, yield about 100 lumens per watt, have a life of about 20,000 hours, and are energy efficient. These lamps are often applied on streets and parking lots, cut through fog, and are designed to allow the eyes to see more detail at greater distances.
- *Low-pressure sodium* lamps are gaseous, produce 150 lumens per watt, have a life of about 15,000 hours, and are even more efficient than high-pressure sodium. These lamps are expensive to maintain.

Each type of lamp has a different color rendition, which is the way the output of a lamp affects human perceptions of color. This also impacts what is viewed through CCTV systems. Incandescent, fluorescent, and certain types of metal halide lamps provide excellent color rendition. Mercury vapor lamps provide good color rendition but are heavy on the blue. High-pressure sodium lamps, which are used extensively outdoors, provide poor color rendition, making things look yellow. Low-pressure sodium lamps make color unrecognizable and produce a yellow-gray color on objects. People find sodium vapor lamps, sometimes called "anticrime lights," to be harsh because they produce a strange yellow haze. Claims are made that this lighting conflicts with aesthetic values and that it affects sleeping habits. In many instances, when people park their vehicles in a parking lot during the day and return to find their vehicle at night, they are often unable to locate it due to poor color rendition from sodium lamps; some report their vehicle as being stolen. Another problem is the inability of witnesses to describe offenders accurately.

Mercury vapor, metal halide, and high-pressure sodium take several minutes to produce full light output. If they are turned off, even more time is required to reach full output because they first have to cool down. This may not be acceptable for certain security applications. Incandescent, halogen, and quartz halogen have the advantage of instant light once electricity is turned on. Manufacturers provide information on a host of lamp characteristics, including the "strike" and "restrike" time. Two additional sources for information on lighting are the National Lighting Bureau and the International Association of Lighting Management Companies.

SECURITY OFFICERS

Security officers are an essential part of security programs. Officers normally are assigned to stationary (fixed) posts or to patrol. A stationary post is at a door or gate where people, vehicles, and objects are observed and inspected. Stationary posts also involve directing traffic or duty at a command post where communications, CCTV, and alarms are monitored. Foot or vehicle patrols conducted throughout the premises and along perimeters identify irregularities while deterring offenders. Examples of unusual or harmful conditions that should be reported are damaged security devices, holes in perimeter fences or other evidence of intrusion, unattended vehicles parked inappropriately, keys left in vehicles, blocked fire exits, cigarette butts in no-smoking areas, accumulations of trash, and odors from fuels or hazardous materials. In contrast to public police officers, private security officers act in primarily a preventive role and observe and report.

Before security officers are employed, farsighted planning ensures optimum effectiveness of this service. What are the unique characteristics of the location? What assets need protection? How many hours per day is the facility open? How many employees? How many visitors and vehicles are admitted daily? What are the particular vulnerabilities? How will security officers interact with other loss prevention measures?

Security officers are expensive. Wages, insurance, uniforms, equipment, and training add up to a hefty sum per officer per year. If each officer costs $40,000 per year for a proprietary force and 5 officers are required for the premises at all times, to maintain all shifts 7 days per week requires approximately 20 officers. The cost would be about $800,000 per year. To reduce costs, many companies switch to contract security services and/or consider technological solutions.

Several specific steps can be taken to improve the effectiveness of officers. Three of the most critical are *applicant screening, training,* and *supervision*. Management should ensure that officers know what is expected of them. Policies, procedures, and day-to-day duties are communicated via verbal orders, memos, and training programs. Policies should ensure that supervisors check on officers every hour. Irregular, unpredictable patrols by all officers hinder offenders. Rotating officers reduces fatigue while familiarizing them with a variety of duties. Providing inspection lists for adverse conditions will keep them mentally alert; the formal list should be returned with a daily report. Courtesy and a sharp appearance command respect from employees and visitors.

PROTECTIVE DOGS

Classified as an animal barrier, a dog can strengthen security around a protected location. An alarm dog patrols inside a fenced area or building and barks at the approach of a stranger, but makes no attempt to attack. These dogs retreat when threatened, but continue to bark. Such barking may become so alarming to an intruder that he or she will flee. A guard or attack dog is similar to an alarm dog with an added feature of attacking the intruder. To minimize the possibility of a lawsuit, these dogs should be selectively applied and adequately fenced in. The posting of warning signs also reduces liability. An experienced person on call at all times is needed to respond to emergencies. Another type of attack dog is the sentry dog. This dog is kept on a leash and responds to commands while patrolling with a uniformed officer. The advantages are numerous. These animals protect officers. Their keen sense of hearing and smell is a tremendous asset when trying to locate a hidden offender (or explosives or drugs). Dogs can distinguish multiple odors at the same time and can discern the slightest perspiration from people under stress, enabling the dog to sense those individuals who are afraid of them. An ingredient in stress perspiration irritates dogs, which makes frightened persons more susceptible to attack. When an "attack" command is given, a German shepherd has the strength in its jaws to break a person's arm.

In addition to the possibility of a lawsuit if a dog attacks someone, there are other disadvantages to the use of dogs. If a proprietary dog is part of the protective team, personnel and kennel facilities are needed to care for the dog. These costs and others include the purchase of dogs and their training, medical care, and food. Using a contract service would probably be more feasible. Another disadvantage is the possibility that dogs may be poisoned, anesthetized, or killed. An offender may also befriend a dog. Dogs should be taught to accept food only from the handler. Neighbors near the protected premises often find dogs noisy or may perceive them as offensive for other reasons.

In addition to the security topics of this chapter, an enormously important part of the total security picture is information technology security, one of the topics in the next chapter.

DISCUSSION QUESTIONS

1. Is improved security the answer to the problem of terrorism? Why or why not?
2. What are your views of U.S. government domestic and international security to protect U.S. citizens and assets from terrorism?
3. How can security programs meet organizational and customer needs?
4. Can all U.S. citizens and assets be protected from terrorism by the public and private sectors? Why or why not?
5. What three security strategies do you view as most helpful for protection against terrorism?
6. What three security strategies do you view as least helpful for protection against terrorism?
7. What innovative security strategies do you suggest to improve protection against terrorism?

APPLICATIONS

9A YOU BE THE DIRECTOR OF SECURITY

You are a newly appointed director of security for a high-rise office building in a major urban setting. You work for a property management company that oversees the entire building. There is a diversity of tenants, mostly businesses, and several tenants maintain their own security departments and/or contract security to a service firm. What five tasks do you focus on initially? Prioritize your list.

9B YOU BE THE DIRECTOR OF LOSS PREVENTION

You are the director of loss prevention for a major global corporation based in the United States. Upon conducting a security survey of a large corporate building in a medium size city in the United States, you listed the following vulnerabilities. Prepare solutions for each vulnerability and prioritize the list so the most serious items are corrected as soon as possible.

- Item A: The building contains an underground garage with minimal controls (i.e., an access gate opened by an employee access card).
- Item B: The front of the building is on Main Street, close to the street, and any vehicles can park at the front on the street. The three other sides of the building contain parking lots close to the building and are accessible through an access gate opened by an employee access card.
- Item C: The rear lobby of the building is at ground level and at the ending point of a straight road one-eighth mile long.

- Item D: In the last 12 months, two employees were robbed at night right outside the building in the parking lots.
- Item E: Corporate offices, functions, assets, and utilities are clearly marked by signs inside and outside of the building.
- Item F: Air intakes for the building are at ground level at the rear of the building.
- Item G: Although employees use a card key to access the building, tailgating is a problem.
- Item H: A minimum number of security officers on the premises result in gaps in security and at access points as they are called off-post to obtain mail and conduct other errands.
- Item I: Executive staff have their names on designated parking spaces.
- Item J: Two garbage dumpsters are located up against the rear of the building.
- Item K: The rear of the building faces nearby hills containing a variety of buildings.

9C   YOU BE THE CHIEF SECURITY OFFICER

As a chief security officer you are at corporate headquarters and receive an emergency telephone call from a frantic administrative assistant who just fled from the human resources (HR) office. She states that a recently retired employee was able to talk his way past a security officer and access controls to speak with someone in the HR office about benefits, but when he reached the director of HR, he demanded to see his ex-wife, an employee presently working. The retiree is supposedly holding a gun pointed at the director of HR, demanding to see his ex-wife. As the CSO, what do you do? List and prioritize the first five tasks you would accomplish.

9D   YOU BE THE SECURITY OFFICER

As an unarmed, uniformed security officer at a corporate location, what do you do in each of the following situations? Which of the situations is most serious and why? Which of the situations is least serious and why?

- Item A: A city police officer walks into the lobby where you are on post at an access point and requests your immediate assistance with an arrest outside.
- Item B: You are on foot patrol in a warehouse, smell and taste a foul odor, and see dead insects in the area.
- Item C: While on foot patrol, you spot a person walking on the premises with a pistol in his hand.
- Item D: While on foot patrol, you observe a HVAC crew working on the building ventilation system. The service company name on the van is different than the usual company, there are more technicians present than usual, and the technicians are standing as if they were guarding the system rather than servicing it.
- Item E: You are assigned to a shipping and receiving dock and a truck driver asks you to "look the other way" and leave your post for $500 cash.

WEB SITES

American Institute of Architects, Security Resource Center: www.aia.org/security
ASIS, International: www.asisonline.org
Federal Emergency Management Agency: www.fema.gov/hazards
International Foundation for Protection Officers: www.ifpo.org
Technical Support Working Group: www.tswg.gov
U.S. Department of Defense: http://www.defenselink.mil/
U.S. Department of Homeland Security: www.dhs.gov
U.S. General Services Administration: www.gsa.gov
U.S. Marshals Service: http://www.usdoj.gov/marshals

NOTES

ASIS, International (2003). *General Security Risk Assessment Guideline.* www.asisonline.org, retrieved January 3, 2005.
ASIS, International (2004). *Chief Security Officer Guideline.* www.asisonline.org, retrieved January 3, 2005.

Clark, R. (1983). "Situational Crime Prevention: Its Theoretical Basis and Practical Scope." In M. Tonry and N. Morris (Eds.), *Crime and Justice,* 4. Chicago: University of Chicago Press.

Collins, P., *et al.* (2005). "The ASIS Foundation Security Report: Scope and Emerging Trends." Alexandria, VA: ASIS, International.

Crawford, J. (1995). "Security, Heal Thyself." *Security Management* (May).

CSO (2004). "What is a Chief Security Officer?" *CSO* (September 13). http://www.csoonline.com/research/leadership/cso_role.html, retrieved November 30, 2005.

Ellis, D. (1991). *Becoming a Master Student,* 6th ed. Rapid City, SD: College Survival, Inc.

Ferris, N. (2005). "RFID: The (radio) wave of the future." *Homeland Protection Professional,* 4 (March).

Harowitz, S. (2005). "The Very Model of a Modern CSO." *Security Management,* 49 (April).

Jacobson, R. (2000). "What Is a Rational Goal for Security?" *Security Management,* 44 (December).

Kessinger, R. (2004). "From Jericho to Jersey Barrier." *Security Management,* 48 (August).

Lab, S. (2004). *Crime Prevention: Approaches, Practices and Evaluations,* 5th ed. www.lexisnexis.com/anderson/criminaljustice

Merrifield, M. (2005). "Surveillance On The Go." *Security Products,* 9 (March).

Murphy, P. (2000). "Grounds for Protection." *Security Management,* 44 (October).

National Institute of Justice (1999). *Appropriate and Effective Use of Security Technologies in U.S. Schools.* Washington, DC: U.S. Department of Justice (September).

Newman, O. (1972). *Defensible Space.* New York: Macmillan.

Owen, D. (2003). *Building Security: Strategies and Cost.* Kingston, MA: Reed.

Philpott, D. (2005). "Physical Security: Biometrics." *Homeland Defense Journal,* 3 (May).

Piazza, P. (2005). "The Smart Cards Are Coming ... Really." *Security Management,* 49 (January).

Post, R., and Kingsbury, A. (1977). *Security Administration: An Introduction,* 3rd ed. Springfield, IL: Charles C Thomas.

Purpura, P. (2002). *Security and Loss Prevention,* 4th ed. Boston, MA: Butterworth-Heinemann.

Purpura, P. (2003). *The Security Handbook,* 2nd ed. Boston, MA: Butterworth-Heinemann.

Radford, D. (2004). "The U.S. Economy: A Prime Terrorism Target." *Security Products,* 8 (August).

Reddick, R. (2005). "What You Should Know About Protecting a Perimeter." *Security Products,* 9 (April).

Reuters News Service (2005). "Bombs found at U.S. companies in Argentina." http://abcnews.go.com, retrieved June 6, 2005.

Revell, O. (2003). "Protective Blast and Anti-Ramming Wall Development." *Security Technology & Design* (November).

Saflex, Inc. (2005). "Introduction to Security Glazing." www.saflex.com, retrieved June 1, 2005.

Shaw, E., Post, J., and Ruby, K. (2000). "Managing the Threat from Within." *Information Security,* 3 (July).

Stinson, J. (1984). "Assessing Terrorist Tactics and Security Measures." Paper presented at the Detroit Police Department Conference on "Urban Terrorism: Planning or Chaos?" (November). In J. White (2003), *Terrorism: An Introduction,* 4th ed. Belmont, CA: Wadsworth/Thomson.

Stromberg, S. (2005). "Addressing the Fundamentals." *Security Products,* 9 (May).

U.S. Army (2001). *Physical Security* (FM 3-19.30). Washington, DC: HQ, Department of the Army.

U.S. Department of Homeland Security (2003). *Reference Manual to Mitigate Potential Terrorist Attacks Against Buildings,* FEMA 426 (December). Washington, DC: FEMA.

U.S. Department of Homeland Security, Science and Technology Directorate and the Executive Office of the President, Office of Science and Technology Policy (2004). *The National Plan for Research and Development In Support of Critical Infrastructure Protection.* www.dhs.gov, retrieved June 13, 2005.

U.S. Government Accountability Office (2005). *Homeland Security: Actions Needed to Better Protect National Icons and Federal Office Buildings from Terrorism* (June). www.gao.gov/cgi-bin/getrpt?GAO-05-681, retrieved July 12, 2005.

Wailgum, T. (2005). "Where the Metrics Are." *CSO* (February). www.csoonline.com, retrieved February 9, 2005.

Zwirn, J. (2003). "Alarm Design that Rings True." *Security Management* (April).

CHAPTER 10

PROTECTING CRITICAL INFRASTRUCTURES AND KEY ASSETS

OBJECTIVES

The study of this chapter will enable you to:
1. Define critical infrastructure and key assets.
2. Explain federal government action to protect critical infrastructures and key assets.
3. List and describe the five-step critical infrastructure protection risk management framework.
4. Examine eight critical infrastructure sectors, how each is unique, what government body facilitates protection, and protection issues and strategies of each.
5. Examine four categories of key assets, how each is unique, what government body facilitates protection, and protection issues and strategies of each.

KEY TERMS

complex terrorism
critical infrastructure
critical infrastructure protection (CIP)
key assets
sector-specific agencies
sector-specific plans
CIP risk management framework
Homeland Security Operations Center
Information Sharing and Analysis Centers
Intelligence Reform and Terrorism Protection
   Act of 2004
The Infrastructure Security Partnership
bioterrorism
agroterrorism

Public Health Security and Bioterrorism
   Preparedness and Response Act of 2002
Project BioShield Act of 2004
model food security plans
penetration test
Johnstown flood
Teton dam
Chernobyl
Three-Mile Island
Bhopal, India
Texas City, Texas
Exxon Valdez
Emergency Planning and Community
   Right-to-Know Act of 1986

KEY TERMS

spam	information security
phishing	Information Systems Audit and Control
social engineering	Association
keylogging programs	Information Systems Security Association
spyware	National Industrial Security Program
malware	General Services Administration
blended cyber threats	Federal Protective Service
blended cyber-physical attack	U.S. Marshals Service
corporate intelligence	

HOW VULNERABLE IS OUR CRITICAL INFRASTRUCTURE?

Homer-Dixon (2002) presents the scenario of a sweltering summer night in July when U.S. power plants struggle to produce enough electricity for millions of air conditioners. Using a coordinated, well-timed plan, groups of men and women on the east and west coasts use rented vans to travel to specific electrical substations and high-voltage transmission lines. They unload their equipment from the vans. Those near the substations prepare simple mortars made from items purchased at hardware stores, while those at the transmission lines use helium to fill weather balloons with long silvery tails. At a set time, the mortars are fired to send aluminum chaff to the substations. The balloons are released and make contact with the transmission lines. The result is an electrical system that is massively short-circuited, leading to a cascade of power failures on a national scale. The horror of unbearable conditions in buildings from the heat, huge traffic jams, disabled water and sewage systems, among other problems, becomes a reality. The national economy is unable to function.

Homer-Dixon claims that his scenario is not far-fetched because of the growing technological ability of small terrorist groups and the increasing vulnerability of our economic and technological systems. He calls the combination of these two trends **complex terrorism** and views it as operating like jujitsu—"it redirects the energies of our intricate societies against us."

Homer-Dixon sees two major vulnerabilities of advanced nations: (1) the growing complexity and interconnectedness of modern societies and (2) the increasing geographic concentration of high-value assets in small locations. He refers to critical complex networks, including energy, information, water, food, transportation, and healthcare. His solutions refer to not only security, but decentralizing networks to reduce the "cascade effect" and dispersal of high-value assets.

WHAT IS CRITICAL INFRASTRUCTURE?

Two major questions concerning **critical infrastructure** (CI) are (1) what is it and (2) how can it be protected? CI is an evolving concept. Because it is impossible and too expensive to protect all the elements of all the sectors of CI, prioritization is required. Risk management and risk analysis tools serve to aid this task. The Department of Homeland Security (DHS) is tasked with assessing and mitigating risks to CI in cooperation with all levels of government and the private sector.

Quirk and Fernandez (2005: 2) define infrastructure as

> ... a collection of interdependent networks that comprises industries, institutions, and distribution systems. These systems provide an essential flow of products and services to ensure the functioning of the government and society as a whole. The national infrastructures are highly interconnected, both physically and through a cyber-based system. The term "interdependent" reflects all types of influences that the behaviors of infrastructures have on one another.

In 1996, President Bill Clinton (Executive Order 13010, 1996: 37347) defined critical infrastructure as those that are "so vital that their incapacity or destruction would have a debilitating impact on the defense or economic security of the United States."

The *National Strategy for Homeland Security* (Office of Homeland Security, 2002: ix) states

> Our society and modern way of life are dependent on networks of infrastructure—both physical networks such as our energy and transportation systems and virtual networks such as the Internet. If terrorists attack one or more pieces of our critical infrastructure, they may disrupt entire systems and cause significant damage to the Nation. We must therefore improve protection of the individual pieces and interconnecting systems that make up our critical infrastructure. Protecting America's critical infrastructure and key assets will not only make us more secure from terrorist attack, but will also reduce our vulnerability to natural disasters, organized crime, and computer hackers. America's critical infrastructure encompasses a large number of sectors. The U.S. government will seek to deny terrorists the opportunity to inflict lasting harm to our Nation by protecting the assets, systems, and functions vital to our national security, governance, public health and safety, economy, and national morale.

This strategy identifies eight major **critical infrastructure protection** (CIP) initiatives

- Unify America's infrastructure protection effort in the DHS.
- Build and maintain a complete and accurate assessment of America's critical infrastructure and key assets.
- Enable effective partnership with state and local governments and the private sector.
- Develop a national infrastructure protection plan.
- Secure cyberspace.
- Harness the best analytic and modeling tools to develop effective protective solutions.
- Guard America's critical infrastructure and key assets against "inside" threats.
- Partner with the international community to protect our transnational infrastructure.

Key assets represent a variety of unique facilities, sites, and structures that require protection (White House, 2003a: 71). Examples are nuclear power plants, national monuments, government buildings, commercial centers, and sports stadiums.

The *National Strategy for The Physical Protection of Critical Infrastructures and Key Assets* (White House, 2003a: 9) identifies the following CI sectors (Figure 10-1) and key assets for protection.

Agriculture and food: 1,912,000 farms; 87,000 food-processing plants

Water: 1800 federal reservoirs; 1600 municipal wastewater facilities

Public health: 5800 registered hospitals

Emergency services: 87,000 U.S. localities

Continued

Defense industrial base: 250,000 firms in 215 distinct industries

Telecommunications: 2 billion miles of cable

Energy

- Electricity: 2800 power plants
- Oil and natural gas: 300,000 producing sites

Transportation

- Aviation: 5000 public airports
- Passenger rail and railroads: 120,000 miles of major railroads
- Highways, trucking and busing: 590,000 highway bridges
- Pipelines: 2 million miles of pipelines
- Maritime: 300 inland/coastal ports
- Mass transit: 500 major urban public transit operators

banking and finance: 26,600 FDIC insured institutions

Chemical industry and hazardous materials: 66,000 chemical plants

Postal and shipping: 137 million delivery sites

Key assets

- National monuments and icons: 5800 historic buildings
- Nuclear power plants:104 commercial nuclear power plants
- Dams: 80,000 dams
- Government facilities: 3000 government owned/operated facilities
- Commercial assets: 460 skyscrapers

Figure 10-1 ■ How many infrastructure sectors can you identify in this photograph?

GOVERNMENT ACTION TO PROTECT CRITICAL INFRASTRUCTURES AND KEY ASSETS

A major mission area of the *National Strategy for Homeland Security* is protecting critical infrastructures and key assets. In December 2003, President George W. Bush issued HSPD-7, establishing a policy for federal departments and agencies to identify and prioritize CI and protect them from terrorist attacks. A major purpose of this policy is to ensure the coverage of the CI sectors identified in the *National Strategy for Homeland Security*. HSPD-7 designates a sector-specific department or agency for each sector to coordinate and collaborate with relevant agencies, state and local government, and the private sector. The DHS is responsible for (1) developing a national CIP plan consistent with the Homeland Security Act of 2002; (2) recommending CIP measures in coordination with public and private sector partners; and (3) disseminating information.

The term **sector-specific agencies** (SSAs) has been used to identify federal departments and agencies with protection responsibilities for specific sectors of CI. SSAs are required to develop **sector-specific plans** (SSPs). SSAs are listed next [U.S. Government Accountability Office (USGAO), 2005a: 75–76; U.S. Department of Homeland Security, 2005: 3; U.S. Department of Homeland Security, 2006a: 20].

Department of Homeland Security: responsible for emergency services, government facilities, information and telecommunications, transportation systems (with Department of Transportation), chemicals, postal and shipping sectors, dams, commercial facilities, and nuclear reactors, materials and waste [with the Department of Energy and the Nuclear Regulatory Commission (NRC)]. Examples of specific functions include protection of federal property throughout the country by the Federal Protective Service, the Secret Service's role in coordinating site security at designated special events, and the National Cyber Response Coordination Group's role in coordinating national cyber emergencies.

Department of Defense: responsible for defense industrial base and physical security of military installations, activities, and personnel.

Department of Energy: responsible for developing and implementing policies and procedures for safeguarding power plants (except for commercial nuclear power facilities), oil, gas, research laboratories, and weapons production facilities.

Department of Justice: through its criminal division and the FBI, the DOJ works to prevent the exploitation of the Internet, computer systems, or networks.

Department of State: responsible for matters of international CIP, given its overseas mission.

Department of Health and Human Services: responsible for public health, healthcare, and food (other than meat, poultry, and egg products).

Environmental Protection Agency: responsible for drinking water and wastewater treatment systems.

Department of Agriculture: responsible for agriculture and food (meat, poultry, and egg products).

Department of the Treasury: responsible for banking and finance.

Department of the Interior: responsible for national monuments and icons.

For fiscal year 2005, the funding request for CIP was $14 billion. The DOD had the largest share at $7.6 billion (54%). The DHS accounted for $2.6 billion (18%) of 2005 funding. Other agencies reported funding to protect their own assets and to work with states, localities, and the private sector.

According to the U.S. Government Accountability Office (2005a: 78), all eight CIP initiatives are being addressed by federal agencies. The DHS, DOD, and HHS cited activity in each of the eight initiatives. Specific examples cited by the USGAO include the following: DHS began the Transportation Worker Identification Credential Program to enhance access security in the nation's transportation system; the Food and Drug Administration, within HHS, issued security guidance to the food industry, including employee background checks; the DOS developed diplomatic agreements with Mexico and Canada to permit background checks of truck drivers; and the DOE conducted polygraph examinations and financial disclosures of employees in the energy field.

The U.S. Government Accountability Office (2005a: 81) reported challenges to CIP efforts and noted an almost infinite number of potential terrorist targets. A major challenge is the federal government's management and planning of CIP. This entails delineating the roles and responsibilities of federal and nonfederal entities, establishing objectives and milestones, setting time frames for reaching objectives, and preparing performance measures. Other concerns included the need for better training and procedures to detect counterfeit documents and identity fraud. The USGAO reported numerous challenges within specific infrastructure sectors: government facilities, postal system, financial services, agriculture and food, drinking water utilities, chemical plants, nuclear power plants, and nuclear weapons sites.

The *Interim National Infrastructure Protection Plan* (NIPP) (U.S. Department of Homeland Security, 2005) was released by the DHS pursuant to HSPD-7. It takes the *National Strategy for Homeland Security* to the next level through an identification of assets, assessment of vulnerabilities, and prioritization of assets to guide protection programs. The Interim NIPP represents the federal piece of a national plan. It is the starting point for SSAs to initiate dialogue with all levels of government and the private sector to obtain their perspectives on CIP as a foundation to implement the SSPs.

NIPP objectives include protecting critical infrastructure and key resources (CI/KR); vulnerability assessment; prioritization; maintaining a national inventory of CI/KR; mapping interdependencies among assets; articulating security partner roles and responsibilities; identifying incentives for voluntary action by the private sector; facilitating best practices, information exchange, training, and metrics; strengthening linkages between physical and cyber efforts; and promoting CI/KR cooperation among international partners.

In January 2006, the DHS released a revised NIPP in response to nearly 7000 public comments. Changes include an explanation of requirements pertaining to the risk management framework and clarification of all-hazards linkages (i.e., terrorism, natural and man-made disasters, and emergencies). The DHS seeks additional input and a collaborative effort to enhance the NIPP (U.S. Department of Homeland Security, 2006b). The final plan was released on June 30, 2006 (U.S. Department of Homeland Security, 2006a).

HSPD-7 requires that the NIPP be integrated with other national plans. The NIPP states that it will support the national response plan (NRP) during the prevention phase by providing information on CI/KR, vulnerabilities, and protection programs. During incident response, NIPP information will be shared through the national incident management system (NIMS) established communications mechanisms.

"ON PAPER" THE FEDERAL GOVERNMENT'S ACTION TO PROTECT CRITICAL INFRASTRUCTURE HAS BEEN CORRECT

Kochems (2005: 3) describes the responsibilities of the federal government and the private sector to protect against terrorism:

> The federal government—not the private sector—is responsible for preventing terrorist acts through intelligence gathering, early warning, and domestic counterterrorism. The private sector is responsible for taking reasonable precautions, much as it is expected to take reasonable safety and environmental

"ON PAPER" THE FEDERAL GOVERNMENT'S ACTION TO PROTECT CRITICAL INFRASTRUCTURE HAS BEEN CORRECT—Cont'd

precautions. The federal government also has a role in defining what is "reasonable" as a performance-based metric and facilitating information sharing to enable the private sector to perform due diligence (e.g., protection, mitigation, and recovery) in an efficient, fair, and effective manner.

Kochems (2005: 3) writes that, "on paper," the federal government's action to protect critical infrastructure has been correct as a risk-based approach with responsibilities shared between the federal government and the private sector. Kochems adds that to move from plans on paper to a functional system, three actions must occur: (1) the DHS should reorganize to include an undersecretary for protection and preparedness; (2) Congress and the administration should strengthen the Protected Critical Infrastructure Information Program to encourage the private sector to share information about CI with the federal government; and (3) the DHS should develop effective means of sharing information among all levels of government and the private sector.

CRITICAL THINKING:

What is your opinion of Kochems' views of protecting infrastructure?

CIP RISK MANAGEMENT FRAMEWORK

In Chapter 7, risk management was covered, including efforts of the USGAO, a strong proponent of risk management as an important element in the national strategy to combat terrorism. The USGAO emphasized the importance of quantifying security investments in monetary terms. Chapter 7 also explained and illustrated the USGAO risk management elements: threat assessment, vulnerability assessment, and criticality assessment. Here we build upon this foundation and introduce the five-step process of the **CIP risk management framework** (U.S. Department of Homeland Security, 2005: 9–10).

1. *Identifying critical assets.* The first step is the identification of CI/KR. This is an ongoing process carried out by both the SSAs and the DHS. It involves maintaining an active inventory of CI/KR assets. This step includes the protected critical infrastructure information (PCII) program. It collects voluntary information on CI/KR from the public and private sectors and the information is "protected from public disclosure to the maximum extent permitted by law." The voluntary information includes security methods from the private sector.
2. *Identifying and assessing vulnerabilities.* Vulnerability assessments are conducted to identify both areas of weakness and protective measures to mitigate weaknesses. A key challenge is understanding interdependencies among assets and sectors, both nationally and internationally, so that cascading impacts can be minimized.
3. *Normalizing, analyzing, and prioritizing study results.* The DHS and SSAs must align the results of many different assessment methodologies used to assess vulnerabilities and then prioritize across assets from multiple sectors. Normalizing allows comparisons of risk across sectors.
   Part of the process of "normalizing" across sectors is a *crucial analysis of interdependencies* among sectors, especially since the failure of one sector may cause cascading impacts throughout other sectors. For example, nearly all sectors depend on energy, information technology, telecommunications, and transportation sectors. Dependency may also be localized,

such as firefighting services relying on a local water supply. Interdependencies can be exploited by, for instance, using one sector to attack another. Transportation, shipping, and mail delivery systems can be used to disperse WMD.

By assessing risk in terms of intersector vulnerabilities, the DHS enhances security planning. "This drives increased efficiency in the deployment of protective measures, better use of resources, and lower overall risk to the Nation through a better understanding of how to protect the ways the infrastructures work together to drive the American economy" (U.S. Department of Homeland Security, 2005: 20).

4. *Implementing protective programs.* Using information generated from steps 1 to 3, protective programs are implemented for the highest priority assets. The DHS will work with all levels of government and the private sector to identify cost-effective incentives or strategies for enhanced security investments. The DHS will also work with the U.S. Department of State to develop international efforts to protect U.S. interests.

5. *Measuring performance.* This step measures protection program effectiveness through performance metrics. These measurements drive improvements across the risk management framework.

Both output and outcome metrics will be used by SSAs and the DHS to track progress on specific activities outlined in the SSPs. Output metrics include the number of vulnerability assessments performed by a certain date. Outcome metrics include a reduced number of facilities

Figure 10-2 ■ Vunerability reduction program. Source: U.S. Department of Homeland Security (2005). http://www.deq.state.mi.us/documents/deq-wb-wws-interim-nipp.pdf

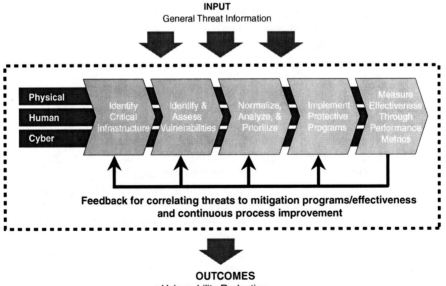

assessed as high risk, following the implementation of protective measures. The DHS notes that selecting outcome metrics for protection programs is challenging because risk reduction is not directly observable. For example, it is difficult to measure the prevention of a terrorist attack or the extent of mitigation from a potential attack.

Examples of metrics include the total number of assets in each sector, the percentage of high-consequence assets to total assets (to determine which sectors should receive a higher priority), and the percentage of high-consequence assets that have been assessed for readiness, response, and recovery capability.

The NIPP risk management framework is implemented in two ways.

1. *Vulnerability reduction program.* The five steps are implemented under the general threat environment (i.e., without a specific threat) to reduce vulnerabilities and improve overall preparedness (Figure 10-2).
2. *Threat-initiated actions.* Based on specific threat information, the DHS reviews CI/KA vulnerabilities and established protection programs and, in consultation with relevant SSAs, issues threat warnings and recommends or undertakes certain protective actions. (The figure for this action is similar to Figure 10-2, except the input is "specific threats" and the outcomes are "protective actions" and "preparedness.")

Reality Check: Where Are We with Sharing Information on CI?

A variety of information-sharing programs have been established as part of counterterrorism efforts. The **Homeland Security Operations Center** (HSOC) serves as a central, national information-sharing and domestic incident management system. It increases coordination among all levels of government and the private sector. The HSOC operates 24 hours a day and provides real-time situational awareness and monitoring of the homeland, coordinates incidents and response, and issues advisories and bulletins on threats and protective measures. The HSOC communicates with its partners through the Homeland Security Information Network (HSIN), an Internet-based counterterrorism tool that uses encryption and a secure network. Another tool, the HSIN-Critical Infrastructure (CI), is designed to communicate real-time information (e.g., alerts and notifications) to CI owners and operators.

The DHS/Information Analysis and Infrastructure Protection Daily Open Source Report is a Monday through Friday e-mail report divided by CI sectors. It is intended to educate and inform personnel engaged in the protection of CI. The content includes a variety of news reports on CI from many media outlets and information bulletins.

The DHS has established **Information Sharing and Analysis Centers** (ISACs) to promote the sharing of information and work among CI sectors. These are voluntary organizations among CI sectors, such as food, electricity, and financial services. Industry associations (e.g., American Chemistry Council) often take the lead in forming ISACs and arrange meetings, establish Web sites, provide technical assistance, and issue warnings. The level of activity of ISACs varies.

Congress has promoted information sharing through the **Intelligence Reform and Terrorism Protection Act of 2004,** also known as the 9/11 Reform Bill. It requires the president to facilitate an "information sharing environment" (ISE) with appropriate levels of government and private entities. An ISE council manages and promotes this effort.

The Infrastructure Security Partnership (TISP) is a private sector group organized to bring together a variety of public and private sector organizations to collaborate on all hazards facing the nation's built environment. TISP facilitates dialogue among those in the design and construction industries. A major goal of TISP is to improve security in the nation's CI. It promotes the transfer of research to codes, standards, and public policy.

Continued

Reality Check: Where Are We with Sharing Information on CI?—Cont'd

Within the states, approaches vary on protecting CI and sharing information (McKay, 2003). However, as the national infrastructure protection plan grows stronger, states will have more guidance. Washington State, for example, began its program from scratch. It addresses CI protection on four levels: physical, personnel, technology, and data. Washington's Department of Information Services provides policy, standards, and guidelines that agency directors are encouraged to follow as they prepare an annual strategic plan and infrastructure portfolio. New Mexico began their effort through the University of New Mexico. Its goals were to share information and work to protect CI, but progress stalled because of a lack of both funding and private sector interest. The effort began as a nongovernmental entity, but the government presence, including the FBI, may have turned off the private sector. One private sector concern was the possibility of a leak of sensitive information from the information-sharing process. For example, if a company reports a cyber attack and the information is reported in the media, profits may suffer. Also, private sector proprietary information must be protected because it is valuable.

CRITICAL THINKING:

Do you think businesses are reluctant to share critical infrastructure information with government? Why or why not?

SECURING CRITICAL INFRASTRUCTURE SECTORS

The remainder of this chapter explains critical infrastructure sectors and key assets as outlined in *The National Strategy for the Physical Protection of Critical Infrastructures and Key Assets* (White House, 2003a). Additional references add to the coverage, especially reports from the USGAO. The USGAO researches weakness of government agencies and offers suggestions for corrective action.

The following critical infrastructure sectors are explained in subsequent pages: agriculture and food, water, energy, chemical industry, telecommunications (including information technology and information security), banking and finance, defense industry base, and government. CI sectors are also explained in other chapters. These include public health and emergency services in Chapter 8, and transportation and postal systems in Chapter 11. Key assets explained in subsequent pages include dams, nuclear power plants, national monuments and symbols, government facilities, and commercial centers.

For the CI sectors and key assets that follow, an emphasis is placed on these topics: brief description, unique characteristics, challenges and vulnerabilities, laws, sector-specific agencies involved in protection, and protection issues and strategies.

AGRICULTURE AND FOOD

The U.S. agriculture and food industry accounts for almost one-fifth of the gross domestic product and a significant percentage of that figure contributes to the U.S. export economy. National and international confidence in the safety of the products of this industry is important. The greatest threats to this industry are disease and contamination. There is an urgent need to improve and validate methods for detecting bioterrorist agents in food products. The White House (2003a: 37) states that although rapid use of threat information could prevent an attack from spreading, serious institutional barriers and disincentives (e.g., economic harm) for sharing such information exist.

"The use of natural agents in attacks on agriculture or directly on people is commonly described as **bioterrorism**" (Congressional Budget Office, 2004: 39). Chalk (2003: 2) defines **agroterrorism** as "the deliberate introduction of a disease agent, either against livestock or into the food chain, to undermine socioeconomic stability and/or generate fear." Terrorism, disease, and disasters in this sector of CI can cause serious health problems, economic losses, and panic.

An attack on the food supply can take place at numerous points between the farm and human consumption. Examples are farms, processing plants, retail stores, and restaurants. Whether domestic or imported, food could be subject to biological or chemical agents. An illustration of a terrorist attack on food occurred in 1984 when members of an Oregon religious group, who followed an Indian-born guru named Bhagwan Shree Rajneesh, secretly applied salmonella bacteria to a restaurant salad bar to poison residents of a community to influence an election. Over 750 people became ill. Disgruntled employees have caused other incidents of food sabotage.

The Centers for Disease Control (CDC) estimates that 76 million illnesses, 325,000 hospitalizations, and 5000 deaths occur annually due to food contaminated from various causes (Mead et al., 1999). Although unintentional, the 2001 outbreak of foot-and-mouth disease in Britain showed the high expense from disease in the food chain. About four million cattle were destroyed and the cost to the British economy (primarily agriculture and tourism) was about $48 billion (Gewin, 2003).

The primary federal regulatory agencies responsible for food safety are the Food and Drug Administration (FDA), the U.S. Department of Agriculture (USDA), and the Environmental Protection Agency (EPA). Inspectors from the DHS's Bureau of Customs and Border Protection assist other agencies with inspecting imports. States also conduct inspections.

The FDA has regulatory authority over about 80% of the nation's food supply. The USDA's Food Safety and Inspection Service regulates the safety, quality, and labeling of most meats, as well as poultry and egg products. The EPA's role is to protect public health and the environment from pesticides and to promote safer pest management (Congressional Budget Office, 2004: 42–43).

The U.S. Government Accountability Office (2005b) recommended that federal agencies responsible for food safety work to correct overlapping activities, such as inspection/enforcement, training, and research. For example, both the FDA and the USDA conduct similar inspections at over 1000 dual jurisdiction businesses that produce foods regulated by both agencies. Also, the FDA and the USDA duplicate training on similar topics for their inspectors that could be shared.

Laws that defend the agriculture and food system against terrorism, disasters, and emergencies include the Homeland Security Act of 2002. It created the DHS, which is responsible for consolidating federal response to emergencies, including agroterrorism, into a single plan called the national response plan (see Chapter 7). Another law, the **Public Health Security and Bioterrorism Preparedness and Response Act of 2002**, also called the Bioterrorism Act, bolstered the FDA's ability to identify domestic and foreign facilities that provide food; inspect food imports; and notify food businesses that become involved in the contamination of food supplies. Regulations under the authority of this law require food businesses in the chain of supply to maintain records to identify the immediate previous sources and subsequent recipients of food. HSPD-9, of January 2004, directed HHS, USDA, and EPA to increase their efforts in prevention, surveillance, emergency response, and recovery. The **Project BioShield Act of 2004** requires action to expand and expedite the distribution of vaccines and treatments to combat potential bioterrorism agents (Congressional Budget Office, 2004: 43).

Protection issues and strategies for the agriculture and food industry include the following (Congressional Budget Office, 2004: 44; Chalk, 2003).

- Use risk management methods.
- Establish more extensive labeling and tracking systems for animals and food products to help pinpoint sources of contamination.

- Establish full tracking of ownership of the most hazardous materials (e.g., nitrates) that can be used as weapons.
- Establish enhanced incentives and protections for reporting new incidents of food contamination, improper sales of hazardous materials, unsafe processing and handling procedures, and incomplete inspections.
- Modify vulnerable practices in the industry.
- Increase the number of inspectors in the food chain and strengthen the capabilities of forensic investigations for early detection and containment.
- Foster improved links among the agriculture, food, and intelligence communities.
- Continue research on vaccinations.
- The FDA established the Office of Food Safety, Defense, and Outreach (OFSDO) to consolidate its educational services with its counterterrorism and chief medical officer responsibilities.
- The USDA Food Safety and Inspection Service (FSIS) offers training and a variety of information, including notices, regulations, emergency resources, and security guidelines. It offers **model food security plans** that are voluntary for egg, meat, and poultry facilities. These plans are risk based and include how to identify threats, such as disgruntled employees or terrorists. The *FSIS Security Guidelines for Food Processors* contain information on food security management; access controls; internal security; and security for slaughter and processing, storage, water and ice, and mail. (Many of the security guidelines are similar to topics in Chapter 9.)
- The Food Products Association (FPA) is the largest trade association serving the food and beverage industry worldwide. It operates a Center for Food Security and Emergency Preparedness (CFSEP), offering on-site vulnerability assessments, training, security plan development, awareness training, and crisis management to members and nonmembers.

TECHNOLOGY IMPROVES EFFICIENCY AND PROTECTS FOOD

The agriculture and food sector, like other sectors, is under increasing pressure to "track and trace" its operations. Businesses in many sectors are trying to balance multiple initiatives, such as planning the use of technology to meet the demands of customers and government regulators (e.g., FDA).

Let us look at one company, fictitiously called the Best Cookie Company (BCC). Although this example illustrates one part of one company's operations, it shows the importance of tracking and tracing as many components of operations as possible in the thousands of companies that exist. The BCC makes cookies and pies for major restaurant chains. In one part of BCC operations, it uses bar code seals that contain the serial number of rail shipments of corn syrup it needs for its products. (One type of seal is similar to a wire and is attached to a door or container opening to prevent tampering. Usually, it can only be used once and it must be cut off.) Prior to using the bar code system, when a rail shipment of corn syrup arrived, an employee had to climb to the top of the rail car to manually record a unique seal number and then type the information in BCC's tracking system. If the seal was broken, the shipment could be rejected and safety testing required. An unusable shipment could cost thousands of dollars. BCC records tens of thousands of seals each year and employees had to walk from the rail cars to the office to type data. To improve efficiency, tracking, and tracing and to reduce the possibility of error, new technology was implemented. Employees carry a handheld computer with special software to scan bar code information from seals on rail cars; hoses used to siphon out the syrup; and tanks holding the syrup. Data are then transmitted wirelessly to a central computer database to record the new shipment that is available for production (Hulme, 2005). RFID (see Chapter 9) is another technology to help meet the demands of customers and regulators, besides assisting with inventory needs and tracking and tracing items in the food chain.

WATER

Driving factors for water infrastructure protection include our basic human need for water, the importance of maintaining a safe water supply, and our economic dependence on a water supply. Furthermore, water has been used as a weapon to defeat enemies through history. Interdependence among infrastructures and the problem of cascading can be illustrated through the water sector. For instance, public water systems (e.g., pumps) are heavily dependent on the energy sector, and other sectors are dependent on the water sector (e.g., emergency services are dependent on water for fire suppression).

The water sector has two major components: fresh water supply and wastewater collection and treatment. The United States has 170,000 public water systems that depend on reservoirs, dams, wells, aquifers, treatment systems, pumping stations, and pipelines. There are 19,500 municipal sanitary sewer systems in the United States, including 800,000 miles of sewer lines. This sector also includes storm water systems that collect storm water runoff (White House, 2003a: 39). The U.S. Government Accountability Office (2005c) reported different numbers: about 52,000 public and private community water systems, with the percentage of each divided equally.

To prioritize protection, the water sector is studying four primary areas of possible attack (White House, 2003a: 39).

- Physical damage to assets and release of toxic chemicals used in water treatment.
- Contamination of the water supply.
- Cyber attack on water information systems.
- Interruption of service from another CI sector.

The U.S. Government Accountability Office (2005a: 87–88) reported similar vulnerabilities. It noted the challenges of protection include a lack of redundancy in vital systems; this increases the probability that an attack will render a water system inoperable. The USGAO recommended that federal funds for utilities focus on high-density areas and those areas serving critical assets (e.g., military bases). Recommendations also included technological upgrades in physical security and monitoring of water systems.

As with other critical infrastructure sectors, water systems should consider terrorist threats under an all hazards, cost-effective, risk management approach that also plans for potential disasters, accidents, and nonterrorist criminals (e.g., vandals).

Threats to water systems are varied. In one community, security was increased when vandals victimized a water reservoir. The offenders broke into a control room, opened two valves, and began to drain the water out of the reservoir. Making matters worse, they opened another valve and flooded the control room. A sensor signaled the drop in the water level of the reservoir. Following this event, an intrusion alarm system was installed at access points. Another threat is the disgruntled employee. This may be a more serious threat than outsiders because employees are knowledgeable of system weaknesses and security measures. However, almost anybody has access to thousands of miles of pipe and an offender can patch into a neighborhood line and introduce a poison after the water has been treated and tested for safety. This type of attack could sicken a neighborhood or people in an office building. Experts argue that to poison a reservoir or other large water source would require truckloads of poisons or biological agents. If an airplane containing anthrax crashed into a water source, this attack is likely to fail because of fire or the inability of the anthrax to diffuse effectively (Winter and Broad, 2001).

WHAT IS DCS/SCADA?

Many industries in the United States have transformed the way in which they control and monitor equipment by using digital control systems (DCS) and supervisory control and data acquisition systems (SCADA). These systems are computer based and are capable of remotely controlling sensitive processes that were once controlled only manually on site. The Internet is used to transmit data, a change from the closed networks of the past. Many sectors use this technology, including water, chemical, transportation, energy, and manufacturing.

In one case an engineer used radio telemetry to access a waste management system to dump raw sewage into public waterways and the grounds of a hotel. The offender worked for the contractor who supplied the remote equipment to the waste management system. In another case, during a **penetration test** (i.e., an authorized test of defenses), service firm personnel were able to access the DCS/SCADA of a utility within minutes. Personnel drove to a remote substation, noticed a wireless network antenna, and without leaving their vehicle, used their wireless radios and connected to the network in 5 minutes. Within 20 minutes they had mapped the network, including SCADA equipment, and accessed the business network and data. CI sectors must understand the risks of wireless communication (U.S. Environmental Protection Agency, Office of Inspector General, 2005). Methods to protect these systems include computer access controls, encryption of communications, virus protection, data recovery capabilities, and manual overrides.

The National Strategy to Secure Cyberspace (White House, 2003b: 32) emphasizes the importance of protecting DCS/SCADA as a national priority because disruption of these systems can result in problems for public health and safety. Security is challenging for several reasons, including the requirement of research and development to implement effective security systems and the possibility that security could impact the performance of processes. The DHS is working with the U.S. Department of Energy to partner with private industry to increase awareness of vulnerabilities, foster training, promote certification of software and hardware, and develop best practices and new technology.

HSPD-7, of December 2003, confirmed the EPA as the lead agency for identifying, prioritizing, and coordinating the protection of drinking water and water treatment systems. Under HSPD-7, the water security division of the EPA has been assigned the responsibility of preparing a water sector plan for the NIPP that the DHS must produce. The plan must identify assets, prioritize vulnerabilities, develop protection programs, and measure effectiveness. Other HSPDs relevant to the EPA are HSPD-8 (strengthens preparedness), HSPD-9 (surveillance program and laboratory network for early warning of an attack), HSPD-10 (a classified document on decontamination), and HSPD-10: Biodefense for the 21st Century (strengthens biodefense).

The Public Health Security and Bioterrorism Preparedness and Response Act of 2002 addresses, in Title IV, drinking water protection. It requires water systems serving over 3300 persons to conduct an assessment of vulnerabilities and to prepare response measures. Other federal laws support safe drinking water.

Protection issues and strategies for the water sector include the following (White House, 2003a: 39–40).

- Several methodologies are available to conduct a vulnerability assessment of water utilities. These are available from the EPA, Sandia National Laboratories, the Association of Metropolitan Sewerage Agencies, and other groups.
- As with all sectors, improve protection of DCS/SCADA.
- Consider new technology, such as small robots placed in pipes to detect tainted water.
- Secure openings (e.g., manhole covers) to prevent the dumping of substances into systems.

- Properly store and secure chemicals.
- Use redundancy to increase the reliability of systems.
- Increase training and awareness.
- The EPA provides helpful information on security at its Web site.
- The DHS and EPA work with the water ISAC to coordinate information on threats and other topics of interest to this sector.
- The American Water Works Association (AWWA) is the largest organization of water supply professionals in the world. It is an international scientific and educational society dedicated to improving drinking water. The group offers training and education opportunities, conferences, and publications on security. Two other related groups are the National Rural Water Association (NRWA) and the Association of State Drinking Water Administrators (ASDWA).

ENERGY

Energy is another critical infrastructure sector (White House, 2003a: 50–53). It supports our quality of life, economy, and national defense. Presidential Decision Directive 63 (PDD 63) and HSPD-3 called for cooperation between government and individual infrastructures for increased protection, and the DOE was designated as the lead agency for the energy sectors. The energy sector is often divided into two industries: (1) electricity and (2) oil and natural gas.

ELECTRICITY

The physical system of electricity consists of three major parts. Generation facilities include fossil fuel plants, hydroelectric dams, and nuclear power plants. Transmission and distribution systems link the national electricity grid while controlling electricity as customers use it. Control and communication systems maintain and monitor critical components. PDD 63 identified the electrical grid as CI.

The electricity industry is highly regulated. Regulators include the Federal Energy Regulatory Commission (FERC) and state utility regulatory commissions. The NRC regulates nuclear plants and related activities.

The DOE designated the North American Electric Reliability Council (NERC) as the sector coordinator for electricity. Following the serious power blackout in New York in 1965, the electric industry established NERC consisting of public and private utilities from the United States and Canada. The aim of this group is to develop guidelines and procedures to prevent disruptions of power. This group also coordinates guidelines on physical and cyber security.

Serious vulnerabilities exist with the equipment used in the production and transmission of electricity and electronic monitoring devices because these assets are outdoors and have minimal protection. The National Research Council reported that an assault on any individual segment of a network would likely result in minimal local disruption, but a coordinated attack on key assets could cause a long-term, multistate blackout.

In December of 2004, the DHS reported that power company employees in Nevada were on routine patrol when they found that nuts, bolts, and supporting cross members had been removed from five transmission line towers. The company noted that if one tower fell, eight more could be brought down at the same time; however, because of redundancy in the transmission system, loss of electricity would not occur.

An example of a broad, regional disruption is the northeast–midwest blackout of August 14, 2003. It affected about 50 million people and took 5 days to fully restore service, although most customers had power within 24 hours. The DOE estimated the total cost of this blackout at $6 billion, mostly from lost income and earnings. This emergency illustrated the importance of preparation. For example, in New York City, many high-rise buildings had no backup generators, traffic lights did not work (causing gridlock), service stations were unable to sell gas (causing vehicles to stop and block traffic), and clean water was in jeopardy because no backup power existed at water facilities. These problems were repeated throughout the region of the blackout, and it has been suggested that codes should be established for emergency backup generators (Congressional Budget Office, 2004: 37).

Protection issues and strategies for the electricity sector include the following (White House, 2003a: 50–53; Congressional Budget Office, 2004: 32–37).

- Many of the assets present unique protection challenges. Examples are power generation facilities and substations.
- The owners and operators of the electric system are a heterogeneous group, and data are needed to conduct analyses of this sector's interdependencies. Such data would help plan protection priorities and strategies.
- One serious issue is the lack of metrics to determine and justify security investments. In the case of natural disasters or accidents, such metrics are more readily available.
- To increase reliability, this sector is seeking to build a less vulnerable grid, while looking to redundancy in its transmission and distribution facilities.
- To improve recovery from equipment failure (e.g., transformer), utilities should maintain adequate inventories of spare parts and the design of parts should be standardized.
- This sector has initiated intraindustry working groups to address security issues and an ISAC to gather incident information and relay alert notices.
- The FERC and the DOE have worked together to enhance physical and cyber security.
- Power management control rooms are perhaps the most protected component of this sector. NERC guidelines require a backup system and security requirements are being formulated.

OIL AND NATURAL GAS

Oil and natural gas businesses are closely integrated. The oil industry includes crude oil transport, pipelines, refining, storage, terminals, ports, ships, trucks, trains, and retail stores. The natural gas industry includes production, transmission, and distribution. There are 278,000 miles of natural gas pipelines and 1,119,000 miles of natural gas distribution lines in the United States (White House, 2003a: 52). The oil and natural gas industries face similar challenges as the electric industry. Examples are issues of reliability, redundancy, risk management, and security.

In addition to the risks of terrorism, other criminal acts, natural disasters, and accidents, critical infrastructure sectors also face the risk of equipment failure that can disrupt vital services.

DAMS

According to the *National Strategy for the Physical Protection of Critical Infrastructure and Key Assets* (White House, 2003a: 76), dams are a key asset and vital to our economy and communities. The Congressional Budget Office (2004: 30–31) reported that about 80,000 dams were listed in the national inventory of dams. These structures are major components of CI sectors that provide electricity and water to population and agricultural areas. Failure of a dam can cause loss of life, property damage, serious economic loss, and the lost value of services (e.g., power, water, irrigation, and recreation). Locations downstream are most vulnerable, as in the **Johnstown flood** of 1889 that caused 2200 deaths. In 1976, the failure of the newly built **Teton dam**, in Idaho, resulted in 11 deaths, 20,000 homes evacuated, and about $800 million in damages (more costly than the dam itself).

DAMS—Cont'd

Most dams are small and the federal government is responsible for roughly 10% of dams. The remaining ones belong to state and local governments, utilities, and the private sector. Under current law, owners are responsible for safety and security. Because of the need to improve the management of risks pertaining to dams, the DHS (i.e., FEMA's national dam safety program) is focusing on the following: (1) partnering on a host of issues (e.g., risk assessment methodologies) with owners, government agencies, the Association of State Dam Safety Officials, and the United States Society of Dams; (2) prioritizing dams for protection; (3) studying security technology (e.g., sensors and barriers to prevent an attack by watercraft); and (4) improving emergency management (White House, 2003a: 76).

NUCLEAR POWER PLANTS

The *National Strategy for the Physical Protection of Critical Infrastructures and Key Assets* (White House, 2003a: 74–75) views nuclear power plants as key assets that represent U.S. economic power and technological advancement. A disruption of these facilities could have a significant impact on the safety and health of citizens and harm the economy.

Nuclear power supplies about 20% of U.S. electricity from 103 commercial nuclear reactors in 31 states. This source of power has created much controversy (Congressional Budget Office, 2004: 9–19; Hebert, 2005). It has been touted as an option to reduce dependence on fossil fuels (i.e., oil, natural gas, and coal) and Middle East oil. Some environmentalists have favored nuclear power to reduce "greenhouse" gases caused by fossil fuels. Opponents refer to nuclear plant disasters. In 1986, the **Chernobyl** nuclear plant, in Ukraine, exploded due to design deficiencies and safety problems not present in U.S. reactors. This disaster spread radioactive substances across northern Europe. Residents of Chernobyl had to permanently relocate, and agricultural lands were permanently contaminated. Thirty-one people died in the fire and meltdown, and cancer rates climbed in the area. The 1979 **Three-Mile Island** partial nuclear meltdown in Pennsylvania resulted in some radioactive material escaping into the atmosphere before the reactor could be shut down. The accident was blamed on feed water pumps that stopped, followed by pressure that began to build, and a safety valve that became stuck. About 150,000 people were forced to evacuate and litigation resulted in damages of about $70 million (mainly from the evacuation). The biggest cost was from the loss of Three Mile Island's Unit 2 that cost ratepayers $700 million to build and $1 billion to defuel and decontaminate. This incident resulted in a halt to nuclear reactor construction in the United States.

Construction costs have been another criticism of nuclear reactors. For example, the Seabrook plant in New Hampshire was projected to cost $850 million in 1976 for two reactors and be completed in 6 years. Fourteen years later the project was finished at a cost of $7 billion and the second reactor was canceled.

In addition to the risk of accidents at nuclear power plants, terrorists find these plants attractive targets because of the potential for mass casualties and long-term environmental damage. Attacks may involve a 9/11 type of strike using an airliner, internal sabotage by an employee, a truck or boat bomb, an assault by a team aiming to plant an explosive, or a combination of these methods. Alternatives to attacking a reactor consist of planting explosives at nuclear waste or fuel locations to spread radioactive materials. Assaults of nuclear plants have occurred in Spain by Basque separatists, in Russia by Chechens, in South Africa during the apartheid era, and a rocket attack targeted a French nuclear plant. Captured al-Qaida documents in Afghanistan contained diagrams of U.S. nuclear plants.

Debate continues over whether the concrete containment structure of a reactor could withstand a crash by a wide-bodied, fully fueled airliner. Reactors have walls 3.5 to 6 feet thick.

The Nuclear Regulatory Commission, an independent agency created by Congress through the Energy Reorganization Act of 1974, regulates security and safety at commercial nuclear facilities. NRC responsibilities include storage, transportation, and disposal of high-level waste.

The Congressional Budget Office (2004: 16) stated: "Despite the many efforts by nuclear plants since September 11, emergency preparedness that would help to contain losses may not fully reflect the realities of the current terrorist threat." The U.S. Government Accountability Office (2005a: 91–92) noted challenges for the NRC. For example, the NRC does not have a system for better utilizing information from security inspections to identify problems that may be common to all plants. Another challenge involves weaknesses in the force-on-force exercises, such as using more defenders than what would be available during an actual attack, not training forces in terrorist tactics, and using unrealistic weapons (rubber guns) that do not simulate actual gunfire. Other issues pertain to the use of automatic weapons, deadly force, and arrest authority.

Protection issues and strategies for nuclear facilities include the following (Congressional Budget Office, 2004: 13–17; White House, 2003a: 74–75).

- The DOE and the EPA maintain programs for the safe disposal of high-level radioactive waste.
- Under agreement with the NRC, states may regulate low-level radioactive materials, such as those used by medical, research, and food irradiation facilities. These locations are sources for a "dirty bomb" and, thus, security is vital.
- The NRC requires strict security and emergency plans at nuclear facilities and for nuclear materials in transit. Information security is also a top priority.
- Security is characterized by layering and redundancy (see Chapter 9).
- Security has been enhanced since the 9/11 attacks, including more restricted site access and improved coordination with law enforcement and military authorities.
- The NRC, the DHS, and other organizations are working together to improve security.
- Options to improve protection include the following: increasing security against both ground and air assaults; adding physical features to better shield containment structures against heavy arms or aircraft; constructing safer storage facilities for spent nuclear materials; and improving protection during transportation of related materials.
- The Price-Anderson Act, a 1957 amendment to the Atomic Energy Act of 1954, provides financial support for the nuclear power industry. It creates insurance limits beyond what is available through commercial insurers. Other sources of federal assistance are available in an emergency.

Nuclear security also entails protection at four nuclear weapons production sites and three national laboratories that design nuclear weapons. The DOE and its National Nuclear Security Administration (NNSA) are responsible for these facilities. The U.S. General Accounting Office (2003) noted that NNSA management problems involve confusion over roles and responsibilities and shortfalls when corrective action was required following security assessments. An example of a security problem at an NNSA-regulated facility is provided in a U.S. Department of Energy (2005) inspector general's report that found foreign construction workers, using false documents and being illegal aliens, had gained access to the DOE's Y-12 complex in Oak Ridge, Tennessee (a national security complex). Some of these workers acquired access badges. Access controls at Y-12 were found to be ineffective or not implemented. When informed of the inspector general's report, Y-12 management took prompt corrective action.

CHEMICAL INDUSTRY

The chemical sector provides another illustration of interdependencies among infrastructures and how a disruption in one sector can have a cascading affect (White House, 2003a: 65–66; Congressional Budget Office, 2004: 21–28). Chemical products depend on raw materials, electricity, and transportation, among other needs. The products from this industry include fertilizer for agriculture, chlorine for water purification, polymers that create plastics from petroleum for many household and industrial products, and a variety of medicines and other health care products. This industry also includes oil and gas production. The chemical sector is the top exporter in the United States, totaling 10 cents out of every dollar. As with other sectors, timely delivery of products is essential for customers. Businesses with "just-in-time" delivery systems maintain a small inventory of chemicals. Municipal water systems often hold only a few days supply of chlorine for disinfecting drinking water.

Protection of the chemical industry is not only important because of our dependence on its products and for economic reasons, but also because of its flammable and toxic substances and the risks of fire, explosion, theft, and pollution. The EPA is the primary federal agency responsible for protecting the public and the environment from chemical accidents. It lists over 300 chemicals as "extremely hazardous," meaning that harm could result in humans from exposure for only a short time. The most hazardous chemicals are largely from three groups.

- *Petrochemicals:* examples in this group are fuels, solvents, and raw materials to make plastic. This group is highly flammable and toxic, and an atmospheric release could lead to cancer and environmental damage.
- *Nitrates:* produced from ammonia or urea, this group is used to make fertilizers, pesticides, and explosives. These substances are pervasive and subject to conversion to WMD. Ammonium nitrate combined with diesel oil was the explosive mixture used against the World Trade Center in 1993 and the federal building in Oklahoma City in 1995.
- *Ammonia and chlorine:* ammonia and its compounds are used as fertilizers and cleaning solutions and for manufacturing chemicals, drugs, and plastics. Chlorine is used to purify drinking water and to produce plastic and medicines. Concern over chlorine is from both its storage and transportation over rail lines through populated areas.

The EPA risk management program monitors facilities that handle hazardous substances beyond a threshold limit. Nearly 15,000 facilities are in the program and many smaller facilities and retailers (e.g., gasoline stations) are excluded. The DHS is concerned about all potential targets and the smaller ones that are dispersed, more difficult to defend, and possibly attractive to terrorists.

Risks and costs from an attack on the chemical sector are from assessments of accidental-release scenarios from the EPA; assessments of attack scenarios from the DHS; and actual accidents. EPA's risk management program requires chemical facility operators to submit analyses of hypothetical worse-case releases for the most hazardous substance present. This program serves as a source of information on the number of potential victims and environmental damage. EPA data indicate that the distance and population threatened are greater for toxic substances than for flammable substances, with the median being 1.6 and 0.4 miles, respectively. However, models show that several variables impact risk. Examples are type of substance and wind direction. The DHS has been working with the EPA on risk models.

A chemical accident that caused widespread losses occurred in 1984 in **Bhopal, India**, where a fatal pesticide was released from a Union Carbide Corporation plant. Nearly 4000 people were killed, and India's courts ordered the company to pay $470 million in compensation to more than 566,000 survivors and dependents, including thousands of victims who were permanently disabled. When the accident occurred, there was no emergency response, the worst atmospheric conditions, inadequate building standards, and no zoning to limit housing near the plant. In the United States, the greatest loss of life from a chemical accident came in 1947 from a ship containing fertilizer that exploded in **Texas City, Texas**, and spread fire to other ships and to industrial facilities. About 600 lives were lost. Another U.S. disaster was the **Exxon Valdez** oil spill in 1989 in Alaska. When this ship ran aground, 240,000 barrels of crude oil, with a value of $25 million, spilled. Exxon paid about $3 billion for mostly cleanup activities.

Safety in the chemical industry has been strengthened through federal laws. The **Emergency Planning and Community Right-to-Know Act of 1986** resulted from the Bhopal accident and was the first federal initiative to promote safety specifically in chemical facilities. It requires plant operators to participate in community emergency planning, provide information to local planners on chemicals on site, and notify local authorities of a release. The Clean Air Act Amendments of 1990 mandated a role for the EPA in risk management planning for the chemical industry. Operators must have programs to prevent, detect, and mitigate releases of chemicals. The Maritime Transportation Security Act of 2002 requires vulnerability assessments for chemical facilities along U.S. waterways. State and local governments are heavily involved in chemical safety through emergency preparedness, and FEMA has provided technical support and training.

Unlike strict federal government security regulations for nuclear plants, chemical plants vary on their security initiatives. The U.S. Government Accountability Office (2005a: 90) noted security challenges facing the chemical industry (Figure 10-3). It wrote that the federal government has not comprehensively assessed the industry's vulnerability to terrorist attacks, no federal law requires *all* chemical facilities to take security actions to protect against terrorism, and the extent of voluntary efforts by the industry is unclear. In 2006, the U.S. Government Accountability Office (2006) reiterated the same points and added the following: while the EPA formerly led federal efforts to ensure chemical facility security, the DHS is now the lead agency to protect these facilities from terrorist attacks; the DHS is developing a chemical sector-specific plan to coordinate all sectors, assess vulnerabilities, and develop protection programs; and Congress should provide the DHS with the authority to *require* the chemical industry to address plant security. (In September, Congress reached a preliminary agreement on legislation requiring security measures and DHS inspections at chemical plants.)

The White House (2003a: 65–66) noted that security is an issue for the chemical industry and listed the following strategies.

- The DHS, the EPA, and the chemical industry are working to improve protection. One example is through the ISAC concept.
- Trade associations have developed security codes. An example is the American Chemistry Council (see Chapter 6). The Web site of this group offers a media kit on security and emphasizes the group's support of "meaningful chemical security legislation."

Figure 10-3 ■ The United States Government Accountability Office noted security challenges facing the chemical industry.

The U.S. Department of Homeland Security, Information Analysis and Infrastructure Protection Directorate (2005) outlined the following principles for a regulatory framework pertaining to chemical security.

- Recognize that not all facilities face the same risk, and attention should focus on facilities that could most endanger public and economic health.
- Develop enforceable, reasonable, clear, and equitable performance standards.
- Set performance standards that fit types and severity of risks and permit facilities to select site-specific security measures.
- Design any new authority to recognize the progress of responsible companies and build on that progress.

The Congressional Budget Office (2004: 26) offers these strategies.

- Establish new regulations for tracking chemicals that could be used as weapons.
- Improve the safety of transporting chemicals and route them away from population centers.
- Create financial disincentives for businesses or residents seeking to locate close to chemical facilities (e.g., higher insurance premiums).
- Establish national property zoning (similar to FEMA's flood-zone mapping) to inform people of local dangers. Set restrictions on what activities can occur near dangerous chemicals.
- Establish enhanced incentives for reporting unsafe practices.

CRITICAL THINKING:

What are your views of the chemical industry's efforts at security? Should the industry be permitted to develop its own security standards, without government involvement?

TELECOMMUNICATIONS

The telecommunications sector is another component of critical infrastructure. It has consistently provided reliable and vital communications and processes to meet the needs of businesses and governments, while subject to technological advances, business and competitive pressures, and changes in government regulations. This sector's cyber and physical assets have faced a challenging threat environment (White House, 2003a: 47–49).

This sector provides voice and data service to public and private customers through the Public Switched Telecommunications Network (PSTN), the Internet, and private enterprise networks. The PSTN includes switched circuits for telephone, data, and leased point-to-point services. Components of the system are connected by nearly two billion miles of fiber optic and copper cable. The physical PSTN is the backbone of this sector, with cellular, microwave, and satellite technologies extending service to mobile customers. Advances in data network technology and increasing demand for data services have helped create the rapid growth of the Internet. Internet service providers (ISPs) enable customers to access the Internet. International PSTN and Internet traffic travel by underwater cables. Enterprise networks support the voice and data needs and operations of large enterprises.

The PSTN and the Internet are becoming increasingly interconnected, software driven, and remotely managed, while the physical assets of this industry are increasingly concentrated in shared facilities. Wireless telecommunications is growing through an infrastructure of base stations and radio-cell towers.

The telecommunications sector is vulnerable to a variety of risks, including adverse weather, unintentional cable cuts, and crime. The 9/11 attacks resulted in significant collateral damage to this sector. However, the damage was offset by diverse and redundant communications capabilities.

As in other sectors, government and business leaders may have different perspectives on risks, security, and reliability. In the telecommunications sector, agreement on these issues remains a challenge. Protection issues and strategies in this sector include the following (White House, 2003a: 48–49).

- As with other sectors, because interdependencies could result in a cascading effect, redundancy and diversity are major concerns.
- Government and industry continue to work together to understand vulnerabilities, develop countermeasures, and raise awareness about physical and cyber threats.
- The DHS works with this industry to define an appropriate security threshold and to develop requirements.
- The DHS works with other nations to consider innovative communications paths to strengthen the reliability of this sector globally.
- Public–private partnerships that influence telecommunications security and reliability include the President's National Security Telecommunications Advisory Committee and Critical Infrastructure Protection Board (PCIPB), the Government Network Security Information Exchanges, the Telecommunications ISAC, and the Network Reliability and Interoperability Council of the FCC.

CYBERSPACE AND INFORMATION TECHNOLOGY (IT)

Cyberspace and information technology are essential components of the telecommunications sector, our economy, and society. The *National Strategy to Secure Cyberspace* (White House, 2003b: iii–vii) states:

> The way business is transacted, government operates, and national defense is conducted have changed. These activities now rely on an independent network of information technology infrastructures called cyberspace.... Cyberspace is composed of hundreds of thousands of interconnected computers, servers, routers, switches, and fiber optic cables that allow our critical infrastructures to work.
>
> This *National Strategy to Secure Cyberspace* is part of our overall effort to protect the Nation. It is an implementing component of the *National Strategy for Homeland Security* and is complemented by a *National Strategy for the Physical Protection of Critical Infrastructures and Key Assets*.

In October of 2001, President Bush issued Executive Order 13231, authorizing a protection program for cyberspace and the physical assets that support such systems. This order was complemented by the Federal Information Security Management Act (FISMA) and the Cyber Security Enhancement Act of 2002. A combination of acts, relevant presidential directives, and statutory authorities provide the legal foundation for action to secure cyberspace.

The following list provides a summary of the *National Strategy to Secure Cyberspace* (White House, 2003b: vii–60).

- The economy is fully dependent on IT and the information infrastructure. The Internet is at the core of these systems. Many components of infrastructure sectors are controlled by these information systems. Examples are water treatment plants, electrical transformers, trains, and stock markets. Of primary concern is the threat of attacks to disrupt CI, the economy, and national security.
- Attack tools and methodologies are becoming widely available, and the sophistication of users is improving. Enhanced cyber threat analysis is needed to address trends related to threats and vulnerabilities.

- In peacetime our enemies may conduct espionage on our government, university research centers, and private companies. They may seek to prepare for cyber strikes by mapping U.S. IT, identifying key targets, and lacing IT with back doors and other means of access.
- The strategy provides direction for the federal government and it identifies steps that can be taken by state and local governments and the private sector to improve collective cybersecurity.
- Strategic objectives are prevent cyber attacks, reduce national vulnerability, and minimize damage and recovery time from attacks that do occur.
- The secretary of the DHS will have responsibility to develop a comprehensive plan for securing cyberspace; provide crisis management and technical assistance; coordinate with other government agencies and the private sector; and support research.
- Five national priorities are (1) a national cyberspace security response system, (2) a national cyberspace security threat and vulnerability reduction program, (3) a national cyberspace security awareness and training program, (4) securing governments' cyberspace, and (5) national security and international cyberspace security cooperation.

In June of 2003, the DHS established the National Cyber Security Division (NCSD) to address cybersecurity issues and to coordinate a cybersecurity strategy. The NCSD also serves to coordinate a public/private partnership supporting the U.S. Computer Emergency Response Team (US-CERT), ISAC partnerships, and the Cyber Warning Information Network, among other initiatives.

BLENDED CYBER THREATS

Cyber attacks offer several advantages to offenders. These include no significant funding, no state sponsor, profit, no physical intrusion, safety for the offender, immense challenges for IT specialists and investigators, and enormous potential harm to victims.

The U.S. Government Accountability Office (2005d) studied spam, phishing, and spyware threats to federal IT systems and its findings have relevance to state and local governments and the private sector. The three threats are among the top emerging cyber threats. Explanations of each follow.

Spam is the distribution of unsolicited commercial e-mail. It has been a nuisance to individuals and organizations by inundating them with e-mail advertisements for services, products, and offensive subject matter. Spammers can forge an e-mail header so the message disguises the actual source. The spam problem is made worse because it is a profitable business. Sending spam is inexpensive and sales do result.

As with other security methods through history, adversaries constantly seek methods to circumvent defenses. This is an ongoing "cat and mouse" competition. Antispam measures have caused spammers to design techniques to bypass detection and filtration. Spammer techniques include using alternate spelling, disguising the addresses in e-mails, and inserting the text as an image so a filter cannot read it. Compromised systems are being used regularly to send spam, making it difficult to track the source of spam.

Phishing is a word coined from the analogy that offenders use e-mail bait to fish for personal information. The origin of the word is from 1996 when hackers were stealing America Online (AOL) accounts by scamming passwords from unsuspecting AOL customers. Hackers have a tendency to replace "f" with "ph," and thus the name phishing developed.

Phishing often uses spam or pop-up messages that trick people into disclosing a variety of sensitive identification information (e.g., credit card and social security numbers and passwords). One ploy is when a phisher sends e-mails appearing as a legitimate business to potential victims. The e-mail requests an "update" of ID information or even participation in "enhanced protection against hackers, spyware, etc." Phishing applies a combination of technical methods and **social engineering** (i.e., using human interaction or social skills to trick a person into revealing sensitive information). Examples of social engineering are when a person is convinced to open an e-mail attachment or visit a malicious Web site or when a hacker telephones a corporate employee and claims to be a corporate IT technician needing an access code to repair the system.

Zeller (2006) reports that keylogging programs are gaining in popularity and replacing phishing by groups of global cybercriminals. **Keylogging programs** copy the keystrokes of computer users and send the information to offenders. These programs exploit security weaknesses and examine the path that carries information from the keyboard to other parts of the computer. Sources of the keylogging programs include Web pages, software downloads, and e-mail attachments. Because these programs are often hidden inside other software and infect computers, they are under the category of Trojan horses.

Spyware lacks an accepted definition by experts and even proposed legislation (U.S. Government Accountability Office, 2005d: 31). The definitions vary depending on whether the user consented to the downloading of the software, the types of information the spyware collects, and the nature of the harm. It is grouped into two major purposes: advertising and surveillance. Often in exchange for a free service (e.g., allegedly scanning for threats), spyware can deliver advertisements. It can collect Web surfing history and online buying habits, among other information. Other types of software are used for surveillance and to steal information. Consumers find it difficult to distinguish between helpful and harmful spyware.

Spyware is difficult to detect and users may not know their system contains it. Spyware typically does not have its own uninstall program and users must remove it manually or use a separate tool. Some types of spyware will install multiple copies and it can disable antispyware and antivirus applications and firewalls.

Malware (malicious software) are programs that create annoying or harmful actions. Often masquerading as useful programs or embedded into useful programs so users activate them, malware can include spyware, viruses, and worms.

Cyber threats are a serious problem for public and private sector organizations, besides individuals. Threats include the breach of confidentiality, integrity and availability of information, theft and manipulation of sensitive information, identity theft, distribution of malware, offensive material, lower productivity, denial-of-service attacks (i.e., a user takes up so much of a shared resource that others cannot use the resource), and liability for organizations.

The potential for financial gain has caused spammers, malware writers, and hackers to combine their methods into blended cyber threats. Security analysts are seeing an increase in blended threats and destructive payloads. **Blended cyber threats** combine the characteristics of different types of malicious code to bypass security controls (Figure 10-4). According to the U.S. Government Accountability Office (2005d: 44–45), several federal agencies found that current

Figure 10-4 ■ Blended threats may bypass traditional security controls. *Source:* U.S.Government Accountability Office (2005d).

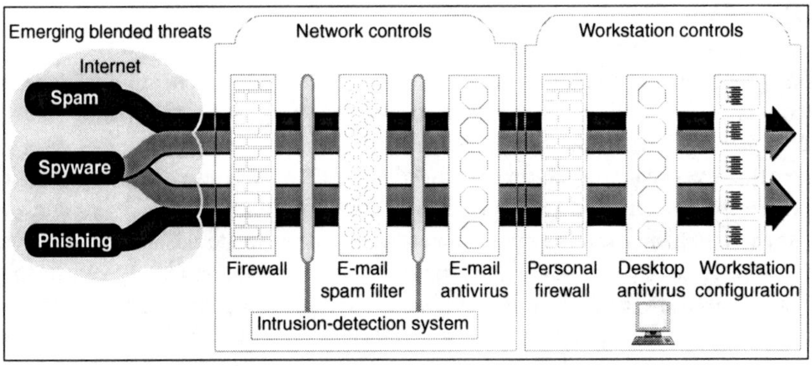

Figure 10-5 ■ Layered security mitigates the risk of individual cybersecurity threats. Source: U.S. Government Accountability Office (2005d).

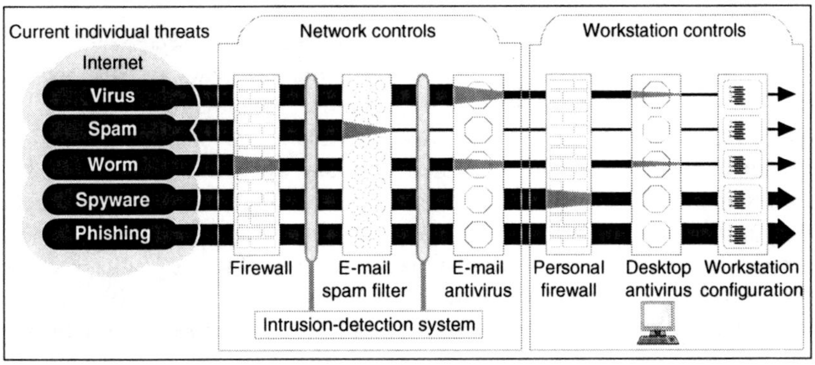

enterprise tools from vendors that protect against cyber threats are inadequate and impede efforts to detect, prevent, remove, and analyze incidents. In the DOJ, for example, IT specialists could gain greater control over systems by implementing tighter security controls, such as limiting users' rights to modify and change certain features on their computers. The USGAO and the National Institute of Standards and Technology have advised agencies to *use a layered security (defense-in-depth) approach, including strong passwords, patches, antivirus software, firewalls, software security settings, backup files, vulnerability assessments, and intrusion detection systems.* Figure 10-5 shows an example of how organizations can use layered security controls to mitigate the risk of individual cyber threats.

The DHS Red Cell Program also anticipates blended cyber threats. (This program provides alternative assessments of threats, especially those not necessarily derived from specific threat reporting. The program involves conducting interviews of government, industry, and academic experts.) Not only could a blended cyber attack cause harm, but a **blended cyber–physical attack** can aggravate damage and hamper recovery. Probable targets are CI, companies supporting U.S. policies, response and recovery assets, and security systems. An example of a blended cyber–physical attack is the detonation of several bombs in a city's mass transit system, followed by simultaneous attacks on key electrical transformers and transmission lines, and a cyber denial-of-service attack on the city's 911 emergency services.

A blended cyber attack or a blended cyber–physical attacks are serious threats.

INFORMATION SECURITY

In our information age, information is often extremely valuable to organizations. It may represent the lifeblood of an organization. Examples are product design, a secret formula, a customer list, and marketing plans. Certain types of information (e.g., credit, medical, educational) require protection under various laws.

Corporate intelligence involves gathering information about business competitors either legally or illegally. Competitive intelligence specialists view their vocation as an honorable profession and follow a code of ethics as they research public information. It makes good business sense to know what the competition is doing in our highly competitive world. However, unethical and illegal acts of acquiring information occur by certain people and organizations in business. Espionage and spying methods are varied and include social engineering, hacking, loss from wireless communications, electronic surveillance, wiretapping, hiring a competitor's employee, stealing a competitor's garbage, and blackmail. Also, governments actively collect information for national security (Purpura, 2002: 435–439).

From a homeland security perspective, select public and private sector information must be protected from terrorists and other offenders. Al-Qaida training materials have pointed to public information on the Internet as a rich source for intelligence gathering. Following the 9/11 attacks, organizations reevaluated their public information available via the Internet, the news media, periodicals, in brochures, etc. For example, for decades, businesses and local governments have publicized the location of natural gas lines to prevent explosions from construction projects, vehicles, and other sources. Now, the trend is to try to suppress the information (Urbina, 2004).

Information security applies numerous strategies to ensure the availability, accuracy, authenticity, and confidentiality of information (Curtis and McBride, 2005: 107–108). Availability ensures that users can access information and not be blocked by, for example, a denial-of-service attack. Accuracy addresses issues of errors (e.g., by an employee) and the integrity of information (e.g., a hacker remotely accesses an IT system to manipulate data). Authenticity means that information and its sender are genuine. Phishing, for instance, can lead to identity theft and loss of sensitive information. Confidentially ensures that information is accessed by only authorized individuals.

Numerous strategies are available to protect information. The first step is to identify and classify it according to its value and the harm that can occur if it is compromised. Further strategies include job applicant screening, policies and procedures, awareness training, IT security, encryption, physical security, controlled destruction, and recovery from disasters, attacks, and other potential threats (Purpura, 2002: 439–448).

SOURCES OF CYBERSECURITY THREATS

The U.S. Government Accountability Office (2005d) conducted an analysis of cybersecurity threats and formulated the following list of threats with a description of each.

- *Terrorists* may use phishing scams or spyware/malware in order to generate funds or gather sensitive information.
- *Criminal groups* are increasingly using cyber intrusions that attack systems for monetary gain; further, organized crime groups are using spam, phishing, and spyware/malware to commit identity theft and online fraud.
- *Foreign intelligence services* use cyber tools as part of their information-gathering and espionage activities.
- *Spyware/malware authors* carry out attacks against users by producing and distributing spyware and malware.
- *Hackers* sometimes break into networks for the thrill of the challenge or for bragging rights in the hacker community. While remote cracking once required a fair amount of skill or computer knowledge, hackers can now download attack scripts and protocols from the Internet and launch them against victim sites. Thus, while attack tools have become more sophisticated, they have also become easier to use.
- *Insider threats* include the disgruntled organization insider as a principal source of computer crimes. Insiders may not need a great deal of knowledge about computer intrusions because their knowledge of a target system often allows them to gain unrestricted access to cause damage to the system or to steal system data. The insider threat also includes outsourcing vendors. Employees who accidentally introduce malware into systems also fall into this category.

SOURCES OF CYBERSECURITY THREATS—Cont'd

- *Botnet operators* are hackers; however, instead of breaking into systems for the challenge or bragging rights, they take over multiple systems to enable them to coordinate attacks and distribute malware, spam, and phishing scams. The services of these networks are sometimes made available on underground markets (e.g., purchasing a denial-of-service attack; servers to relay spam or phishing scams).
- *Phishers* are individuals or small groups that execute phishing scams in an attempt to steal identities or information for monetary gain. Phishers may also use spam and spyware/malware to accomplish their objectives.
- *Spammers* are individuals or organizations that distribute unsolicited e-mail with hidden or false information in order to sell products, conduct phishing scams, distribute spyware/malware, or attack organizations.

THE INFORMATION TECHNOLOGY SECURITY PROFESSION

Several organizations work to improve the IT security profession. ASIS, International has joined with the **Information Systems Audit and Control Association** (ISACA) and the **Information Systems Security Association** (ISSA) to form an alliance to seek solutions to enterprise security risks (ASIS, International, 2005: 8–9). This alliance brings together over 80,000 security professionals from around the world who possess a variety of backgrounds capable of protecting enterprises from increasingly complex risks.

The ISACA is a global leader in information governance, security, and assurance. It sponsors conferences, offers training, publishes a journal and standards, and administers the certified information systems auditor and the certified information security manager designations. The ISSA is a global organization that provides educational forums, training, and publications.

The International Information Systems Security Certifications Consortium certifies information security professionals worldwide. The group's certifications are the certified information systems security professional (CISSP) and the System Security Certified Practitioner (SSCP).

BANKING AND FINANCE

This sector includes banks, insurance companies, mutual funds, pension funds, and other financial entities. Traditionally, financial institutions faced threats from robbery, burglary, larceny, fraud, and embezzlement. The Bank Protection Act of 1968 mandated minimum security measures for protection against robbery, burglary, and larceny, primarily. Today, the threat environment and the legal responsibilities of this CI sector are immense. In addition to traditional crimes, the challenges include cyber crimes, identity theft, money laundering, and terrorism. A host of laws and regulations place considerable responsibilities on this sector. The laws include the Bank Secrecy Act of 1986 and the Anti-Drug Abuse Act of 1988, both aimed at money laundering and financial sector transaction reporting requirements. The Gramm-Leach Bliley Act of 1999, which has broad application, requires safeguards on the privacy and security of customer information. The USA Patriot Act of 2001 contains measures against money laundering and the financing of terrorism. The Sarbanes-Oxley Act of 2002, passed in the wake of major corporate scandals, requires public companies to assess internal controls over financial reporting to ensure accuracy.

The banking and finance CI sector is at the heart of the U.S. economy and al-Qaida has publicly acknowledged that the U.S. economy is a primary target. Most of the banking and finance sector's activities take place in large commercial office buildings that house retail or wholesale operations, financial markets, regulatory institutions, and physical repositories for documents and securities. Although some assets in this sector are transferred physically, most of the business takes place electronically. Financial institutions hold only a small portion of depositors' assets in cash, and a disaster resulting in a rush to withdraw assets could present problems for the financial system. Also, like other sectors, banking and finance rely on other sectors, especially energy, telecommunications, transportation, and public safety services. Thus, public confidence and recovery from a disruption of services are primary concerns (White House, 2003a: 63–64).

Another serious vulnerability of this sector (and other sectors) is the outsourcing of services. Banks, for instance, obtain security officers from temporary agencies and permit outside companies to service online credit-card applications. Improved investigations of outside services and their employees offer greater protection (Buxbaum, 2005: 24–27).

Protection issues and strategies for the banking and finance sector include the following (White House, 2003a: 63–64).

- The U.S. Department of the Treasury (the lead agency for this sector) and federal and state regulatory agencies maintain emergency communications plans for this sector.
- Substitutability characterizes this sector. In other words, one type of payment mechanism or asset can replace another (e.g., cash, checks, or credit cards).
- This industry is highly regulated, vulnerabilities are identified, protective measures are taken, and sanctions can result from institutions not meeting standards.
- Redundancy and backup characterize this sector. Multiple sites have full functionality and each site can perform operations without other sites (Buxbaum, 2005: 24).
- The U.S. Department of the Treasury established the Financial and Banking Information Infrastructure Committee (FBIIC). It is made up of representatives from federal and state financial regulatory agencies and it works with the Financial Services ISAC. Major goals of these groups are to improve information dissemination and the protection of cyberspace.
- The U.S. Department of the Treasury is working the DHS and representatives of various CI sectors to address the banking and finance sector's dependencies on electronic networks and telecommunications services.

DEFENSE INDUSTRY BASE

Private sector defense industries play a crucial role in supporting the U.S. military (White House, 2003a: 45–46). These industries manufacture a wide variety of weapons (e.g., fighter jets, tanks, ships, and small arms), support equipment, and supplies essential to national defense and military operations. Also, many companies provide important services (e.g., IT, maintenance, security, and meals) to the military. Chapter 6 explained the extent of U.S. government outsourcing to private companies to support military operations.

For several decades the Department of Defense (DOD) has identified its own critical assets and those it depends on in the private sector. For example, private utilities service many military bases. The U.S. Government Accountability Office (2005a: 93) acknowledged that the DOD has taken steps to protect military installations. However, the USGAO claims the DOD lacks a single organization with authority to manage and integrate installation preparedness and prepare a comprehensive plan.

Because of market competition and attrition, the DOD now relies on a single or limited number of private sector suppliers to fulfill essential needs. These circumstances require enhanced risk management and security.

The DOD, the DHS, and the private sector work to identify CI and protection requirements. These groups, and the intelligence and law enforcement communities, are working to establish policies and mechanisms to improve the exchange of security-related information. The DOD is also working with defense industry contractors to address national emergency situation requirements, such as response time and supply and labor availability.

The DOD operates the **National Industrial Security Program** (NISP). This program integrates information, personnel, and physical security to protect classified information entrusted to contractors. The goal is to ensure that contractors' security programs deter and detect espionage and counter the threat posed by adversaries seeking classified information. According to DOD's Defense Security Service (DSS), which administers the NISP, attempts by foreign agents to obtain information from contractors have increased over the last several years and are expected to increase further. The U.S. General Accounting Office (2004: 2–4) found that the DSS cannot provide adequate assurances to federal government agencies that its oversight of contractors reduces the risk of information compromise and it is unable to provide this assurance because its performance goals and measures do not relate directly to the protection of classified information. Furthermore, the DSS maintains files on contractor facilities' security programs and their security violations, but it does not analyze this information. By not analyzing information on security violations and how well classified information is being protected across all facilities, DSS cannot identify systemic vulnerabilities and make corrective changes to increase protection. As a result, government agencies are not being kept informed of possible compromises of their information. Remedies include establishing results-oriented performance goals and measures to assess whether DSS is achieving its mission.

Outsourcing and complex mergers and acquisitions of domestic and foreign companies have produced challenges for the DOD in ensuring that its prime contractors' second-, third-, and fourth-tier subcontractors fulfill supply and security requirements in a national emergency and during peacetime. The U.S. Government Accountability Office (2005e: 3) noted that the DSS oversight of contractors under foreign ownership, control, or influence (FOCI) depends on contractors self-reporting. DSS then verifies the extent of the foreign relationship and works with the contractor on protective measures. The USGAO found that the DSS cannot ensure that its approach under FOCI is sufficient to reduce the risk of a foreign nation gaining unauthorized access to U.S. classified information. Violations of FOCI policies were found by the USGAO. Remedies include central collection and analysis of information, use of counterintelligence data, research tools, training for DSS staff, and lower turnover.

CRITICAL THINKING:

Why is classified information important? What are your views of the DOD efforts at protecting classified information?

GOVERNMENT

According to *The National Strategy for the Protection of Critical Infrastructures and Key Assets* (White House, 2003a), government is a CI sector and it contains key assets. The government CI sector is broad based and includes the defense industrial base, emergency services, public health care, public utilities, public transportation, and the postal system. The government's key assets are numerous. Examples are government buildings, national monuments, and dams. The present chapter, and others, contains numerous topics on government.

KEY ASSETS

In contrast to CI, key assets represent a variety of unique facilities, sites, and structures that require protection (White House, 2003a: 71). One category of key assets consists of facilities and structures of technological and economic power. Examples of these key assets are nuclear power plants and dams that were explained under the energy CI sector.

Another category of key assets includes national monuments and symbols that have historical significance and represent U.S. traditions, values, and political power. These sites attract tourists and media attention. The U.S. Department of the Interior (DOI) is the lead agency responsible for the security and safety of 70,000 employees, 200,000 volunteers, 1.3 million daily visitors, and over 507 million acres of public land that includes several national monuments, dams, and reservoirs (U.S. Government Accountability Office, 2005f: 5). Protection challenges for the DOI are balancing security and public access, securing assets in remote areas, and addressing jurisdictional issues among federal, state, and local jurisdictions and, in some cases, private foundations. The DOI has improved security at high-profile sites, created a central security office, and developed a risk management and ranking methodology as a foundation for security spending priorities. The DOI works with numerous law enforcement agencies, including the DHS, especially during high-profile events. State and local governments are also involved in the protection of monuments, symbols, and icons.

Government facilities are categorized as key assets (White House, 2003a: 77). This category includes buildings owned and leased by the federal government for use by federal entities. Government buildings (Figures 10-6 and 10-7)—whether federal, state, or local—are subject to a variety of serious internal and external threats, similar to commercial high-rise buildings, and they require comprehensive protection (see Chapters 7 through 9).

In the federal system, the **General Services Administration** (GSA) is a primary agency charged with managing federal facilities; however, other government organizations are involved in protecting facilities (e.g., DOD). The GSA controls over 8000 buildings, including office buildings, courthouses, and border stations. It owns most of the major departmental headquarters in Washington, DC (e.g., Departments of State, Justice, and Interior) and most of the key multi-agency federal office buildings in major cities. The GSA has developed security standards and works with other groups (e.g., DHS) to enhance protection. It faces similar challenges as the DOI, namely balancing security and public access. The **Federal Protective Service** (FPS), transferred from the GSA to the DHS, serves as a law-enforcement and security service to federal buildings. The FPS offers a broad range of services, such as patrol, security, investigative, canine, and WMD response. The FPS and the **U.S. Marshals Service** provide law enforcement and security services to federal buildings that house court functions. Both of these groups have worked together to enhance protection. Numerous private security companies also protect federal facilities. Privately owned buildings that house federal tenants present unique challenges that may create friction between the government and nonfederal occupants. The GSA must work with lessors to implement security enhancements. In federally owned buildings, federal laws and regulations are enforced. In buildings shared by federal and nonfederal tenants, federal laws and regulations that, for example, prohibit weapons apply only to those spaces occupied by federal tenants.

Commercial centers, office buildings, sports stadiums, and theme parks comprise another category of key assets (White House, 2003a: 78–79). A large number of people congregate at these locations to conduct business, shop, and enjoy restaurants and entertainment. Life safety and public safety are important objectives at these sites for protection against all hazards, besides terrorist attacks. Day-to-day protection is the responsibility of private sector proprietary and contract security personnel with the assistance of physical security technology. The federal government, especially the DHS, provides assistance through advisories and alerts; efforts to bring groups together to enhance protection; and designating an event (e.g., Superbowl) as a national security special event, resulting in federal law enforcement participation and aid. Various guidelines,

Figure 10-6 ■ Government buildings are key assets that require protection.

Figure 10-7 ■ Courthouse screening. Walk-through metal detector, left; X-ray scanner, right.
Courtesy: Wackenhut Corp.

standards, codes and regulations involving private sector organizations and government agencies also play an important role in protecting people and assets.

DISCUSSION QUESTIONS

1. Of the critical infrastructure sectors, which ones do you view as necessitating the highest priority for protection?
2. Of the key assets, which ones do you view as necessitating the highest priority for protection?
3. What can be done about the problem of cascading?
4. What are your views of blended cyber attacks and blended cyber–physical attacks? What protection strategies do you recommend?
5. Do you think government and businesses are doing enough to protect critical infrastructures and key assets? Explain your views on both groups.

APPLICATIONS

10A   YOU BE THE TERRORIST PLANNER
As a terrorist, how would you attack the food chain to cause as many deaths as possible? Include the target and the method of attack.

10B   YOU BE THE DIRECTOR OF SECURITY
As director of security for a breakfast cereal company, how do you protect the product from contamination by terrorists or a disgruntled employee? List at least 10 protection strategies.

10C   YOU BE THE TERRORIST PLANNER
As a terrorist in your locale, how would you attack infrastructure and/or key assets to cause a cascading effect in your community? How would you do the same to impact the state in which you live? For each attack, include the target, the method of attack, and how your attack would cause a cascading effect.

10D   YOU BE THE CHIEF SECURITY OFFICER
As a CSO for a manufacturing company, how do you protect your employer (i.e., its employees and company assets) from the cascading effect from a variety of types of terrorist attacks? List at least 10 protection strategies that can be applied by manufacturers in general.

WEB SITES

American Bankers Association: www.aba.com
American Chemistry Council: www.americanchemistry.com
American Water Works Association: www.awwa.org
ASIS, International: www.asisonline.org
Department of Homeland Security: www.dhs.gov
DHS Critical Infrastructure Daily Report: dhsdailyadmin@mail.dhs.osis.gov
Food Products Association: www.fpa-food.org
Government Web sites on food safety: www.foodsafety.gov
Information Systems Audit Control Association: www.isaca.org
Information Systems Security Association: www.issa.org
International Information Systems Security Certifications Consortium: www.isc2.org
The Infrastructure Security Partnership: http://www.tisp.org
U.S. Department of Agriculture, Food Safety and Inspection Service: www.fsis.usda.gov

U.S. Environmental Protection Agency: http://cfpub.epa.gov/safewater/watersecurity/index.cfm

U.S. Food and Drug Administration, Food Safety, Defense, and Outreach: www.cfsan.fda.gov

NOTES

ASIS, International (2005). "ASIS, ISACA, and ISSA Unite." *ASIS Dynamics,* 176 (May/June).

Buxbaum, P. (2005). "Critical Infrastructure: Security Under Wraps." *Homeland Security,* 2 (May/June).

Chalk, P. (2003). "Agroterrorism: What Is the Threat and What Can Be Done about It?" Santa Monica, CA: Rand Corp.

Congressional Budget Office (2004). *Homeland Security and the Private Sector* (December). Washington, DC: Congress of the United States.

Curtis, G., and McBride, R. (2005). *Proactive Security Administration.* Upper Saddle River, NJ: Pearson Prentice Hall.

Executive Order 13010 (1996). "Critical Infrastructure Protection." *Federal Register,* 61 (July 17).

Gewin, V. (2003). "Agriculture Shock." *Nature* (January).

Hebert, H. (2005). Associated Press. "Interest rises in nuclear plants for first time since disasters." (June 12).

Homer-Dixon, T. (2002). "The Rise of Complex Terrorism." *Foreign Policy* (January 15).

Hulme, G. (2005). "Security Tools Play Role in Protecting Food Chain." *Security Pipeline* (May 23). www.securitypipline.com, retrieved May 25, 2005.

Kochems, A. (2005). "Who's on First? A Strategy for Protecting Critical Infrastructure." *Backgrounder,* 1851 (May 9) www.heritage.org, retrieved June 20, 2005.

McKay, J. (2003). "Critical Strategies." *Government Technology* (January). www.govtech.net, retrieved June 16, 2004.

Mead, P., *et al.* (1999). "Food-Related Illness and Death in the United States: Reply to Dr. Halberg." *Emergency Infectious Diseases,* 5 (November–December).

Office of Homeland Security (2002). *National Strategy for Homeland Security* (July). www.whitehouse.gov, retrieved September 14, 2004.

Purpura, P. (2002). *Security and Loss Prevention,* 4th ed. Boston, MA: Butterworth-Heinemann.

Quirk, M., and Fernandez, S. (2005). "Infrastructure Robustness for Multiscale Critical Missions." *Journal of Homeland Security and Emergency Management,* 2.

U.S. Department of Energy (2005). *Inspection Report: Security Access Controls at the Y-12 National Security Complex* (June). www.ig.doe.gov/pdf/ig-0691.pdf, retrieved June 22, 2005.

U.S. Department of Homeland Security (2005). *Interim National Infrastructure Protection Plan* (February). www.dhs.gov, retrieved February 11, 2005.

U.S. Department of Homeland Security (2006b). *Revised Draft NIPP V2.0* (January). Nipp@dhs.gov, retrieved January 24, 2006.

U.S. Department of Homeland Security, Information Analysis and Infrastructure Protection Directorate (2005). *Fact Sheet: Protecting America's Critical Infrastructure—Chemical Security* (June 15). www.dhs.gov/dhspublic/display?content=4543, retrieved June 20, 2005.

U.S. Environmental Protection Agency, Office of Inspector General (2005). *EPA Needs to Determine What Barriers Prevent Water Systems from Securing Known Supervisory Control and Data Acquisition (SCADA) Vulnerabilities* (January 6). www.epa.gov/oig, retrieved January 13, 2005.

U.S. General Accounting Office (2003). *Nuclear Security: NNSA Needs to Better Manage Its Safeguards and Security Program* (May). www.gao.gov/cgi-bin/getrpt?GAO-03-471, retrieved June 22, 2005.

U.S. General Accounting Office (2004). *Industrial Security: DOD Cannot Provide Adequate Assurances That Its Oversight Ensures the Protection of Classified Information* (March). www.gao.gov/cgi-bin/getrpt? GAO-04-332, retrieved July 20, 2005.

U.S. Department of Homeland Security (2006a). *National Infrastructure Protection Plan.* www.dhs.gov/internet/assetlibrary/NIPP_plan.pdf, retrieved June 30, 2006.

U.S. Government Accountability Office (2005a). *Homeland Security: Agency Plans, Implementation, and Challenges Regarding the National Strategy for Homeland Security* (January). www.gao.gov/cgi-bin/getrpt?GAO-05-213, retrieved February 15, 2005.

U.S. Government Accountability Office (2005b). *Federal Agencies Should Pursue Opportunities to Reduce Overlap and Better Leverage Resources* (March). www.gao.gov/cgi-bin/getrpt?GAO-05-213, retrieved June 1, 2005.

U.S. Government Accountability Office (2005c). *Protection of Chemical and Water Infrastructure: Federal Requirements, Actions of Selected Facilities, and Remaining Challenges* (March). www.gao.gov/cgi-bin/getrpt?GAO-05-327, retrieved June 1, 2005.

U.S. Government Accountability Office (2005d). *Information Security: Emerging Cybersecurity Issues Threaten Federal Information Systems* (May). www.gao.gov/new.items.do5231.pdf, retrieved May 16, 2005.

U.S. Government Accountability Office (2005e). *Industrial Security: DOD Cannot Ensure Its Oversight of Contractors under Foreign Influence Is Sufficient* (July). www.gao.gov/cgi-bin/getrpt?GAO-05-681, retrieved July 18, 2005.

U.S. Government Accountability Office (2005f). *Homeland Security: Actions Needed to Better Protect National Icons and Federal Office Buildings from Terrorism* (June). www.gao.gov/cgi-bin/getrpt?GAO-05-681, retrieved July 12, 2005.

U.S. Government Accountability Office (2006). *Homeland Security: DHS Is Taking Steps to Enhance Security at Chemical Facilities, but Additional Authority Is Needed* (January). www.gao.gov/new.items/d06150.pdf, retrieved March 1, 2006.

Urbina, I. (2004). "Mapping Natural Gas Lines: Advise the Public, Tip off the Terrorists." *The New York Times* (August 29). www.nytimes.com/2004/08/29/nyregion/29pipeline.html, retrieved August 30, 2004.

White House (2003a). The *National Strategy for the Physical Protection of Critical Infrastructures and Key Assets* (February). www.whitehouse.gov, retrieved September 14, 2004.

White House (2003b). *The National Strategy to Secure Cyberspace* (February). www.whitehouse.gov, retrieved July 17, 2003.

Winter, G., and Broad, W. (2001). "Added Security for Dams, Reservoirs and Aqueducts." www.waterindustry.org, retrieved April 25, 2002.

Zeller, T. (2006). "Cyberthieves silently copy keystrokes." *News.Com.* (February 27). http://news.com, retrieved February 28, 2006.

CHAPTER 11

BORDER AND TRANSPORTATION SECURITY

OBJECTIVES

The study of this chapter will enable you to:

1. List and discuss the major initiatives of the federal government to improve border and transportation security.
2. Name and describe the federal agencies with major roles in border and transportation security.
3. Outline the major functions of U.S. Customs and Border Protection.
4. Outline the major functions of U.S. Immigration and Customs Enforcement.
5. Outline the major functions of the U.S. Citizenship and Immigration Services.
6. Outline the major functions of the Transportation Security Administration.
7. Understand the reality of border security and immigration policies.
8. Examine eight transportation security sectors, how each is unique, and protection strategies for each.

KEY TERMS

Aviation and Transportation Security
  Act of 2001
U.S. Customs and Border Protection
U.S. Immigration and Customs Enforcement
U.S. Citizenship and Immigration Services
Transportation Security Administration
U.S. Coast Guard
U.S. Department of State
visa
Container Security Initiative
Advanced Manifest Rule
Customs-Trade Partnership Against Terrorism

Immigration and Nationality Act
Visa Waiver Program
secure border initiative
expedited removal
guest-worker program
Intelligence Reform and Terrorism Prevention
  Act of 2004
national strategy for transportation security
Federal Aviation Administration
Secure Flight
Explosives Detection Canine Team Program
Federal Flight Deck Officer Program

KEY TERMS

Alien Flight Student Program
Man-Portable Air Defense Systems
Association of American Railroads
Federal Transit Administration
Federal Railroad Administration
transportation choke points

American Trucking Association
International Ship and Port Facility
   Security Code
Maritime Transportation Security
   Act of 2002
anthrax attacks

THE HIJACKING OF AMERICAN AIRLINES FLIGHT 11 ON SEPTEMBER 11, 2001

American Airlines Flight 11 provided nonstop service from Boston to Los Angeles. On September 11, Captain John Ogonowski and First Officer Thomas McGuinness piloted the Boeing 767. It carried its full capacity of nine flight attendants. Eighty-one passengers boarded the flight with them (including the five terrorists).

The plane took off at 7:59. Just before 8:14, it had climbed to 26,000 feet, not quite its initial assigned cruising altitude of 29,000 feet. All communications and flight profile data were normal. About this time the "Fasten Seatbelt" sign would usually have been turned off and the flight attendants would have begun preparing for cabin service. At that same time, American 11 had its last routine communication with the ground when it acknowledged navigational instructions from the FAA's air traffic control (ATC) center in Boston. Sixteen seconds after that transmission, ATC instructed the aircraft's pilots to climb to 35,000 feet. That message and all subsequent attempts to contact the flight were not acknowledged. From this and other evidence, we believe the hijacking began at 8:14 or shortly thereafter.

Reports from two flight attendants in the coach cabin, Betty Ong and Madeline "Amy" Sweeney, tell us most of what we know about how the hijacking happened. As it began, some of the hijackers—most likely Wail al Shehri and Waleed al Shehri, who were seated in row 2 in first class—stabbed the two unarmed flight attendants who would have been preparing for cabin service.

We do not know exactly how the hijackers gained access to the cockpit; FAA rules required that the doors remain closed and locked during flight. Ong speculated that they had "jammed their way" in. Perhaps the terrorists stabbed the flight attendants to get a cockpit key, to force one of them to open the cockpit door, or to lure the captain or first officer out of the cockpit. Or, the flight attendants may just have been in their way. At the same time or shortly thereafter, Atta—the only terrorist on board trained to fly a jet—would have moved to the cockpit from his business-class seat, possibly accompanied by Omari. As this was happening, passenger Daniel Lewin, who was seated in the row just behind Atta and Omari, was stabbed by one of the hijackers, probably Satam al Suqami, who was seated directly behind Lewin. Lewin had served 4 years as an officer in the Israeli military. He may have made an attempt to stop the hijackers in front of him, not realizing that another was sitting behind him.

The hijackers quickly gained control and sprayed Mace, pepper spray, or some other irritant in the first-class cabin in order to force the passengers and flight attendants toward the rear of the plane. They claimed they had a bomb.

About 5 minutes after the hijacking began, Betty Ong contacted the American Airlines southeastern reservations office in Cary, North Carolina, via an AT&T airphone to report an emergency aboard the flight. This was the first of several occasions on 9/11 when flight attendants took action outside the scope of their training, which emphasized that in a hijacking, they were to communicate with the cockpit crew. The emergency call lasted approximately 25 minutes, as Ong calmly and professionally relayed information about events taking place aboard the airplane to authorities on the ground.

THE HIJACKING OF AMERICAN AIRLINES FLIGHT 11
ON SEPTEMBER 11, 2001—Cont'd

At 8:19, Ong reported: "The cockpit is not answering, somebody's stabbed in business class—and I think there's Mace—that we can't breathe—I don't know, I think we're getting hijacked." She then told of the stabbings of the two flight attendants.

At 8:21, one of the American employees receiving Ong's call in North Carolina, Nydia Gonzalez, alerted the American Airlines operations center in Fort Worth, Texas, reaching Craig Marquis, the manager on duty. Marquis soon realized this was an emergency and instructed the airline's dispatcher responsible for the flight to contact the cockpit. At 8:23, the dispatcher tried unsuccessfully to contact the aircraft. Six minutes later, the air traffic control specialist in American's operations center contacted the FAA's Boston air traffic control center about the flight. The center was already aware of the problem. Boston center knew of a problem on the flight in part because just before 8:25 the hijackers had attempted to communicate with the passengers. The microphone was keyed, and immediately one of the hijackers said, "Nobody move. Everything will be okay. If you try to make any moves, you'll endanger yourself and the airplane. Just stay quiet." Air traffic controllers heard the transmission; Ong did not. The hijackers probably did not know how to operate the cockpit radio communication system correctly, and thus inadvertently broadcast their message over the air traffic control channel instead of the cabin public-address channel.

Also at 8:25, and again at 8:29, Amy Sweeney got through to the American Flight services office in Boston but was cut off after she reported someone was hurt aboard the flight. Three minutes later, Sweeney was reconnected to the office and began relaying updates to the manager, Michael Woodward.

At 8:26, Ong reported that the plane was "flying erratically." A minute later, Flight 11 turned south. American also began getting identifications of the hijackers, as Ong and then Sweeney passed on some of the seat numbers of those who had gained unauthorized access to the cockpit.

Sweeney calmly reported on her line that the plane had been hijacked; a man in first class had his throat slashed; two flight attendants had been stabbed—one was seriously hurt and was on oxygen while the other's wounds seemed minor; a doctor had been requested; the flight attendants were unable to contact the cockpit; and there was a bomb in the cockpit. Sweeney told Woodward that she and Ong were trying to relay as much information as they could to people on the ground.

At 8:38, Ong told Gonzalez that the plane was flying erratically again. Around this time Sweeney told Woodward that the hijackers were Middle Easterners, naming three of their seat numbers. One spoke very little English and one spoke excellent English. The hijackers had gained entry to the cockpit, and she did not know how. The aircraft was in a rapid descent.

At 8:41, Sweeney told Woodward that passengers in coach were under the impression that there was a routine medical emergency in first class. Other flight attendants were busy at duties such as getting medical supplies, while Ong and Sweeney were reporting the events.

At 8:41, in American's operations center, a colleague told Marquis that the air traffic controllers declared Flight 11 a hijacking and "think he's [American 11] headed toward Kennedy [airport in New York City]. They're moving everybody out of the way. They seem to have him on a primary radar. They seem to think that he is descending."

At 8:44, Gonzalez reported losing phone contact with Ong. About this same time, Sweeney reported to Woodward, "Something is wrong. We are in a rapid descent ... we are all over the place." Woodward asked Sweeney to look out the window to see if she could determine where they were. Sweeney responded: "We are flying low. We are flying very, very low. We are flying way too low." Seconds later she said, "Oh my God we are way too low." The phone call ended.

At 8:46:40, American 11 crashed into the north tower of the World Trade Center in New York City. All on board, along with an unknown number of people in the tower, were killed instantly.

THE HIJACKING OF AMERICAN AIRLINES FLIGHT 77 ON SEPTEMBER 11, 2001

American Airlines Flight 77 was scheduled to depart from Washington Dulles for Los Angeles at 8:10. The aircraft was a Boeing 757 piloted by Captain Charles F. Burlingame and First Officer David Charlebois. There were four flight attendants. On September 11, the flight carried 58 passengers. American 77 pushed back from its gate at 8:09 and took off at 8:20. At 8:46, the flight reached its assigned cruising altitude of 35,000 feet. Cabin service would have begun. At 8:51, American 77 transmitted its last routine radio communication.

The hijacking began between 8:51 and 8:54. As on American 11 and United 175, the hijackers used knives (reported by one passenger) and moved all the passengers (and possibly crew) to the rear of the aircraft (reported by one flight attendant and one passenger). Unlike the earlier flights, the Flight 77 hijackers were reported by a passenger to have box cutters. Finally, a passenger reported that an announcement had been made by the "pilot" that the plane had been hijacked. Neither of the firsthand accounts mentioned any stabbings or the threat or use of either a bomb or Mace, although both witnesses began the flight in the first-class cabin.

At 8:54, the aircraft deviated from its assigned course, turning south. Two minutes later the transponder was turned off and even primary radar contact with the aircraft was lost. The Indianapolis air traffic control center repeatedly tried and failed to contact the aircraft. American Airlines dispatchers also tried, without success.

At 9:00, American Airlines Executive Vice President Gerard Arpey learned that communications had been lost with American 77. This was now the second American aircraft in trouble. He ordered all American Airlines flights in the northeast that had not taken off to remain on the ground. Shortly before 9:10, suspecting that American 77 had been hijacked, American headquarters concluded that the second aircraft to hit the World Trade Center might have been Flight 77. After learning that United Airlines was missing a plane, American Airlines headquarters extended the ground stop nationwide.

At 9:12, Renee May called her mother, Nancy May, in Las Vegas. She said her flight was being hijacked by six individuals who had moved them to the rear of the plane. She asked her mother to alert American Airlines. Nancy May and her husband promptly did so.

At some point between 9:16 and 9:26, Barbara Olson called her husband, Ted Olson, the solicitor general of the United States. She reported that the flight had been hijacked and that the hijackers had knives and box cutters. She further indicated that the hijackers were not aware of her phone call and that they had put all the passengers in the back of the plane. About a minute into the conversation, the call was cut off. Solicitor General Olson tried unsuccessfully to reach Attorney General John Ashcroft. Shortly after the first call, Barbara Olson reached her husband again. She reported that the pilot had announced that the flight had been hijacked and asked her husband what she should tell the captain to do. Ted Olson asked for her location and she replied that the aircraft was then flying over houses. Another passenger told her they were traveling northeast. The solicitor general then informed his wife of the two previous hijackings and crashes. She did not display signs of panic and did not indicate any awareness of an impending crash. At that point, the second call was cut off.

At 9:29, the autopilot on American 77 was disengaged; the aircraft was at 7000 feet and approximately 38 miles west of the Pentagon. At 9:32, controllers at the Dulles Terminal Radar Approach Control "observed a primary radar target tracking eastbound at a high rate of speed." This was later determined to have been Flight 77.

At 9:34, Ronald Reagan Washington National Airport advised the Secret Service of an unknown aircraft heading in the direction of the White House. American 77 was then 5 miles west–southwest of the Pentagon and began a 330° turn. At the end of the turn, it was descending through 2200 feet,

THE HIJACKING OF AMERICAN AIRLINES FLIGHT 77 ON SEPTEMBER 11, 2001 — Cont'd

pointed toward the Pentagon and downtown Washington. The hijacker pilot then advanced the throttles to maximum power and dove toward the Pentagon.

At 9:37:46, American Airlines Flight 77 crashed into the Pentagon, travelling at approximately 530 miles per hour. All on board, as well as many civilian and military personnel in the building, were killed (National Commission on Terrorist Attacks Upon the United States, 2004).

BORDER AND TRANSPORTATION SECURITY

The borders of the United States (Figure 11-1) include a 5525 mile border with Canada and a 1989 mile border with Mexico. Another component of the U.S. border is 95,000 miles of shoreline and navigable waterways. All people and goods legally entering the United States must be processed through an air, land, or sea port point of entry. Over 500 million people legally enter the United States each year and 330 million are noncitizens. Eight-five percent enter via land, often as a daily commute. The trade across U.S. borders amounted to $1.35 trillion in imports and $1 trillion in exports in 2001 (Office of Homeland Security, 2002: 21).

As we know, terrorists are elusive, crafty, and patient as they search for vulnerabilities in potential targets. The proliferation of WMD has created opportunities for terrorists to become more lethal and inflict mass casualties and severe economic harm. Consequently, the global transportation system that crosses borders, and has access to all communities, must be protected against terrorists who may use this system as a means of delivering WMD. The protection challenges are enormous. The National Strategy for Homeland Security (Office of Homeland Security, 2002: 22–23 and 59–61) promotes the following major initiatives to improve border and transportation security.

- Consolidate principal border and transportation security agencies in the DHS.
- Create "smart borders" through improvements in management systems, databases, coordination, intelligence, and international cooperation. Increase the information available on inbound goods and passengers so border agencies can apply risk-based management tools.
- Increase the security of shipping containers that move about 90% of the world's cargo. This initiative includes identifying high-risk containers, prescreening containers, using technology to inspect, designing containers with security features, and, when possible, placing inspectors at foreign ports to screen U.S.-bound containers.
- Implement the **Aviation and Transportation Security Act of 2001** (ATSA). The goals of this act are to secure the air travel systems; recognize the importance of security for all forms of transportation; strengthen partnerships among federal, state, and local governments and the private sector; and protect critical transportation assets such as ports, pipelines, rail, and highway bridges.
- Recapitalize the U.S. Coast Guard. Increase funding to improve the aging fleet, command and control systems, shore facilities, and multiple missions.
- Reform immigration services within the DHS to improve administration and enforcement of laws.
- Pursue a sustained international agenda to counter global terrorism and improve homeland security.
- Work with key trading partners to create systems to verify the legitimacy of people and goods entering the United States.
- Seek international support on many fronts, such as intensified law enforcement cooperation and improved security standards for travel documents (e.g., passports and visas).

Figure 11-1 ■ Map of North America and United States borders with Canada and Mexico. Courtesy: Central Intelligence Agency. http://www.cia.gov/cia/publications/factbook/reference_maps/north_america.html

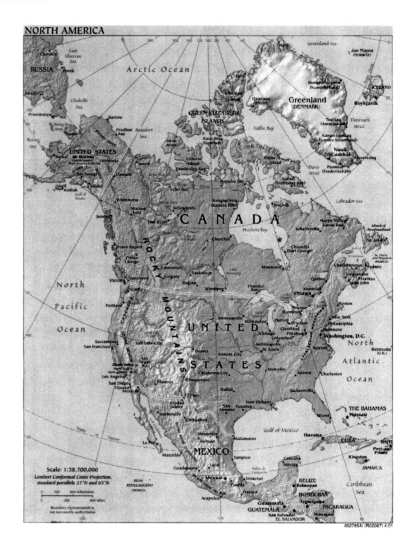

AGENCIES WITH MAJOR ROLES IN BORDER AND TRANSPORTATION SECURITY

The Department of Homeland Security and the Department of State have major roles in border and transportation security. Within the DHS is the **U.S. Customs and Border Protection** (CBP) that conducts inspections at land borders and ports of entry to prevent and detect people and goods from entering the United States illegally (Figure 11-2). The **U.S. Immigration and Customs Enforcement** (ICE), also within the DHS, concentrates on interior customs and immigration law enforcement to curb the unlawful presence of people and goods within the United States. The **Transportation Security Administration** (TSA), another major component of the DHS, focuses on aviation security activities and security measures for nonaviation modes of transportation. Also within the DHS is the **U.S. Coast Guard**, which is the lead organization for the protection of seaports and waterways.

The **U.S. Department of State** (DOS), often referred to as "State," is separate from the DHS. It administers the visa program to prevent terrorists and other offenders from traveling to

Figure 11-2 ■ CBP conducts check at border crossing. Photo by Gerald Nino. http://www.customs.gov/xp/cgov/newsroom/photo_gallery/afc/homeland_security/homeland_security_11.xml

the United States. A **visa** is an official approval of a passport so the holder can enter a particular country. The DOS works with the DHS and the DOJ to screen visitors to the United States, while striving to share information on security risks and changes in the status of individual visas.

The Office of Management and Budget reported that funding requests for border and transportation security was about $17 billion for fiscal year 2005. The majority was for the DHS ($16 billion), largely for CBP, TSA, and the Coast Guard. These figures exclude funding for the DOD, HHS, and DOE, which have related border and transportation security activities underway (U.S. Government Accountability Office, 2005d: 44).

On November 25, 2002, the Homeland Security Act was signed into law and the Immigration and Naturalization Service (INS) was transferred to the DHS, where its functions were assigned to other agencies and the INS ceased to exist.

U.S. CUSTOMS AND BORDER PROTECTION

U.S. Customs and Border Protection, established on March 1, 2003, is the unified border agency of the DHS (U.S. Customs and Border Protection, n.d.). The CBP contains the inspectional workforce and border authorities of legacy (i.e., predecessor agency) U.S. Customs, legacy Immigration and Naturalization Service (INS), legacy USDA Animal and Plant Health Inspection Service (APHIS), and the entire U.S. Border Patrol. This united force, often promoted as "one face at the border," consists of over 40,000 employees.

The priority mission of CBP is homeland security. It is charged with managing, securing, and controlling the U.S. borders. CBP has six primary strategic goals.

1. Detecting and preventing terrorists and their weapons, including WMD, from entering the United States *at* ports of entry.

2. Strengthening national security *between* ports of entry to prevent the illegal entry of terrorists, weapons, contraband, and illegal aliens into the United States.
3. Merging and unifying all U.S. border agencies.
4. Facilitating the efficient movement of legitimate cargo and people while maintaining security.
5. Protecting citizens by prohibiting the introduction of contraband (i.e., anything illegal), including illegal drugs and other harmful materials and organisms, into the United States.
6. Continue to build a modern management infrastructure that assures the achievement of business results.

CBP priorities include the following.

- "Pushing U.S. borders outward." In other words, protect the global supply chain early in the transport process by cooperating with other countries to improve the security of shipments.
- Plug gaps in security at and between borders.
- Improve targeting and analysis to permit better collection and analysis of passenger and trade data prior to arrival.
- Leverage technology to enhance security at ports of entry.
- Improve IT so information is available to those needing it most.
- Secure resources to ensure adequate training to respond to the changing environment and organization. Use cross training to handle terrorism and other homeland security responsibilities. Leverage technology to meet training needs.
- Improve management effectiveness and efficiency, internalize core values, and reward outstanding performance.
- Strengthen partnerships with other law enforcement agencies, especially with ICE, trade and travel communities, and the public.

CBP Initiatives

ONE FACE AT THE BORDER
Historically, travelers at U.S. borders were required to make two or three separate stops. These stops included immigration inspection, customs inspection, and, if they were carrying food or plants, agriculture inspection. Creation of the CBP officer position is aimed at maximizing efficiency for travelers and those involved in trade. One-stop processing seeks to continue traditional missions, such as interdicting illegal drugs and other contraband, enforcing trade and immigration laws, and protecting the United States from harmful pests and diseases. CBP agriculture specialists support other CBP officers in the analysis of agriculture imports.

CONTAINER SECURITY INITIATIVE
The **Container Security Initiative** (CSI) extends the zone of security outward so that U.S. borders are the last line of defense, not the first. Maritime containers that present a risk for terrorism are identified and inspected at foreign ports before they are shipped to the United States. This initiative involves using intelligence and automated advance information to identify and target high-risk containers; detection technology; and smarter, tamper-evident containers. Teams of CBP officials work with host nations in the screening process. This initiative is important because 90% of global trade is transported in cargo containers, half of incoming trade to the United States arrives by containers onboard ships, and nine million cargo containers arrive on ships and are offloaded at U.S. seaports annually (Figure 11-3).

Are all maritime containers that arrive in U.S. ports inspected? The CBP argues that contrary to media reports that the CBP only pays attention to 2% of entering containers, the "CBP actually employs a multilayered process that scrutinizes virtually all incoming sea cargo and targets those shipments that pose the highest risk" (U.S. Customs and Border Protection, n.d.).

Figure 11-3 ■ Containerized cargo presents a security risk and the possibility that it will be exploited to smuggle WMD into the United States.

ADVANCED MANIFEST RULE

The CBP receives electronic information on over 95% of all U.S.-bound sea cargo before it arrives. Under the **Advanced Manifest Rule**, all sea carriers, with few exceptions (e.g., bulk carriers), must provide cargo descriptions and valid consignee addresses 24 hours before cargo is loaded at the foreign port for shipment to the United States. Under the Sea Automated Manifest System, data include cargo type, manufacturer, shipper, country of origin, routing, and the terms of payment. Using computer systems to analyze data, the CBP assigns a numeric score to each shipment indicating its level of risk. High-risk containers are flagged to receive a security inspection.

INDUSTRY PARTNERSHIP PROGRAMS

Because CBP resources are limited, the trade community has been brought into the process of homeland security. In addition to terrorism, other threats are money laundering and smuggling contraband that can enter legitimate commerce to use it as a vehicle. CBP strategies include automation, risk management, and industry awareness.

Customs-Trade Partnership Against Terrorism (C-TPAT) seeks to engage the trade community into a voluntary partnership with customs. This initiative is part of the extended border strategy and entails customs working with importers, carriers, brokers, and other businesses to improve supply chain security. America's Counter Smuggling Initiative (ACSI) is a component of C-TPAT and is designed to counter the smuggling of drugs and the possible introduction of WMD in cargo and conveyances. ACSI concentrates on each part of the commercial transportation process and seeks a comprehensive approach to curb smuggling. The Business Anti-Smuggling Coalition (BASC) is a private sector led coalition, without government mandates, that focuses on the challenges of preventing the concealment of contraband in trade. Businesses follow BASC security standards. The Carrier Initiative Program (CIP) offers CBP antidrug smuggling training to air, sea, and land transport companies. The CIP trains employees of carriers with transportation routes that are high risk for drug smuggling. Carriers sign agreements with the CBP that offer benefits to both groups. Carriers agree to prevent smuggling by securing their facilities and conveyances, and the CBP conducts security surveys followed by recommendations to improve security. A carrier's cooperation and compliance may become a mitigating factor if narcotics are found on board a conveyance and authorities are assessing a fine. The Free and Secure Trade (FAST) initiative offers expedited clearance of low-risk shipments to carriers and importers enrolled in C-TPAT. This program is established between the United States and Mexico and the United States and Canada. It is designed to promote free and secure trade through risk management principles, supply chain security, industry partnerships, and advanced technology. FAST aims to streamline and integrate registration for drivers, carriers, and importers, while reducing paperwork. The program offers dedicated lanes at major crossings to FAST participants and minimum frequency of inspections of cargo.

TECHNOLOGY

The CBP continues to rely on technology as an important component of border security. It does not rely on any single technology or inspection process. Instead, it applies multiple technologies in different combinations to increase the likelihood that a WMD will be detected. The technology includes large-scale X-ray and gamma-imaging systems, mobile truck X-ray, and a variety of portable and handheld radiation detection technologies.

Reality Check: Can Customs and Border Protection Stop Illegal Radioactive Materials from Crossing into the United States?

During 2005, the U.S. Government Accountability Office (2006a), at the request of the U.S. Senate, conducted an undercover investigation to test whether CBP could stop radioactive materials from entering the United States at its borders. The investigation was conducted in accordance with quality standards for investigations as established by the president's council on integrity and efficiency. Investigators purchased a small quantity of radioactive material, enough to construct a "dirty bomb," from a commercial source by posing as an employee of a phony company. This showed the ease of obtaining radioactive material because suppliers are not required to exercise due diligence to ascertain whether the buyer is legitimate and suppliers are not required to request, from the buyer, a Nuclear Regulatory Commission (NRC) document when purchasing small quantities. Simultaneous crossings occurred at the U.S.–Canadian border and the U.S.–Mexican border. The investigation focused on two questions: Are radiation portal monitors capable of detecting the radioactive material? These monitors consist of large stationary equipment that the CBP uses to detect the presence of radioactive material by screening people, vehicles, and cargo as they pass through ports of entry. Do CBP inspectors exercise due diligence to determine the authenticity of documents presented by individuals seeking to transport radioactive materials across borders? Results showed that the radiation portal monitors properly signaled the presence of radioactive material in vehicles. However, the undercover investigators successfully crossed the borders with the radioactive material using counterfeit documents. As employees of a bogus company, the undercover investigators presented a counterfeit bill of lading and a counterfeit NRC document authorizing them to acquire, receive, possess, and transfer radioactive material. An Internet search and off-the-shelf computer software helped produce the counterfeit documents. Following the undercover investigations, corrective action briefings were conducted by the USGAO with CBP and NRC officials.

One further question: How can we improve the security of radioactive material already in the United States and used by several industries?

In addition to using roads, fencing, and vehicle barriers along the borders, a variety of technologies improve surveillance capabilities. Examples are outdoor sensors, CCTV, night-vision equipment, and aircraft, including unmanned aerial vehicles (UAV).

Biometric verification is another helpful and growing technology. For example, both the Mexican border and the Canadian border contain entry points that are equipped with the biometric verification system. It is designed to read the fingerprint encoded on a border crossing card and compare it to the fingerprint of the person presenting the card to detect imposters. Border crossing cards are often used to replace passports and visas.

Another technology applied by the CBP is the automated biometric identification system (IDENT)/integrated automated fingerprint identification system (IAFIS). IDENT/IAFIS was implemented to integrate the IDENT database with the FBI criminal master file (CMF) known as IAFIS. A full set of fingerprints is recorded on a person and the prints are sent simultaneously to both IDENT and IAFIS databases. IDENT searches for wants and warrants and the recidivist database that holds the names of subjects previously encountered by the CBP. IAFIS searches the CMF, which contains millions of criminal records.

The CBP employs many other technologies to accomplish its goals. These include its improving communication infrastructure (e.g., land mobile radio, cellular coverage, and satellite communication capabilities), remote access to national law enforcement databases, mobile alien processing capabilities, and computer-based training.

MULTILAYERED STRATEGIES AND INVESTIGATIONS TO PROTECT AGAINST WMD

The CBP employs multilayered strategies to protect the United States against weapons of mass destruction. U.S. adversaries frequently seek to illegally obtain sensitive technology, and the CBP serves as the lead agency for enforcing U.S. export control laws. CBP strategies include strategic investigations, intelligence, and outbound examinations to prevent sensitive technology from being exported illegally. Also, the CBP partners with manufacturers to guard items sought by adversaries. Hundreds of schemes have been targeted for investigation by the CBP. For example, in April 2002, Richard Smyth, a former NATO advisor and president of Milco International, was sentenced for exporting nuclear trigger devices to Israel. He had been charged in 1985 for exporting 800 such devices without obtaining the required export license. Before trial, Smyth fled, but after 16 years on the run, he was arrested in Spain in 2001 and extradited to Los Angeles where he pleaded guilty to charges in the original 1985 indictment.

In June 1995, CBP investigators in New York arrested three men on charges of attempting to smuggle seven tons of nuclear-grade zirconium to Iraq. CBP undercover agents posed as Iraqi military officers. The zirconium had been smuggled in multiple shipments from Ukraine, through Germany, to New York and Cyprus, where it awaited export to Iraq.

Since the early 1990s, the CBP has provided nonproliferation training and equipment to thousands of border guards in many nations to prevent the spread of WMD. The U.S. State and Defense Departments have funded CBP advisors and training in eastern Europe, the Caucuses, the Middle East, and Asia. The CBP delivers high-tech (e.g., personal radiation detectors; X-ray vans) and low-tech (e.g., fiber-optic scopes, drills, mirrors) equipment to other countries to conduct searches at borders. An example of one seizure occurred in March 2000 when Uzbekistan customs authorities at the Gisht Kuprink border crossing were alerted by radiation pagers and found 10 highly radioactive lead containers concealed in 23 tons of scrap metal in a truck entering from Kazakhstan. The Iranian driver had documents indicating delivery to Pakistan.

ORIGINS OF THE U.S. BORDER PATROL

The border patrol has provided many years of service to the United States (U.S. Customs and Border Protection, 2003). In 1904, mounted watchmen of the U.S. Immigration Service patrolled the border with Mexico and were based out of El Paso, Texas. The patrols to protect against illegal crossings were irregular and undertaken only when resources permitted. Although the mounted guards never exceeded 75, they patrolled as far west as California as they tried to restrict the flow of illegal Chinese immigration.

Continued

ORIGINS OF THE U.S. BORDER PATROL — Cont'd

In March 1915, Congress authorized a separate group of mounted guards, also called mounted inspectors, who rode horseback and used cars and boats. Again, their patrols were irregular and they pursued Chinese immigrants trying to avoid the Chinese exclusion laws. These inspectors were also assigned to inspection stations. Military troops and Texas Rangers also sporadically patrolled the border with Mexico.

In the early part of the 20th century, custom violations and watching for "the enemy" were higher priorities than enforcing immigration regulations. The difficulty of protecting the border was growing and it became worse when, in 1917, a higher head tax and literacy requirement were imposed, prompting more people to cross the border illegally.

Greater attention to border enforcement resulted from Prohibition (i.e., the 18th amendment to the U.S. Constitution prohibited the importation, transport, manufacture, or sale of alcoholic beverages), in 1920, and passage of the Immigration Acts of 1921 and 1924, which specified numerical limits on immigration to the United States. On May 28, 1924, Congress established the U.S. Border Patrol, and in 1925, its duties were expanded to patrol seacoasts. Agents were initially provided with a badge and revolver, oats and hay for their horses, and an annual salary of $1680. They furnished their own horse and saddle. Uniforms were not supplied until 1928. During this period, most of the 450 officers were assigned to the Canadian border. Whiskey bootlegging was a major concern and it often accompanied alien smuggling. In 1933, President Franklin D. Roosevelt combined the Bureau of Immigration and the Bureau of Naturalization into the Immigration and Naturalization Service (INS).

During the world wars, border security increased and saboteurs were sought. Through the 1950s, tens of thousands of illegal immigrants were transported by air, train, and bus to the Mexican interior, but many deportees returned to recross the seriously undermanned border. Illegal immigration continued through subsequent decades and it is a serious problem today. Following the 9/11 attacks, concern over border security intensified.

NATIONAL BORDER PATROL STRATEGY

The border patrol (BP) is an important operational component of the CBP. The *National Border Patrol Strategy* (U.S. Customs and Border Protection, 2004) complements the national strategy for securing U.S. ports of entry. The BP's strategy consists of six elements:

1. Securing a combination of personnel, technology, and infrastructure.
2. Improving mobility and rapid deployment to quickly counter and interdict based on changing smuggling routes and intelligence, and to protect against intrusion.
3. Deploying defense depth by using interior checkpoints to deny successful migration.
4. Coordinating and partnering with other law enforcement agencies.
5. Improving border awareness and intelligence, and responding to that intelligence, is critical to mission success.
6. Strengthening the headquarters command structure to evaluate overall situations and rapidly deploying resources from one sector to another.

THE THREAT AND ENVIRONMENT

The 9/11 attacks prompted the CBP to develop the priority mission of preventing terrorists and WMD from entering the United States. Prior to the attacks, the primary focus of the BP was illegal aliens, alien smuggling, and illegal drug interdiction. Each year, the BP arrests over one million illegal aliens and seizes over one million pounds of marijuana and 15–20 tons of cocaine.

Figure 11-4 ■ Smugglers' methods, routes, and modes of transportation can be exploited by terrorists. CBP locates hidden drug money. Photo by James Tourtellotte. http://www.customs.gov/xp/cgov/newsroom/photo_gallery/afc/concealment_methods/concealment_methods_01.xml

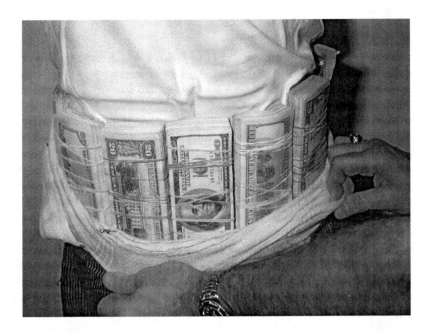

The smugglers' methods, routes, and modes of transportation are vulnerabilities that can be exploited by terrorists and possibly result in WMD entering the United States (Figure 11-4). The BP's expertise can serve to protect the United States from this threat (U.S. Customs and Border Protection 2004: 4).

The BP faces differing threat locations, as explained next. The response to these threats depends on numerous variables, including geography, population, routes of ingress and egress from the border, economic stability of neighboring countries, and migration patterns.

The *southern (United States–Mexico) border* contains some harsh terrain. Hundreds of aliens die each year trying to cross this border. Three primary smuggling corridors along this border are south Texas corridor; west Texas/New Mexico corridor; and California/Arizona corridor. These corridors are dictated by transportation routes, geography, and population centers. Over 90% of the one million plus annual arrests that the BP makes occur along these three corridors. *Although the BP has experienced success in some border areas, many other areas along the southwest border are not yet under operational control, and the daily attempts to cross into the United States by thousands of illegal aliens from countries around the world present a threat to U.S. national security.* Most of these aliens have been referred to as "economic migrants" who seek a better life and higher paying jobs than what they find in their native country. Terrorists can possibly blend into alien groups to enter the United States illegally and bring WMD.

The *northern (United States–Canada) border* contains some water boundary such as the Great Lakes. Certain waterways freeze during the winter and create the threat of adversaries walking or using a vehicle to cross the border. Over 90% of Canada's population lives within 100 miles of the border, and intelligence indicates that some adversaries represent a threat to U.S. national security. This border has well-organized smuggling operations. *The BP's ability to detect, respond to, and interdict illegal cross-border penetrations along this border is limited.*

The *coastal (Caribbean) borders* are subject to maritime smuggling and migrations. The BP works with a variety of law enforcement agencies, including the U.S. Coast Guard. To address the threats in coastal sectors, the CBP seeks investments in air and maritime assets and partnerships with other DHS components.

STRATEGIC OUTCOME MEASURES

The CBP seeks to improve its efficiency and effectiveness, which includes a results-oriented focus. It is also working to develop an integrated planning methodology that is supported by performance measures. At the same time, the CBP realizes that measuring program effectiveness in law enforcement is complex (U.S. Customs and Border Protection 2004: 21). For example, how can the CBP measure its effectiveness in preventing terrorism? How many terrorists has the BP deterred from crossing borders into the United States? The direct impact being made on unlawful activity is typically unknown and quantitative measurement is difficult. The CBP has developed a mix of qualitative and quantitative measures. Workload statistics (e.g., pedestrians, passengers, and conveyances processed; contraband seized) augment these measures because the CBP sees them as preventing crimes. The CBP is continuing to refine its metrics through, for example, increasing area-specific apprehensions and increasing and deploying border technology.

The U.S. Government Accountability Office (2005d) studied the challenges facing government as it secures borders. The USGAO reminds us of the long-standing effort to balance security and commercial needs while facilitating the efficient flow of people, goods, and conveyances across borders. Challenges involving the efficient flow of people are detecting false documents, unifying and enhancing inspector training, providing timely intelligence to the field, and successfully implementing new entry-exit systems. In reference to cargo, the CBP selects and inspects high-risk incoming cargo while facilitating other cargo to be cleared in a timely manner.

The USGAO reports that although biometrics curbs document fraud, it may cause offenders to shift their entry into the United States to other than official entry points. Other challenges related to biometric technology are technology's effect on border control procedures and people; its cost benefit; and the impact on privacy, convenience, the economy, and relations with other countries.

The acquisition and deployment of radiation detection equipment are other challenges. The USGAO found that present equipment has limitations and a comprehensive plan is needed for all border crossings and ports of entry to enhance risk analyses, identify what complement of radiation detection equipment is best and where, and ensure maintenance and effective training in radiation science and response to alarms.

U.S. IMMIGRATION AND CUSTOMS ENFORCEMENT

Immigration and Customs Enforcement (ICE) is the largest investigative arm of the DHS and it focuses on immigration and customs law enforcement *within* the United States (U.S. Immigration and Customs Enforcement, 2005a). ICE seeks to prevent acts of terrorism by targeting the people, money, and materials that support terrorists and other criminals. ICE also aims to identify and shut down vulnerabilities in the nation's border, economic, transportation, and infrastructure security.

The Office of Detention and Removal (DRO) is a division of ICE that removes unauthorized aliens from the United States. DRO resources and expertise transport aliens, manage them while they are in custody and their cases are pending, and remove aliens from the United States when ordered. DRO's primary customers are the CBP and the U.S. Citizenship and Immigration Services. In fiscal year 2004, 157,281 aliens were removed from the United States, an increase of about 8% over the previous fiscal year. Nearly 53% were criminal aliens (i.e., aliens who are eligible for removal based on a criminal conviction in the United States).

The **Immigration and Nationality Act** (INA) provides aliens the right to a removal hearing before an immigration judge who decides both inadmissibility and deportability. Removal of aliens can result from health, criminal status, economic well-being, national security risk, and other reasons specified in the act. An immigration judge weighs evidence presented by both the alien and the DHS. A decision can be appealed to the board of immigration appeals. When an alien is ordered to depart, DRO facilitates the process by coordinating with the respective foreign government and embassy to obtain travel documents and country clearances, planning transportation to repatriate the alien, and, when required, providing escort.

DRO established the National Fugitive Operations Program (NFOP) to apprehend, process, and remove aliens from the United States who have failed to surrender for removal or to comply with a removal order. NFOP teams focus on fugitive cases, especially cases involving criminal aliens. The "ICE Most Wanted" program publicizes the names, faces, and other ID features of the 10 most wanted fugitive criminals sought by ICE.

ICE contains an office of investigations that concentrates on many types of violations, including those pertaining to national security, the transfer of WMD and arms, critical technology, commercial fraud, human trafficking, illegal drugs, child pornography/exploitation, and immigration fraud. Also, ICE special agents conduct investigations involving the protection of critical infrastructure industries that may be victimized by attack, sabotage, exploitation, or fraud. In the financial sector, for example, ICE investigates illegal money laundering, insurance schemes, bulk cash smuggling, intellectual property rights, counterfeit goods smuggling, and other crimes.

ICE maintains an office of intelligence that collects, analyzes, and shares information on homeland security vulnerabilities. The intelligence professionals in this office provide assessments of patterns, trends, and new developments in a variety of law enforcement areas.

The Federal Protective Service is also a component of ICE. It protects federal buildings as explained at the end of Chapter 10. The Federal Air Marshal Service was transferred from ICE to the Transportation Security Administration during the Fall 2005 reorganization of the DHS.

The U.S. Government Accountability Office (2005c) reported that although the functions of the INS were transferred to the DHS in 2003 and placed in the newly created ICE and CBP, many similar management challenges found at the INS were still present in the new agencies. The USGAO questions whether ICE and CBP currently have good management frameworks in place, including a clear mission, a strategic planning process, a good organizational structure, performance measures, accountability, and leadership. Another concern is whether ICE and CBP have developed systems and processes to support the management frameworks in place. A third concern is that management challenges exist in the larger context of the evolution of the DHS. Transformation and integration at DHS may take 5–7 years to accomplish, and some management challenges might be resolved in this process.

CRITICAL THINKING:

Do you think U.S. Customs and Border Protection and U.S. Immigration and Customs Enforcement should be merged? Why or why not?

DO INVESTIGATIONS OF THE ILLEGAL DRUG TRADE IMPACT HOMELAND SECURITY?

ICE reported in September 2005 that 22 members of two Colombian drug-trafficking organizations were arrested for conspiring to import massive quantities of narcotics through seaports in New York and California (U.S. Immigration and Customs Enforcement, 2005b). The investigation began in December 2000 when police learned that Jose Escobar Orejuela was managing an international narcotics operation from the Federal Correctional Center in Allenwood, Pennsylvania, where he was serving a

Continued

DO INVESTIGATIONS OF THE ILLEGAL DRUG TRADE IMPACT HOMELAND SECURITY?—Cont'd

30-year sentence for importing cocaine into Port Newark, New Jersey. Several law enforcement agencies participated in the investigation, including ICE, DEA, CBP, and New York/New Jersey Port Authority Police. Code named "Operation Pier Pressure," evidence was developed through court-authorized wire and oral intercepts, informants, physical surveillance, and review and analysis of prison telephone calls, correspondence, and visitor logs. Escobar enlisted the assistance of longshoremen in Brooklyn and Staten Island, New York, by ensuring that cargo containers holding cocaine were placed in easily accessible locations and by informing the organization if police were nearby. The plan called for a "break-in team" that sneaked into the port terminal during the night, located the right container, removed the cocaine, and delivered it to associates waiting in vehicles outside the terminal. During one such operation, authorities made arrests. Following the arrests, Escobar and his associates decided to move the operation to another port. They selected the ports of San Francisco and Oakland. However, at a meeting at the visiting room of Allenwood, Escobar and his associates agreed that those ports were also under heavy surveillance by authorities and security was so tight that cocaine could not be successfully imported there.

The authorities noted that the port investigation was particularly difficult because some of the conspirators (i.e., insiders employed at the port) had the right to enter cargo areas and observe how law enforcement agencies conduct inspections of containerized cargo. Also, the insiders had the ability to move containers to areas of convenience for the "break-in team." This conspiracy illustrates the serious dangers from insider threats. One strategy to counter the insider threat is to assign undercover investigators to various jobs at the ports.

CRITICAL THINKING:

In reference to the nearby box on illegal drug smuggling at ports, what do you think the drug traffickers will do since the ports cited were too secure for smuggling? Do you think the methods applied by drug smugglers should be studied to understand how terrorists might smuggle WMD into the United States? Since the smuggling of contraband into the United States can never be completely eliminated, do you think WMD will eventually penetrate U.S. border security?

CITIZENSHIP AND IMMIGRATION SERVICES

In 2003, the **U.S. Citizenship and Immigration Services** (CIS), within the DHS, also played a role in taking over services formerly performed by the INS (U.S. Citizenship Immigration Services, 2005). The CIS mission is to grant immigration and citizenship benefits, promote awareness and understanding of citizenship, ensure the integrity of the U.S. immigration system, and contribute to the security of the United States. This agency works with the U.S. Department of State, CBP, and ICE. It processes all immigrant and nonimmigrant benefits provided to visitors of the United States. The CIS, with its thousands of federal employees and contractors working worldwide, are responsible for establishing policies and procedures, and immigration and naturalization adjudication, such as the adjudication of immigrant visa petitions. Its focus includes the following.

- *Family-based petitions* to facilitate the process for close relatives to immigrate, gain permanent residency, work, etc.
- *Employment-based petitions* to facilitate the process for current and prospective employees to immigrate or stay in the United States temporarily.

- *Asylum and refugee processing* to adjudicate asylum and processing of refugees.
- *Naturalization* to approve citizenship of eligible persons who wish to become U.S. citizens.
- *Special status programs* to adjudicate eligibility for U.S. immigration status as a form of humanitarian aid to foreign nationals.
- *Document issuance and renewal*, including verifying eligibility and producing and issuing immigration documents.

TRANSPORTATION SECURITY ADMINISTRATION

The **Transportation Security Administration** (TSA) was created following the 9/11 attacks under the Aviation and Transportation Security Act of 2001 (ATSA) (U.S. Transportation Security Administration, n.d.). Originally, the TSA was in the Department of Transportation, but it was transferred to the DHS in March 2003. *The mission of the TSA is to protect the U.S. transportation system while facilitating freedom of movement of people and commerce.* Although the 9/11 attacks resulted in the airline industry being a top priority for protection by the TSA, this agency recognizes the importance of securing all forms of transportation.

The TSA issues and administers transportation security regulations (TSRs), which are codified in Title 49 of the Code of Federal Regulations (CFR), Chapter XII. Many TSRs are former rules of the Federal Aviation Administration (FAA) that were transferred to TSA when it assumed FAA's civil aviation security role in 2002.

The TSA has developed numerous initiatives to increase protection in the transportation sector. TSA programs and strategies are discussed in subsequent pages under the various transportation modes.

U.S. VISITOR AND IMMIGRATION STATUS INDICATOR TECHNOLOGY (US-VISIT)

The US-VISIT program aims to enhance the security of both the United States and visitors while facilitating legitimate travel and trade. It begins overseas and continues through a visitor's arrival and departure from the United States. The program involves eligibility determinations by the Departments of Homeland Security and State. Originally, it applied to all visitors (with limited exemptions) holding nonimmigrant visas, regardless of country of origin. Later, it was expanded to countries under the **visa waiver program** (i.e., mostly western Europe, but also Japan and Singapore, whose citizens can visit for 90 days without a visa, provided their passports contain biometric identifiers). Most Canadians are not subject to the program. Mexicans who cross the border regularly with a border-crossing card, called a "laser visa," are also exempt.

The process begins when an overseas U.S. consular office, of the Department of State, issues a visa and the visitor's biometrics (i.e., digital finger scans and photographs) are collected and checked with a database of terrorists. When the visitor arrives at the port of entry, the same biometrics are collected and checked to ensure the person arriving is the same person who received the visa. The CBP screens visitors through a digital finger scan and photograph and checks/scans travel documents (i.e., visa and passport). The ultimate goal of the program is to check all people entering and departing the United States.

The information collected through the US-VISIT program can be of immense help to all levels of law enforcement. Ideally, even on the local level, a police officer on patrol that stops a vehicle, and has computer access to such information, can check if the subject entered the United States legally, traveled to where the subject noted on the visa, and whether the subject is on schedule for departure. Also, with biometric technology reaching the patrol officer on the street, verification of identity is improving. The speed at which both the US-VISIT program is fully utilized and law enforcement access to it at all levels remains to be seen.

Continued

U.S. VISITOR AND IMMIGRATION STATUS INDICATOR TECHNOLOGY (US-VISIT)—Cont'd

Fotos (2005: 34) writes that "developing a system to track the entry and exit into the United States of the millions of foreigners who visit America each year is proving to be a daunting task." Fotos explains the challenges as described next. He notes that the system will have to handle entries and exits at all air, sea, and land borders. Many government agencies will rely on a DHS-wide initiative to develop an "enterprise architecture." This entails a model that a variety of data and systems feed into. For example, the State Department submits biometrics on an individual's initial contact, the Department of Labor grants a nonresident employment visa, the Department of Justice uses its watch lists, and CBP examines the traveler on arrival. Another challenge is data coordination with other countries and getting all of them to adopt biometrics. The ideal system is when people can fly, for instance, from New York to Paris to Athens under the same registered travel system. Another issue is privacy and its many questions, such as how will data be protected and who will have access to it. Privacy laws that protect U.S. citizens and legal residents do not necessarily apply to other nationals.

The U.S. Government Accountability Office (2005d: 54–55) recognizes that part of the effort to reform immigration services and create a "border of the future" is the implementation of the US-VISIT program. The USGAO views the successful implementation of this program as challenging because of the way it is being managed, its complexity, and its enormous cost. Implemented in 2004, the program challenges include the need for DHS to institute rigorous management controls, specifically testing, typically associated with successful programs.

O'Harrow and Highman (2005) offer interesting reporting on the US-VISIT contract between the DHS and the global consulting firm Accenture. In 2004, the contract was awarded and estimated to be valued up to $10 billion. Although US-VISIT is in its infancy, the program has been criticized because of its alleged speculative technology, while neglecting basic procedures to ensure that taxpayers receive full value from the contract. The contract is unique, without a clear idea of how the final system will work or when it will be completed. The government can cancel the project at any point. The contractor is paid for specific tasks as the project progresses, even if the overall system fails to work. One problem is the controversy over how many fingerprints should be used for verification. A two-fingerprint system is claimed to not be as accurate and compatible with other databases as using all 10 prints.

The U.S. Government Accountability Office (2005d: 51–54) reported on other challenges involving the screening of foreign visitors. For example, there is a need for refining the interagency visa revocation process. This is important for preventing terrorists from entering the United States and for identifying terrorists who have arrived. The USGAO found delays in notifying immigration authorities of the need to investigate individuals with revoked visas who may be in the United States. The USGAO noted challenges with the visa waiver program under the Departments of Justice and State. The program presents several issues related to national security, whether the program should be eliminated, relations with other countries, U.S. tourism, and costs. Another challenge is reducing the time required to adjudicate visas for science students and scholars. Security checks in this area are designed to protect against sensitive technology transfers. One problem is interoperability between the State Department's and FBI's computer systems.

CRITICAL THINKING:

As the United States makes it more difficult for people to enter the country legally, do you think illegal entry will increase? Explain your answer.

Reality Check: Border Security and Immigration Policies

Despite the positive efforts of dedicated law enforcement authorities at U.S. borders and "challenges" repeatedly echoed by USGAO reports, serious problems remain with border security and U.S. immigration policies. Hall (2005) reports that despite an influx of new technology at the U.S.–Mexican border, agents do not have the capabilities to apprehend many of the people who cross the border illegally each year. Although most of those who cross illegally are poor Mexican laborers searching for work, authorities are alarmed at the growing number from other countries, such as Syria and Iran. According to the border patrol, in 2003, they arrested 39,214 so-called "OTMs," meaning other-than-Mexicans. The number increased to 65,814 in 2004. Authorities believe that al-Qaida may see advantages in operatives paying their way into the United States illegally than entering legally. U.S. intelligence seems to think that terrorists are living south of the Mexican border, assimilating the culture and learning the language, to eventually blend in with Mexicans to cross the border. *Essentially, the U.S. government does not know who is crossing the Mexican border.* Similar problems face other U.S. borders.

Because the U.S. government (i.e., ICE's Office of Detection and Removal) has limited space to house OTMs while they wait for a deportation hearing and they are too far from their native land to be quickly transported home, many are released with a notice to show up in immigration court. Before OTMs are released, they are screened by checking their name and ID in databases. However, bogus information may be used by an OTM. Many never appear in court for their hearing and become part of the millions of undocumented migrants living in the United States. It is not unusual for OTMs, who are struggling across the border, to seek border patrol agents to be taken into custody for amenities.

Another problem is alien smuggling, a $7 billion a year business. The United Nations sees it as the fastest growing organized crime enterprise. About 500,000 people enter the United States illegally each year. This figure is similar for the number illegally entering the European Union annually. Migrants may pay thousands of dollars for illegal passage or they are bought and sold as commodities (Naim, 2003).

Border patrol agents face increasingly sophisticated smugglers who maintain counterintelligence operations. Although agents have new technology, so do smugglers who use two-way radios, cell phones, global positioning systems, infrared night-vision goggles, and other technology to monitor agents and their movements.

Violence along the Mexican border is another serious problem. Border patrol agents are subject to being shot at, assaulted, rammed with vehicles, and pelted with rocks by immigrants and smugglers. Accusations of excessive use of force by agents have strained U.S.–Mexican relations. Forsyth (2006) reported on federal raids of homes in the Texas border city of Laredo where illegal drugs, automatic weapons, grenades, and IEDs were seized. A DHS spokesperson found no connection to terrorists following the raids. The weaponry is related to the ongoing gang war over the lucrative illegal drug and immigrant trade.

Because federal authorities are overburdened with law enforcement duties along the border with Mexico, should state, local, and tribal police enforce immigration laws? The International Association of Chiefs of Police (IACP) offers a position on this question (Polisar, 2005: 16–27). The IACP recognizes differences of opinion on this matter. Many police contend that state and local police should not enforce immigration laws, as such action would impede illegal aliens from reporting crime or assisting with investigations. Other police see the importance of enforcing immigration laws against individuals who are in the United States illegally and should be treated as other offenders. The IACP argues that the decision should be made at the local level, with the police executive working with elected officials, community leaders, and citizens. State, tribal, and local police are not required to enforce federal immigration laws. However, if such legislation is proposed, the IACP recommends the following elements: it should be a local, voluntary decision; the federal government should clarify the legal authority of state, tribal, and local police; funding for immigration enforcement; a liability shield; and training resources.

Continued

Reality Check: Border Security and Immigration Policies—Cont'd

A look at the U.S. border with Canada also shows problems. Numerous terrorist groups have some presence in Canada, including al-Qaida, Hezbollah, and Hamas. Also, such groups raise money from legal and illegal operations to support their causes. Although this border is over twice as long as the U.S.–Mexican border, it has about one-tenth the border patrol force found at the U.S.–Mexican border. In addition to numerous supervised border crossings, large forests and waterways make this border easy to smuggle contraband and people. The historic openness of the U.S.–Canadian border and busy commerce make tight security a difficult challenge.

Returning to the topic of the U.S.–Mexican border, it is commonly agreed that immigration is a national security, humanitarian, and economic crisis. *Interestingly, through history, Mexican immigration to the United States has been encouraged and discouraged, with extremes depending on economic conditions.* During the Great Depression, Mexicans were more likely to be deported, but during World War II, when workers were needed to replace soldiers fighting overseas, U.S. programs encouraged immigration. Ngai (1998) writes that immigration policy was deeply implicated in the reorganization of the political economy of the southwest.

Passel (2006), a researcher with the Pew Hispanic Center, reports that the number of illegal immigrants in the United States is as many as 12 million, with Mexicans making up 56% of illegal immigrants. About 850,000 illegal immigrants have arrived in the United States each year since 2000. Undocumented workers account for 5% (7.2 million) of the U.S. work force. Passel notes that efforts to reduce illegal immigration have not only failed, but people entering illegally from Mexico remain in the United States longer because security has increased the difficulty of traveling back across the border.

Leiken (2002) notes that after the 9/11 attacks, immigration was viewed through a security lens. He describes pre- and post-9/11 immigration policy debate. Before the 9/11 attacks, the debate focused on how many illegal immigrants would be legalized, how to safeguard the lives of those crossing the border illegally, and whether or when to "open" the border entirely. Following the attacks, the economy suffered, unemployment increased, and public support for legalization waned. National security and lax immigration enforcement became major issues. Leiken's solutions include closer U.S.–Mexican partnerships on immigration and security issues, adequate funding for border agencies, the screening (through a database) of everyone who crosses the border, all immigrants brought into the system, and for the system to work, *Mexico must patrol its border*.

In November 2005, a top priority of the DHS became known as the **secure border initiative** (SBI). It consists of the following strategies:

- Increase funding for additional border patrol officers and ICE criminal investigators.
- Increase funding to ICE for additional detention bed spaces.
- Increase funding for border barriers, integrated video and sensor surveillance systems, lighting, and aerial assets, including unmanned aerial vehicles.
- Increase interior enforcement of immigration laws, including worksite enforcement.
- Creation of border enforcement and security task forces that consist of teams of federal, state, and local police that share information, develop prioritized targets, and coordinate operations.
- Expand **expedited removal**. This strategy permits undocumented immigrants apprehended within 100 miles from the Mexican border, within 14 days of their crossing, to be ordered returned to their home country as soon as possible, without a hearing before an immigration judge, unless they have a legitimate fear of returning.
- Immigration policy. Various policy changes have been proposed. For example, in 2004, President Bush offered the **guest-worker program** that would provide workers legal status for 3-year renewable periods, but requires them to return to their homeland when their work is done. Critics argued, "nothing is more permanent than a temporary worker." Another proposal, from Congress, entailed illegal immigrants receiving 3-year visas, renewable once, followed by an application for permanent legal residency. On one side of the issue, businesses want workers, while on the other side, conservatives want tighter immigration controls and security.
- Implement the SBI with appropriate dialogue between the Departments of State and Homeland Security and the governments of Mexico, Canada, and other countries.

TRANSPORTATION SECURITY SECTORS

As written in Chapter 10, *The National Strategy for the Physical Protection of Critical Infrastructures and Key Assets* (White House, 2003) identifies transportation as one of several critical infrastructure (CI) sectors. It consists of several key modes: aviation; passenger rail and railroads; mass transit systems; highways, trucking, and intercity busing; maritime; postal and shipping; and pipelines. Interdependencies exist between the transportation sector and nearly every other sector, and a disruption of this sector can have a cascading affect on other sectors. For example, the agriculture and food sector is dependent on the transportation sector to ship goods to customers. The transportation sector is vital to our economy and national security, including mobilization and deployment.

As explained in Chapter 10, HSPD-7 designated certain federal agencies as lead federal points of contact for protection activities in their assigned infrastructure sectors. A major goal of these federal agencies is to coordinate and collaborate with relevant federal, state, and local governments and the private sector to enhance the protection of CI. The lead agencies for the transportation sector are the DHS in collaboration with the Department of Transportation (DOT).

The **Intelligence Reform and Terrorism Prevention Act of 2004** directly impacts the security of public transportation. It requires the DHS to develop a **national strategy for transportation security**. This includes the identification of the transportation infrastructure, risk-based security priorities, protection strategies, and research and development.

AVIATION

The aviation system is vast and made up of thousands of entry points. In the United States, it consists of two main parts: (1) airports, aircraft, and supporting personnel and assets and (2) aviation command, control, communications, and IT systems to support and maintain safe use of airspace.

There are 19,000 general aviation airports, 453 commercial airports (Figure 11-5), 211,000 active aircraft, and 550,000 active pilots and instructors. General aviation airports involve primarily recreational flying, but also include such activities as medical services, aerial advertising, and aerial application of chemicals (U.S. Government Accountability Office, 2004: 57).

The **Federal Aviation Administration**, within the DOT, regulates civil aviation to promote safety and air traffic control. It issues airport operating certifications depending on the type of aircraft served. The FAA also issues certifications for aviation employees, aircraft, airlines, and other purposes.

Security varies at airports and depends on the type of airport and aircraft. *General aviation airports present a serious security vulnerability.* Here the emphasis is on commercial airports.

Prior to the 9/11 attacks, security at airports was the responsibility of private carriers and state and local airport owners. Following the attack, Congress passed the ATSA, establishing the TSA as the responsible authority for aviation security. In other words, the TSA is charged with federalizing security at commercial airports in the United States and replacing private screeners with federal screeners.

Aviation is vital to the economy and it provides an opportunity for many people to travel great distances quickly. It is one of the marvels of our age. At the same time, aviation presents unique security challenges (White House, 2003: 55).

- U.S. carriers transport millions of passengers daily and about twice as many bags and other cargo.
- Many businesses rely on "just-in-time" delivery of cargo to meet production goals. A delay in processing or transporting such cargo could harm the economy.
- Airports are open to the public, near roads, and connected to a variety of other modes of transportation. Maintaining security in such an environment of mass transportation, while limiting congestion and delays, and not creating economic harm, is a huge challenge.

Figure 11-5 ■ Commercial airport and aircraft.

- Because terrorists view aviation as a potential target with a substantial payoff (e.g., 9/11 attacks), security must be formidable. Consequently, the aviation industry faces concern over the costs of security enhancements.
- Airport security failures on September 11, 2001 placed the industry under intense scrutiny and pressure to maintain customers.
- To improve security, risk assessments have identified vulnerabilities, research has focused on new methods of identifying human threats, security has been tightened at access points and other locations, and new technologies are being developed to improve baggage screening, detection of explosives, and other protection priorities (Figure 11-6).

The TSA applies several layers of security to protect the air transportation sector. These include the following measures.

PRESCREENING PASSENGERS

The U.S. Government Accountability Office (2005d: 55–56) noted that the computer-assisted passenger prescreening program (CAPPS II) was DHS's solution to prescreening passengers before they even arrive at airports. CAPPS II was aligned with the goals of the ATSA and it was designed to identify passengers requiring additional security attention. The USGAO recognized several challenges facing CAPPS II. These included developing international cooperation to obtain passenger data and ensuring that identity theft cannot be used to render the system useless. Persistent problems caused the TSA to scrap CAPPS II and replace it with Secure Flight, but the USGAO stated that the new program could face similar challenges as CAPPS II. **Secure Flight** involves the comparison of passenger name records (PNRs) from domestic flights to names in the terrorist screening database (TSDB) established by the terrorist screening center (TSC). The U.S. Government Accountability Office (2006b) has been critical of TSA and its Secure Flight

Figure 11-6 ■ Passenger and baggage screening. Source: U.S. Government Accountability Office (2005a).

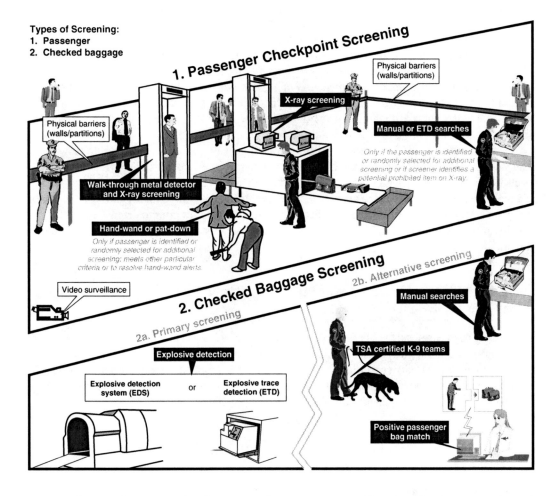

Types of Screening:
1. Passenger
2. Checked baggage

1. Passenger Checkpoint Screening

Physical barriers (walls/partitions)

X-ray screening

Manual or ETD searches

Only if the passenger is identified or randomly selected for additional screening or if screener identifies a potential prohibited item on X-ray.

Physical barriers (walls/partitions)

Walk-through metal detector and X-ray screening

Hand-wand or pat-down

Only if passenger is identified or randomly selected for additional screening; meets other particular criteria or to resolve hand-wand alerts.

Video surveillance

2. Checked Baggage Screening

2a. Primary screening

2b. Alternative screening

Manual searches

TSA certified K-9 teams

Explosive detection

Explosive detection system (EDS)   or   Explosive trace detection (ETD)

Positive passenger bag match

program for out of sequence planning, uncertainty over costs, and how it will enhance security and protect personal information on passengers.

SCREENING PASSENGERS AND BAGGAGE

Another challenge is effective and efficient screening of passengers and baggage arriving at airports for flights. The USGAO emphasized that this has been a long-standing concern where actions have been taken, but challenges remain, such as hiring, training, and deploying screeners and measuring performance of screeners and operations. Testing of screeners has shown weaknesses in their ability to detect threat objects. Deploying and leveraging screening equipment and technologies is another challenge as the TSA seeks to achieve a mandate to screen all baggage using explosive detection systems.

The TSA partners with industry to deploy and test technology at airports to detect contraband and to verify a person's identity. Detection is aimed at people and their belongings, including luggage. A variety of technologies are applied to detect explosives, weapons, metals, and plastics. Examples include X-ray systems, metal detectors, biometrics, explosive trace detection (ETD) systems, and body scanning. An ETD whole-body portal detects and identifies microscopic quantities of explosives by puffing air onto a person and analyzing the particles dislodged and collected from the person's clothing and skin. Body scanning applies a form of X-rays or wave radiation to produce an image of a person; however, the technology is being refined prior to widespread use because it is capable of "seeing" through clothes, creating a privacy issue. Technology is increasingly being integrated, such as ETD portals containing a metal detector. Technology serves as another strategy to detect contraband, besides the use of patdowns, which are time-consuming and unpopular. The problems associated with screening technology include false alarms, ineffectiveness in detecting certain items, and personnel costs and performance.

The screening of cargo transported on commercial passenger aircraft is another serious concern and vulnerability that does not receive enough attention. Calls to eliminate this practice face opposition from the passenger airline business that sees it as a source of income in an industry confronted with tight profit margins. A major issue is the source of funding for a thorough screening system for such cargo.

In August of 2006, Pakistani and British intelligence units uncovered a plot to blow up as many as ten airliners over the Atlantic Ocean while flying from Britain to the U.S. Over twenty suspects were arrested, many with Pakistani backgrounds. The terrorists were linked to al-Qaida. They planned to use their hand luggage to smuggle liquid explosives aboard airliners, and with the use of common electronic devices, assemble the bombs in aircraft lavatories prior to detonation. Following the discovery of the plot, airline passengers were prohibited from bringing liquids and gels aboard aircraft.

THE COMPLEXITY OF SCREENING PASSENGERS AND THEIR POSSESSIONS

Screening passengers and their possessions at controlled access points at modes of transportation is a complex undertaking that entails careful planning, policies, procedures, training, and evaluation. While maintaining security, consideration is also required for constitutional issues, privacy, and respect for individuals and their possessions. The balancing process is difficult. What follows here is an example of this challenge from the TSA Web site.

TSA Funeral Homes

Become a TSA Funeral Home Partner and become part of this important initiative (http://www.tsa.gov/public/interapp/editorial/editorial_1698.xml)

Funeral Home Partners

The Transportation Security Administration has implemented a new procedure affecting those passengers attempting to transport a crematory container on airplanes as carry-on baggage. Passengers are still allowed to carry on a crematory container, but the container **must** first pass through the X-ray machine. If the container is made of a material that generates an opaque image and prevents the security screener from clearly being able to see what is inside, then the container will **not** be allowed through the security checkpoint. In respect to the deceased, under **no** circumstances will a screener open the container even if the passenger requests that this be done. Documentation from the funeral home is no longer sufficient to carry a crematory container through security and onto a plane.

As a result of this policy the TSA would like to partner with funeral homes throughout the country to accommodate passengers transporting remains via air travel. To ensure that a TSA screener can X-ray the crematory container's contents successfully the TSA recommends that remains be transported in containers constructed of light-weight materials such as cardboard, plastic, or wood. We realize that containers made of these materials may not be desirable as the container used to permanently house the remains of a passenger's loved ones; however, it can be used as a temporary container to transport the remains to their final destination. Using such a solution, passengers are ultimately faced with the dilemma of how to transfer the remains from the temporary container to the permanent container.

THE COMPLEXITY OF SCREENING PASSENGERS AND THEIR POSSESSIONS—Cont'd

The TSA Solution

Form a voluntary partnership with willing funeral homes. TSA funeral home partners agree to offer a complementary "Remains Transfer Service" at no charge to the traveler. This allows the passenger to obtain a temporary "security friendly" container for transporting the remains via air travel and, in addition, purchase a permanent container that can be made of any material they desire. Once the passenger reaches their final destination they can contact their local "TSA Funeral Home Partner" and have the remains transferred free of charge.

Please share this program and the new TSA crematory container policy with your patrons to help extend TSA's public outreach and education efforts.

Benefits to Our Funeral Home Partners

- Your business will be listed as a funeral home partner on our Web site and will include a link to your Web site.
- You may post the TSA Web site link on your Web site and advertise that you are a TSA partner to encourage those seeking this service to visit your establishment.
- Funeral home and cremation Web sites that list area or nationwide funeral homes can advertise that your establishment offers this service and that you are a TSA partner.
- This partnership allows you to get possible buyers in the door where you can sell the traveler a permanent crematory container at the point of their final destination.
- You will be performing a service for the public that will be appreciated, remembered, and possibly reflected in future funeral service or crematory container purchases.

Thank you for your support!

TSA EXPLOSIVES DETECTION CANINE TEAM PROGRAM

On March 9, 1972, a Trans World Airlines jet took off from JFK International airport in New York bound for Los Angeles. Initially, the flight was normal, but then the airline received an anonymous telephone call warning of a bomb on the flight. The aircraft returned to JFK, passengers were evacuated, and a bomb-sniffing dog named Brandy conducted a search of the aircraft. Brandy found the bomb 12 minutes before it was set to explode. This successful conclusion of a dangerous situation resulted in the establishment of the FAA **Explosives Detection Canine Team Program**, designed to place certified teams at strategic locations in the United States so aircraft with a possible bomb can be diverted quickly to an airport with such a program. Because the teams are characterized by excellent mobility and reliable detection rates, they search luggage, cargo, vehicles, airport terminals, and aircraft.

The program is a partnership with industry in which airports voluntarily participate and are supported by federal funds. The TSA pays for the dogs, training, and other costs. The breeds used include Labradors, Chesapeake Bay retrievers, and golden retrievers. These breeds are selected for their gentle temperament and keen sensory capabilities. The TSA and the DOD operate a training program at Lackland Air Force Base, San Antonio, Texas. Puppies are raised in "foster families" in the San Antonio area until they enter the program. TSA dogs are kenneled at the homes of their handlers and are retired to these homes after 10 to 12 years of service.

CREW MEMBER SELF-DEFENSE

Airlines are required to provide basic security training for all aircrew members. The TSA is required by law to provide optional, hands-on self-defense training if crew members request it.

Under the **Federal Flight Deck Officer Program**, a pilot, flight engineer, or navigator is authorized to use firearms to defend the aircraft. Crew members are trained in the use of force and firearms, defensive tactics, psychology of survival, and legal issues.

Self-defense in an aircraft is extremely important not only for crew members, but also passengers. As we know from the 9/11 attacks, terrorists may try to deceive passengers into thinking that they will not be harmed if they follow terrorist demands. Crew members and passengers must consider the option of being creative with available items to be used as weapons and using force to survive.

FEDERAL AIR MARSHAL SERVICE

The Federal Air Marshal Service (FAMS) began in 1968 as the FAA Sky Marshal Program. This was a time when the Palestine Liberation Organization (PLO)-affiliated Popular Front for the Liberation of Palestine (PFLP) attracted world attention by introducing the hijacking of aircraft, which spawned subsequent hijackings (Poland, 1988: 103–104).

The mission of the FAMS is to detect, deter, and defeat hostile acts targeting U.S. air carriers, passengers, and crews. The training requirements are stringent and include behavioral observation, intimidation tactics, close-quarters self-defense, and a higher standard for handgun accuracy than officers of any other federal law enforcement agency. The number of federal air marshals is classified information. During the Fall 2005 reorganization of the DHS, FAMS was transferred from ICE to TSA to improve coordination of aviation security.

ALIEN FLIGHT STUDENT PROGRAM

Another TSA measure of protection is the **Alien Flight Student Program**. This program began in 2001 with the ATSA. Under Section 113 of ATSA (49 USC 44939), specific aviation training entities are prohibited from offering flight training to aliens and other individuals in the operation of aircraft with a maximum takeoff weight (MTOW) of 12,500 pounds or more unless the trainer notified the attorney general of the identity of the student and the attorney general did not notify the trainer within 45 days that the student presented a security threat. If it was determined that the student was a threat more than 45 days after receiving notification from the trainer, the attorney general was required to notify the trainer and the trainer was required to terminate the student from flight training. In December 2003, Congress made changes to 49 USC 44939, including transferring threat assessment of flight students from the attorney general to the secretary of homeland security; expanding the population of flight students subject to assessment to aircraft having an MTOW of 12,500 pounds or less; specifying ID information from flight students (e.g., fingerprints, passport, visa); and requiring the training of trainers on awareness of suspicious circumstances.

PARTNERING WITH THE PRIVATE SECTOR

The TSA partners with the private sector through various initiatives. For example, the Aviation Security Advisory Committee partnered with the TSA to develop general aviation security recommendations entitled Security Guidelines for General Aviation Airports (Publication A-001). Another initiative is the airport watch program, which includes a "hotline" in coordination with the Aircraft Owners and Pilots Association. This program promotes the reporting of suspicious behavior. The TSA also partnered with the National Business Aviation Association to develop security guidelines for corporate flight departments (U.S. Government Accountability Office, 2004: 57–58).

ADDITIONAL CONCERNS

The ATSA also mandates improvements in airport perimeter security and access controls. Compliance inspections and vulnerability assessments serve as a foundation for funding priorities, planning new technologies, and reducing the security threats of airport employees.

Airport security and law enforcement personnel are vital for protection, besides the application of various technologies. The strategies include various forms of patrol (e.g., visible, undercover, foot, and vehicles) and surveillance. Training is essential. Behavioral-pattern recognition is important during observations of people and is based on studies of patterns of criminal suspects (see Chapter 5 under legal profiling).

Another concern, specifically against aircraft, is **man-portable air defense systems** (MAN-PADS). These handheld missile systems have been fired by terrorists against commercial aircraft in the past (see Chapter 2). A countersystem faces the establishment of system requirements, the development of technology, cost effectiveness, and funding. Furthermore, improvement is needed in U.S. efforts to keep MANPADS out of the hands of terrorists. The state department has made progress to control the proliferation of MANPADS, even though the DOD has sold thousands of Stinger missiles to 18 countries and monitoring is inconsistent (U.S. Government Accountability Office, 2005d: 57).

Despite increased aviation security, concerns remain. For example, certain technologies do not work as intended or touted, there is little explosive screening for passengers and employees, and the quality of airport and aircraft security varies worldwide.

Between 2003 and 2005 the USGAO published several reports on the quality of TSA aviation security efforts. One criticism of the TSA was that it has not consistently implemented a risk management program or conducted the systematic analysis needed to improve decisions and prioritize security. Several USGAO reports noted TSA challenges with airport screener training and performance. These included the need for improved training, covert testing, and performance measures of screeners. The U.S. Government Accountability Office (2005a) claimed that TSA officials have no formal policies or methods of monitoring the completion of required training for screeners. The USGAO added that the TSA has implemented and strengthened its efforts to measure and improve screener performance. It has increased the number of covert tests to gauge screeners' ability to detect threats from passengers, carry-on baggage, and checked baggage. The tests showed that weaknesses and vulnerabilities remain.

The many small airports nationwide present a serious vulnerability in the air transportation industry. Minimal security, no screening of passengers, and unsecured aircraft create dangerous risks. Furthermore, flights from such airports are connected to large airports. One solution to "watch" aircraft at small airports is to apply RFID technology. An RFID tag can be installed in an aircraft, and if the aircraft is moved without an access card held by the owner, readers at the airport will alert a monitoring company. Aircraft equipped with GPS transponders will enable them to be tracked globally. RFID technology is applicable to large airports and can be installed on numerous items (Pervola, 2005: 78–79). Costs and testing are important considerations to ensure a cost-effective investment in technology.

The 9/11 attacks resulted in improvements in physical security inside aircraft. For example, commercial airlines contain reinforced cockpit doors that remain locked during flight. Right outside the door, CCTV cameras are installed in some aircraft.

PASSENGER RAIL AND RAILROADS

Trains play an important role in our economy by linking raw materials to manufactures and carrying a wide variety of fuels and finished goods. Over 20 million intercity travelers ride the rail system annually, and 45 million passengers ride trains and subways operated by local transit authorities. Securing the rail sector is important to ensure the safety of passengers and to protect U.S. commerce (White House, 2003: 56).

The U.S. rail system is vast and contains numerous entry points. It is complex because of differences in design, structure, and purpose. The differences result in disadvantages and advantages for security. For example, the size of the rail system makes responding to various threat scenarios difficult. At the same time, trains must follow specific routes, so if one were hijacked, for example, it could be diverted off a mainline. Similarly, if a bridge or tunnel were destroyed, the rail line would suffer disruption; however, national-level disruptions would be limited. A serious risk in this sector is the transportation of hazardous materials, especially through populated areas, and industry and government coordination is necessary for decision making. Security and safety of containerized cargo are other challenges. Controversy has developed over the markings of containers to indicate the type of hazardous materials being transported. Although placards on rail cars provide helpful information to first responders during an emergency, the information can also assist terrorists planning an attack. Another concern of the rail sector is the cost of security. The increased threat environment means expenses for additional security personnel and overtime (White House, 2003: 56).

Rail mode protection initiatives include the following (White House, 2003: 57).

- The rail mode has been working with the DOT to assess risk.
- A surface transportation information sharing and analysis center has been formed to exchange information related to both cyber and physical threats.
- The DHS and the DOT are coordinating with other federal agencies, state and local governments, and industry to improve the security and safety of hazardous materials.
- The DHS and the DOT are working with the rail sector to identify and explore technologies and processes to efficiently screen rail passengers and baggage and to secure containers and detect threatening content.
- The DHS and the DOT are working with industry to delineate infrastructure protection roles and responsibilities for surge requirements during emergencies.

The railroad industry works with all levels of government and maintains police and security forces for its individual railroad entities. The **Association of American Railroads** (n.d.) uses a multistage alert system and open lines of communications with DHS and DOD officials. This group's railroad security task force applied national intelligence community "best practices" to develop a security plan consisting of the following strategies.

- A focus on hazardous materials, operations, infrastructure, IT and communications, and military movements.
- A database on critical assets.
- Risk management.
- Increased security and random inspections.
- Improved protective housings, valves, and fittings to increase security in the transportation of hazardous materials and to prevent sabotage.
- Protection against signal tampering.

Reality Check: The Vulnerability at Rail Yards

Rail yards illustrate the difficulty of protecting so many potential terrorist targets. An investigative reporter and photographer observed a rail depot not far from New York City and described unlocked and unguarded gates and easy access to tracks where rail cars contained deadly chlorine, ammonia, and other chemicals. The sight of graffiti-covered tank cars illustrated unauthorized access by others. They also noticed that switching devices were unlocked, which could allow an offender to redirect a train and cause an accident. The journalists were unchallenged in their observations. They wrote that when rail yards are located near fuel storage tanks, losses might be greater from an attack. Additionally, although efforts are under way to improve chemical plant security, vulnerabilities include the rail cars that enter and depart the plants (Kocieniewski, 2006).

Reality Check: The Vulnerability at Rail Yards—Cont'd

The news article covered other vulnerabilities described by railroad industry officials and unions and "finger pointing" among government leaders as to why corrective action is so slow. *A major point of the article is the difficulty of increasing security and safety for a glaring vulnerability that can harm millions of residents who live nearby in an urban area where emergency managers and first responders are working hard to protect residents.* Because so many potential terrorist targets exist, protection depends on the priorities established by public and private sector leaders and the reaction following a disaster that brings the vulnerability to the forefront.

MASS TRANSIT SYSTEMS

About 9.5 billion trips are made on mass transit systems (e.g., urban subway and rail; buses) in the United States each year. Mass transit carries more passengers each day than air or rail (i.e., between cities) transportation (White House, 2003: 61).

Mass transit systems are typically funded and operated at the local level as nonprofit government agencies. Although these systems are unique in size and design among cities, they are open and convenient to the public with minimal access controls. This makes protection difficult, challenging, and expensive (Figure 11-7).

The DHS, the DOT, and all levels of government seek to improve guidelines and standards to protect mass transit systems. Initiatives include design and engineering standards for rail and bus vehicles; improved screening and training for operators; security standards; and emergency and continuity of operations planning.

The U.S. Government Accountability Office (2005e) reports that the numerous stakeholders involved in securing rail transportation can lead to communication challenges, duplication of effort, and confusion of roles and responsibilities. Key federal stakeholders include the TSA and the Office for Domestic Preparedness (ODP), both within the DHS. The ODP provides grants to rail operations and conducts risk assessments for passenger rail agencies. Two other federal agencies, both within the DOT, are the **Federal Transit Administration** (FTA), and the **Federal Railroad Administration** (FRA). The FTA conducts nonregulatory safety and security activities, such as training, research, technical assistance, and demonstration projects. The FRA has regulatory authority over rail safety for commuter rail lines and Amtrak; it employs over 400 rail inspectors. Other important stakeholders are state and local agencies and rail operators.

The U.S. Government Accountability Office (2005d: 58) notes that whereas the aviation system is housed in a closed and controlled system, mass transit systems are open so large numbers of people can be moved quickly. Mass transit systems are characterized by multiple access points, sometimes no barriers, the inability of officials to monitor or control who enters or leaves, and, depending on the system, high ridership, expensive infrastructure, and economic importance. Security features that limit access, cause delays, increase fares, or result in inconvenience could make automobiles more attractive. At the same time, those mass transit systems located in large urban areas or tourist spots make them attractive targets because of the potential for mass casualties and economic damage.

Jenkins (2004: 2) writes: "For those determined to kill in quantity and willing to kill indiscriminately, trains, subways and buses are ideal targets. They offer terrorists easy access and escape." He notes that an analysis of nearly 1000 terrorist attacks on transportation found that the percentage of fatalities was much higher than the percentage for terrorist attacks in general.

In 2004, following the Madrid rail attacks, the TSA issued directives containing required security measures for passenger rail operators and Amtrak. The security measures produced controversy over limited dialogue to ensure that industry "best practices" were included in the measures. Examples of the TSA security measures are listed next (U.S. Government Accountability Office, 2005e: 22).

Figure 11-7 ■ Passenger rail security. Source: U.S. Government Accountability Office (2005e).

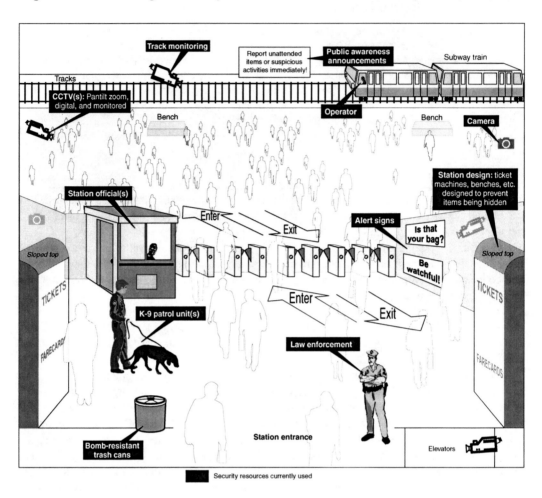

- Designate coordinators to enhance security-related communication.
- Provide TSA with access to security assessments and plans.
- Reinforce employee watch programs.
- Ask passengers to report unattended property and suspicious behavior.
- Use clear plastic or bomb-resistant containers.
- Use canine explosive detection teams to screen passenger baggage, terminals, and trains.
- Allow TSA canine teams access to rail operations.
- Conduct frequent inspections of facilities and assets.
- Use surveillance systems.
- Ensure appropriate levels of policing and security that correlate with DHS threat levels.
- Lock all doors that allow access to train operators.
- Require Amtrak to request that adult passengers provide ID at the initial point where tickets are checked.

Additional measures from a variety of sources are emergency planning and drills, quality intelligence systems, visible and undercover patrols, behavioral observation skills of police and security, emergency call boxes, research and testing of WMD detection equipment, ventilation systems that remove toxic smoke, and windows that blow out to reduce both the destructive force of a blast and smoke.

Many security methods applied to trains are also applicable to buses. Examples are training drivers to recognize suspicious behavior, watch programs for drivers and passengers, CCTV, sensors for WMD, and emergency procedures and communication. The U.S. Department of Transportation, Federal Transit Administration (2004) provides an illustration of transit security by highlighting bus security in the Worcester (Massachusetts) Regional Transit Authority (WRTA). The majority of transit agencies in the United States are small or mid sized. The WRTA is mid sized. Central to its service area is its Union Station, a multimodal transportation hub providing commuter rail, Amtrak, regional bus, local transit service, and is next to freight rail lines. Each transit bus contains a standard two-way radio with dispatch, plus a "red phone" that is a dedicated link to the Worcester Police Department for dealing with passenger or medical emergencies. CCTV is also installed in several transit buses with images stored either onboard or via a wireless network to the WRTA dispatch center. The WRTA distributes within its system a brochure entitled, "See Something? Say Something." It contains security awareness tips and information on reporting threats. To protect the transit bus yard and other facilities, the WRTA is improving security through CCTV, gates, and alarms. Training is also increasing and includes the distribution of the National Transit Institute pamphlet entitled, "Employee Guide to System Security." The WRTA partners with local first responders and participates in emergency drills.

HIGHWAYS, TRUCKING, AND INTERCITY BUSING

Trucking and intercity busing are essential components of the transportation infrastructure to move people, goods, and services. Related components include highways and roads. The White House (2003: 57–58) notes that the trucking and intercity busing industries present several protection challenges because these industries are heterogeneous in size and operations, span numerous government jurisdictions, and operate under many owners.

Transportation choke points (TCPs) are another challenge. These points include bridges, tunnels, highway interchanges, terminals, and border crossings that are crucial to transportation routes. TCPs are vulnerabilities in the transportation sector because they connect roads and modes of transportation. If subject to attack and destruction, traffic could be blocked at TCPs and the vulnerabilities of people, vehicles, and vehicle contents would be compounded.

The White House (2003: 58) pointed to the need for coordination in assessing TCP vulnerabilities and evaluating risk and funding to promote communications, planning, and security criteria. Initiatives aimed at improving the protection of highways, trucking, and intercity busing include cooperation among the DHS, the DOT, and sector stakeholders on

- risk management
- development of criteria for identifying and mitigating TCPs
- technological solutions for increased protection
- national operator security education and awareness.

Two major types of TCPs, bridges and tunnels, present complex challenges as other critical infrastructures and key assets. There are about 600,000 bridges in the United States, with about 1000 subject to substantial casualties and economic disruption if attacked. Similarly, the 337 highway tunnels and 211 transit tunnels, many of which are beneath waterways, pose additional vulnerabilities. Threats to TCPs include damage, catastrophic failure, and contamination. In addition to risk management, emergency management, security, and other protection methods, issues of importance for bridges and tunnels include structural components and their behavior to blast loads and mitigation through structural design and retrofit. Additional recommendations can be found through the American Association of State Highway and Transportation Officials (2003).

The TSA implemented a program for checking the backgrounds of truck drivers hauling hazardous materials. The first phase consisted of name-based threat assessments on 2.7 million licensed HAZMAT drivers to see if any presented a potential terrorist threat. The second phase added fingerprint-based criminal history FBI checks and immigration checks for new applicants. The third phase focuses on drivers seeking to renew or transfer their current hazardous materials endorsement by requiring a fingerprint-based assessment. Critics argue that it will take years to check all the drivers, and if all the drivers are registered, terrorists could seek help from a registered driver through cash, trick, or extortion or steal or hijack a truck.

The **American Trucking Association**, with cooperation and funding from the DHS, promotes a "watch" program that seeks to include the millions of drivers of commercial and public trucks, buses, and other vehicles to recognize safety and security threats and avoid becoming a target. Drivers can become intelligence gatherers, report suspicious behavior, and extend the reach of homeland security. Training is provided on observation methods and how to report safety and security concerns. For example, the hundreds of thousands of school bus drivers in the United States should not only be alert to youths with weapons and drivers with road rage, but also watchful for terrorists and other offenders who may be casing their routes and observing their routines.

SOFT TARGETS: PUBLIC TRANSPORTATION, SCHOOLS, THEATERS, ETC.

Terrorists often focus on "soft" targets to increase the likelihood of their success. "Hard" targets include military bases and fortified government buildings. Examples of "soft targets" are public transportation (Figure 11-8), schools, theaters, houses of worship, and shopping malls. The Associated Press (12-5-03 and 2-6-04) provides a glimpse of the carnage from two terrorist attacks on commuters in Russia. In one attack, a suicide bomber blew himself up and destroyed part of a commuter train near Chechnya, killing 40 people and injuring 177. The Federal Security Service stated that a man triggered the shrapnel-filled bomb as the train approached a station near Yessentuki, about 750 miles south

Figure 11-8 ■ Public transportation is one of many "soft targets" favored by terrorists.

SOFT TARGETS: PUBLIC TRANSPORTATION, SCHOOLS, THEATERS, ETC.—Cont'd

of Moscow. Passengers were thrown out, as the train was ripped open like a sardine can, while others were trapped in the burning, twisted wreckage. Police found the dead bomber who still had grenades strapped to what remained of his legs.

In another attack, a suicide bomber killed 39 commuters and wounded 120 as a subway train in Moscow was destroyed. Following the explosion, the train traveled for several hundred more feet as the tracks became littered with body parts. Inside the train, bodies covered in soot and debris sat side by side and remained seated. Because Moscow's subways are very deep, the injured were brought to the surface on stretchers carried on the escalators and then to waiting ambulances. Victims with minor injuries and other passengers including those from a train coming from the opposite direction were forced to walk through smoke to another exit about a mile along the track. Passengers complained that initially they could not open the train doors following the explosion, but they were able to eventually pry the doors open.

Russian President Vladimir Putin blamed Chechen rebels and said that "Russia doesn't negotiate with terrorists—it destroys them." Russia has fought an insurgency in the breakaway republic of Chechnya since the 1990s, a time when the former Soviet Union collapsed.

Several other bombings occurred in Russia and Chechnya. Examples include the 2002 suicide truck bombing that destroyed the headquarters of Chechnya's Moscow-backed government and killed 72 people. In the same year, 50 people were killed in a similar type of attack on a military hospital containing Russian soldiers wounded in Chechnya. Another target was a rock concert in Moscow where 16 died.

One of the most controversial actions by the Russians in dealing with terrorists occurred in October of 2002 when Chechen rebels seized a Moscow theater and 800 hostages and set explosives. After 3 days, authorities sprayed a powerful gas into the building and 120 were killed, many from the gas. The dead rebels in the theater were shown on television with bullet holes in their heads.

In 2004, Russia faced more attacks by Chechen rebels: bombs exploded on two jets in-flight killing all passengers, a suicide bombing occurred outside a Moscow subway station, and an elementary school was seized and bombed. The 3-day hostage standoff at the elementary school in Beslan, where the Chechen rebels rigged bombs around 1200 hostages, ended in gunfire, explosions, and 338 deaths, mostly children. Each side blamed the other for the battle in the school that caused more controversy over Chechen terrorism and Russian responses.

On March 11, 2004 Spain suffered its worse terrorist attack when passenger trains in Madrid were targeted (Dickey, 2004; Associated Press, 4-7-04). Many called this attack Spain's 9/11. The creativity and resourcefulness of terrorists were illustrated when 13 backpacks and gym bags, each containing 25 pounds of high explosives, were left lying around trains as they reached three crowded stations. Detonators on each bomb were wired to cell phones so when the terrorists called the phones when the trains arrived, 10 of the bombs exploded. The slaughter left 200 people dead or dying. With 1500 injured, and many bleeding and staggering away from the wreckage, emergency services were overwhelmed. Ironically, loved ones and friends used the same technology used to detonate the bombs as they frantically tried to check on people. One eerie aspect of the tragedy was that cell phones rang not only on the injured bodies, but also on the disfigured corpses.

It was a cell phone again that surfaced when Spanish investigators broke the case by finding a cheap Trium phone and phone card in one of the bombs that failed to explode. Three Moroccan Arabs and two Indians were linked to the evidence. Then, a videotape was found near a mosque in Madrid that contained a recording of a man speaking Arabic, with a Moroccan accent, who stated that he was the military leader of al-Qaida in Europe and responsible for the attack. Interestingly, the attack occurred about 3 days before general elections in Spain, and it is thought that the attack influenced citizens in voting out a government that supported the U.S.-led coalition efforts in Iraq.

Continued

SOFT TARGETS: PUBLIC TRANSPORTATION, SCHOOLS, THEATERS, ETC.—Cont'd

The fanaticism of the terrorists who bombed the trains in Madrid was illustrated when Spanish special forces prepared to storm their hideout in an apartment building when they blew themselves up. As forensic doctors and police scientists tried to identify the dead, they found 200 body parts, including 11 legs. Within a month of the attack, Spanish police had arrested 16 suspects, mostly Moroccan. The focus of the investigation was on the Moroccan Islamic Combatant Group, which has links to al-Qaida.

In another example of terrorists attacking mass transit, explosions occurred in three subway trains and one double-decker bus in London during July of 2005. The explosions occurred at the morning rush hour and killed 55 and wounded 700 in the worst attacks on London since the Nazi air blitz of World War II. One victim in a train described a massive bang that was deafening. Then a flash and flame engulfed the train as windows shattered. Another witness described the floor of the train as blown out. As the train filled with smoke, passengers escaped the London underground covered in blood and soot. The roof of the red double-decker bus flew into the air from the explosion in the back of the bus that killed 14, including the suicide bomber. Survivors streamed away from the bus to seek help from first responders as specialists in protective suits searched for evidence of WMD. The secret organization of al-Qaida in Europe claimed responsibility and said the attacks were in retaliation for Britain's support of the wars in Iraq and Afghanistan (Bryson, 2005). (In 2006, British government reports concluded the terrorists were homegrown and not at the direction of a foreign group.) Two weeks later four similar attacks occurred simultaneously on three subway trains and one double-decker bus. However, this time the explosive devices were either faulty or too small to do damage, and the bombers did not perish. Two arrests were made soon after the second wave of attacks and more arrests were expected. Authorities and the public were shocked by the second wave of attacks because Britain was still on alert, an intense investigation was in progress from the first attacks, and subsequent attacks are usually foiled. Following the first attacks, police released CCTV images showing all four terrorists entering public transit systems on the morning of the attacks. The investigation also focused on those who financed, recruited, and coordinated the operation (Kole, 2005).

On July 11, 2006 eight bombs exploded in packed Bombay (India) commuter trains, killing about 200 people and injuring about 800. The well-coordinated terror attack was alleged to be linked to a Kashmiri militant group.

CRITICAL THINKING:

- How can the problem of terrorists detonating explosives on trains or buses be prevented and controlled?
- What is your opinion of the actions of Russian authorities when Chechen rebels seized the theater in Moscow during October of 2002? What are your views of the outcome of the seizure of the elementary school in Beslan in 2004?

MARITIME

The maritime shipping infrastructure is another vital component of the economy. It consists of ports, ships that carry cargo and passengers, waterways, locks, dams, canals, and a network of transportation modes, such as railroads and pipelines, that connect to ships in port. The 361 seaports in the United States are diverse in size and characteristics. They are owned and operated by either private corporations or state and local governments. Ships are primarily owned and operated by the private sector. The DOD has designated certain seaports as strategic seaports for military purposes (White House, 2003: 60).

Annually, the U.S. maritime industry manages over two billion tons of freight, three billion tons of oil, more than 134 million ferry passengers, and about seven million cruise ship travelers. Furthermore, about 7500 foreign ships, operated by 200,000 sailors, enter U.S. ports each year (Maxwell and Blanda, 2005: 22).

The delivery and activation of a WMD on a ship near a port, in port, or in transit from a port would be a catastrophe. Also, knowing the creativity and patience of terrorists, one possible scenario is the use a fuel-laden supertanker as a WMD.

As with other transportation systems, maritime shipping faces the huge challenge of access controls. The inspection of all vessels and cargo that enter ports is impossible, and security concerns must be balanced with efficient access to ports by passengers and cargo. Compounding the need for improved security are international agreements and multinational authorities. The U.S. Department of State, the diplomatic arm of the U.S. government, is responsible for the negotiation of maritime rules and practices with other countries.

The **International Ship and Port Facility Security Code** takes a risk management approach and seeks global standardization of security of port facilities and ships. Similar to U.S. Coast Guard rules, the code requires minimal requirements, such as port security plans, a port security officer, ship security plans, a ship security officer, and training. Failure to comply with the code has resulted in ships being detained or denied entry by the U.S. Coast Guard.

Various government agencies work to improve protection in this industry. The DHS and the DOT work with other government agencies, the private sector, foreign governments, and international organizations to improve maritime security. Primary concerns are to identify threats at ports of embarkation and monitor ships, cargo, and passengers heading to the United States. The DHS and the DOT are also involved in enhanced port-facility design, workforce ID measures, vessel hardening, standards for container seals, research and development of security and monitoring systems for ships and cargo, trace-back systems for containers, prescreening processes for high-risk containers, and reviewing the best practices of other countries.

The DOT is working with the CBP to ensure security in the shipping supply chain. Those shippers who are unable to comply with rules and regulations are subject to increased attention and delay when seeking entrance to U.S. ports.

In addition to the CBP, the U.S. Coast Guard is another primary agency involved in port security (Figure 11-9). It was transferred to the DHS intact in 2003. Because the 9/11 attacks hit the U.S. mainland, the Coast Guard has had its missions expanded and its capabilities strained. Three major priorities of the Coast Guard are (1) implementing a maritime strategy for homeland security; (2) enhancing performance; and (3) recapitalizing the Coast Guard. This third priority includes the Deepwater Program, which replaces or upgrades cutters and aircraft that are capable of performing missions far out at sea (U.S. Government Accountability Office, 2005b). The **Maritime Transportation Security Act of 2002** (MTSA) charged the Coast Guard with numerous responsibilities, such as assessing port vulnerabilities, ensuring that vessels and ports have security plans, and promoting uniform standards of security. Homeland security missions also include waterways and coastal security; drug interdiction; migrant interdiction; and defense readiness to assist the U.S. Navy. Nonhomeland security missions include marine safety; search and rescue; aids to navigation (e.g., buoys); marine resources (e.g., fishing treaties); environmental protection; and ice operations (Office of Inspector General, 2004). Critics argue that increased security tasks by the Coast Guard hinder their traditional duties, such as boating safety and rescue.

The MTSA is a major law promoting maritime security. The act mandates a national maritime transportation security plan and contingency plans in response to terrorist attacks; an increase in security personnel and screening equipment; a grant program to support security upgrades; security regulations to be developed through the DOT, such as access controls and identification cards; training and certification; a maritime intelligence system; and the establishment of local port security committees to coordinate federal, state, and local law enforcement agencies and private security.

Figure 11-9 ■ U.S. Coast Guard helicopter rescue and local police

In September 2005, the Departments of Homeland Security, Defense, and State collaborated to approve *The National Strategy for Maritime Security* (U.S. Department of Homeland Security, 2005). This first-ever national maritime security plan, with contributors from over 20 government agencies and the private sector, contains supporting plans involving awareness, intelligence, layered security, threat response, domestic and international outreach, and recovery. This national strategy considers threats from WMD, transnational crime and piracy, and environmental destruction.

The U.S. Government Accountability Office (2005d: 59–61) describes the following challenges of the maritime sector. The USGAO sees the automatic vessel identification system, called for by the MTSA, as a major challenge for maritime security. Implemented by the Coast Guard, the system is designed to allow port authorities to determine the identity and position of vessels entering or operating within the harbor area and to provide early warning of an unidentified vessel or one that was in a location where it should not be. An effective system calls for land-based equipment and other infrastructure that is lacking at many ports.

Another challenge, and MTSA requirement, is that the DHS must approve security plans for all vessels operating in U.S. waters. These plans include assessing vulnerabilities and correcting them, designating security officers, conducting training and drills, and preventive measures. According to the USGAO, the process of approval of vessel plans requires refinement.

Coast Guard security assessments and security planning of ports as mandated by the MTSA are additional issues. This protection effort is intended to include conditions throughout a port and nearby that pose a potential threat. Refinements in assessments are needed in the scope, quality, and usefulness to port stakeholders.

The CBP faces continued challenges with inspections of oceangoing cargo containers. A national system for reporting and analyzing inspection statistics should be made available by risk level (e.g., low, medium, and high). The system should be uniformly reported, easy to interpret, and complete. Space limitations and safety concerns about inspection equipment have impacted the efficiency of inspections.

The USGAO noted challenges with CBP's implementation of both the CSI and the C-TPAT. As covered earlier in this chapter, the former seeks to permit CBP officials to screen for high-risk containers at key overseas ports, whereas the latter aims to improve global supply chain security in the private sector. For these programs to be successful, the challenges that must be overcome include the development of human capital plans that delineate recruitment, training, and retention of staff that are assigned to other countries; strategic plans that describe goals, objectives, and strategies; and improved performance measures.

The initiatives to reduce maritime vulnerabilities are varied as illustrated in the following list (U.S. Department of Homeland Security, 2004).

- *Ship Security Alert System*: a silent alarm system that enables a ship operator to alert author-ities that a threat faces the ship. The International Ship and Port Facility Security Code requires installation of this equipment on large passenger and cargo ships.
- *Smart Box Initiative*: security for cargo containers through a "tamper evident" seal that reveals attempted entry or entry through the cargo door. The seal serves to deter and detect tampering.
- *Automated Targeting System*: a CBP system that evaluates risks from cargo and passengers arriving by sea, truck, air, and rail. The system relies on prearrival information and input from the intelligence community.
- *National Targeting Center (NTC)*: this center provides tactical targeting and analytical research support for CBP antiterrorism efforts. The NTC also supports container security ini-tiative personnel assigned to foreign ports worldwide.
- *High Interest Vessels Boarding*: prior to entering port, high-risk ships are targeted for offshore boarding to address security issues. Specially trained Coast Guard teams board the ships.
- *Maritime Safety and Security Teams*: a rapid response force of the Coast Guard prepared for a variety of terrorist threats.
- *America's Waterways Watch*: an awareness and reporting program to combat terrorism and other crimes by enlisting the help of the maritime and recreational industries, and the general public, to recognize and report suspicious activity to the Coast Guard.

POSTAL AND SHIPPING

The U.S. Postal System (USPS) handles about two-thirds of a billion pieces of mail each day as more than 300,000 postal carriers deliver mail to more than 137 million delivery addresses nation-wide. Total employment in the USPS is about 749,000. The USPS consists of a headquarters in Washington, DC, tens of thousands of postal facilities, and hundreds of thousands of official drop boxes. The system is dependent on the transportation infrastructure and its trucks, aircraft, rail-roads, and ships. Annual revenue from the USPS is over $60 billion. Private industry mailing and shipping revenues exceed $140 billion (White House, 2003: 67).

The networks of the USPS and private shipping companies present complex protection challenges. The Fall 2001 **anthrax attacks** through the USPS illustrate the impact of a serious disruption to this system. This attack resulted in five deaths and contamination at postal facilities and equipment, other government offices, and businesses (see Chapter 2).

The USPS identified five areas of concern.

- Numerous points of entry into the system complicate protection. An option is effective, cost-effective technology to scan mail and provide early warning.
- Because the USPS relies on many independent contractors to transport mail, the USPS does not always maintain control of the mail during its chain of custody. To increase protection, USPS purchasing requirements include criminal (e.g., fingerprinting) and drug background checks of vendors, subcontractors, and related employees.
- Fourth amendment prohibitions against unreasonable search and seizure, and the sanctity of the postal seal, require justification of scanning or X-ray of a parcel for contraband.
- Improvements are needed in the coordination of the USPS, other government agencies, and the private shipping industry in response to emergencies.

- Through research and standards, the USPS and the private shipping industry can improve their selection of quality products for detecting, decontaminating, and remediating the impact of hazardous substances.

The USPS has developed six core initiatives in its emergency preparedness plans: prevention, protection and health-risk reduction, detection and identification, intervention, decontamination, and investigation. The USPS and the DHS seek to work with all levels of government for coordinated emergency response; increase stockpiles of equipment and materials for contamination events; conduct risk analyses of high-risk facilities; and coordinate the security of mail transiting U.S. borders with the U.S. Customs Service.

The U.S. Government Accountability Office (2005f) noted that since the Fall 2001 anthrax attacks, over 16,000 incidents involving suspicious packages or powder spills have occurred at postal facilities. This dramatic increase resulted from greater caution and hoaxes. Also, in October 2003, the biotoxin ricin was discovered at an airmail facility in Greenville, South Carolina (see Chapter 2), and, in November 2003, an envelope, initially suspected of being ricin, was discovered at a White House mail processing facility. These two incidents prompted Congress to request that the USGAO study the government emergency response to these incidents. The USGAO recommended that the USPS (1) provide improved guidance to employees on response actions to suspicious mail and mail containing hazardous material; (2) expand related training for managers and supervisors; and (3) provide explicit guidance to managers on communicating with employees and unions regarding incidents in which a mail piece is being tested.

The USGAO also suggested consistency and simplicity in guidance to USPS employees for suspicious packages. Characteristics of suspicious packages include the following.

- Lopsided or uneven
- Powdery substance on the outside
- Odors, discoloration, or oily stains
- Excessive postage or tape
- No return address
- Handwritten or poorly typed address
- Marked with restrictions, such as "Personal, Confidential," or "Do Not X-Ray."
- Threatening message

Simplified guidance on identifying suspicious mail includes "SLAP": unusual shape, look, address features, or packaging. The "three Ps" of response are package—do not handle it and isolate the area; people—evacuate the area around the package and notify your supervisor; and plan—contact the postal inspection service, police, and community first responders.

PIPELINES

According to *The National Strategy for the Physical Protection of Critical Infrastructures and Key Assets* (White House, 2003: 58), pipelines are considered part of the transportation CI sector. Chapter 10 included a discussion of oil and natural gas businesses as part of the energy CI sector. Here, we emphasize the pipeline industry. It moves a variety of substances, such as crude oil, refined petroleum products, and natural gas within many hundreds of thousands of miles of pipelines that are mostly underground. This industry has a commendable record of safety, contingency plans, and the capabilities to repair or bypass localized disruptions. However, protection is an important issue because of the volatile nature of the products that pipelines deliver. Pipelines cross local, state, and international jurisdictions, and numerous businesses and other entities depend on a reliable flow of fuel. The problem of cascading is evident with pipelines, as it is with other CI sectors. The Departments of Homeland Security, Energy and Transportation, state and local governments, and the private sector collaborate to improve protection measures and emergency response plans.

DISCUSSION QUESTIONS

1. What do you think is the most vulnerable part of border and transportation security and why? What are your suggestions to reduce this vulnerability?
2. What do you think is the most secure part of border and transportation security and why? Should resources from the part you selected be shifted to less secure parts and why?
3. How can security be improved along the Mexican and Canadian borders?
4. How do you think terrorist plans and tactics have changed since modifications in U.S. border and transportation security following the 9/11 attacks?
5. What are your suggestions for improving immigration laws and policies?
6. What can be done about the availability of so many soft targets for terrorists?
7. If you were to choose an employment position or specialization in border and transportation security, what would you select and why?

APPLICATIONS

11A   YOU BE THE AIRLINE PASSENGER

You are a passenger on an airliner and 15 minutes into the flight four terrorists take action to try to control the aircraft. In their quick, surprising moves, one uses thin wire to choke a flight attendant, while another slashes at a passenger. At the same time, two other terrorists protect the assailants by holding plastic knives and an item they say is a bomb that they will detonate if attacked. They state that no one else will be harmed if everyone follows their instructions. What do you do?

11B   YOU BE THE BORDER PATROL AGENT

As an experienced border patrol agent working along the U.S. border with Mexico, you have discretion in your job and you must prioritize your daily activities. Prioritize the following items and explain why you placed them in your particular order of importance.

- Item A: You and your partner apprehend two illegal alien Mexicans on a road about one mile inside the U.S. border. One is in possession of a few grams of marijuana.
- Item B: The two illegal alien Mexicans that you and your partner apprehended tell you that a woman is having a baby nearby and she is in desperate need of assistance.
- Item C: You and your partner are scheduled to meet two other officers in 30 minutes for assignment to a stationary post to conduct surveillance of possible drug smugglers who are due to cross the border soon.
- Item D: About 15 minutes ago, your supervisor requested a meeting as soon as possible to discuss important information that she does not want to transmit over the radio.
- Item E: Two officers about 3 miles away radio you for assistance upon apprehending five Pakistanis trying to cross the border.
- Item F: Your "check engine" light in your vehicle has just come on.

11C   YOU BE THE SECURITY OFFICER

You are a security officer at a wholesale food distribution facility. Today, you are assigned to the main gate and control access of people, trucks, and other vehicles. The other security officer on duty is assigned to the shipping and receiving dock, but she has been taken off her assigned post periodically to help with the mail. She is presently off the premises at lunch and picking up lunch orders. As you perform your duties, you are faced with several tasks. Prioritize the following items and explain why you placed them in your particular order of importance.

- Item A: About 10 minutes ago the security officer on lunch break from the facility called you for help with her dead auto battery. She is at a fast food restaurant a short distance away. She wants you to leave your post for just a few minutes, locate jumper cables, and drive to her.

- Item B: A manager, who cannot find the other security officer, telephoned you 15 minutes ago and requested that you leave your post and go to the post office to pick up an important package as soon as possible.
- Item C: You are presently checking a truck and truck driver seeking access. The driver's license, other documents, and paperwork look legitimate. However, something just does not seem right, but you cannot pinpoint the problem. The truck seems to have a strange odor that you cannot identify. The truck has all new tires and you have never seen all new tires on a truck at the same time. The tires, mud flaps, and under the truck have red dirt scattered about. The dirt looks like it came from the region where you grew up, but the truck supposedly traveled through another region that does not contain red dirt. The driver is growing impatient and asks if you could speed things up. Three other trucks are waiting in line.
- Item D: You hear a vehicle alarm go off in the employee parking lot. Last month, two employee vehicles had windows broken and items were stolen. At that time, an employee saw two juveniles running away, climbing the fence, and disappearing into the woods. Thereafter, management ordered that at least one security officer patrol the parking lot.
- Item E: A man you have never seen before walks up to the guardhouse, claims he is having chest pain, and then collapses in front of you on the premises. You are trained in CPR, first aid, and how to use a defibrillator. You know that a one-way mask and a defibrillator are located in the main office nearby.

11D YOU BE THE TERRORIST

As a terrorist cell leader in the United States, you have narrowed numerous attack plans down to three. Which of the following plans do you execute and why did you select the particular plan?

1. Order your cell members to obtain employment with crews that clean commercial passenger airliners and creatively plant bombs on large passenger aircraft prior to flight.
2. Using uniforms, ID, weapons, and trained dogs similar to TSA canine teams, enter a commuter subway system from multiple points and introduce WMD.
3. Order your cell members to follow applicable laws and regulations to obtain a job as a truck driver of hazardous materials. When cell members are assigned the task of driving a truck containing a hazardous and dangerous chemical, attach explosives to the truck and use it as a powerful bomb on a bridge or at a school.

WEB SITES

Airports Council International: www.airports.org
American Association of Airport Executives: www.aaae.org
American Bus Association: www.buses.org
American Public Transportation Association: www.apta.com
American Trucking Association: http://www.truckline.com/index
Association of American Railroads: www.aar.org/
International Council of Cruise Lines: www.iccl.org
Metropolitan Transportation Authority, State of New York: www.mta.nyc.ny.us/
United Motorcoach Association: www.uma.org
U.S. Citizenship and Immigration Services: www.uscis.gov
U.S. Coast Guard: www.uscg.mil/USCG.shtm
U.S. Customs and Border Protection: www.cbp.gov
U.S. Department of Homeland Security: www.dhs.gov
U.S. Department of Transportation: www.dot.gov
U.S. Immigration and Customs Enforcement: www.ice.gov
U.S. Transportation Security Administration: www.tsa.gov

NOTES

American Association of State Highway and Transportation Officials (2003). *Recommendations for Bridge and Tunnel Security* (September). Washington, DC: AASHTO.
Associated Press (December 5, 2003). "40 killed in train blast near Chechnya."

Associated Press (February 6, 2004). "Moscow subway explosion kills 39; terror is suspected."

Associated Press (April 7, 2004). "Prosecutor seeks more arrest warrants in Madrid bombings."

Association of American Railroads (n.d.). "Freight Railroad Security Plan." www.aar.org, retrieved October 23, 2005.

Bryson, D. (2005). Associated Press. "Terrorist attack brings out best in ordinary Britons" (July 8).

Dickey, C. (2004). "From 9/11 to 3/11." *Newsweek* (March 22).

Forsyth, J. (2006). "IED's among Weapons Seized in Laredo Raids." *San Antonio News* (February 3).

Fotos, C. (2005). "The Challenges of US-VISIT." *Homeland Security,* 2 (May/June).

Hall, M. (2005). "Despite new technology, Border Patrol overwhelmed." *USA Today* (February 22). www.usatoday.com/news/nation/2005-02-22-border-patrol_x.htm, retrieved February 23, 2005.

Jenkins, B. (2004). "Terrorism and the Security of Public Surface Transportation" (April). Santa Monica, CA: RAND. Testimony presented to the Senate Committee on Judiciary on April 8, 2004.

Kocieniewski, D. (2006). "Despite 9/11 Effect, Railyards Are Still Vulnerable." *The New York Times.* www.nytimes.com/2006/03/27/nyregion, retrieved March 28, 2006.

Kole, W. (2005). Associated Press. "Prime Minister warns against the spread of terrorism" (July 17).

Leiken, R. (2002). "Enchilada Lite: A Post-9/11 Mexican Migration Agreement." Center for Immigration Studies. www.cis.org/articles/2002/leiken.html, retrieved October 19, 2005.

Maxwell, C., and Blanda, T. (2005). "Terror by Sea: The Unique Challenges of Port Security." *FBI Law Enforcement Bulletin,* 74 (September).

Naim, M. (2003). "The Five Wars of Globalization." *Foreign Policy* (January/February).

National Commission on Terrorist Attacks Upon the United States (2004). *The 9/11 Commission Report.* www.9-11commission.gov/, retrieved July 26, 2004.

Ngai, M. (1998). "The Architecture of Race in American Immigration Law: A Reexamination of the Immigration Act of 1924." *The Journal of American History,* 86.

Office of Homeland Security (2002). *National Strategy for Homeland Security.* Washington, DC: The White House (July).

Office of Inspector General (2004). *FY 2003 Mission Performance United States Coast Guard* (September). Washington, DC: DHS.

O'Harrow, R., and Highman, S. (2005). "U.S. Border Security at a Crossroads." *Washington Post* (May 23). www.washingtonpost.com, retrieved May 25, 2005.

Passel, J. (2006). "Size and Characteristics of the Unauthorized Migrant Population in the U.S." Pew Hispanic Center. http://pewhispanic.org, retrieved March 8, 2006.

Pervola, F. (2005). "Airport Security: The Industry That Never Rests." *Security Products,* 9 (March).

Poland, J. (1988). *Understanding Terrorism: Groups, Strategies, and Responses.* Englewood Cliffs, NJ: Prentice Hall.

Polisar, J. (2005). "Enforcing Immigration Law: The Role of State, Tribal, and Local Law Enforcement." The *Police Chief,* LXXII (April).

U.S. Citizenship and Immigration Services (2005). "This is USCIS" (July 26). http://uscis.gov, retrieved October 5, 2005.

U.S. Customs and Border Protection (n.d.). "Combating the Threat of Nuclear Smuggling at Home and Abroad." www.customs.gov, retrieved October 5, 2005.

U.S. Customs and Border Protection (2003). "U.S. Border Patrol History" (July 15). www.customs.gov, retrieved October 5, 2005.

U.S. Customs and Border Protection (2004). *National Border Patrol Strategy* (September). www.customs.gov, retrieved October 5, 2005.

U.S. Department of Homeland Security (2004). *Secure Seas, Open Ports: Keeping Our Waters Safe, Secure and Open for Business* (June 21). www.dhs.gov/interweb/assetlibrary/DHSPortSecurityFactSheet-062104.pdf, retrieved March 24, 2006.

U.S. Department of Homeland Security (2005). *National Strategy for Maritime Security* (September). www.dhs.gov/interweb/assetlibrary/HSPD13_MaritimeSecurityStrategy.pdf, retrieved October 25, 2005.

U.S. Department of Transportation, Federal Transit Administration (2004). "Transit Security." *Safety & Security Newsletter* (Spring).

U.S. Government Accountability Office (2004). *General Aviation Security: Increased Federal Oversight Is Needed, but Continued Partnership with the Private Sector Is Critical to Long-Term Success* (September). www.gao.gov/cgi-bin/getrpt?GAO-05-144, retrieved December 13, 2004.

U.S. Government Accountability Office (2005a). *Aviation Security: Screener Training and Performance Measurement Strengthened, but More Work Remains* (May). www.gao.gov/cgi-bin/getrpt?GAO-05-457, retrieved May 4, 2005.

U.S. Government Accountability Office (2005b). *Coast Guard: Observations on Agency Priorities in Fiscal Year 2006 Budget Request* (March 17). www.gao.gov/cgi-bin/getrpt?GAO-05-364T, retrieved March 18, 2005.

U.S. Government Accountability Office (2005c). *Department of Homeland Security: Addressing Management Challenges That Face Immigration Enforcement Agencies* (May 5). www.gao.gov/new.items/d05664t.pdf, retrieved May 6, 2005.

U.S. Government Accountability Office (2005d). *Homeland Security: Agency Plans, Implementation, and Challenges Regarding the National Strategy for Homeland Security* (January). www.gao.gov/cgi-bin/getrpt?GAO-05-33, retrieved February 15, 2005.

U.S. Government Accountability Office (2005e). *Passenger Rail Security: Enhanced Federal Leadership Needed to Prioritize and Guide Security Efforts* (October). www.gao.gov/cgi-bin/getrpt?GAO-06-181T, retrieved October 21, 2005.

U.S. Government Accountability Office (2005f). *U.S. Postal Service: Guidance on Suspicious Mail Needs Further Refinement* (July). www.gao.gov/new.items/d05716.pdf, retrieved August 12, 2005.

U.S. Government Accountability Office (2006a). *Border Security: Investigators Transported Radioactive Sources across Our Nation's Borders at Two Locations* (March 28). www.gao.gov/new.items/d06583t.pdf, retrieved March 29, 2006.

U.S. Government Accountability Office (2006b). *Aviation Security: Significant Management Challenges May Adversely Affect Implementation of the Transportation Security Administration's Secure Flight Program* (February 9). www.gao.gov/cgi-bin/getrpt?GAO-06-374T, retrieved February 10, 2006.

U.S. Immigration and Customs Enforcement (2005a). "About ICE" (October 4). www.ice.gov, retrieved October 5, 2005.

U.S. Immigration and Customs Enforcement (2005b). "22 Members of Two Colombian Drug Trafficking Organizations Charged with Conspiring to Import Massive Quantities of Narcotics through Seaports in New York and California" (September 28). www.ice.gov, retrieved October 5, 2005.

U.S. Transportation Security Administration (n.d.). "About TSA." www.tsa.gov/public/display?theme=7, retrieved September 30, 2005.

White House (2003). *The National Strategy for the Physical Protection of Critical Infrastructures and Key Assets* (February). www.whitehouse.gov, retrieved September 14, 2004.

PART IV

THE FUTURE

CHAPTER 12

ANTICIPATING THE FUTURE: TERRORISM, TECHNOLOGY, RESEARCH, AND EDUCATION

OBJECTIVES

The study of this chapter will enable you to:

1. Examine how futurists anticipate future events.
2. Discuss multiple viewpoints on the problem of terrorism and countermeasures.
3. List the five wars of globalization and why these wars are so difficult to win.
4. Discuss WMD and the future.
5. List and explain technologies to counter terrorism.
6. Describe how terrorists use technology to further their cause.
7. Explain how research is assisting the Department of Homeland Security and the war against terrorism.
8. Discuss how homeland security education is evolving.

KEY TERMS

wild cards
backcasting
threat framework
two-front strategy
three-front strategy
Nunn-Lugar program
new terrorism
lethal violence sequence
geospacial information systems

autodidactic
basic research
applied research
national common operating picture
American National Standards Institute's
    Homeland security standards panel
Homeland Security Act of 2002
DHS centers of excellence
National Strategy for Homeland Security

ANTICIPATING TERRORISM

Although we marvel at the capabilities of our modern technology, no system, model, method, or person is capable of accurately and consistently predicting future events. This author makes no such claim, except to state that terrorism will continue in the future. It would be wonderful if we had the capability of accurately predicting terrorist attacks, but this is not the case.

Edward Cornish (2003), a noted futurist and author, offers guidance for anticipating future events. He refers to the term, **wild cards,** used by futurists to describe events that are startling and have important consequences for the majority of people. Wild cards are powerful because they disrupt our everyday life and radically change our way of thinking and planning. Most people experience multiple wild cards in their lifetime. Common wild cards in people's lives include being unexpectedly dismissed by an employer or lover, or the unexpected death of a loved one. Another example is being victimized by a natural disaster. Cornish writes that wild cards are not always bad. Beneficial wild cards are an occupational promotion and winning a contest like the lottery. Cornish views the year 1941 as being the most memorable for wild cards. During that year, Nazis troops invaded the Soviet Union and Japan attacked the United States. Both attacks were a surprise and the victims were unprepared, although each victim received warnings that were ignored.

Cornish (2003) refers to the work of futurist John L. Petersen, who wrote the book, *Out of the Blue: How to Anticipate Big Future Surprises.* Petersen's future wild cards include the collapse of the United Nations and a terrorist attack on the United States with the use of a nuclear device. Cornish also cites future wild cards from Rockfellow and his colleagues who claim Hong Kong will dominate China's economy, the European nation state will collapse, and life expectancy will approach 100. Rockfellow argues that business managers should think about wild cards to free up their thinking. They rarely think about the possibility of the organization's market coming to a surprising end, such as suggesting to toy makers that children of the future may not play with toys. Rockfellow points out that deconstructing our perception of reality facilitates creative thinking. Also, the most successful products throughout history could only have been anticipated through wild-card thinking, according to Rockfellow.

Cornish writes that Petersen believes mankind can *anticipate* wild cards and *prepare* for them. These undertakings are vital because wild cards can threaten the capabilities of human systems and trigger a chain of events that may be worse than the initial event itself. (An example is the cascading effect as covered in Chapter 10.) Petersen suggests three basic rules for dealing with wild cards: (1) thinking about a wild card before it happens is valuable because the more that is known about a potential event, the less threatening it becomes and the easier it is to formulate a solution; (2) sophisticated and effective information gathering and analysis is important to identify early warning signs, understanding the structure of a wild card, and planning responses; and (3) because we have reached a period when potential events may overwhelm our ability to understand and respond to them, and our current methods of problem solving are weak, new approaches are required. Cornish supports Petersen's contentions by referring to the 9/11 attacks. Most people would have laughed at the idea that terrorists might destroy the World Trade Center's twin towers by crashing hijacked airliners into them. However, *The Futurist* published articles that provided warnings. Brian Jenkins, a terrorism expert, mentioned in a 1987 article the possibility of aerial suicide attacks. Marvin J. Cetron, a futurist, specifically stated, in a 1994 article, the World Trade Center as a terrorist target. Cetron stressed that for terrorist groups to succeed, they will likely mount multiple, simultaneous attacks to overtax responders and demonstrate their capabilities.

Cornish (2003) describes the technique of backcasting to analyze warnings of terrorist attacks and to provide a method to anticipate attacks. He presents the situation of security officers charged with preventing terrorist attacks who just read Jenkins' article warning of aerial suicide attacks. The first step is to obtain the views of experts on the likelihood of such an attack, the method of attack, and the possible targets. (This step is similar to a focus group.) Second, **backcasting** is applied as a technique to anticipate future events by "forecasting backward from a possible future rather than forward from the present." Once it is anticipated that terrorists might attack by air, scenarios are created, each showing a sequence of events leading to an attack. Cornish provides sample questions to consider: How could terrorists gain control of an aircraft? How could they smuggle a weapon onto an aircraft? Because Cornish's illustration is related to the 9/11 attacks and they are easier to backcast, let us apply his technique in anticipation of some potential future event. A dirty bomb attack (see Chapter 2) will serve as an example. Suppose numerous experts anticipate a dirty bomb attack on a port as the most likely WMD attack. Now that the potential attack has been narrowed, various scenarios can be created and questions posed: How can a dirty bomb be detonated at a port? How can it be smuggled into a port? What security methods must be overcome? Where can the components of a dirty bomb be obtained? What types of weapons, equipment, vehicles, and other support are required for the attack to succeed? How many cell members are needed and what types of skills are necessary? How will cell members be recruited? How will the operation be financed? What are the goals of the attack?

Cragin and Daly (2004) offer a framework to help U.S. policymakers place parameters around the threat of terrorism. Their **threat framework** is based on analyses of terrorist groups' *intentions* and *capabilities*. They claim that terrorism analysis rarely combines the two. Cragin and Daly place intentions on an x axis with a range from benign to hostile and capabilities on a y axis with a range from low to high. The purpose of their matrix is to measure terrorist groups against each other for prioritizing threats and refining counterterrorism. Al-Qaida would represent the highest degree of both intentions and capabilities, whereas a group such as the Liberation Tigers of Tamil Eelam (LTTE) has a high degree of capabilities, but they have not expressed anti-U.S. sentiment.

CRITICAL THINKING:

If several terrorism experts claim that a particular type of attack at a specific type of location has a high likelihood of occurring, and protection methods are improved for the probable targets, do you think terrorists would apply this information and choose another type of weapon and target?

Petersen (2001) writes that we have an old problem in a new context because of population and technology. He notes that we are living in a time when the rich are getting richer faster than at any time in history. Also, as population increases are producing multitudes of poor people, they have access to television and see how the rest of the world lives, while the have/have not divide broadens. Petersen espouses the dangers of WMD and he refers to comments by Defense Secretary Donald Rumsfeld who suggested that terrorist groups would eventually acquire nuclear weapons. Petersen also cites investor Warren Buffett who claims that the war against terrorism will never be won and a major nuclear event will occur in the United States.

Petersen (2001) explains that a **two-front strategy** is best to deal with terrorism: a short-term component to confront current terrorists and a long-term component to seek solutions to problems that produce and encourage terrorism. He argues that government typically focuses on short-term problems. This leads to the continued growth of the underlying causes of terrorism. Petersen emphasizes that short-term solutions (e.g., new initiatives in defense and intelligence) are not enough, and proactive approaches and incentives are needed that are based on an understanding of our global system with shared responsibility. His suggestions include the following.

- There is a need to systematically learn how to think about the future. Governments should do more to prepare scenarios about potential future events.
- Seek nonviolent alternatives to armed conflict and economic sanctions.

- The United States is the most influential world player and has the responsibility to be involved in major global problems.
- Numerous studies show that education, especially of girls, is the best long-term approach to problems in developing countries. Educated mothers raise their families differently, they have different values and goals, and they have fewer children.

Lloyd (2002) advocates "war" against terrorism based on a **three-front strategy**. First, increased security must be considered with issues of effectiveness, cost, and restrictions on freedom. Second, Lloyd views addressing the causes of terrorism as probably the most important and difficult front. He discusses these relevant issues: the definition of terrorism; injustice; use and abuse of power; greed; giving; and concern for others. Lloyd concedes that there is little prospect of ridding the world of evil, but we should expect to reduce evil through millions of small positive "good" acts and our commitment to a better future. Third, it is necessary to reduce the impact of any terrorist event if it occurs. He refers indirectly to a cascading effect and the need for mitigation. Also, he reminds us that a WMD can be delivered through a minivan or sailing yacht more easily than through a missile.

Hoffman (2003: 429–442) presents an assessment of al-Qaida and the future of terrorism. He writes that although progress has been made against global terrorism, it would be imprudent to think that al-Qaida was dead, since it has the ability to mutate into a new, more dangerous form. He offers six reasons to support his views.

1. *Disagreement over the definition of al-Qaida.* Is it a franchise with local representatives? Is it an army or an ideology? Does it function with a centralized command structure? How can it be affected by events when there is disagreement over what it is?
2. *The propaganda value of bin Laden's foresight.* As early as 1996 bin Laden argued that the "Crusader military forces" of the United States and the United Kingdom had established a "beachhead" in Saudi Arabia to impose imperialism on the Middle East to control the huge oil reserves in the region. Current events have added weight to bin Laden's argument, and al-Qaida's propaganda has sought to rejuvenate the movement and recruit and motivate supporters.
3. *The imperative of individual jihad fused with collective revenge.* Bin Laden has long advocated jihad as an individual responsibility to destroy all anti-Islamic forces so Islam can take over the whole world. This appeal may gather strength in light of humiliation and resentment over the conquest of Iraq by the West and American power and influence in the region. Because of Muslim defeats by the West, al-Qaida advocates revenge, and a single, dramatic terrorist attack could breathe new life into al-Qaida.
4. *The operational possibilities in Iraq.* Al-Qaida has advocated the asymmetric virtues of guerrilla warfare as a way to continue the conflict with the crusader enemy and it sees the deployment of American forces in the Mideast as creating a "target-rich environment."
5. *The competence and determination of the remaining al-Qaida leadership cadre.* Although al-Qaida has been hunted and weakened, a "corporate succession" plan seems to function.
6. *The resiliency of al-Qaida and the likelihood of a post-bin Laden al-Qaida.* This group's resiliency and longevity are strongly influenced by its continued ability to recruit and mobilize.

Hoffman offers the following additional points on al-Qaida and future potentialities.

- The success of the 9/11 attacks was based on three capabilities that al-Qaida likely still retains: (1) the ability to identify vulnerabilities of the enemy (i.e., the West) that could be mercilessly exploited; (2) the effective use of deception (e.g., the 9/11 passengers were lulled into believing that if they cooperated, they would not be harmed); and (3) the use of suicide attacks to ensure success.

- As counterterrorism improves, al-Qaida constantly adapts itself; there will be continued attacks against soft targets.
- Local causes will be exploited to extend the power and influence of al-Qaida.
- Al-Qaida operatives will continue to recruit young Muslims in Western countries, even though it may be assumed that such youth are assimilated into the culture of the new host country. In this way, new recruits are unlikely to be under scrutiny of police.
- Terrorism against Israel holds clues and insight into possible threats to Western countries. Examples are suicide bombings of mass transit; an attempt to bomb a large gasworks near Tel Aviv; and use of a SAM-7 missile in an attempt to shoot down an Israeli passenger aircraft as it took off from Mombasa, Kenya, airport.
- In the post-9/11 environment, terrorism's power (i.e., to coerce and intimidate, to force changes in behavior, and to influence government policies and how money is spent) has increased enormously.
- The metric of success for government is to prevent, preempt, and deter attacks. For terrorists, the metric of success is simply the ability to act.
- Because al-Qaida sees America locked in a global "war on Islam," the movement is greater than ever.

CRITICAL THINKING:

Do you think the next major terrorist attack against the United States will come from al-Qaida or another terrorist group? Do you think the next major terrorist attack will be in the United States or overseas?

Reality Check: The Big Picture of Global Wars

Naim (2003) compares the global war on terrorism to global wars against the illegal trade in drugs, arms, intellectual property, people, and money. He takes a macrocosmic perspective on these wars and uses the term "five wars of globalization." Naim notes that the intense media coverage of the war on terrorism obscures the other five global wars. He emphasizes that religious zeal or political goals drive terrorists, whereas profit drives the other wars, and all of the wars result in murder, mayhem, and global insecurity.

According to Naim, governments have been fighting the five wars for centuries and losing them. He does not include terrorism in this statement. *Although Naim writes about "five wars of globalization," it is important to draw a connection between these wars and terrorist financing.*

Naim explains why governments cannot win the five wars of globalization:

- Criminal cartels can manipulate weak governments by corrupting politicians and police.
- International law, including embargoes, sanctions, and conventions, offer criminals opportunities to profit from illegal goods.
- Al-Qaida members are stateless and so are criminal networks involved in the five wars. Whereas terrorists and other criminals can seek refuge in and take advantage of porous borders, traditional notions of sovereignty frustrate governments.
- These wars pit governments against market forces. Thousands of independent, stateless organizations are motivated by large profits gained by exploiting international price differentials, unsatisfied demand, or the cost advantages resulting from theft (i.e., no cost to produce the product).

Continued

Reality Check: The Big Picture of Global Wars—Cont'd

- These wars pit bureaucracies against networks. The same network that smuggles illegal drugs may be involved in counterfeit watches that are sold on the streets of Manhattan by illegal immigrants. Highly decentralized networks can act swiftly and flexibly, while often lacking a headquarters and central leadership to be targeted. Governments often meet the challenge by forming task forces or creating new bureaucracies.

  Naim claims that governments may never be able to completely eliminate the international trade from the five wars, but they can and should do better. He offers four areas capable of producing ideas to meet the challenges from these wars.

- Negotiate more flexible notions of sovereignty. Because stateless networks regularly violate laws and cross borders to trade illegally, nations should develop agreements to "manage" sovereignty to combat criminal networks.
- Naim calls for stronger multilateral institutions (e.g., multinational police efforts such as Interpol). However, nations do not trust each other, some assume that criminals have infiltrated the police agencies of other countries, and today's allies may become tomorrow's enemies.
- The five wars render obsolete many institutions, legal frameworks, military doctrines, weapons systems, and law enforcement techniques that have been applied for numerous years. Rethinking and adaptation are needed to develop, for instance, new concepts of war "fronts" defined by geography and new functions for intelligence agents, soldiers, and enforcement officers.
- In all five wars, government agencies battle networks motivated by profits created by other government agencies that create an imbalance between demand and supply that makes prices rise and profits skyrocket. Because beating market forces is next to impossible, reality may force governments, in certain illegal markets, to change from repressing the markets to regulating them. Also, creating market incentives may be better than creating bureaucracies to curb the excesses of markets. In certain instances, technology can possibly be used to replace government policies (e.g., encryption to protect software on CDs).

CRITICAL THINKING:

Compare and contrast the war against terrorism with the "five wars of globalization."

ANTICIPATING THE USE OF WMD

Terrorists will continue to use weapons of mass destruction in the future. Chapter 2 explains past attacks involving WMD. It is impossible to predict the type of WMD that will be used by terrorists in the next attack, what delivery system will be employed, the target, and the date. The WMD threat is compounded by the creativity, long-term planning, and patience of terrorists, plus numerous soft targets.

An unclassified Central Intelligence Agency (2003a) report noted that al-Qaida's end goal is to use WMD to cause mass casualties. However, the report added that "most attacks" by this group and other extremists would likely be small scale, using crude delivery methods and easily produced or obtained chemicals, toxins, or radiological substances. The report goes on to state that the number of casualties from an attack would depend on many factors and most scenarios could cause panic and disruption. Of concern in this report is reference to "most attacks," which leaves the door open to one or more attacks that could possibly be horrendous.

SOURCES OF WMD

Opinions differ as to the source of WMD that will be used in the next attack. Much has been stated about the accountability of WMD in the former Soviet Union that became 15 independent states containing thousands of nuclear weapons, vast quantities of chemical and biological materials, and thousands of missiles. Although Russia worked to secure its own WMD arsenals, it was also responsible for WMD in other states. Efforts by the Russian and U.S. governments brought nuclear weapons to Russia for storage and disposal. However, various reports point to the possibility of missing WMD. In 2003, a leading Ukrainian politician stated that only 2200 of the 2400 warheads in the Ukrainian territory were transferred at the time of the Soviet disintegration, and the fate of the other 200 is unknown. The Russian government was also having problems accounting for part of its own arsenals. Media reports out of Germany and Finland reported that organized crime groups were trying to sell warheads. Chechen separatists are also believed to possess WMD, but the types of WMD they possess are difficult to ascertain. This group tipped off the media to a lead container at a Moscow park that contained radioactive cesium-137. The U.S. Departments of Energy and Defense, and other U.S. government agencies, have spent billions of dollars on nuclear security programs, otherwise known as the **Nunn-Lugar program** (see Chapter 3), in the former Soviet Union (Saradzhyan, 2005).

Although the nuclear arsenals of the former Soviet Union present a serious threat, a broader picture of sources of WMD should be considered. This includes not only nuclear weapons, but also radiological, chemical, and biological weapons. We know from Chapter 2 that radiological material, a major component of a dirty bomb, is used in many industries and is widely available. Waterman (2005) notes that the knowledge and skill set required to build WMD have become more and more dispersed. Also, rogue states such as Iran and North Korea have developed their own WMD.

According to Risk Management Solutions (RMS) (2003: 7), terrorist obstacles to obtaining WMD are twofold. First, specialized materials and equipment are required. Radiological weapons require radioactive source material, biological weapons need initial cultures, and chemical weapons require special ingredients. Second, knowledge and skill are prerequisites to producing successful weapons, and al-Qaida is recruiting scientists to fill this need. RMS experts estimate that it could take between 9 months to 3 years for a technical team to become an effective unit. They claim that U.S. intelligence analysts believe authorities will be lucky to interdict these preparations and that a WMD attack has a high probability of occurring soon.

RMS may have been shortsighted in its explanation of terrorist access to WMD. For instance, Strohm (2005) refers to an EPA report in June of 2005 that about 600 U.S. chemical facilities could each impact over 100,000 people from a "worst-case" attack and about 2200 other facilities could each threaten 10,000 to 100,000 residents. The report noted that the risk of terrorists using chemicals or attacking a chemical facility is low, but the risk is increasing. The report added that terrorist expertise is no longer a limiting factor in chemical weapon development because terrorists affiliate loosely with others possessing scientific skills, the level of higher education is rising worldwide, and the Internet has facilitated communications, training, and cooperation on a global scale.

The Central Intelligence Agency (2003a) sees a wide range of industrial chemicals that are not as toxic as cyanide, mustard, or nerve agents, but can be used in much larger quantities to compensate for their lower toxicity. The CIA reported that chlorine and phosgene are transported in multiton shipments by road and rail and rupturing the container can release these gases that are similar to the effects of mustard agents. Pesticides were also mentioned and referred to as being in the same chemical class as nerve agents.

The Canadian Security Intelligence Service (1995) reported on the ease of producing chemical agents. For example, it refers to one of the deadliest chemicals known, VX nerve gas, that can be produced with books from the local library and no special materials or knowledge. Also, crude World War I-era poison gases can be made from common commercial ingredients or items from around the home. Several authors warn of the hazards of amateurs manufacturing chemical agents and that some instructions are even published with deliberate errors in quantity, temperature, or process to cause serious problems. The Canadian Security Intelligence Service (1995) concludes their report with numerous authors who view chemical, rather than biological or nuclear, as the most likely WMD that will be used by terrorists in the future.

In an unclassified Central Intelligence Agency (2003b) report, entitled *The Darker Bioweapons Future*, a panel of life science experts revealed that advances in biotechnology, coupled with the difficulty in detecting nefarious agents, have created a more dangerous biological warfare threat than in the past. The panel's comments are summarized next. This threat has grown more serious because of a knowledge explosion in the life sciences based on improved insight of genes and how they work. The same science applied to our worst diseases could be directed toward producing engineered biological agents with frightening capabilities. The wave front of knowledge in this area will be so broad, complex, and widely available to the public that traditional means of monitoring WMD development could prove inadequate. Because the processes, techniques, equipment, and know how for agents are dual use, it will be difficult to distinguish between legitimate and nefarious development. This contrasts with detecting nuclear weapons that have surveillance and detection "observables," such as highly enriched uranium or obvious production equipment. Unconventional pathogens that may be developed include binary agents that only become effective when two components are combined (e.g., a mild pathogen combined with its antidote becomes highly infectious); "designer" agents that are antibiotic resistant or evade immune response; gene agents that change a victim's genetic makeup; or a "stealth" virus triggered at a later time. The diversity of agents creates a broad range of attack scenarios and difficulty and lag time in developing effective biodefense. To counter the bioweapons threat, more specific human intelligence is necessary, coupled with a closer working relationship between the intelligence and the biological sciences communities. Another strategy is government–life sciences community cooperation in developing "standards and norms" to expose nefarious research and development of biological agents.

WILL TERRORISTS CONTINUE TO USE WMD?

Martin (2003: 250) explains that the **new terrorism** differs from previous models because "it is characterized by vaguely articulated political objectives, indiscriminate attacks, attempts to achieve maximum psychological and social disruption, and the potential use of weapons of mass destruction."

Stern (1999: 70) offers some reasons why terrorists would use high-yield weapons.

- Attracting attention to the movement. A high body count gets attention.
- Pleasing God, such as killing those whose beliefs differ, or to hasten the apocalypse.
- Damaging economies. For example, doctoring with food or other consumer products.
- Influencing enemies. Mass casualties may result in a loss of confidence in a government and consideration of terrorist grievances by the citizenry.

Here are additional points from the Democratic Members of the House Select Committee on Homeland Security (2004).

- There are hundreds of tons of unsecured nuclear, chemical, and biological weapons and materials worldwide. Securing them is critical.
- Although the largest stock of unsecured nuclear material is in Russia and some of its former republics, the problem extends beyond these geographic areas. Nuclear materials exist at 130 civilian research facilities in 40 countries and security is often inadequate.
- The United States, the former Soviet Union, and sites worldwide contain dangerous pathogens and the expertise to use them.
- The anthrax attacks of 2001 provide an example of how bioterrorism can be used to murder, spread fear, and paralyze infrastructure. Serious gaps in protection still remain.

Although the topic of whether nations will use WMD internally or externally in the future is not considered here, the anticipated use of WMD by terrorists is based on the following reasons.

- WMD have been used in the past by nations against external enemies (United States against Japan during World War II) and internal enemies (Iraq against the Kurds). These facts can help terrorists rationalize their use of WMD.
- The "war on terror" is not a conventional war and the rules of engagement facilitate innovation on both sides of the conflict.
- The use of WMD is a viable option for terrorists, especially when limited or no progress is being made on grievances.
- Terrorist groups possess various degrees of fanaticism and those groups possessing extreme fanaticism may be more likely to use WMD.
- Because of the war on terror, nations are seeking to distance themselves from terrorists to avoid being labeled as a state sponsor of terrorism. Consequently, terrorists may be under less restraint. Their acquisition of WMD may become much more secretive, leading to more difficulties for authorities seeking to prevent and investigate such cases.
- The collapse of the Soviet Union, and the black market, creates a climate for profiteers willing to sell WMD.
- Mideast terrorists' background, logic, political perspectives, religion, values, sense of justice, and views are so different from Westerners that limited progress on issues may lead to frustration on both sides and escalating violence. Although each side may label the other as irrational, the truth of the matter is that each side *is* rational.
- The enormous success of the 9/11 attacks and the Tokyo subway attack show that determined terrorists, who are patient and capable of long-term planning, can execute successful WMD attacks.
- With the war on terror focused heavily on Mideast terrorists, non-Mideast terrorists (e.g., domestic; South American narcoterrorists) may opt to execute surprise WMD attacks.
- Certain WMD can result in consequences abhorrent or unanticipated by terrorists. Use of a biological weapon can spread disease to one's own group. A nuclear weapon can cause excessive death and destruction and lay waste a geographic area for several years. Because nuclear weapons are typically under a high level of security and require significant resources and expertise to produce, terrorists may opt for loosely controlled radiological materials or choose those chemical weapons that are easiest to procure or produce and deliver.

The United Nations, Office on Drugs and Crime (n.d.) offers the following reasons why terrorists may be reluctant to use WMD.

- Fear of using unfamiliar weapons, including possible harm to user.
- Fear that it would not work or work too well.
- Fear of alienating constituencies and supporters on moral grounds.
- Fear of strong government response and retaliation.
- Lack of need for indiscriminate, high-casualty attacks for the goals of the terrorist group.
- Lack of funds to procure WMD.

Palfy (2003) researched the question as to why those terrorists seeking to produce high casualties continue to employ conventional weapons rather than WMD? He found that terrorists seeking to cause high casualties prefer conventional weapons and that terrorists focusing on causing fear, panic, and general disruption, regardless of casualties, may be more tempted to use WMD.

Laqueur (2003: 155–156) offers his views of terrorist use of WMD.

- Numerous technical problems are inherent in the production, manufacture, storage, and delivery of nuclear, radioactive, biological, and chemical WMD.
- A nuclear device is more complicated to produce than obtaining radioactive material to make a "dirty bomb."
- Terrorists are less likely to use nuclear devices than chemical agents, and least likely to use biological weapons.
- Terrorists may refrain from using WMD if their traditional weapons are successful. However, what if, after years of struggle with limited success, a last desperate attempt to reach their goals is made by using a WMD?

CRITICAL THINKING:

What are your views of terrorist use of WMD in the future?

PREDICTING USE OF WMD

Paltin (2003: 41–68) writes of predictive behavior patterns of not only violent offenders and genocidal murderers, but also terrorists and rogue leaders who use chemical and biological weapons (CW/BW). He notes that profiling may be helpful for capability analysis and early identification of offenders, but it lacks the advantage of predicting the sequence and construction of a CW/BW terrorist attack. Paltin (2003: 46) writes that "capability analyses combine scientific data on chemical and biological weapons properties with intelligence about the characteristics, size, and organizational level of potential weapons users."

Paltin applies the **lethal violence sequence** (LVS) to understand common behavioral patterns that precede and follow the use of CW/BW. The LVS consists of group baseline, preconflict, lethal violence, and recovery. Paltin examined data from lethal incidents and uses the LVS as a model for understanding common behavior patterns.

1. *Measuring the group baseline.* This is the beginning point of the LVS for terrorists or rogue states. It seeks information on the number of prior violent acts that targeted the general population, detailed planning, accusations of actively seeking CW/BW, use of CW/BW, responsibility for mass casualties, attacks without warning, and involvement in ethnic purges or genocide followed by official denial or hiding of evidence.
2. *Preconflict phase.* The first step in this phase is the acquisition of CW/BW technology and materials, which may occur long before the group decides to use CW/BW in an attack. Paltin (2003: 54) writes that germ spores, such as anthrax, and chemical elements, such as fertilizers, are available from underground and "legitimate" sources. This phase is also characterized by efforts to acquire multiple types of CW/BW, establishment of a "research program" so group members can become familiar with weapons and use, bargaining with the opposition (e.g., a religious or ethnic group or government) for demands (e.g., elections, freeing political prisoners), selection of a target (e.g., ethnic or religious group), and rehearsal and drills.
3. *Lethal violence phase.* Factors that may trigger a CW/BW attack are failure of negotiations, a significant anniversary for the offender or victim (e.g., death of a political prisoner; national holiday), or the availability of victims/target. This phase includes no warning to victims, simultaneous (favored by terrorist cells) or wide time frame (Iran–Iraq war) attacks, hiding evidence of the attack by perpetrators (e.g., mass graves), mass casualties, and horrible physical and mental health problems for surviving victims.

4. *Recovery phase.* This phase involves denial by the perpetrators even though evidence exists to the contrary. State perpetrators are especially prone to deny CW/BW attacks. The motivation for denial is to prevent retaliation. There is a return to earlier phases to renegotiate political issues, reduce global sanctions if instituted, confront international organizations seeking an investigation, and when criticism has abated, seek additional weapons.

Paltin (2003) writes of the following noteworthy points.

- Earlier research of individual factors that contribute to prediction models analyzed behavior of regimes involved in weapons stockpiling.
- It was once thought that terrorist attacks involving CW/BW required a skilled, team effort to implement a sophisticated plan. The anthrax attack in the United States in 2001 changed such thinking.
- Sponsorship by a country increases the potential of a CW/BW attack. Covert transfers of CW/BW weapons may take the form of "agricultural" or "medical" supplies to provide an opportunity for the sponsor to deny involvement.
- Large terrorists groups may have more than one LVS at the same time and each LVS may be at a different phase of the sequence. Also, each LVS may involve a different type of weapon. Al-Qaida's innovative attack of 9/11 resulted in a military response from the United States that disrupted its CW/BW LVS.

Paltin (2003: 62–65) offers recommendations for intervening in the CW/BW LVS. He favors multidimensional participation of individual citizens, national leaders, multinational corporations, and world councils. Law enforcement should learn to identify the phases of the LVS, associated behaviors, and interventions for each phase. Industries and governments should monitor export sales of items related to CW/BW.

TECHNOLOGY

TECHNOLOGIES TO COUNTER TERRORISM

Carafano (2005) supports a proactive approach to technological innovation to meet the challenges of terrorism. He calls for technologies that go beyond evolving dangers and changing tactics of terrorists. He writes that we need to get ahead of terrorists and develop "overmatching" security systems that protect people, safeguard liberties, and do not hinder travel and commerce. To accomplish these goals, Carafano argues for clear requirements, prioritizing needs, establishing cooperative means for the development of technologies, and building human and financial capital. The criteria offered by Carafano for selecting the most promising technological investments are (1) seeking technologies that build a true national system covering a broad spectrum of challenges from intelligence and early warning to counterterrorism and response; (2) adopting cost-effective technologies that provide the most security for the investment and address a broad spectrum of threats; and (3) developing "breakthrough" technologies that stop the cycle of innovation of counterterrorism and terrorism (i.e., each side responding to the other's new methods) and place terrorists in a position whereby they can no longer compete.

CRITICAL THINKING:

Do you think "breakthrough" technologies can stop terrorists? Explain your answer.

Carafano sees six technologies offering the greatest promise for combating terrorism.

1. *System integration technologies.* This approach is often called "network-centric" operations and consists of increasing operational effectiveness at all levels of the public and private sectors by networking important information, sensors, decision makers, and first responders to increase efficiency, safety, and security. The technologies include IT systems that permit the sharing of data, integrate disparate databases, and link various communication systems.
2. *Biometrics.* These technologies are used for verification or identification. They have become increasingly important since the 9/11 attacks, especially for visa and immigration documentation and government-issued ID cards. (See Chapter 9.)
3. *Nonlethal weapons.* When civilians and terrorists are together, safety of civilians is a serious concern. Nonlethal weapons can incapacitate terrorists and their materiel while minimizing civilian casualties and property damage. Examples include malodorants, antitraction materials, high-power microwave for stopping vehicles, and nonpenetrating munitions.
4. *Data mining and link analysis technologies.* The trail of terrorists is typically combined with the general population in the form of a massive amount of bills, license applications, telephone records, etc. Traditional law enforcement begins with a suspect and then information is obtained on the individual. Data mining is a technology that analyzes historical and current online data to develop patterns and anomalies. Whereas data mining focuses on anomalies, link analysis seeks commonalties (e.g., relationships among people and organizations).
5. *Nanotechnology.* Although this technology is in its infancy, it involves developing materials and systems at the atomic, molecular, or macromolecular levels. It enables the creation of devices from the atom up, rather than having to shrink materials. The applications are very broad and include nanoscale electronics that reduce the size of computer circuits, biomedical nanostructures that interact with people for targeted drug delivery, and high temperature protective materials. Coleman (2003) writes about the applications for homeland security. He anticipates microscopic self-powered reconnaissance and surveillance devices, high-sensitivity sensors for biological and chemical detection, nanofabrics applied to building materials to absorb bomb blasts, and micropower-generating devices, among other advances.
6. *Directed-energy weapons.* These technologies include lasers and microwave radiation emitters that deposit energy on a target to inflict casualties or damage equipment. Whereas conventional weapons rely on the kinetic or chemical energy of a projectile, directed-energy weapons strike a target with subatomic particles or electromagnetic waves that travel at about the speed of light.

Businessweek ("The State Of Surveillance," 2005) notes that each advance in protection against terrorism results in more intrusion into the privacy of ordinary people and they do not seem to mind. *Businessweek* envisions a host of advances in surveillance as described next. Smart cameras that identify people at a distance by their gait or the shape of their ears. A sensor that analyzes the sweat, body odor, and skin flakes in the human thermal plume (i.e., the halo that surrounds each person). Sensors that recognize faint traces of explosives on a pedestrian. Tiny sensors floating in a drinking water reservoir that detect deadly microbes and signal an alarm. Radio-frequency identification tags implanted under people's skin to broadcast their ID and medical data. (Some people have had this done.) Superscanners that can be tuned to receive images from another person's computer. *Businessweek* claims that many technologies are presently "too green;" it may take years before a terrorist can be picked out of a crowd by a camera, or a network of sensors blanketing a city can accurately detect WMD. "For now, only a combination of electronic monitoring and human intelligence stands a chance of holding radicals at bay."

Geospacial information systems (GIS) are becoming increasingly helpful to authorities responsible for preventing, detecting, and responding to terrorism and other hazards. The future of GIS is promising. It has come a long way from paper and basic computer maps. The old wall-mounted pin map identified trouble spots (e.g., crimes) though color-coded pins. GIS identify the location and characteristics of natural features, buildings, and boundaries on earth. GIS consist of computer-based tools that perform a variety of functions, including the creation of a pin map or three-dimensional map, viewing of data related to geographic features, querying, analyzing information, and performing statistical functions. GIS offer numerous uses for homeland security, such as assisting with risk management, pinpointing locations vulnerable to attack, and planning and executing a response to an attack or disaster. GIS were employed following the 9/11 attacks in New York City to assess damage and to aid in the recovery. With thousands of miles of borders to protect, plus ports, and many other high-risk targets, GIS offer another strategy to watch and protect these locations. Geospatial data, when linked with intelligence and other data, provide helpful input to the DHS for command, control, and situational awareness.

The trend for the present and future is fusing information with geographic references. This includes a convergence of GIS with data mining and link analysis technologies. Philpott (2004: 47) offers an example:

> ... the threat could be an inbound ship suspected of carrying materials used in bio-chemical production while other locations might be sites in the United States where radio messages to the ship have been intercepted. The ship can be tracked and detained when it makes port and those people in contact with it can be kept under surveillance and then rounded up. As a result, a terrorist attack has been averted and a terrorist cell eliminated.

The DOD has consistently led efforts to develop new technologies for the war fighter and the battles against terrorism. The 9/11 attacks and the wars in Iraq and Afghanistan have led to innovative technologies such as the phraselator (a paperback-book-sized device containing computer chips that act as a translator of many languages), the water purification pen, improved body armor, a redesign of armored vehicles to deflect roadside bombs, the thermobaric bomb (to blast caves in Afghanistan), improved unmanned aerial vehicles, and improved countermortar radar systems. Also, we read earlier of Carafano's anticipation of directed-energy weapons, improved nonlethal weapons, and the potential of nanotechnology.

Similar to the military, public police benefit from new technologies. Public police can expect improvements in body armor, protection against WMD, nonlethal weapons, surveillance equipment, communications systems, and information accessible "from the street." A growing number of police officers will have instant access to vast databases via handheld wireless devices. This is coupled with improvements in street-level digital fingerprint technology that will facilitate widespread use of devices to enable police to verify the identification and identity presented by subjects when stopped. "Smart cruisers" will also be more widespread. Because police must perform so many functions while driving, what may seem as a simple car stop entails action to activate emergency lights, siren, and camera while ascertaining location coordinates to communicate to dispatch via the radio. "Smart cruisers" include voice recognition to automatically perform a variety of functions, rather than the officer, for example, picking up the radio or typing requests into a computer. Information received from a request can be projected on the windshield so the officer can avoid another distraction (i.e., looking at a computer) while driving (Associated Press, 2003).

IT security constantly battles adversaries and seeks new technology. Hofmeyr (2004: 244–246) writes that to improve IT security, we must shift from traditional approaches to security that are knowledge intensive and requiring expertise and control at all stages of the process. The shift should be to automated systems that learn and react independently to counter attacks.

Hofmeyr refers to the human immune system to explain that it secures the human body against numerous, ever-changing threats autonomously with no centralized control and no human input. Hofmeyr realizes that we are some distance from implementing such an approach for IT systems, but we can learn from the immune system. The immune system is self-learning and adaptive and this is called **autodidactic**. It "learns to distinguish self (the body) from nonself (everything else)." Although a scientific challenge, future IT security systems will "learn to distinguish between acceptable (legitimate) behavior and unacceptable (illegitimate) behavior." Hofmeyr notes that "the trick is determining how to define what constitutes acceptable behavior." Looking to the immune system again, Hofmeyr writes that the body uses peptides (short protein fragments) to provide a stable basis for the definition of self (acceptable behavior). He sees other key properties of the immune system that scientists should emulate for IT systems.

CRITICAL THINKING:

Many ideas are being advanced to combat terrorism. One idea calls for installing sensors in all portable electronic devices (e.g., cell phones) to detect and report WMD, by radio frequency, to achieve decentralized surveillance (Page, 2005: 11). What are your views of this idea?

USE OF TECHNOLOGY BY TERRORISTS

Technology is a double-edged sword—it is applied against terrorists and applied by terrorists. Any technology has the potential of being exploited by terrorists as well as other criminals. Terrorists use vehicles, cell phones, surveillance equipment, computers, the Internet, explosives, and WMD. Furthermore, terrorists are creative in their use of technology. An example is the successful 9/11 attacks, whereby commercial passenger jets, loaded with fuel, were used like missiles with devastating results.

Multimedia technology has been a tremendous asset to al-Qaida propaganda efforts. This includes videotapes, audiotapes, CD-ROMs, DVDs, and the Internet. The messages are communicated for motivational and recruitment value while promoting the virtues of martyrdom. Three basic themes are that the West is hostile to Islam, the only way to address the threat and the only language the West understands is the logic of violence, and *jihad* is the only option (Hoffman, 2003: 435).

As the Taliban were displaced by U.S. forces in Afghanistan in 2001, al-Qaida training camps were destroyed. However, fixed sanctuaries have not disappeared and terrorist cells operate globally. At the same time, *al-Qaida became the first terrorist movement in history to migrate from physical space to cyberspace* (Coll and Glasser, 2005: A1). The laptop computer is supplementing the AK-47 as essential terrorist equipment. In secret hideouts and at Internet cafes, al-Qaida members are using computers to advance their cause, preach, recruit, train, and communicate. Attackers in Iraq and elsewhere routinely use the Internet to train and to plan bombings. Al-Qaida and its loosely affiliated groups have published a huge training library on the Web that provides guidance on planning attacks, surveillance, constructing bombs, preparing poison, how to infiltrate through a border, and how to shoot at U.S. soldiers.

When Professor Gabriel Weimann of the University of Haifa in Israel began to track terrorist-related Web sites in 1997, he found 12. Eight years later he was tracking over 4500 sites (Coll and Glasser, 2005: A16). Terrorists have found that they are safer when working on the Internet and they change their methods as they are being pursued. Because fixed Internet sites have become vulnerable, terrorists have turned to sites that offer free upload services for file storage, bulletin boards, chat rooms, and the use of encryption.

Mark Rasch, former head of the U.S. Department of Justice's computer crime unit, warns that terrorist groups, such as al-Qaida, and foreign governments are seeking to hire hackers to access federal government and commercial IT systems to commit sabotage or to steal information. He claims that a massive cyber attack on our infrastructure would hinder services, but not inspire terror. Rasch sees recruitment being conducted via chat rooms, anonymous outsourcing, and anonymous remailers that hide the original source of the message. His protection strategies include disaster recovery and business continuity technology, redundant systems, and exchange of information (Tsuruoka, 2005).

The terrorist bombings in London during 2005 illustrate how terrorists apply technology and how technology can also be a source of investigative leads for authorities. Following the bombings, investigators gained evidence on the movement and training of suspects through cell phones and computers. Suspects even tried to mislead authorities by changing the electronic chip in cell phones. One suspect admitted using Internet tutorials to learn methods of making bombs. Terrorists are known to plan attacks and explain techniques on a Web page that is set up and taken down in a few hours before investigators can discover and trace the Web page (Harrington, 2005: A7). Loy (2006) reported that a Web site purportedly connected to al-Qaida called for jihadists in the United States, Canada, or Mexico to form four- or five-member cells to shoot "piercing bullets" or plant explosives at the Alaska oil pipeline and Valdez tanker dock. The author of the Web site argued that by targeting U.S. energy sources globally, the economy of the "American devils" could be brought down. The Web site provided 10 pages of detailed maps, links, and other information about the pipeline. It noted that, in 2001, a bullet hole in the pipeline caused a loss of 300,000 gallons of crude oil and that the pipeline is largely above ground and close to a highway. [The perpetrator of this crime was sentenced to 16 years in state prison.]

RESEARCH AND HIGHER EDUCATION

RESEARCH

Universities have two primary missions: research and teaching. Two types of research are basic and applied. **Basic research** seeks an improved understanding of a subject and the research results may have no practical use. **Applied research** seeks a solution to a problem and the research results can be applied quickly. Applied research is more common because of its practical implications (e.g., business, health, homeland security, defense). However, basic research can provide a foundation for applied research. For example, basic research on toxic substances provides a foundation for applied research on medical and emergency responses to chemical attacks. Universities have been actively fulfilling the applied research needs of homeland security and defense, besides conducting basic research. Funding for university research for homeland security and defense is provided by federal departments (e.g., DHS, DOD) and agencies (e.g., CIA, EPA) and also the private sector and state governments.

The DHS is involved in numerous research initiatives through its office of science and technology. The DHS partners with other government agencies, universities, and industry to find and develop innovative ideas. A major area of focus is protection against catastrophic terrorism that could result in large-scale loss of life and major economic harm.

Homeland Security Presidential Directive-7 (HSPD-7) calls for a national critical infrastructure protection research and development (R&D) plan. *The National Plan for Research and Development in Support of Critical Infrastructure Protection* (The Executive Office of the President, Office of Science and Technology Policy and The Department of Homeland Security Science and Technology Directorate, 2004) is essentially a road map for investment and protection that integrates cyber, physical, and human elements. This R&D plan was developed in coordination with the *National Infrastructure Protection Plan* (see Chapter 10). The R&D plan consists of science and technology themes as a way of organizing and pursuing advances and breakthroughs for critical infrastructure protection (CIP). These themes are summarized next.

Theme 1. Detection and sensor systems. A **national common operating picture** (COP) for CI assists in learning status, condition, needs, concerns, actions, and behaviors of all assets and participants. This theme includes protection and sensors to detect intruders to physical and cyber CI and the presence of WMD.

Theme 2. Protection and prevention. Security and safety measures to protect physical and cyber CI from a host of threats (e.g., explosives, directed energy weapons, fire, WMD).

Theme 3. Entry and access portals. This theme includes physical and cyber access controls for CI, plus access controls at borders, ports, and other important locations.

Theme 4. Insider threats. A major objective of this theme is to develop systems to detect rogue behavior in a trusted resource or anticipate their threat to CI.

Theme 5. Analysis and decision support systems. This theme focuses on risk management, modeling, simulation, IT, and other tools to aid responders and leaders in emergency management decisions.

Theme 6. Response, recovery, and reconstruction. This theme involves emergency management before, during, and following a serious event.

Theme 7. New and emerging threats and vulnerabilities. The focus of this theme is to anticipate the next generation of threats, such as new explosives, innovative cyber attacks, and nano-delivery methods of WMD.

Theme 8. Advanced infrastructure architectures and systems design. This theme includes COP systems to provide automated responses for CI protection and next-generation security for the Internet. An all hazards protection approach is an essential part of this theme.

Theme 9. Human and social issues. This theme addresses a host of social and economic issues, including anticipating the reactions and actions of victims of a serious event, economic results of attacks and disasters, public and private sector interaction, and computer and human interaction.

One avenue to facilitate quality in the development of new technologies is through standards. The DHS, for example, works to develop and approve standards that help public safety agencies select equipment and tools (e.g., radios, protective equipment, and procedures) that are effective and reliable. The DHS is assisted by the **American National Standards Institute's Homeland Security Standards Panel** (ANSI-HSSP). Its mission is to promote, accelerate, and coordinate the development of standards to meet DHS needs and communicate standards to the public and private sectors.

Through the **Homeland Security Act of 2002**, Congress mandated the DHS to enhance U.S. leadership in science and technology aimed at homeland security issues. This goal is supported through DHS funding of undergraduate and graduate fellowships and scholarships and establishing **DHS Centers of Excellence** (HS-centers). HS-centers (i.e., universities) are overseen by the office of university programs within the science and technology directorate and are designed to create learning and research environments that bring together experts who focus on numerous topics, including WMD, risk analysis related to the economic consequences of terrorism, and the behavioral aspects of terrorism and its consequences. Here is a list of HS-centers and their research activities.

- In 2003, the University of Southern California (partnering with the University of Wisconsin at Madison, New York University, North Carolina State University, Carnegie Mellon University, Cornell University, and others) was awarded $12 million over 3 years to house the first HS-center, known as the Homeland Security Center for Risk and Economic Analysis of Terrorism Events (CREATE). This HS-center focuses on the study of risk analysis related to the economic consequences of terrorist threats and events.

- In 2004, Texas A&M University and its partners were awarded $18 million over 3 years for the Homeland Security National Center for Foreign Animal and Zoonotic Disease Defense. Texas A&M University assembled a team of experts from across the country, including partnerships with the University of Texas Medical Branch, University of California at Davis, University of Southern California, and University of Maryland. This HS-center works closely with partners in academia, industry, and government to address potential threats to animal agriculture, including foot and mouth disease, Rift Valley fever, avian influenza, and brucellosis. The research on foot and mouth disease is carried out in close collaboration with Homeland Security's Plum Island Animal Disease Center.

- In 2004, the University of Minnesota and its partners were awarded $15 million over 3 years for the Homeland Security Center for Food Protection and Defense, which addresses agrosecurity issues related to postharvest food protection. This HS-center includes partnerships with major food companies, as well as other universities, including Michigan State University, University of Wisconsin at Madison, North Dakota State University, Georgia Institute of Technology, Rutgers University, Harvard University, University of Tennessee, Cornell University, Purdue University, and North Carolina State University.

- In 2005, the University of Maryland and its major partners, the University of California at Los Angeles, the University of Colorado, the Monterey Institute of International Studies, the University of Pennsylvania, and the University of South Carolina, were awarded $12 million over 3 years for the Homeland Security Center of Excellence for Behavioral and Social Research on Terrorism and Counter-Terrorism. This HS-center addresses a set of broad, challenging questions on the causes of terrorism and strategies to counter terrorism, developing the tools necessary to improve our understanding of, and response to, the magnitude of the threat, examining the psychological impact of terrorism on society, and strengthening the population's resilience in the face of terrorism.

- In 2005, Michigan State University was awarded $10 million over 5 years to house the Center for Advancing Microbial Risk Assessment, funded jointly by the DHS and the EPA. The purpose is to provide policy makers and first responders with the information they need to protect human life from biological threats and to set decontamination goals by focusing on two primary objectives. The first objective is a technical mission to develop models, tools, and information that can be used to reduce or eliminate health impacts from the deliberate indoor or outdoor use of biological agents. The second objective is a knowledge management mission to build a national network for information transfer about microbial risk assessment among universities, professionals, and communities.

- In 2005, Johns Hopkins University and its partners were awarded $15 million over 3 years for the Center for the Study of High Consequence Event Preparedness and Response. This HS-center studies deterrence, prevention, preparedness, and response, including issues such as risk assessment, decision making, infrastructure integrity, surge capacity, and sensor networks. It also studies interactions of networks and the need to use models and simulations.

Larger sources of research on homeland security issues are the over 700 federally funded research and development laboratories and centers throughout the United States. These sites include federal laboratories, college and university laboratories, and private industry laboratories. In addition to the DHS, other federal agencies involved in homeland security research include the Departments of Health and Human Services, Defense, and Agriculture. Each year billions of dollars support homeland security R&D. The DHS is using grants and contracts to secure R&D projects, and under the Homeland Security Act of 2002, it may enlist the services of any federal laboratory as needed. Because the DHS must deal with WMD, three major national federal laboratories are assisting the DHS. They are the Lawrence Livermore, Los Alamos, and Sandia National Laboratories. Examples of other laboratories assisting the DHS include Brookhaven National Lab on Long Island, New York, that is researching, for example, a variety of WMD sensors, and the U.S. Navy's Office of Naval Research that is studying, for example, a robotic snake for examining damaged spaces too confining for humans to search (White, 2004: 17–25).

HIGHER EDUCATION

Since the 9/11 attacks, hundreds of new academic and training programs have been implemented. Universities, 4-year colleges, and 2-year colleges have increased their offerings of degree programs, certificates, and courses in homeland security (HS), emergency management (EM), and related disciples. Other sources of education and training include proprietary schools, corporations, government agencies, unions, and associations. Despite an increase in education and training programs relevant to HS, there is no consensus of what constitutes a common body of knowledge to establish HS as an academic discipline. Furthermore, course content in this field of study varies among institutions and training programs. HS in higher education is being developed in a wide variety of academic disciplines and focusing on various audiences and needs. Part of the problem is that the DHS is continuously developing its mission under changing circumstances and events. Also, public and private sectors are trying to determine what knowledge and skills are required for HS. In addition, perspectives on HS differ among specialists. As examples, first responders maintain an interest in protection against WMD attacks, IT specialists view protection against cyber attacks as a high priority, and engineers may study building construction to resist bomb blasts. Furthermore, the study of HS involves many issues involving numerous disciplines, including agriculture, architecture, business, computer science, criminal justice, engineering, fire protection, history, international relations, law, military science, politics, public health and medicine, religion, risk management, the sciences, and security, among other fields of study.

Academic programs in EM have a longer history than academic programs in HS, yet both are evolving at an erratic pace with no uniformity, while being influenced by catastrophic events followed by government action. Phillips (2003), an EM educator, provides insight applicable to the development of not only EM, but also HS. She asks: "Is emergency management a discipline? Or a multidisciplinary endeavor? Or a truly interdisciplinary field, integrated into something greater than the sum of its parts?" In contemplating the future of EM, Phillips draws on the development of other fields, such as public administration, criminal justice, and women's studies. She refers to four development phases.

1. Independent programs develop.
2. Programs move into the "mainstream" driven by curriculum transformation projects.
3. "Difficult dialogues" erupt over key questions.
4. Programs are infused by new ideas and directions (e.g., graduate programs, internationalization, links to new disciplines).

Phillips offers the following topics commonly found within disciplines and reflecting core issues often found in accreditation.

- Naming the field.
- Defining the field.
- Concepts. What are the key concepts and definitions? What is the core curriculum and does it serve both student and employer needs?

- What is the history of the field?
- Theory. What are the theories, paradigms, and philosophies of the field?
- Methods. Which methods should be taught to students?
- Practice. What are the roles and relationships between educators and practitioners?
- Student outcomes assessment. What types of recruitment and retention work best with students? What are the demographic backgrounds of students? What do graduates do with their new education? What are employer views of graduates?
- Faculty roles. What are the roles of faculty? How can faculty be evaluated?

Darlington (n.d.) writes the following on her:

> What the nation currently has is not a vision of needs, but rather a reactionary mix of courses that have been assembled to respond to specific laws aimed at specific hazards and specific responses. Curriculums are not holistic, but an accumulation of topics related to hazards and disasters. We need to harness this misdirected energy in a new direction. Leadership is needed with a vision of how to link theory and performance based training within a core curriculum of emergency management education.

Marks (2004: 3) adds to the unsettled questions surrounding EM and HS academic programs. He writes:

> Since Sept. 11, the higher education offerings for emergency management have morphed to include the now household term, "homeland security." In fact, DHS, seeing the phenomenal success of Dr. Blanchard's Higher Education Project at FEMA, has replicated that office to create homeland security textbooks and courses. Some see "terrorism," and "homeland security" as pushing aside traditional emergency management issues. It will be the educators who either stop or foster this trend.

McEntire (2004: 8), in discussing competing theoretical perspectives in EM, writes:

> Homeland security is a step back from the proactive approaches being recommended today, and it de-emphasizes all hazards other than terrorism. Waugh points out that "even within the Homeland Security apparatus, minimal attention is being paid to matters beyond prevention of terrorism-related disasters, as [former] Secretary Ridge himself has stated" [Waugh, 2004: 11]. This rivalry among divergent and incomplete paradigms has created confusion for a discipline that so desperately needs both inclusion and direction.

The many issues of HS were discussed and debated at the 2005 ASIS Academic-Practitioner Symposium, whose attendees worked to enhance education and research in the discipline of security. David Gilmore, a security practitioner and educator who chairs the annual event, expressed the sentiment of most participants that the concept of HS is not clearly defined and its meaning varies (Davidson, 2005: 74). Dr. Wayne Blanchard, who hopes to make EM a legitimate academic discipline, spoke at the symposium. He noted that most EM academic programs are oriented toward the public sector, but the private sector is larger, and perhaps academia should offer more programs on preventing and responding to emergencies in the private sector. He was asked how HS differs from EM. "Dr. Blanchard observed that since EM covers all hazards, all actors, and all phases, a program dealing only with terrorist threats would not be considered an EM program. However, such distinctions and definitions change over time. The work done by FEMA used to be called civil defense, then emergency management, and perhaps one day might be called homeland security" (ASIS International, 2005: 23).

Over several years, a HS body of knowledge and standardization of curricula will evolve to strengthen HS as an academic discipline. At the same time, diverse academic departments will continue to clash as decisions are made as to which department will house HS. EM has been going through such an evolutionary process for a longer period of time and it will continue. Although a major source of direction for HS education and training is the **National Strategy for Homeland**

Security (see Chapter 4 under "critical mission areas"), future events, challenges, legislation, and government policy will shape curriculum design.

CRITICAL THINKING:

Do you think research, higher education, and training are meeting the needs of homeland security? What can be done to more precisely fulfill the needs?

DISCUSSION QUESTIONS

1. Although we cannot accurately predict when and where terrorists will attack, what can be done to anticipate and prepare for attacks?
2. Do you think terrorism will increase or decrease in the near future?
3. Of the various types of WMD, which one do you think will be used next by terrorists?
4. Which technologies do you think hold the most promise to counter terrorism?
5. What can be done by authorities to reduce the use of technology by terrorists?
6. What two topics should be at the top of the list for research pertaining to the war against terrorism?
7. Would you seek a degree in homeland security? Why or why not?

WEB SITES

ASIS International: www.asisonline.org

Central Intelligence Agency: www.cia.gov

Department of Homeland Security, Research & Technology: www.dhs.gov FEMA (link to higher education): www.training.fema.gov/emiweb/cgi-shl/college/display_by_degree.cfm?degree=28

FEMA Emergency Management Institute: http://www.training.fema.gov/emiweb/edu/

National Academic Consortium for Homeland Security: http://homelandsecurity.osu.edu/NACHS/index.html

The Homeland Security/Defense Education Consortium: www.hsdec.org

World Future Society: www.wfs.org

NOTES

ASIS International (2005). "Proceedings of the 2005 Academic/Practitioner Symposium." Alexandria, VA: ASIS International.

Associated Press (2003). "Police cruisers go high-tech." October 26.

Canadian Security Intelligence Service (1995). "Chemical and Biological Terrorism: The Threat According to the Open Literature" (November 1). www.csis-scrs.gc.ca/eng/miscdocs/tebintr_e.html, retrieved August 15, 2005.

Carafano, J. (2005). "The Future of Anti-Terrorism Technologies" (June 6). www.heritage.org/Research/HomelandDefense/h1885.cfm, retrieved August 11, 2005.

Central Intelligence Agency (2003a). *Terrorist CBRN: Materials and Effects* (May). www.cia.gov/cia/reports/terrorist_cbrn/CBRN_threat.pdf, retrieved August 15, 2005.

Central Intelligence Agency (2003b). *The Darker Bioweapons Future* (November 3). www.securitymanagement.com, retrieved January 16, 2004.

Coleman, K. (2003). "NanoTechnology and the Fight Against Terrorism." *Direction Magazine* (June 11). www.directionsmag.com, retrieved October 1, 2004.

Coll, S., and Glasser, S. (2005). "Terrorists Turn to the Web as Base of Operations." *The Washington Post* (August 7).

Cornish, E. (2003). "The wild cards in our future: Anticipating wild cards—unexpected, life-changing events–is important in preparing for the future and coping with surprise." *The Futurist,* 37 (July–August).

Cragin, K., and Daly, S. (2004). *The Dynamic Terrorist Threat: An Assessment of Group Motivations and Capabilities in a Changing World.* Santa Monica, CA: RAND Corp.

Darlington, J. (n.d.). "The Profession of Emergency Management: Educational Opportunities and Gaps." www.training.fema.gov/EMIWeb/edu/highpapers.asp, retrieved February 14, 2006.

Davidson, M. (2005). "A Matter of Degrees." *Security Management,* 49 (December).

Democratic Members of the House Select Committee on Homeland Security (2004). *America at Risk: Closing the Security Gap* (February). www.house.gov/hsc/democrats/, retrieved July 27, 2004.

Harrington, M. (2005). "Leaving a trail of tech." *Newsday* (August 2).

Hoffman, B. (2003). "Al Qaida, Trends in Terrorism, and Future Potentialities: An Assessment." *Studies in Conflict & Terrorism,* 26.

Hofmeyr, S. (2004). "Can IT Defenses Work Like the Body's?" *Security Management,* 48 (September).

Israel, S. (2005). "In Search of New Solutions for a New Type of War." *Homeland Security,* 2 (March/April).

Laqueur, W. (2003). "Postmodern Terrorism." In C. Kegley (Ed.), *The New Global Terrorism: Characteristics, Causes, Controls.* Upper Saddle River, NJ: Prentice-Hall.

Lloyd, B. (2002). "Terrorism, Today and Tomorrow." *World Future Society Home Page.* www.wfs.org/eslloyd.htm, retrieved August 11, 2005.

Loy, W. (2006). "Web post urges jihadists to attack Alaska pipeline." *Anchorage Daily News* (January 19). www.and.com/front/v-printer/story/7371578p-7283808c.html, retrieved January 20, 2006.

Marks, C. (2004). "Eye on Education." *IAEM Bulletin,* 21 (May). www.training.fema.gov/EMIWeb/edu/highpapers.asp, retrieved February 14, 2006.

Martin, G. (2003). *Understanding Terrorism: Challenges, Perspectives, and Issues.* Thousand Oaks, CA: Sage.

McEntire, D. (2004). "The Status of Emergency Management Theory: Issues, Barriers, and Recommendations for Improved Scholarship." Paper presented at the FEMA Higher Education Conference, Emmitsburg, MD, June 8. www.training.fema.gov/EMIWeb/edu/highpapers.asp, retrieved February 14, 2006.

Naim, M. (2003). "The Five Wars of Globalization." *Foreign Policy* (January/February).

Page, D. (2005). "Think tank attempts to remove terror from terrorism." *Homeland Protection Professional,* 4 (May).

Palfy, A. (2003). "Weapon System Selection and Mass-Casualty Outcomes." *Terrorism and Political Violence,* 15 (June).

Paltin, D. (2003). "Chemical and Biological Violence: Predictive Patterns in State and Terrorist Behavior." In Harold Hall (Ed.), *Terrorism: Strategies for Intervention.* Binghamton, NY: The Haworth Press.

Petersen, J. (2002). "The Future of Terrorism." *World Future Society Home Page.* www.wfs.org/petersen.htm, retrieved August 11, 2005.

Phillips, B. (2003). "Disasters by Discipline: Necessary Dialogue for Emergency Management Education." A presentation made at the workshop "Creating Educational Opportunities for the Hazards Manager of the 21st Century." Denver, Colorado, October 22. www.training.fema.gov/EMIWeb/edu/highpapers.asp, retrieved February 14, 2006.

Philpott, D. (2004). "Geospacial Information Systems: The New Frontier." *Homeland Defense Journal,* 2 (September).

Risk Management Solutions (2003). *Managing Terrorism Risk in 2004.* www.rms.com, retrieved August 13, 2004.

Saradzhyan, S. (2005). "Nuclear Accounting in the Age of Terror." *Homeland Defense Journal,* 3 (June).

Stern, J. (1999). "The Ultimate Terrorist." In G. Martin, *Understanding Terrorism: Challenges, Perspectives, and Issues.* Cambridge, MA: Harvard University Press.

Strohm, C. (2005). "Report cites increased risk of terrorist attack using chemicals" (August 10). *GOVEXEC.* www.govexec.com/story-page.cfm?articleid=31976&dcn=e_hsw, retrieved August 18, 2005.

The Executive Office of the President, Office of Science and Technology Policy and the Department of Homeland Security Science and Technology Directorate (2004). *The National Plan for Research and Development in Support of Critical Infrastructure Protection.* www.dhs.gov, retrieved June 13, 2005.

"The State of Surveillance" (2005). www.businessweek.com/magaznie/content/05-32/b3946001_mz001.htm, retrieved August 8, 2005.

Tsuruoka, D. (2005). "Al-Qaida Recruiting Target: Skilled Hackers." *Inventor's Business Daily* (August 19).

United Nations, Office on Drugs and Crime (n.d.). *Why Terrorists Have Not Used Weapons of Mass Destruction.* www.unodc.org/unodc/terrorism, retrieved April 21, 2004. [Note: Terrorists have used WMD. The UN list offers reasons why terrorists may be reluctant to use WMD.]

Waterman, S. (2005). "Motive, Means and Opportunity: Where do the Terrorists Stand?" *Homeland Defense Journal,* 3 (June).

Waugh, W. (2004). "The All-Hazards Approach Must Be Continued." *Journal of Emergency Management,* 2. In D. McEntire, "The Status of Emergency Management Theory: Issues, Barriers, and Recommendations for Improved Scholarship."

White, C. (2004). "Mining a National Treasure: Federal Laboratories in Homeland Security." *Homeland Defense Journal,* 2 (July).

Glossaries

Source: Federal Emergency Management Agency (2003). *Insurance, Finance, and Regulation Primer for Terrorism Risk Management in Buildings* (FEMA 429) http://www.fema.gov/fima/rmsp429.shtm and U.S. Department of Homeland Security (2004). *National Incident Management System* (March 1) www.fema.gov/pdf/nims.nims_appendix.pdf. Terms and definitions from the NIMS are noted with an asterisk.

GENERAL GLOSSARY

Access controls   Procedures and controls that limit or detect access to minimum essential infrastructure resource elements (people, technology, applications, data and/or facilities), thereby protecting these resources against loss of integrity, confidentiality accountability, and/or availability.

Accountability   The explicit assignment of responsibilities for oversight of areas of control to executives, managers, staff, owners, providers, and users of minimum essential infrastructure resource elements.

Acoustic eavesdropping   The use of listening devices to monitor voice communications or other audibly transmitted information with the objective to compromise information.

Active vehicle barrier   An impediment placed at an access control point that may be deployed manually or automatically in response to detection of a threat.

Aerosol   Fine liquid or solid particles suspended in a gas, e.g., fog or smoke.

Aggressor   Any person seeking to compromise a function or structure.

Airborne contamination   Chemical or biological agents introduced into and fouling the source of supply breathing or conditioning air.

Airlock   A building entry configuration with which airflow from the outside can be prevented from entering a toxic-free area. An airlock uses two doors, only one of which can be opened at a time, and a blower system to maintain positive air pressures and purge contaminated air from the airlock before the second door is opened.

Alarm assessment   Verification and evaluation of an alarm alert through the use of closed circuit television or human observation. Systems used for alarm assessment are designed to respond rapidly, automatically, and predictably to the receipt of alarms at the security center.

Alarm priority   A hierarchy of alarms by order of importance. This is often used in larger systems to give priority to alarm with greater importance.

Annunciation   A visual, audible, or other indication by a security system of a condition.

Antiterrorism   Defensive measures used to reduce the vulnerability of individuals, forces, and property to terrorist acts.

Area command*   (unified area command) An organization established (1) to oversee the management of multiple incidents that are each being handled by an ICS organization or (2) to oversee the management of large or multiple incidents to which several incident management teams have been assigned. Area command has the responsibility to set overall strategy and priorities, allocate critical resources according to priorities, ensure that incidents are managed properly, and ensure that objectives are met and strategies followed. Area command becomes unified area command when incidents are multijurisdictional. Area command may be established at an emergency operations center facility or at some location other than an incident command post.

Area commander   A military commander with authority in a specific geographical area or military installation.

Areas of potential compromise   Categories where losses can occur that will impact either a department or agency's minimum essential infrastructure and its ability to conduct core functions and activities.

Assessment   The evaluation and interpretation of measurements and other information to provide a basis for decision making.

Assessment system elements   Detection measures used to assist guards in visual verification of intrusion detection system alarms and access control system functions and to assist in visual detection by guards. Assessment system elements include closed-circuit television and protective lighting.

Asset   A resource of value requiring protection. An asset can be tangible, such as people, buildings, facilities, equipment, activities, operations, and information, or intangible, such as processes or a company's information and reputation.

Asset value The degree of debilitating impact that would be caused by the incapacity or destruction of an asset.

Audible alarm devices An alarm device that produces an audible announcement (bell, horn, siren, etc.) of an alarm condition.

Balanced magnetic switch A door position switch utilizing a reed switch held in a balanced or center position by interacting magnetic fields when not in alarm condition.

Ballistics attack Attack in which small arms (such as pistols, submachine guns, shotguns, and rifles) are fired from a distance and rely on the flight of the projectile to damage the target.

Bar code Black bars printed on white paper or tape that can be read easily with an optical scanner.

Biological agents Living organisms or the materials derived from them that cause disease in or harm to humans, animals, or plants or cause deterioration of material. Biological agents may be used as liquid droplets, aerosols, or dry powders.

Biometrics The use of physical characteristics of the human body as a unique identification method.

Biometric reader A device that gathers and analyzes biometric features.

Blast curtains Heavy curtains made of blast-resistant materials that could protect the occupants of a room from flying debris.

Blast-resistant glazing Window opening glazing that is resistant to blast effects because of the interrelated function of the frame and glazing material properties frequently dependent on tempered glass, polycarbonate, or laminated glazing.

Blast vulnerability envelope The geographical area in which an explosive device will cause damage to assets.

Bollard A vehicle barrier consisting of a cylinder, usually made of steel and sometimes filled with concrete, placed on end in the ground and spaced about 3 feet apart to prevent vehicles from passing, but allowing entrance of pedestrians and bicycles.

Boundary penetration sensors Interior intrusion detection sensors that detect an attempt by individuals to penetrate or enter a building.

Building hardening Enhanced construction that reduces vulnerability to external blast and ballistic attack.

Business continuity program An ongoing process supported by senior management and funded to ensure that the necessary steps are taken to identify the impact of potential losses, maintain viable recovery strategies and recovery plans, and ensure continuity services through personnel training, plan testing, and maintenance.

Cable barrier Cable or wire rope anchored to and suspended off the ground or attached to chain link fence to act as a barrier to moving vehicles.

Capacitance sensor A device that detects an intruder approaching or touching a metal object by sensing a change in capacitance between the object and the ground.

Card reader A device that gathers or reads information when a card is presented as an identification method.

Chain of command* A series of command, control, executive, or management positions in hierarchical order of authority.

Chimney effect Air movement in a building between floors caused by differential air temperature (differences in density), between the air inside and outside the building. It occurs in vertical shafts, such as elevator, stairwell, and conduit/wiring/piping chase. Hotter air inside the building will rise and be replaced by infiltration with colder outside air through the lower portions of the building. Conversely, reversing the temperature will reverse the flow (down the chimney). Also know as stack effect.

Chemical agent A chemical substance that is intended to kill, seriously injure, or incapacitate people through physiological effects. Generally separated by severity of effect: lethal, blister, and incapacitating.

Clear zone An area that is clear of visual obstructions and landscape materials that could conceal a threat or perpetrator.

Closed circuit television (CCTV) An electronic system of cameras, control equipment, recorders, and related apparatus used for surveillance or alarm assessment.

CCTV pan-tilt-zoom camera (PTZ) A CCTV camera that can move side to side, up and down, and zoom in or out.

CCTV pan-tilt-zoom control The method of controlling the PTZ functions of a camera.

CCTV switcher A piece of equipment capable of presenting any of multiple video images to various monitors, recorders, and so forth.

Collateral damage Injury or damage to assets that are not the primary target of an attack.

Components and cladding   Elements of the building envelope that do not qualify as part of the main wind-force resisting system.

Confidentiality   The protection of sensitive information from unauthorized disclosure and sensitive facilities from physical, technical, or electronic penetration or exploitation.

Consequence management   Measures to protect public health and safety, restore essential government services, and provide emergency relief to governments, businesses, and individuals affected by the consequences of terrorism. State and local governments exercise primary authority to respond to the consequences of terrorism.

Contamination   The undesirable deposition of a chemical, biological, or radiological material on the surface of structures, areas, objects, or people.

Continuity of services and operations   Controls to ensure that, when unexpected events occur, departmental/agency minimum essential infrastructure services and operations, including computer operations, continue without interruption or are promptly resumed and critical and sensitive date are protected through adequate contingency and business recovery plans and exercises.

Control center   A centrally located room or facility staffed by personnel charged with the oversight of specific situations and/or equipment.

Controlled lighting   Lighting illumination of specific areas or sections.

Controlled perimeter   A physical boundary at which vehicle and personnel access is controlled at the perimeter of a site. Access control at a controlled perimeter should demonstrate the capability to search individuals and vehicles.

Conventional construction   Building construction that is not specifically designed to resist weapons, explosives, or chemical, biological, and radiological effects. Conventional construction is designed only to resist common loadings and environmental effects such as wind, seismic, and snow loads.

Counterintelligence   Information gathered and activities conducted to protect against espionage, other intelligence activities, sabotage, or assassinations conducted for or on behalf of foreign powers, organizations, or persons; or international terrorist activities, excluding personnel, physical, document, and communications security programs.

Counterterrorism   Offensive measures taken to prevent, deter, and respond to terrorism.

Covert entry   Attempts to enter a facility by using false credentials or stealth.

Crash bar   A mechanical egress device located on the interior side of a door that unlocks the door when pressure is applied in the direction of egress.

Crime prevention through environmental design (CPTED)   A crime prevention strategy based on evidence that the design and form of the built environment can influence human behavior. CPTED usually involves the use of three principles: natural surveillance (by placing physical features, activities, and people to maximize visibility); natural access control (through the judicial placement of entrances, exits, fencing, landscaping, and lighting); and territorial reinforcement (using buildings, fences, pavement, signs, and landscaping to express ownership).

Crisis management   Measures taken to identify, acquire, and plan the use of resources needed to anticipate, prevent, and/or resolve a threat or act of terrorism.

Critical assets   Those assets essential to the minimum operations of the organization, and to ensure the health and safety of the general public.

Critical infrastructure   Primary infrastructure systems (utilities, telecommunications, transportation, etc.) whose incapacity would have a debilitating impact on the organization's ability to function.

Damage assessment   The process used to appraise or determine the number of injuries and deaths, damage to public and private property, and the status of key facilities and services such as hospitals and other health care facilities, fire and police stations, communications networks, water and sanitation systems, utilities, and transportation networks resulting from a man-made or natural disaster.

Data gathering panel   A local processing unit that retrieves, processes, stores, and/or acts on information in the field.

Data transmission equipment   A path for transmitting data between two or more components (such as a sensor and alarm reporting system, a card reader and controller, a CCTV camera and monitor, or a transmitter and receiver).

Decontamination   The reduction or removal of a chemical, biological, or radiological material from the surface of a structure, area, object, or person.

Defense layer   Building design or exterior perimeter barriers intended to delay attempted forced entry.

Defensive measures Protective measures that delay or prevent attack on an asset or that shield the asset from weapons, explosives, and CBR effects. Defensive measures include site work and building design.

Delay rating A measure of the effectiveness of penetration protection of a defense layer.

Design basis threat The threat (tactics, and associated weapons, tools, or explosives) against which assets within a building must be protected and upon which the security engineering design of the building is based.

Design team A group of individuals from various engineering and architectural disciplines responsible for the protective system design.

Detection layer A ring of intrusion detection sensors located on or adjacent to a defensive layer or between two defensive layers.

Detection measures Protective measures that detect intruders, weapons, or explosives; assist in assessing the validity of detection; control access to protected areas; and communicate the appropriate information to the response force. Detection measures include detection system, assessment system, and access control system elements.

Disaster An occurrence of a natural catastrophe, technological accident, or human-caused event that has resulted in severe property damage, deaths, and/or multiple injuries.

Disaster field office (DFO) The office established in or near the designated area of a presidentially declared major disaster to support federal and state response and recovery operations.

Disaster recovery center (DRC) Places established in the area of a presidentially declared major disaster, as soon as practicable, to provide victims the opportunity to apply in person for assistance and/or obtain information relating to that assistance.

Domestic terrorism The unlawful use, or threatened use, of force or violence by a group or individual based and operating entirely within the United States or Puerto Rico without foreign direction committed against persons or property to intimidate or coerce a government, the civilian population, or any segment thereof in furtherance of political or social objectives.

Door position switch A switch that changes state based on whether or not a door is closed. Typically, a switch mounted in a frame that is actuated by a magnet in a door.

Door strike, electronic An electromechanical lock that releases a door plunger to unlock the door. Typically, an electronic door strike is mounted in place of or near a normal door strike plate.

Dose rate (radiation) A general term indicating the quantity (total or accumulated) of ionizing radiation or energy absorbed by a person or animal per unit of time.

Dosimeter An instrument for measuring and registering total accumulated exposure to ionizing radiation.

Dual technology sensors Sensors that combine two different technologies in one unit.

Duress alarm devices Also known as panic buttons, these devices are designated specifically to initiate a panic alarm.

Effective standoff distance A standoff distance at which the required level of protection can be shown to be achieved through analysis or can be achieved through building hardening or other mitigating construction or retrofit.

Electromagnetic pulse (EMP) A sharp pulse of energy radiated instantaneously by a nuclear detonation that may affect or damage electronic components and equipment. EMP can also be generated in lesser intensity by nonnuclear means in specific frequency ranges to perform the same disruptive function.

Electronic emanations Electro-magnetic emissions from computers, communications, electronics, wiring, and related equipment.

Electronic-emanations eavesdropping Use of electronic-emanation surveillance equipment from outside a facility or its restricted area to monitor electronic emanations from computers, communications, and related equipment.

Electronic security system An integrated system that encompasses interior and exterior sensors, closed-circuit television systems for assessment of alarm conditions, electronic entry control systems, data transmission media, and alarm reporting systems for monitoring, control, and display of various alarm and system information.

Emergency Any natural or man-caused situation that results in or may result in substantial injury or harm to the population or substantial damage to or loss of property.

Emergency alert system A communications system of broadcast stations and interconnecting facilities authorized by the Federal Communication Commission. The system provides the president and other national, state, and local officials the means to broadcast emergency information to the public before, during, and after disasters.

Emergency environmental health services
Services required to correct or improve damaging environmental health effects on humans, including inspection for food contamination, inspection for water contamination, and vector control; providing for sewage and solid waste inspection and disposal; cleanup and disposal of hazardous materials; and sanitation inspection for emergency shelter facilities.

Emergency medical services Services including personnel, facilities, and equipment required to ensure proper medical care for the sick and injured from the time of injury to the time of final disposition, including medical disposition within a hospital, temporary medical facility, or special care facility, release from site, or declared dead. Further, emergency medical services specifically include those services immediately required to ensure proper medical care and specialized treatment for patients in a hospital and coordination of related hospital services.

Emergency mortuary services Services required to assure adequate death investigation, identification, and disposition of bodies; removal, temporary storage, and transportation of bodies to temporary morgue facilities; notification of next of kin; and coordination of mortuary services and burial of unclaimed bodies.

Emergency operations center The protected site from which state and local civil government officials coordinate, monitor, and direct emergency response activities during an emergency.

Emergency operations plan* The "steady-state" plan maintained by various jurisdictional levels for responding to a wide variety of potential hazards.

Emergency planning zones (EPZ) Areas around a facility for which planning is needed to ensure that prompt and effective actions are taken to protect the health and safety of the public if an accident or disaster occurs. In the radiological emergency preparedness program the two EPZ's are (1) **plume exposure pathway (10-mile EPZ)**, which is a circular geographic zone (with a 10-mile radius centered at the nuclear power plant) for which plans are developed to protect the public against exposure to radiation emanating from a radioactive plume caused as a result of an accident at the nuclear power plant, and (2) **ingestion pathway (50-mile EPZ)**, which is a circular geographic zone (with a 50-mile radius centered at the nuclear power plant) for which plans are developed to protect the public from the ingestion of water or food contaminated as a

result of a nuclear power plant accident. In the chemical stockpile emergency preparedness program (CSEPP), the EPZ is divided into three concentric circular zones: (1) **Immediate response zone (IRZ)**, which is a circular zone ranging from 10 to 15 kilometers (6 to 9 miles) from the potential chemical event source, depending on the stockpile location on-post. Emergency response plans developed for the IRZ must provide for the most rapid and effective protective actions possible, as the IRZ will have the highest concentration of agent and the least amount of warning time. (2) **Protective action zone (PAZ)** is an area that extends beyond the IRZ to approximately 16 to 50 kilometers (10 to 30 miles) from the stockpile location. The PAZ is that area where public protective actions may still be necessary in case of an accidental release of chemical agent, but where the available warning and response time is such that most people could evacuate. However, other responses (e.g., sheltering) may be appropriate for institutions and special populations that could not evacuate within the available time. (3) **Precautionary zone (PZ)** is the outermost portion of the EPZ for CSEPP, extending from the PAZ outer boundary to a distance where the risk of adverse impacts to humans is negligible. Because of the increased warning and response time available for implementation of response actions in the PZ, detailed local emergency planning is not required, although consequence management planning may be appropriate.

Emergency public information Information that is disseminated primarily in anticipation of an emergency or at the actual time of an emergency and, in addition to providing information, frequently directs actions, instructs, and transmits direct orders.

Emergency response team advance element (ERT-A) For federal disaster response and recovery activities under the Stafford Act, the portion of the ERT that is first deployed to the field to respond to a disaster incident. The ERT-A is the nucleus of the full ERT.

Emergency response team national (ERT-N) An ERT that has been established and rostered for deployment to catastrophic disasters where resources of the FEMA region have been, or are expected to be, overwhelmed. Three ERT-Ns have been established.

Emergency support function (ESF) In the federal response plan (FRP), a functional area of response activity established to facilitate the delivery of federal assistance required during the immediate response phase of a disaster to save lives, protect property and public health, and to maintain public safety. ESFs represent those types of federal assistance that the state will most likely need because of the impact of a catastrophic or significant disaster on its own resources and response capabilities or because of the specialized or unique nature of the assistance required. ESF missions are designed to supplement state and local response efforts.

Emergency support team (EST)   An interagency group operating from FEMA headquarters. The EST oversees the national-level response support effort under the FRP and coordinates activities with the ESF primary and support agencies in supporting federal requirements in the field.

Entity-wide security   Planning and management that provide a framework and continuing cycle of activity for managing risk, developing security policies, assigning responsibilities, and monitoring the adequacy of the entity's physical and cyber security controls.

Equipment closet   A room where field control equipment such as data-gathering panels and power supplies are typically located.

Evacuation, spontaneous   Residents or citizens in the threatened areas observe an emergency event or receive unofficial word of an actual or perceived threat and without receiving instructions to do so, elect to evacuate the area. Their movement, means, and direction of travel are unorganized and unsupervised.

Evacuation, voluntary   This is a warning to persons within a designated area that a threat to life and property exists or is likely to exist in the immediate future. Individuals issued this type of warning or order are *not* required to evacuate; however, it would be to their advantage to do so.

Evacuation, mandatory or directed   This is a warning to persons within the designated area that an imminent threat to life and property exists and individuals *must* evacuate in accordance with the instructions of local officials.

Exclusive zone   An area around an asset that has controlled entry with highly restrictive access.

Explosives disposal container   A small container into which small quantities of explosives may be placed to contain their blast pressures and fragments if the explosive detonates.

Facial recognition   A biometric technology that is based on features of the human face.

Federal coordinating officer   The person appointed by the FEMA director to coordinate federal assistance in a presidentially declared emergency or major disaster.

Federal on-scene commander   The FBI official designated upon joint operations center (JOC) activation to ensure appropriate coordination of the overall U.S. government response with federal, state, and local authorities until such time as the attorney general transfers the LFA role to FEMA.

Federal response plan (FRP)   The FRP establishes a process and structure for the systematic, coordinated, and effective delivery of federal assistance to address the consequences of any major disaster or emergency.

Fence sensors   Exterior intrusion detection sensors that detect aggressors as they attempt to climb over, cut through, or otherwise disturb a fence.

Fiber optics   A method of data transfer by passing bursts of light through a strand of glass or clear plastic.

Field of view   The visible area in a video picture.

First responder   Local police, fire, and emergency medical personnel who first arrive on the scene of an incident and take action to save lives, protect property, and meet basic human needs.

Forced entry   Entry to a denied area achieved through force to create an opening in fence, walls, doors, etc., or to overpower guards.

Fragment retention film   A thin, optically clear film applied to glass to minimize the spread of glass fragments when the glass is shattered.

Frame rate   In digital video, a measurement of the rate of change in a series of pictures, often measured in frames per second.

Frangible construction   Building components designed to fail to vent blast pressures from an enclosure in a controlled manner and direction.

Function*   Refers to the five major activities in ICS: command, operations, planning, logistics, and finance/administration. Function is also used when describing the activity involved, e.g., the planning function. A sixth function, intelligence, may be established, if required, to meet incident management needs.

Glare security lighting   Illumination projected from a secure perimeter into the surrounding area making it possible to see potential intruders at a considerable distance while making it difficult to observe activities within the secure perimeter.

Glass-break detector   Intrusion detection sensors that are designed to detect breaking glass through either vibration or acoustics.

Glazing   A material installed in a sash, ventilator, or panes such as glass, and plastic, including material such as thin granite installed in a curtain wall.

Governor's authorized representative   The person empowered by the governor to execute, on behalf of the state, all necessary documents for disaster assistance.

Grid wire sensors   Intrusion detection sensors that use a grid of wires to cover a wall or fence. An alarm is sounded if the wires are cut.

Hand geometry   A biometric technology based on characteristics of the human hand.

Hazard   A source of potential danger or adverse condition.

Hazard mitigation   Any action taken to reduce or eliminate the long-term risk to human life and property from hazards. The term is sometimes used in a stricter sense to mean cost-effective measures to reduce the potential for damage to a facility or facilities from a disaster event.

Hazardous material   Any substance or material that when involved in an accident and released insufficient quantities poses a risk to people's health, safety, and/or property. These substances and materials include explosives, radioactive materials, flammable liquids or solids, combustible liquids or solids, poisons, oxidizers, toxins, and corrosive materials.

High-hazard areas   Geographic locations that for planning purposes have been determined through historical experience and vulnerability analysis to be likely to experience the effects of a specific hazard (e.g., hurricane, earthquake, hazardous materials accident) resulting in vast property damage and loss of life.

High-risk target   Any material resource or facility that, because of mission sensitivity, ease of access, isolation, and symbolic value, may be an especially attractive or accessible terrorist target.

Human-caused hazard   Human-caused hazards are *technological hazards* and *terrorism*. These are distinct from natural hazards primarily in that they originate from human activity. Within the military services, the term *threat* is typically used for human-caused hazard.

Hurricane   A tropical cyclone, formed in the atmosphere over warm ocean areas, in which wind speeds reach 74 miles per hour or more and blow in a large spiral around a relatively calm center or "eye." Circulation is counterclockwise in the Northern Hemisphere and clockwise in the Southern Hemisphere.

Impact analysis   A management level analysis that identifies the impacts of losing the entity's resources. The analysis measures the effect of resource loss and escalating losses over time in order to provide the entity with reliable data upon which to base decisions on hazard mitigation and continuity planning.

Incident action plan*   An oral or written plan containing general objectives reflecting the overall strategy for managing an incident. It may include the identification of operational resources and assignments. It may also include attachments that provide direction and important information for management of the incident during one or more operational periods.

Incident command system (ICS)*   A standardized on-scene emergency management construct specifically designed to provide for the adoption of an integrated organizational structure that reflects the complexity and demands of single or multiple incidents, without being hindered by jurisdictional boundaries. ICS is a combination of facilities, equipment, personnel, procedures, and communications operating within a common organizational structure designed to aid in the management of resources during incidents. It is used for all kinds of emergencies and is applicable to small as well as large and complex incidents. ICS is used by various jurisdictions and functional agencies, both public and private, to organize field-level incident management operations.

Insider compromise   A person authorized to access a facility (an insider) compromises assets by taking advantage of that accessibility.

Intercom door/gate station   Part of an intercom system where communication is typically initiated, usually located at a door or gate.

International terrorism   Violent acts or acts dangerous to human life that are a violation of the criminal laws of the United States or any state or that would be a criminal violation if committed within the jurisdiction of the United States or any state. These acts appear to be intended to intimidate or coerce a civilian population, influence the policy of a government by intimidation or coercion, or affect the conduct of a government by assassination or kidnapping. International terrorist acts occur outside the United States or transcend national boundaries in terms of the means by which they are accomplished, the persons they appear intended to coerce or intimidate, or the locale in which their perpetrators operate or seek asylum.

Intrusion detection sensors   Devices that initiate alarm signals by sensing the stimulus, change, or condition for which they were designed.

Jersey barrier   A protective concrete barrier initially and still used as a highway divider and now functions as an expedient method for traffic speed control at entrance gates and to keep vehicles away from buildings.

Joint information center (JIC)   A central point of contact for all news media near the scene of a large-scale disaster. News media representatives are kept informed of activities and events by public information officials who represent all participating federal, state, and local agencies that are collocated at the JIC.

Joint interagency intelligence support element (JIISE)   An interagency intelligence component designed to fuse intelligence information from the various agencies participating in a response to a WMD threat or incident within an FBI JOC. The JIISE is an expanded version of the investigative/intelligence component, which is part of the standardized FBI command post structure. The JIISE manages five functions, including security, collections management, current intelligence, exploitation, and dissemination.

Joint information system (JIS)   Under the FRP, connection of public affairs personnel, decision makers, and news centers by electronic mail, fax, and telephone when a single federal/state/ local JIC is not a viable option.

Joint operations center   Established by the LFA under the operational control of the Federal OSC as the focal point for management and direction of on-site activities, coordination/establishment of state requirements/priorities, and coordination of the overall federal response.

Jurisdiction   Typically counties and cities within a state, but states may elect to define differently in order to facilitate their assessment process.

Laser card   A card technology that uses a laser reflected off of a card for uniquely identifying the card.

Layers of protection   A traditional approach in security engineering using concentric circles extending out from an area to be protected as demarcation points for different security strategies.

Lead federal agency (LFA)   The agency designated by the president to lead and coordinate the overall federal response is referred to as the LFA and is determined by the type of emergency.

In general, an LFA establishes operational structures and procedures to assemble and work with agencies providing direct support to the LFA in order to provide an initial assessment of the situation, develop an action plan, monitor and update operational priorities, and ensure that each agency exercises its concurrent and distinct authorities under U.S. law and supports the LFA in carrying out the president's relevant policy. Specific responsibilities of an LFA vary according to the agency's unique statutory authorities.

Liaison   An agency official sent to another agency to facilitate interagency communications and coordination.

Line of sight   Direct observation between two points with the naked eye or hand-held optics.

Line-of-sight sensor   A pair of devices used as an intrusion detection sensor that monitor any movement through the field between the sensors.

Line supervision   A data integrity strategy that monitors the communications link for connectivity and tampering. In intrusion detection system sensors, line supervision is often referred to as two-, three-, or four-state in respect to the number of conditions monitored. The frequency of sampling the link also plays a big part in the supervision of the line.

Local government   Any county, city, village, town, district, or political subdivision of any state, Indian tribe or authorized tribal organization, or Alaska Native village or organization, including any rural community or unincorporated town or village or any other public entity.

Logistics*   Providing resources and other services to support incident management. The logistics section is responsible for providing facilities, services, and material support for the incident.

Magnetic lock   An electromagnetic lock that unlocks a door when power is removed.

Magnetic stripe   A card technology that uses a magnetic stripe on the card to encode data used for unique identification of the card.

Mantrap   An access control strategy that uses a pair of interlocking doors to prevent tailgating. Only one door can be unlocked at a time.

Mass care   Actions that are taken to protect evacuees and other disaster victims from the effects of the disaster. Activities include providing temporary shelter, food, medical care, clothing, and other essential life support needs to those people that have been displaced from their homes because of a disaster or threatened disaster.

Mass notification   Capability to provide real-time information to all building occupants or personnel in the immediate vicinity of a building during emergency situations.

Microwave motion sensors   Intrusion detection sensors that use microwave energy to sense movement within the field of view of the sensor. These sensors work similar to radar by using the Doppler effect to measure a shift in frequency.

Minimum essential infrastructure resource elements   The broad categories of resources, all or portions of which constitute the minimal essential infrastructure necessary for a department, agency, or organization to conduct its core mission(s).

Minimum measures   Protective measures that can be applied to all buildings regardless of the identified threat. These measures offer defense or detection opportunities for minimal cost, facilitate future upgrades, and may deter acts of aggression.

Mitigation   Those actions taken to reduce the exposure to and impact of an attack or disaster.

Motion detector   Intrusion detection sensor that changes state based on movement in the sensors field of view.

Mutual-aid agreement*   Written agreement between agencies and/or jurisdictions that they will assist one another on request by furnishing personnel, equipment, and/or expertise in a specified manner.

National   Of a nationwide character, including the federal, state, local, and tribal aspects of governance and polity.

Natural hazard   Naturally occurring events such as floods, earthquakes, tornadoes, tsunami, coastal storms, landslides, and wildfires that strike populated areas. A natural event is a hazard when it has the potential to harm people or property (FEMA 386-2, *Understanding Your Risks*). The risks of natural hazards may be increased or decreased as a result of human activity. However, they are not inherently human induced.

Natural protective barriers   Natural protective barriers are mountains and deserts, cliffs and ditches, water obstacles, or other terrain features that are difficult to traverse.

Nonexclusive zone   An area around an asset that has controlled entry but shared or less restrictive access than an exclusive zone.

Nonpersistent agent   An agent that, upon release, loses its ability to cause casualties after 10 to 15 minutes. It has a high evaporation rate, is lighter than air, and will disperse rapidly. It is considered to be a short-term hazard; however, in small, unventilated areas, the agent will be more persistent.

Nuclear, biological, or chemical weapons   Also called weapons of mass destruction (WMD). Weapons that are characterized by their capability to produce mass casualties.

On-scene coordinator   The federal official predesignated by the EPA and U.S. Coast Guard to coordinate and direct response and removals under the national oil and hazardous substances pollution contingency plan.

Open system architecture   A term borrowed from the IT industry to claim that systems are capable of interfacing with other systems from any vendor, which also uses open system architecture. The opposite would be a proprietary system.

Operator interface   The part of a security management system that provides that user interface to humans.

Organizational areas of control   Controls consist of the policies, procedures, practices, and organization structures designed to provide reasonable assurance that business objectives will be achieved and that undesired events will be prevented or detected and corrected.

Passive infrared motion sensors   Devices that detect a change in the thermal energy pattern caused by a moving intruder and initiate an alarm when the change in energy satisfies the detector's alarm criteria.

Passive vehicle barrier   A vehicle barrier that is permanently deployed and does not require response to be effective.

Perimeter barrier   A fence, wall, vehicle barrier, landform, or line of vegetation applied along an exterior perimeter used to obscure vision, hinder personnel access, or hinder or prevent vehicle access.

Persistent agent   An agent that, upon release, retains its casualty-producing effects for an extended period of time, usually anywhere from 30 minutes to several days. A persistent agent usually has a low evaporation rate and its vapor is heavier than air; therefore, its vapor cloud tends to hug the ground. It is considered to be a long-term hazard. Although inhalation hazards are still a concern, extreme caution should be taken to avoid skin contact as well.

Physical security   The part of security concerned with measures/concepts designed to safeguard personnel; to prevent unauthorized access to equipment, installations, material, and documents; and to safeguard them against espionage, sabotage, damage, and theft.

Planter barrier   A passive vehicle barrier, usually constructed of concrete and filled with dirt (and flowers for aesthetics). Planters, along with bollards, are the usual street furniture used to keep vehicles away from existing buildings. Overall size and the depth of installation below grade determine the vehicle-stopping capability of the individual planter.

Plume   Airborne material spreading from a particular source; the dispersal of particles, gases, vapors, and aerosols into the atmosphere.

Polycarbonate glazing   A plastic glazing material with enhanced resistance to ballistics or blast effects.

Predetonation screen   A fence that causes an antitank round to detonate or prevents it from arming before it reaches its target.

Preliminary damage assessment (PDA)   A mechanism used to determine the impact and magnitude of damage and the resulting unmet needs of individuals, businesses, the public sector, and the community as a whole. Information collected is used by the state as a basis for the governor's request for a presidential declaration and by FEMA to document the recommendation made to the president in response to the governor's request. PDAs are made by at least one state and one federal representative. A local government representative familiar with the extent and location of damage in the community often participates; other state and federal agencies and voluntary relief organizations also may be asked to participate, as needed.

Preparedness   Establishing the plans, training, exercises, and resources necessary to enhance mitigation of and achieve readiness for response to and recovery from all hazards, disasters, and emergencies, including WMD incidents.

Pressure mat   A mat that generates an alarm when pressure is applied to any part of the mat's surface, as when someone steps on the mat. Pressure mats can be used to detect an intruder approaching a protected object or they can be placed by doors and windows to detect entry.

Primary asset   An asset that is the ultimate target for compromise by an aggressor.

Primary gathering building   Inhabited buildings routinely occupied by 50 or more personnel. This designation applies to the entire portion of a building that meets the population density requirements for an inhabited building.

Probability of detection   A measure of an intrusion detection sensor's performance in detecting an intruder within its detection zone.

Probability of intercept   The probability that an act of aggression will be detected and that a response force will intercept the aggressor before the asset can be compromised.

Progressive collapse   A chain reaction failure of building members to an extent disproportionate to the original localized damage. Such damage may result in upper floors of a building collapsing onto lower floors.

Protective barriers   Define the physical limits of a site, activity, or area by restricting, channeling, or impeding access and forming a continuous obstacle around the object.

Protective measures   Elements of a protective system that protect an asset against a threat. Protective measures are divided into defensive and detection measures.

Proximity sensors   Intrusion detection sensors that change state based on the close distance or contact of a human to the sensor. These sensors often measure the change in capacitance as a human body enters the measured field.

Public information officer   A federal, state, or local government official responsible for preparing and coordinating the dissemination of emergency public information.

Qualification and certification*   This subsystem provides recommended qualification and certification standards for emergency responders and incident management personnel. It also allows the development of minimum standards for resources expected to have an interstate application. Standards typically include training, currency, experience, and physical and medical fitness.

Radiation   High-energy particles or gamma rays that are emitted by an atom as the substance undergoes radioactive decay. Particles can be either charged alpha or beta particles or neutral neutron or gamma rays.

Radiation sickness   The symptoms characterizing the sickness known as radiation injury, resulting from excessive exposure of the whole body to ionizing radiation.

Radio frequency data transmission   A communication link using radio frequency to send or receive data.

Radiological monitoring   The process of locating and measuring radiation by means of survey instruments that can detect and measure (as exposure rates) ionizing radiation.

Recovery The long-term activities beyond the initial crisis period and emergency response phase of disaster operations that focus on returning all systems in the community to a normal status or to reconstitute these systems to a new condition that is less vulnerable.

Request-to-exit device Passive infrared motion sensors or push buttons that are used to signal an electronic entry system that egress is imminent or to unlock a door.

Resolution The level to which video details can be determined in a CCTV scene is referred to as resolving ability or resolution.

Resource management Those actions taken by a government to identify sources and obtain resources needed to support disaster response activities; coordinate the supply, allocation, distribution, and delivery of resources so that they arrive where and when most needed; and maintain accountability for the resources used.

Response Executing the plan and resources identified to perform those duties and services to preserve and protect life and property as well as provide services to the surviving population.

Response force The people who respond to an act of aggression. Depending on the nature of the threat, the response force could consist of guards, special reaction teams, military or civilian police, an explosives ordnance disposal team, or a fire department.

Response time The length of time from the instant an attack is detected to the instant a security force arrives onsite.

Retinal pattern A biometric technology that is based on features of the human eye.

Risk The potential for loss of, or damage to, an asset. It is measured based on the value of the asset in relation to the threats and vulnerabilities associated with it.

Rotating drum or rotating plate vehicle barrier An active vehicle barrier used at vehicle entrances to controlled areas based on a drum or plate rotating into the path of the vehicle when signaled.

Sacrificial roof or wall Walls or roofs that can be lost in a blast without damage to the primary asset.

Safe haven Secure areas within the interior of the facility. A safe haven should be designed such that it requires more time to penetrate by aggressors than it takes for the response force to reach the protected area to rescue the occupants. It may be a haven from a physical attack or air-isolated haven from WMD contamination.

Scramble keypad A keypad that uses keys on which the numbers change pattern with each use to enhance security by preventing eavesdropping observation of the entered numbers.

Secondary asset An asset that supports a primary asset and whose compromise would indirectly affect the operation of the primary asset.

Secondary hazard A threat whose potential would be realized as the result of a triggering event that of itself would constitute an emergency. For example, dam failure might be a secondary hazard associated with earthquakes.

Secure/access mode The state of an area monitored by an intrusion detection system regarding how alarm conditions are reported.

Security analysis The method of studying the nature of and the relationship among assets, threats, and vulnerabilities.

Security console Specialized furniture, racking, and related apparatus used to house the security equipment required in a control center.

Security engineering The process of identifying practical, risk-managed short- and long-term solutions to reduce and/or mitigate dynamic man-made hazards by integrating multiple factors, including construction, equipment, manpower, and procedures.

Security engineering design process The process through which assets requiring protection are identified, the threat to and vulnerability of those assets is determined, and a protective system is designed to protect the assets.

Security management system database In a security management system, a database that is transferred to various nodes or panels throughout the system for faster data processing and protection against communication link downtime.

Security management system distributed processing In a security management system, a method of data processing at various nodes or panels throughout the system for faster data processing and protection against communication link downtime.

Segregation of duties Policies, procedures, and an organizational structure established so that one individual cannot control key aspects of physical and/or computer-related operations and thereby conduct unauthorized actions or gain unauthorized access to minimum essential infrastructure resource elements.

Senior FEMA official The official appointed by the director of FEMA, or his representative, that is responsible for deploying to the JOC to

(1) serve as the senior interagency consequence management representative on the command group and (2) manage and coordinate activities taken by the consequence management group.

Shielded wire Wire with a conductive wrap used to mitigate electromagnetic emanations.

Situational crime prevention A crime prevention strategy based on reducing the opportunities for crime by increasing the effort required to commit a crime, increasing the risks associated with committing the crime, and reducing the target appeal or vulnerability (whether property or person). This opportunity reduction is achieved by management and uses policies such as procedures and training, as well as physical approaches, such as alteration of the built environment.

Smart card A newer card technology that allows data to be written, stored, and read on a card typically used for identification and/or access.

Software level integration An integration strategy that uses software to interface systems. An example of this would be digital video displayed in the same computer application window and linked to events of a security management system.

Span of control* The number of individuals a supervisor is responsible for, usually expressed as the ratio of supervisors to individuals. (Under the NIMS, an appropriate span of control is between 1:3 and 1:7.)

Specific threat Known or postulated aggressor activity focused on targeting a particular asset.

Staging area* Location established where resources could be placed while awaiting a tactical assignment. The operations section manages staging areas.

Standoff distance A distance maintained between a building or portion thereof and the potential location for an explosive detonation or other threat.

Standoff weapons Weapons such as antitank weapons and mortars that are launched from a distance at a target.

State coordinating officer The person appointed by the governor to coordinate state, commonwealth, or territorial response and recovery activities with FRP-related activities of the federal government, in cooperation with the FCO.

State liaison A FEMA official assigned to a particular state who handles initial coordination with the state in the early stages of an emergency.

Stationary vehicle bomb An explosive-laden car or truck stopped or parked near a building.

Storm surge A dome of seawater created by strong winds and low barometric pressure in a hurricane that causes severe coastal flooding as the hurricane strikes land.

Strain-sensitive cable Transducers that are uniformly sensitive along their entire length and generate an analog voltage when subject to mechanical distortions or stress resulting from fence motion. They are typically attached to a chain-link fence about halfway between the bottom and the top of the fence fabric with plastic ties.

Structural protective barriers Man-made devices (such as fences, walls, floors, roofs, grills, bars, roadblocks, signs, or other construction) used to restrict, channel, or impede access.

Superstructure The supporting elements of a building above the foundation.

Supplies-bomb delivery Bombs or incendiary devices concealed and delivered to supply or material handling points such as loading docks.

System events Events that occur normally in the operation of a security management system. Examples include access control operations and changes of state in intrusion detection sensors.

System software Controls that limit and monitor access to the powerful programs and sensitive files that (1) control the computer hardware and (2) secure applications supported by the system.

Tactics The specific methods of achieving the aggressor's goals to injure personnel, destroy assets, or steal material or information.

Tamper switch Intrusion detection sensor that monitors an equipment enclosure for breach.

Tangle-foot wire Barbed wire or tape suspended on short metal or wooden pickets outside a perimeter fence to create an obstacle to approach.

Taut-wire sensor An intrusion detection sensor utilizing a column of uniformly spaced horizontal wires, securely anchored at each end and stretched taut. Each wire is attached to a sensor to indicate movement of the wire.

Technical assistance The provisioning of direct assistance to states and local jurisdictions to improve capabilities for program development, planning, and operational performances related to responses to WMD terrorist incidents.

Technological hazard Incidents that can arise from human activities such as manufacture, transportation, storage, and use of hazardous materials. For the sake of simplicity, it is assumed that technological emergencies are accidental and that their consequences are unintended.

TEMPEST   An unclassified short name referring to investigations and studies of compromising emanations. It is sometimes used synonymously for the term "compromising emanations," e.g., TEMPEST tests, TEMPEST inspections.

Terrorism   The unlawful use of force and violence against persons or property to intimidate or coerce a government, the civilian population, or any segment thereof in furtherance of political or social objectives.

Thermally tempered glass   Glass that is heat treated to have a higher tensile strength and resistance to blast pressures, although a greater susceptibility to airborne debris.

Threat   Any indication, circumstance, or event with the potential to cause loss of or damage to an asset.

Threat analysis   A continual process of compiling and examining all available information concerning potential threats and human-caused hazards. A common method to evaluate terrorist groups is to review the factors of existence, capability, intentions, history, and targeting.

Time/date stamp   Data inserted into a CCTV video signal with the time and date of the video as it was created.

TNT equivalent weight   The weight of TNT (trinitrotoluene) that has an equivalent energetic output to that of a different weight of another explosive compound.

Tornado   A local atmospheric storm, generally of short duration, formed by winds rotating at very high speeds, usually in a counterclockwise direction. The vortex, up to several hundred yards wide, is visible to the observer as a whirlpool-like column of winds rotating about a hollow cavity or funnel. Winds may reach 300 miles per hour or higher.

Toxicity   A measure of the harmful effects produced by a given amount of a toxin on a living organism.

Toxic-free area   An area within a facility in which the air supply is free of toxic chemical or biological agents.

Triple-standard concertina wire   This type of fence uses three rolls of stacked concertina. One roll will be stacked on top of two rolls that run parallel to each other while resting on the ground, forming a pyramid.

Tsunami   Sea waves produced by an undersea earthquake. Such sea waves can reach a height of 80 feet and can devastate coastal cities and low-lying coastal areas.

Twisted pair wire   Wire that uses pairs of wires twisted together to mitigate electromagnetic interference.

Two-person rule   A security strategy that requires two people to be present in or gain access to a secured area to prevent unobserved access by any individual.

Unified area command*   A unified area command is established when incidents under an area command are multijurisdictional. (See area command.)

Unity of command*   The concept by which each person within an organization reports to one and only one designated person. The purpose of unity of command is to ensure unity of effort under one responsible commander for every objective.

Vault   A reinforced room for securing items.

Vertical rod   Typical door hardware often used with a crash bar to lock a door by inserting rods vertically from the door into the door frame.

Vibration sensors   Intrusion detection sensor that changes state when vibration is present.

Video intercom system   An intercom system that also incorporates a small CCTV system for verification.

Video motion detection   Motion detection technology that looks for changes in the pixels of a video image.

Video multiplexer   A device used to connect multiple video signals to a single location for viewing and/or recording.

Visual displays   A display or monitor used to inform the operator visually of the status of the electronic security system.

Visual surveillance   The aggressor uses ocular and photographic devices (such as binoculars and cameras with telephoto lenses) to monitor facility or installation operations or to see assets.

Voice recognition   A biometric technology that is based on nuances of the human voice.

Volumetric motion sensors   Interior intrusion detection sensors designed to sense aggressor motion within a protected space.

Vulnerability   Any weakness in an asset or mitigation measure than can be exploited by an aggressor (potential threat element), adversary, or competitor. It refers to the organization's susceptibility to injury.

Warning   The alerting of emergency response personnel and the public to the threat of extraordinary danger and the related effects that specific hazards may cause.

Watch   Indication in a defined area that conditions are favorable for the specified type of severe weather (e.g., flash flood watch, severe thunderstorm watch, tornado watch, tropical storm watch).

Waterborne contamination   Chemical, biological, or radiological agent introduced into and fouling a water supply.

Weapons-grade material   Nuclear material considered most suitable for a nuclear weapon. It usually connotes uranium enriched to above 90% uranium-235 or plutonium with greater than about 90% plutonium-239.

Weigand protocol   A security industry standard data protocol for card readers.

Zoom   The ability of a CCTV camera to close and focus or open and widen the field of view.

CHEMICAL, BIOLOGICAL, AND RADIOLOGICAL GLOSSARY

CHEMICAL TERMS

Acetylcholinesterase   An enzyme that hydrolyzes the neurotransmitter acetylcholine. The action of this enzyme is inhibited by nerve agents.

Atropine   A compound used as an antidote for nerve agents.

Blister agents   Substances that cause blistering of the skin. Exposure is through liquid or vapor contact with any exposed tissue (eyes, skin, lungs). Examples are distilled mustard (HD), nitrogen mustard (HN), lewisite (L), mustard/lewisite (HL), and phenodichloroarsine (PD).

Blood agents   Substances that injure a person by interfering with cell respiration (the exchange of oxygen and carbon dioxide between blood and tissues). Examples are arsine (SA), cyanogens chloride (CK), hydrogen chloride, and hydrogen cyanide (AC).

Casualty (toxic) agents   These produce incapacitation, serious injury, or death. They can be used to incapacitate or kill victims. These agents are the choking, blister, nerve, and blood agents.

Central nervous system depressants
Compounds that have the predominant effect of depressing or blocking the activity of the central nervous system. Primary mental effects include the disruption of the ability to think, sedation, and lack of motivation.

Central nervous system stimulants   Compounds that have the predominant effect of flooding the brain with too much information. The primary mental effect is loss of concentration, causing indecisiveness and the inability to act in a

sustained, purposeful manner. Examples of depressants and stimulants include agent 15 (suspected Iraqi BZ), BZ (3-quinulidinyle benzilate), canniboids, fentanyls, LSD (lysergic acid diethylamide), and phenothiazines.

Chemical agent   A chemical substance that is intended for use in military operations to kill, seriously injure, or incapacitate people through its physiological effects. Excluded from consideration are riot control agents and smoke and flame materials. The agent may appear as a vapor, aerosol, or liquid; it can be either a casualty/toxic agent or an incapacitating agent.

Choking/lung/pulmonary agents   Substances that cause physical injury to the lungs. Exposure is through inhalation. In extreme cases, membranes swell and lungs become filled with liquid. Death results from lack of oxygen; hence, the victim is "choked." Examples are chlorine (CL), diphosgene (DP), cyanide, nitrogen oxide (NO), perflourorisobutylene (PHIB), phosgene (CG), red phosphorous (RP), sulfur trioxide-chlorosulfonic acid (FS), Teflon and perfluororisobutylene (PHIB), titanium tetrachloride (FM), and zinc oxide (HC).

Cutaneous   Pertaining to the skin.

G-series nerve agents   Chemical agents of moderate to high toxicity developed in the 1930s. Examples are tabun (GA), sarin (GB), soman (GD), phosphonofluoridic acid, ethyl-1-methylethyl ester (GE), and cyclohexyl sarin (GF).

Incapacitating agents   These produce temporary physiological and/or mental effects via action on the central nervous system. Effects may persist for hours or days, but victims usually do not require medical treatment. However, such treatment speeds recovery.

Industrial agents   Chemicals developed or manufactured for use in industrial operations or research by industry, government, or academia. These chemicals are not primarily manufactured for the specific purpose of producing human casualties or rendering equipment, facilities, or areas dangerous for use by humans. Hydrogen cyanide, cyanogen chloride, phosgene, chloropicrin, and many herbicides and pesticides are industrial chemicals that also can be chemical agents.

Liquid agent   A chemical agent that appears to be an oily film or droplets. The color ranges from clear to brownish amber.

Nerve agents   Substances that interfere with the central nervous system. Exposure is primarily through contact with the liquid (skin and eyes) and secondarily through inhalation of the vapor. Three distinct symptoms associated with nerve agents are pin-point pupils, an extreme headache, and severe tightness in the chest. Also see G-series and V-series nerve agents.

Nonpersistent agent   An agent that upon release loses its ability to cause casualties after 10 to 15 minutes. It has a high evaporation rate, is lighter than air, and will disperse rapidly. It is considered to be a short-term hazard. However, in small unventilated areas, the agent will be more persistent.

Organophosphorous compound   A compound, containing the elements phosphorus and carbon, whose physiological effects include inhibition of acetylcholinesterase. Many pesticides (malathione and parathion) and virtually all nerve agents are organophosphorous compounds.

Percutaneous agent   Able to be absorbed by the body through the skin.

Protection   Any means by which an individual protects his body. Measures include masks, self-contained breathing apparatuses, clothing, structures such as buildings, and vehicles.

Tear (riot control) agents   These agents produce irritating or disabling effects that disappear rapidly within minutes after exposure ceases. Examples are bromobenzylcyanide (CA), chloroacetophenone (CN or commercially as Mace), chloropicrin (PS), CNB (CN in benzene and carbon tetrachloride), CNC (CN in chloroform), CNS (CN and chloropicrin in chloroform) CR (dibenz-(b,f)-1,4-oxazepine, a tear gas), CS (tear gas), and Capsaicin (pepper spray).

Vapor agent   A gaseous form of a chemical agent. If heavier than air, the cloud will be close to the ground. If lighter than air, the cloud will rise and disperse more quickly.

Volatility   A measure of how readily a substance will vaporize.

Vomiting agents   Substances that produce nausea and vomiting effects, can also cause coughing, sneezing, pain in the nose and throat, nasal discharge, and tears. Examples are adamsite (DM), diphenylchloroarsine (DA), and diphenylcyanoarsine (DC).

V-series nerve agents   Chemical agents of moderate to high toxicity developed in the 1950s. They are generally persistent. Examples are VE (phosphonothioic acid, ethyl-S-[2-(diethylamino)ethyl]-O-ethyl ester), VG (phosphorothioic acid, S-[2-(diethylamino)ethyl]-O,O-diethyl ester), VM (phosphonothioic acid, methyl-S-[2-(diethylamino)ethyl]-O-ethyl ester),

VS (phosphonothioic acid, ethyl-S-[2-[bis (1-methylethyl)amino]ethyl]-O-ethyl ester), and VX (phosphonothioic acid, methyl-S-[2-[bis (1-methylethyl)amino]ethyl]-O-ethyl ester).

BIOLOGICAL TERMS

Antibiotic   A substance that inhibits the growth of or kills microorganisms.

Antisera   The liquid part of blood containing antibodies that react against disease-causing agents such as those used in biological warfare.

Bacteria   Single-celled organisms that multiply by cell division and that can cause disease in humans, plants, or animals.

Biochemicals   Chemicals that make up or are produced by living things.

Biological warfare agents   Living organisms or the materials derived from them that cause disease in or harm to humans, animals, or plants or cause deterioration of material. Biological agents may be used as liquid droplets, aerosols, or dry powders.

Biological warfare   The intentional use of biological agents as weapons to kill or injure humans, animals, or plants or to damage equipment.

Bioregulators   Biochemicals that regulate bodily functions. Bioregulators produced by the body are termed "endogenous." Some of these same bioregulators can be synthesized chemically.

Causative agent   The organism or toxin responsible for causing a specific disease or harmful effect.

Contagious   Capable of being transmitted from one person to another.

Culture   A population of microorganisms grown in a medium.

Fungi   Any of a group of plants mainly characterized by the absence of chlorophyll, the green-colored compound found in other plants. Fungi range from microscopic single-celled plants (such as molds and mildews) to large plants (such as mushrooms).

Host   An animal or plant that harbors or nourishes another organism.

Incapacitating agent   Agents that produce physical or psychological effects, or both, that may persist for hours or days after exposure, rendering victims incapable of performing normal physical and mental tasks.

Infectious agents   Biological agents capable of causing disease in a susceptible host.

Infectivity   (1) The ability of an organism to spread. (2) The number of organisms required to cause an infection to secondary hosts. (3) The capability of an organism to spread out from the site of infection and cause disease in the host organism. Infectivity also can be viewed as the number of organisms required to cause an infection.

Line-source delivery system   A delivery system in which the biological agent is dispersed from a moving ground or air vehicle in a line perpendicular to the direction of the prevailing wind. (See also Point-source delivery system.)

Microorganism   Any organism, such as bacteria, viruses, and some fungi, that can be seen only with a microscope.

Mycotoxin   A toxin produced by fungi.

Nebulizer   A device for producing a fine spray or aerosol.

Organism   Any individual living thing, whether animal or plant.

Parasite   Any organism that lives in or on another organism without providing benefit in return.

Pathogen   Any organism (usually living) capable of producing serious disease or death, such as bacteria, fungi, and viruses.

Pathogenic agents   Biological agents capable of causing serious disease.

Point-source delivery system   A delivery system in which the biological agent is dispersed from a stationary position. This delivery method results in coverage over a smaller area than with the line-source system. (See also Line-source delivery system.)

Route of exposure (entry)   The path by which a person comes into contact with an agent or organism, e.g., through breathing, digestion, or skin contact.

Single-cell protein   Protein-rich material obtained from cultured algae, fungi, protein, and bacteria; often used as food or animal feed.

Spore   A reproductive form some microorganisms can take to become resistant to environmental conditions, such as extreme heat or cold, while in a "resting stage."

Vaccine   A preparation of killed or weakened microorganism products used to artificially induce immunity against a disease.

Vector   An agent, such as an insect or rat, capable of transferring a pathogen from one organism to another.

Venom   A poison produced in the glands of some animals, e.g., snakes, scorpions, or bees.

Virus   An infectious microorganism that exists as a particle rather than as a complete cell. Particle sizes range from 20 to 400 manometers (one-billionth of a meter). Viruses are not capable of reproducing outside of a host cell.

RADIOLOGICAL TERMS

Acute radiation syndrome   This consists of three levels of effects: hernatopoietic (blood cells, most sensitive); gastrointestinal (GI cells, very sensitive); and central nervous system (brain/muscle cells, insensitive). The initial signs and symptoms are nausea, vomiting, fatigue, and loss of appetite. Below about 200 rems, these symptoms may be the only indication of radiation exposure.

Alpha particle   The alpha particle has a very short range in air and a very low ability to penetrate other materials, but has a strong ability to ionize materials. Alpha particles are unable to penetrate even the thin layer of dead cells of human skin and consequently are not an external radiation hazard. Alpha-emitting nuclides inside the body as a result of inhalation or ingestion are a considerable internal radiation hazard.

Beta particles   High-energy electrons emitted from the nucleus of an atom during radioactive decay. They normally can be stopped by the skin or a very thin sheet of metal.

Cesium-137 (Cs-137)   A strong gamma ray source that can contaminate property, entailing extensive clean-up. It is commonly used in industrial measurement gauges and for irradiation of material. The half-life is 30.2 years.

Cobalt-60 (Co-60)   A strong gamma ray source that is used extensively as a radiotherapeutic for treating cancer, food and material irradiation, gamma radiography, and industrial measurement gauges. The half-life is 5.27 years.

Curie (Ci)   A unit of radioactive decay rate defined as 3.7×10^{10} disintegrations per second.

Decay   The process by which an unstable element is changed to another isotope or another element by the spontaneous emission of radiation from its nucleus. This process can be measured by using radiation detectors such as Geiger counters.

Dose   A general term for the amount of radiation absorbed over a period of time.

Gamma rays   High-energy photons emitted from the nucleus of atoms; similar to X-rays. They can penetrate deeply into body tissue and many materials. Cobalt-60 and cesium-137 are both strong gamma emitters. Shielding against gamma radiation requires thick layers of dense materials, such as lead. Gamma rays are potentially lethal to humans.

Half-life   The amount of time needed for half of the atoms of a radioactive material to decay.

Highly enriched uranium (HEU)   Uranium that is enriched to above 20% uranium-235 (U-235).

Weapons-grade HEU is enriched to above 90% in U-235.

Ionize   To split off one or more electrons from an atom, thus leaving it with a positive electric charge. The electrons usually attach to one of the atoms or molecules, giving them a negative charge.

Iridium-192   A gamma-ray emitting radioisotope used for gamma radiography. The half-life is 73.83 days.

Isotope   A specific element always has the same number of protons in the nucleus. That same element may, however, appear in forms that have different numbers of neutrons in the nucleus. These different forms are referred to as "isotopes" of the element. For example, deuterium (2H) and tritium (3H) are isotopes of ordinary hydrogen (H).

Lethal dose (50/30)   The dose of radiation expected to cause death within 30 days to 50% of those exposed without medical treatment. The generally accepted range is from 400 to 500 rem received over a short period of time.

Nuclear reactor   A device in which a controlled, self-sustaining nuclear chain reaction can be maintained with the use of cooling to remove generated heat.

Plutonium-239 (Pu-239)   A metallic element used for nuclear weapons. The half-life is 24,110 years.

Rad   A unit of absorbed dose of radiation defined as deposition of 100 ergs of energy per gram of tissue. A rad amounts to approximately one ionization per cubic micrometer.

Radiation   High-energy alpha or beta particles or gamma rays emitted by an atom as the substance undergoes radioactive decay.

Radiation sickness   Symptoms resulting from excessive exposure to radiation of the body.

Radioactive waste   Disposable, radioactive materials resulting from nuclear operations. Wastes are generally classified into two categories: high level and low level.

Radiological dispersal device   A device (weapon or equipment), other than a nuclear explosive device, designed to disseminate radioactive material in order to cause destruction, damage, or injury by means of the radiation produced by the decay of such material.

Radioluminescence   The luminescence produced by particles emitted during radioactive decay.

REM or rem   A Roentgen Man Equivalent is a unit of absorbed dose that takes into account the relative effectiveness of radiation that harms human health.

Index

CPSIA information can be obtained at www.ICGtesting.com
Printed in the USA
BVOW03*1340280115

385338BV00005B/40/P